3rd Edition

Legal Update for Teachers: The Complete Principal's Guide

- Harassment and Bullying
- Dress Codes and Appearance
- Student Search and Seizure

- Freedom of Speech and Association
- Cell Phones and Electronic Devices
- Students with Disabilities

Legal guidance and real-life dramatizations that help teachers make the right decisions – and prevent legal trouble.

Center for Education & Employment Law

Center for Education & Employment Law
P.O. Box 3008
Malvern, Pennsylvania 19355

Copyright © 2011 by Center for Education & Employment Law.
All rights reserved. No part of this publication may be reproduced by any means, electronic or mechanical, including photocopying, without prior written permission from the publisher.
Printed in the United States of America.

> "This publication is designed to provide accurate and authoritative information in regard to the subject matter covered. It is sold with the understanding that the publisher is not engaged in rendering legal, accounting or other professional service. If legal advice or other expert assistance is required, the services of a competent professional person should be sought."—
> *from a Declaration of Principles jointly adopted by a Committee of the American Bar Association and a Committee of Publishers and Associations.*

ISBN 978-1-933043-55-5

Published 2011   by: Center for Education & Employment Law

Library of Congress Control Number: 2009939224

Cover Design by Patricia Jacoby

Other Titles Published By
Center for Education & Employment Law:

Deskbook Encyclopedia of American School Law
Higher Education Law in America
Keeping Your School Safe & Secure: A Practical Guide
Private School Law in America
Students with Disabilities and Special Education
Deskbook Encyclopedia of Employment Law
Deskbook Encyclopedia of Public Employment Law

TABLE OF CONTENTS

Page

INTRODUCTION i
ABOUT THE EDITORS iii
HOW TO USE YOUR DESKBOOK v

CHAPTER ONE
School Liability and Safety

I. NEGLIGENCE 3
   A. Elements 3
   B. Defenses 4
      1. Immunity 4
      2. Comparative and Contributory Negligence 5

II. SCHOOL ATHLETICS 6
   A. Participants 6
      1. Duty of Care 6
      2. Governmental Immunity 7
      3. Assumption of Risk and Waiver 8
   B. Spectators, Employees and Parents 9

III. OTHER SCHOOL ACTIVITIES 10
   A. Physical Education Classes 10
      1. Duty of Care 10
      2. Governmental Immunity 11
   B. Shop Class Injuries 11
      1. Duty of Care 11
      2. Governmental Immunity 12
   C. Field Trips 12
   D. Other Supervised Activities 13
      1. Duty of Care 13
      2. Governmental Immunity 14

IV. UNSUPERVISED ACCIDENTS 14
   A. On School Grounds 15
      1. Duty of Care 15
      2. Governmental Immunity 15
   B. Off School Grounds 16
      1. Duty of Care 16
      2. Governmental Immunity 18

V. LIABILITY FOR INTENTIONAL CONDUCT..18
   A. Employee Misconduct 18
      1. Types of Misconduct 18
      2. Governmental Immunity 20
   B. Student Misconduct 21
      1. Types of Misconduct 21
      2. Bullying 22
      3. Governmental Immunity 23
   C. Parent Misconduct 24
      1. Sign-Out Policies 24
      2. Parental Liability 25

TABLE OF CONTENTS

- D. Duty to Report Abuse and Neglect 26
- E. Suicide 28
- F. Defamation 28

VI. SCHOOL BUS ACCIDENTS 30
- A. Duty of Care 30
- B. Governmental Immunity 31

VII. SCHOOL SECURITY 32
- A. Duty of Care 32
- B. Governmental Immunity 33
- C. Building and Grounds 34
  1. Visitors and Intruders 34
  2. Building Entry Policies 34

VIII. TEACHER SCENARIOS 35

CHAPTER TWO
Religion and the Public Schools

I. RELIGIOUS ESTABLISHMENT 61
- A. Prayer and Religious Activity 61
- B. Instruction of Students 63
  1. Curriculum 63
  2. Textbooks 65
  3. School Music Performances 65
- C. Commencement Ceremonies 66
- D. School Policies 67
  1. The Pledge of Allegiance 67
  2. Other Policies 69
  3. Immunization 70

II. USE OF SCHOOL FACILITIES 71
- A. Assemblies and School-Sponsored Events 71
- B. Student Groups 72
- C. The Equal Access Act 73
- D. Non-Student Use 74
- E. Religious Literature and Symbols 75

III. LIMITATIONS ON EMPLOYEE RELIGIOUS ACTIVITY 78

IV. FINANCIAL ASSISTANCE AND VOUCHER PROGRAMS 79

V. TEACHER SCENARIOS 81

CHAPTER THREE
Freedom of Speech and Association

I. STUDENTS 97
- A. Protected Speech 98
  1. Disciplinary Cases 98
  2. Threats and Bullying 99
  3. Internet and Technology Cases 101
  4. Confederate Flags 103
- B. Student Publications and Expression 104
- C. Non-School Publications 105
- D. Personal Appearance and Dress Codes 106
  1. Dress Codes 106
  2. Hair Length and Appearance 109
  3. Gang Affiliation 110

TABLE OF CONTENTS

- II. EMPLOYEES 111
  - A. Protected Speech...111
  - B. Personal Appearance and Dress Codes 114
  - C. Association Rights 115

- III. ACADEMIC FREEDOM 116
  - A. Library Materials..116
  - B. Textbook Selection 117
  - C. School Productions 118

- IV. PARENTAL SPEECH AND ASSOCIATION RIGHTS 118
  - A. Access to School Campuses 118
  - B. Curriculum 120

- V. USE OF SCHOOL FACILITIES 121
  - A. Student Organizations and Demonstrations 121
  - B. Non-Student Groups 123

- VI. TEACHER SCENARIOS 125

CHAPTER FOUR
Harassment and Discrimination

- I. SEXUAL HARASSMENT 165
  - A. Texting, Sexting and Electronic Harassment 165
  - B. Sexual Harassment by Students 166
  - C. Sexual Harassment by Staff..168
  - D. Sexual Orientation 169
  - E. Students with Disabilities 170

- II. RACE AND NATIONAL ORIGIN DISCRIMINATION 172

- III. RELIGIOUS DISCRIMINATION 174

- III. TEACHER SCENARIOS 175

CHAPTER FIVE
Student Discipline

- I. EXPULSIONS AND SUSPENSIONS..183
  - A. Due Process..183
    - 1. Notice and Procedural Protections 183
    - 2. Alternative Placements 186
    - 3. Zero-Tolerance Policies 187
  - B. Misconduct..188
    - 1. Sexual Harassment 188
    - 2. Drugs, Alcohol and Weapons Possession..189
    - 3. Extracurricular and Co-Curricular Events 192
    - 4. Fighting and Violence 193
    - 5. Cell Phones and Electronic Devices 194
  - C. Academic Expulsions or Suspensions 196

- II. STUDENT SEARCH AND SEIZURE 197
  - A. Fourth Amendment "Reasonable Suspicion" 197
    - 1. Searches Based on Individualized Suspicion 197
    - 2. Off-Campus Searches 200
    - 3. Locker Searches 201
    - 4. Strip Searches 201
    - 5. State Constitutional Cases 204
  - B. Random Testing Policies 205

TABLE OF CONTENTS

  C. Police Involvement 206
   1. *Miranda* Warnings 206
   2. Police-Assisted Searches 208
   3. Drug-Sniffing Dogs 208
   4. Liability Issues 209

III. CORPORAL PUNISHMENT 210
  A. Student Due Process Rights 211
  B. Teacher Liability Protection 212

IV. TEACHER SCENARIOS 215

CHAPTER SIX
Academic Practices

I. REFORM LEGISLATION 237
  A. The No Child Left Behind Act of 2001 237
  B. State Reform Acts 239
  C. Charter Schools 240
   1. Legislation 240
   2. Applications 241
   3. Operations and Finance 243

II. CURRICULUM AND GRADING..245
  A. Curriculum 246
  B. Bilingual Education..247
  C. Grading 248

III. STUDENT RECORDS 249
  A. Student and Parental Rights 249
  B. Media Requests 252
  C. Electronic and Video Records 254

IV. TESTING 256

V. EDUCATIONAL MALPRACTICE 257

VI. ADMISSIONS AND ATTENDANCE 258
  A. Race, Admission and School Assignment 258
  B. Age and Residency Requirements...260

VII. COMPULSORY ATTENDANCE 262
  A. Compulsory Attendance and Truancy 262
  B. Home Study Programs 263
  C. Attendance Policies 264

VIII. TEACHER SCENARIOS 266

CHAPTER SEVEN
Students with Disabilities

I. THE IDEA..271
  A. IDEA Substantive Requirements 271
  B. Procedural Protections..272
   1. IEPs and Team Meetings...272
   2. Notice and Hearing Requirements 274
  C. Implementation of IEPs 275

II. DISCIPLINE OF STUDENTS WITH DISABILITIES 275
  A. Discipline as a Change in Placement..276

TABLE OF CONTENTS

- B. Manifestation Determinations 276
- C. Delinquency and Juvenile Justice 278

III. PLACEMENT OF STUDENTS WITH DISABILITIES 279
- A. Identification and Evaluation 279
- B. Child Find Obligation 281
- C. Least Restrictive Environment 282
- D. Change in Placement and the 'Stay-Put' Provision 283
- E. Other Placement Issues 285
  - 1. Behavior Problems 285
  - 2. Extended School Year Services 285
  - 3. Transfer Students 286
- F. Residency Issues 287

IV. RELATED SERVICES 288
- A. Generally 288
- B. Level or Location of Services 289
- C. Provision of Related Services at Private Schools 290

V. TUITION REIMBURSEMENT 290
- A. Private School Tuition Claims 291
- B. Parental Conduct 292

VI. TRANSITION AND GRADUATION 293
- A. Transition Plans 293
- B. Graduation 294

VII. SCHOOL LIABILITY 295
- A. IDEA Claims 295
  - 1. Compensatory Education 295
  - 2. Monetary Damages, Costs and Fees 296
- B. Discrimination Claims 297
- C. Negligence and Civil Rights Claims 298
- D. Abuse and Neglect 300

VIII. TEACHER SCENARIOS 302

CHAPTER EIGHT
Interscholastic Athletics

I. HIGH SCHOOL ATHLETICS 315
- A. Eligibility Rules and Restrictions 315
  - 1. Transfer Students 315
  - 2. Other Rules 316
- B. Athletic and Extracurricular Suspensions 317
- C. Drug Testing 318

II. DISCRIMINATION AND EQUITY 319
- A. Gender Equity 319
- B. Race Discrimination 321
- C. Students with Disabilities 322

III. ISSUES IN COACHING 323
- A. Employment 323
- B. Defamation 325
- C. Liability 326
- D. Misconduct 328

REFERENCE SECTION

INDEX 329

INTRODUCTION

Legal Update for Teachers: The Complete Principal's Guide is a unique resource created for the busy education professional. This easy-to-use deskbook presents a combination of materials designed to help principals stay up to date on relevant legal decisions and formulate sound school policies. Case summaries, real-life teacher scenarios and practical guidance are organized into chapters by subject area for easy reference. The teacher scenarios, a convenient training tool that helps teachers learn how to react to various difficult classroom situations, are organized in a way that makes them easy to use and share with your staff. A comprehensive index makes it easy to quickly find the information you need.

Rely on ***Legal Update for Teachers: The Complete Principal's Guide*** with confidence as a valuable tool to avoid legal problems and keep your school running smoothly.

ABOUT THE EDITORS

Curt J. Brown is the Group Publisher of the Center for Education & Employment Law. Prior to assuming his present position, he gained extensive experience in business-to-business publishing, including management of well-known publications such as *What's Working in Human Resources, What's New in Benefits & Compensation, Keep Up to Date with Payroll, Supervisors Legal Update,* and *Facility Manager's Alert.* Mr. Brown graduated from Villanova School of Law and graduated magna cum laude from Bloomsburg University with a B.S. in Business Administration. He is admitted to the Pennsylvania bar.

James A. Roth is the editor of *Legal Notes for Education* and *Special Education Law Update.* He is a co-author of *Students with Disabilities and Special Education Law* and an adjunct program assistant professor at St. Mary's University in Minnesota. Mr. Roth is a graduate of the University of Minnesota and William Mitchell College of Law. He is admitted to the Minnesota bar.

Thomas D'Agostino is a managing editor at the Center for Education & Employment Law. He graduated from the Duquesne University School of Law and received his undergraduate degree from Ramapo College of New Jersey. He is a past member of the American Bar Association's Section of Individual Rights and Responsibilities as well as the Pennsylvania Bar Association's Legal Services to Persons with Disabilities Committee. Mr. D'Agostino is admitted to the Pennsylvania bar.

Elizabeth A. Wheeler is editor of the monthly newsletter *Private Education Law Report* and the *Private School Law in America* deskbook. She's also a contributing editor for the newsletters *Higher Education Legal Alert* and *School Safety and Security Alert.* A graduate of Macalester College and Capital University Law School, she's a member of the Massachusetts bar. Before joining the Center for Education and Employment Law, she was a legal editor for a South Boston publisher, where she edited employment law and education law newsletters.

Carol Warner is the editor *EducationTechNews.com* and two monthly newsletters: *School Safety & Security Alert* and *Legal Update for Teachers.* She is also a contributing editor for *HigherEdMorning.com* and *Higher Education Legal Alert.* Before joining the Center for Education & Employment Law, she was an editor for two employment law newsletters: *What's Working in Human Resources* and *What's New in Benefits & Compensation.* Carol is a graduate of The New York Institute of Technology and holds a Bachelor of Arts in English with an emphasis in professional writing.

HOW TO USE YOUR DESKBOOK

We have designed *Legal Update for Teachers: The Complete Principal's Guide* in an accessible format to provide guidance for principals on how to train teachers to react to classroom situations in a way that keeps students safe and the school out of legal trouble. This complete guide is unique as it provides two tools: a research tool and a training tool.

How Chapters Are Organized

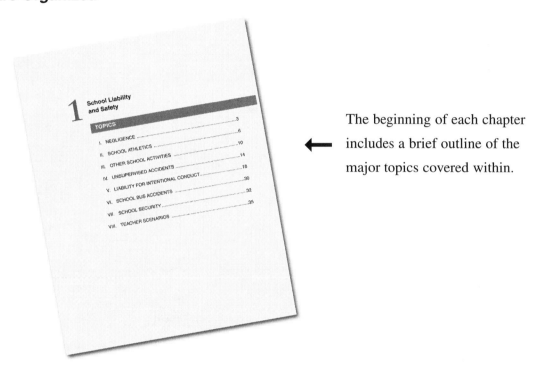

The beginning of each chapter includes a brief outline of the major topics covered within.

Within chapters, an overview of each new major topic is followed by page references to relevant teacher scenarios and then by summaries of relevant court decisions.

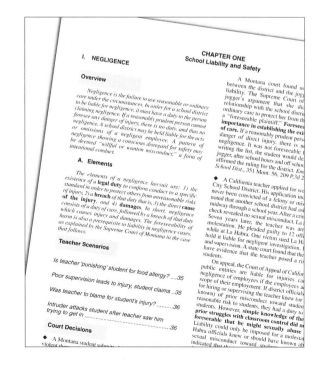

How to Use Your Deskbook

The teacher scenarios, which consist of half-page and full-page dramatizations of actual court cases, are positioned at the end of each chapter so they can be easily shared with your staff.

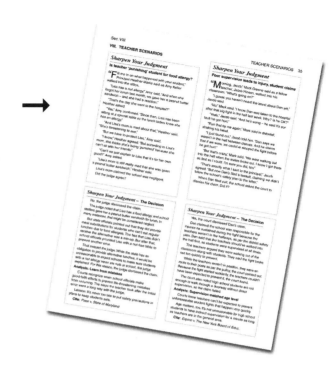

Research Tool

As a research tool, our guide book allows you to research by topic.

If you have a general interest in a particular **topic** area, our **table of contents** provides descriptive chapter headings containing detailed subheadings from each chapter.

> **Example:**
>
> For more information on cell phones, the table of contents indicates that a discussion about cell phones takes place beginning on page 194 of Chapter Five:
>
> **CHAPTER FIVE**
> **Student Discipline**
>
> I. EXPULSIONS AND SUSPENSIONS 183
>   A. Due Process 183
>   1. Notice and Procedural Protections 183
>   2. Alternative Placements 186
>   3. Zero-Tolerance Policies 187
>   B. Misconduct 188
>   1. Sexual Harassment 188
>   2. Drugs, Alcohol and Weapons Possession 189
>   3. Extracurricular and Co-Curricular Events 192
>   4. Fighting and Violence 193
>   ➤ 5. Cell Phones and Electronic Devices 194
>   C. Academic Expulsions or Suspensions 196

How to Use Your Deskbook

If you have a specific interest in a particular **issue**, our comprehensive **index** collects all of the relevant page references to particular issues

> **Example:**
>
> For more specific information on freedom of speech and association, the index provides references to specific cases dealing with Internet and technology cases, so you don't have to sort through all of Chapter Three to find the topic of interest:
>
> Freedom of speech and association, 97-124
>   academic freedom, 116-118
>   bullying, 99-101
>   Confederate flags, 103-104
>   dress code, 106-111
>   employees, 111-116
>   gang affiliation, 110-111
> →   Internet and technology cases, 101-103
>   non-school publications, 105-106
>   parents, 118-121

Training Tool

As a training tool, our guide book offers real-life classroom scenarios to share with teachers.

The **teacher scenarios** provide real-life classroom situations that escalated into legal disputes. Based on court rulings, the scenarios provide teachers with specific examples of ways they should – and should not – react during several typical classroom situations. The teacher scenarios section is the ideal training tool for several reasons. The scenarios are:

- based on real decisions held by the courts
- presented in dramatized settings that teachers can relate to and in which they may see themselves
- comprehensive accounts of the events that happened, from the initial dispute through the court decision, and
- readily available for principals to share with teachers as specific issues come up.

Scenario topics are included within the book's main index. Simply go to the main heading "Teacher Scenarios" to find a scenario about a topic of interest.

> **Example:**
>
> For more information on how to handle typical everyday challenges in the classroom, such as bullying, the teacher scenarios section of the index lists real instances of bullying turning into legal battles. Teachers learn how they should and shouldn't react:
>
> Teacher scenarios
>   accidents/incidents off school grounds, 50
>   allergies, 35
>   athletics, 38
> →   bullying, 49, 51, 135, 220, 221, 222
>   cell phones, 130

We hope you benefit from the use of the ***Legal Update for Teachers: The Complete Principal's Guide***. If you have any questions about how to use the deskbook, please contact Thomas D'Agostino at tdagostino@pbp.com.

1 School Liability and Safety

TOPICS

I.	NEGLIGENCE	3
II.	SCHOOL ATHLETICS	6
III.	OTHER SCHOOL ACTIVITIES	10
IV.	UNSUPERVISED ACCIDENTS	14
V.	LIABILITY FOR INTENTIONAL CONDUCT	18
VI.	SCHOOL BUS ACCIDENTS	30
VII.	SCHOOL SECURITY	32
VIII.	TEACHER SCENARIOS	35

CHAPTER ONE
School Liability and Safety

I. NEGLIGENCE

Overview

Negligence is the failure to use reasonable or ordinary care under the circumstances. In order for a school district to be liable for negligence, it must have a duty to the person claiming negligence. If a reasonably prudent person cannot foresee any danger of injury, there is no duty, and thus no negligence. A school district may be held liable for the acts or omissions of a negligent employee. A pattern of negligence showing a conscious disregard for safety may be deemed "willful or wanton misconduct," a form of intentional conduct.

A. Elements

*The elements of a negligence lawsuit are: 1) the existence of a **legal duty** to conform conduct to a specific standard in order to protect others from unreasonable risks of injury, 2) a **breach** of that duty that is, 3) the direct **cause of the injury**, and 4) **damages**. In short, negligence consists of a duty of care, followed by a breach of that duty which causes injury and damages. The foreseeability of harm is also a prerequisite to liability in negligence cases, as explained by the Supreme Court of Montana in the case that follows.*

Teacher Scenarios

Is teacher 'punishing' student for food allergy? 35

Poor supervision leads to injury, student claims ..35

Was teacher to blame for student's injury? 36

Intruder attacks student after teacher saw him trying to get in 36

Court Decisions

◆ A Montana student submitted a list of resolutions with violent themes for a school assignment. Among the themes were to "get a drivers license so I can do those horrible things people like to read about in the paper," and "kill the tooth fairy." A teacher reported the list, and his parents were contacted. In a meeting, the principal stated that although the list was inappropriate, the student was "a normal kid." Meeting attendees felt the list was "a teenage attempt at black humor" that he knew was inappropriate, so no action was taken. While driving near the high school some 17 months later, the student intentionally ran over a jogger. Before doing so, he told a passenger he planned to run her over and commit necrophilia with her corpse. The jogger sued the district for negligence.

A Montana court found no "special relationship" between the district and the jogger so as to give rise to liability. The Supreme Court of Montana rejected the jogger's argument that she did not need a special relationship with the school district for it have a duty of ordinary care to protect her from the student. She was not a "foreseeable plaintiff." **Foreseeability is of primary importance in establishing the existence of a legal duty of care.** If a reasonably prudent person cannot foresee any danger of direct injury, there is no duty, and thus no negligence. It was not foreseeable that 17 months after writing the list, the student would deliberately run over a jogger, after school hours and off school grounds. The court affirmed the ruling for the district. *Emanuel v. Great Falls School Dist.*, 351 Mont. 56, 209 P.3d 244 (Mont. 2009).

◆ A California teacher applied for work at the La Habra City School District. His application indicated that he had never been convicted of a felony or misdemeanor, but he noted that another school district had asked him to resign midway through a school year. After a criminal background check revealed no sexual misconduct, La Habra hired him. Seven years later, the teacher was arrested for child molestation. He pleaded guilty to 12 offenses occurring while at La Habra. One victim sued La Habra, seeking to hold it liable for negligent investigation, hiring, training and supervision. A state court found that the school did not have evidence that the teacher posed a risk of harming students.

On appeal, the Court of Appeal of California stated that public entities are liable for injuries caused by the negligence of employees if the employees act within the scope of their employment. If district officials responsible for hiring or supervising the teacher knew (or should have known) of prior misconduct toward students, or of a reasonable risk to students, they had a duty to protect the students. However, **simple knowledge of the teacher's prior struggles with classroom control did not make it foreseeable that he might sexually abuse students.** Liability could only be imposed for a molestation if La Habra officials knew or should have known about prior sexual misconduct toward students. As no evidence indicated that the teacher might sexually abuse students, the court affirmed the judgment for La Habra. *Ryan W. v. La Habra City School Dist.*, No. G040704, 2009 WL 1581499 (Cal. Ct. App. 6/5/09).

◆ A California student was attacked by eight males while he walked past the school gymnasium. Another student was assaulted by a group of three others while approaching a school exit. Both students suffered substantial injuries, and their guardian sued their school district, board of education and school principal for negligence. She also asserted violation of a duty to supervise students, claiming that officials were indifferent to reports of threats against the students, and that daily brawls and rampant gang activity were present at the school. The court held for the district and officials, and the guardian appealed to the Court of

Appeal of California. It noted that "causation" is one element of a negligence claim. The court agreed with the school district that the guardian had failed to show that officials caused the injuries to the students arising from the third-party attacks. She did not show it was more probable than not that additional security precautions would have prevented the attacks. **School districts are not the insurers of the physical safety of students.** To hold a district liable for negligence, a student must prove the elements of the claim, including causation. Claims of abstract negligence cannot survive. The court affirmed the judgment for the district and officials. *Castaneda v. Inglewood Unified School Dist.*, No. B198829, 2008 WL 2720631 (Cal. Ct. App. 7/14/08).

B. Defenses

◆ An 11-year-old New York student fell from a banister at school while unsupervised and suffered serious injuries. When his parents sued the district for negligence, it asserted that he had assumed the risk of harm by engaging in horseplay when he slid down the banister. The case reached the Court of Appeals of New York, which found that **assumption of risk is typically raised in cases involving athletic and recreational activities**. Allowing the defense here would have unfortunate consequences and could not be used to nullify the district's duty. If assumption of risk was allowed, students would be deemed to consent in advance to the risks of their own misconduct. Children often act impulsively and without good judgment. This does not mean they consent to assume the resulting danger. If the student's injury was attributable to his own conduct, this could be handled by allocating comparative fault. The court returned the case to a lower court for more proceedings. *Trupia v. Lake George Cent. School Dist.*, 927 N.E.2d 547 (N.Y. 2010).

1. Immunity

Immunity protects school districts and their employees from liability in many cases. Sovereign or "governmental" immunity precludes district liability in cases where school employees are performing "discretionary duties" within the scope of their employment. State laws define the scope of school and official immunity in specific cases. "Discretionary" or "official" immunity protects school employees and officials from liability when they perform "discretionary" (as opposed to "ministerial") duties. A "ministerial act" leaves nothing to discretion and is a simple or definite duty. Public officials whose duties require them to exercise judgment or discretion are not personally liable for damages unless they act intentionally. Discretionary or official immunity ensures that public officials who are charged by law with duties calling for the exercise of judgment or discretion are not held personally liable for damages, if they act in the scope of their employment and not intentionally, wilfully or with malice.

Teacher Scenarios

Mom sues after student suffers eye injury during science experiment 37

Court Decisions

◆ On a February day, an Indiana teacher took her students to a middle school for enrichment classes. She slipped and fell on a walkway. While there had been no precipitation for at least two days, a witness later described the area as "slick and wet looking." The teacher sued the district for negligence, and a jury awarded her $90,000. The Supreme Court of Indiana upheld the verdict. It held **the state tort claims act confers immunity on government units for injuries caused by temporary conditions on "a public thoroughfare" resulting from weather**. However, there is a common law duty to maintain roads and sidewalks in a reasonably safe condition. In this case, the school district claimed that the accident was due to normal thawing and freezing of a thin layer of ice. But because there had been no precipitation for a few days before the accident, the court found there was no "temporary conditions" immunity. *Gary Community School Corp. v. Roach-Walker*, 917 N.E.2d 1224 (Ind. 2009).

◆ A Kansas parent entered a school gymnasium to pick up his stepson. He then left the gym through double doors leading to a commons area. One of the doors came off a closing mechanism and fell on the parent's head. He sued the school district in the state court system for negligence. A trial court agreed with the district that the Kansas Tort Claims Act (KTCA) provided immunity. It applied the KTCA's "recreational use exception" to liability. After the state court of appeals affirmed the decision, the Supreme Court of Kansas agreed to hear the case. It held the legislative purpose of the KTCA was to immunize government entities to encourage them to build recreational facilities without fear of lawsuits. The court found that while the commons was not exclusively used for recreational purposes, it was an integral part of the gymnasium's use.

The commons was used to sell tickets and concessions during events and was not "incidentally connected to the gymnasium." And the court found the commons was necessarily connected to the gymnasium as a principal means of access and for purchasing tickets and concessions. **A school would be discouraged from opening a gymnasium for recreational use if liability was permitted in an area that was an integral part of its recreational usage.** Accordingly, the school district was immune from liability under the recreational use exception to the KTCA. *Poston v. Unified School Dist. No. 387, Altoona-Midway, Wilson County*, 189 P.3d 517 (Kan. 2008).

◆ An Illinois eighth-grader participated in an extracurricular tumbling class during lunch periods in his school gymnasium. The teacher who supervised the class had a physical education degree, but little mini-trampoline experience. After taking a forward flip off the mini-trampoline, the student seriously injured his neck and became quadriplegic. He and his mother sued the school board and teacher. They claimed that the teacher failed to provide any spotters and did not watch students while they used the mini-trampoline. The complaint also named the Chicago Youth Centers (CYC), which ran the tumbling class. The family asserted that use of a mini-trampoline was a hazardous recreational activity, and that the CYC and the teacher could not claim state law immunity because they acted willfully and wantonly. The trial court granted immunity to the teacher, the CYC and the board. Appeal reached the Supreme Court of Illinois. It held the Illinois Local Governmental and Governmental Employees Tort Immunity Act contained exceptions to immunity for hazardous recreational activities.

Trampolining was listed in the act as a hazardous recreational activity. The risk of spinal cord injuries from the improper use of a mini-trampoline was well known. Evidence indicated the CYC tumbling/trampoline program was not supervised by an experienced instructor and was not taught properly, as trained spotters and safety equipment were often not provided. Genuine issues of fact existed regarding whether the board, CYC and teacher were guilty of willful and wanton conduct, and the case required a trial. *Murray v. Chicago Youth Center*, 224 Ill.2d 213, 864 N.E.2d 176 (Ill. 2007).

2. Comparative and Contributory Negligence

Under comparative negligence principles, courts may apportion negligence among parties by their degree of fault. For example, a jury may find a student who slipped on a bar of soap in a school locker room 40% negligent, and the district whose employee left out the bar of soap 60% negligent. If the damages were $10,000, the student would recover $6,000 from the district.

"Contributory negligence" is a defense barring any recovery by a plaintiff in a negligence case when the plaintiff is at fault in any measure for the injury. A 1985 Indiana amendment adopted a "modified comparative fault system." In Penn Harris Madison School Corp. v. Howard, *861 N.E.2d 1190 (Ind. 2007), below, the Indiana Supreme Court held contributory negligence principles still applied in actions against school districts. State law recognized a presumption that children between the ages of seven and 14 are incapable of contributory negligence.*

Court Decisions

◆ A 13-year-old Indiana student blacked out during a basketball practice. Later, his mother told the coach he could walk through plays but could not run or perform strenuous activities. The student attended school for the next two days without incident. Although a doctor did not clear him to practice, he did so without restrictions at a practice two days after the blackout. During a running drill, the student collapsed and died. His parents sued the school district in the state court system. There, the district argued the student's own negligence was a contributing factor in his death. A jury returned a verdict for the parents, and the district appealed. The case reached the Supreme Court of Indiana, which held **a child between ages seven and 14 is required to exercise due care for his or her own safety**. Indiana law recognized a presumption that children between ages seven and 14 are incapable of contributory negligence. In this case, the district failed to overcome that legal presumption. *Clay City Consolidated School Corp. v. Timberman*, 918 N.E.2d 292 (Ind. 2009).

◆ A deaf Florida student left her school bus near her home on a two-lane residential street with a 25 mile-per-hour speed limit. The bus driver activated the bus' flashing lights and waited for her to cross the street. The driver heard a pickup truck speeding down the street and tried to signal the student. However, the pickup struck the student and knocked her to the ground. The pickup truck driver pleaded no contest to criminal conduct and was sentenced to five years in prison for reckless driving. The student's family sued the school board for negligence. In pre-trial activity, the bus driver said, "in my heart, yes, I feel like I hurt her a lot." A jury found the board 20% at fault for the student's injuries, the pickup driver 70% at fault, and the student 10% at fault. The family appealed to a Florida District Court of Appeal, arguing that the pickup driver acted intentionally (removing him from the negligence calculations), and that the school board should have been liable for a greater share of liability. The court of appeal affirmed, noting that **although the pickup driver had been fleeing police, he never intended to injure the student**. The percentage of fault had been properly calculated. *Petit-Dos v. School Board of Broward County*, 2 So.3d 1022 (Fla. Dist. Ct. App. 2009).

◆ An Indiana high school student helped an elementary school music teacher produce the play "Peter Pan." He had rock climbing experience, and he designed and built a pulley mechanism to allow the Peter Pan character to "fly." The teacher held a ladder for the student as he connected himself to the mechanism during a dress rehearsal for the play. When the student jumped from the ladder, the mechanism failed and he fell to the gym floor, suffering serious injuries. He and his mother sued the school district for negligence. A jury awarded him $200,000, but the Court of Appeals of Indiana held that the trial court gave the jury improper instructions. The student appealed. The Supreme Court of Indiana reinstated the jury's award. Although the jury instruction had been inaccurate, it hadn't prejudiced the school. **Under contributory negligence principles, the school could not defend its negligence by asserting the student's negligence.** *Penn Harris Madison School Corp. v. Howard*, 861 N.E.2d 1190 (Ind. 2007).

◆ A Washington student and her family sued a teacher, district and principal for sexual abuse by the teacher. The claims included negligent supervision and hiring. The principal and district sought to have any potential damage award reduced in part based on the student's alleged consent to have sexual relations with the teacher. The case reached the Supreme Court of Washington. It noted that the state Tort Reform Act required comparing the fault of the parties in negligence cases. However, contributory fault did not apply in this case. **Washington schools have a "special relationship with students" and a duty to protect them from reasonably anticipated dangers.** Because of the vulnerability of students, they had no duty to protect themselves from sexual abuse by teachers. This result was consistent with cases from Indiana, South Carolina, Colorado, Oregon, and Pennsylvania. The school district could not rely on the defense of contributory negligence. *Christensen v. Royal School Dist. #160*, 156 Wash.2d 62, 124 P.3d 283 (Wash. 2005).

II. SCHOOL ATHLETICS

Overview

Student-athletes assume the inherent risks of sports participation. Absent a showing of gross negligence or intentional conduct by a coach, league or school, they may not recover damages. The cases in this section involve district or school board liability.

A. Participants

1. Duty of Care

State laws require a showing that the school or its staff acted recklessly or intentionally to overcome the defense of governmental immunity.

Teacher Scenarios

Must cheerleader cheer for alleged attacker? 37

Did school do enough to stop track meet injury? 38

School faces suit for fight on basketball court 38

Cheerleader hurt at practice – is school responsible? 39

Court Decisions

♦ An Iowa high school basketball player elbowed an opposing player on the court. The opponent suffered from postconcussion syndrome, and his family sued the player in a state court for assault and battery, adding a claim against the player's district for negligent supervision. The court awarded damages against the player but refused to award the opponent's family any punitive damages. It also dismissed the claims against the district. The Supreme Court of Iowa found no error in the compensatory damage award against the player. **Under Iowa law, school districts have a duty of reasonable care. But there was no foreseeable risk in this case.** The assaulting player had only committed one previous technical foul, and it was for using profanity. While he was regarded as an intense player, his school district was not held liable because it could not have foreseen he would commit a battery during a game. *Brokaw v. Winfield-Mt. Union Community School Dist.*, 788 N.W.2d 386 (Iowa 2010).

♦ A California community college baseball player was hit in the head by a pitch, possibly in retaliation for a pitch thrown by his teammate the previous inning. After being hit, the student staggered, felt dizzy, and was in pain. His manager told him to go to first base. The student did so, but complained to his first-base coach, who told him to stay in the game. Soon after that, the student was told to sit on the bench. He claimed no one tended to his injuries. The student sued the host college for breaching its duty of care by failing to supervise or control its pitcher and failing to provide umpires or medical care. The court dismissed the case, and appeal reached the Supreme Court of California. It noted that in sports, the doctrine of assumption of risk precludes liability for injuries deemed "inherent in a sport." **Athletic participants have a duty not to act recklessly or outside the bounds of the sport.** Coaches and instructors have a duty not to increase the risks inherent in sports participation. Being hit by a pitch is an inherent risk of baseball. Colleges are not liable for the actions of their student-athletes during competition. The failure to provide umpires did not increase risks inherent in the game. The student's own coaches, not the host college, had the responsibility to remove him from the game for medical attention. The court reversed the judgment. *Avila v. Citrus Community College Dist.*, 38 Cal.4th 148, 41 Cal.Rptr. 299, 131 P.3d 383 (Cal. 2006).

♦ A Louisiana football player injured his back in a weight training session. His physician diagnosed him with a lumbar strain and dehydrated disc, and gave him a medical excuse from football for a week with instructions for "no weightlifting, squats or power cleans." Coaches interpreted the weightlifting limitation to be for only one week, and a coach instructed the student to do a particular lift. He did the lift, suffered severe back pain, and was diagnosed with a disc protrusion and a herniated disc. He lost interest in school, failed classes and transferred to an alternative school. He sued the school board for personal injury. A state trial court awarded him less than $7,500 for medical expenses, but awarded him $275,500 for pain and suffering, future medical expenses and loss of enjoyment of life. On appeal, the Louisiana Court of Appeal reviewed testimony that the student continued to experience severe back pain and often could not sleep. It held the trial court did not commit error in awarding the student damages for pain and suffering. **Evidence supported the trial court's findings that he had been severely injured and would experience recurring pain that would limit his daily activities indefinitely.** The court affirmed the damage award for loss of enjoyment of life, based on evidence that the student lost the opportunity to play varsity baseball and football. *Day v. Ouachita Parish School Board*, 823 So.2d 1039 (La. Ct. App. 2002).

2. Governmental Immunity

In some cases, a claim arising from a sports-related injury will face the challenge of overcoming the defense that the claim is blocked by governmental immunity. The following cases demonstrate how the governmental immunity defense comes into play and how courts resolve the question of whether the defendant is entitled to the benefit of the defense.

Court Decisions

◆ A 17-year-old Mississippi student collapsed during football practice on a hot August day. Emergency responders were unable to revive him, and he later died at a hospital. His survivors sued the school district for negligence. A state trial court denied pretrial judgment on the negligence claim. On appeal, the Supreme Court of Mississippi noted the Mississippi Tort Claims Act (MTCA) is the exclusive remedy in a negligence action against a governmental entity or employee. The MTCA provides immunity to state and political subdivisions whose employees act in the course and scope of their employment while performing discretionary acts. **Acts are discretionary if they require officials to use their own judgment and discretion. Coaching is a discretionary act.** Nothing indicated that the district or its coaches violated any statute, ordinance or regulation concerning practices, and the district was entitled to immunity. *Covington County School Dist. v. Magee*, 29 So.3d 1 (Miss. 2010).

◆ An Illinois school district operated a summer football camp. A student was hurt when he tripped over a grass-concealed shot-put bumper on the route he was told to take. His parent sued the district in a state court for over $50,000 in damages for negligence and willful and wanton conduct. Applying a recreational immunity provision of Illinois law, the court dismissed the action against the district. Before the Appellate Court of Illinois, the parent argued that the football facility was educational and not recreational in nature. This would preclude a recreational immunity defense. **The appellate court noted that immunity depended upon the character of the property, not the activity performed.** The property was on school grounds and was being used for a summer camp – by inference an educational purpose. As the lower court did not fully explore the property's character, dismissal was improper. *Peters v. Herrin Community School Dist. No. 4*, 928 N.E.2d 1258 (Ill. App. Ct. 2010).

◆ A Wisconsin varsity basketball cheerleading squad practiced a stunt in their high school commons area without mats. A spotter failed to stop a cheerleader from falling backward and striking her head. The cheerleader sued the spotter and school district for negligence. Evidence indicated that the cheerleaders were practicing a stunt they had not previously performed together, and that the spotter was not positioned to prevent the injury. The cheerleading coach was working with others about ten feet away at the time of the fall. The court held that the spotter and the school district were entitled to immunity, but the state court of appeals reversed the judgment against the spotter. On appeal to the state supreme court, the cheerleader argued that state law gave immunity only to athletes in "contact sports," and that cheerleading was neither a team nor a contact sport. However, the court held that cheerleading was a "contact sport."

The court found no evidence that the spotter was "reckless," which would defeat his claim to statutory immunity. He was simply standing in the wrong place. His conduct was characterized as "discretionary," not ministerial. In this case, the cheerleading squad operated under "spirit rules" that did not eliminate the coach's discretion. Spirit rules did not mandate a spotter for this exercise, and the coach had discretion to use mats. **The district was entitled to immunity.** *Noffke v. Bakke*, 315 Wis.2d 350, 760 N.W.3d 156 (Wis. 2009).

◆ A disagreement arose between a Texas faculty cheerleading sponsor and a principal over the punishment of varsity cheerleaders who were accused of disrespect, leaving school grounds, violating the school dress code and making obscene gestures toward staff. They were also accused of drinking at off-campus parties and being photographed in suggestive poses. After the cheerleading sponsor lost her job, she sued the school district, superintendent, principal and others for breach of contract, wrongful termination and defamation. The principal claimed sovereign immunity. After amending her petition to add claims for interference with her contract and denial of due process, the cheerleading sponsor filed a notice of non-suit, which had the effect of voluntarily dismissing her case. Before entering a non-suit order, the court held for the principal, based on her defense of immunity. It also awarded her $14,071 for her attorneys' fees and costs. The court then dismissed the case.

The cheerleading sponsor appealed to the Court of Appeals of Texas, asserting that her non-suit notice mooted the case and relieved her from paying the principal's attorneys' fees. **The court agreed that the notice of non-suit made the principal's claim to immunity moot.** But she was still entitled to her attorneys' fees under the state Education Code, since she was acting within her discretionary authority regarding student punishment. *Ward v. Theret*, No. 08-08-00143-CV, 2009 WL 2136299 (Tex. Ct. App. 7/15/09).

◆ An Ohio student injured his forehead and wrist during a pole vault at a high school track meet. He landed on improper padding near the landing pad that was later identified as in violation of National Federation of State High School Associations rules. The student sued the school district, coach and other officials for negligence. A state court held for the district and officials. The Court of Appeals of Ohio held the trial court had improperly granted immunity under the state recreational user statute. The student was not a "recreational user." The trial court also committed error by finding he assumed the risk of injury by the inherent dangers of pole vaulting. The court held **the sponsor of a sporting event has a duty not to increase the risk of harm over and above any inherent risks of the sport**. The court rejected the district's claim to immunity, as there was no discretionary, policymaking, planning or enforcement activity. But the coach was entitled to immunity under state law, as he did not act recklessly, with malice, or in bad faith. *Henney v. Shelby City School Dist.*, No. 2005 CA 0064, 2006 WL 747475 (Ohio Ct. App. 2006).

♦ A Maine high school wrestling team ran timed drills in school hallways in its warm-up routine. A wrestler was seriously injured after being bumped into a window by a teammate during a drill. The school had no policy prohibiting athletic training in school hallways at the time. The student sued the school district in the state court system for personal injury. A court held that the district and officials were protected by discretionary immunity. The Maine Supreme Judicial Court agreed, and held **government entities are generally entitled to absolute immunity from suit in any tort action for damages**. An exception to this rule imposes liability on government entities for the negligent operation of a public building. Here, allowing relay races in the school hallway was not the "operation of a public building." To impose liability under the public building exception to immunity, the claim must implicate a building's physical structure. The district and officials were protected by discretionary immunity. *Lightfoot v. School Administrative Dist. No. 35*, 816 A.2d 63 (Me. 2003).

♦ A Kansas school football team held its first practice on a hot August day. A student reported feeling ill after completing his first two stations. An assistant coach instructed him to drink some water, which he did. He then asked to sit out further drills and was told again to get water. As the team left practice, the student collapsed and was taken to a hospital, where he died the next day. His estate sued the school district and head coach for negligence. A state court granted the estate's motion to prevent the district and coach from relying on the "recreational use" exception to the Kansas Tort Claims Act (KTCA). On appeal, the Supreme Court of Kansas found a rational basis existed for distinguishing between injuries occurring on public recreational property and those occurring elsewhere. **The discretionary function exception protects government entities and employees from claims based on the exercise of discretion or the failure to exercise it.** The recreational use exception eliminated liability for ordinary negligence and barred all the claims. The court reversed the judgment and returned the case to a lower court for a determination of whether the district or coach acted with gross or wanton negligence. *Barrett v. Unified School Dist. No. 259*, 32 P.3d 1156 (Kan. 2001).

3. Assumption of Risk and Waiver

When student-athletes are injured while participating in school-related sports activities, it is common for the defendant to raise the argument that it should not be held liable because the student-athlete assumed the risk of participating in the activity and thus gave up the right to sue for any resulting injuries.

Court Decisions

♦ A New York student said he contracted herpes in a school wrestling match. He sued his school district, high school, wrestling opponent and the opponent's school in a state court for negligence. The case reached the New York Supreme Court, Appellate Division, which explained that **athletes consent to commonly appreciated risks inherent in the sport**. Athletes indicate their consent to injury-causing events by participating in them when risks are known, apparent or reasonably foreseeable, and are not assumed, concealed or unreasonably increased risks. Wrestling involved close contact between athletes, and diseases transmitted through skin-to-skin contact could result. The wrestling coach had identified communicable diseases as an "inherent danger of the sport." Even the student's expert admitted that herpes may exist in 29.8% of high school wrestlers. And the lower court had found that the possibility of contracting communicable diseases such as herpes is well known to coaches and officials.

Contrary to the student's argument, school officials informed him of the specific risk of contracting herpes, as well as the general risk of contracting skin diseases through wrestling. He was instructed to shower after each practice, and to use strong soap and shampoo to limit the possibility of contracting skin diseases including staph, ringworm, impetigo and herpes simplex virus. The court rejected all the student's arguments and reversed the judgment. *Farrell v. Hochhauser*, 65 A.D.3d 663, 884 N.Y.S.2d 261 (N.Y. App. Div. 2009).

♦ An Indiana student-athlete who weighed over 250 pounds had "dry heaves" early in a morning school football practice session. He stopped his activity for a minute, then told two coaches he felt better. The student ate lunch during a team rest period. He spent time lying on the locker room floor. The head coach asked the student how he felt, and the student again said he was okay. Near the end of the afternoon session, the student told a coach he did not feel well. The coach told him to get water, but he soon collapsed. The coaches took him to the locker room and placed him in a cool shower. He lost consciousness and the coaches called for an ambulance. He died at a hospital the following day. His parents sued the school district in the state court system for negligence.

After a trial, a jury returned a verdict for the school district. The parents appealed to the Court of Appeals of Indiana, which held that they did not submit sufficient evidence to find the district negligent as a matter of law. The head coach responded to hot weather by shortening parts of the schedule and adding more water breaks. Coaches emphasized the importance of drinking fluids, and several of them checked on the student. They had no indication that he was ill until he collapsed, when they called 911. **To negate a legal duty of care and avoid any finding of negligence, a participant must have "actual knowledge and appreciation of the specific risk involved and voluntarily acceptance of that risk."** But the release forms did not refer to "negligence." Since the release forms did not contain the word "negligence," the district was not released from negligence claims. The trial court should have granted the parents' request for a jury instruction stating that they had not released the district from negligence. The court reversed the judgment and remanded the case for a new trial. *Stowers v. Clinton Cent. School Corp.*, 855 N.E.2d 739 (Ind. Ct. App. 2006).

◆ A Massachusetts school district required a signed parental release for all students seeking to participate in extracurricular activities. For four years, the father of a high school cheerleader signed a release form before each season. During her fourth year, she was injured during a practice. When the cheerleader reached age 18, she sued the city in a state court for negligence. She added claims for negligent hiring and retention of the cheerleading coach. The court held for the city on the basis of the parental release, finding the father had released the city from any and all actions and claims. The cheerleader appealed to the Massachusetts Supreme Judicial Court, asserting the release was invalid. The court held that **enforcement of a parental release was consistent with Massachusetts law and public policy**. There was undisputed evidence that the father read and understood the release before signing it, and that the form was not misleading. It was not contrary to public policy to require parents to sign releases as a condition for student participation in extracurricular activities. To hold the release unenforceable would expose public schools to financial costs and risks that would lead to the reduction of extracurricular activities. *Sharon v. City of Newton*, 437 Mass. 99, 769 N.E.2d 738 (Mass. 2002).

B. Spectators, Employees and Parents

Unfortunately, not only student-athletes sustain injuries at school sporting events. As shown by the cases below, claims are also brought by spectators, employees and parents of participants. The cases in this section demonstrate the kinds of claims that typically arise in these situations and the legal analysis that courts utilize to resolve them.

Court Decisions

◆ The Supreme Court of Delaware denied a request for relief from a pretrial order that required a private cheerleading organization to defend and indemnify a school district for injuries to a spectator who was attending a cheerleading event at a district high school. The organization had leased the school gymnasium from the school district for a cheerleading competition. After the spectator fell from the bleachers, the organization claimed gross negligence by school staff who failed to install guard rails. In pretrial proceedings a state trial court dismissed negligence claims against the school board and officials but allowed the claims for gross or wanton negligence to proceed. As the supreme court found no reason to allow an appeal at this stage of the case, **the organization had to provide legal defense to the school board and indemnify it for any loss**. *Diamond State Wildcats v. Boyle*, 986 A.2d 1164 (Table) (Del. 2010).

◆ A patron at an Alabama high school basketball game fell from the bleachers where he had been sitting, and was injured. He sued the school board for negligence and contract claims. A trial court held for the school board on the negligence claims, but allowed a breach-of-implied contract claim to survive. On appeal to the Supreme Court of Alabama, the patron argued that county education boards can be sued for an implied breach of contract for failing to provide safe premises for athletic contests. In contrast, the board argued that it was an agency of the state entitled to the same immunity as any state agency enjoyed. The court found that immunity was conferred by the Constitution, and it affirmed the judgment for the board. **Absolute immunity extended to all arms or agencies of the state, including county education boards.** *Ex parte Hale County Board of Educ.*, 14 So.3d 844 (Ala. 2009).

◆ An Alabama five-year-old fell from bleachers at a quarterfinal football playoff game held at a high school by the Alabama High School Athletic Association (AHSAA). The child fell through an opening in the seats and broke both her wrists. Her parents sued the school board for breach of an implied contract and breach of implied warranty of safe premises. The case reached the Supreme Court of Alabama, which stated that **Alabama county education boards are considered state agencies, and are immune from tort actions**. The court agreed with the school board that the AHSAA sponsored and controlled the game, defeating any contract claim. The parents' claim was barred by an absolute immunity provision of the state constitution. *Ex Parte Jackson County Board of Educ.*, 4 So.3d 1099 (Ala. 2008).

◆ A Louisiana child fell on bleachers at a football game at a high school stadium. Her family claimed the fall was caused by a lack of adequate traction tape or guards on the bleachers. A school custodial supervisor submitted a statement that he witnessed the fall. He stated that the child was being chased by another child and that the family did nothing to stop her. The family sued the school board for negligence. A state court found insufficient evidence for a trial. The family appealed to the Court of Appeal of Louisiana, which affirmed the judgment. School employees indicated that there was no defect in the bleachers, steps or guard rails, or in the design or construction of the stadium. **To impose liability on a public entity, the entity must know of "a particular vice or defect" that caused the damage, yet fail to fix the defect after having a reasonable opportunity to do so.** Not every imperfection or irregularity is a "defect" resulting in liability for a school board. There was no evidence that the board knew of any defect. There was also no evidence that the bleachers were slippery or that similar incidents had occurred there. The absence of traction tape was not a defect that created an unreasonable risk of harm. *Mason v. Monroe City School Board*, 996 So.2d 377 (La. Ct. App. 2008).

◆ A West Virginia spectator slipped and fell on ice and snow on school grounds while trying to reach a high school basketball game. She sued the board in a state court, arguing it was negligent to hold a basketball game on a day when the entire school system was closed due to weather. The board claimed immunity under the state Governmental Tort Claims and Insurance Reform Act. The case reached the Supreme Court of Appeals of West Virginia, which rejected the spectator's argument that the decision to hold the basketball game was an affirmative act that was not immunized. **While the act of holding the game may have encouraged her to venture out into the snow, it did not cause the conditions at the school.** The Tort Act provided immunity for losses or claims resulting from snow or ice on public ways resulting from the weather. *Porter v. Grant County Board of Educ.*, 633 S.E.2d 38 (W.Va. 2006).

III. OTHER SCHOOL ACTIVITIES

Overview

Courts have held schools liable for injuries during school events which resulted from the failure to provide a reasonably safe environment, failure to warn participants of known hazards (or to remove known dangers), failure to properly instruct participants in the activity, and failure to provide supervision adequate for the type of activity and the ages of the participants involved. Schools and their staff members are not liable for unforeseeable harms, as schools are not the insurers of student safety. The fact that each student is not personally supervised at all times does not itself constitute grounds for liability.

A. Physical Education Classes

1. Duty of Care

Teacher Scenarios

Student gets hurt in PE: Mom blames teacher 39

Student injured during PE: Was teacher at fault? 40

Was boy hurt because teacher wasn't there? 40

Student dies after teacher supposedly ignored 'warning signals' – now parents place blame 41

Was teacher responsible for phys ed class injury? 41

Court Decisions

◆ A California school district was not liable for injuries to a student who was hit by a golf club swung by a classmate in their physical education class. According to the student, the teacher did not give a whistle command for the classmate to hit the ball, as was her usual practice. The student sued the school district for negligence. A state court found that the district did not breach its limited duty of care and held for the district. The student appealed to the Court of Appeal of California, which held that the lower court applied the wrong legal standard. **The Supreme Court of California has applied the "prudent person" standard of care to cases involving students injured during school hours.** This simply requires persons to avoid injuring others by using due care. As the lower court should have applied the prudent person standard, the court reversed the judgment and remanded the case. *Hemady v. Long Beach Unified School Dist.*, 143 Cal.App.4th 566, 49 Cal. Rptr.3d 464 (Cal. Ct. App. 2006). The Supreme Court of California denied review of this case in 2007.

◆ During a gym class, an Ohio eighth grader with a history of mild asthma obtained his teacher's permission to retrieve his prescription inhaler from his locker. Minutes later, another teacher found the student unconscious and not breathing on the locker room floor. Despite the administration of medical treatment, he died. The student's estate sued the school board for wrongful death. A jury found for the school board, and the Court of Appeals of Ohio affirmed. The trial court had allowed a physician to testify that the death of a student previously recognized as having "mild asthma" was "one in a million." **According to the physician, not even medical professionals could have foreseen the death.** The court rejected the estate's additional arguments and affirmed the judgment. *Spencer v. Lakeview School Dist.*, No. 2005-T-0083, 2006 WL 1816452 (Ohio Ct. App. 2006).

◆ A New York student was playing football in a physical education class when a classmate threw a football tee that hit her in the eye. Her parents brought a negligence action against the school district in a state court. A state appellate division court held the district had a duty to adequately supervise and instruct students, and was liable for foreseeable injuries caused by their negligence. But **school districts are not insurers of student safety and will not be held liable for every spontaneous, thoughtless or careless act by which one student injures another**. The degree of care required is what a reasonably prudent parent would exercise under similar circumstances. Here, the teacher had not instructed students on how to properly handle the tee and never told them not to throw it. The evidence differed as to whether students had previously thrown the tee or seen the teacher throw it. In affirming a judgment for the student, the court held that the trial court would have to determine if the injury causing conduct was reasonably foreseeable and preventable. *Oakes v. Massena Cent. School Dist.*, 19 A.D.3d 981, 797 N.Y.S.2d 640 (N.Y. App. Div. 2005).

◆ A 16-year-old Louisiana student who weighed 327 pounds collapsed and began having seizures during a PE class. The class was conducted by a substitute art teacher in a gym that was not air-conditioned, and the temperature inside was at least 90 degrees. After the student collapsed, he was taken to a hospital, where he later died. His teacher had played in the game instead of monitoring students. The student's parent sued the school board and its insurer in a state court for wrongful death, and the court awarded her $500,000. The Court of Appeal of Louisiana found no error in trial court findings that the board had breached its duty to exercise reasonable care and supervision. The lower court was also entitled to hear the testimony of a physical education professor and to consider reliable medical testimony. **Teachers have a duty to exercise reasonable care and supervision over students in their custody, and to avoid exposing them to an unreasonable risk of injury.** As physical education classes may involve dangerous activities, due care must be used in them to minimize the risk of student injury. *James v. Jackson*, 898 So.2d 596 (La. Ct. App. 2005). The state supreme court denied the board's appeal. *James v. Jackson*, 902 So.2d 1005 (La. 2005).

2. Governmental Immunity

Although state laws grant varying degrees of immunity to school districts in negligence cases, the general rule is that government agencies and employees have immunity from civil liability based on "discretionary actions." An Illinois court held immunity is allowed for "policy decisions," which require the balancing of competing interests so that there must be a "judgment call."

Court Decisions

◆ After a Wisconsin student expressed fear about performing a beginning parallel bar exercise, her physical education teacher moved the bars to their lowest setting. Another student demonstrated the exercise, and the teacher positioned herself to spot the student. However, the teacher's attention was diverted by another student who asked a question. The student caught her leg on the bar and seriously injured her knee. She was the first student injured during the teacher's 32-year career. In the student's negligence action against the teacher and the school district, a state trial court held that the teacher deserved governmental immunity. On appeal, the Court of Appeals of Wisconsin held that **Wisconsin law immunizes government agencies and employees from liability for "discretionary actions."** There was no statute, rule or regulation specifying how the teacher should teach gymnastics. Since any directives she received did not eliminate her discretion, immunity protected her. *Krus v. Community Insurance Corp.*, 324 Wis.2d 306 (Wis. Ct. App. 2010).

◆ Two Minnesota students were injured in a darkened school gym while playing "flashlight tag." Their parents sued the district for negligence, and it asserted immunity under a state law requiring each school district in the state to purchase liability insurance if it was available at a cost of $1.50 or less per student per year. The statutory dollar amount was never changed after 1970, and no school district could now obtain liability insurance for $1.50 per student. The case reached the Supreme Court of Minnesota, which explained that the law had expired in 1974. **Had the legislature intended to completely immunize school districts for tort immunity, it would have drafted a statute announcing such immunity.** The district had been self-insured for tort claims since 1990, and had paid out claims it deemed meritorious. So the court held the district was not entitled to immunity. *Granville v. Minneapolis Public Schools, Special School Dist. No. 1*, 732 N.W.2d 201 (Minn. 2007).

B. Shop Class Injuries

1. Duty of Care

Schools are required to provide their students with a safe environment. Known shop class dangers must be minimized, and safety devices are to be in place and working. Failure to supervise, warn students of known dangers, or maintain safety devices can result in school liability.

Teacher Scenarios

Accident in shop: Mom sues teacher personally 42

When student gets injured, teacher gets blame 42

Student injured by tire – is it school's fault? 43

Court Decisions

◆ A Minnesota student amputated a finger in a wood shop class accident. He had experience using the saw, which was equipped with a blade guard. Before students could use the saw, they had to pass a test on a protocol for its use. The protocol stated that the best practice for cutting small strips of wood was to disengage the blade guard and use a push stick to guide the strips through the saw. On the day of the accident, the teacher instructed the student to cut small wood strips using a push stick with the blade guard disengaged. After watching the student cut some strips, he moved to another part of the room. The student then reached over the blade to remove a piece of scrap wood and lost a finger.

The student sued the teacher and school district for negligence. A state court denied the teacher's claim to official immunity, and the school district's motion for statutory immunity. The Supreme Court of Minnesota explained that teachers did not forfeit official immunity because their conduct was "ministerial," if that conduct was established by a policy or protocol that was created though the exercise of discretionary judgment. Both the decision to establish a protocol and the protocol itself involved the exercise of professional judgment. **The teacher was entitled to common law official immunity because his liability was based on compliance with the protocol.** The court reversed the judgment against the teacher and held that the school district was entitled to vicarious immunity.

Anderson v. Anoka Hennepin Independent School Dist. 11, 678 N.W.2d 651 (Minn. 2004).

2. Governmental Immunity

Court Decisions

◆ An Ohio student lost fingers on his dominant hand when he tried to operate a jointer machine in his high school shop class. Prior to the accident, the teacher had demonstrated its use and instructed the students on safety issues. Neither the student nor the teacher could later say for sure what had happened. After the accident, the machine was taken out of operation and stored. The student sued the school board in a state court for negligence. An inspection of the machine about a year after the incident revealed that its guard was locked open. The court considered testimony from the teacher that it "would probably take five years" for the guard to remain in the open position. The teacher believed the machine was purchased in 1964 and had been broken and repaired since that time. He believed the guard was functioning properly, and he adjusted it weekly. The court denied the board's motion for state political subdivision immunity. On appeal, the Court of Appeals of Ohio held **employees of political subdivisions are immune from liability unless their actions or omissions are manifestly outside the scope of employment or their official duties**. A jury would have to decide whether the teacher's conduct was reckless, and consider inconsistencies in his statements. *Bolling v. North Olmsted City Schools Board of Educ.*, No. 90669, 2008 WL 4599670 (Ohio Ct. App. 10/16/08).

C. Field Trips

School districts do all they can to ensure absolute safety on field trips, such as by setting clear rules with students beforehand and choosing capable parent chaperones in appropriate numbers. Despite these best efforts, accidents can and do happen. As a result, some lawsuits seek recovery based on the alleged failure of school officials to ensure proper supervision on field trip excursions. The following cases demonstrate some of the issues that arise in these circumstances.

Teacher Scenarios

Can school be blamed for field trip injury? 43

Court Decisions

◆ A California student with asthma went on a field trip to a science camp operated by her school district. When she suffered an asthma attack, camp counselors gave her an asthma inhaler and performed CPR until paramedics arrived. She died as she was being airlifted to a hospital. Her parents sued the school district for negligent failure to provide adequate medical staff and misrepresenting the level of medical staffing that would be available at the camp. A state court held for the district, as did the Court of Appeal of California. **It held the district was entitled to immunity because any person on a school field trip was deemed to have waived all claims against a school district,** charter school or the state for injury, accident, illness or death occurring "during or by reason of the field trip or excursion." The court held this broad grant of immunity was designed to encourage the use of field trips. *Sanchez v. San Diego County Office of Educ.*, 182 Cal.App.4th 1580, 106 Cal.Rptr.3d 750 (Cal. Ct. App. 2010).

◆ A California school held a year-end field trip for seventh-graders to a waterpark. It notified families that the event would be "a closed party" supervised by teaching staff. The notice also advised families that waterpark lifeguards would be present. A student drowned during the event, and his family sued the waterpark for wrongful death. The waterpark in turn sought to apportion part of the liability to the school district and indemnify it for any loss. According to the waterpark, the district failed to comply with its own policy requiring a minimum ratio of one adult chaperone for every 13 students.

According to the waterpark, district chaperones caused the death because they failed to determine the student's swimming ability, warn him of risks or watch him while he attempted to swim. The superior court dismissed the district from the case, and the waterpark appealed. The California Court of Appeal held that the district was shielded from liability by the California Education Code, which created "field trip immunity" for California school districts. All persons making a field trip or excursion in connection with a school-related activity were deemed to have waived all claims against a school district for injury, accident, illness or death. **Under the law, the student was deemed to have waived all claims against the district arising from the excursion to the waterpark.** It was irrelevant that the student's parent or guardian had not signed a school permission slip. The court affirmed the judgment for the school district. *Windsor R/V Waterworks Park Co. v. Santa Rosa City Schools*, No. A118090, 2008 WL 4601138 (Cal. Ct. App. 10/16/08).

◆ An autistic Ohio eighth-grader weighed 150 pounds and had a history of behavior problems. A teacher's aide agreed to supervise her on school buses, even though she knew the child had previously hurt others. The child hit and bit the aide on one occasion while they were on a bus. Despite this, the aide agreed to supervise her on a field trip to a bowling alley. The aide received additional pay for this assignment. While at the bowling alley, the child wandered onto a lane and tried to hit a student from another school. When the aide intervened, the child hit and choked her. As a result, the aide suffered two herniated disks in her neck. She sued the school board, its superintendent, and the child's parents. The parents settled the case and the aide appealed a judgment for the board and superintendent to the U.S. Court of Appeals, Sixth Circuit.

The court held the board was charged by the federal Individuals with Disabilities Education Act (IDEA) with providing autistic children a free appropriate public education in the least restrictive environment. Here, the board was attempting to discharge its duties under the IDEA. A more restrictive setting might have violated the IDEA. According to the court, **it would not create "a Catch 22 situation by imposing substantive due process liability for failure to do an act that might itself have exposed the actor to liability on another theory."** The district could not simply decline to educate the child on the basis of behavior that was a manifestation of her disability. In any event, the aide was entirely aware of the child's history and accepted additional pay for extra assignments that required her to control her actions. The board did not act arbitrarily, and the judgment in its favor was upheld. *Hunt v. Sycamore Community School Dist. Board of Educ.*, 542 F.3d 529 (6th Cir. 2008).

◆ A profoundly mentally disabled Kentucky student broke his ankle during a school field trip to a roller rink. An adult supervisor was on the floor taking pictures of students at the time of the accident. The student fell when he leaned over to kiss one of his peer tutors for a picture. His parents sued the school board and teacher for personal injury. A state trial court held that the board was entitled to governmental immunity, and the teacher had qualified immunity. On appeal, the state court of appeals held **qualified official immunity applies when public employees perform acts involving the exercise of discretion and judgment, if they are made in good faith and within the scope of their employment authority**. According to the court, there is no "bright line" rule of demarcation between discretionary and ministerial acts. There was no clear error by the trial court, as the teacher had to exercise her personal judgment and deliberation numerous times during the day of the field trip. This included how best to implement the student's individualized education program and how to supervise him. As the teacher's actions required deliberation and judgment, and she acted in good faith and within the course and scope of her employment, the court affirmed the judgment. *Pennington v. Greenup County Board of Educ.*, No. 2006-CA-001942-MR, 2008 WL 1757209 (Ky. Ct. App. 4/18/08).

D. Other Supervised Activities

1. Duty of Care

School districts have a duty to use reasonable care to supervise and protect students against hazards on school property that create an unreasonable risk of harm. Liability may also exist if supervision is negligently performed.

Teacher Scenarios

Teacher followed emergency drill procedure – so why's Mom suing?...44

Did teacher do enough to prevent student's injury? Mom says, 'No!'...45

Chemistry explosion injures student: Did teacher explain safety measures?...45

Tardy students' horseplay causes accident..........46

Girl hurt playing football: Is it school's fault?........46

They charge teacher wasn't paying attention......47

Should school be blamed for fall from monkey bars?..47

Court Decisions

◆ A 16-year-old Iowa student collapsed while listening to guest speeches as she stood at attention following a band performance at an outdoor bandshell. Two and a half years later, she sued the school district in a state court, claiming that the band director negligently failed to supply water and failed to recognize the signs of heat stroke, heat exhaustion and/or dehydration. She also asserted claims against the school district. A state trial court held the action was untimely under the state's two-year statute of limitations. The Supreme Court of Iowa rejected the student's claim that she had up to a year after her eighteenth birthday to initiate a lawsuit. Instead, Iowa Code Chapter 670 is the exclusive remedy for tort actions against municipalities and their employees. That law provided that every action against a municipality must be filed within six months, or within two years if the person seeking damages files a notice of a claim of loss with the government. In this case, **the student had not filed a notice with the school district**. The court commented that the legislature had now simplified the law by removing the notice requirement. It also changed the statute so that minors will now have one year from the attainment of majority within which to file a complaint, but that did not help the student here. *Rucker v. Humboldt Community School Dist.*, 737 N.W.2d 292 (Iowa 2007).

◆ A Montana high school freshman rode home from an out-of-town school basketball game on a pep band bus. The driver teased students by pumping the brakes and jarring the bus. The student asked for a restroom break, but the band instructor denied the request. Many students threw food and candy during the trip. As the bus neared the school, the band instructor announced that no one could leave the bus until it was cleaned up. The student told the instructor twice "you let me off this fucking bus." The driver pumped the brakes while stopping the bus, and the student wet himself. The school suspended the student for using profanity and placed him on detention. Eight days later, the student was hospitalized with ketoacidosis. After remaining in a life-threatening condition for several days, he recovered but was diagnosed with Type I diabetes and post-traumatic stress disorder (PTSD). The student and his parents sued the district, band instructor and driver for causing or accelerating his diabetes and PTSD.

A state trial court held for the school district. On appeal, the Supreme Court of Montana explained that **to impose liability on a school district in a negligence case, it must first be shown the district had a duty of care**. In this case, the trial court had erroneously found that the district owed no duty to the student. But the trial court had been unable to determine if the student's diabetes was caused or accelerated by the events resulting from the bus trip. Even his doctor could not establish that diabetes was a likely result of the bus trip or its aftermath. Since the family could not prove the injuries were caused by the district's conduct, the court affirmed the judgment. *Hinkle v. Shepherd School Dist. #37*, 322 Mont. 80, 93 P.3d 1239 (Mont. 2004).

◆ A North Dakota school district operated a middle school in a building owned by the U.S. Bureau of Indian Affairs (BIA). The district and BIA had an agreement to jointly operate the school, which was primarily attended by American Indian students. The principal was a BIA employee who supervised both BIA and district staff. BIA teachers supervised the lunchroom under a plan created through a collective bargaining agreement. A BIA teacher tried to break up a fight between two students during her lunchroom supervision period and suffered a disabling, traumatic brain injury. The teacher sued the district for personal injury, alleging negligent failure to maintain a safe environment. A state court held for the district, finding that it did not own, supervise or control the building at the time of the injury, and thus owed the teacher no duty of care.

The teacher appealed to the Supreme Court of North Dakota. On appeal, the court found no evidence to show district control over the lunchroom, lunchroom supervision plan or teacher. This was true even assuming the district maintained some control over the school through state funding, accreditation and the arrangement with the BIA. The teacher was a BIA employee performing her lunchroom duties under the collective bargaining agreement. **As she did not show a relationship between herself and the district that imposed a legal duty to provide her with a safe working environment, the trial court had correctly held for the school district.** *Azure v. Belcourt Public School Dist.*, 681 N.W.2d 816 (N.D. 2004).

2. Governmental Immunity

As discussed in the immunity sections of other areas in this chapter, state laws typically grant immunity to school districts and their employees when a claim is based on an injury that was sustained as a result of the exercise of discretion by a school official. When immunity is available, the injured party cannot recover damages.

Teacher Scenarios

Was teacher liable for student's Field Day injury? 48

Court Decisions

◆ A North Dakota teacher held a "60s Day" as part of a unit of study for her history class curriculum each year. She showed a video of another student who had ridden a bicycle off the school auditorium stage and onto the floor during a 60s Day event two years earlier. A student believed that the video meant he was allowed to perform the stunt. After school, he and another student went to the auditorium to practice the stunt. They ran into the teacher, who told them she thought it was not a good idea. However, they snuck in a side door anyway. The student was injured when he crashed and struck his head on the auditorium floor. His father sued the school district and teacher in the state court system for negligence. A state trial court ruled for the district, but the Supreme Court of North Dakota allowed the lawsuit to proceed. Although the incident occurred after classes had ended, administrators and teachers were still present and the "school day had not come to an end." **The state's recreational use immunity statutes did not bar the lawsuit.** As for the claims against the teacher, the student's viewing of the video of the previous bicycle stunt could be seen as implying that the stunt would be permissible. *M.M. v. Fargo Public School Dist. No. 1*, 783 N.W.2d 806 (N.D. 2010).

◆ An Idaho school district held a carnival to celebrate the last day of the school year. A contractor provided the activities. Participants in a "bungee run" wore harnesses tethered to a fixed object by a bungee cord. They raced over an inflated rubberized surface until the cord snapped them backward. A student was injured on the bungee run. She sued the district and contractor in a state court for negligence. The court found the school's conduct was not reckless and held it was therefore immune from liability under the Idaho Tort Claims Act.

On appeal, the state supreme court held the Tort Claims Act generally made governmental entities liable for monetary damages to the same extent that a private person would be under the circumstances. Schools generally have a duty to supervise student activities, including extracurricular and school-sponsored events, and a duty to protect students from reasonably foreseeable risks. The court found the student had stated valid claims based on allowing her to participate in an unreasonably hazardous activity, failing to supervise her during the activity, and failing to supervise the contractor to ensure it provided adequate instruction and supervision. **The district court had correctly found the district was immune from liability for negligent supervision and failing to inspect the bungee equipment.** But the student should have been allowed to pursue a theory of direct liability for planning and sponsoring an unreasonably dangerous activity, and the court returned the case to the trial court. *Sherer v. Pocatello School Dist. #25*, 143 Idaho 486, 148 P.3d 1232 (Idaho 2006).

IV. UNSUPERVISED ACCIDENTS

Overview

Schools are required to exercise reasonable care in maintaining safe buildings, grounds and facilities. They can be found liable for negligently maintaining buildings or tolerating hazardous structures, fixtures or grounds.

A. On School Grounds

1. Duty of Care

Teacher Scenarios

Disabled student dies on the playground: Parents ask, 'Did teacher follow the IEP?' 48

Could teacher have protected student from bully? 49

Student falls at school bake sale: Is district responsible? 49

Court Decisions

◆ A New York child fractured her clavicle and femur after falling off a slide on a playground maintained by a city and school district. According to the child's family, the playground used no protective ground cover and was grass and dirt. Other playgrounds operated by the city and district had protective ground cover such as pea stone to lessen injuries, as recommended by the U.S. Consumer Product Safety Commission (CPSC). The family sued the school district and city. After the trial court denied pretrial dismissal, a state appellate division court held that the school's expert witness established that lack of adequate ground cover was not the legal cause of the injuries. On appeal, the New York Court of Appeals held the expert had calculated the force of the child when she landed on the ground, relying on prior tests in which he had used rubber mats. By contrast, CPSC and similar guidelines were based on use of various ground covers. **The expert witness did not provide a scientific or mathematical foundation to substantiate his opinion that the type of ground cover did not cause injury.** So the court reinstated the claims. *Butler v. City of Gloversville*, 12 N.Y.3d 902, 885 N.Y.S.2d 245 (N.Y. 2009).

◆ A California student joined other children on school property who were picking oranges from a tree on the other side of the fence. He placed a bike next to the fence and poked the handlebar through the fence for stability. However, the bike slipped, and he fell and cut his arm on the fence. The student's parents sued the school district for negligence. A state superior court awarded pretrial judgment to the district, and the family appealed. The Court of Appeal of California noted that for at least 16 years prior to the accident, there had been no complaints about the fence. The state Government Code makes a public entity liable for injuries caused by dangerous conditions on public property. A "dangerous condition" is one that creates a substantial risk of injury when the property is used with due care, and in the manner intended. **The student could not show that he was using "due care" while using the fence in a way that was reasonably foreseeable to the school district.** The danger was obvious since "fences are not meant to be climbed, they are meant to keep people out." Common sense would demonstrate that even a nine-year old child could see the danger of injury created by attempting to use a bike as a ladder to reach over a chain link fence. The lower court had properly found the metal tines on the top of the fence were not a "dangerous condition of public property." The court affirmed the judgment. *Biscotti v. Yuba City Unified School Dist.*, 158 Cal.App.4th, 69 Cal.Rptr.3d 825 (Cal. Ct. App. 2007).

2. Governmental Immunity

Court Decisions

◆ At recess, a Massachusetts student chased a first-grader around an enclosed area and pushed him. The first-grader fell against the corner of a bench wall, suffering a severe injury. The principal had directed that first-graders have recess in the enclosed area, despite its sharp-cornered concrete bench-walls. In a state court action against the school system for negligence, school officials claimed immunity under the Massachusetts Tort Claims Act (MTCA). The Appeals Court of Massachusetts explained that the MTCA prevents liability for claims asserting an act (or failure to act) to prevent or diminish harmful acts by a third person "not originally caused by the public employer." In this case, the principal had ordered that first-grade recess be held in the concrete courtyard. According to the court, the causal link between the decision to hold recess in the enclosure and the injury was "not so remote" as to hold that the principal's decision was not an "original cause" of the injury. **The principal's decision to hold recess in the courtyard was not a "policymaking decision," and it was not entitled to discretionary immunity.** *Gennari v. Reading Public Schools*, 933 N.E.2d 1027 (Mass. App. Ct. 2010).

◆ The Court of Appeals of Wisconsin affirmed a trial court order granting immunity to a school district in a preschool student's negligence action. The parents sued the district after their child fell from play equipment in her classroom. The court held that the district was not required to transfer her to a new room based on a special education evaluation indicating that she required speech/language services. **The classroom teacher had exercised her discretion and judgment in creating classroom safety rules.** State law conferred immunity on political subdivisions and school officials for their discretionary acts. *Nagel v. Green Bay Area Public School Dist.*, 293 Wis.2d 362, 715 N.W.2d 240 (Table) (Wis. Ct. App. 2006).

◆ A 10-year-old Georgia student's teacher instructed her to get paper from heavy, eight-foot-high rolls standing upright in a storage garage. The student was killed when the roll fell on her as she tried to get paper from it. Her parents sued the district, its board and the teacher for wrongful death and intentional misconduct. A state trial court awarded pretrial judgment against the parents, finding the teacher and board were entitled to immunity. On appeal, the Georgia Court of Appeals stated that **the Georgia Supreme Court has previously held that supervising and disciplining students involves discretionary acts**. The teacher was found to be exercising her discretionary authority to monitor, control and supervise students when she sent fourth-graders to the garage. Because she was entitled to immunity, she could be liable only if her actions were motivated by actual malice or intent to cause injury. As there was no evidence of malice or intentional conduct, the court affirmed the judgment. *Aliffi v. Liberty County School Dist.*, 578 S.E.2d 146 (Ga. Ct. App. 2003).

B. Off School Grounds

1. Duty of Care

Courts have disagreed about the duty of a school to supervise students after they are dismissed from school. The age of the student plays a role in whether school liability exists. In a case involving an elementary student, New Jersey's Supreme Court held that "dismissal is part of the school day," creating a legal duty for schools to supervise dismissal. On the other hand, a Florida court recently found no duty to supervise high school students from unforeseen off-campus hazards. Courts in Louisiana and California have imposed a duty to supervise student safety at dismissal. And New York's highest court held that if a student is injured off school grounds, a school district could not be held liable because the district's duty of care only extended to its own boundaries.

Teacher Scenarios

Student falls asleep at the wheel on way home from post-prom party..50

Parent fails to supervise student who got hurt – but teacher must defend himself against charge........50

Court Decisions

◆ The New York Court of Appeals held that a school district was not liable for injuries suffered by a tenth-grader who was struck by a vehicle while crossing a street off school property. The district was not responsible for any hazardous condition off school grounds where the student was injured. A school's duty to its students "is co-extensive with the school's physical custody and control over them ..., and **when a student is injured off school premises the school district cannot be held liable for the breach of a duty that generally extends only to the boundaries of the school property**." The accident in this case occurred after school and off school property, and the municipality that owned the road was responsible for warning of any hazards on it. *Hess v. West Seneca Cent. School Dist.*, 15 N.Y.3d 813 (N.Y. 2010).

◆ Two female students in Idaho reported that two males were planning a Columbine-style attack at school. The principal confronted one of the male students, who said he was "going to have a school shooting" on a specified date. The two male students were warned about their threatening conduct, and they agreed not to make further statements. But one month later, the students were accused of threatening to shoot guns at a school dance. Two years after these incidents, one of the male students wrote threatening notes that were viewed by his locker partner. Although the threats were brought to the attention of the school resource officer and a vice principal, they were "dismissed." The same month as the notes were found, the student and a male accomplice murdered a female student at the house of her friend. When her parents sued the school district in a state trial court, it was found that the district owed no duty to protect the student off school grounds and after school hours. On appeal, the Supreme Court of Idaho affirmed the judgment. Nothing in the record convinced the court that the district knew that one of the male students would commit a murder based on information received about him some 30 months earlier. **As the murder was not foreseeable, the district had no duty to prevent it.** *Stoddart v. Pocatello School Dist. #25*, 239 P.3d 784 (Idaho 2010).

◆ A six-year-old California student took the bus irregularly, due to his parents' schedules. About a month after starting school, he got on his bus, but soon told the driver that he saw his father's car. The driver grabbed him by the arm and asked if he was sure, and he said he was. When the student left the bus, he could not find his father and began walking with other students. He was later struck by a car as he tried to cross a busy street. The family sued the school district, bus driver and car driver for personal injuries. A state superior court held for the district under the California Education Code, which provided immunity for accidents occurring off campus and after school hours.

The case reached the Court of Appeal of California, which recited the general rule in the state that **"a school district owes a duty of care to its students because a special relationship exists between the students and the district."** Once a district agreed to provide transportation for its students, it had a legal duty to exercise reasonable care. It rejected the district's claim that "transportation" occurred only while a bus was in motion. In this case, the district had undertaken a duty of care to its students for some time after dismissal. During the loading process, students were still on school premises, and under school supervision. As a result, the fact that the injury took place later and off-campus did not decide the case. The lower court should have considered whether there had been a duty of supervision, and whether the duty was breached. Once the child was on the bus, the district had a duty to exercise ordinary care over him. The case was returned to the superior court to consider questions such as the foreseeability of harm and whether the bus driver should have done more to help the student. *Eric M. v. Cajon Valley Union School Dist.*, 174 Cal.App.4th 285, 95 Cal.Rptr.3d 428 (Cal. Ct. App. 2009).

◆ Washington high school seniors bought six kegs of beer for an off-campus party at a remote location without adult supervision. At the party, three seniors confronted the only junior class member who attended. One of the seniors hit him on the forehead with a beer mug. Although the wound appeared minor, the junior collapsed and fell into a coma four months later. After surviving four years in a persistent vegetative state, the junior died. His estate sued the seniors who had bought the beer, the students who confronted him at the party, and the beer distributor that made the beer kegs available. The Court of Appeals of Washington held that **the non-assailant seniors could not be held liable for the attack on the junior without evidence that they knew the assailants had violent tendencies.** A state law forbidding the purchase of alcohol by minors did not give rise to a duty of care because the law was not intended to protect against assaults. *Cameron v. Murray*, 214 P.3d 150 (Wash. Ct. App. 2009).

♦ A nine-year-old New Jersey student was left quadriplegic after being struck by a car several blocks from school and about two hours after school dismissal. His family sued the car driver, the school principal and the board of education. They asserted that the district and principal breached their duty of reasonable supervision during dismissal. The complaint claimed the parents did not have advance notice on the day of the accident that it was an early-dismissal day. The family settled its claims against the car driver. But a state trial court then held that the board's duty did not apply to an accident that occurred two hours after dismissal and several blocks from school. A state appellate division court reversed the judgment, holding that school boards have a duty of reasonable care to supervise children at dismissal. The case was returned to the trial court.

The school district appealed to the Supreme Court of New Jersey, which explained that dangers to students continued at dismissal time because they were susceptible to numerous risks. It was foreseeable that young students leaving school grounds without parental supervision were vulnerable. A school's duty to exercise reasonable care for students was integral to the state's public education system. **"Dismissal is part of the school day." The school's duty of supervision did not disappear when the school bell rang.** The duty required school districts to create a reasonable dismissal supervision policy, provide notice to parents, and to comply with the policy and with parental requests concerning the dismissal of students from school. The court affirmed the decision of the appellate division court, and returned the case to the trial court for further proceedings. *Jerkins v. Anderson*, 191 N.J. 285, 922 A.2d 1279 (N.J. 2007).

♦ A New York kindergartner with asthma attended an early childhood center. His mother gave the school nurse asthma medication, an inhaler, and an authorization and directive from his pediatrician. A teacher and an aide noticed he was coughing and decided he should see the nurse. The aide walked him to the office, where the nurse gave him his medication. The student was reported as "breathing, alert and in no distress." He returned to class, and his mother was notified. When the mother arrived at school one hour later, the student was still able to breathe, walk and talk. She planned to take him to his pediatrician, but he became hot and ill in the car and she went home instead. The mother called 911, and emergency personnel treated the student without success. He was pronounced dead at a hospital emergency room. The mother sued the school district. A New York appellate division court noted that the student had been released to his mother's custody prior to his death. **Since she had removed him from the geographic boundaries of the district and the control of district staff, no legal duty existed that would create district liability.** *Williams v. Hempstead School Dist.*, 46 A.D.3d 550 (N.Y. App. Div. 2007).

♦ A Florida student died in an automobile crash after skipping class with several other eleventh-graders who simply walked to their cars and left school grounds. The car in which she was riding was driven at over 70 miles per hour. This occurred on wet roads in a residential area with a 35-mile-an-hour speed limit. The car crashed into a tree, killing the student. The student's estate sued the driver of the vehicle and the school board for negligence. A state trial court rejected the estate's argument that the board had a duty to prevent students from leaving campus, and that there was no duty to lessen the risk of injury off campus by preventing students from leaving campus. The estate appealed, claiming that lax enforcement of truancy rules made the death foreseeable.

A Florida District Court of Appeal found that none of the students had accumulated 15 unexcused absences, so they were not "habitually truant." **The court held that even if they were deemed habitually truant, there was no duty of the school board to protect them from unforeseen off-campus hazards.** The primary purpose of Florida truancy laws was to promote academic success, not to enhance student safety. School attendance rules did not impose a legal duty of care on the district to protect students from off-campus traffic injuries. The court found that "the decision whether to have an open campus, a 'fortress,' or something in-between, is a policy decision that should be left to school professionals and not second-guessed by civil juries." The court affirmed the judgment for the school board. *Kazanjian v. School Board of Palm Beach County*, 967 So.2d 259 (Fla. Dist. Ct. App. 2007).

♦ Two emotionally disturbed North Carolina students rode a public school bus to a program for violent students. A bus attendant overheard them speak about committing robbery and murder with a gun one of them had at home. The attendant reported their conversation to the bus driver, but neither employee informed school officials, the school board or the police department. A week later, the students and two other youths stopped cars at an intersection between 7:00 p.m. and 8:15 p.m. A student shot a driver in the head and severely injured her. The victim sued city and county education officials for personal injuries. A state trial court held for the board, and the victim appealed. The Supreme Court of North Carolina said school personnel who overheard students planning criminal conduct had a moral and civic obligation to report it. But this did not create a legal duty which afforded the victim relief. **No legal duty exists unless an injury "was foreseeable and avoidable through due care."** The board could not be held liable for actions by students without a "special relationship" with them. The victim was attempting to hold the board liable for the actions of students who were outside its control at 8:15 p.m. and not on school property. *Stein v. Asheville City Board of Educ.*, 626 S.E.2d 263 (N.C. 2005).

2. Governmental Immunity

In the next case, the Supreme Court of Alabama restated a general rule that an agent of the state is immune from civil liability for conduct based on the formulation of plans, policies or designs.

Court Decisions

◆ An Alabama sixth-grade student told her teacher she was sick and wanted to go home. The teacher instructed her to telephone her mother and she went to the office to do so. Later, an 18-year-old former student arrived at the office and identified himself as the student's brother. An instructional assistant who had been assigned to check students in and out from school allowed the student to leave with the former student. Staff members realized she had left school under false pretenses, and left school to search for her. After the former student sexually assaulted the student in a car, the student's family sued the school board, principal, instructional assistant, and secretary for negligence. A state trial court held the school board and the secretary were entitled to immunity.

But the court denied state-agent immunity to the teaching assistant and the principal. On appeal, **the Supreme Court of Alabama stated the general rule that an agent of the state is immune from civil liability for conduct based on the formulation of plans, policies or designs**. State agents are immune for claims based on the exercise of judgment in the discharge of duties imposed by statute, rule or regulation when educating students. The school's standard checkout procedure allowed students to leave with an older sibling, and the incident occurred while the principal and assistant were "discharging their official duties." The student did not show they acted "willfully, maliciously, fraudulently, in bad faith, or beyond their authority." The trial court should not have denied pretrial judgment to the principal and the teaching assistant. *In re T.W. v. Russell County Board of Educ.*, 965 So.2d 780 (Ala. 2007).

◆ The Court of Appeal of Florida held that a school board had sovereign immunity in a negligence lawsuit filed by a parent whose 13-year-old son was killed while walking home from school. The death occurred at an intersection with no crossing guard. The student was the fourth child to die in transit to or from the school in a seven-year period. The mother asserted that the decision to operate the school from 9:00 a.m. to 4:00 p.m. negligently exposed students to rush-hour traffic. **The court found the scheduling of school hours was a planning-level decision that deserved immunity.** The board did not create a hidden or dangerous condition for which there was no proper warning. Traffic hazards at the site were readily apparent, and court held the school board had no authority over the regulation of traffic. *Orlando v. Broward County, Florida*, 920 So.2d 54 (Fla. Dist. Ct. App. 2005).

V. LIABILITY FOR INTENTIONAL CONDUCT

Overview

"Willful or wanton misconduct" refers to intentional conduct. A finding of intentional, willful or wanton misconduct typically defeats immunity. Courts have found school districts liable for intentional acts of third parties on or near school grounds. In such cases, a court must find the district should have foreseen the potential misconduct.

A. Employee Misconduct

1. Types of Misconduct

Teacher Scenarios

Teacher follows policy – but gets
sued personally 51

Court Decisions

◆ A Georgia teacher was accused of shoving a disabled student's head into a trash can and then pulling him out by his legs. The principal investigated and, after finding that the teacher and student had often engaged in horseplay prior to the trash can incident, determined it was only horseplay. He found no evidence that the teacher acted maliciously. Although the teacher was counseled to end this type of conduct with students, the parents decided to sue. A federal court awarded pretrial judgment to the school district and officials, finding they were all entitled to qualified immunity. The Eleventh Circuit affirmed the judgment, finding the trash can incident did not violate the student's substantive due process rights. **Only intentional actions by officials that shock the conscience may be found to violate the Constitution.** As the lower court had found, the student did not suffer physical injury and there was no evidence that the teacher acted with malice or intent to harm him. Not all injuries to a student by a teacher amounted to corporal punishment. *Mahone v. Ben Hill County School System*, 377 Fed.Appx. 913 (11th Cir. 2010).

◆ A Louisiana high school teacher twice assaulted a student who had volunteered to work with special education students. Others complained about him and criminal charges were filed. He pleaded guilty to simple battery, was fined small amounts and served 30 days in jail. After settling claims against the teacher in a state court civil action, the student pursued the school board for further damages. A jury found the board should pay her $45,000, and the board appealed to the Court of Appeal of Louisiana. There, the board claimed it could not be held liable because the teacher was "merely dealing with a student-at-large who was not one of his students" at the time. The court held **the teacher was engaged in business so closely related to his teaching duties that the board was liable for his conduct.** The state supreme court has held employers should be held liable for employee misconduct if a wrongful act was rooted in employment, reasonably incidental to employment duties, occurred on the employer's premises and occurred during work hours. As the teacher's conduct met this test, and the damages were not excessive, the judgment was affirmed. *T.S. v. Rapides Parish School Board*, 11 So.3d 628 (La. Ct. App. 2009).

◆ A Michigan elementary school student claimed that classmates assaulted him at school twice within a few days. He said that he reported both incidents to the principal's secretary, who failed to notify the principal. The student's parent sued the school district and principal for negligence and gross negligence in a state trial court, which held for the school district. The parent appealed to the Court of Appeals of Michigan. The court explained that the operation of a school or a school system constitutes a governmental function. For this reason, the district had immunity from tort liability for any negligence or gross negligence. Accordingly, the lower court had correctly dismissed the tort action.

Government employees also enjoy immunity from tort liability if the injury is caused while they act in the course of their employment, or in the reasonable belief they are acting within the scope of their employment. On the other hand, a governmental employee is not immune from tort liability if an injury is caused by the employee's gross negligence. **"Gross negligence" is conduct so reckless that it demonstrates a substantial lack of concern for whether an injury results. It is an almost willful disregard for safety or precautions.** The student could not show gross negligence by the district or employees. He did not report either incident to his teacher. While the student claimed he reported the first incident to the principal's secretary, this did not show that she relayed the message to the principal. As the student failed to present evidence that the principal knew or should have known of the first fight, the court found no reasonable person could find her negligent, much less grossly negligent, for failure to investigate. The judgment was affirmed. *Reynolds v. Detroit Public Schools*, No. 276369, 2008 WL 2389492 (Mich. Ct. App. 6/12/08).

◆ The U.S. Court of Appeals, Fifth Circuit, affirmed a damage award for two Mississippi students who claimed a school bus driver arbitrarily excluded them from their bus based on their odor. A federal magistrate judge found the driver drove off while one student had his hand trapped in the bus door. On another occasion, the driver directly sprayed a student with deodorizer. The magistrate judge found the driver had arbitrarily suspended the children from their bus privileges. The Fifth Circuit agreed, finding that **"the bus driver acted preemptively and offensively rather than to control or discipline the children." This satisfied state Tort Claims Act standards.** As there was evidence of damages, the court affirmed the judgment for the students. *Turner v. North Panola School Dist.*, 299 Fed.Appx. 330 (5th Cir. 2008).

◆ In 2001, a California parent's 15-year-old daughter attended the same high school that the parent had attended about 25 years earlier. The daughter began to encounter an English teacher who had taught at the high school when her parent attended. The parent became upset, claiming that when she was 15 years old, the English teacher engaged her in sexual conduct both on and off school grounds for over two years. The parent did not notify the school district of the contact until 2003. A licensed mental health practitioner interviewed the parent and concluded that she still suffered from psychological injury from the sexual abuse. She sued the school district and the English teacher. The Court of Appeal of California found that a party is required to present a timely written claim for damages before suing a public entity. **The deadline for filing a lawsuit against a public entity is the statute of limitations for presenting claims against an entity such as a school district.** The parent was required to make a claim against the district by May 1980, six months after the last molestation. As the parent did not make a timely claim, the case was barred. *Shirk v. Vista Unified School Dist.*, 42 Cal.4th 201, 54 Cal.Rptr.3d 210, 164 P.3d 630 (Cal. 2007).

◆ A Missouri school district assigned a substitute to an elementary school classroom. He grabbed a student by the neck and lifted him off the ground. The teacher later pleaded guilty in state criminal court proceedings to third degree criminal assault and endangering the welfare of a child. The family accepted $20,000 in settlement of negligence claims against the district and board members, and agreed to settle claims against the teacher for $100,000. The agreement provided that any judgment would be sought from the district's insurer. The district had liability coverage through the Missouri United School Insurance Council (MUSIC), a pool of self-insuring school districts. After MUSIC declined to pay the judgment, the family sued for coverage. A state trial court awarded pretrial judgment to MUSIC. The case reached the Supreme Court of Missouri, which affirmed the judgment. It held that **the assault was an intentional act, and not a covered "occurrence" under the policy**. *Todd v. Missouri United School Insurance Council*, No. 223 S.W.3d 156 (Mo. 2007).

◆ An Arkansas student attended a band competition in Atlanta with his school band. He became ill and missed the entire competition while remaining in his hotel room. Shortly after the student returned home, his mother took him to a medical center. He suffered a cardiac arrest and died of a diabetic condition the next day. His mother sued the school district and officials for negligence and deliberate indifference to her son's medical needs. A federal court dismissed her constitutional claims, and the case went before the U.S. Court of Appeals, Eighth Circuit. It held the Due Process Clause does not confer affirmative rights to government aid. States assume a constitutional duty to protect safety only when they have restrained an individual's liberty through incarceration, institutionalization or a restraint that renders the individual incapable of self care. That did not happen here. **School officials have no duty to care for students who participate in voluntary school-related activities such as school band trips.** *Lee v. Pine Bluff School Dist.*, 472 F.3d 1026 (8th Cir. 2007).

2. Governmental Immunity

Court Decisions

◆ An Alabama fifth-grader repeatedly disrupted his class. An education board policy required the presence of a witness whenever corporal punishment was administered. When the student avoided his teacher's attempts to hit his palms with two taped-together rulers, she retrieved a paddle and hit him with it. She claimed this was the end of the incident. But the student claimed she kept hitting him, causing injury. He enrolled in another school and then sued the school board and teacher for negligence. A state court denied claims by both the education board and the teacher for judgment based on absolute immunity. On appeal, the Supreme Court of Alabama held the board had been wrongly denied immunity. It reversed that part of the judgment. But the board's policy required the presence of a witness whenever corporal punishment was administered. **The teacher's rationale for deviating from the policy was that she could not leave her other students alone to find a witness.** While this was supported by her statement and those of her supervisors, further inquiry by the trial court was necessary. *Ex Parte Monroe County Board of Educ.*, 48 So.3d 621 (Ala. 2010).

◆ A disabled Ohio student rode a bus with three middle school boys with special needs. An aide on the afternoon route saw a male student with his hand up the student's dress. They were immediately separated. When questioned, the female student said the male student had sexually molested her each day on the afternoon route. The parents claimed that the assaulting student had serious behavior problems and exhibited physical and verbal aggression. They sued the school board and officials in the state court system, asserting negligence and related claims. A trial court denied the board's motion for state law immunity.

The case reached the Supreme Court of Ohio, which noted that state law barred immunity for injuries arising from the "operation of any motor vehicle," but did not define the term "operation." According to the family, the term meant all the essential functions that a driver is trained or required to do by law, not just driving. A dictionary definition of "operate" is to "control or direct the functioning of." This suggested to the court that the term is limited to driving the vehicle itself. **The court held the exception to immunity for negligent operation of a motor vehicle applied only to negligence in driving the vehicle.** It held for the school board. *Doe v. Marlington Local School Dist. Board of Educ.*, 122 Ohio St.3d 124, 907 N.E.2d 706 (Ohio 2009).

◆ A Tennessee alternative school student repeated grade nine at another school in the same system. His disciplinary record was not forwarded from the alternative school. At his new school, the student began harassing a female student, and his name-calling and "unpleasant noises quickly escalated." An assistant principal received repeated reports from the female, her parents and others about the male student, and told the male student to avoid contact with the female. But he later knocked her unconscious in a school hallway and broke her jaw. She was hospitalized and underwent surgery. Her father sued the male student, his mother, the assistant principal and the school board in a Tennessee court. The assistant principal was dismissed from the case, but the court found the assault foreseeable and the school board negligent for failing to protect the female student. She received $75,000 for emotional distress, pain and suffering, and her parents won over $10,000 for medical costs. The state court of appeals rejected the board's claim to immunity under the doctrine of public duty. **School systems, teachers and administrators have a duty of reasonable care to supervise and protect students.** The board had a duty to protect students from foreseeable intentional acts of third parties such as the male student. As a result, the judgment was affirmed. *Dean v. Weakley County Board of Educ.*, No. W2007-00159-COA-R3-CV, 2008 WL 948882 (Tenn. Ct. App. 4/9/08).

◆ An Indiana high school student was shot to death before school started, in an area where students congregated prior to classes. The shooter was a former student with aggressive behavior and homicidal ideation. He was convicted of murder. At the time of the shooting, the school's security officers were inside the building, attending to other duties. The student's parents sued the school corporation for negligence. A state court held a jury trial and allowed evidence of several prior acts of violence involving district schools, including a drive-by shooting. After the trial, a jury awarded a verdict to the parents. On appeal, the Court of Appeals of Indiana agreed with the school corporation's argument that the prior incidents were not similar enough to the shooting to be admitted as evidence of school negligence. **Evidence of a dangerous condition and notice about the condition must be similar to the one at issue in order to be admissible.** But the court rejected the school corporation's claim to immunity under the state tort claims act. Officials did not show they made any policy decision regarding the placement of security staff. A new trial would be held. *Gary Community School Corp. v. Boyd*, 890 N.E.2d 794 (Ind. Ct. App. 2008).

◆ The parents of a 14-year-old South Carolina student learned a substitute had sexual relations with their child. The substitute was convicted of criminal sexual conduct with a minor. The parents sued the school district in a separate action, and a state court held for the district. On appeal, the Supreme Court of South Carolina affirmed the judgment on a claim for infliction of emotional distress. But it agreed with the parents that their claim for negligent supervision had been wrongly dismissed. The state Tort Claims Act precluded government liability for losses resulting from any responsibility or duty such as the supervision, protection, control, confinement, or custody of a student, except where the responsibility or duty was exercised in a "grossly negligent manner." Here, **the parents had alleged gross negligence by the district.** As a result, that claim had been improperly dismissed. The case had to be reconsidered. *Doe v. Greenville County School Dist.*, 375 S.C. 63, 651 S.E.2d 305 (S.C. 2007).

B. Student Misconduct

1. Types of Misconduct

In Dailey v. Los Angeles Unified School Dist., 2 Cal.3d 741, 87 Cal.Rptr. 376 (1970), the Supreme Court of California held school authorities are to "supervise at all times the conduct of the children on school grounds and to enforce those rules and regulations necessary to their protection." The standard of care for supervising students is that which a "person of ordinary prudence" would exercise when performing comparable duties.

Court Decisions

◆ A California student sued his school district for injuries caused by another student who beat him with a baseball bat off school grounds after school hours. According to the student, the district allowed his assailant to carry a bat around school during school hours, in view of teachers and administrators. He claimed the assailant threatened others with violence and had a history of violence and discipline at school. The district claimed discretionary immunity and argued it could not be held liable for an injury taking place off school grounds after school hours. The Court of Appeal of California agreed, finding **neither school districts nor their employees are liable for the conduct or safety of any student when not on school property, unless there is a specific undertaking by a school district** or a sponsored activity, which was not the case here. *Cortinez v. South Pasadena Unified School Dist.*, No. 2352046, 2010 WL 2352046 (Cal. Ct. App. 6/14/10).

◆ A 185-pound Louisiana student with autism began to hit himself on the head. His teacher was pushed into a wall while trying to keep a mat under him to prevent injury. During the 45-50 minute struggle, the teacher was "twisting and sliding the entire time" but was not hit, knocked down or bitten by the student. She reported injuries to her hand, knee and buttocks. Claiming entitlement to "assault pay" under a state law provision, the teacher sued the school board. A state trial court granted pretrial judgment to the board, but the Court of Appeal of Louisiana held that a trial was required. **"Assault pay" is available to teachers injured or disabled while acting in an official capacity as a result of an assault or battery.** Under the assault pay provision, injured or disabled teachers receive sick pay with no reduction in pay or accrued sick leave days while disabled as the result of the assault or battery. A separate provision covers teachers who are injured as a result of "physical contact" while assisting students. Here, the facts would determine if the teacher's injuries resulted from an "assault" by the student. *Miller v. St. Tammany Parish School Board*, Nos. 2008 CA 2582-2583, 2009 WL 3135208 (La. Ct. App. 9/11/09).

◆ A California school district operated a free after-school program on a school playground. Between 200 and 300 children participated, with two adults typically present to supervise them. One day, only one supervisor was present to watch over 113 participants. A second-grade girl was led by an older girl to an unlocked shed on campus that was off-limits to program participants. The older girl forced a boy to have sexual contact with the second-grader. Both the boy and the second-grader later said the girl held them against their wills and threatened to hit them. The second-grader's mother sued the school district for negligent supervision, claiming the district and employees knew for some time that some of the children had been kissing and engaging in other inappropriate activity. The case reached the state court of appeal, which noted that the after-school program was voluntary. A question remained regarding whether the absence of a supervisor from her post contributed to the injury. As a result, the case required further fact-finding. **If the supervisor allowed dangerous conduct to go on, liability could be imposed.** *J.H. v. Los Angeles Unified School Dist.*, 183 Cal.App.4th 123, 107 Cal.Rptr.3d 182 (Cal. Ct. App. 2010).

◆ A 14-year-old California student with multiple disabilities functioned in her public school on a "borderline basis." During a lunch period, a male special needs student led her from the cafeteria to a hidden alcove under a stairway and sexually assaulted her. A parent observed the students from a sidewalk and reported them to the school office. In the resulting negligence action against the district, a state court noted that the alcove was hidden from anyone on campus but visible from the sidewalk. The alcove was marked as off-limits by a yellow chain. While there had been no reported sexual assaults or other illicit activity in the alcove during school hours, it was considered a "problem area." A "tardy sweep" of the campus should have been conducted six minutes after every lunch period. But the students were found about 14 minutes after the final check of the alcove. The court held for the school district, and the student appealed.

The Court of Appeal of California held that **school officials had a special relationship to special needs students and had to adequately supervise them due to the foreseeability of harm**. School officials were on notice that the alcove was a problem area. As the district had an affirmative duty to protect the student based on a "special relationship" with her, it could be held liable. It also had potential liability for maintaining a dangerous condition of public property, since a yellow chain would not keep out a child who could not appreciate danger. *Jennifer C. v. Los Angeles Unified School Dist.*, 168 Cal.App.4th 1320, 86 Cal.Rptr.3d 274 (Cal. Ct. App. 2008).

◆ A Washington school district declared a school safe for a student who had been named on a "2 kill list" written by two others. The student's parents wanted one of the list writers suspended for the rest of the school year, and they sued the school district for negligence. A trial court held for the school district, and the parents appealed to the Court of Appeals of Washington. The court explained that school districts must protect students from reasonably anticipated dangers. **A duty to use reasonable care only extends to risks of harm that are foreseeable.** The court rejected the parents' claim that the list writer had to be expelled for the rest of the school year. The district had to consider his educational needs. The district acted within its authority by first expelling the writer on an emergency basis, then suspending him, and ultimately reducing the suspension on the basis of a psychiatrist's report. **The district was not obligated to impose discipline to accommodate the student's family.** It acted reasonably and according to the law and its own policies by relying on the psychiatrist's judgment. The judgment was affirmed. *Jachetta v. Warden Joint Consolidated School Dist.*, 142 Wash.App. 918, 176 P.3d 545 (Wash. Ct. App. 2008).

◆ Montana high school boys worked as towel boys and secretly watched and videotaped female students undressing in the school locker room over a period of almost two years. They showed the tapes to classmates during school hours. A teacher and the superintendent heard reports of possible videotaping, but took limited action. After a janitor discovered the boys' activity, several criminal and civil actions were filed. In one case, the female students sued the school district for privacy rights violations and interference with family relationships. A federal court held against the female students. To impose municipal liability, there must be a policy of inaction that is more than just negligence. The hiring of towel boys to serve in locker rooms for females was not a "state-created danger." **The failure to be more attentive or to supervise the boys may have been negligent, but it did not create any constitutional liability.** On appeal, the U.S. Court of Appeals, Ninth Circuit, cited a long-standing rule of federal law: a state's failure to protect persons from private violence does not create a constitutional injury. The district and officials were not deliberately indifferent to student rights and were not the "moving force" behind any violation of rights. *Harry A. v. Duncan*, 234 Fed.Appx. 463 (9th Cir. 2007).

◆ A Michigan teacher lined up most of her students in a hallway and led them to a computer class. She left five students in the classroom because they had not completed their work. One of the students who remained took a pistol out of his desk, put bullets into it, then shot and killed a classmate. The teacher was in the hallway at the time. The classmate's parent claimed the student was involved in several behavior incidents in the months before the shooting, including beating up other students and stabbing another student with a pencil. The parent sued the teacher, principal and school district in a federal district court for a variety of civil rights violations. The court held for the district and school employees, and the parent appealed. The U.S. Court of Appeals, Sixth Circuit, held **the teacher's act of leaving five students unsupervised in the classroom was not an "affirmative act" creating a specific risk to the classmate.** She would have been in about the same degree of danger had the teacher remained. The danger was the student's possession of the gun, not the teacher's positioning. The district was not liable for a civil rights violation because there was no evidence of a district policy or custom of depriving persons of constitutional rights. *McQueen v. Beecher Community Schools*, 433 F.3d 460 (6th Cir. 2006).

◆ A Tennessee student had a history of aggressive behavior and fighting in classes, but was not identified as having a disability. Soon after an assessment team evaluated him, he struck his teacher. The principal suspended him for 10 days and prepared to expel him. She then arranged an individualized education program (IEP) team meeting. The IEP team found the student ineligible for special education. But it found he had a "suspected disability" and that his case should be reopened. The principal decided to return the student to his classroom with a teacher's aide. On his first day back, he assaulted his teacher and the aide.

The teacher sued the school board in a state court. It granted the board immunity, and appeal went to the state court of appeals. According to the court, a school official's decision deserved immunity if it was based on a discretionary function. In this case, the principal was not bound by state and local zero-tolerance policies. She had to balance these mandates against conflicting IDEA requirements. While the student had not yet been declared eligible for special education, the IEP team indicated that further evaluation was warranted. **A federal "stay-put" rule did not allow the principal to expel the student.** Her testimony showed she exercised discretion in balancing competing policies. The judgment was affirmed. *Babb v. Hamilton County Board of Educ.*, No. E2004-00782-COA-R3-CV, 2004 WL 2094538 (Tenn. Ct. App. 2004).

2. Bullying

In Mirand v. City of New York, *84 N.Y. 44, 637 N.E.2d 263 (1994), New York's highest court held* **a school is liable for student-on-student violence only if it had "specific, prior knowledge of the danger that caused the injury." A student's acts must have been foreseeable by the district to impose liability.**

Teacher Scenarios

Teacher sent bullies to office: Was that enough? 51

'You let them harass my kid!' Mom's claim ends up in court..52

Court Decisions

◆ An Arizona parent called school administrators to report that a classmate was threatening her seventh-grade daughter. But the bullying and threats by the classmate escalated. A teacher called the mother to report rumors that the classmate was planning to attack the daughter. That afternoon, the classmate assaulted the daughter at school. Her family sued the school district and school and law enforcement officers in a federal court for civil rights violations. One of the claims alleged a deprivation of federal due process rights, while others asserted state law negligence and failure to train employees under Arizona's Anti-Bullying law. The court noted that under *DeShaney v.*

Winnebago County Dep't of Social Services, 489 U.S. 189 (1989), the Fourteenth Amendment does not generally require the government to prevent private citizens from harming each other. **No special relationship existed in this case that imposed an affirmative duty on school officials to protect the daughter from the classmate.** As Arizona courts had yet to interpret the anti-bullying statute, that claim was sent to a state court. *O'Dell v. Casa Grande Elementary School Dist. No. 4*, No. CV-08-0240-PHX-GMS, 2008 WL 5215329 (D. Ariz. 12/12/08).

◆ An Ohio student said that he was assaulted by a classmate he described as a "known bully." The classmate had been suspended before for fighting, but the district superintendent overturned the discipline after determining he did not instigate the fight. He was evaluated for a disability, but that was interrupted by a brief transfer to another school district. When he returned, he had disciplinary problems based on minor misconduct such as improper language and horseplay. The classmate attacked the student after gym class without provocation. The student was seriously injured, and his parents sued the school district in a state court for negligent supervision. The court granted the district immunity, and the parents appealed. The state court of appeals found earlier incidents involving the classmate were not unprovoked attacks. Staff members testified that he was not viewed as a bully or a disciplinary problem. While the classmate was disruptive at times, earlier incidents only showed he might be involved in horseplay or a provoked fight. **The classmate's prior disciplinary incidents did not make it foreseeable that he would commit an unprovoked criminal assault on the student.** The fact that he had been incarcerated was not enough to put the school on notice that he might attack the student. The court affirmed the judgment for the district. *Aratari v. Leetonia Exempt Village School Dist.*, No. 06 CO 11, 2007-Ohio-1567, 2007 WL 969402 (Ohio Ct. App. 3/26/07).

◆ Connecticut students persistently harassed and bullied a ninth-grade student with attention deficit hyperactivity disorder (ADHD) who was under five feet tall and weighed only 75 pounds. He claimed school employees knew of the harassment and bullying, but did nothing about it. He withdrew from school, and his family sued the school board in a federal court. They asserted claims under the IDEA, conspiracy to deprive the student of his due process and equal protection rights, and negligence. The court dismissed the case, and the family appealed. The Second Circuit held that the Due Process Clause of the Fourteenth Amendment creates no affirmative right to government protection. **Failure of school employees to respond to harassment and bullying conduct, while "highly unfortunate," did not create constitutional liability.** The lower court also properly dismissed the student's equal protection claim. He did not allege that school employees treated him differently because of his size or his ADHD. But the Second Circuit has recognized monetary claims based on IDEA violations under 42 U.S.C. § 1983, and the lower court would have to reconsider that claim. State law negligence claims were also reinstated. *Smith v. Guilford Board of Educ.*, 226 Fed.Appx. 58 (2d Cir. 2007).

◆ An Illinois student was reluctant to go to school after being bullied, shoved and kicked. His mother complained to the principal but did not identify the bullies. She later called a school social worker to obtain counseling for her son. She told the social worker the names of the bullies and said that her son did not wish them to be revealed. The social worker agreed not to disclose their names but soon provided them to the principal. The principal then met with the bullies and revealed the student's name before assigning them to detention. The student claimed to suffer emotional distress from the disclosure of his name to the bullies. He transferred schools and filed a state court privacy rights violation action against the principal, social worker, school board and the rural special education cooperative that employed the social worker. The Appellate Court of Illinois held the social worker was protected by state law, which **permits a good-faith disclosure to protect a person against a clear, imminent risk of serious injury.** He had discretion to decide whether disclosing confidential information was necessary to protect the student and relayed this information to the principal in the belief there was a risk of further harm. And the principal's handling of bullying fell within the definition of "discretionary" action. *Albers v. Breen*, 346 Ill.App.3d 799, 806 N.E.2d 667 (Ill. App. Ct. 2004).

3. Governmental Immunity

Court Decisions

◆ Parents of an Ohio student with Down syndrome claimed he was sexually assaulted at school by a school district employee. Their state court complaint said the assault occurred under circumstances that showed recklessness and "an extreme lack of teacher oversight" in a classroom. The parents claimed the school knew one of the attackers had a history of psychological problems and that dangerous students were recklessly placed in the classroom. Also, regular and substitute teachers were reckless in monitoring class activities. The Court of Appeals of Ohio noted that school employees were accused of failing to monitor student behavior. This activity was within the scope of their official job duties. **An assault under circumstances of recklessness and "an extreme lack of teacher oversight" was sufficient to establish potential liability.** *E.F. v. Oberlin City School Dist.*, No. 09CA009640, 2010 WL 1227703 (Ohio Ct. App. 3/31/10).

◆ A Nebraska student claimed that she was sexually assaulted by a classmate at their high school during school hours. She claimed he had a history of physical and/or sexual misconduct toward other students, but that school officials took no steps to restrain him. The family sued the school district for negligence. A court held that the district was immunized from liability by the Nebraska Political Subdivisions Tort Claims Act (PSTCA). The family appealed to the Supreme Court of Nebraska, which explained that the PSTCA eliminated in part the traditional immunity of school districts for the negligent acts of their employees. **Districts are now generally liable for wrongful acts to the same extent as a private individual** *in a similar case.* The complaint alleged that the district had prior knowledge of specific behavior by the classmate that made violent conduct reasonably foreseeable. The court therefore rejected the district's sovereign immunity defense. *Doe v. Omaha Public School Dist.*, 273 Neb. 79, 724 N.W.2d 447 (Neb. 2007).

◆ A Mississippi cheerleader claimed male students surreptitiously videotaped her changing into a swimsuit at an off-campus pool party. Her mother sued the parents of the male students and obtained a restraining order against the boys. Juvenile court proceedings were also instituted. But the principal found no evidence of harassment. The school was unable to place one of the boys in a separate accelerated biology class, as it was the only such class offered at the time. The mother claimed that the boys and their parents harassed the cheerleader at sporting events. She sued the school system for negligence.

A state trial court found much of her testimony about harassment concerned off-campus conduct. It found the school system took reasonable steps to prevent the harassment and was immune from suit under the Mississippi Tort Claims Act (MTCA). The mother appealed to the Court of Appeals of Mississippi. It held the evidence did not support a finding that the school system breached a duty to the student. Instead, there was "substantial proof that the district met and exceeded any duty owed" the student. **The school system was not responsible for any harassment the student suffered outside of school that was linked to the videotaping.** The school system took reasonable steps to investigate the cafeteria incident, and the teacher monitored the students in class. The school system was immune from any liability under the MTCA. *Beacham v. City of Starkville School System*, 984 So.2d 1073 (Miss. Ct. App. 2008).

C. Parent Misconduct

Teacher Scenarios

Drawing the line when dealing with difficult students – and parents 53

Court Decisions

1. Sign-Out Policies

◆ After a Kentucky child was picked up from school by an unauthorized individual, the parent sued the education board and superintendent for negligence. The case reached the Court of Appeals of Kentucky, which stated that immunity applied to the board if it was performing a "governmental function." Here, the board's after-school pick-up and drop-off policy directly furthered the education of students, which was a governmental function. So the board was entitled to immunity. According to the parent, the superintendent did not investigate, take disciplinary action or enact policies to prevent future incidents. But the court held these alleged failures did not strip the superintendent of immunity. **Nothing in the complaint alleged any failure by the superintendent to exercise personal discretion, in good faith and within the scope of his authority.** Both the school board and superintendent were entitled to immunity. *Breathitt County Board of Educ. v. Combs*, No. 2009-CA-000607-MR, 2010 WL 3515747 (Ky. Ct. App. 9/10/10).

◆ A Louisiana father gave his children's middle school documentation that he had their sole "provisional custody." He claimed that they could only be released to him. School policy allowed only the persons listed on a check out form to sign a student out of school. When the children's mother appeared at their school prior to a holiday break, the principal telephoned the father. He stated that under no circumstances could they be released to her, and that he would come to the school. But when the father arrived at school 20 minutes later, the principal had already released the children to the mother. The father sued the school board, principal and insurer. After the case was dismissed, the Court of Appeal of Louisiana held that the father's claims for out-of-pocket expenses could proceed if the school officials owed him a duty to refrain from allowing the mother to check the children out of school. **Schools have a "duty to make the appropriate supervisory decisions concerning a student's departure from campus during regular school hours."** As the father asserted violation of the policy on checking-out students, and claimed the sole authority to do so, the principal had violated the policy and her duty to the children and father. *Peters v. Allen Parish School Board*, 996 So.2d 1230 (La. Ct. App. 2008).

◆ A Tennessee couple began divorce proceedings. The wife obtained a temporary restraining order splitting custody of the children. She told school staff not to release the children to their father, but a staff member told her that would require a court order. The husband signed the children out of school early the next day, giving as a reason: "keeping promise by mother" for the daughter and "pay back" for the son. A staff member read the reasons for early dismissal on the sign-out sheet after the father left, and she told the principal. Police were called. They arrived at the father's house to find it ablaze. The father brandished a knife, and the police shot him to death. The children's bodies were found inside the house. Later, the mother sued the school board for negligence in the state court system. A trial court held for the board, and the mother appealed.

The state court of appeals held that the board was not liable for negligently violating its own sign-out policy. There was no evidence that staff knew of a dispute until the mother called the day before the murders. The trial court had correctly held that a **school has no legal duty to follow the instruction of one parent not to release a child to the other parent without a court order to this effect**. But failure to read the father's reasons for signing out the children was evidence of breach of the duty to exercise ordinary care for safety. The court rejected a claim that the board had no duty to examine the reason for signing out a child. The trial court was to further consider this claim.

Haney v. Bradley County Board of Educ., 160 S.W.3d 886 (Tenn. Ct. App. 2004).

◆ An Alaska father had legal custody of his son, and the child's mother had visitation during the Christmas and summer vacations. The father warned the principal that the mother would attempt an abduction. A state court stayed enforcement of the parties' custody order pending investigations in Alaska and Washington. Just before Christmas vacation, the mother arrived at school to pick up the student, accompanied by a police officer. The principal noted that the custody order provided by the father did not specify visitation terms. The mother produced her copy of a previous order granting her visitation rights. The principal called the father, who objected to releasing the student. However, the principal released the student to the mother after a discussion with the police officer. The mother refused to return the student to the father after the Christmas break and he was unable to regain custody for over five months. The father sued the district and principal for interference with his custodial rights.

A state trial court held the principal and district were entitled to qualified immunity. On appeal, the Supreme Court of Alaska held state law established official immunity for "discretionary actions," which require personal deliberation, decision and judgment. The court found **the principal's actions were discretionary, since he acted with deliberation and made a considered judgment** after speaking with the father, verifying the mother's identification, reviewing legal documents and consulting with the police. His actions were not malicious, corrupt or in bad faith and were not subject to any exception to immunity. *Pauley v. Anchorage School Dist.*, 31 P.3d 1284 (Alaska 2001).

2. Parental Liability

Section 316 of the Restatement of Torts (a legal encyclopedia) states there is no legal duty for parents to prevent harm by their children unless "they are in a position to exercise immediate control over their children to prevent some foreseeable harm." Parents have no duty "to take precautionary disciplinary measures or to regulate their children's behavior on an ongoing basis."

Court Decisions

◆ A Minnesota teacher had several confrontations with a parent. Eventually, the teacher obtained a restraining order against the parent and sent a copy of the order to her principal. The school district's counsel determined the order did not prohibit the parent from entering the school. It only prevented her from coming near the teacher's classroom. Within three months, the teacher saw the parent in the school and called 911 to report a violation of the order. She then left school for the rest of the day. The district maintained that the parent had not violated the harassment order and suspended the teacher without pay for three days.

Near the end of the school year, the teacher saw the parent while she was escorting her class to a school bus. She left school for the day and later sued the district and the parent for negligence. A state court held that the district was entitled to official immunity. The teacher won a judgment against the parent for $32,205 for assault, then appealed the decision for the school district to the state court of appeals. The court found the teacher's whistleblowing was not a "report" within the meaning of Minnesota law. Also, a state law requirement for schools to adopt anti-harassment policies did not concern parents; it applied only to students, teachers, school employees and administrators. **The parent's harassment did not violate any contractual obligation of the district.** The judgment for the district was affirmed. *Ellison-Harpole v. Special School Dist. No. 1*, No. A07-1070, 2008 WL 933537 (Minn. Ct. App. 4/8/08).

◆ An Illinois teacher claimed that a student charged at her with scissors and threatened to stab her while screaming obscenities. She was able to disarm the student, who ran out of the room, kicked the door, and slammed it shut on her finger. The teacher sued the school district and the student's mother. She claimed that the parent had prior knowledge of the student's arrest record, mental illness, conduct disorder, character, and history of outbursts in class. A federal court held the parent could not be held liable simply because she was the student's mother. Liability required proof that the parent did not adequately control or supervise her son. To state a claim for negligent supervision, the teacher had to show the parent was aware of specific prior conduct that put her on notice that the assault was likely to occur, and had the opportunity to control the student. **Parents have a duty to exercise "reasonable care" to control their minor children and prevent them from intentionally harming others.** The court found no duty of parents to "take precautionary disciplinary measures or to regulate their children's behavior on an ongoing basis." Since parental liability may result only if parents are in position to exercise immediate control over their children to prevent some foreseeable harm, the court granted the parent's motion to dismiss the teacher's claim against her. *Bland v. Candioto*, No. 3:05-CV-716RM, 2006 WL 2735501 (N.D. Ill. 2006).

◆ Under Louisiana law, parents are legally accountable for the acts of their children. An 11-year-old student with impulsivity and aggression problems pointed a toy gun at a teaching assistant (TA). The TA did not know the gun was a toy and claimed to be emotionally and mentally traumatized. The TA received workers' compensation benefits for psychological injuries. The school board sued the student's mother, claiming that the student was negligent and that the mother was personally liable for his actions. A trial court held for the mother. On appeal, the state court of appeal held **Louisiana parents of minor children can be liable for harm caused by a child's conduct even where a parent is not personally negligent**. But the student could be deemed negligent only if a court found that he violated the applicable standard of care. Here, given the student's maturity level, lack of awareness of risks and his inclination to be impulsive and aggressive, he did not breach the standard. As the student was not negligent, his mother could not be held liable for his actions. *Lafayette Parish School Board v. Cormier*, 901 So. 2d 1197 (La. Ct. App. 2005).

D. Duty to Report Abuse and Neglect

State laws require the reporting of suspected child abuse or neglect by teachers and other mandatory reporters and afford immunity for good-faith reports. New York recently amended its child abuse reporting law to clarify that mandated reporters who work for a school must report suspected child abuse or maltreatment **themselves.** *Schools are not to designate an agent to make reports on behalf of a mandated reporter and are prohibited from putting any conditions upon child abuse or maltreatment reports by mandated reporters. New York's highest court has suggested that teachers and other state-mandated reporters of child abuse and neglect "ought to err on the side of caution and make a report" if they reasonably suspect child abuse or neglect.*

Teacher Scenarios

School gets caught up in
parental-abuse case 53

Teacher spots a bruise on a student: Parent insists,
'It's none of your business' 54

Principal and teacher follow policy over
report of sexual abuse: Should they have
done more? 54

Good student suddenly starts acting up in class –
what's going on? 55

Court Decisions

◆ A Texas court acquitted a teacher of charges of indecency with a child. He then sought expunction (erasure) of records relating to the charges. Some of the records were in the possession of the Texas Education Agency (TEA). A court ordered the TEA to return all files and records pertaining to the teacher "arising out of the transaction of indecency with a child" and his subsequent arrest. The Court of Appeals of Texas noted that an agency may possess and retain documents related to an acquitted defendant that are not subject to expunction. Child abuse reports and internal investigations were subject to expunction if they referenced police records and files relating to the arrest. **The TEA could have files pertaining to the teacher that were separate from those relating to his criminal investigation, arrest and prosecution.** State law did not intend to erase all evidence of underlying misconduct. While evidence of a criminal investigation, arrest and prosecution was to be expunged, TEA documents from its internal investigation were not. *Texas Education Agency v. T.G.F.*, 295 S.W.2d 398 (Tex. Ct. App. 2009).

◆ California first-graders claimed a substitute molested them at a Central School District (CSD) school. The students sued CSD and three other school districts that formerly employed the substitute, claiming each failed its mandatory duty to report suspected child abuse. One of those districts argued that it had no duty to protect students not in its district from potential abuse in the future. The district argued the Supreme Court of California refused to find such a broad duty under the state Reporting Act in *Randi W. v. Muroc Joint Unified School Dist.*, 14 Cal.4th 1066, 60 Cal.Rptr. 263 (1997). After considering 2000 amendments to the Reporting Act, the court held that the legislature did not intend to overcome the *Randi W.* rule that **"future victims were not within the class of persons intended to be protected by the statute."**

On appeal, the Court of Appeal of California noted that the first-graders did not attend the former district at the time of the misconduct. Nor was the substitute under the former district's supervision at that time. The Reporting Act protected children in the custodial care of the person charged with abuse, not all those who might be abused by the same offender in the future. According to the court, *Randi W.* was not intended to extend liability to all children who might conceivably be harmed, even years later, for a reporter's failure to report suspected injury to a child. *P.S. v. San Bernardino City Unified School Dist.*, 94 Cal.Rptr. 788 (Cal. Ct. App. 2009).

◆ A Kentucky kindergartner reported to her mother that another girl in her class had "put her finger up my butt" while they were at school. The mother called the teacher, who assured her the girls would be separated. But the kindergartner later reported that the other girl had been "up my butt" during a classroom reading group. The teacher immediately questioned the other girl, who admitted touching the kindergartner. The teacher was unable to find an administrator for advice at this time, so she carried on with her instructional duties. That evening, the kindergartner told her aunt that the girl had fingered her genitals. The kindergartner's mother reported the improper touching to the school principal the next day. After a conference, the other girl admitted she had "accidentally touched" the kindergartner between the legs.

The principal deemed the incidents to be accidents and did not report them to child protection authorities. The kindergartner reported more conduct by the other girl of a sexual nature. A physical examination of the kindergartner found she had some irritation of the vagina. Medical personnel then reported their observations to the police. The mother sued the school district, teacher and district's insurer for negligently failing to report and investigate. A state court found the teacher's supervision of the children was in good faith and was a discretionary function. The board and teacher were entitled to state law immunity. On appeal, the Court of Appeals of Kentucky held that **it is well-established state law that public school teachers may be held liable for negligent supervision of students**. As the lower court had given no analysis of the discretionary acts issue, the court vacated the judgment and returned the case to the trial court. *Nelson v. Turner*, 256 S.W.3d 37 (Ky. Ct. App. 2008).

◆ New York parents sought the names of school employees who reported them for suspected child abuse and maltreatment to the statewide central register. In response to the report, the parents sued the school district and an employee in a state court, asserting claims for defamation and intentional infliction of emotional distress. They sought to compel the disclosure of the names of the persons who reported the incidents. The court granted the motion and the district appealed. The New York Supreme Court, Appellate Division, stated Social Services Law Section 422 makes reports to the central register confidential and available only to persons and agencies listed by statute.

The court stated the parents, as the subjects of the report, were entitled to see the report, but not the names of the reporters. It rejected the trial court's reasoning that because a court could obtain these names, it had an implied right to release them to the subject. While the parents might encounter difficulty in bringing their civil action against the reporters, **Social Services Laws Sections 419 and 422 did not permit the release of reporter names based on allegations that the reporters acted with wilful misconduct or gross negligence**. This holding was consistent with the intent of Section 422 to protect the confidentiality of reporters of suspected child abuse. Disclosure of the names might have a chilling effect on reporting and hamper agency efforts to help families. The court reversed the trial court order. *Selapack v. Iroquois Cent. School Dist.*, 794 N.Y.S.2d 547 (N.Y. App. Div. 2005).

◆ A student who attended a private school in Massachusetts claimed the 22-year-old brother of a classmate forced her to have sex with him when she was 15. The incident occurred off school grounds. The brother had previously sexually abused another student and his own sister. The student sued the school in a Massachusetts court for negligently failing to report the brother's history of sexually abusing other students to the state Department of Social Services. The court held for the school, and the student appealed. The Court of Appeals of Massachusetts held that to prove the school was negligent, the student had to first show it had a duty to protect her. She was not on school property and was under her parents' control at the time of the assault. **The state child abuse reporting statute created no duty for the school to protect unnamed, potentially at-risk children in the abstract.** It was instead intended to protect specific children that a reporter had reasonable cause to believe were at risk. The court affirmed the judgment for the school. *S.I. v. Sennott*, 65 Mass. App. Ct. 1102, 836 N.E.2d 350 (Table) (Mass. App. Ct. 2005).

◆ An Ohio teacher was investigated for inappropriately touching and making sexual remarks to a ninth-grader. The principal determined the student was lying and took no action. The allegation was not reported to the police or a child services agency. Three years later, the teacher sexually assaulted another ninth-grader in a school athletic equipment room. The student and her parents sued the school board, alleging that its failure to report the first incident violated mandatory state abuse and neglect reporting requirements. A court held that the board was entitled to sovereign immunity. The Court of Appeals of Ohio affirmed the sovereign immunity ruling and determined that state law created a duty only to a specific child. Failure to report the 1996-97 incident could result in liability to that child, but not a different one. The Supreme Court of Ohio found that **teachers and school officials have a special responsibility to protect students committed to their care and control**. They should appreciate that all students are in danger when an abuse report is received about a teacher. A school board could be held liable for failing to report sexual abuse of a minor student by a teacher, when the failure caused the abuse of another minor student by the same teacher. *Yates v. Mansfield Board of Educ.*, 102 Ohio St.3d 205, 808 N.E.2d 861 (Ohio 2004).

◆ A New Jersey principal covered his school office windows in violation of a state law and always kept the door locked. The district superintendent did not monitor this and other violations, and the school board took no action to ensure he complied with the law. A school secretary frequently heard the principal taking pictures of students in his office but failed to report it because he was her "superior." Other staff observed many questionable incidents involving the principal and male students, but no one reported him. Law enforcement investigators arrested the principal for suspected child abuse and found 176 photographs in his office of male students with their legs spread in a chair. The parents of two student victims sued him, and a jury returned a verdict of $275,000 for each student, adding over $100,000 for their parents.

The court entered a judgment of over $775,000 against the board, and the case reached the Supreme Court of New Jersey, which upheld the trial court's liability finding against the board. Here, the **board did not fulfill its most basic obligation of protecting students and did not implement even rudimentary reporting procedures**. The board "grossly disregarded critical information" requiring scrutiny of the principal's activities. School nurses and others breached their independent state law obligation to report child abuse to the appropriate state agency. *Frugis v. Bracigliano*, 827 A.2d 1040 (N.J. 2003).

◆ A South Dakota elementary school counselor met several times with a third-grader, who said that her father had asked her to touch his penis. The counselor discussed the student's statements with a high school guidance counselor and decided the third-grader's reports were probably untrue, based on the student's tendency to fabricate or exaggerate. District policy forbade employees from speaking with parents about abuse allegations, but the counselor discussed the child's statements with the parents. Over a year later, the father pled guilty to sexually assaulting a neighbor child.

The sheriff's office questioned the counselor, who admitted contacting the parents. The state then brought criminal charges against the counselor for failing to report child abuse. The charges were eventually dismissed, but the district notified the counselor of its intent to fire her. The

Supreme Court of South Dakota found no evidence to support the district's conclusion that the failure to report child abuse was a breach of the counselor's contract. When the board nevertheless voted to discharge the counselor without making additional findings of fact, the supreme court noted that the board failed to make the required findings of fact in support of its decision. **In the absence of a finding in the record that the counselor suspected child abuse, the board action was arbitrary, capricious and an abuse of discretion.** *Hughes v. Stanley County School Dist.*, 638 N.W.2d 50 (S.D. 2001).

E. Suicide

Teacher Scenarios

Expelled student commits suicide, mom blames teacher: Was she liable? 55

What seemed like an innocent case of teasing turned into a school's worst nightmare 56

Court Decisions

◆ A New Hampshire student with learning disabilities was having problems at his middle school. During his seventh-grade year, a teacher's aide overheard him say he "wanted to blow his brains out." A guidance counselor called the student's mother, and had the student sign a contract for safety, but she took no other action. Several weeks later, the mother claimed that a special education teacher made a false and knowing attempt to impose discipline on her son. The next day, the student was reported to the vice principal and suspended. After the suspension, the student returned home, went to his room and hanged himself.

The mother sued the school administrative unit, a teacher and the guidance counselor for negligence, intentional infliction of emotional distress and wrongful death. A court dismissed the case, and the Supreme Court of New Hampshire affirmed. **It rejected the mother's claim that the counselor and administrative unit had a special duty to prevent the suicide** and that the counselor voluntarily assumed a duty to prevent it. There was no intentional or malicious conduct in this case that might create a duty to prevent the suicide. The administrative unit did not have actual physical custody over the student in such a manner that liability could be imposed. A false statement by the teacher leading to the student's discipline did not satisfy the high standard of "extreme and outrageous conduct" for infliction of emotional distress claims. *Mikell v. School Administrative Unit #33*, 972 A.2d 1050 (N.H. 2009).

◆ A Minnesota student killed himself after returning home from school. The student used a gun and ammunition he found in the house. A suicide note and his mid-term grades were found next to his body. The family sued the school district, claiming the suicide was a foreseeable consequence of bullying and school negligence that the district had a duty to prevent. A court held for the district, as did the state court of appeals. While Minnesota schools have a duty to protect students, they are not liable for sudden, unanticipated misconduct. Here, the suicide was not foreseeable. School staff had no reason to know of the student's continuing problems with bullying, because he did not report them. As there was no foreseeable harm, there was no duty to protect him. The court rejected claims by the estate that the principal should have proactively intervened with the bullies. **There was no evidence that a school bullying policy would have prevented the tragedy.** *Jasperson v. Anoka-Hennepin Independent School Dist. No. 11*, No. A06-1904, 2007 WL 3153456 (Minn. Ct. App. 10/30/07).

◆ A student who formerly attended an Idaho high school committed suicide. His estate tried to hold the Idaho district liable because an essay he wrote for a class showed that he had contemplated suicide in the past. He also wrote that he had "turned his life around" and was currently happy. The state legislature had enacted a law providing that **neither a school district nor a teacher had a duty to warn of a student's suicidal tendencies "absent the teacher's knowledge of direct evidence of such suicidal tendencies."** The law stated that "direct evidence" included "unequivocal and unambiguous oral or written statements by a student" that would not cause doubts in a reasonable teacher. The legislature adopted the new provision specifically to narrow the duty of a teacher to warn of a student's suicidal tendencies. The student's words provided an opposite conclusion to the one urged by his parents. *Carrier v. Lake Pend Oreille School Dist. No. 84*, 142 Idaho 804, 134 P.3d 655 (Idaho 2006).

F. Defamation

As teachers are deemed "public officials," they must show a false statement has been published to a third party, with "actual malice" and damages in order to recover in a defamation case. The actual malice standard is difficult to meet. A person seeking recovery in a defamation suit must prove the publication has caused damage to his or her reputation. Privilege is a defense to certain defamation claims. Persons with a common interest in the subject matter of speech (such as a teacher's performance) may enjoy a privilege to discuss their common interest in protecting students.

Teacher Scenarios

'Vulgar' reference to student makes it into print: Now, parents want to know who's responsible 56

Court Decisions

◆ Most of the students attending a Minnesota charter school were Somali Muslims. The American Civil Liberties Union of Minnesota (ACLU) sued the charter school, its directors and state education officials in a federal court to halt the school's allegedly religious practices – such as the posting of prayers, school prayer sessions, the enforcement of a school dress code, dietary practices and the bus schedule. In responding to the lawsuit, the school filed five counterclaims against the ACLU, including defamation and interference with its business relationships with the parents of students. These claims were based on comments made by the ACLU outside of the litigation. However, the court refused to allow the claims to move forward. The Charter School Law made charter schools a part of the state system of public education. And **established law prohibited government bodies from suing for libel, defeating the defamation claim**. Since the claim for interference with business relationships only duplicated the defamation claim, the ACLU was entitled to dismissal of both claims. *ACLU of Minnesota v. Tarek Ibn Ziyad Academy*, No. 09-138, 2009 WL 4823378 (D. Minn. 12/9/09).

◆ A South Carolina special education teacher formed a close bond with a student and let him use her car, unaware that he did not have a license. She also gave him school computer passwords and wrote him excuses from his classes. The principal fired her after learning of this. She was also arrested and charged with contributing to the delinquency of a minor. Later, the principal told a staff member that the teacher had "cleaned [them] out," referring to the fact that when she left, she took a great deal of equipment that she had purchased. She sued the principal for defamation and raised other claims. The state court of appeals held that she could pursue the defamation claim against the principal because **she was accused of a crime involving moral turpitude**. *McBride v. School Dist. of Greenville County*, 698 S.E.2d 845 (S.C. Ct. App. 2010).

◆ An Indiana principal notified a parent that his access to the school where his three children attended would be restricted because he was a convicted sex offender. After the parent supplied proof that he was not the sex offender, the principal wrote him a formal apology. But the parent stated that school officials continued to treat him as a sex offender and spread this belief throughout the community. He and his wife sued the school board, school officials and the city, alleging slander, civil rights violations and other claims. The defendants sought to have the case dismissed. But a federal court refused to do so. The parents alleged intentional treatment different from other parents regarding the pick-up and drop-off of their children, without a rational basis. **The parents also raised an issue of false allegations by the principal "accusing them of being on the run from Florida law enforcement."** *Luera v. City of Ft. Wayne*, 2010 No. 1:09-CV-136 JVB, 2010 WL 3021514 (N.D. Ind. 7/29/10).

◆ A Maine student left a ham sandwich on a cafeteria table where Somali Muslim students were sitting. The school suspended the student for 10 days and classified the incident as a hate crime/bias offense. A reporter contacted the superintendent and quoted him as saying that work had to be done to bring the community together. A user of a website platform called "Associated Content" posted an Internet article that mischaracterized facts and described the response to the incident by a Somali community center as an "anti-ham response plan." Fox Network staff members retrieved the user's contrived article, read the reporter's original article, and based a three-hour cablecast on the incident. Two Fox co-hosts repeatedly ridiculed the superintendent and attributed a contrived anti-Somali statement to him. Fox later issued a retraction and apology, but the superintendent sued one of the cohosts and others for defamation.

A federal court held the statements were protected, and appeal went to the U.S. Court of Appeals, First Circuit. It held discussions of public officials such as the superintendent deserved "breathing space" under the Constitution. **A conditional privilege of free speech may only be overcome by clear and convincing evidence that a speaker made a defamatory statement with actual knowledge of its falsity.** Courts describe this as the "actual malice" standard. While some statements were defamatory, they did not meet the actual malice standard. The "anti-ham response plan" statement was not defamatory, as the court found it "imaginative expression" or "rhetorical hyperbole." It was not suggested that the co-hosts knew the Associated Content posting was false. While the cohosts carelessly relied on the Associated Content posting, this was negligence, not actual malice. *Levesque v. Doocy*, 560 F.3d 82 (1st Cir. 2009).

◆ A West Virginia school employee learned he would be transferred due to declining enrollment. He requested a hearing, posted the location and date of the hearing and wrote "This is the night to expose the cockroaches." He accused the board treasurer and superintendent of being "thieves," and implied that another board member lived with "his mistress." He claimed that funds for the school golf team were "stolen" for team travel, although this claim had been investigated and no impropriety found. At his hearing, the employee reasserted his accusations against board members and the superintendent, never reaching the substance of his own transfer. The superintendent advised the employee he would be recommending employment termination based on insubordination. In response, the employee called the superintendent more epithets. The board then voted to fire the employee for insubordination. After a grievance board upheld the action, a state court ordered him reinstated, finding his speech protected.

On appeal, the Supreme Court of Appeals of West Virginia noted the grievance board had found the employee's conduct was insubordinate. A school board's need to conduct its affairs far outweighed any right to make personal and potentially unfounded and damaging remarks against school officials. **Statements that are knowingly false, or made with reckless disregard of whether they are true, are unprotected** by the First Amendment. The employee's speech was not protected. *Alderman v. Pocahontas County Board of Educ.*, 223 W.Va. 431, 675 S.E.2d 907 (W.Va. 2009).

◆ A Nevada school administrator obtained an evaluation of courses offered by a distance learning software seller and found that they did not comply with salary enhancement provisions of the relevant collective bargaining agreement. The seller demanded recognition of its classes and threatened legal action. The administrator wrote to the seller that its courses were not "credit bearing toward any degree" offered by three universities. She noted that some courses could be completed in three to five hours and that tests could be passed without reading the material. According to the letter, no safeguards assured a candidate actually took the test. The administrator then emailed three different teachers to explain that the seller's courses were not credit-bearing toward a degree. She said some courses were not eligible for elective credit at the universities offering them.

The seller sued the district for defamation and related claims in a state court. A jury found some of the administrator's comments were defamatory and awarded the seller over $340,000. On appeal, the Supreme Court of Nevada explained that **an absolute privilege protected the administrator's letter because the seller had already demanded that the district recognize its courses and threatened legal action if it did not**. This privilege extended to non-lawyers as well as lawyers. At the trial court level, the seller attempted only to show that its business was down, and did not link this claim to the letter or emails. The administrator's writings did not impugn the seller's fitness for trade. The communications concerned the fitness of the seller's products, and the administrator had no intent to harm the seller's business interests. As she did not show reckless disregard for the truth, the judgment was reversed. *Clark County School Dist. v. Virtual Educ. Software*, 213 P.3d 496 (Nev. 2009).

◆ A former temporary teacher lost his defamation action against a Louisiana school board. A high school principal sent the board's human resources office a brief letter stating the teacher's dates of employment and noting only that "it is recommended that Mr. Tatum not be returned to Cohen School." The Court of Appeal of Louisiana affirmed a trial court's dismissal of the case. It held that **a communication is defamatory if it tends to harm one's reputation in the community**, deters association with others, or exposes the person to contempt or ridicule. The principal's recommendation against rehiring the teacher was not defamatory. Expression of opinion is actionable only if it implies false factual assertions, is defamatory, and is made with actual malice. *Tatum v. Orleans Parish School Board*, 982 So.2d 923 (La. Ct. App. 2008).

◆ A California high school principal served with distinction at several inner city schools before being assigned to Jefferson High School in Los Angeles. Jefferson significantly improved its traditionally low-achievement standing, but a series of violent disturbances occurred that resulted in several student injuries and arrests. The superintendent of schools was quoted in the media as saying "stronger leadership was needed at Jefferson," and that the principal had "retirement plans that did not fit with the district's needs." The principal was removed from the school and reassigned to a "desk job." He retired six months later and sued the school district and two superintendents in a state court for defamation and invasion of privacy. The case reached the state court of appeal. It held **the superintendent "had an official duty to communicate with the press about matters of public concern."** His duty was to inform the public about how the district would respond to the violence, and these statements were privileged. The principal's leadership was a subject of legitimate public concern, and none of the statements divulged private information. The superintendent's statements were privileged in his capacity as chief executive officer for the district. The court upheld the judgment and held the school officials were entitled to their attorneys' fees. *Morrow v. Los Angeles Unified School Dist.*, 149 Cal.App.4th 1424, 57 Cal.Rptr.3d 885 (Cal. Ct. App. 2007).

◆ A 74-year-old Massachusetts foreign language teacher filed a defamation and discrimination lawsuit against her principal. The principal had criticized the teacher's handling of a class trip to Germany, alleging that she left a sick child unattended while she visited another town. A state trial court dismissed the case, but the court of appeals held that the teacher raised valid concerns about the principal's statements to a group of parents concerning her performance. **His statements and his "ongoing antagonistic relationship" with her were enough to allow the defamation claim to proceed.** While the principal was entitled to discuss the teacher's performance with parents, this privilege would be lost if the teacher showed that he spoke with malice. *Dragonis v. School Committee of Melrose*, 64 Mass. App. Ct. 429, 833 N.E.2d 679 (Mass. App. Ct. 2005). The Supreme Judicial Court of Massachusetts denied further review.

VI. SCHOOL BUS ACCIDENTS

Overview

Courts have found school bus drivers and districts liable for injuries to students resulting from the failure to exercise reasonable care in the operation of a vehicle or the design of a bus route. Districts are not liable for injuries caused by sudden and unforeseeable attacks of students on school buses.

A. Duty of Care

School boards are not insurers of school safety. While a school board's duty to students regarding transportation extends from when a bus picks up the student at a bus stop to when the student reaches the school door, some accidents and injuries simply cannot be fairly attributed to action or inaction by school district employees.

Teacher Scenarios

School sued after student gets off bus,
skips school..57

Court Decisions

◆ A Florida middle school student was killed while crossing a street to get to her bus stop. She was using the stop because of problems she had with other students at the stop on her side of the road. Her school counselor told her to use the stop across the street. Her family sued the board in a state court. Appeal reached the state court of appeal. It found that if a student was harmed before reaching a designated bus stop (or after leaving one), the student was outside the board's duty of care. Florida regulations placed the burden on parents to ensure the safe travel of students to and from home, when they were not in school custody. **Since the student was under the exclusive control of her parents while she walked to the bus stop, the school district had no duty to ensure her safe arrival.** The court affirmed the judgment for the board. *Francis v. School Board of Palm Beach County*, 29 So.3d 441 (Fla. Dist. Ct. App. 2010).

◆ A nine-year-old North Carolina student was seated on a school bus next to another student who was poking holes in paper with a pencil. The driver told the other student to put the pencil away and told the student to turn around in the seat and stay out of the aisle. When the bus went over a dip in the road, the driver heard a scream. The student's left eye was punctured by the other student's pencil, causing a serious injury. In a State Tort Claims Act proceeding before the North Carolina Industrial Commission, the student's parents claimed the bus driver's failure to supervise the other student was the cause of the eye injury. The commission found the student's injuries resulted from the driver's negligence and awarded the student $150,000 in damages. The state court of appeals upheld the award. **Evidence supported the commission's finding that the driver had a duty of care to enforce school safety policies but failed to do so.** And this failure was the legal cause of the student's eye injury. *Lucas v. Rockingham County Schools*, 692 S.E.2d 890 (N.C. Ct. App. 2010).

◆ A 15-year-old Louisiana student asked her school bus driver if she could exit a bus a few blocks from home. She had no written permission slip as required by school board policy, but the driver allowed her to leave as she was not a behavior problem. The student spent the day with her 18-year-old boyfriend and had sex with him. The principal called the family home during the school day to report her absence. The student did not return home, fearing consequences from her parents. Law officers found her a few days later in an abandoned building where she had been hiding. The student's family sued the school board for negligence. A trial court found that the board breached a duty owed to the student, but that this did not cause the harm she alleged.

The Court of Appeal of Louisiana reviewed evidence that the two students had been observed displaying affection at school, and that the principal had warned the student of the possible legal consequences of attempting a relationship with an 18-year-old. He had also issued her a three-day suspension for her conduct at school. There was evidence that the student's parents knew of the relationship. While they claimed that the truancy incident would not have occurred if the driver had not let her off the bus, the court disagreed. The driver's conduct was not the cause-in-fact of any harm. **The injury was not within the scope of any school board duty because of the lack of its foreseeability.** Accordingly, the court affirmed the judgment for the school board. *J.M. v. Acadia Parish School Board*, 7 So.3d 150 (La. Ct. App. 2009).

◆ A four-year-old Florida child with disabilities endured a four-hour bus ride on his first day of school because the driver lost his way. The child's father took him to a pediatrician, who found no signs of abuse or injury. But the child began having nightmares and wetting his bed. His parents sued the school board for negligence and false imprisonment. Appeal reached the state court of appeal. It held **the "impact rule" requires a personal injury plaintiff to show that any emotional distress must "flow from the physical injuries" suffered from an impact.** Neither the pediatrician nor the psychologist who examined the child found any physical or emotional injury. As the impact rule barred recovery for emotional injury, the court reversed the judgment on the negligence claim. It affirmed the appeal on the false imprisonment claim. There was no evidence of any intent to confine the child or keep him on the bus. *School Board of Miami-Dade County, Florida v. Trujillo*, 906 So.2d 1109 (Fla. Dist. Ct. App. 2005).

◆ A Washington school bus driver dropped a student off past her usual stop, but closer to her home and on the same side of the street as her house. After the bus pulled away, the student started walking across the street to get her mail and was severely injured when struck by another vehicle. She sued the school district and bus driver for negligence. A court held for the district and driver, and the state court of appeals affirmed. The accident was not caused by the drop-off location. The only proof offered to show that the drop-off point was dangerous was the accident itself. The bus driver did not violate a legal duty towards the student. **State rules governing school bus drivers required drivers to take reasonable action to assure a student crosses a road safely, but only if the student must cross the road.** The student did not need to cross the street to get home, and the driver was unaware that she intended to cross it. *Claar v. Auburn School Dist. No. 408*, 125 Wash. App. 1048 (Wash. Ct. App. 2005).

B. Governmental Immunity

Court Decisions

◆ A seven-year-old Alabama student with disabilities attended an intensive therapeutic placement center for students with behavioral and emotional problems. Each day, he rode a five-seat special education bus about 30 miles to the center. According to the student, a classmate sexually assaulted him on a day when a substitute driver drove the bus. The classmate claimed that the two boys had only exposed themselves to each other. The student's parents sued the board and school officials for negligence and civil rights violations. A court held that the assault did not result from a school board policy. The substitute driver was entitled to immunity, as driving the bus was a discretionary duty. The parents appealed to the Eleventh

Circuit, which held public schools do not generally have any constitutional duty to protect students from violent acts by third parties. The student's special education status did not form a "special relationship" creating a duty to protect him. The parents failed to show any board policy was the "moving force" behind the incident. There was no evidence that the classmate had previously committed sexual assault or was a known threat to do so. The Alabama Supreme Court has repeatedly held that **the supervision of students involves discretion and judgment**. Persons who supervise students are entitled to immunity in negligence cases. *Worthington v. Elmore County Board of Educ.*, 160 Fed.Appx. 877 (11th Cir. 2005).

◆ A Texas pre-kindergartner fell asleep on her school bus and was locked inside it for a full afternoon. After arriving at school, the driver and bus monitor failed to check the bus before locking it. The child's parents sued the school district for negligence. The district claimed sovereign immunity, and the case reached the Court of Appeals of Texas. It explained that the Texas Code waives immunity for property damage, personal injury and death that "arises from the operation or use of a motor-driven vehicle." The court noted that in an earlier case, **the Supreme Court of Texas had found that the unloading of a school bus was part of the transportation process**. Here, the family's claim was based on the "use of the bus." Since the locking of bus doors was distinguished from negligent supervision, sovereign immunity was waived. *Elgin Independent School Dist. v. R.N.*, 191 S.W.3d 263 (Tex. Ct. App. 2006).

◆ After an accident between a school bus and a car, the car driver sued the school board and bus driver in a Virginia trial court. The bus driver and the board asserted the defense of sovereign immunity, and the court granted their request, ruling the bus driver was entitled to sovereign immunity for simple negligence and that the board's liability was entirely dependent upon and derived from his negligence. Because the car driver did not allege gross negligence against the bus driver and the board, the court held that the board was entitled to judgment. The car driver appealed to the state supreme court, which observed that **state law abrogated school board immunity for acts of simple negligence up to the amount of a board's insurance coverage**. The statute imposed liability on school boards for simple negligence, even where their employees were liable only for gross negligence. The court reversed the judgment, as transportation of students on school buses was a governmental function over which the district exercised significant control. Transportation of students involved discretion and judgment by bus drivers. *Linhart v. Lawson*, 540 S.E.2d 875 (Va. 2001).

VII. SCHOOL SECURITY

State legislatures have enacted laws regarding school safety, but to this date, most of the lawsuits arising from breaches of school security remain rooted in negligence principles. School districts owe their students a duty of reasonable care, and the duty of teachers and administrators to supervise and protect their students is well-established. In A.W. v. Lancaster County School District 0001, *784 N.W.2d 907 (Neb. 2010), below, the Supreme Court of Nebraska held that foreseeability questions in negligence cases are generally for juries to determine. It found that questions of foreseeability are not "legal" questions, but involve common sense, common experience, and the application of community standards and behavioral norms. So juries, rather than judges are typically entitled to review questions of foreseeability in negligence cases.*

A. Duty of Care

Court Decisions

◆ A Nebraska school policy required visitors to check in at the main office of the school. However, an intruder entered the school without being observed by school secretaries. Teachers asked the intruder if they could help him, but he ignored them. One teacher directed him to a restroom and told him to report to the office after he was finished. Another teacher reported him to the office, but she did not continue observing him. After the teachers lost sight of the intruder, he went to another restroom and sexually assaulted a five-year-old student. The student's mother sued the school district for negligence. A state court awarded pretrial judgment to the district, but on appeal, the Supreme Court of Nebraska stated that a trial was required. In this case, the district owed the student a duty of reasonable care. But the question of whether the assault was reasonably foreseeable involved a fact-specific inquiry for a jury. **As the teachers had permitted the intruder to evade them, reasonable minds could differ as to whether the assault was foreseeable.** It had been improper for the lower court to award judgment to the district, and the case was returned to it for further proceedings. *A.W. v. Lancaster County School District 0001*, 784 N.W.2d 907 (Neb. 2010).

◆ Four Michigan teachers and their union brought a lawsuit against their school board, asserting it improperly failed to expel students who had assaulted them. They maintained that state law required the expulsion of students who assaulted others, and argued that school administrators who failed to follow the law should have their contracts cancelled. The Court of Appeals of Michigan ruled against them, holding that they did not have standing to pursue the case. On further appeal, the Michigan Supreme Court held that the teachers had standing to pursue their action. They were likely to suffer an injury that other members of the public wouldn't face. Thus, **the teachers had a substantial and distinct interest in enforcing the law that a student be expelled for assaulting a teacher**. *Lansing Schools Educ. Ass'n MEA/NEA v. Lansing Board of Educ.*, 487 Mich. 387, 792 N.W.2d 686 (Mich. 2010).

◆ An Iowa student used a BB gun to shoot a classmate on a sidewalk outside their high school at dismissal time. Law officers arrested the student and two other boys later in the day when they used the same BB gun during a theft. Although the student claimed the shooting was accidental, he was placed in juvenile detention and expelled. Dissatisfied with the school's handling of the matter, the classmate's mother sued the school district and officials for negligence. A jury returned a verdict for the school district and officials.

The mother appealed to the Court of Appeals of Iowa, which noted that **schools must exercise the same care as a parent of ordinary prudence would in comparable circumstances**. In the month before the shooting, the student had been involved in three fights at school. The school had responded with a student responsibility plan and placed him on "full escort" by a staff member at all times. In addition, the student was suspended and recommended for alternative placement the next year. The court found evidence from which the jury could find the school had responded appropriately to the prior incidents. School administrators followed district disciplinary policies in dealing with the student. Moreover, the fights may have been provoked and were "mutual" in nature. The judgment for the district and officials was affirmed. *Herrig v. Dubuque Community School Dist.*, 772 N.W.2d 15 (Iowa Ct. App. 2009).

◆ In 2005, an Oregon school district adopted a policy that any employee having a firearm in school or at a school event would face discipline up to and including termination. A teacher had an ex-husband whom she feared might turn violent. She sought to bring a handgun to school, asserting that she was licensed to carry a concealed weapon and that she needed it for self-defense. The district's human resources department warned her that she could be fired for bringing the gun to school, and she sued. She claimed that the policy was illegal because Oregon law states that only the legislature can "regulate" firearms or pass ordinances concerning them. A court dismissed her claim, holding that the law didn't apply to workplace policies, and the Oregon Court of Appeals affirmed. The state law was only intended to prevent cities and counties from creating a patchwork of conflicting laws concerning firearms. It was not intended to reach as far as internal employment policies. *Doe v. Medford School Dist. 549C*, 221 P.3d 787 (Or. Ct. App. 2009).

B. Governmental Immunity

As in other tort liability areas, public officers and employees enjoy qualified official immunity if they are performing discretionary acts involving the exercise of judgment or personal deliberation. It is further required that the government official or employee be acting in good faith and within the scope of their authority.

Court Decisions

◆ A Minnesota kindergartner said that he did not want to go outside with his class for recess. He stayed in a supervised detention room in the school office, but an aide instructed him to use a lavatory down the hallway instead of the one in the detention area. While in the lavatory, the kindergartner was sexually assaulted by a recent high school graduate who had been inside the school several times in the days before the assault to do janitorial work. On the day of the assault, he entered the school through a side door without signing in and obtaining a visitor badge. The kindergartner's mother sued the school district for negligent supervision and failure to have and enforce a specific policy on school security. A court denied pretrial judgment on the negligent supervision claim, and the Court of Appeals of Minnesota agreed that a trial was required on that issue. The aide had let the kindergartner go unaccompanied to a restroom outside a detention room equipped with its own lavatory, and the graduate somehow got in the school building without signing in and wearing a badge. But **the school district was entitled to immunity for not having a specific policy to protect elementary children from intruders**. These decisions took place at the planning level and involved the evaluation of financial, political, economic and social factors. *Doe v. Independent School Dist. No. 2154*, No. A09-2235, 2010 WL 3545585 (Minn. Ct. App. 9/14/10).

◆ A Georgia student was severely beaten by a classmate after they left their classroom. The principal and vice principal found the student unconscious and bleeding profusely in the hallway. According to the student's parents, the school's only effort to assist him was taking him to the school clinic, where a nurse cleaned his wounds. They claimed he was placed in an intensive care unit for traumatic brain injury due to the lack of immediate treatment. The parents filed a negligence action against the district, asserting that the school knew of the classmate's extensive history of violence and that a teacher ignored his threats against the student. The court awarded judgment to the district, and the parents appealed. The Supreme Court of Georgia found a state constitutional provision requires schools to prepare safety plans to address violence in schools, and to provide a safe environment. But qualified immunity protects officials for their discretionary actions taken within the scope of their official authority. **Public officials and employees may be held personally liable only for ministerial acts that are negligently performed, and for those acts performed with malice or intent to injure.** School officials had exercised discretion in how they created a school safety plan. Their alleged malice in not providing the student immediate medical care did not deprive them of immunity. *Murphy v. Bajjani*, 282 Ga. 197, 647 S.E.2d 54 (Ga. 2007).

◆ A student at Philadelphia's Olney High School was punched by an unknown attacker who was trying to hit someone else. The attack occurred on the stairwell, where there were no surveillance cameras or security staff. The intended victim ducked, and the attacker hit the student in the eye, severely injuring him. Neither the attacker nor the intended victim was ever identified. The student's mother sued the school district and school officials in a federal court, asserting due process violations and willful misconduct. The court rejected the claims, including one alleging that school officials had created the danger leading to the injury. On appeal, the U.S. Court of Appeals, Third Circuit, affirmed. Although the school was short four security officers that day, and had been short of a full security staff on 83 of the previous 85 school days, **the injury to the student was not foreseeable**. The atmosphere of violence at the school did not make it foreseeable that he would be attacked. Additional surveillance or security might have helped apprehend the attacker, but it was speculation to say this would have prevented the attack. *Mohammed v. School Dist. of Philadelphia*, 196 Fed.Appx. 79 (3d Cir. 2006).

C. Building and Grounds

1. Visitors and Intruders

Court Decisions

◆ Washington school employees identified a former student as the person who broke into a junior high school and damaged it, based on their review of surveillance camera video. After police arrested him and charged him with criminal conduct, fingerprint analysis showed he was not the offender. By the time the fingerprint analysis exonerated him, the former student had spent 19 days in jail. He sued the school district in the state court system for malicious prosecution. The state court of appeals held the former student did not satisfy the legal requirements for a malicious prosecution claim. **He had to show more than just a mistake by proving "evil intent," but he failed to do so.** *Hubbard v. Eastmont School Dist. No. 206*, 152 Wash.App. 1040 (Wash. Ct. App. 2009).

◆ A Kansas jogger was approached by a municipal police officer because her dog was running loose on school grounds. She had an unloaded handgun with her. A state court acquitted the jogger of a criminal charge of possessing a firearm on school property, since there were no classes in session and no school-sponsored activities at the time. The Court of Appeals of Kansas noted **state law declared that possession of a firearm by any person (other than a law enforcement officer) in or on any school property or grounds was a criminal offense**. None of the exceptions to the law applied here. Whether school was in session was irrelevant, and the court reversed the judgment. *State of Kansas v. Toler*, 41 Kan.App.2d 986, 206 P.3d 548 (Kan. Ct. App. 2009).

◆ A Louisiana high school student was stabbed in a hallway by an intruder who was leaving the school office, where he had been denied a visitor's pass. Staff members watched him exit the building but did not escort him out as he walked to a school parking lot. He re-entered the building unobserved through an unlocked side door. The intruder apparently recognized the student as a person who had laughed at him some years earlier about a personal slight. The student and her parents sued the school board for negligence. A state trial court dismissed the case, and appeal went to the state court of appeal. It held school boards have a duty of reasonable supervision over their students. Supervision must be reasonable and competent, according to the circumstances of the case. But school board were not insurers of children's safety. **"Constant supervision of all students is not possible nor required for educators to discharge their duty to provide adequate supervision."** Before liability may be imposed, there must be proof of negligent supervision and a causal connection between the lack of supervision and the accident. *Boudreaux v. St. Tammany Parish School Board*, No. 2007 CA 0089, 2007 WL 4480703 (La. Ct. App. 12/21/07).

2. Building Entry Policies

Court Decisions

◆ After a sex offender entered a Texas school and exposed himself to a child, the district implemented a regulation requiring every visitor to produce a state-issued photo identification as a condition of entering secure areas where students were present. Under the regulation, pictures were taken of visitor identification cards but no other information was taken. The system enabled schools to check visitor names and birth dates to determine if they were listed on national registered sex-offender databases. A parent refused to allow her child's school to either scan her driver's license or permit manual entry of her information. As a result, she was denied access to areas of the school. She and her husband sued, challenging the policy as a violation of their constitutional rights. A federal court held for the district, and the Fifth Circuit affirmed. **The regulation addressed a compelling state interest and was not overly intrusive.** The system took only the minimal information needed to determine sex offender status. *Meadows v. Lake Travis Independent School Dist.*, 397 Fed.Appx. 1 (5th Cir. 2010).

◆ A Chicago third-grader had conflicts with another girl at school. The other girl's mother and a companion threatened the student's mother at her home. The school principal set up a meeting between the families. Near the end of a school day, the other girl's parent and an adult cousin fought the student's mother and grandmother in a school office. The principal called police and swore out criminal complaints for disorderly conduct against all four adults. Criminal charges were dismissed, and the principal later said he had made a mistake and should have only had two of the women arrested. The parent and grandparent sued. The U.S. Court of Appeals, Seventh Circuit, noted the issue was not whether a parent or grandparent had actually committed disorderly conduct. **It was only necessary to show a reasonable person in the principal's position had probable cause to believe there was disorderly conduct.** The principal entered a chaotic situation and could easily have viewed the mother to be an equal participant in the fight. Each of the family's civil rights claims failed. *Stokes v. Board of Educ. of City of Chicago*, 599 F.3d 617 (7th Cir. 2010).

VIII. TEACHER SCENARIOS

Sharpen Your Judgment

Is teacher 'punishing' student for food allergy?

"Fill me in on what happened with your student," Principal Heather Marks said as Amy Keller walked into the office.

"Lisa has a nut allergy," Amy said. "And when she forgot her lunch last month, we gave her a peanut butter sandwich – and she had a reaction."

"That's the day she went to the hospital?" Heather asked.

"Yes," Amy confirmed. "Since then, Lisa has been sitting at a special table so the lunch ladies know she has an allergy."

"And Lisa's mom is mad about that," Heather said. "She's threatening to sue."

"But we have to protect Lisa," Amy said.

"I know," Heather agreed. "But according to Lisa's mom, she thinks she's being 'punished' because she can't sit with her friends."

"Can't we just explain to Lisa that it's for her own good?" Amy asked.

"Lisa's mom is still really mad that she was given a peanut butter sandwich," Heather said.

Lisa's mom claimed the school was negligent.

Did the judge agree?

Sharpen Your Judgment – The Decision

No, the judge dismissed the claim.

The judge noted that Lisa has a food allergy, and school staffers gave her a peanut butter sandwich for lunch. In many instances, that might be considered neglect.

But state officials pointed out that they did provide meal substitutions for students who can't eat regular lunches due to food allergies. The fact that Lisa didn't receive the alternative was a mix-up. But after that, school officials provided Lisa with a nut-free table to prevent another error.

That swayed the judge. While the state has an obligation to provide alternative lunches, it would be unreasonable to expect schools to make sure students with a nut allergy never ate nuts at school, the judge explained. For this reason, the judge dismissed the claim.

Analysis: Learn from mistakes

Courts recognize when school officials make good-faith efforts to prevent life-threatening mistakes from recurring. The steps the teacher took after the initial error went a long way with the judge.

Lesson: It's never too late to put safety precautions in place to keep students safe.

Cite: *Pace v. State of Maryland.*

Sharpen Your Judgment

Poor supervision leads to injury, student claims

"Morning, Jacob," Mark Greene said as a fellow teacher, Jacob Hinson, walked into his classroom. "What's going on?"

"I guess you haven't heard the latest about Dan yet," Jacob said.

"No," Mark said. "I know Dan was taken to the hospital after that big fight in the hall last week. Why? Is he OK?"

"Yeah," Jacob said. "And he's suing – he said it's our fault he got hurt."

"Run that by me again," Mark said in disbelief, shaking his head.

"I just found out," Jacob told him. "Dan says we weren't in the hall between classes. And he claims that if we were, we could've stopped the fight before he got hurt."

"But that's crazy," Mark said. "We were walking out into the hall when the melee broke out. I know I got there as fast as I could. I'm sure you did, too."

"That's exactly what I said to the principal," Jacob agreed. "But now Dan's filed a lawsuit, claiming we didn't follow the school's safety plan to the letter."

When Dan filed suit, the school asked the court to dismiss his claim. Did it?

Sharpen Your Judgment – The Decision

Yes, the court dismissed Dan's claim.

Dan claimed the school was responsible for the injuries he sustained during the fight because the teachers weren't in the hallways, as per the district safety plan. Dan said that the teachers should've walked into the hall first, so students were supervised at all times.

The teachers argued they were walking out of the classroom along with students. They said the fight broke out too quickly to prevent.

While the teachers weren't in position, they were en route to their posts as per the policy, the court pointed out. Because the fight started suddenly, the teachers couldn't have been expected to prevent it, the court found.

The court also noted high school students are old enough to walk through a doorway without direct supervision, so the claim failed.

Analysis: Supervision matched age level

Courts know teachers can't be expected to prevent unforeseeable student fights that happen very quickly.

Age matters, too. It's not unreasonable for high school students to have indirect supervision for a minute as long as teachers are in the general area.

Cite: *Espino v. The New York Board of Educ.*

Sharpen Your Judgment
Was teacher to blame for student's injury?

"Oh boy," said teacher Heather Marks, seeing the look on Principal Mary Salinger's face as she sat down in her office. "Is everything OK?"

"Not exactly," said Mary. "Karen Wright's parents are suing us for that fall she took on the way to the nurse."

"But I had no idea Karen might faint," said Heather. "She didn't say she felt light-headed. If I'd known she thought she might faint, I would've sent someone with her."

"Karen's parents say we know she has a tendency to faint when she gets sick," said Mary. "They say if she'd been escorted to the nurse, she wouldn't have been hurt by falling."

"Karen's mom did tell us about the fainting," agreed Heather. "That's why we told Karen to sit down on the floor and tell a teacher if she ever felt faint. She never said anything to me about feeling faint."

"Well, I guess they're saying we were just supposed to know," said Mary. "I mean, you did say she looked pale, right?"

Karen's parents sued the teacher for negligence. The school's lawyer asked the judge to throw out the case. Did the judge agree?

Sharpen Your Judgment – The Decision

Yes, the judge agreed to throw out the parents' lawsuit.

Heather argued her decision to send the student to the nurse without an escort was reasonable because Karen never said anything about feeling light-headed. Heather also pointed out that Karen had been told to tell her if she felt faint, but hadn't.

Karen's parents said the teacher should have known Karen needed an escort, but the court sided with the school.

Since Karen didn't say she felt faint, Heather had to use her best judgment to decide if the student needed an escort to the nurse's office. This teacher wasn't liable for the student's injury because she made a reasonable decision based on what she knew.

Analysis: Tell students to communicate

It's important to be sure students with chronic health conditions understand they need to clearly tell a teacher if they feel an episode coming on. Teachers can only respond appropriately to a potential health crisis if they understand one is likely.

Teachers care very much about students' health – but they're not mind readers.

Cite: *Hughes v. Christina School Dist.*

Intruder attacks student after teacher saw him trying to get in

Should teacher have raised the alarm?

"What do you mean I can't have a visitor's pass?"

The yelling made teacher John Garcia stop and look. A red-faced man was standing in front of the check-in desk.

"Is there a problem here?" asked John, walking over.

"Do you know this gentleman, Mr. Garcia?" asked the guard.

"No," said John.

The guard turned back to the angry man. "Sorry, sir. It's like I said. I can't issue you a pass unless you show me an ID – or someone on staff can vouch for you."

"Fine!" said the man. He turned and stormed off toward the front door.

The guard slipped around the desk to follow, quietly explaining to John, "I just want to make sure he leaves." John nodded and joined the guard. They watched the man leave.

Later that day, the guard delivered bad news to John, "Did you hear that guy from this morning snuck in by a side door and stabbed a girl student?"

"What?" cried John. "Is she OK?"

"They're keeping her overnight, but yeah. She says she never saw that guy before. And one of the cops told me he just stabbed her on impulse. Thought she was laughing at him, or something."

The student's parents sued the school, saying it didn't properly supervise their daughter. Did they win?

Decision: No, the case was dismissed.

Schools aren't responsible for things that no one can predict and prevent.

Here, nothing like this had ever happened at the school before, no one knew the man (let alone knew he might turn violent) and the guard and teacher couldn't have known he was coming back.

Key: This teacher did all that could be expected of him under the circumstances. It would have been different if he'd heard threats or if he'd seen an obviously dangerous intruder. Here, his response to the situation he saw was reasonable.

Cite: *Boudreaux v. St. Tammany Parish Board.*

Mom sues after student suffers eye injury during science experiment

Teacher didn't follow school policy, Mom claims

Teacher Diane Price looked up from the tests she was grading when her classroom door opened. "Hi, Ms. Bryan," she said. "How is Joey doing?"

"You know how he is," Ms. Bryan said sarcastically. "He's hurt because of your science experiment, remember?"

"Ms. Bryan," Diane assured her. "I'm very concerned about the well-being of my students. I'm sorry about Joey's eye, but it was a fluke accident."

Did teacher follow the policy?

"An accident that should have been prevented by this," Ms. Bryan said as she held up the paper in her hand.

"This policy says when students work with explosives in science, they have to wear eye protection," she said. "Joey wasn't, so you will hear from my lawyer!"

"Ms. Bryan, the class experiment was to launch two-liter bottles, but we didn't use explosives," Diane explained. "We only used air and water pressure for the launch.

"Joey just happened to get hit in the eye," Diane continued. "It really was just an unfortunate accident."

"This is ridiculous," Ms. Bryan said. "I'm not going to split hairs over details. Joey said you warned the kids the bottle might explode. I'll see you in court!"

Joey's mom sued Diane personally, claiming negligence. Did the judge agree?

Decision: No, the judge ruled that Diane was entitled to qualified immunity.

Key: In order to prove the teacher was negligent, Joey's mom had to show the teacher failed to follow school policy or acted with malice or an intent to injure.

The court found that wasn't the case here because the science experiment didn't include explosives, so the teacher followed policy. In addition, Joey's mom couldn't show Diane acted with malice, such as aiming the bottle at Joey.

For these two reasons, the claim failed and the teacher was entitled to qualified immunity, the court explained.

Cite: *Grammens v. Dollar.*

Sharpen Your Judgment

Must cheerleader cheer for alleged attacker?

"Why do I teach and coach the student teams?" Jayson Fuller asked, sighing as he stirred his coffee.

Fellow teacher Amy Keller laughed. "Why? What happened at the game last night?"

"One of the cheerleaders, Maddy Wilson, refused to cheer for Ray Dean," Jayson said.

"Wait? Isn't Ray one of the best players on the team?" Amy asked.

"Yes," Jayson said. "Maddy refused to cheer because Ray supposedly assaulted her at a party. But her accusations didn't hold up, and those charges were dismissed a while back.

"Her non-participation when Ray had the ball was obvious, so I told her to cheer or she was off the squad – and she left," Jayson continued. "Now her mom's mad that I 'chose Ray over Maddy' and she's threatening to sue."

"What are you going to do?" Amy asked.

"I don't know," Jayson said. "This feels like it's a no-win situation."

Maddy's mother sued the school, claiming it deprived Maddy of a property right – an interest in her position on the school cheerleading squad.

Did the judge agree?

Sharpen Your Judgment – The Decision

No, the school won.

Maddy's mother claimed that releasing Maddy from the cheerleading squad deprived her of a property right, which is protected by the Fourteenth Amendment.

School officials argued that cheerleaders have a contractual obligation to cheer for the entire team. While there was a questionable history between Maddy and Ray, the school said Ray wasn't found guilty of criminal charges. School officials said they required both athletes to perform as expected.

The judge agreed, noting that it was reasonable to remove Maddy from the squad if she failed to cheer correctly. Participating in extracurricular activities isn't a constitutionally protected right, so the school didn't deprive her of a property interest, the court ruled.

Analysis: Everything isn't a 'right'

Sometimes it seems as if today's students have an "entitlement mentality."

As this case shows, students don't always have a constitutional right to participate in extracurricular activities.

Lesson: Schools can establish rules and expect athletes to follow those rules if they want to participate.

Cite: *Doe v. Silsbee Independent School Dist.*

Sharpen Your Judgment

Did school do enough to stop track meet injury?

"It's been quite a ceremony so far, wouldn't you agree?" teacher Heather Marks said to principal Mary Salinger during the school graduation. "Everyone looks so nice."

"Yes, yes, I guess so ... " Mary's voice quickly trailed off.

"What's the matter?" Heather asked. "Haven't got your summer vacation plans set yet?"

"Oh, it's not that," Mary said. "It's just this Timmy Tresh case. I found out today he's suing the school, and I'm a bit preoccupied."

Student hurt at shot put event

"That's the student who got hurt at the school track meet last year, isn't it?" Heather recalled.

"That's right," Mary confirmed. "He got hit with a shot put by a student from another school. Now he's suing us for his injuries."

"A student from another school accidentally hits him and it's our fault?" Heather asked.

"That's basically what he's saying," Mary said. "I don't get it either. There's always a chance for injury when it comes to school sports. I don't think we did anything that made it more dangerous."

"I agree," Mary remarked. "I sure hope the court sees it our way."

Tresh sued the school district, claiming it was responsible for the injuries he sustained. The district tried to have the case against it dismissed. Was it successful?

Sharpen Your Judgment – The Decision

Yes, the school district was able to have the case against it dismissed.

The injured student said the school district violated a duty of care it owed to him when it allowed him to be injured by the shot put at the track meet. He said the district should be required to compensate him for the personal injuries he sustained.

The district argued that there were inherent risks associated with the shot put event. It pointed out that the injured student had participated in more than 10 meets before the accident and had thrown the shot at least 100 times before. It also noted that the student had admitted at his deposition that he understood all the rules and procedures that applied to the shot put event.

The court agreed with the district and dismissed the case. The student assumed the risk of participating in the event, and the district did not do anything to make the meet or the event unusually dangerous.

Analysis: Limit liability for sports injuries

When it comes to sports, the key is to make sure you don't increase the inherent risk associated with participation. This means making sure students have the right equipment, coaching, facilities, etc.

Cite: *Gerry v. Commack Union Free School Dist.*

Sharpen Your Judgment

School faces suit for fight on basketball court

"I'm sure glad the election's finally over," said teacher Heather Marks as she poured her morning coffee. "Those political ads were getting to be a bit much."

"I'm glad it's over too," said principal Mary Salinger. "But I'm afraid having a new president won't do much to help us with this Pat Dobson case."

"That's the boy who was injured by one of our players during the basketball playoffs last year, right?" Heather remembered.

"That's right," Mary said. "Our player, Bill Henry, got thrown out of the game right after he threw that elbow.

"But now the Dobsons have sued us, saying we should have known something like that would happen."

Did prior incidents give warning?

"I talked to Coach Bauer after that game," Heather said. "He said Bill just plays hard. He did get a technical foul earlier in the year, but that was for cursing, not fighting."

"He had an argument with another player in an earlier game," Mary said. "But the coach didn't think he needed to be kicked off the team, and neither did I."

"I can't imagine losing that case," Heather said. "It's not like Bill was constantly getting into fights."

"Let's just hope things go our way," Mary sighed.

A lower court ruled for the school. On appeal, was the school held responsible for the player's injuries?

Sharpen Your Judgment – The Decision

No, the school was not responsible for the opposing player's injuries. The appeals court agreed with the lower court and upheld the ruling for the school.

The injured student's parents said school officials had enough information to know the aggressor was likely to commit the attack, based on his prior conduct. They accused the school of failing to do enough to prevent further aggressive behavior.

The school said it could not have predicted the assault, noting that the boy who threw the elbow did not have any history of physically aggressive behavior.

The appeals court agreed. To win, the injured player needed to show the school could have foreseen that its player would physically attack an opponent during a game. There was not enough of a history of aggression to put the school on notice that the player was likely to commit an attack, the court said.

Analysis: Prior history a good indicator

The deciding issue in this case was whether the attack was reasonably foreseeable. Because there was no history of similar problems, it wasn't. The flip side is that you need to be ready to step in and remove a player if he or she engages in a pattern of physically aggressive behavior.

Cite: *Brokaw v. Winfield-Mt. Union School Dist.*

Sharpen Your Judgment

Cheerleader hurt at practice – is school responsible?

"Good afternoon," principal Heather Marks said cheerfully as she answered her office phone.

But she could tell right away that it was not a good afternoon for the voice on the other end of the line, teacher Rick Anderson.

"You need to get down to the gym right away," Anderson said. "There's been an accident at cheerleading practice."

Marks rushed to the gym to find cheerleader Susan Watson resting on a bleacher and grimacing in pain.

"We'll take care of you and call your parents," Marks assured her. "Just tell me what happened."

Cheerleading stunt led to injury

Watson told Marks she was hurt after a routine cheerleading stunt went wrong, causing her to fall.

Later, Marks discussed the incident with a visibly upset Anderson.

"I hope we don't get blamed for this," Anderson said. "I've already heard some of the other girls saying we should have had mats down on that bare wood floor."

"Cheerleading can be dangerous, and accidents happen," Marks said. "The girls know that."

Watson's parents sued the school district, claiming it unreasonably increased the risk involved with the sport of cheerleading by failing to provide mats.

The district argued that Watson assumed the risk involved. Did it win?

Sharpen Your Judgment – The Decision

Yes, an appeals affirmed a lower court's ruling in favor of the school district.

The girl's parents claimed the district was liable because it allowed the cheerleaders to practice on a bare wood floor instead of a matted surface. They argued that the bare wood floor unreasonably increased the risk of participating in cheerleading.

The district said it was not at fault for the girl's injuries because she assumed the risk of participating in cheerleading. It argued that the risks involved are obvious, and it is up to students and their parents to decide whether to take the chance of getting hurt.

The court agreed with the district. The risk of participating in cheerleading, including the risk of practicing on a bare wood floor, was obvious. Therefore, the district wasn't liable.

Analysis: Don't increase the risks

Courts recognize that some school-related activities, like cheerleading and football, involve a risk of injury. School districts usually won't be held liable when the risk is obvious and an accident happens. As this ruling points out, the key is to make sure you don't do anything to unreasonably increase a risk that comes with the territory.

Cite: *Williams v. Clinton Cent. School Dist.*

Sharpen Your Judgment

Student gets hurt in PE: Mom blames teacher

"Bet you're holding PE inside today," teacher Diane Price said to gym teacher Vinny Travo as she took off her coat.

"I am," Vinny said as he held out a cup of coffee. "Here, this will warm you up."

"Thanks," Diane said. "So did Cindy break her leg during that kickball game?"

"Yeah," Vinny said, sighing. "But she's back in school, which is the good news."

"Uh-oh," Diane said. "There's bad news?"

"Yep," Vinny said. "Her mom is suing. She said it's my fault that Cindy got hurt."

"But it was an accident," Diane said. "The kids ran into each other."

"Yeah," Vinny agreed. "But her mom thinks if I'd blown my whistle in time, Cindy wouldn't have gotten hurt."

"I know it's tough," Diane said. "But don't beat yourself up about this. Cindy's accident wasn't your fault."

"Thanks," Vinny said. "I hope you're right."

Cindy's mom sued, claiming Vinny was negligent during PE class.

Did the judge agree?

Sharpen Your Judgment – The Decision

No, the judge dismissed the claim.

The judge looked at how the accident happened – two students collided during a kickball game – and ruled that the teacher wasn't negligent in supervising the game.

But what about Cindy's broken leg? Didn't that injury prove that the teacher wasn't paying attention to the game?

No, the judge ruled. Even though Cindy broke her leg during PE class, that didn't prove the teacher was negligent, the judge said.

The court noted when students participate in athletic games, they often run into each other. Therefore, it wouldn't be reasonable to expect the teacher to blow the whistle to stop the game before an unforeseeable collision occurred, the court ruled.

Analysis: Minimize the risk

It's natural for parents to get upset if their child gets hurt. But courts know that accidents do not prove teachers are negligent. To reduce the likelihood of accidents, take precautions to thwart injuries that can be prevented.

For example, teach good sportsmanship, keep play surfaces in good repair and check equipment for wear and tear regularly.

Cite: *Lizardo v. Board of Educ. of the City of New York.*

Sharpen Your Judgment

Student injured during PE: Was teacher at fault?

Teacher Rich Wells walked into Principal Heather Marks' office. "I got your message. What's going on?"

"I have some bad news," Heather told him. "Jesse Wilson's parents are suing."

"Why, because he hurt his elbow in PE?" Rich asked. "You've got to be kidding."

"I wish it were a joke," Heather said, sighing. "Jesse's parents say it's too dangerous for students to take martial arts in PE."

"That's ridiculous," Rich said. "I've taught martial arts classes before. Jesse landed on his elbow wrong. It was an accident."

"I wonder if any other schools in the area teach martial arts classes," Heather said.

"I don't know," Rich admitted. "But his parents did sign a safety rules form."

"Good, but I'm still not sure on this one," she said. "We'll see what happens in court."

Jesse's parents sued, claiming the school was negligent. School officials asked for dismissal.

Did the judge agree?

Sharpen Your Judgment – The Decision

Yes, the judge sided with the school.

The judge noted Jesse's parents raised a valid question: Should martial arts be taught in PE classes? But in this case, that's not what the court had to decide.

The court had to determine whether the student's accident resulted from the teacher's reckless teaching methods.

The judge pointed out all that the teacher did right, such as:

- instructing students on safety maneuvers to help prevent injuries
- distributing safety guidelines to students
- requiring signed consent forms, and
- teaching the previous martial arts class without incident or injury.

Good-faith efforts were evident, ruled the court, so the school wasn't negligent.

Analysis: Risk can't be eliminated

Courts recognize PE classes carry elements of risk that are "never completely eliminated," as this judge put it.

Best practice: Do what you can to reduce the risks in PE.

Cite: *Noble v. Clermont Local School Dist.*

Sharpen Your Judgment

Was boy hurt because teacher wasn't there?

"Hey!" shouted PE teacher Jim Kelly. His class's volleyball game had gotten so boisterous that the boys didn't hear him – but they heard the blast from his whistle.

"Good to see you playing hard," said Jim when he had their attention. "But it's time to go change now. Hey, no pushing!" he added as he started to follow the boys into the locker room. "What's gotten into you guys today?"

"Spring fever?" guessed a student who was hanging back. "Listen, could I talk to you privately about my scholarship application?"

"Only if you're quick," said Jim. "I obviously need to keep an eye on this rowdy crew."

"Two minutes. I promise."

But two minutes was too long

The student was as brief as he'd promised. But when the teacher got to the locker room, one of the boys was stunned and bleeding.

His parents sued, saying horseplay got out of hand because the teacher wasn't there to keep the students in check. A judge dismissed the case, but the parents appealed.

Did the appellate court agree the accident wasn't the teacher's fault?

Sharpen Your Judgment – The Decision

No, the court decided the accident might be the teacher's fault, so a trial was needed.

To get a trial, the parents had to show it was predictable their son would be hurt if a teacher wasn't on hand to supervise the class.

They did, showing: 1) students are likelier to act up in the locker room than the gym, and 2) kids were getting out of control by the end of class – prompting the teacher to realize he had to keep a closer eye on them than usual.

Analysis: Keep students calm

As a teacher, you know there are days when kids are more rambunctious than others – and you'll probably be seeing more days like that whenever the weather gets nicer and vacation closer.

When students are more excitable than usual, you have a heightened duty to keep a close eye on them and make sure they don't hurt themselves – or each other.

With so much attention on bullying and the intentional ways kids hurt each other, it's easy to forget students also get hurt by preventable accidents. That's why it's important for teachers to make sure high-spirited kidding around doesn't get out of hand.

Cite: *Flanagan v. Canton Cent. School Dist.*

Student dies after teacher supposedly ignored 'warning signals' – now parents place blame

Could anyone have foreseen the fatal heart attack?

"I know you feel terrible about Matt Thernstrom's death, but we have to discuss it," Principal Jeanne Agar said. "Let's get right to what happened, step by step, in your class."

"It was my first-period phys-ed class, and the kids were jogging in place to warm up," Richard Smalley explained while reviewing his notes. "Matt jogged for a while and then told me he felt 'upset,' maybe because he'd skipped breakfast."

The principal made some notes of her own while asking, "Was that the first time he'd complained about not feeling good?"

Richard thought for a moment and then replied: "I'm pretty sure he'd mentioned something like that once or twice before. And of course his mother had sent in that note mentioning that he came home complaining a couple of times about having an upset stomach and shortness of breath in phys-ed."

"And so what did you say to Matt on the day he collapsed?"

"When he first complained, I told him to jog a little more and if he still felt bad, he should sit down," the teacher recalled.

"And that's when he collapsed, right?" the principal asked.

"Right," Richard nodded. "I administered CPR right away, but I couldn't feel his pulse. They said it was a massive heart attack."

"OK," the principal said. "It looks as if you took the right steps."

What the judge said

However, the student's parents sued for negligence, saying that the teacher had warnings about the boy's health, plus a note from home citing some danger signals about his health.

Did the school win the suit?

Decision: Yes. A judge said the teacher couldn't have been expected to diagnose the problem and that he took every precaution he could, given his training and expertise.

Key: In this case, the teacher didn't "push" the student or make extraordinary demands, and he took reasonable steps to assist the student.

Cite: *Badajosz v. ABC Unified School Dist.*

Sharpen Your Judgment
Was teacher responsible for phys ed class injury?

Teacher Ron Samuels poked his head into principal Mary Salinger's office. "Got a minute?" Samuels asked. "I have a quick question."

"Come on in," motioned Salinger. "Now's as good a time as any."

"It's about Tad Johnston," Samuels said. "I noticed he hasn't been back to school since he got hurt lifting weights in my phys ed class. How's he doing?"

"I just found out he's suing us," Salinger said.

Student claims lack of supervision

"What did we do wrong?" Samuels asked.

"He's saying you weren't there to supervise, and that's why he got hurt," Salinger explained.

"Half the class was in the weight room and the other half was in the gym," Samuels said. "I had to move back and forth between the rooms to supervise. I wasn't in there when he got hurt, but I can't be in two places at once.

"Besides, the accident happened so fast I couldn't have stopped it even if I was in there."

"You and I both know that," Salinger said. "Let's just hope the court sees it the same way."

A lower court refused to throw out the student's negligence claim, and the school appealed.

Did the appeals court dismiss the case?

Sharpen Your Judgment – The Decision

No, the court did not dismiss the case. Instead, it decided the student's claim should proceed.

The student claimed that the school district and teacher were negligent because they failed to provide enough supervision over the phys ed class. This lack of supervision caused the student's injury, they said.

The school district and teacher claimed that the level of supervision they provided for the phys ed class was adequate. They also insisted that the student failed to show he wouldn't have been hurt even if a greater level of supervision had been provided.

The court refused to dismiss the student's claims. The teacher admitted he was not in the room when the student was injured, and it was too soon to tell whether more supervision would have prevented the accident.

Analysis: Better safe than sorry

How closely must students be supervised? Several factors come into play, including the age of the students and the activity they are engaged in. In a gym class involving weightlifting, the risk is relatively high and more supervision is needed. As this case shows, it's risky to take chances by relying on a single staff member to supervise separate locations during a phys ed class.

Cite: *Murphy v. Fairport Cent. School Dist.*

Sharpen Your Judgment

Accident in shop: Mom sues teacher personally

"Sorry to interrupt your planning period, but was Tina using a homemade safety guard when she cut her hand on the saw blade?" Principal Heather Marks asked as she walked into teacher Rich Wells' classroom.

"Yeah," Rich said. "How's she doing? Have you heard? I'm worried about her hand."

"Hmmm, that might be a problem," Heather said, leaning against one of the desks.

"Well," she continued. "I have good news and bad: Tina's cut is healing, but her mother's suing you – personally."

"What?" Rich exclaimed in shock. "That doesn't make sense. It was an accident, and I did everything I could have done: I trained her, I tested her, and I documented everything!"

"Here's the thing," Heather explained, "Tina's mom claims the homemade safety guard was an accident waiting to happen. And it violated OSHA rules because you should've bought the manufactured safety guard."

"The one I made had the right specs," Rich said. "I was just trying to save some money."

Heather sighed. "I don't know about this."

Tina's mom sued Rich personally, claiming he was negligent. Did the judge agree?

Sharpen Your Judgment

When student gets injured, teacher gets blame

As the ambulance pulled away with student Greg Chambers inside, industrial-arts teacher Karl Aiken and principal Brenda Jackson walked back toward the school.

"Tell me what happened," Brenda began.

"We had just started working on the scenery for the school play," Karl explained. "I assigned Greg the job of using the shop table saw to cut pickets for the scene with the fence in it. Next thing I know, I turned my back for a second and he sliced his hand."

"Why'd you pick Greg?" Brenda asked.

"I've had him in class, and he was one of the best at using the saw," Karl replied.

She asked her next question: "Did he ever ignore safety rules?"

"Well, you know how kids are," Karl shook his head. "They're always trying to take shortcuts, and Greg was no different. But he was trained in safety to the point that I had a lot of confidence in him."

"OK," Brenda concluded. "Write up a report. We'll need some documentation if there are questions later."

In fact, there were questions. And the student's parents eventually sued Karl personally for negligence.

Did the teacher win the case?

Sharpen Your Judgment – The Decision

No, the judge sided with the school.

The judge acknowledged Tina's mother's concern: This teacher didn't provide students with the manufacturer's safety guard. Instead, he offered them a homemade replica. In many instances, this might be considered negligent.

But the teacher pointed out that he used the manufacturer's specs to make the safety device. None of the safety features on the OSHA-approved guard were omitted from the homemade version.

The judge also noted the teacher trained students on how to use equipment, tested them to make sure they understood safety rules and documented the results.

Because the homemade guard was modeled after the manufactured tool's specs, Tina's mom couldn't show Tina's injury would've been prevented if she'd used the manufactured guard. That meant the teacher's actions weren't negligent, the court explained.

Analysis: Train, test, document

As this case shows, courts generally recognize that accidents will happen. But it's always a good idea to document how you teach safety lessons to students.

Cite: *Fields v. Talawanda Board of Educ.*

Sharpen Your Judgment – The Decision

Yes. The teacher won.

In court, two factors weighed heavily in favor of the teacher and his decisions:

- He made sure a qualified student operated the saw. If he'd picked someone with no experience or training – or someone with whom he had no familiarity – the negligence claim would have been a lot stronger, and
- None of the teacher's actions surrounding the activity seemed out of the ordinary. They fell within the normal course of how a teacher operates in a school setting.

What would be "out of the ordinary"? Possibly, for instance, if he had left the room while the student was operating the saw.

Given those two points in the teacher's favor, the judge dropped the negligence claim.

Your best protection

Even though every classroom doesn't have a power saw or similar implements, students do get injured.

Here's what's considered the key factor when that happens: Did the teacher follow procedures and manage the classroom in a way that showed reasonable judgment?

Cite: *Anderson v. Anoka Hennepin Independent School Dist.*

Sharpen Your Judgment

Student injured by tire – is it school's fault?

"Have you seen Tom Gorman today?" teacher Heather Marks asked principal Mary Salinger. "Ever since that accident in his class, he's not the same upbeat teacher he used to be."

"It's been almost a year already since it happened, but he's still shook up about it," Salinger said. "That student got hurt pretty bad when that tire exploded."

"I heard the story," Marks said. "The student was inflating the tire when it exploded in his face.

"But Tom chained the tire to the rim as a safety precaution. Wasn't it just an unavoidable freak accident?"

Did teacher do enough?

"Not according to the boy's parents," Salinger said. "They say we're not careful enough about screening donations like that tire. They say the accident's our fault."

"But Tom had that chain wrapped completely around the tire to keep it from separating in case it burst," Marks said. "What else was he supposed to do?"

"I can't tell you exactly why they think it's our fault," said Salinger. "I just hope the court doesn't blame Tom for what happened. He's beaten himself up over this enough as it is."

A lower court issued a ruling against the boy's parents. On appeal, did the court find the teacher and district were responsible for the boy's injuries?

Sharpen Your Judgment – The Decision

No, the court did not hold the teacher or district legally responsible for the boy's injuries.

The parents claimed the teacher, the school and the district created an unreasonable risk of harm. They also said the district had an unconstitutional policy of accepting equipment from anonymous donors and having students inflate tires without the right safety equipment.

The school district and other defendants said the parents failed to prove their case. They argued that the parents needed to show the teacher acted in a way that "shocks the conscience."

The court agreed with the school officials. The teacher took safety precautions by using a chain to secure the tire. Because he was not "deliberately indifferent" to the student's safety, there was no constitutional violation.

Analysis: Make sure precautions are followed

Unfortunately, taking safety precautions doesn't always guarantee that no one will get hurt. But it's critical to train your teachers on what precautions need to be taken, and to make sure they're followed. Doing so can keep you from being held legally responsible if something goes wrong.

Cite: *Brown v. Farrell.*

Sharpen Your Judgment

Can school be blamed for field trip injury?

"So are you all set for the start of another school year?" teacher Heather Marks asked as she finished stocking her desk on the first day of school.

"I'm as ready as I can be," principal Mary Salinger said. "But it hasn't taken long for the excitement to start. I just found out we're being sued over that accident that happened on the field trip to the farm last year!"

"Are you talking about the little boy who poked himself in the eye with a wire?" asked Marks.

"Yes," Salinger said. "He ended up losing the eye."

"That's terrible," Marks said. "But he wasn't even one of our students. How can we be blamed?"

School nurse offered help

"The nurse we brought along for the trip offered to look at the boy's eye that day," Salinger said. "Now his family says she failed to give him proper care. And they say we're at fault too."

"But that woman wasn't a school nurse," Marks said. "And if she wasn't a school employee, the school shouldn't be blamed for anything she did. Besides, isn't there some kind of Good Samaritan law that says she can't be sued?"

"I really don't know how it will end up," Salinger said.

Did the court find the school and the nurse were legally responsible for the boy's injury?

Sharpen Your Judgment – The Decision

No, the court held the school and nurse were not legally responsible for the boy's injury.

According to the boy's mother, the nurse failed to provide her son with proper medical care. The parent also claimed the school was responsible for the boy's injury because the nurse was acting at its direction.

But the nurse said she was not liable because of a nursing Good Samaritan statute. Under that law, nurses who volunteer to help in an emergency can't be sued unless they are grossly negligent. The nurse said the statute applied because she was not grossly negligent.

There was no liability on the part of the school, it argued, because the nurse was an independent contractor. And it added that if the Good Samaritan statute applied, it couldn't be held liable.

The court sided with the school and nurse because the Good Samaritan law applied.

Analysis: Check your state's laws

When arranging for medical help on a school field trip, you'll need to make it clear to the nurse or health care provider whether they should limit assistance to your students only. You also need to be aware of whether your state has a similar Good Samaritan statute.

Cite: *McDaniel v. Keck.*

Teacher followed emergency drill procedure – so why's Mom suing?

Did teacher do enough to prevent accident?

Time to call it a day, teacher Diane Price thought as she surveyed the stack of papers that still needed to be graded.

Diane reached for her coat as a parent walked into the classroom. "Good afternoon, Ms. Booth. How are you?"

"I'm not happy," Ms. Booth said, pulling off her gloves.

"My daughter Claire told me she got knocked down yesterday during the fire drill," she continued, "and now her wrist hurts. How could you let this happen?"

"Let it happen?" Diane repeated as she forced a smile. "Claire fell down – "

"Those boys ran into her and knocked her down," Ms. Booth interrupted.

An accident?

"But it was an accident. Why don't we talk about what happened?" Diane suggested calmly.

"Claire has already filled me in. Two boys knocked her down," she said. "You should've kept those kids under control."

"Students weren't out of control," Diane explained. "The boys accidentally ran into Clair and she fell. She didn't even tell me her wrist hurt."

"Well, Claire told me that kids always get hurt during fire drills," Ms. Booth said.

"I'm not aware of students always getting hurt," Diane said.

"Of course not," she snapped. "Just like you weren't 'aware' of what was going on when my daughter fell!"

Diane took a deep breath, wondering if she could respond without losing her temper.

"Why didn't you watch them?" Ms. Booth asked.

Led the line

"I was watching my students," Diane said. "I led students outside and across the street – as per school policy."

"If you're at the front of the line, how do you properly supervise students at the end of the line?" Ms. Booth asked pointedly. "What about students like Claire who are in the back of the line?"

"I looked back to check on them several times," Diane told her.

"But it wasn't enough, was it? Seems to me you should stay in the middle – so you can take care of all your students," Ms. Booth argued. "If you had been watching everyone, Claire wouldn't have gotten hurt."

"I led students to a safe area. I explained that they needed to walk quickly, but not run," Diane said. "I instructed them to walk in pairs, and I looked back to check on them several times."

"Claire got hurt because you didn't do your job," Ms. Booth said.

"I'm sorry about this, but it was an accident," Diane stressed.

"I know it's frustrating," she continued, "I can't change what happened. What can I do now?"

"You've done enough already." Ms. Booth shook her head and walked out.

'See you in court'

Ms. Booth sued, claiming the teacher didn't watch students carefully enough, which caused Claire to get hurt.

School officials argued that the teacher properly supervised students during the fire drill. They insisted Claire's fall was an accident. When a lower court ruled against the school, it appealed. Did the court overturn the ruling?

Decision: Yes, the appellate court reversed the decision.

Key: The teacher stood at the front of the line, which is the logical place to be when students have to cross the street, the court explained.

The court also noted that she gave clear instructions before the drill. Even if the teacher had walked in the middle of the line, it would be unlikely that she could've prevented this unforeseeable accident, the court ruled.

Cite: *Esponda v. City of New York.*

Discussion points for teachers and principals:

Accidents can happen – even during drills designed to keep students safe.

To help reduce the chance of an accident during a fire drill, remind students to:

- remain calm
- listen for further instructions
- walk quickly, but do not run
- pair up with a classmate, and
- stay with the class.

Did teacher do enough to prevent student's injury? Mom says, 'No!'

Student injured in class – and parent blames the teacher

"Walk me through it," Principal Heather Marks said to teacher Olivia Neal. "Mike Lane's mom is upset."

"I understand that she's not happy about Mike getting hurt," Olivia said. "But it was an accident."

"Fill me in on the details," Heather sighed. "She wants to know why we had three student injuries in one day."

Three 'injuries'

"We were using scalpels to dissect flowers in our biology lab," Olivia said.

"OK, go on," Heather prodded her.

"The first student cut his hand in the morning, but it was more like a paper cut. He just needed a bandage," Olivia insisted.

"And I didn't even know about the second student's cut until the next day," she continued. "Actually, it was more of a scrape than a cut."

"So Mike was the third student who cut himself with the scalpel?" Heather asked.

"Yes, Mike was in the last lab," Olivia said. "When he yanked the cap off of his scalpel, the blade sliced his thumb pretty bad. But his was the only real injury. We called for help right away."

"What did you do after the first injury? Did you fill out one of the student accident report forms?" Heather asked.

"Of course I did," Olivia replied.

"Good," Heather said, "because Mike's mom is threatening to sue."

Mike's mother did sue, claiming the school was negligent. Did the judge agree?

Decision: Yes, the court ruled the district was negligent and refused to grant immunity, because it had prior knowledge of the danger before Mike was injured.

Key: This teacher knew potential hazards existed because two students had sustained minor injuries. The teacher listed recommendations to prevent similar injuries in the accident report form. But she failed to follow her own suggestions – and her non-action resulted in a more serious student injury.

Cite: *Heuser v. Community Insurance Corp.*

Chemistry explosion injures student: Did teacher explain safety measures?

Parents blame teacher for accident in chemistry lab

Principal Heather Marks put her coffee cup down when teacher Jacob Hinson walked into her office.

"Have you heard from Karen's parents yet?" Jacob asked. "I barely slept last night from worrying about her chin."

"Karen's OK," Heather said. "But her parents are furious. We need to talk about what happened in the chemistry lab."

Lab partner didn't follow the rules

"Karen's lab partner took the stopper out of a flask holding hydrogen – which is extremely flammable," Jacob explained.

"Right," Heather nodded, prompting him to continue.

"Then he lit a match directly over the flask. It exploded, and the shattered glass flew up into Karen's face," Jacob said.

"You know the rest," he continued. "That's when we called for help."

Heather sighed. "Karen's parents are threatening to sue you personally."

"Are you serious?" Jacob asked. "I gave the students clear instructions in the lab. Her partner usually follows the lab rules."

Karen's parents did sue the teacher, claiming he was negligent.

School officials argued that the accident wasn't foreseeable. The student who caused the explosion was an upperclassman, and he didn't have a history of behavior problems, so the teacher assumed he'd follow the rules. They asked the court to dismiss the claims, saying the teacher was entitled to governmental immunity.

Did the judge agree?

Decision: No, the judge said a trial was needed to determine if the teacher failed his duty to keep students safe.

Key: The danger was foreseeable, because hydrogen is extremely flammable, the court ruled. The court also noted that it's unwise to assume older students will follow the rules as "teenagers can be just as apt to exercise bad judgment or misbehave" as younger students.

Cite: *Sheehan v. Coventry Board of Educ.*

Sharpen Your Judgment

Tardy students' horseplay causes accident

"I needed a seventh-inning stretch anyway," teacher Jake Hinson said as he put away the paper he was grading.

"Baseball references, already? The season just started!" Principal Heather Marks laughed.

Jake grinned. "Yeah, well don't keep me in suspense. This chat must be about Mike."

"It is," Heather said. "Let's go over it again."

"I took attendance in the lab, as usual. After the tardy bell, we went into the adjoining classroom," he explained.

Heather nodded, waiting for more info.

"A few minutes later, we heard a crash in the lab," he said. "Mike, Brad and Joe were tardy. As they walked in, their horseplay got out of hand. That's how Mike broke his ankle."

"Did you lock the lab to keep students from going in unsupervised?" Heather asked him.

"No," Jake admitted. "But I never do."

"Hmmm," Heather said. "Well, Mike's mom is saying you didn't supervise the students who were in the lab. She's threatening to sue."

Mike's mother did sue, claiming Jake failed his duty to protect her son while he was in the school's lab. Did the judge agree?

Sharpen Your Judgment

Girl hurt playing football: Is it school's fault?

"The NFL playoffs have been really exciting this year," teacher Heather Marks said to principal Mary Salinger as they chatted in Salinger's office. "Who do you think will win the big game?"

"I'm not sure," Mary replied. "To tell you the truth, I'm kind of soured on football right now."

"But our school team had a great season," Marks pointed out. "They were undefeated this year."

"They were great," Salinger agreed. "But we have a football problem that has nothing to do with them.

"Brianna Giles' parents are suing because she got hurt playing football at recess."

Accident happened suddenly

"I heard she lost three teeth," Marks said. "But it happened so fast that I don't think any amount of supervision could have prevented it."

"Brianna's parents are saying we shouldn't have allowed touch football," Salinger said.

"But it was just an accident," Marks said.

"Let's hope the court sees it that way," Salinger said.

The girl's parents sued the school district for negligent supervision, claiming touch football was an improper recess activity.

Did they win?

Sharpen Your Judgment – The Decision

No, the judge sided with the school.

The judge noted Mike's mom had a logical argument: The teacher wasn't even in the lab when the accident happened, so he didn't protect Mike. Under normal circumstances, that scenario might be enough to prove a teacher failed to protect a student.

But the judge said this case was different: The student and his buddies were tardy. The teacher couldn't be expected to foresee tardy students goofing off as they came in.

The judge pointed to steps the teacher set up to supervise both the lab and the classroom, such as taking attendance in the lab, staying in the lab until after the late bell and teaching in the adjoining classroom with the shared door open.

On the day of the accident, Jake followed those steps, which meant he didn't breach his duty, the court ruled.

Analysis: Follow procedures consistently

As this case shows, courts generally recognize that accidents do happen.

Even so, it's always a good idea to follow safety procedures consistently to keep risks and accidents to a minimum.

Cite: *Medeiros v. Sitrin.*

Sharpen Your Judgment – The Decision

No, an appeals ruled for the school district and dismissed the parents' case.

The girl's parents claimed the district did not provide enough playground supervision while the students were at recess. They also said touch football is an inappropriate recess activity. Allowing boys and girls to play together made it worse, they added, because boys and girls physically mature at different rates.

The district said it couldn't be blamed for the girl's injuries because they resulted from a spontaneous and unintentional accident. It pointed out that neither the girl nor the child who collided with her had any history of disciplinary issues. There was no way to predict or stop the unfortunate accident, it insisted.

The court agreed. Even direct supervision would not have prevented the collision, which could have happened just as easily in a game of tag or any other game in which students run in different directions.

Analysis: Don't let your guard down

It's reassuring when a court issues a common-sense ruling that recognizes unavoidable accidents will happen. But you still need to do all you can to provide an appropriate level of supervision during recess activities.

Cite: *Bellinger v. Ballston Spa Cent. School Dist.*

Sharpen Your Judgment

They charge teacher wasn't paying attention

The district's lawyer began taking notes as he asked the first question: "Did you see Michael Allenwood fall from the monkey bars?"

Teacher Drucie West replied: "Yes, I was standing right next to the monkey bars while supervising recess. I saw the whole thing."

"You understand Michael's parents are suing for negligence as a result of his injuries from the fall?" he explained.

"I know that," the teacher said, "but I don't understand why they say there was negligence involved. I was watching the whole time, and everything was normal. He just slipped."

"Right," the lawyer nodded. "But the issue here, according to the parents, is that you saw Michael fall from the bars two other times. That's correct, isn't it?"

"Yes, it is. There were a couple of other occasions when he fell. As I recall, he had a few minor scrapes from those falls – nothing as serious as the injuries from this last fall."

"OK, I understand," the lawyer said. "We'll have to see where this suit goes."

The parents persisted in filing the suit, and the teacher and the school had to defend against the negligence charge. Did the school win the case?

Sharpen Your Judgment – The Decision

Yes. The school won when a judge found the teacher wasn't negligent in her supervision of the school playground.

In court, the parents contended that, having observed two previous falls, the teacher should have been aware of the danger to the student and taken extra precautions to prevent injuries.

The school pointed out that falls from playground equipment are ordinary events and that no one could predict that a fall resulting in minor injury would lead to another fall resulting in serious injury.

The judge sided with the school and pointed out that the teacher had been diligent in performing her job supervising recess in the school playground.

That's all that could have been required of her.

Analysis: Did teacher do the job?

In general, courts recognize that injuries in schools and on playgrounds often happen as a result of normal circumstances and not because of negligence.

Most times, however, judges want evidence that the teacher was doing his or her job in a consistent and safe manner.

Cite: *Botti v. Seaford Harbor Elementary School Dist.*

Sharpen Your Judgment

Should school be blamed for fall from monkey bars?

"Looks like we're out of sugar again," teacher Heather Marks sighed to principal Mary Salinger as she checked each cabinet in the teacher's lounge. "What do we have to do to keep this place stocked?"

"That's the least of my worries right now," Mary replied. "I just heard there's supposed to be a ruling in the Rose Tafoya case any day now."

"That's the first-grader who fell off the monkey bars, right?" Heather said. "I heard she got hurt pretty bad."

"Yes," Mary said. "She got pushed from behind."

Was school at fault?

"But that happened while Rose was in the after-school program, didn't it?" Heather remembered. "We don't even run that program. How can we get blamed for something that happened after school?"

"I guess they're saying since it happened in our school yard we're responsible," Mary said.

"You just never know how these things are going to turn out," Mary said.

Rose's mother sued the school district, saying its negligence caused her daughter's injuries.

The school district filed a motion for summary judgment, asking the court to throw out the mother's claims against it.

Did the court agree with the district and dismiss the negligence claims?

Sharpen Your Judgment – The Decision

Yes, the court granted the school district's motion.

The student's mother argued the district was liable, even though the accident occurred after the school day had ended and the girl was in the custody of the after-school program. The mother pointed out that the accident happened on school grounds.

The school district relied on the fact that neither the injured child nor the boy who pushed her were under its custody or control when the accident happened. It said the duty to supervise the children had been passed along to the after-school services provider.

The court agreed with the school district. A school's duty to supervise students and keep them safe "is coextensive with its physical custody and control" of them. At the time of the accident, the school did not have custody or control of the injured student.

Analysis: Be clear on custody transfers

Your duty to supervise ends when students leave your custody and control. Just make sure you make that clear to the next link in the chain when students leave their classrooms at the end of the day.

Cite: *Medina v. City of New York.*

Sharpen Your Judgment

Was teacher liable for student's Field Day injury?

"Todd is suing? Are you serious?" Coach Vinny Travo asked as he sat down in Principal Heather Marks' office.

"I'm afraid so," Heather said. "Todd says you shouldn't have asked him to help you set up for Field Day."

"I'm sorry that Todd lost his toe," Vinny said. "But it was a freak accident."

"Walk me through the accident. What happened?" Heather asked.

"Todd was moving one of the volleyball poles across the field," Vinny explained. "The metal base came off and crushed his foot."

"Anything else?" Heather asked.

"Well, we've never had a problem with the poles before," Vinny added.

"Todd's parents claim we were negligent," Heather told him. "They've named you in the suit, too."

"If I had known this would happen, I wouldn't have asked for volunteers to help," Vinny said.

Todd and his parents sued, claiming the school and the teacher were negligent.

Did the judge agree?

Sharpen Your Judgment — The Decision

No, the judge said this wasn't a case of negligence.

The judge looked at how Vinny organized the Field Day preparations: Students were asked to volunteer, and the school didn't have any prior problems with the equipment.

The judge noted that Vinny supervised the Field Day set-up and concluded that the injury happened so fast that Vinny couldn't have prevented Todd's injury.

What about asking for help? Didn't that prove Vinny and the school were responsible for the injury?

No, the judge said. It's not uncommon for students to help set up for special school activities, the judge explained. Todd's injury was unforeseeable, so Vinny was entitled to qualified immunity, the judge ruled.

Analysis: Every accident isn't foreseeable

As this case shows, courts understand that accidents do happen. It's still a good idea for teachers to supervise students and inspect equipment regularly for wear and tear.

Doing so may help prevent foreseeable accidents, keeping special activities – such as Field Day – fun and safe for students.

Cite: *Raef v. Union County Public School Board.*

Disabled student dies on the playground: Parents ask, 'Did teacher follow the IEP?'

Dispute over 'reasonable attention' ends up in court

The school district's attorney, Isaac Akers, began: "I know you're still shaken by the death of Michael Reedle on the school playground, but since his parents have decided to sue over it, we'll need to concentrate on gathering information to prepare our case."

Teacher Glenna Frost nodded.

"Now," he continued, "you were aware from Michael's IEP that he used a breathing tube and required special attention. Is that right?"

"Yes," the teacher confirmed, "I had read the IEP and spoken to Michael's mother about it. I always kept a close eye on him, but the mother insisted that he should go out on the playground 'just like the other children.' Nothing in the IEP prevented him from doing that."

The attorney wrote as he spoke: "And did you see what happened?"

The teacher thought for a moment and then answered: "I didn't see much of anything because I had turned to answer another student's question. That's when I heard shouting and turned around to see Michael on the ground gasping for air."

"What did you do then?"

The family says ...

"I first ran over to check on him. Then I saw the breathing tube was dislodged, so I got our nurse to come out and help."

The attorney made a few more notes and then said, "You're aware the family says you should have been paying closer attention to Michael, since you knew about his IEP and his condition?"

"I am," she replied.

In court, the family charged the teacher with negligence and asked for damages. Did the school and the teacher win?

Decision: Yes. A judge said the teacher had taken reasonable steps to watch over the student and followed the IEP.

Key: The teacher showed that she was aware and considerate of the child's condition but couldn't ignore the needs of the other students to give 100% attention to the child.

Cite: *Ortega v. Bibb County School Dist.*

Sharpen Your Judgment

Could teacher have protected student from bully?

"Stop it," said student Ray Baer, but student Carl Pardo punched him again.

"Ow!" cried Ray. "Why do you always have to pick on me?"

"You wuss," said Carl. "That didn't hurt."

"Stop it," said Ray. "I just want to get this DVD player back to class in one piece."

"Then I think you'd better let me push the cart," sneered Carl.

"Fine," said Ray, backing away before Carl could shove him. "But be careful – OK? Don't break it."

"I hope you're not really trying to tell me what to do," said Carl. "But just in case you are, I'd better knock some sense into you."

Carl grabbed Ray, picked him off the ground, then hurled him down. There was a terrible crack as Ray's leg broke.

Ray's parents sued. They said the teacher shouldn't have sent the boys to run an errand together. Ray was bound to get hurt because Carl was already terrorizing him. But the teacher said she never saw bullying and Ray didn't tell her Carl was bothering him.

The school asked the court to dismiss the case. Did the court agree?

Sharpen Your Judgment – The Decision

No, the court refused to dismiss the case.

A trial is needed so that a jury can hear both sides of the story.

The jury will have to figure out how much the school's staff knew about Carl's bullying before the teacher sent Ray off to run an errand alone with him.

Ray's parents could win their lawsuit if a jury decided the school knew Carl was bullying Ray, and their teacher didn't keep Carl away from him.

Analysis: Keep your students safe

One of the most important things you do in your job is stop students from hurting each other. Protecting kids from bullies can also help keep your school from getting sued.

It's routine to separate students when you know one of them is bothering another – but what if you don't know?

People at school need to work as a team by sharing information.

Bullies often wait until the coast is clear before they strike. That's why you need to encourage students to come forward – and to urge other teachers to speak up if they see even subtle signs of harassment.

Cite: *Johnson v. Ken-Ton Union Free School Dist.*

Sharpen Your Judgment

Student falls at school bake sale: Is district responsible?

"My team was eliminated from the NBA playoffs last night," teacher Ron Samuels sighed as he walked into Principal Heather Marks' office.

"Cheer me up with news about our bake sale numbers," he said.

"We met our goal," Marks shifted gears, "but we have a more pressing issue to discuss. What happened when Jenna Roberts fell down the stairs during the sale?"

"Uh-oh. That doesn't sound good," Samuels said.

"It's not. Her parents are suing us," Marks replied.

How the cookie crumbles ...

"Seriously?" Samuels shook his head. "Jenna tripped. We're supposed to prevent kids from stumbling now?"

"Jenna's parents said kids were running up and down the stairs with cookies. They said some icing must have fallen off, and that's probably why Jenna slipped."

"Well, we didn't find icing on the stairs – or any other food, for that matter," Samuels said. "And no one requested a cleanup. I was there the entire time."

"I know you monitored the area. Were kids running on the stairwell with food?" Marks asked him.

"A little," he said. "But I told them to slow down."

Jenna's parents sued the school district, claiming it failed to maintain a safe environment for students during a school-sponsored event.

Did they win?

Sharpen Your Judgment – The Decision

No, an appeals court affirmed a lower court's ruling in favor of the school district and dismissed the case.

The parents claimed the school failed to keep the stairwell floor safe. They said the fall occurred after one of the children must have dropped food on the stairs.

The district said it couldn't be blamed. It pointed out that a spill was neither found by nor reported to school staff.

The court agreed with the district. For the school to be held liable, the parents had to prove two points.

First, they had to show an actual spill caused the child's fall. Second, they had to prove school personnel knew about the hazard, but failed to clean up the spill.

The parents couldn't prove either of the two.

Analysis: Do what you can – monitor and eliminate

As this case shows, a mere hazard possibility doesn't mean schools aren't maintaining safe environments. School administrators know the potential for risks will always be present. The best practices: Monitor areas vigilantly and take care of reported concerns quickly.

Cite: *Barrera v. City of New York.*

Student falls asleep at the wheel on way home from post-prom party

Parents ask, 'Shouldn't teacher have taken his keys?'

It was the first school day after student Kevin Schaefer's car accident. He'd dozed off and crashed after taking his date home from the post-prom party.

When teacher Judy Kitt saw Kevin's best friend Dan coming down the hall that morning, the anger on his face made her stomach sink.

"What's wrong?" Judy asked him. "Is there bad news from the hospital?"

"No, but Kev's still pretty out of it," said Dan. "It's just that I had a long talk with his folks last night. They're really mad at the school for this."

"Mad at the school?" repeated Judy.

"Sure," said Dan angrily. "An all-night party on top of the dance! Anybody'd drift off at the wheel after that. Why didn't the school arrange for buses?"

"Because the school didn't have anything to do with it," said Judy. "The post-prom was the parents' group's party."

"Then why were you there?" he asked.

"I volunteered as a chaperone. I wanted to help give you kids a safe and fun alternative to parties with alcohol."

"That's nice," retorted Dan, "but if you were so worried about our safety, why didn't you stop Kevin from driving?"

"You were there, Dan," said Judy. "You heard Kevin tell me he felt fine when you two left with your dates."

"Nobody's really fine when they've been up all night," Dan shot back. "You should have known that. I wouldn't be surprised if Kev's parents sued the school. And I wouldn't blame them, either!"

Kevin's parents did sue. They claimed the school created the danger that their son would nod off while driving. Did it?

Decision: No. The all-night party wasn't the school's responsibility. And even if it had been, there was no sign Kevin was too tired to drive when he left.

Key: When it's prom season, we all want to keep students safe. It might be best to be overly cautious. Extra communication with parents could be a good first step.

Cite: *Watson v. Methacton School Dist.*

Parent fails to supervise student who got hurt – but teacher must defend himself against charge

Who was supposed to be in charge when the accident happened?

As soon as he heard the screams, teacher Dan Dykstra dropped his paperwork and sprinted across the meadow and toward the sound on the other side of the hill.

Before he got there, he ran into a sobbing Tracy Wells, who shouted, "Mr. Dykstra, Michael Phister's been hurt. My father called 911."

Later ...

In a conference room, Dan sat with principal Alicia Cruze, who began with, "Your group was chopping wood to sell as part of the after-school fundraiser for the band, right?"

"Correct," Dan nodded. "We were on the land owned by Tracy Wells' father, who agreed to let us do it."

"According to Tracy's father, he turned away for a moment and Michael put his hand into the log splitter," the principal recounted. "That's when he was injured."

"That's the story I got," Dan agreed. "Though, of course, I didn't see it."

"Where were you?" the principal asked.

"I had gone back to my car to grab some forms we were using to keep track of our inventory," Dan explained. "I made sure to tell Tracy's father that I'd be gone for a minute and that he was in charge."

"He acknowledged that?" the principal followed up.

"Definitely," Dan said. "He said, 'OK, I'll watch them.'"

The complaint

The injured student's parents later sued for negligence, arguing that the teacher should have been in charge at all times and was responsible for the accident. Did the teacher win?

Decision: No. A judge ruled there was reasonable evidence that the student wasn't properly supervised. The case went to trial – and a likely expensive settlement.

Key: The ruling was based on the concept that a teacher supervising a school activity – even one after school – is solely responsible for the students and can't delegate that responsibility.

Cite: *Travis v. Bohannon.*

Sharpen Your Judgment

Teacher follows policy – but gets sued personally

As she walked into the teachers' lounge, teacher Amy Hill almost ran into her TA, Kay Harris. "Sorry," Amy muttered.

"What's wrong?" Kay asked.

"Remember that little incident with Gia's abortion T-shirt?" Amy continued without waiting for an answer. "She's suing the school and me personally, too!"

"I know Gia's suing the school over the dress code," Kay said. "But what does that have to do with you?"

"According to Gia, I snatched her arm and dragged her as she was trying to walk to the office," Amy told her.

"That won't fly," Kay reassured Amy. "I saw the whole thing: After I told her to go to the office, you led her by the arm – and it wasn't forced or unreasonable."

"I don't think so either," Amy agreed. "I can't believe I have to deal with this because Gia didn't follow the dress code."

"You'll get this cleared up," Kay said.

Gia and her parents sued the school and Amy personally. She asked the court to dismiss the claim. Did it?

Sharpen Your Judgment

Teacher sent bullies to office: Was that enough?

"Sorry to keep you waiting," teacher Amy Hill said as she walked in Principal Heather Marks' office. "What happened?"

"Just what we expected," Heather said. "Tina Hemby's mother is suing.

"She claims we didn't do enough to stop that group of boys from harassing Tina about her weight," Heather said, sighing.

"But I did everything by the book," Amy said, counting on her fingers. "First, I talked to the kids. When that didn't stop the nasty remarks, I sent them to the guidance counselor and your office."

"I know," Heather agreed. "But now Tina's mother claims the teasing triggered an eating disorder. According to her, if we had stopped the teasing, Tina wouldn't have anorexia."

"This doesn't make sense," Amy said. "Can we really be held accountable for a student developing a medical condition?"

"We're going to fight this," Heather said.

Tina's mother sued, claiming the school condoned a hostile environment by failing to stop the harassment.

School officials asked the court to dismiss the claim. Did it?

Sharpen Your Judgment – The Decision

No, the court didn't dismiss Gia's lawsuit.

The judge acknowledged that Amy followed school policy by sending Gia to the office for a possible dress code violation.

But the court pointed to one undisputed fact: When Amy took Gia by the arm, she was already walking to the office as she'd been instructed.

One question remained:

Did Amy "lead" Gia to the office or did Amy "drag" Gia to the office?

The judge said more info was needed before the court could determine whether the teacher used excessive force when escorting Gia to the office.

For this reason, the case needed to go to trial, the judge explained.

Analysis: Let verbal instructions work

As this case shows, courts recognize when teachers follow school policy. But it also shows the growing concern about student safety.

Best practice: When students follow verbal instructions, it's best to avoid physical contact to prevent misconceptions about your intent.

Cite: *T.A. v. McSwain Union Elementary School.*

Sharpen Your Judgment – The Decision

No, the court refused to dismiss the claim.

Lawyers for the school pointed out that mere teasing and name-calling shouldn't be enough to support a Title IX claim.

But Tina and her mother argued that Tina was subjected to constant teasing "on a daily basis" for an entire school year.

They said the teacher and the principal should've taken further steps to protect Tina.

Because they didn't, the constant bullying triggered an eating disorder. As a result of their "deliberate indifference," Tina was hospitalized for anorexia, her mother said.

The judge said a trial was needed to determine whether school officials acted appropriately under the circumstances.

Follow up on ongoing complaints

Rather than face a costly trial, this district agreed to a hefty $55,000 settlement to resolve the dispute.

School officials can avoid repeat complaints by following up right away to make sure:

- the initial problem was resolved, and
- additional issues aren't lingering.

Cite: *Mary V. v. Pittsburgh Public Schools.*

'You let them harass my kid!' Mom's claim ends up in court

Jury returns $800K verdict against district

When the bell rang, teacher Amy Hill sat down at her desk and watched students file out of the room. Normally Amy looked forward to dismissal time. But not today. She sighed as she re-read the e-mail from Dane Clark's mother.

Ms. Clark's message was to the point. It said: "We have to talk – today! I will be there right after school."

When Amy heard the door open, she closed the e-mail and stood up. "Hello, Ms. Clark. Come inside and have a seat."

"How many times do I have to come to this school?" Ms. Clark asked as she plopped her bag onto an empty desk.

"Dane was extremely upset when he got home from school yesterday," she continued without waiting for an answer. "Tell me exactly what you people plan to do about what happened."

Classmate embarrassed her son

"I understand that Dane was upset yesterday," Amy said.

"Of course he was," Ms. Clark said. "That girl humiliated my son in front of the whole class."

"When I realized what was going on," Amy said, "I stopped Leah."

"Don't sugarcoat it," Ms. Clark said. "Leah embarrassed Dane on purpose. She wrote 'Dane-is-a-fag' on the back of her note cards.

"So when she flipped through her index cards while reading her notes, the whole class saw her 'joke' about Dane," Ms. Clark said. "You let it happen."

Could she have prevented it?

"I'd never 'let' students harass each other in my class," Amy said.

"But you did," Ms. Clark said. "Other students have gotten away with bullying Dane, like spray-painting his locker and calling him 'queer' and 'pig.' And now this? I'm tired of this."

"I know," Amy agreed. "But I want to be very clear – I didn't 'let' this happen.

"When the class started snickering, I knew something was up," Amy explained. "I saw what Leah did, and I stopped the presentation. I also took the cards from her and talked to her about treating people with respect."

"Oh, you talked to her?" Ms. Clark repeated. "Well, I don't think that's going to cut it this time."

"This time?" Amy asked. "Leah has never been in trouble for being mean to Dane before.

"But I still sent her to the principal's office," Amy added. "And I'm sure the principal will take care of it."

"That answer's not going to satisfy me today," Ms. Clark said.

Mom files suit

Ms. Clark sued, claiming the school allowed other students to harass her son.

The district said it didn't allow students to bully each other. The teacher talked to Leah and sent her to the office. Because this was a first offense, Leah received a verbal warning, as per school policy, officials said.

The court ruled for the district, but Ms. Clark appealed.

Did the court side with her?

Decision: Yes, the appellate court reversed the decision, and the jury awarded Dane an $800,000 verdict.

Key: The court noted handling discipline on a case-by-case basis would be correct under normal circumstances.

But the court pointed out a big difference here: Dane was bullied by several students, all of whom received verbal warnings. But those warnings didn't put an end to the systemic pattern of bullying, the court explained.

It's not enough to prevent one student from bullying another. Schools must also make an effort to stop "patterns of harassment" as well, the court ruled.

Cite: *Patterson v. Hudson Area Schools.*

Discussion points for teachers and principals:

Public speaking and anxiety go hand in hand. But this case shows how speakers can cause a member of the audience to have anxiety.

Teachers can prevent bullying during oral presentations by:

- approving visual aids and notes before the presentation, and
- sitting with the class during presentations – to share the audience's vantage point.

Sharpen Your Judgment

Drawing the line when dealing with difficult students – and parents

The parent sat down and got right to the point: "I'd like you to let my daughter Brenda make up the assignments she's missed because of absences, and give her a break on future absences."

Teacher Terri Howland hesitated and then answered: "That's a big request, one I normally don't meet."

"Let me tell you the circumstances," the parent continued. "We're having some problems with Brenda's father. That's what's caused her to miss so much school and so many assignments."

"I'm sorry," the teacher said. "Still, it's not fair to the other students if I just overlook when Brenda doesn't show up or finish her work on time. You see that."

"Look, failing Brenda can only make a bad situation worse for her," the parent replied. "You don't want that, right?"

"Of course not," the teacher said. "We can look at other ways to help …"

"Forget that," the parent snapped. "What she needs is your cooperation."

When the teacher refused, the parent sued, arguing the refusal caused emotional distress for the child.

Did the school win?

Sharpen Your Judgment – The Decision

Yes. A judge ruled that the teacher couldn't be blamed for causing emotional distress just because of a commitment to school standards.

In court, the parent argued that the teacher was being a slave to the rules by failing to account for a special situation at home.

The judge said schools should consider special situations – but that didn't mean the teacher was obligated to lower academic standards or overlook absences.

Decision: The teacher was right to stick to the standards.

Analysis: Help in other ways

It's always difficult when you know a student is mired in a tough situation at home, one that's affecting academic performance.

And of course you want to help. But that doesn't mean you have to give the student a "pass." Instead:

- Take a look at and recommend the resources available to help the student through a tough time, and
- Keep parents and administrators informed at the first sign of problems, so that no one is surprised later when or if the problem reaches crisis stage.

Cite: *Barrino v. East Baton Rouge Parish School Board.*

Sharpen Your Judgment

School gets caught up in parental-abuse case

Bev O'Neill poked her head in the doorway and said, "You wanted to see me?"

Principal Lou Vasquez nodded and said, "Yes, it's about that report you gave me describing the bruises on one of your students, Jeremy Wales, and what he told you about how he got them."

As the teacher sat down, she noted, "When he talked about how his father beat him with a hose, I couldn't let it go."

"And I agree with your decision," the principal said. "We have a problem, however.

"I sent the report on to social services, as the policy dictates, and they're investigating the parents for abuse."

"Where's the problem?" the teacher asked.

"The parents say they want to know who in this school wrote the report," he explained. "As I promised you, when I forwarded the report, I left your name off it."

"What happens if I say it's OK to release my name?" she responded.

"They may sue you for emotional distress."

The parents eventually went to court to get the teacher's name released. Did they win?

Sharpen Your Judgment – The Decision

No. The teacher was not required to release her name.

The court ruled that the parents had a right to a copy of the report so they could mount a defense against the charge of abusive treatment.

However, the source of the report had to remain anonymous.

The parents argued that the court was making it impossible to file a suit against the source if that source remained anonymous.

That's true, the judge agreed.

Still, the name of the person who wrote the report must be kept confidential and out of the public record. Final ruling: The teacher's name stays out.

Courts and agencies agree

Most courts and family-services agencies have agreed on cases like this one: Teachers who report suspected abuse have a right to anonymity.

Here's why:

Courts and agencies realize the threat of going public with a source's name would make teachers hesitant to report abuse, for fear of being dragged into a lawsuit. Generally, in such cases, your name is protected.

Cite: *Selapack v. Iroquois Cent. School Dist.*

Teacher spots a bruise on a student: Parent insists, 'It's none of your business'

What's the right – and legal – move when abuse looks like a possibility?

The "ouch!" from Jason Royer startled teacher Ben Amos.

"Gee, Jason," Ben said, "could brushing against Alex in line really hurt that much?"

"Oh, it wasn't Alex's fault," the student responded. "It's because of my arm."

"Your arm?"

Jason raised his sleeve to reveal an ugly, large bruise.

Later, the teacher took Jason aside and asked, "Did that happen in a fight here?"

The boy hesitated, then answered. "No, it happened at home. My mother did it."

A week later ...

Ben sat with a district social worker, Eileen Sager, and finished up: "So, the story is pretty much what I wrote in my report you saw. Jason said his mother regularly beat him since the parents got divorced."

"Good thing you said something," she noted. "We had Jason examined, and there were more bruises. We've arranged to have him stay with his father until this whole thing gets sorted out by social services and the courts. That'll probably take a few meetings and official hearings."

"But you were able to have him placed with his father without an official hearing?" Ben asked.

"Well, because of the way you described the situation, we were able to have it declared an emergency and skip some of the normal steps," she explained.

"How did his mother react?"

"Not well," Eileen sighed. "She even mentioned filing a lawsuit."

Eventually, the mother did sue the school and social services for invasion of privacy and failure to follow due process.

Did the school win?

Decision: Yes. A judge ruled the teacher and social services took appropriate action under the circumstances.

Key: Depending on state law, courts usually back teachers who take action at the first hint of abuse in the home.

Cite: *Shapiro v. Kronfeld.*

Principal and teacher follow policy over report of sexual abuse: Should they have done more?

Mother insists the school didn't take strong enough action

The district's lawyer, Clive Rusher, began firing off questions as soon as he sat down for the meeting.

"When did you first learn that Janna Pickett was being sexually abused by her brother?"

Principal Dee Dattis gestured to teacher Mara Chastain to go first.

"It was about two months ago, when I saw Janna crying at her desk," Mara said. "I took her aside and asked her what was wrong and if I could help."

"And she told you all about it?" the lawyer asked while making notes.

"Yes, and I immediately told Dee."

"And, Ms. Dattis," he turned to the principal, "you then notified Janna's mother and made a call to the abuse crisis center. Is that correct?"

"That's right," Dee nodded.

He stopped for a minute to write a few more notes, and then looked up at the two of them. "As you know, Janna's mother is suing the school for failing to take appropriate action to prevent the abuse. She says you should have called the police."

'Take care of it'

The principal responded: "She was pretty hysterical when I called her and said she couldn't handle her son, and wanted us to take care of it. I explained that the policy is to call police only when the report involves abuse by a parent or guardian."

"OK, thanks," he concluded. "We'll see what happens from here."

Did the school win the lawsuit?

Decision: Yes. The court considered (a) who was ultimately responsible for the girl's well-being, and (b) whether the school had taken the proper steps upon hearing the abuse complaint. The ruling: The parent was responsible, and the school followed policy and acted appropriately.

Key: While the school may have wanted to take stronger action, policy has to be followed to respect the rights and privacy of the family. Be sure to check those policies in your state.

Cite: *Catherine G. v. County of Essex.*

Good student suddenly starts acting up in class – what's going on?

Educators wonder if moodiness is enough to suggest child abuse

"Have any other teachers noticed something different about Pia Wolfe lately?" teacher Kate Anders asked Assistant Principal Kyle Wing.

"Yes," said Kyle. "She's logged a lot of time in my office lately – blowing up over nothing, starting fights, talking back."

"It's not just me, then," said Kate. "But I'm also worried because she seems so sad. I asked her after class why she's acting like this, and she seemed about to cry."

"I've noticed the sadness, too," said Kyle. "When she's not getting aggressive, it's like she's fighting back tears."

Is there a deeper problem here?

"I wanted to talk to you because I'm worried something bad might be happening to Pia at home," said Kate.

"Like abuse?" asked Kyle.

"That's what I'm afraid of," said Kate. "I know adolescents can be moody – even when everything's fine. She says nothing's wrong. So why is she acting like this?"

"Abuse crossed my mind, too," said Kyle. "But I hate to call the authorities and set off an investigation without something even semi-definite to go on. What if they get it wrong and tear her family apart?"

No call was the wrong call

It turned out Pia's stepfather was sexually abusing her. After she broke down and told her mother, her mom called the police – then sued Kyle and Kate, saying they saw the signs but didn't report abuse.

Did the judge agree to dismiss the suit?

Decision: No, a trial was needed for a jury to decide if the educators behaved recklessly and exposed Pia to continued sexual abuse.

Key: No one wants to make a serious allegation and get it wrong, but educators have a legal duty to report. In Kyle and Kate's state, there's a duty to report if a teacher even suspects abuse. The exact duty varies from state to state. You can check your state law duty at *childwelfare.gov*.

Cite: *Wilson v. Columbus Board of Educ.*

Expelled student commits suicide, mom blames teacher: Was she liable?

Mom sues after suicide note claims teacher lied about behavior problem

Teacher Dana Anderson headed to Principal Heather Marks' office. She hoped today would be less stressful than yesterday. Reid Andrews, the student who caused all the trouble, had been expelled.

She walked into the office. "You needed to see me first thing? What's going on?"

"Well," Heather hesitated, tracing the rim of her coffee cup with her finger, "There's no easy way to say this."

"You're making me nervous," Dana told her.

Note claims teacher lied

"Reid Andrews. He, um, committed suicide yesterday afternoon."

"What?" Dana whispered, allowing the news to sink in. "I mean, I can't believe it. He had problems in school, but – "

"Reid's mom found a suicide note," Heather continued, "and it says you lied about Reid's latest disciplinary issue. She's threatening to sue you personally."

Dana sank back into the chair and stared at the ceiling for a full minute. Then she looked at Heather and whispered, "That's ridiculous. I feel bad, but – "

"I do, too, Dana," Heather told her. "This is a tragedy."

"But here's the issue: Reid was expelled for continuous behavior problems," Heather pointed out. "He threw chairs, called names, used profanity and tipped desks on a regular basis. We have witnesses and documentation."

Reid's mother did sue the teacher, accusing her of intentional infliction of emotional distress and wrongful death. Was she to blame?

Decision: No. In order to prove emotional distress, Reid's mom had to show the way Dana treated Reid exceeded the bounds of decency.

Key: One unproven accusation doesn't show a teacher intentionally caused emotional distress, and the school's thorough documentation recorded Reid's ongoing disciplinary problems.

Cite: *Mikell v. School Administrative Unit No. 33.*

What seemed like an innocent case of teasing turned into a school's worst nightmare

Did the teacher respond strongly enough to prevent a tragedy?

"I know how mean kids can be. But I never thought it would lead to this," explained teacher Mary Walker.

"As you know, Julie's parents are suing you and the school for Julie's suicide," said the district's lawyer, John Kearny.

"But we didn't do anything wrong. How can they blame us?" Mary asked.

John read from his notes as he spoke: "They say several students teased Julie about her weight for months and you didn't stop it. What's been going on?"

"Several students had been teasing Julie for a while. But kids often do that," noted Mary.

"Did you do anything about it?" John asked.

"I followed the standard procedures," she replied. "The first time I saw it happen, I told the kids to stop. When I noticed it a second time, I separated some of them to keep them from ganging up on her."

"Were there any more incidents you remember?" he continued.

"One more time a couple of weeks ago," answered Mary. "I sent three of the children to the principal's office to be disciplined."

Taking the right steps

"Did you notice if Julie seemed depressed or anything?" asked John.

"No. I never saw anything that indicated she'd do something that drastic," Mary said. "If I had, of course I'd have done whatever was necessary to help her."

The parents insisted the teacher and the school were negligent in allowing the teasing to continue.

Did the school and the teacher win?

Decision: Yes. The court said the teacher and the school had no sign the student was thinking of suicide, and responded correctly.

Key: Use appropriate measures of discipline when you think the teasing is abusive. That's usually a strong defense against charges of negligence. Of course, if a student makes a direct suicide threat, make sure to follow procedures mandated by state and local regulations.

Cite: *Smith v. Lincoln Park Public School.*

'Vulgar' reference to student makes it into print: Now, parents want to know who's responsible

They say teacher and school fell asleep on the job

Principal Donna Tomlinson tried to lighten the mood: "I guess this comes under the category of, 'No good deed goes unpunished.'"

English teacher Mark Allenberg managed a smile as he spoke, "I don't know how I missed that vulgar reference to Amy Sweet in the holiday list of student names we handed out."

"It was something that was easy to overlook," the principal noted. "It's a busy time of year."

'We did everything right'

"Thanks for your understanding," the teacher said. "But I guess we should talk about where we're headed on this."

"Yes, we have to," the principal nodded. "Amy Sweet's parents are very angry about it, and I don't think they're just going to let it go."

"Are they aware Robert Miller slipped it into the list, and that we've disciplined him for it?" the teacher asked.

"Yes, I went over all the details with them, including a recall of the list and the deletion of the reference to Amy in the updated copies."

The teacher responded: "And they're still not satisfied?"

"When I met with them, they were still angry that the reference hadn't been caught before the list went out, and they said the six days it took to do the recall was too long.

"They say Amy is so embarrassed she can't show her face. I just hope they don't decide to sue us."

The parents did sue, charging the teacher and the school with defamation leading to emotional stress for the student.

Did the school win?

Decision: Yes. A court found the school had taken appropriate action to remedy the situation and that the failure to catch a reference was an ordinary mistake.

Key: Quick action by the school convinced the court that everything reasonably possible had been done to fix the problem.

Cite: *Price v. Boyceville Community School Dist.*

Sharpen Your Judgment

School sued after student gets off bus, skips school

"Congrats on getting the job as principal!" teacher Ron Samuels said as he greeted Heather Marks as the two entered the building at the start of another school day. "How's it going so far?"

"I'm hitting the ground running to say the least," Marks said. "There's so much to learn. And yesterday I found out Susan Brion's mother is suing us."

"What?" Samuels asked. "Her bus driver obviously shouldn't have let her off the bus before it got to school. But nobody could have predicted what happened next."

"The principal who was here at the time had an idea she went to her boyfriend's house, but when Susan's mother called she wouldn't give her the boy's address."

Student missing for three days

"It was three days before they finally found her," Marks continued. "And he's 18, and she's only 15."

"What a nightmare for the mother," Samuels said. "Thank goodness Susan's all right. But I don't see how it's our fault. She basically decided to run away."

"Well, we do require a written permission slip if a student wants to get off the bus before their stop," Marks said. "And Susan didn't have one."

"I know," Samuels said. "But even so, I just don't see how we could have predicted she was going to take off like she did."

Did Susan's mother win?

Sharpen Your Judgment — The Decision

No, Susan's mother lost the case.

The girl's mother said it was the school's fault that her daughter went missing for three days. She claimed the school breached a duty it owed to her daughter when the driver let the girl get off the bus without a permission slip.

The school didn't dispute that the driver failed to get a permission slip as required by school policy. But it said the bus driver's action, while a breach of duty, was not what caused the student to go missing for three days.

The court agreed with the school. To win, the mother had to show not only that the bus driver breached a duty but also that the breach caused the harm. The school couldn't have known Susan would get off the bus and disappear for three days. So the mother lost the case.

Analysis: Exceptions to policy spell trouble

The school avoided liability, but only after a costly lawsuit. It got dragged into court because the bus driver failed to follow established policy and decided to make an exception to the permission slip rule. But policy exceptions that can put students in danger are always a bad idea.

Cite: *J.M. v. Acadia Parish School Board.*

2 Religion and the Public Schools

TOPICS

I. RELIGIOUS ESTABLISHMENT 61

II. USE OF SCHOOL FACILITIES 71

III. LIMITATIONS ON EMPLOYEE RELIGIOUS ACTIVITY 78

IV. FINANCIAL ASSISTANCE AND VOUCHER PROGRAMS 79

V. TEACHER SCENARIOS 81

CHAPTER TWO
Religion and the Public Schools

I. RELIGIOUS ESTABLISHMENT

Overview

The Establishment Clause of the First Amendment to the U.S. Constitution prohibits Congress from making any law respecting the establishment of a religion. Because public schools and administrators are subject to this mandate by operation of the Fourteenth Amendment, the courts have struck down practices that improperly entangle public schools with religion.

The U.S. Supreme Court has set forth various tests in Establishment Clause cases, but has held **"the touchstone for our Establishment Clause analysis is the principle that the First Amendment mandates government neutrality between religion and religion, and between religion and non-religion."*

A. Prayer and Religious Activity

Teacher Scenarios

When students' 'rights' create a disruption: Where to draw the line 81

Court Decisions

◆ Illinois' "Silent Reflection and Student Prayer Act" allowed a voluntary moment of silence in public school classrooms. In 2007, an amendment to the act provided that "the teacher in charge **shall** observe a brief period of silence" at the start of every school day, "with the participation of all the pupils" in the classroom. It further provided that the period "shall not be conducted as a religious exercise but shall be an opportunity for silent prayer or for silent reflection on the anticipated activities of the day." A public high school student sued her school district and state officials in a federal district court, which held the amended act invalid.

On appeal, the U.S. Court of Appeals, Seventh Circuit, reviewed Supreme Court precedents including *Wallace v. Jaffree*, 472 U.S. 38 (1985), which involved an Alabama moment of silence act. **The court found the Illinois act served the secular purpose of helping calm students and prepare them for their school day.** No evidence indicated this purpose was a sham, as the student claimed. In *Wallace*, Alabama legislators openly admitted a legislative intent to "return prayer to the public schools." But review of the Illinois legislative debate confirmed a secular purpose and an intent to create uniformity across the state. Nothing indicated the act was motivated by a religious purpose. A review of moment of silence laws in other states revealed that federal courts had upheld similar laws in Georgia, Virginia and Texas. As the state argued, student prayer is permissible, and language in the act negated an impression that students could not pray silently during a moment of silence. A lack of specifics did not make the act so vague that guesswork was required. As a result, the court upheld the act. *Sherman v. Koch*, 623 F.3d 501 (7th Cir. 2010).

◆ A New Jersey head football coach led his teams in pre-game prayers for many years. In 2005, parents began to complain, and administrators told him he could not lead, encourage or participate in student prayers. District guidelines emphasized student rights to pray on school property or at school events, so long as it did not interfere with school operations. However, the guidelines barred school representatives from participating in student-initiated prayers.

After temporarily resigning, the coach agreed to abide by the district's policy. He then sued the district and its superintendent. He emailed team co-captains and asked them if they would like to resume pre-game and pre-meal team prayers. After players voted to continue team prayers, the coach stood with them and bowed his head during pre-meal team prayers. He also knelt during pre-game prayers. A federal district court found "nothing wrong with remaining silent and bowing one's head and taking a knee as a sign of respect for his players' actions and traditions." The school district appealed to the U.S. Court of Appeals, Third Circuit, which noted that the coach's silent expression of support and respect for the team was "not a matter of public concern." His conduct violated the Establishment Clause. In *Board of Educ. of Westside Community Schools v. Mergens*, 496 U.S. 226 (1990), this chapter, the U.S. Supreme Court held that faculty involvement in student religious groups was limited to a "nonparticipatory capacity." **The relevant question is whether a school official has improperly endorsed religion based on what a reasonable observer, familiar with the context and history of the display, would believe.** Here, the coach's prayer activities with his teams were well known. His conduct over 23 years signaled an unconstitutional endorsement of religion to any reasonable observer. The judgment was reversed. *Borden v. School Dist. of Township of East Brunswick*, 523 F.3d 153 (3d Cir. 2008).

◆ A Pennsylvania parent selected 10 Bible verses for her kindergartener to share with his class, including Psalms 118, Verse 14 which states, "The Lord is my strength and my song, and is become my salvation." However, the principal informed the parent that reading the Bible to the class would be "against the law of separation of church and state." The parent sued for speech rights violations under the state and federal constitutions. A court held for the district, and the U.S. Court of Appeals, Third Circuit, affirmed. **A kindergarten class is a "unique forum" that is not a place for debate about issues of public importance.** Age and context are relevant, as "the age of the students bears an important inverse relationship to the degree and kind of control a school may exercise." The younger the student, the more control over speech a school could exercise. *Busch v. Marple Newton School Dist.*, 567 F.3d 89 (3d Cir. 2008).

◆ A New York school district with a Mohawk Indian majority permitted the saying of "Ohen: Ton Karihwatehkwen," also referred to as "the Thanksgiving Address," over the school's public address (PA) system. The address acknowledged people, Mother Earth, plants, fruits, grasses, water, fish, medicine, animals, trees, birds, Grandfather Thunders, Four Winds, Elder Brother Sun, Grandmother Moon, stars, Four Beings and a concept sometimes interpreted as "Creator." A parent who was not Mohawk complained that "the address could be a prayer." A district lawyer agreed, but stated that the school could allow student-initiated recitation of the address at a location chosen by students. The superintendent then let students go to the school auditorium for recitation of the address instead of having it said over the PA system. The saying of the address was also discontinued at pep rallies and at school lacrosse games. Mohawk students sued the school district, superintendent and other officials, asserting that discontinuing the address at school events violated their Equal Protection rights. A federal district court rejected their claim that they were treated differently than students who recited the Pledge of Allegiance.

Thanksgiving is not a religious holiday and is unrelated to a specific group or culture. The district did not broadcast Christmas carols or hymns over the PA system or at pep rallies or games. **Here, the district had attempted to promote diversity, pluralism and tolerance for culture, including Mohawk tradition.** The district continued to celebrate Mohawk culture in many ways. Students could still say the address in the auditorium, and their flag and traditional forms of dress were displayed on some occasions. The address' references to "the life forces of creation" resembled religious belief, as it described the relationship between Mohawks and the earth, using a word frequently translated as "creator." As the district acted reasonably by ending the recitation of the address at rallies, lacrosse games and over the PA system, the court ruled in its favor. On appeal, the U.S. Court of Appeals, Second Circuit, affirmed the judgment. *Jock v. Ransom*, No. 07-3162, 2009 WL 742193 (2d Cir. 3/20/09).

◆ A Louisiana parent claimed that his children's school permitted prayers to be said over the PA systems at sporting events and in school. Student-athletes prayed before and after games, and the school board opened its meetings with a prayer. The parent sued the school board in a federal court for Establishment Clause violations. The parties resolved challenges to most of the practices by consent judgment, but could not agree on the issue of prayers before board meetings. The court then held that these prayers violated the Establishment Clause under the traditional analysis of *Lemon v. Kurtzman*, 403 U.S. 602 (1971). The prayers fell outside a limited exception allowing prayers before legislative sessions found in *Marsh v. Chambers*, 463 U.S. 783 (1983).

The school board appealed to the Fifth Circuit. A three-judge panel of the court held that allowing Christian prayers was unconstitutional. The full court reheard the case and held that the parent did not have standing to bring the challenge. There was no evidence that the parent's own children were exposed to the prayers said at the school board meetings. **"Abstract knowledge" that the prayers were being said was not enough to grant standing to bring an Establishment Clause challenge.** As there was no proof that the parent or his children had ever attended school board meetings where prayers were said, the court vacated the judgment and instructed the lower court to dismiss the case. *Doe v. Tangipahoa Parish School Board*, 494 F.3d 494 (5th Cir. 2007).

◆ A New York school board directed a principal to have a prayer read aloud by each class in the presence of a teacher at the beginning of the school day. The procedure was adopted on the recommendation of the state board of regents. State officials had composed the prayer and published it as part of their "Statement on Moral and Spiritual Training in the Schools." The parents of 10 students sued the board, insisting that use of an official prayer in public schools violated the Establishment Clause of the First Amendment. The New York Court of Appeals upheld the practice as long as schools did not compel pupils to join in the prayer over the parents' objections. On appeal, the U.S. Supreme Court held that the practice was wholly inconsistent with the Establishment Clause. **There could be no doubt that the classroom invocation was a religious activity.** Neither the fact that the prayer was denominationally neutral nor that its observance was voluntary served to free it from the Establishment Clause. *Engel v. Vitale*, 370 U.S. 421, 82 S.Ct. 1261, 8 L.Ed.2d 601 (1962).

◆ Pennsylvania law required that "[a]t least ten verses from the Holy Bible shall be read, without comment, at the opening of each public school on each school day. Any child shall be excused from such Bible reading, or attending such Bible reading, upon written request of his parents or guardian." A family sued school officials to enjoin enforcement of the laws as violative of the First Amendment. The school commissioner of Baltimore had also adopted a rule that mandated the reading of a chapter of the Bible or the Lord's Prayer at the start of each school day without comment. That rule was also challenged. The U.S. Supreme Court consolidated the cases and held that both rules violated the Establishment Clause. The Court reiterated the premise of *Engel v. Vitale*, above, that **neither the state nor the federal government can constitutionally force a person to profess a belief or disbelief in any religion**. Nor can it pass laws that aid all religions as against nonbelievers. The primary purpose of the statutes and rule was religious. The compulsory nature of the ceremonies was not mitigated by the fact that students could excuse themselves. *Abington School Dist. v. Schempp*, 374 U.S. 203, 83 S.Ct. 1560, 10 L.Ed.2d 844 (1963).

◆ **The U.S. Supreme Court invalidated an Alabama statute allowing meditation or voluntary prayer in public school classrooms.** The case was initiated in 1982 by the father of three elementary students who challenged the validity of two Alabama statutes: a 1981 statute that allowed a period of silence for "meditation or voluntary prayer," and a 1982 statute authorizing teachers to lead "willing students" in a nonsectarian prayer composed by the state legislature. After a lower court found both statutes unconstitutional, the U.S. Supreme Court agreed to review only the portion of the lower court decision invalidating the 1981 statute that allowed "meditation or voluntary prayer." The Court concluded that the intent of the Alabama legislature was to affirmatively reestablish prayer in the public schools. Inclusion of the words "or voluntary prayer" in the statute indicated that it had been enacted to convey state approval of a religious activity and violated the First Amendment's Establishment Clause. *Wallace v. Jaffree*, 472 U.S. 38, 105 S.Ct. 2479, 96 L.Ed.2d 29 (1985).

◆ Two Texas students challenged a number of their school district's practices, including one allowing overtly Christian prayers at graduation ceremonies and football games. The district permitted nondenominational prayers at graduation ceremonies, read by students selected by vote of the graduating class. In response to the complaint, the district revised its policies for prayer at school functions by requiring them to be nonsectarian and non-proselytizing. Shortly thereafter, the district enacted new policies deleting the nonsectarian, non-proselytizing requirements for pre-game invocations and graduation prayers. A federal district court ordered the school district to enact a more restrictive policy, allowing only nonsectarian and non-proselytizing prayers.

The case reached the U.S. Supreme Court, which ruled that student-led, pre-game prayers violated the Establishment Clause. Although the district asserted that students determined the content of the pre-game message without review by school officials and with approval by the student body, school officials regulated the forum. **The majoritarian process for selecting speakers guaranteed that minority candidates would never prevail and that their views would be effectively silenced.** The degree of school involvement in the pre-game prayers created the perception and actual endorsement of religion by school officials. *Santa Fe Independent School Dist. v. Doe*, 530 U.S. 290, 120 S.Ct. 2266, 147 L.Ed.2d 295 (2000).

B. Instruction of Students

1. Curriculum

Teacher Scenarios

Did teacher's response to difficult parent help head off a lawsuit? 82

*Group charges teacher with promoting religion....*82

Court Decisions

◆ A California non-profit organization called Islamic Relief sponsored a charter school with two Minnesota campuses. For the 2008-09 school year, the academy expected $3.8 million in funds from the state of Minnesota. A vast majority of the academy's students were Somali Muslims. The ACLU claimed the academy violated the Establishment Clause by permitting prayer sessions during school hours in which parents, volunteers and teachers participated. The academy was accused of endorsing Islamic dress codes and dietary practices, and providing bus transportation only at the end of an after-school religious program. The ACLU sued academy officials, Islamic Relief and the Minnesota Department of Education in a federal district court, asserting that the academy preferred "Muslim" religious practices. The court found Islamic Relief was not a state actor, but had potential liability under the Establishment Clause due to its role in the traditionally exclusive function of public education.

Minnesota charter schools are a part of the public school system under state law, and the state Charter School Law required each school sponsor to assure compliance with nonsectarian requirements. The court rejected arguments for pretrial dismissal. Issues raised by the academy and Islamic Relief were factual in nature and should not be resolved at this stage of the litigation. For example, **religious entanglement created by the academy's dress code and the busing schedule required a factual inquiry**. The role played by Islamic Relief in the academy's operations also required further scrutiny. As a result, the case required a trial. *American Civil Liberties Union of Minnesota v. Tarek Ibn Ziyad Academy*, Civil No. 09-138 (DWF/JJG) (D. Minn. 7/21/09).

◆ A New York kindergartener made a poster for a class assignment with his mother's help. She wrote statements on the poster such as "prayer changes things" and "Jesus loves children." The student's teacher did not hang the poster, and the school principal later told her to have the student make a new one. After the mother helped her son make a new poster that also had religious themes, the teacher and principal folded it to obscure the religious content. The mother sued the school district and several officials for speech and religious rights violations in a federal district court. The court held for the district, and appeal reached the U.S. Court of Appeals, Second Circuit. In a 2005 decision, the court found the poster was a class assignment given under specific parameters which the school could regulate in a reasonable manner. **Schools may reasonably regulate speech and activities that are part of the school curriculum.** The Establishment Clause claim had been properly dismissed. *Peck v. Baldwinsville Cent. School Dist.*, 426 F.3d 617 (2d Cir. 2005).

The case was returned to the district court, which entered a judgment for the school district and officials. In 2009, the Second Circuit noted the case had been filed 10 years earlier. It held the student now lacked standing to pursue the case because he was seeking an injunction relying on a past, not a future injury. *Peck v. Baldwinsville Cent. School Dist.*, 351 Fed.Appx. 477 (2d Cir. 2009).

◆ A Michigan elementary school held a simulated marketplace event in the school gymnasium. Fifth-graders made products under assignment guidelines for sale at booths in the school gymnasium. Other students at the school visited the booths and purchased goods with faux school currency. A student accepted his mother's suggestion to sell Christmas candy cane-shaped tree ornaments made of pipe cleaners and beads. His father offered to make cards to attach to the canes, which bore a religious message. The student did not attach a sample card when he submitted his required prototype ornament, and he never told the school he intended to attach the cards. On the day of the marketplace event, the student's teacher learned about the card for the first time. She halted sales of the card, and the school principal informed the family that the student could not sell ornaments with the card. The principal stated that the marketplace event was considered instructional time and that the cards could not be attached due to their religious message. However, the student was permitted to sell cards in a school parking lot. Instead, the student sold the ornaments without the cards. He earned an A for the assignment and was not disciplined in any way.

The parents sued the school district and principal for speech rights violations. A court held for the school district, and the U.S. Court of Appeals, Sixth Circuit, affirmed. The marketplace event was part of the fifth-grade curriculum. **Educators do not offend the First Amendment by exercising editorial control over student speech in school-sponsored events.** The school's desire to avoid a curricular event that might offend parents and other children at the school qualified as a valid educational purpose, and the principal's decision to stop the sales of the religious card was based on her reasonable evaluation of legitimate pedagogical concerns. *Curry v. Hensiner*, 513 F.3d 570 (6th Cir. 2008).

◆ A Virginia high school Spanish teacher posted items with religious content on his classroom bulletin board. Following a complaint by a visitor, the principal took down five items, including a "National Day of Prayer" poster depicting George Washington kneeling in prayer, and four newspaper clippings discussing the Bible and religion. The school board had no written policy on teacher use of classroom bulletin boards and it relied on principals to decide which postings were appropriate. The principal's primary criterion for assessing postings was relevancy to the curriculum being taught by the particular teacher.

The teacher sued the board in a federal court, which held that the removed items were "curricular" in nature and that his speech was unprotected. On appeal, the U.S. Court of Appeals, Fourth Circuit, rejected his assertion that he could post any materials he wished in the classroom. His material was curricular in nature, and not a matter of public concern. **School boards have the right to regulate speech within a compulsory classroom setting.** The school had an interest in preventing in-class teacher speech that interfered with day-to-day operations. If speech is curricular in nature, it is not speech on a matter of public concern. Since the materials were likely to be attributed to the high school, the principal had the authority to remove them, and the court affirmed the judgment. *Lee v. York County School Division*, 484 F.3d 687 (4th Cir. 2007).

◆ Dover (Pennsylvania) area residents elected two Fundamentalist Christians to their school board. One became the board's president. He sought to include creationism and prayer in the district curriculum and recommended purchasing a textbook advocating "intelligent design." The board accepted 60 copies and forced teachers to use it as a reference text. The board then voted to change the district's ninth-grade biology curriculum so that "students will be made aware of gaps/problems in Darwin's theory and of other theories of evolution, including but not limited to intelligent design." Resident parents sued the board in a federal district court, asserting Establishment Clause violations.

The court held that **the intelligent design policy conveyed a message of religious endorsement**. None of the experts who testified at trial could explain how intelligent design "could be anything other than an inherently religious proposition." The disclaimer singled out evolution from everything else being taught in the district, suggesting evolution was a "highly questionable opinion or hunch." While evolution was "overwhelmingly accepted" by the scientific community, intelligent design had been refuted in peer-reviewed research papers. The conduct of the board members conveyed a strong message of religious endorsement. The court entered a permanent order preventing the district from maintaining the intelligent design policy and from requiring teachers to denigrate or disparage evolutionary theory. *Kitzmiller v. Dover Area School Dist.*, 400 F.Supp.2d 707 (M.D. Pa. 2005).

◆ **The U.S. Supreme Court let stand a decision by lower courts that a school district's Islam program did not violate the Establishment Clause of the First Amendment.** Prior to the Court's order denying review, the U.S. Court of Appeals, Ninth Circuit, held that the program activities were not "overt religious exercises that raise Establishment Clause concerns." The action was brought by two families who alleged that a middle school world history teacher asked them to choose Muslim names, learn prayers, simulate Muslim rituals and engage in other role-playing exercises. The Ninth Circuit held that the school district and individual school employees were entitled to qualified immunity "because they did not violate any constitutional right, let alone a clearly-established one." *Ecklund v. Byron Union School Dist.*, 549 U.S. 942 (U.S. cert. denied 10/2/06).

◆ In 1981, the Louisiana legislature enacted "Balanced Treatment for Creation Science and Evolution Science in Public School Instruction," an act providing that any school offering instruction in evolution must include equal time for instruction in "creation science." The act required that curriculum guides be developed and research services supplied for creation science but not for evolution. The stated purpose of the act was to protect academic freedom. A group of parents, teachers, and religious leaders challenged the law's constitutionality. A federal court and the Fifth Circuit both held that the act was an unconstitutional establishment of religion, and Louisiana state officials appealed to the U.S. Supreme Court. The Court addressed the issue of whether the Creationism Act was enacted for a clear secular purpose. It noted that **because the act provided for sanctions against teachers who chose not to teach creation science, it did not**

promote its avowed purpose of furthering academic freedom. The Court ruled that "[b]ecause the primary purpose of the Creationism Act is to advance a particular religious belief, the Act endorses religion in violation of the First Amendment." The Creationism Act was therefore declared unconstitutional. *Edwards v. Aguillard*, 482 U.S. 578, 107 S.Ct. 2573, 96 L.Ed.2d 510 (1987).

2. Textbooks

Court Decisions

◆ Massachusetts parents objected to their school district's presentation of books portraying diverse families to their children. This included depictions of families in which both parents were of the same gender. Massachusetts law required notification to parents and an opportunity to exempt their children from curriculums that primarily involved human sexuality. State law also mandated that academic standards include respect for cultural, ethnic and racial diversity, but did not mention or provide for notice to parents when a school curriculum included any discussion of homosexuality. Two families sued the school district, claiming that the exposure of their children to books describing diverse families violated a core belief of their religion that homosexual behavior and gay marriage are immoral and violate God's law. They claimed that two books were part of an effort by the public schools to systematically indoctrinate young children into the belief that homosexuality and homosexual marriage are moral and acceptable conduct. The court dismissed the case.

The U.S. Court of Appeals, First Circuit, found "Given that Massachusetts has recognized gay marriage under its state constitution, it is entirely rational for its schools to educate their students regarding that recognition." **Exposure to the books would not prevent the parents from raising their children in their religious beliefs.** Parental rights in the public school context are not absolute, and parents lack constitutional rights to control each and every aspect of their children's education. No federal case had recognized a due process right to allow parents an exemption from exposure to particular books used in the public schools. Requiring a student to read a particular book is not coercive, and public schools are not obligated to shield students from ideas that are potentially offensive. *Parker v. Hurley*, 514 F.3d 87 (1st Cir. 2008).

◆ A Georgia school district's textbook review committee recommended purchasing *Biology* by Miller and Levine as the best available text. School board members were concerned that their constituents wanted texts with "alternate theories of the origin of life." The board adopted a new policy and regulation providing that evolution would be taught in county science classes, and that religion would not be taught. A school attorney drafted a statement that was eventually written on stickers placed on each textbook. The stickers said: "This textbook contains material on evolution. Evolution is a theory, not a fact, regarding the origin of living things. This material should be approached with an open mind, studied carefully, and critically considered." Parents who believed the stickers endorsed religion sued the school board. A federal district court held that **an informed, reasonable observer would believe the stickers sent a message of approval to creationists.** As the board impermissibly entangled itself with religion, the court ordered it to remove the stickers.

The board appealed to the Eleventh Circuit. It found the lower court had improperly relied on a letter from a parent who objected to teaching evolution and a petition that she allegedly submitted to the board prior to its vote to place the stickers on the new textbooks. The lower court had relied on the timing of events in finding the stickers had the effect of endorsing religion. However, the record did not establish that the letter and petition were submitted to the board before the vote. The court recommended that the lower court issue new findings of fact and conclusions of law. Of particular importance would be what petition, if any, was submitted prior to the board's vote. The court vacated and remanded the decision. *Selman v. Cobb County School Dist.*, 449 F.3d 1320 (11th Cir. 2006). In late 2006, the board voluntarily agreed to refrain from placing any stickers or labels disclaiming evolutionary theory in textbooks.

3. School Music Performances

In Nurre v. Whitehead, *below, a school district's tradition of letting seniors pick music for their graduation ceremonies was held to be a "limited public forum." But in* Stratechuk v. Board of Educ., South Orange-Maplewood School Dist., *below, a New Jersey holiday concert was not deemed a public forum. Schools are not public forums unless they are intentionally designated as such.*

Court Decisions

◆ A Washington school district received complaints about religious music selections at a 2005 high school graduation ceremony. As the 2006 graduation approached, administrators rejected the school wind ensemble's selection of "Ave Maria," believing it created a risk of new complaints. They asked the ensemble to make another selection. A student member of the wind ensemble sued the school district and superintendent for constitutional violations. A federal district court held the district did not violate the student's rights. On appeal, the U.S. Court of Appeals, Ninth Circuit, held that **instrumental music was "speech" for First Amendment analysis.** Schools are not considered public forums for speech unless they are opened up by officials for indiscriminate use. A limited public forum for expression had been opened in this case because of the district's tradition of letting seniors select the music for their graduation ceremonies. In a limited public forum, restrictions can be based on subject matter, so long as any distinctions are reasonable in light of the purpose of the forum. Here, the school district acted reasonably to avoid repeating the prior year's controversy. The court affirmed the judgment for the district. *Nurre v. Whitehead*, 580 F.3d 1087 (9th Cir. 2009).

◆ A New Jersey school holiday activity policy stated that "special effort must be made to ensure the activity is not devotional and that pupils of all faiths and beliefs can join without feeling they are betraying their own faiths." After receiving complaints about religious music at a school concert, the policy was reexamined. A school fine arts director issued a memo clarifying that music selections representing religious holidays would be avoided. A parent complained this conveyed a message that Christianity was disfavored, and sued.

A federal court ruled for the school district, and the U.S. Court of Appeals, Third Circuit, affirmed the judgment. Applying the test from *Lemon v. Kurtzman*, 403 U.S. 602 (1971), the court found no Establishment Clause violation. As the lower court held, the district's intent was to avoid government endorsement of religious holidays and potential Establishment Clause violations. Although the parent maintained this was a "sham" purpose, the court held **the Constitution did not require schools to promote religion to the maximum extent allowed**. Failure to do so did not make the district "anti-religious," as he claimed. The policy did not preclude religious songs from classrooms or concerts, unless they were specific to a holiday. **School concerts are not public forums**, and as the lower court had correctly found the policy was reasonably related to legitimate pedagogical concerns, the judgment for the school district was affirmed. *Stratechuk v. Board of Educ., South Orange-Maplewood School Dist.*, 587 F.3d 597 (3d Cir. 2009).

C. Commencement Ceremonies

Important factual differences led two courts to reach opposite results in challenges to decisions to hold graduation ceremonies at churches. A Wisconsin school district had a new facility where future ceremonies would be held. But a Connecticut district did not use a cheaper alternate site, and the court found a reasonable observer would see religious endorsement when the board voted to hold ceremonies at school sites, then changed course under pressure.

Teacher Scenarios

Could teacher have stopped student from 'preaching' at graduation? 83

Teacher has to break bad news to class – then a disappointed student sues 84

Court Decisions

◆ After denying a motion for a preliminary order that would have halted a Wisconsin school district from holding 2009 graduation ceremonies at a church, a federal district court considered a permanent order. It reviewed evidence that the church was near both of the district's high schools, had air-conditioning, was accessible to disabled people, and had ample parking and a seating capacity of near 3,000. Observers would see many religious articles throughout the church. Some religious items could be covered or removed for graduation ceremonies, but the church was unwilling to remove or cover permanent structures. Alternate sites were suggested over the years, but senior classes had always voted to hold graduation ceremonies at the church. According to the court, **the purpose of the Establishment and Free Exercise Clauses "is to prevent, as far as possible, the intrusion of either the church or the state into the precincts of the other."** Total separation of church and state "is not possible in an absolute sense." The students and parents claimed that holding graduation ceremonies at the church had no secular purpose, but the history and context of the case showed otherwise. It appeared to the court that the ceremonies had been held at the church because it was convenient and cost-effective. This secular purpose was seen in the district's assertion that it would be holding future ceremonies in its new 3,500-seat field house. The objectors did not show rental of a church site created excessive religious entanglement. There was no attempt to "cleanse the Church of religious symbols and items" for ceremonies. The case was dismissed. *Does 1, 7, 8 and 9 v. Elmbrook Joint Common School Dist. No. 21*, No. 09-C-0409, 2010 WL 2854287 (E.D. Wis. 7/19/10).

◆ A Connecticut school district held its high school graduation ceremonies at a cathedral. Before the 2010 graduation ceremony, the school board voted to hold the ceremony on school grounds after learning of a threatened lawsuit. But the board later rescinded its vote after lobbying by a religious organization that promised free legal representation if the board agreed to hold the ceremonies at the cathedral. Alternative sites were rejected, including a symphony hall that would cost a total of $5,000 less than the cathedral. A federal district court case was filed to obtain an order prohibiting the board from holding 2010 graduation ceremonies at the cathedral. Among the court's findings was that many large crosses, banners and other religious items would be in view at the cathedral.

The court held **a reasonable observer would find selection of the cathedral for graduation ceremonies conveyed a message that the board embraced one religious view**. Observers would see religious objects, symbols and messages in the cathedral. Even with modifications, the cathedral remained a religious environment. By selecting the cathedral, the board sent a message that it was closely linked with a religious mission, and that it favored "the religious over the irreligious, and that it prefers Christians" over others. Any consideration of alternate sites did not appear to be open-minded. No precise criteria were stated, and the board rejected a cheaper site. And "the uneasy process of attempting to 'secularize' First Cathedral by covering some of its religious imagery" created excessive government entanglement with religion. Government coercion was found, since graduating seniors had no real choice to skip graduation. As the board failed the relevant Establishment Clause tests, the court issued a preliminary order for the students and parents. *Does 1, 2, 3, 4 and 5 v. Enfield Public Schools*, 716 F.Supp.2d 172 (D. Conn. 2010).

◆ A graduating Nevada high school senior was denied Supreme Court review of lower court decisions that rejected her claims against school officials who turned off her microphone when she deviated from her valedictory speech to talk about her faith in Christ. In a brief memorandum, **the U.S. Court of Appeals, Ninth Circuit, held school officials did not violate the student's rights under the Speech and Free Exercise Clauses of the first Amendment by "preventing her from making a proselytizing graduation speech."** It was also not an equal protection violation, as officials did not allow any other speakers to proselytize. *McComb v. Crehan*, 320 Fed.Appx. 507 (9th Cir. 2009). *McComb v. Crehan*, No. 08-1566, 130 S.Ct. 622 (U.S. cert. denied 11/16/09).

◆ A Colorado high school valedictorian submitted a speech for review by her school principal that did not mention religion. But at the ceremony, she encouraged attendees to learn about Jesus Christ and "the opportunity to live in eternity with Him." After the ceremony, the valedictorian learned she would not receive her diploma unless she publicly apologized. Instead of apologizing, she prepared a statement explaining that her speech reflected her beliefs and that it was made without the principal's prior approval. Although the valedictorian submitted the statement and received a diploma, she sued the school district in a federal district court. After the court held for the school district, she appealed to the U.S. Court of Appeals, Tenth Circuit. It applied *Hazelwood School Dist. v. Kuhlmeier*, 484 U.S. 260 (1988), which held **educators do not offend the First Amendment by exercising editorial control over student speech in school-sponsored expressive activities**, "so long as their actions are reasonably related to legitimate pedagogical concerns." Greater control over student speech was appropriate in school-sponsored events because the school community might reasonably perceive them to bear the school's approval. The valedictory speeches were supervised by faculty and were clearly school-sponsored.

An order to apologize was reasonably related to learning, and did not violate the valedictorian's rights. There was no substantial burden on the valedictorian's free exercise or equal protection rights, as she was held to the same religion-neutral policies as others. The judgment was affirmed. *Corder v. Lewis Palmer School Dist. No. 38*, 566 F.3d 1219 (10th Cir. 2009).

◆ A Rhode Island student and her father sued their school district in a federal district court to prevent an annual graduation prayer performed by clergy members of various faiths. The court held the clergy-led prayers violated the Establishment Clause of the First Amendment. The defendants appealed to the U.S. Court of Appeals, First Circuit, which also held the prayers violated the Establishment Clause. The First Circuit affirmed the judgment.

On appeal, the U.S. Supreme Court held the district violated the Establishment Clause by selecting clergy members to say prayers as part of an official public school graduation ceremony. **The government may not coerce anyone to support or participate in religion, or otherwise act in any way that establishes a state religion or religious faith, or tends to do so.** In this case, state officials directed the performance of a formal religious exercise. The principal decided that a prayer should be given, selected the clergy participant, and directed and controlled the prayer's content. The district's supervision and control of the graduation ceremony placed subtle and indirect public and peer pressure on attending students to stand as a group or maintain respectful silence during the invocation and benediction. The state may not force a student dissenter to participate or protest. The argument that the ceremony was voluntary was unpersuasive, and the Court affirmed the judgment for the student and her parent. *Lee v. Weisman*, 505 U.S. 577 (1992).

D. School Policies

1. The Pledge of Allegiance

In Croft v. Perry, *a federal court held recitation of the Texas state pledge is a patriotic exercise, and it is made no less so by the acknowledgment of Texas's religious heritage via the inclusion of the phrase "under God."*

Nearly 70 years ago, the U.S. Supreme Court held the states cannot compel citizens to recite the Pledge of Allegiance in West Virginia State Board of Educ. v. Barnette, *319 U.S. 624 (1943). The Court held the First Amendment protects both the right to speak freely and the right to refrain from speaking at all.*

Teacher Scenarios

Does student need a permission slip to skip the pledge? Parents say, 'No!' 85

Dissent vs. order in class: Did teacher make right choice? 85

Student: 'I don't pledge allegiance to the flag' – and his parents sue when he's disciplined for it 86

Court Decisions

◆ In 2007, Texas legislators added "under God" to the state pledge, which now declares "Honor the Texas flag, I pledge allegiance to thee, Texas, one state under God, one and indivisible." A group of parents sued the governor to challenge inclusion of the phrase "under God" in the pledge. A federal district court upheld the pledge. On appeal, the Fifth Circuit reviewed the legislative history of the bill and found it was intended to mirror the national pledge. The Supreme Court has never ruled on the constitutionality of the national pledge, but the Fifth Circuit has previously found it is a "patriotic exercise designed to foster national unity and pride" and is not a religious exercise.

Using the Establishment Clause tests applied by federal courts, the court found the amendment satisfied each of them. It found the Establishment Clause is not violated by "nonsectarian references to religion." Describing the term "God" as "adequately generic," the court said its use was a "tolerable attempt at acknowledging religion without favoring a particular sect or belief." Under *Lemon v. Kurtzman*, the amendment had a secular purpose. The legislature believed that conformity with the U.S. Pledge was the "safest and smoothest means" to acknowledge "our religious heritage." The court found the bill had permissible secular purposes and was not enacted as a sham to advance Christianity. **The court found no reasonable observer would understand the purpose of the pledge to be religious endorsement.** Use of the words "under God" acknowledged but did not endorse religion. Applying the test from *Lee v. Weisman*, the court held the pledge did not coerce students to engage in a religious exercise and was not "prototypical religious activity." The court held for the governor, finding even with the addition of "under God," the pledge remained a patriotic exercise with a minimal religious component. *Croft v. Perry*, 624 F.3d 157 (5th Cir. 2010).

◆ California teachers led willing students in daily recitations of the Pledge of Allegiance, as permitted by California Education Code Section 52720. A parent claimed the phrase "under God" in the Pledge offended her disbelief in God, interfered with her parental rights and indoctrinated her child. She filed a federal district court case against the school district, alleging Establishment Clause violations. The court held for the parent, and the district appealed to the U.S. Court of Appeals, Ninth Circuit. On appeal, she pursued only claims based on state law and the school district policy. The court held not every mention of God or religion by the government is a constitutional violation. **Complete separation of church and state was not required.** Instead, the court found **the Constitution "affirmatively mandates accommodation, not merely tolerance, of all religions, and forbids hostility towards any."** The child had never recited the Pledge but was seeking to prohibit others from doing so.

As the Supreme Court found in *Elk Grove Unified School Dist. v. Newdow*, this chapter, "the Pledge is a patriotic exercise designed to foster national unity and pride." Finding that Congress had an "ostensible and predominant purpose" to inspire patriotism, the court held the Pledge was predominantly a patriotic exercise. For this reason, the phrase "one Nation under God" did not convert the Pledge from a patriotic exercise into a religious one. While California Education Code Section 52720 permitted teachers to lead Pledge recitations, the court noted objectors could sit or stand quietly. Under each of the tests used by the Supreme Court in Establishment Clause cases, the court found no violation. "One nation under God" described the Republic, and it was not an expression of the speaker's particular theological beliefs. The court held neither the state law nor the district policy violated the Establishment Clause. *Newdow v. Rio Linda Union School Dist.*, 597 F.3d 1007 (9th Cir. 2010).

◆ Florida's Pledge Statute requires Pledge recitation at all public schools and requires that "civilians must show full respect to the flag by standing at attention." The law exempts students from Pledge recitation upon presenting a signed, written statement from a parent. An eleventh-grade student challenged the law in a federal court, asserting speech rights violations. The court agreed with the student. State education officials appealed. The U.S. Court of Appeals, Eleventh Circuit, upheld the student's claim that the "standing at attention" provision of the law could not be enforced. **There is a well-established constitutional right to remain seated and silent during Pledge recitations.** While the "standing at attention" provision was unconstitutional, the remainder of the statute did not violate the First Amendment. Parents had a fundamental right to control their children's upbringing. Thus, they could excuse their children from reciting the Pledge, and school officials would have to honor that request even if the students wished to recite the Pledge. Parents could refuse to excuse their children, and those rights would also be honored. According to the court, parental rights to interfere with the wishes of their children trumped school officials' rights to interfere on behalf of the school's interest. *Frazier v. Winn*, 535 F.3d 1279 (11th Cir. 2008).

◆ Virginia law provides for the daily, voluntary recitation of the Pledge and placement of the U.S. flag in each public school classroom. Loudoun County Public Schools implemented the provision through a policy allowing students to remain seated quietly during Pledge recitation if their parents objected on religious, philosophical or other grounds. An Anabaptist Mennonite parent asserted that the Pledge indoctrinated his children with a "'God and Country' religious worldview" and violated the Mennonite Confession of Faith. He sued the school system, asserting that the inclusion of the words "under God" in the Pledge made it a religious exercise that violated the Establishment Clause. A federal district court dismissed the case, finding recitation of the Pledge was a secular activity that neither advanced nor inhibited religion. On appeal, the U.S. Court of Appeals, Fourth Circuit, stated **the Establishment Clause does not require separation of church and state "in every and all aspects."** It rejected the parent's assertion that Pledge recitation was like a prayer. The Supreme Court ruled "fleeting references to God" in a classroom are not unconstitutional. The Establishment Clause "does not extend so far as to make unconstitutional the daily recitation of the Pledge in public school." The court held for the school system. *Myers v. Loudoun County Public Schools*, 418 F.3d 395 (4th Cir. 2005).

◆ The non-custodial father of a California student sued state, local and federal officials in a federal court, claiming that a 1954 Act of Congress adding the words "under God" to the Pledge violated the Establishment Clause. He also claimed a state law requiring elementary schools to open the day with patriotic exercises and the school district's use of daily Pledge recitations violated the Constitution. The court dismissed the case, but the U.S. Court of Appeals, Ninth Circuit, held the 1954 Act and district policy violated the Establishment Clause.

The court denied a motion by the child's mother to intervene in the case, even though a state family court order granted her the child's exclusive legal custody. She alleged that her daughter was a Christian who did not object to recitation of the Pledge. The Ninth Circuit reconsidered the standing issue and noted that the father no longer claimed to represent his daughter. It held that he retained a state law right to expose her to his particular religious views, even if they contradicted those of the mother. The U.S. Supreme Court then rejected the father's claim to unrestricted rights to inculcate his daughter in his atheistic beliefs. His rights could not be viewed in isolation from the mother's parental rights. Nothing done by the mother or the school board impaired his right to instruct the child in his religious views. **State law did not authorize the father to dictate what others could say or not say to his daughter about religion.** The Court reversed the judgment. *Elk Grove Unified School Dist. v. Newdow*, 542 U.S. 1, 124 S.Ct. 2301, 159 L.Ed.2d 98 (2004).

◆ An Alabama student raised his fist and remained silent while the rest of his class recited the Pledge. The principal told him he could not receive a diploma unless he served three days of detention and apologized to the class. The student sued the teacher, principal and school board in a federal court for First Amendment violations. The case reached the U.S. Court of Appeals, Eleventh Circuit, which noted that *West Virginia State Board of Educ. v. Barnette*, 319 U.S. 624 (1943), established a clear right for students to refuse to say the Pledge. Any reasonable person would have known that disciplining the student for refusing to recite the Pledge violated his First Amendment rights. **Officials may only regulate student expression that materially and substantially interferes with school activities or discipline.** Here, the student was being punished for his unpatriotic views, not for being disruptive. *Holloman v. Harland*, 370 F.3d 1252 (11th Cir. 2004).

2. Other Policies

Courts have upheld released time programs, policies prohibiting harassment based on sexual orientation, and mandatory anti-harassment training for students. Courts have allowed schools to set limits on the time and manner the Gideons may distribute Bibles at school.

Court Decisions

◆ In 2006, the South Carolina legislature enacted the Released Time Credit Act, which permitted school districts to award high school students "no more than two elective Carnegie units for the completion of released time classes in religious instruction." Prior law authorized districts to release students from school to attend classes in religious instruction conducted by a private entity. The Spartanburg County School District adopted a released time program permitting students to receive instruction in a Bible education program. Their grades were sent to the school district by a private religious school and treated as coming from the school "without further inquiry" for entry on student transcripts.

Parents and a public interest group sued the district in a federal district court for Establishment Clause and equal protection violations. The court found **released time programs allowing students to leave campus during school hours for religious instruction have been upheld as constitutional**, notably by the Supreme Court in *Zorach v. Clausen*, 343 U.S. 306 (1952). While the court denied the district's motion to dismiss the Establishment Clause claim, it found no equal protection violation. There was no evidence that students were treated differently based on participation in the released time program. *Moss v. Spartanburg County School Dist. No. 7*, 676 F.Supp.2d 452 (D.S.C. 2009).

The parents and organization sought to join the state of South Carolina as a party. The court held an absent party must be joined when complete relief cannot be awarded among existing parties or if the absence of a party might impair that party's ability to protect an interest or expose the party to a substantial risk of inconsistent obligations. The court held the state was not a required party because its absence would not preclude the parents and organization from obtaining complete relief. *Moss v. Spartanburg County School Dist. No. 7*, No. 7:09-1586-HMH, 2010 WL 2136642 (D.S.C. 5/25/10).

◆ A Missouri school allowed the Gideons to distribute Bibles to fifth-grade classrooms during the school day in the presence of a teacher or administrator. Objecting parents sued the school district. The school board then passed a new policy on the distribution of literature at school. The case reached the U.S. Court of Appeals, Eighth Circuit, which noted that the amended policy required organizations to obtain approval from the superintendent prior to distributing literature. If material was approved by the superintendent, it could be distributed in front of school offices or at a table in the cafeteria during non-class times. If a request was denied, the policy specified that the organization could appeal to the school board. **The amended policy was reasonable and did not prohibit the district from neutrally facilitating private Bible distributions.** *Roark v. South Iron R-1 School Dist.*, 573 F.3d 556 (8th Cir. 2009).

◆ A Kentucky school board implemented a new speech rights policy after being sued by a group of students who petitioned for a gay/straight alliance club. See *Boyd County High School Gay Straight Alliance v. Board of Educ. of Boyd County*, 258 F.Supp.2d 667 (E.D. Ky. 2003).

The board then adopted policies prohibiting harassment based on sexual orientation, and providing mandatory anti-harassment training to all students. A student believed it was his Christian responsibility to "tell others when their conduct does not comport with his understanding of Christian morality." He said he refrained from commenting about his beliefs to avoid punishment under the school's anti-harassment policy, then sued the board for speech rights violations. The board revised its policy to allow anti-homosexual speech unless the speech was sufficiently severe or pervasive that it adversely affected a student's education or created a climate of hostility or intimidation. The student appealed to the U.S. Court of Appeals, Sixth Circuit, arguing that he had refrained from telling of his beliefs to avoid discipline, and that the new policy "chilled" speech in violation of the First Amendment. The Sixth Circuit ruled against him. Here, **the** student's claim that his rights were chilled under the board policy was insufficient to establish standing in a federal court. It was speculative whether he would have been punished under the new policy. *Morrison v. Board of Educ. of Boyd County*, 521 F.3d 602 (6th Cir. 2008).

◆ A Louisiana elementary school principal informed fifth-grade teachers at his school that the Gideon society would distribute Bibles to the fifth-grade class outside his office. He said that while students did not have to take a Bible, he was acting on instructions from the school board. A student accepted a Bible but claimed she felt pressured to do so because of potential name-calling and teasing from peers if she refused. Her parent sued the school board. A court ruled that **the Bible distribution violated the Establishment Clause**. The student feared peers would say she did not believe in God and call her a "devil worshipper" or "Goth" if she refused a Bible. Concern for religious coercion in elementary grades is strong, based on the impressionability of young students. Elementary students may not fully appreciate the difference between official and private speech, and a school board policy might be misperceived as endorsement. Allowing the Gideons to have access to an elementary school during a school day to hand out Bibles was "unquestionably religious." The board had no secular purpose for the practice, and it created an impression of religious preference that violated the Establishment Clause. *Roe v. Tangipahoa Parish School Board*, Civ. No. 07-2908, 2008 WL 1820420 (E.D. La. 4/22/08).

◆ A New York school district released Catholic and Protestant students to nearby programs at designated times during the school day. Others remained in classrooms with nothing to do until the released students returned. A family claimed the program led to "abusive religious invective directed against those who did not participate and that the district did not adequately train teachers and principals to protect non-participants from the taunts of program participants."

The family sued the district, asserting the "released time" program violated the Establishment Clause by promoting Christianity over other religions and non-religion. A court held for the school district, and the family appealed. The Second Circuit noted the released-time program authorized by New York Education Law permitted districts to release students, with parental permission, for one hour per week for religious instruction. The U.S. Supreme Court had upheld this law in *Zorach v. Clauson*, 343 U.S. 306 (1952). The Second Circuit noted that the program used no public funds and involved no on-site religious instruction. Schools simply adjusted their schedules to accommodate student religious needs. **The court rejected the argument that the school's imprimatur was placed on a program of religious instruction and that churches used the schools in support of their religious missions.** Nothing here suggested that the released time program was administered in a coercive manner. *Pierce v. Sullivan West Cent. School Dist.*, 379 F.3d 56 (2d Cir. 2004).

3. Immunization

Court Decisions

School districts and state educational agencies have a compelling state interest in requiring the immunization of all students in an effort to prevent and control communicable diseases.

◆ A New York high school denied a student's request for a waiver allowing him to attend school without undergoing immunization pursuant to New York Public Health Law Section 2164(9). The section exempts students from state immunization requirements if their parents hold "genuine and sincere religious beliefs" which are contrary to immunization. The student appealed the district's decision to forbid him from competing or practicing with the lacrosse team, which he had done in years past without obtaining an immunization. While the appeal was pending before the state commissioner of education, he sued the district for violating his religious free exercise rights. He claimed that the district's policy had a discriminatory impact on students whose religious convictions prohibited immunization. The court disagreed, finding that **the district's responsibility for ensuring student safety was rationally based**. It was "firmly established that there is no constitutional right to participate in extracurricular sporting activities." The district did not violate the student's equal protection or religious free exercise rights. *Hadley v. Rush Henrietta Cent. School Dist.*, No. 05-CV-6331T, 2007 WL 1231753 (W.D.N.Y. 4/25/07).

◆ New York parents refused immunizations based on their religious beliefs, asserting that their genuine and sincere beliefs fulfilled the legal requirements for a state law religious exemption. School officials met with the family to discuss their position. The parents stated that use of aborted fetal tissue made immunization unholy and violated God's supreme authority. However, they cited no biblical authority for this claim. The school district denied the request, and its decision was upheld by the New York State Commissioner of Education.

A federal court noted the parents did not know the basis for their religious objection. The district sought pretrial judgment on that ground. The court found the Second Circuit has emphasized the limited function of the judiciary in determining whether beliefs are to be accorded First Amendment protection. To assess a person's religious sincerity, the Second Circuit used a subjective test under which the person's claim must be given great weight. **So long as the person conceived of his or her beliefs as religious in nature, the subjective test was met.** It was not appropriate to award pretrial judgment when a person's subjective state of mind was at issue. Since the family had presented evidence of a sincerely held religious belief against immunization, the court denied pretrial judgment. *Moses v. Bayport Bluepoint Union Free School Dist.*, No. 05 CV 3808 (DRH) (ARL), 2007 WL 526610 (E.D.N.Y. 2/13/07).

Sec. II   USE OF SCHOOL FACILITIES   71

♦ Arkansas law prevented schools from admitting students without a certification of immunization for specified diseases. An exemption was granted to families who objected to immunization on religious grounds if they were members of a "recognized church or religious denomination." Four Arkansas students filed lawsuits against state and local officials, asserting the law violated the Establishment Clause by limiting the exemption from immunization to those who objected on religious tenets and practices of a "recognized" church or denomination. The students claimed they had sincere religious beliefs even though they did not belong to a religion "recognized" by the state. The courts held that the exemption violated the Establishment Clause, agreeing with the students that the exemption had a discriminatory impact on religious groups not officially recognized by the state. But **the unconstitutional part of the law could be separated from the rest of the law** and the students had to be immunized. On appeal, the Eighth Circuit noted the Arkansas legislature had by then amended the law to omit the references to "recognized religions." The exemption was now available to any family with religious or philosophical objections to immunization. As a result, the case was moot and the court dismissed it. *McCarthy v. Ozark School Dist.*, 359 F.3d 1029 (8th Cir. 2004).

II. USE OF SCHOOL FACILITIES

Overview

Courts use a "forum analysis" when considering the use of school facilities by students, clubs and non-students. A "limited public forum" exists whenever a government agency voluntarily opens up its facilities or programs for public use. The "forum" may be a bulletin board, public address system, or the use of classrooms for meetings during noninstructional time. Once a district makes the decision to open a limited public forum, any restriction it places on speech must be reasonable in view of the purposes of the forum. There can be no discrimination on the basis of viewpoint. The nature of the forum determines the limits that may be placed on speech by intended users.

The No Child Left Behind (NCLB) Act requires school districts to certify to their state educational agencies "that no policy of the local educational agency prevents, or otherwise denies participation in, constitutionally protected prayer in public elementary schools and secondary schools." The requirement is a condition of receiving federal funds, and is codified at 20 U.S.C. § 7904.

Court Decisions

♦ A Tennessee elementary school student said staff members told him not to read and discuss the Bible with his friends on the playground during recess. He said he was told he could discuss the Bible only during his "free time," which staff said did not include recess. The student's parent sued the school board in a federal district court for constitutional rights violations. In pretrial activity, **the court held recess was non-instructional time to which full First Amendment speech protections applied**. And it held the student had a clearly established constitutional right to read and study the Bible in a nondisruptive manner. A jury returned a verdict for the school board and officials. The student sought a post-trial judgment or a new trial, but the court found a jury verdict can be overturned only if the jury had "reached a seriously erroneous result."

According to the court, sufficient evidence supported the verdict. While the student claimed he only wanted to read the Bible with his friends, the school principal testified during the trial that she had rejected a request for an adult-led Bible study class. She said she did not learn of the informal playground Bible study until later. As a result, the court found the principal had misunderstood the student's intent. Testimony by the superintendent corroborated the belief that an adult-led Bible study class was being sought. There was testimony that no parents approached the school about a Bible club. **It was reasonable for the jury to find there had been a misunderstanding about the nature of a Bible club, and the court found no First Amendment violation.** Since the court found the verdict was not a "seriously erroneous result," the court denied the student's request for a judgment in his favor or a new trial. *L.W. v. Knox County Board of Educ.*, No. 3:05-CV-274, 2010 WL 3632208 (E.D. Tenn. 9/9/10).

A. Assemblies and School-Sponsored Events

Teacher Scenarios

Parents say school is culturally insensitive and excluding their child 86

Students put teacher on hot seat over carol-free holiday concert 87

Did outside speaker promote religion in class? 88

Court Decisions

♦ A New Jersey school district hosted after-school talent shows called "Frenchtown Idol." The shows were held at 7:00 p.m. in the school auditorium and were entirely voluntary. Students were invited to develop their own performances at home and received no school credit for participating. Three teachers reviewed all song lyrics, skits, and acts. A student submitted "Awesome God" as her talent show selection. The district superintendent found this inappropriate for the show because of its "overtly religious message and proselytizing nature." She found the song was "the musical equivalent of a spoken prayer." The music teacher informed the student that she could not sing "Awesome God" at the show and offered her two songbooks to select a replacement song, even if it was a religious one. The student sued the board in a federal district court for constitutional rights violations. The court found the talent show was not a "school-sponsored production." **Speech taking place in the show "was the private speech of a student and not a message conveyed by the school itself."** The board could not engage in viewpoint discrimination.

Any restrictions on speech had to be viewpoint neutral and reasonable in view of the purposes served by the forum. Here, the exclusion of speech simply because it was controversial or divisive was "viewpoint discrimination." The court rejected the school board's argument that it had to exclude the song to avoid an Establishment Clause violation. It was unlikely an audience would perceive the student's song to be the expression of anyone's view but her own. The court awarded pretrial judgment to the student. *Turton v. Frenchtown Elementary School Dist. Board of Educ.*, 465 F.Supp.2d 369 (D.N.J. 2006).

◆ Ohio high school students had a band that performed mostly Christian songs. The father of one student was a school board member and the band's manager. He sought approval for a band performance at a school-wide assembly during school hours. The district superintendent first approved the performance but cancelled it after a school attorney warned her of Establishment Clause problems. The board member appeared in a television interview. He said "together we can bring religion back into the schools." The board then asked another band that performed secular music to perform at the assembly. Band members sued the school district in a federal court, asserting their appearance was cancelled because of disapproval of their Christian message.

The court rejected the band members' claim that the assembly was a public forum in which the district had to maintain viewpoint neutrality. The assembly was not a "forum" of any kind, and for that reason, the district was not subject to any neutrality requirement. The school district "was entitled to exercise editorial control" over it. When the school itself was the speaker, educators were entitled to exercise greater control to assure the views of speakers were not erroneously attributed to the school. **The school district could discriminate against the band members because of their Christian religious identity.** The court awarded pretrial judgment to the school district. *Golden v. Rossford Exempted Village School Dist.*, 445 F.Supp.2d 820 (N.D. Ohio 2006).

B. Student Groups

Teacher Scenarios

Secular item or religious symbol: Was teacher's choice of class material OK?..............................88

Court Decisions

◆ A New York student submitted a request to use school facilities for private religious club meetings after school hours. The superintendent denied the request, stating that this use of facilities amounted to school support of religious worship. The club sued the school in a federal district court, which issued an order preventing the school from prohibiting the club's use of school facilities. The U.S. Court of Appeals, Second Circuit, later held that the school's denial of access was permissible because it was based on content rather than viewpoint.

The club appealed to the U.S. Supreme Court, which observed that **the nature of the forum determines the limits that a school may place on speech taking place in the forum.** The school had established a limited public forum in which it could reasonably seek to avoid identification with a particular religion. While the school was not required to allow all speech, limits on speech could not be based upon viewpoint and had to be reasonable in light of the purpose of the forum. The school's policy broadly permitted speech about the moral and character development of children. The school had excluded the club from its facilities solely because of its religious viewpoint. This resulted in unconstitutional viewpoint discrimination. "Speech discussing otherwise permissible subjects cannot be excluded from a limited public forum on the ground that the subject is discussed from a religious viewpoint." Club meetings took place after school hours and were not school sponsored. No risk of coercion was present, because students had to obtain permission from their parents to attend meetings. The school failed to show any risk of school endorsement of religion. The Court reversed the judgment. *Good News Club v. Milford Cent. School*, 533 U.S. 98 (2001).

◆ A South Carolina school district charged the Child Evangelism Fellowship of South Carolina fees to use its facilities for Good News Club meetings after school. Many other users had free access to school facilities, including parent-teacher and district organizations, booster clubs, political parties, the SADD, 4-H, FFA and FHA. After paying the district over $1,500 during a two-year period, the Good News Club sought a waiver from the fee. The district denied the request, and the club sued it in a federal district court. The board eliminated a "best interest of the district" waiver provision from the policy. A new provision waived fees for organizations that had used its facilities for at least 20 years. Only scouting groups met this requirement. The case reached the Fourth Circuit, which held the provision unconstitutional. The government may not regulate speech based on its content or the message it conveys. **Once government facilities are opened for private speech, an agency may not discriminate based upon the viewpoint of the speaker.** The "best interest of the district" provision was subjective and "a virtual prescription for unconstitutional decision making." And the revised provision incorporated the viewpoint discrimination built into the earlier "best interest" provision, under which the scouting groups initially got access. *Child Evangelism Fellowship of South Carolina v. Anderson School Dist. Five*, 470 F.3d 1062 (4th Cir. 2006).

◆ An Oregon school district let Boy Scout representatives make presentations during school lunch periods when students were required to be present. School employees helped the Scouts by quieting children, directing attention to the Scout representative and helping fasten hospital-style bracelets on students with information on Scout meetings. Staff also distributed Scout flyers in classes and put Scout information in school newsletters. An atheist parent objected to these practices and filed a discrimination complaint against the district under an Oregon statute. The state superintendent of public instruction investigated the complaint, but found no substantial evidence of discrimination. A state circuit court reversed the decision, and the Court of Appeals of Oregon affirmed.

The Supreme Court of Oregon reviewed the case, and noted that the parent did not challenge the decision to allow Boy Scout recruiting at school, but only sought to determine whether the district had discriminated under the statute. Under the statute, there could be no discrimination on the basis of religion or other protected grounds in any public school program, service or school activity. Class time and lunch periods were "school activities." However, handing out Boy Scout flyers and making presentations did not amount to discrimination against the student because it did not treat him differently than others because of religion. **The flyers and other information were distributed to all students, with no mention of a religious affiliation.** The lunchroom presentations were neutral, making no mention of religion. The court reversed the judgment. *Powell v. Bunn*, 341 Or. 306, 142 P.3d 1054 (Or. 2006).

C. The Equal Access Act

The federal Equal Access Act (EAA), 20 U.S.C. §§ 4071-4074, governs student use of secondary school facilities during noninstructional time. It makes it unlawful for a public secondary school to deny equal access to facilities, if the school maintains a "limited open forum." A limited open forum exists where student groups have been accorded the right to meet in noncurricular groups on school grounds during noninstructional time.

Court Decisions

◆ A Nebraska high school student wanted permission to begin a Christian Club. The school permitted its students to join, on a voluntary basis, a number of groups and clubs that met after school. Each of these clubs had faculty sponsors. However, the student who wished to start the Christian Club did not have a faculty sponsor. School administrators denied her request because she did not have a sponsor and because they believed a religious club at the school would violate the Establishment Clause. The student sued the school board and administrators in a federal district court. She alleged a violation of the EAA. The district court ruled in favor of the school, holding that the other clubs at the school related to the school's curriculum and thus, the school did not have a "limited open forum" as defined by the EAA.

The student appealed to the Eighth Circuit, which ruled in her favor. The school then appealed to the U.S. Supreme Court, which stated the other clubs did not relate to the school's curriculum. **The school had to provide a limited open forum to all students wishing to participate in groups.** The EAA provided that schools could limit activities that substantially interfered with their orderly conduct. The Court also stated **the EAA did not violate the Establishment Clause because it had a secular purpose and limited the role of teachers who work with religious clubs**. The Court affirmed the decision, holding the school violated the EAA. *Board of Educ. of Westside Community School v. Mergens*, 496 U.S. 226, 110 S.Ct. 2356, 110 L.Ed.2d 191 (1990).

◆ A Minnesota school district classified a gay tolerance organization as "noncurricular." The organization claimed the district violated the EAA by denying it access to school facilities enjoyed by other noncurricular groups like cheerleading and a synchronized swimming club. A federal court granted the organization's request for a preliminary order, finding that cheerleading and synchronized swimming, like the tolerance group, were "noncurricular."

The district appealed to the U.S. Court of Appeals, Eighth Circuit, which explained that a limited open forum exists under the EAA when at least one noncurriculum-related group is allowed to meet on school grounds during non-instructional time. The EAA is triggered even if a school permits only one noncurriculum group. The court agreed with the gay tolerance group that cheerleading and the synchronized swimming club were not curriculum-related. The school offered no courses for these activities, and they were not required for a particular course. Accordingly, the gay tolerance group was on the same ground as they were and could use the facilities they enjoyed. **A district could legitimately categorize cheerleading and synchronized swimming classes as "curriculum related" by awarding P.E. credits to participants.** A more drastic option would be to "wipe out all of its noncurriculum-related student groups and totally close its forum." The court affirmed the district court's preliminary order for the gay tolerance group. *Straights and Gays for Equality v. Osseo Area Schools-Dist. No. 279*, 471 F.3d 908 (8th Cir. 2006).

The case returned to the lower court, which issued a permanent order for the gay tolerance club to have the same access to meetings, communications and other school facilities as recognized curricular groups. The district appealed again to the Eighth Circuit, which held that the district had violated the EAA by denying the club access to school facilities on the same terms as provided to other noncurricular clubs. And **the placement of favored student groups as student government subgroups did not automatically make them "curriculum related."** This would make it far too easy for a school to circumvent the EAA. The lower court had properly awarded permanent relief to the club, and the judgment was affirmed. *Straights and Gays for Equality v. Osseo Area Schools-Dist. No. 279*, 540 F.3d 911 (8th Cir. 2008).

◆ A Washington school district required student clubs to submit their proposals for official recognition to the Associated Student Body (ASB) council for approval. Students attempted to form a Bible club for several years and submitted three different applications. The ASB denied the application based on the club's proposal to make announcements over the public address system and decorate the school in a biblical theme. The ASB later rejected applications by the club based on its name – "Truth," and its restriction of voting membership to those who professed belief in the Bible and Jesus Christ. After the ASB voted down a second application, the club sued the school district and school officials. A federal court awarded pretrial judgment to the district, finding club membership restrictions were a legitimate reason to deny recognition.

The club appealed to the Ninth Circuit, which ordered the district court to reconsider several claims. It noted that many of the 30 ASB-recognized student clubs had selective membership criteria, including the Earth Club, Gay-Straight Alliance and National Honor Society. Significantly, two honor clubs at the school had gender-exclusive memberships. **The Bible club's membership restrictions inherently excluded non-Christians in violation of the district's non-discrimination policies, making denial of recognition consistent with the EAA.** The club did not show the district's nondiscrimination policy restricted ASB status on the basis of religion or the content of speech. To the extent that the district allowed waivers to other groups, there remained an issue of fact to consider. The court reversed and remanded the case for further review. *Truth v. Kent School Dist.*, 542 F.3d 634 (9th Cir. 2008).

◆ A Pennsylvania school district established an "activity period" after homeroom and prior to the first class of the day. During this time, students had to remain on school grounds but could participate in club meetings, go to study hall, attend student activities or relax. The district recognized three student groups as "curriculum-related" and allowed them to meet during the activity period, post signs and use the public address system. When a student Bible Club was not allowed to meet during the activity period, a club member sued the school board for violating the EAA and her First Amendment speech rights. The court denied her request for a preliminary order, finding the activity period was not "noninstructional time" under the EAA.

The student appealed to the Third Circuit, which explained that "noninstructional time" could include the activity period, even though it was neither before the start of the school day, nor after its conclusion. The district had set aside the activity period as noninstructional time. **The court rejected an interpretation of the EAA that would allow districts to evade application of the Act by describing an otherwise "limited open forum" as time that counted toward student instruction.** The district violated the EAA by forbidding Bible club meetings during the activity period. The court remanded the case to determine damages and attorneys' fees. *Donovan v. Punxsutawney Area School Board*, 336 F.3d 211 (3d Cir. 2003).

D. Non-Student Use

Court Decisions

◆ The Good News Club (GNC) held after-school evangelical programs for elementary school students in public schools. Students could only participate if they had prior written parental permission. Meetings were free and students did not raise funds for the GNC. A Virginia school board adopted a new facilities use policy in response to legislation allowing the Boy Scouts to use school facilities. The policy gave the superintendent discretion to waive facilities use fees, and the board waived fees for city or county agencies and groups affiliated with those agencies. All school groups and school-sponsored activities were granted a waiver, as were Boy and Girl Scouts and other patriotic organizations. Local charitable organizations and partners were also exempted from the fee. By contrast, the GNC paid $12.50 per hour to use school facilities. After paying to use school facilities for about six months, the GNC sued.

A federal court noted that the **government does not have to allow all speech on all its property at all times, but once it has opened up facilities to private speech, there can be no discrimination based on the viewpoint of a speaker**. Here, the policy gave the superintendent "complete unfettered discretion in deciding who benefits from the fee-waiver." This improperly allowed the superintendent to decide which organizations could have a fee waiver. As a result, the GNC was entitled to a preliminary order waiving the fees. *Child Evangelism Fellowship of Virginia v. Williamsburg-James City County School Board*, Civ. No. 4:08cv4, 2008 WL 3348227 (E.D. Va. 8/08/08).

◆ A Maryland school district allowed many nonprofit groups to distribute flyers to teachers, who then placed them in student cubbies. The district did not let the Child Evangelism Fellowship distribute flyers for student meetings of the Good News Club through this forum. The club sued. A federal district court granted the club's request for preliminary relief concerning bulletin boards, open houses and other events, but denied its request to distribute flyers based on the risk of an Establishment Clause violation. On appeal, the U.S. Court of Appeals, Fourth Circuit, reviewed evidence that the district had allowed over 225 groups to distribute flyers in 18 months. Other religious groups, such as the Salvation Army, Jewish Community Center and YMCA were allowed to circulate flyers. **Here, the role of teachers in placing the materials in student cubbies during school hours did not create an Establishment Clause risk.** The risk of religious endorsement was no greater than the risk of a perception of hostility toward religion if the group was not allowed to distribute its flyers. The court reversed the lower court order. *Child Evangelism Fellowship of Maryland v. Montgomery County Schools*, 373 F.3d 589 (4th Cir. 2004).

The board then revised its take-home mail policy. Under the revised policy, materials and announcements of five organizations could be approved for display or direct distribution to students. The case returned to the Fourth Circuit, which found that the new policy gave too much discretion to the school district to control the take-home flyer forum. As the new policy did not require viewpoint neutrality, the court again reversed the judgment. The district could restrict the number or content of messages in the forum in a viewpoint neutral or reasonable manner. It could also eliminate the flyer forum by reserving it solely for government messages. *Child Evangelism Fellowship of Maryland v. Montgomery County Public Schools*, 457 F.3d 376 (4th Cir. 2006).

◆ A New Jersey school district policy reserved the superintendent's right to approve materials from community groups to be sent home with students. Teachers placed approved materials from community organizations in student mailboxes at the close of the school day. Community materials had to meet five requirements, including approval by the superintendent and some relationship to the school or its students. Partisan and election materials were not allowed, nor could students "be exploited" by profit-makers. The policy applied to requests by community groups to post information on school walls, and to "Back to School nights." The district rarely excluded groups from these events.

An evangelical organization sponsored weekly Good News Club meetings after school. The meetings included activities such as Bible lessons and learning games. The superintendent approved the club's request to meet in an elementary school classroom after school hours but rejected its request to distribute flyers and parent permission slips through student mailboxes, citing Establishment Clause concerns. The organization sued the district and its officials for constitutional violations. The case reached the Third Circuit, which held that the district created "limited open public forums" by allowing community groups to use school channels for communication on particular topics. It could not exclude speech unreasonably or discriminate based on viewpoint. The club's materials satisfied all district requirements. The rejection of religious groups which attempted to recruit members was viewpoint discrimination. **Since the district permitted discussion of topics from a secular perspective, it could not shut out speech on the same topics with a religious perspective.** The court rejected the claim that allowing the club to use school facilities would violate the Establishment Clause. *Child Evangelism Fellowship of New Jersey v. Stafford Township School Dist.*, 386 F.3d 514 (3d Cir. 2004).

◆ A New York school district issued regulations allowing social, civic, or recreational uses of its property as well as limited use by political organizations, but provided that the school not be used for religious purposes. An evangelical church sought permission to use school facilities to show a film series on traditional Christian family values. The district denied permission to use its facilities because the film was religious. The church filed a lawsuit in a federal court alleging the district violated the First Amendment. The court found the district's action "viewpoint neutral," and the U.S. Court of Appeals, Second Circuit, agreed. The church appealed to the U.S. Supreme Court, which **held the exclusion of subject matter based on its religious content would impermissibly favor some viewpoints or ideas at the expense of others. Therefore, the regulation discriminated on the basis of viewpoint.**

The exclusion of the church from using school property was not viewpoint neutral. Next, the Court determined that since the film series was not to be shown during school hours and was to be open to those outside the church, the public would not perceive the district to be endorsing religion. Since use of school facilities by the church did not violate the test from *Lemon v. Kurtzman*, permission by the district would not violate the Establishment Clause. The film had a secular purpose, its primary effect did not advance religion, and the showing of the film would not "foster excessive state entanglement with religion." Thus, speech about "family and child related issues" from a religious perspective could be aired on public school grounds. The Court reversed the lower court decisions. *Lamb's Chapel v. Center Moriches Union Free School Dist.,* 508 U.S. 384, 113 S.Ct. 2141, 124 L.Ed.2d 352 (1993).

◆ An Ohio elementary school let community groups place flyers in student mailboxes advertising activities sponsored by the American Red Cross, 4-H Club, sports leagues and local churches. Some of the flyers described religious activities. The principal reviewed the flyers to ensure sponsoring organizations were nonprofit groups serving children in the community, did not advocate any particular religion and did not seek to use flyers as a recruiting tool. Approved flyers were distributed to teachers, who then placed them in student mailboxes with official school papers. Teachers did not discuss the flyers with students. A parent claimed the distribution of flyers advertising religious activities violated the Establishment Clause. He sued the school district in a federal district court.

The court ordered the school to stop distributing flyers that advertised activities at which proselytizing would occur. The district appealed to the Sixth Circuit, which held **no reasonable parent observing the flyers would perceive religious endorsement by the school**. There was no risk of religious coercion, as the activities advertised in the flyers were not school-sponsored and did not take place on school grounds. If the school refused to distribute flyers advertising religious activities while continuing to distribute other flyers, students might suspect disapproval of religion. The court reversed the judgment. *Rusk v. Crestview Local School Dist.*, 379 F.3d 418 (6th Cir. 2004).

E. Religious Literature and Symbols

In McCreary County v. American Civil Liberties Union of Kentucky*, 545 U.S. 844 (2005), the U.S. Supreme Court struck down the display of the Ten Commandments at county courthouses in Kentucky. In* McCreary County, *the Supreme Court held it would look to the events leading up to a Ten Commandments display to assess its constitutionality. It found substantially religious objectives by the Kentucky counties. In another 2005 case,* Van Orden v. Perry, *545 S.Ct. 677 (2005), the Supreme Court allowed a display of the Ten Commandments on a monument at the Texas Capitol. The Court explained the display was "a far more passable use of those texts than was the case in* Stone, *where the text confronted elementary school students every day."*

Teacher Scenarios

Religious symbolism during the holidays:
How far is too far? 89

Invitations have a religious tone: Should teacher take action? 90

Is longstanding tradition OK? Parent says 'No!' 91

Defining the limits on mixing school and religion 91

Student's 'Jesus pencil' gifts put teacher on the spot: Now what? 92

Teacher protected students' faith ... Didn't she? 94

Court Decisions

◆ A Kentucky statute required the posting of the Ten Commandments on the wall of each public school classroom in the state. A group of citizens sought an injunction against the statute's enforcement, claiming it violated the First Amendment's Establishment and Free Exercise Clauses. The Kentucky state courts upheld the statute, finding it was secular and did not advance or inhibit any religion and did not entangle the state with religion. Utilizing the test from *Lemon v. Kurtzman*, **the U.S. Supreme Court struck down the statute. The Court held the posting of the Ten Commandments had no secular purpose.**

Kentucky state education officials insisted the statute served the secular purpose of teaching students the foundation of western civilization and the common law. The Court stated, however, the pre-eminent purpose was plainly religious in nature. **The Ten Commandments undeniably came from a religious text**, despite the legislative recitation of a secular purpose. The Court noted the text of the Commandments was not integrated into a course or study of history, civilization, ethics, or comparative religion, but simply posted to induce children to read, meditate upon, and perhaps, to venerate and obey them. The Court held it made no difference that the cost of posting the commandments was paid for through private funds and that they were not read aloud. *Stone v. Graham*, 449 U.S. 39, 101 S.Ct. 192, 66 L.Ed.2d 199 (1981).

◆ Four Texas families claimed an elementary school would not let their children hand out religious materials. They sued their school district in a federal court for First Amendment violations. While the case was pending, the school district adopted a new policy that allowed students to distribute materials 30 minutes before or after school, during recess and at annual school parties. Under the new "2005 Policy," middle and secondary school students could hand out literature in hallways and cafeterias during non-instructional time and in cafeterias during lunch. Stated reasons for the policy were to decrease disruption, increase learning time and improve the educational process. After the 2005 Policy was approved, the families sought pretrial judgment.

The court found a challenge to the policy in effect in 2004 was moot and upheld the 2005 Policy. On appeal, the U.S. Court of Appeals, Fifth Circuit, held **a time, place and manner regulation on student speech must be "content and viewpoint neutral," be "narrowly tailored to serve a significant government interest" and allow ample alternative channels for communication**. Under this test, the court upheld the 2005 Policy as content neutral and supported by the district's legitimate interests. Regulation of student speech during and immediately before classes began was intended to facilitate education. Restrictions on hallway and cafeteria distributions of literature were intended to help students move between classes and during lunch and to reduce littering. There was evidence that the 2005 Policy was a positive response to past disruption. Students had ample alternative communication channels under the 2005 Policy. Elementary school students needed more guidance than older students, so it was permissible to limit when they could hand out literature. The court returned claims involving the 2004 policy to the district court for further review. *Morgan v. Plano Independent School Dist.*, 589 F.3d 740 (5th Cir. 2009).

◆ The group of parents from the case summarized above claimed elementary principals "interrogated" their children and searched their gift bags for religious materials. One parent said students were forbidden from using the term "Christmas" for school events. Another claimed a principal threatened to call the police if she tried to hand out religious materials. In pretrial activity, the principals argued they were entitled to qualified immunity. The court denied the request, and the case came before a three-judge panel of the Fifth Circuit.

The panel explained that **qualified immunity shields government officials who are performing discretionary functions from any liability for civil damages if their conduct does not violate clearly established rights of which a reasonable person would have known**. The panel held the principals had "fair warning" that viewpoint-based suppression of student distribution of literature was unconstitutional. It denied immunity to the principals. But the opinion was soon withdrawn and a request for a rehearing before all judges of the Fifth Circuit was granted. *Morgan v. Swanson*, 628 F.3d 705 (5th Cir. 2010).

◆ Las Cruces Public Schools employed an insignia incorporating three crosses that was used on official vehicles and other school district property. A taxpayer challenged the use of the crosses in a federal court, which noted that "Las Cruces" is Spanish for "the crosses." The city had long used crosses in its official insignia, as did non-religious and private entities. The crosses were in a part of the insignia that was less than two inches wide. And the school district did not use the symbol to proselytize. The insignia was locally recognized as having a secular purpose, and it did not advance religion or entangle the government with religion. The taxpayer appealed to the Tenth Circuit, which noted that the insignia was also used by the area chamber of commerce and many private businesses. **The "Establishment Clause enshrines the principle that government may not act in ways that aid one religion, aid all religions or prefer one religion over another."** Of primary importance was whether the government intended to endorse religion or had the effect of endorsing religion. An objective observer would not conclude that the city adopted the logo with the purpose of endorsing Christianity. Compelling evidence established that the symbol was not religious. The policy ensured compliance with Establishment Clause principles, and the court affirmed the lower court judgments. *Weinbaum v. City of Las Cruces, New Mexico*, 541 F.3d 1017 (10th Cir. 2008).

◆ New York City's holiday display policy did not permit creches (nativity scenes). The policy allowed the display of secular holiday symbols, including "Christmas trees, Menorahs, and the Star and Crescent." Displays could not "appear to promote or celebrate any single religion or holiday." The Catholic League for Religious and Civil Rights protested the absence of creches from holiday displays in city schools. After the city refused to change the policy, a Catholic parent of two elementary students sued. She claimed that the policy promoted Judaism and Islam and disapproved of Christianity. After a federal court upheld the policy, the U.S. Court of Appeals, Second Circuit, held the decision to represent Christmas with secular symbols, rather than creches, did not show hostility to Christianity. **The menorah and the star and crescent were religious symbols, but they did not depict a deity while a nativity scene did.** The policy had a secular purpose "to teach the lesson of pluralism." Promoting tolerance and respect for diverse customs did not violate the Religion Clauses of the First Amendment. The policy avoided a religious message by requiring any symbol or decoration to be displayed simultaneously with others reflecting different beliefs or customs. Objective observers would perceive the promotion of pluralism, not religion. The court affirmed the judgment for the city. *Skoros v. City of New York*, 437 F.3d 1 (2d Cir. 2006).

◆ A Florida student painted murals with religious messages or symbols for a school project, without informing the teacher who supervised the project. The student placed them in conspicuous locations in the school, where they caused a commotion. The teacher instructed the student to paint over the overt religious words and sectarian symbols, but allowed other images and messages to remain. Other students were also instructed to edit their murals due to profanity, gang symbols or satanic images. The student complied with the instructions, but sued for First Amendment violations. A federal district court held that the school did not create a public forum when it invited students and staff to paint murals.

The U.S. Court of Appeals, Eleventh Circuit, held that the project was a nonpublic forum. The school did not display an intent to open the project for indiscriminate use, and the principal explicitly forbade profane or offensive content, while the teacher maintained supervision of the project. **The mural project was a nonpublic forum, over which the school could exert editorial control.** Schools can regulate expression in nonpublic forums, so long as their regulations are viewpoint neutral and reasonable in light of the purpose of the forum. The murals were curricular in nature and were "school-sponsored speech" under *Hazelwood School Dist. v. Kuhlmeier*, 484 U.S. 260 (1988). Curricular expression did not have to occur in a classroom. The school had a legitimate pedagogical concern in avoiding disruption, and the court affirmed the judgment. *Bannon v. School Dist. of Palm Beach County*, 387 F.3d 1208 (11th Cir. 2004).

◆ A ministerial association donated monuments inscribed with the Ten Commandments to an Ohio school board and agreed to indemnify the board for any resulting litigation costs. Once the monuments were accepted, the board resolved to dedicate the grounds on which they stood as areas for structures of symbolic history. It erected the monuments at four new high schools and installed signs reciting that the board had incurred no costs and intended no endorsement of religion. Two county residents sued the board to prohibit the display. The board modified the display to add excerpts from the Justinian Code, the Preamble to the U.S. Constitution, the Declaration of Independence and the Magna Carta. The board stated that the Ten Commandments provided the "moral background of the Declaration of Independence and the foundation of our legal tradition." A federal district court held that the display violated the Establishment Clause, and the U.S. Court of Appeals, Sixth Circuit, affirmed. **The original display had no secular purpose. Acceptance of the monuments from a religious organization implied the opposite.** *Baker v. Adams County/Ohio Valley School Board*, 86 Fed.Appx. 104 (6th Cir. 2004).

◆ A New Jersey preschool student tried to distribute pencils stamped with the message "Jesus [heart symbol] The Little Children" at a class party. His teacher confiscated them because of their religious message. The next year, a teacher stopped him from handing out candy canes with a religious story. After the student's mother contacted the school, officials allowed him to distribute candy canes at recess or after school. When the student reached first grade, officials again stopped him from distributing candy canes with a religious story. The student sued the school board and superintendent. The case reached the Third Circuit, which held age and context are key considerations in school speech cases. **A student's age bore an inverse relationship to the degree and kind of control a school could exercise.** Class parties were part of the curriculum, not a place for student advocacy. In an elementary classroom, the line between school-endorsed speech could be blurred for young, impressionable students and their parents. It was appropriate for school officials to set these boundaries, and for the courts to afford them leeway to create an appropriate learning environment and to restrict student messages intending to promote religion. It was within the school's authority to stop the distribution. In any event, the school had allowed him to distribute the message outside class time. *Walz v. Egg Harbor Township Board of Educ.*, 342 F.3d 271 (3d Cir. 2003).

III. LIMITATIONS ON EMPLOYEE RELIGIOUS ACTIVITY

Overview

The Free Exercise Clause of the First Amendment provides that Congress shall make no law prohibiting the free exercise of religion. Courts examining the rights of school employees to engage in religious speech follow the First Amendment analysis from Garcetti v. Ceballos *and* Pickering v. Board of Educ., *with the additional consideration of the employee's right to freely exercise religion.*

Teacher Scenarios

How far do you have to go to keep religion out of school now? 93

Court Decisions

◆ Employees of the Texas Education Agency (TEA) provided support to the state board of education. The board set curricular and graduation requirements for state public schools and determined which textbooks to purchase. TEA staff members were told "not to advocate a particular position on curriculum issues" and to refrain from participating in matters under deliberation. A TEA Director of Science for the Curriculum Division directed the state K-12 science program. Her supervisor instructed her not to communicate with people outside the TEA regarding the state education board's science curriculum deliberations. But she disobeyed the order when she forwarded an email to 36 teachers and teacher organizations concerning a presentation critical of teaching creationism in public schools. Finding the director had violated TEA's neutrality policy, the supervisor recommended employment termination, and she resigned.

The director sued the TEA and state education commissioner in a federal district court, which held for the TEA and the commissioner. On appeal, the U.S. Court of Appeals, Fifth Circuit, held the First Amendment mandates government neutrality among various religions and non-religion. The director claimed the TEA neutrality policy established religion by deeming creationism to be a subject matter for the board to consider in setting the state science curriculum. But the court found no evidence of religious advancement. **A TEA policy against employee speech about possible subjects to be included in the curriculum did not primarily advance religion.** The court held the policy preserved the role of TEA staff to support the board. As the court found no circumstances under which a TEA director's inability to speak about potential subjects for the state curriculum could be perceived as state endorsement of religion, it affirmed the judgment. *Comer v. Scott*, 610 F.3d 929 (5th Cir. 2010).

◆ A Wisconsin guidance counselor prayed with students and destroyed school literature on condom usage without consulting her supervisor. She then ordered literature advocating abstinence. The school superintendent informed her, during her three-year probationary employment contract, that her contract would not be renewed. The counselor sued, asserting that her non-renewal was based on hostility to her religious beliefs in violation of Title VII of the Civil Rights Act and the Free Exercise Clause of the First Amendment. A court awarded pretrial judgment to the school district, and the counselor appealed. The U.S. Court of Appeals, Seventh Circuit, affirmed, noting that the counselor was let go because of her conduct, not her religious beliefs. It was easy to understand the imprudence of retaining a guidance counselor who threw out school materials and substituted her own without asking permission. U.S. Department of Education guidelines prohibit teachers, administrators and other school employees from "encouraging or discouraging prayer, and from actively participating in such activity with students." Finding that **"teachers and other public school employees have no right to make the promotion of religion a part of their job description,"** the court held that the Constitution is not a license for uncontrolled teacher expression. *Grossman v. South Shore Public School Dist.*, 507 F.3d 1097 (7th Cir. 2007).

◆ A South Dakota school district let the Good News Club hold meetings on school grounds under its community use policy. A teacher attended the club's first meeting at her school. The principal told her she could not attend future meetings, warning that her participation might be perceived as an establishment of religion. She sued. A court held that the district had engaged in viewpoint discrimination by excluding her from meetings. While the district could bar the teacher from club meetings at her own school, no Establishment Clause concerns applied to meetings at other schools. The court issued a permanent order allowing the teacher to attend meetings at schools other than her own. The U.S. Court of Appeals, Eighth Circuit, held that **the teacher's participation in after-school club meetings was private speech that did not put the district at risk of violating the Establishment Clause.** Nonparticipants left the building by the time meetings were held, and student participants had parental permission. No reasonable observer would perceive the teacher's presence at club meetings in her own school or any other school to be a state endorsement of religion. The court reversed the decision in part and affirmed it in part, holding for the teacher on all issues appealed. *Wigg v. Sioux Falls School Dist. 49-5*, 382 F.3d 807 (8th Cir. 2004).

◆ A Pennsylvania instructional assistant often wore a small crucifix to work over a six-year period without disruption or controversy. Her supervisor saw her a few times each week but did not notice the crucifix until "someone in the teachers union" reported it. The district suspended the assistant for violating its policy and state law prohibiting public school teachers from wearing religious dress, marks, emblems or insignia while performing their duties. The assistant declined her supervisor's instruction to remove or hide the crucifix.

The school district suspended the assistant, and she

sued for reinstatement and a declaration that the policy was unconstitutional. A federal district court noted that although district policy forbade employees from wearing religious symbols, it allowed them to wear nonreligious decorative jewelry. The district's policy was overtly averse to religion, because it punished religious content or viewpoints while "permitting its employees to wear jewelry containing secular messages or no messages at all." **The policy constituted impermissible viewpoint discrimination because it was directed only at religious speech.** It had a discriminatory purpose and effect that was not justified by any countervailing government interest. The court rejected the district's arguments based on potential criminal liability and threatened violations of the Establishment Clause. The section did not apply to the instructional assistant, since she was not a certificated teacher. No reasonable observer would perceive the district as endorsing religion if it allowed employees to wear unobtrusive crucifixes or similar jewelry. The assistant was entitled to reinstatement and an order preventing the district from enforcing its policy. *Nichol v. ARIN Intermediate Unit 28*, 268 F.Supp.2d 536 (W.D. Pa. 2003).

IV. FINANCIAL ASSISTANCE AND VOUCHER PROGRAMS

Overview

The U.S. Supreme Court upheld an Ohio law authorizing public funding of a private school voucher program in Zelman v. Simmons-Harris, *below. The case may be contrasted to cases like* Committee for Public Educ. and Religious Liberty v. Nyquist, *413 U.S. 756 (1973), where the Court held direct aid from states to sectarian schools "in whatever form is invalid."*

While Zelman *found no Establishment Clause violation in the Ohio program, the case did not resolve the constitutionality of voucher programs under state constitutional provisions, which is for state courts to decide.*

Court Decisions

♦ The Ohio General Assembly adopted the Ohio Pilot Scholarship Program in 1995 in response to a federal court order to remedy problems in the Cleveland School District. The program made vouchers of up to $2,500 available for Cleveland students to attend public or private schools, including schools with religious affiliations. The Supreme Court of Ohio struck down the program on state constitutional grounds in 1999. The general assembly cured the state constitutional deficiencies and reauthorized the program for 1999-2000.

A new lawsuit was commenced in a federal court, which permanently enjoined the state from administering the program. The Sixth Circuit affirmed the judgment, and state officials appealed. The U.S. Supreme Court reversed the judgment, finding no Establishment Clause violation. It held the program allowed government aid to reach religious institutions only because of the deliberate choices of the individual recipients. Any incidental advancement of religion, or perceived endorsement of a religious message, was attributable to the individual recipients, not to the government. The New York program struck down in *Committee for Public Educ. and Religious Liberty v. Nyquist* gave benefits exclusively to private schools and the parents of private school enrollees. Ohio's program offered aid directly to a broad class of individual recipients defined without regard to religion. **Where government aid is religiously neutral and provides direct assistance to a broad class of citizens that in turn directs funds to religious schools through genuine and independent private choices, the program is not readily subject to an Establishment Clause challenge.** *Zelman v. Simmons-Harris,* 536 U.S. 639, 122 S.Ct. 2460, 153 L.Ed.2d 604 (2002).

♦ An Arizona statute provided a tax credit for any corporation contributing cash to a school tuition organization (STO). An STO is a charitable organization exempt from federal tax that allocates 90% of its annual revenue for scholarships or tuition grants to students to attend any qualified school of their parents' choice. A group opposed to the tax credit sued for a declaration that the statute was unconstitutional. A court held for the state, and the opponents appealed. The Court of Appeals of Arizona found that **the statute supported the secular purpose of encouraging Arizona businesses to direct funds to STOs to improve education in the state**. The state had a legitimate interest in facilitating high-quality education for all students, regardless of the school chosen by their parents. As the U.S. Supreme Court has held, "programs of true private choice do not offend the Establishment Clause." The tax credit did not provide direct aid to religious schools, and was neutral with respect to religion, making no distinction between sectarian and nonsectarian schools or STOs. The law created no financial incentive for a student to attend a religious school. As no religious entanglement was present, the law was upheld. *Green v. Garriott*, 221 Ariz. 404, 212 P.3d 96 (Ariz. Ct. App. 2009).

♦ Arizona's Scholarships for Pupils with Disabilities allowed students with disabilities to attend a private school or a school outside their residence school district. Legislators also enacted a Displaced Pupils Choice Grant Program, which permitted children in foster care to attend a private school of their choice. Under the Disabilities Program, parents of a disabled student could apply for scholarships if they were not satisfied with their child's progress in a public school the prior year. After the parents selected a school, they received checks from the state that were restrictively endorsed to their school of choice. The program allowed both sectarian and nonsectarian schools to participate, and schools were "not required to alter their creed, practices or curriculum" to do so. Objectors to the programs sued the state superintendent of public instruction for violating two provisions of the state constitution.

The Supreme Court of Arizona agreed to review the case. It explained that Arizona Constitution Article 9, Section 10, the "Aid Clause," has no equivalent under the U.S. Constitution. The Aid Clause was "aimed at placing restrictions on the disbursement of public funds to specified institutions, both religious and secular." The court distinguished the voucher programs from a state tax credit program for contributions to school tuition organizations. The Aid Clause was primarily designed to protect the public fisc and public schools, and **the scholarship programs provided aid to private schools in violation of the Aid Clause**. *Cain v. Horne*, 220 Ariz. 77, 202 P.3d 1178 (Ariz. 2009).

◆ Opponents of Florida's Opportunity Scholarship Program (OSP) sued state officials in a Florida court for violating three state constitutional provisions. The Supreme Court of Florida held that the OSP was unconstitutional under the "no aid" provision, Article I, Section Three of the Florida Constitution. The OSP violated the state constitution's uniformity requirement by diverting public funds into "separate private systems parallel to and in competition with the free public schools that are the sole means set out in the Constitution for the state to provide for the education of Florida's children." Paying tuition for students to attend private schools was a substantially different manner than the one prescribed in the state constitution. OSP funding was taken directly from each school district's appropriated funds, reducing the funds available to the district. No OSP provision ensured private schools were "uniform." While public schools were held accountable for teaching certain state standards and to teach all basic subjects, private schools were not required to do so and could even hire teachers who did not possess bachelor's degrees. **"Because voucher payments reduce funding for the public education system, the OSP by its very nature undermines the system of 'high quality' free public schools."** The court struck down the OSP program. *Bush v. Holmes*, 919 So.2d 392 (Fla. 2006).

◆ Swan's Island, Maine, had no high school of its own and did not contract with another district to educate resident secondary students as permitted by state law. Two Swan's Island students went to a private religious school at their parents' expense. The Town of Swan's Island then adopted a policy for a monthly tuition subsidy for year-round residents with children enrolled in private high schools. The parents received monthly subsidies for a full school year under the policy, until the Maine Attorney General's Office found the policy violated Maine Revised Statutes Section 2951(2). The town suspended the program, and the parents sued Maine officials in the state court system.

A trial court held for the state, which argued the policy was "nothing more than an attempt to do an end run around the words and the will of the Legislature." On appeal, **the Supreme Judicial Court held Section 2951(2) barred the payment of any public funds, whether state or municipal, from reaching sectarian schools**. The legislature had considered and rejected a bill that would have repealed Section 2951(2) after the court's 2006 decision in *Anderson v. Town of Durham*, below. This reaffirmed the state's public policy against the public funding of sectarian schools. The court affirmed the judgment. *Joyce v. State of Maine*, 951 A.2d 69 (Me. 2008).

◆ Maine law authorizes public funding to pay private school tuition on behalf of students living in school districts that do not operate their own high schools. Districts may contract with other school districts or private schools meeting state criteria to satisfy their obligation to educate resident high school students. In 1980, the state added a provision limiting public funding to nonsectarian schools for school districts that contract with private schools to educate their high school students. The Supreme Court of Maine upheld the provision against a challenge by parents who sought public funding for their children to attend religious schools. *Bagley v. Raymond School Dep't*, 782 A.2d 172 (Me. 1999).

After the U.S. Supreme Court upheld the Ohio voucher program in *Zelman v. Simmons-Harris*, this chapter, a bill to repeal the provision was introduced in the Maine Legislature. The bill failed, and another group of parents seeking public funding for their children to attend religious schools sued. The U.S. Court of Appeals, First Circuit, held that even after *Zelman*, **the Constitution did not require Maine to fund tuition at sectarian schools**. *Eulitt v. State of Maine*, 386 F.3d 344 (1st Cir. 2004).

Another group of parents filed a challenge to the provision in a state court. They sent their children to private schools that were not "nonsectarian schools" under the law. The case reached the Supreme Court of Maine, which noted that the state had decided to exclude sectarian schools from the tuition program based on a 1980 attorney general's opinion. The state was not motivated by religious discrimination, and the provision did not burden or inhibit the free exercise of religion in any constitutionally significant way. The court upheld the provision. *Anderson v. Town of Durham*, 895 A.2d 944 (Me. 2006).

◆ The Colorado Opportunity Contract Pilot Program was enacted to meet the educational needs of low-achieving students in the state's highest poverty areas. Participation was mandatory for any district that had at least eight schools with poor academic ratings. Voucher opponents sued the state in a case that reached the Supreme Court of Colorado. It found local boards retained no authority under the pilot program to determine which students were eligible to participate or how much funding to devote to it. In fact, the program deprived school districts of all local control over instruction. And it violated the local control provision of the state constitution by requiring districts to pay funds, including some locally raised tax revenues, to parents who paid them to nonpublic schools in the form of vouchers. The program violated the state constitution, as **"local control" required school districts to maintain discretion over any instruction paid for with locally raised funds**. *Owens v. Colorado Congress of Parents, Teachers and Students*, 92 P.3d 933 (Colo. 2004).

V. TEACHER SCENARIOS

When students' 'rights' create a disruption: Where to draw the line

How far can teacher go in handling religious conflict?

This was one of teacher Pam Veso's favorite parts of the high school "crafts fair" assignment. Elementary students were shuffling into the high school gym and being given the pretend money to "buy" the products Pam's students had spent the semester developing.

This was a great project on so many levels. The high school students enjoyed creating their own businesses, and the younger kids loved playing customer.

Just then, Pam heard sophomore Rajan Singh shouting, "This isn't OK, Todd!"

Pam hurried over to Rajan and Todd's table. "Let's settle down," she whispered. "What's wrong?"

Rajan whispered, "Todd wants to put these cards on our fish ornaments. Look."

Pam took a card from Rajan and read: "Thanks for choosing our fish. This simple wire shape, which we've strung with beads, is an ancient symbol of Jesus. Hang it anywhere as a reminder of your faith."

Pam sighed and looked up at the boys.

"Please tell Todd he can't put that card on our fish," Rajan insisted. "Honestly, my parents would kill me. We're Sikhs!"

"We need to talk about this, Todd," said Pam. "But let's step away from your table, OK? We don't want to scare any customers away. A big part of this assignment is finding out which products make the most money."

"OK," said Todd. He followed Pam to a quiet corner of the gym.

"Todd," said Pam, "were the cards attached when you did market surveys in Ms. Lu's class?"

"No," said Todd. "I made them last night."

"Oh," said Pam. "Well, it's not fair to spring this on Rajan. How would you like it if he tried to turn your fish into a Sikh product at the last minute?"

Todd looked annoyed.

"Apart from that," Pam went on quietly, "it sounds like you're trying to sell a product that wasn't approved for the crafts fair."

"No, I'm not," argued Todd. "They're exactly the same fish."

"Actually," said Pam calmly, "I think there's a big difference between a plain fish versus a fish with a card that explains it's religious. I'm worried about giving your card to elementary students."

"But why?" asked Todd.

"Because it makes it look like we're trying to push religion to little kids. I'm not sure their parents want them hearing about that on a field trip to the high school. And I'm not sure Principal Higgins wants that, either. Let's go talk to him about it."

Cards not allowed

The principal decided a religious message wasn't appropriate for a school project – especially when it would be read by younger children.

Todd and his parents sued. They said not letting Todd use the card violated his free speech rights.

Did it?

Decision: No. This was school-sponsored speech, and the school had good reasons to forbid it.

The cards were school-sponsored speech because the school had control over the class project for which they were made. Other students and their parents would assume the school endorsed the cards' religious message.

Schools only need a valid educational reason to censor school-sponsored speech. Here, the school had two: the risk of offending students of other faiths, and the importance of not giving visiting elementary school students a religious message that might clash with what they learned at home.

Key: Focus on age when deciding what's appropriate for the classroom. The teacher here was right to be especially careful with much younger – therefore much more impressionable – students involved.

Cite: *Curry v. Hensiner.*

Discussion points for teachers and principals:

Even when students' religious expression could be seen as coming from the school, some think:

- students have an absolute right to express their faith, even in class or at a school event.

But others think:

- bringing up religion at school virtually always leaves someone feeling disrespected, angry – or even discriminated against.

Did teacher's response to difficult parent help head off a lawsuit?

Parent wants minister to talk to class

Despite staying up late and then getting up early, teacher April Jovan still hadn't finished the grading. She suddenly realized she couldn't mark even one more paper until she'd had a cup of coffee.

But just then, an angry woman rushed into her classroom. It was Tim's mother, waving the reading list for the class's upcoming comparative religion section.

"American Indian Spiritualism!" said Mrs. Duffy. "What's next – astrology?"

"Hi," said April, forcing herself to smile and stay calm. "What can I do for you?"

"More than your principal, I hope! I've just come from him. I proposed two reasonable solutions to this problem, but -"

"I'm sorry," April interrupted quietly. "What problem is this?"

"Exposing children to destructive religious lies, of course! What you should be teaching is the Bible. Have one in every classroom. And I want my pastor to speak to your class, too."

"I'm sure I'd like him," said April carefully. "But I'm guessing Principal Ford told you why that's not possible. We can only teach religion as an academic subject at public school – not as a belief."

"Then what do you call this?" roared Mrs. Duffy, shaking the reading list hard.

"We're learning about cultures," said April, "not personal faith."

"Oh, you're so sweet," said Mrs. Duffy. "But so naive. I'll be back," she warned, turning to go. "And I'll bring my pastor!"

April worried about this for days, but Mrs. Duffy didn't sue the school. She sued the U.S. government, arguing it violated her rights by excluding Bible-based beliefs from school. What did the judge say?

Decision: The judge said she didn't have a case. He dismissed her lawsuit.

Key: Teachers need diplomatic skills. Here, the parent may have sued the school, too, if the teacher had thrown more fuel on the fire. Because she didn't, she may have saved the school from an expensive and time-consuming lawsuit.

Cite: *Edwards v. U.S.*

Sharpen Your Judgment
Group charges teacher with promoting religion

History teacher Ed Dunlap nodded toward the sheets of paper and said, "It's all there in my lesson plan."

Principal Heather Berg said, "I've seen it, Ed, but let me make sure I have everything straight. You had the students perform a Native American religious dance as a way of teaching them about the culture?"

"That's right," he replied. "It's called 'The Sun Dance' and was part of an American Indian spiritual ceremony."

"Have you used religious ceremonies to teach about other cultures, too?"

"Not often," he shook his head as he spoke. "This sort of case is special, though, because religious ceremonies are so much a part of the overall culture. One is tied to the other."

"OK that helps," the principal said. "I'm going to explain it to the church group that's saying we're teaching about one religion but not about theirs."

"Are they really that upset?" Ed asked.

"They're talking about suing," she replied.

The group eventually sued. Did the school win the case?

Sharpen Your Judgment – The Decision

Yes. The school won the case.

The court ruled that having students act out or learn about a religious ceremony didn't necessarily mean that religion was being taught in the school.

The key to the decision came in the teacher's explanation that the lesson was about cultures, not religions; that the lesson would've been incomplete without covering the religious aspects; and that there was no endorsement of one religion.

What's 'excessive entanglement'?

Of course, you're always walking a narrow line when you bring religion into a lesson, but courts consistently have ruled that religion in the proper context is an acceptable topic and subject of study in schools, as long as the teaching doesn't clash with state regulations about curriculum.

What courts warn about is what they term "the excessive entanglement with religion." That generally includes teaching one religion is superior to others or one is inferior to another.

While some schools have skirted the problem by avoiding any mention of religion, courts often allow the topic when it's part of a larger lesson and done without endorsing one set of beliefs.

Cite: *Brown v. Woodland Unified School Dist.*

Could teacher have stopped student from 'preaching' at graduation?

Restricting student speech: How far you can (and can't) go

Sitting in the audience at commencement, teacher Cheri Blakely beamed with pride as cap-and-gowned valedictorian Gina Gencer walked up to the microphone.

Cheri had loved helping Gina with her speech – but it hadn't always been easy. The worst part was when Gina insisted she had to tell graduates Jesus was the answer to any challenge they faced after high school. It took forever to make Gina understand why she couldn't "preach" at graduation.

But once they ironed that out, work on the speech had been a joy. And when the principal screened the speeches, she said Gina's was the best she'd ever heard.

Cheri had to agree. As many times as she'd heard it, she was excited to hear it "for real" now.

But instead of the opening Cheri expected, Gina said, "We're saying a lot of goodbyes today. So isn't it good to know we never have to lose our lord Jesus Christ?"

That's not the speech we agreed on!

The rest of the ceremony was a blur to Cheri. As soon as it was over, she rushed over to Gina.

"I can't believe you did this! This is not what we discussed."

"I'm sorry I had to go behind your back," said Gina. "But I knew you'd be mad."

Giving student the bigger picture

"It doesn't matter if I'm mad," said Cheri. "What does matter is this could cause big problems for the school – and you."

"You told me!" said Gina irritably. "But I had a higher purpose to serve."

"That doesn't impress me, Gina," said Cheri, "not when you went about 'serving it' in such a dishonest way.

"Gina, You could have given this speech at your church, like I suggested. Didn't you understand why you couldn't give it at graduation?"

"Because people could get angry and might even sue," said Gina impatiently. "You told me!"

"Right. That's why the principal had to prescreen the speeches – to make sure speakers weren't saying anything that could get the school in trouble. Oh, no. The principal! We need to see her right away."

Student faces the consequences

The principal decided Gina wouldn't get her diploma without a public apology that made it clear:

- the speech expressed only Gina's personal beliefs
- Gina didn't give the school any warning she'd be doing that, and
- the school wouldn't have OK'd her speech if she had.

Gina e-mailed out her apology. Then she sued.

Did apology violate her rights?

Gina claimed that forcing her to apologize for talking about Jesus violated her free speech and religious rights.

But the school said Gina didn't have the right to proselytize at its commencement. It asked the judge to dismiss her lawsuit.

Did he?

Decision: Yes. Gina's rights weren't violated.

The school had the right to control what its graduation speakers said – so it could require an apology when a student evaded this control.

The apology, itself, also didn't violate Gina's rights.

First, the school didn't discipline her for exercising her constitutional rights – because graduation speakers don't have a right to "preach." Second, the school only asked for a factual apology. If it had asked her to lie or betray her faith in order to get a diploma, that would have been another matter.

Key: Some students are going to break the rules. That's just a fact of life at school. You can't control their choices. What you can do is make sure they understand the likely consequences of their actions.

Cite: *Corder v. Lewis Palmer School Dist. No. 38.*

Discussion points for teachers and principals:

The apology here wasn't just for discipline – it clarified the school hadn't broken the law by endorsing religion. But what about when it's only about discipline. Do "forced apologies" work?

■ Some educators say yes: they make students sit down and think about what they've done.

■ Others say no: they only put words in students' mouths that they don't really mean.

Teacher has to break bad news to class – then a disappointed student sues

"Good morning," said teacher Meg Parry to music director Radha Bhola in the teacher's lounge. "I just heard the superintendent and principal vetoed the music your orchestra picked to play at graduation. I'm sorry."

"It was the right call," said Radha. "But I'm not looking forward to telling the kids. They were so excited about that piece. Hey, maybe *you* could tell them we have to find a new one. Want to be my sub today?"

"You know I couldn't find middle C if I had a GPS tracking device," said Meg. "But count on me for moral support later."

When Radha walked into her music room, she heard a cheerful buzz of conversation. Looking up from their semi-circle of chairs, the young musicians smiled and said hello to her. The bell hadn't rung yet, but they had their instruments ready and the sheet music for *Ave Maria* open on their music stands.

Radha's stomach sank because the kids were so excited to play this music.

When the bell rang, she took a deep breath and said, "I have something to tell you. The principal and superintendent didn't approve *Ave Maria* for our graduation performance."

They stared at her for a moment. Then violist Pegi Caprio said, "But they just can't do that!"

"They can. We've known all along they have the final say," said Radha. "And they've decided *Ave Maria* isn't right for graduation."

Graduation Day is special

"Why do non-musicians get to decide? They're probably tone deaf," said Pegi.

"Let's keep the conversation civilized," said Radha. "Because that day has to be for everyone."

"But how could beautiful music leave anybody out?" asked Pegi.

"By sending a religious message in the program," said Radha. "*Ave Maria* is Latin for 'Hail Mary' – a Catholic prayer."

The students all began to talk at once, but Pegi's voice was loudest. "It has nothing to do with religion!" she shouted. "And besides: It's only music, no words."

"Shh," said Radha. "You don't see it as a religious song, but other people might. And administration has decided the ceremony can't include anything religious because that issue's so sensitive it could lead to all kinds of problems. They don't want trouble on a day that's supposed to be special."

"Wait," said Pegi. "Did you say the only real problem is putting *Ave Maria* in the program? Then why don't we call it something else? How about, Graduation Song?"

"No," said Radha. "If we can't do it openly, we can't do it at all. It's about being honest."

"Really?" said Pegi. "Because I think it's about stamping out artistic expression for no good reason. This is about music, not religion. They just can't do this!"

After the school approved the orchestra's second choice, Suite in F, Pegi sued.

She said barring the performance of *Ave Maria* violated her free speech. Did it?

Decision: No, although music can qualify as protected speech.

The school could veto this performance based on its decision to keep all religion out of the ceremony.

It would have been illegal to bar *Ave Maria* to discriminate against Catholics. But the school could forbid it to avoid giving the impression that it was illegally endorsing religion.

The judge found this a valid reason, noting that everything in a graduation ceremony is understood to be endorsed by the school.

Key: Teachers sometimes have the thankless task of delivering bad news. A good rule of thumb is to remain matter-of-fact and tell students only as much as they really need to know before moving on and getting everybody back into the regular routine.

Cite: *Nurre v. Whitehead.*

Discussion points for teachers and principals:

The above case shows that free speech doesn't have to mean actual speech.

Students express themselves in all kinds of ways: dancing, painting, miming, sculpting ... Also by playing music and wearing images.

Teachers need to remember that students' freedom of "speech" doesn't always include words.

Instead, it can encompass just about any kind of self-expression or communication.

Does student need a permission slip to skip the pledge? Parents say, 'No!'

Student refuses to recite pledge – and refuses to bring in required note

Teacher Jacob Hinson asked, "We didn't dodge the legal bullet, did we?"

"I'm afraid not," Principal Heather Marks said. "Ryan Gray's parents filed a lawsuit. They say our Pledge of Allegiance policy violates his speech rights."

"I got nervous as soon as I saw your e-mail," Jacob said.

"Let's review it again," she said.

Student ignores school policy

"Ryan refused to stand and say the pledge," Jacob explained. "I told Ryan he needed a note from his parents to be excused from reciting it."

"You explained why?" Heather asked.

"Yes, I told Ryan it was perfectly OK if he chose not to participate in the morning pledge," Jacob said. "And I explained that I needed the note from his parents, but he never brought one in."

"What happened next?" Heather prodded him for more information.

"Well, I reminded Ryan a few times, but then I gave up on him," Jacob said. "I called his parents and explained that I just needed a note – as per our school policy."

"How did they respond?" Heather asked. "Did they agree to send a note?"

"They acted as if I were inconveniencing them," Jacob told her. "They didn't send a note, and Ryan still refused to participate. That's when I brought you into the loop."

"I see," Heather said, sighing. "And we know what happened next."

Ryan's parents sued, claiming his speech rights were violated. Did the court agree?

Decision: Yes, the court ruled that Ryan's speech rights were violated.

Key: The judge noted that school officials asked for a note to comply with school policy. In most instances, that's enough to stay out of trouble.

But in this case, the policy itself violated students' speech rights – because requiring parents' permission violates students' speech rights, the court explained.

Cite: *Frazier v. Smith.*

Dissent vs. order in class: Did teacher make right choice?

Student refuses to follow the school's rule

Teacher Andy Resnick hoped his chat the previous day with student Dane Melstrom would have some effect.

But as the other students stood for the Pledge of Allegiance, Dane sat at his desk and turned his face away as a form of protest.

The other students tried to stifle their giggles.

At the end of the period, the teacher said, "Dane, I'd like to talk to you a minute."

"Remember the talk we had yesterday about the Pledge?" the teacher began.

"Sure. You said I didn't have to recite it if I didn't want to, but I'd have to stand like the other students do."

"You know why?" the teacher asked.

The student nodded and said, "So there's no disruption in class."

"Right," the teacher said. "Now, if you don't want to stand, please bring in a note from your parents asking that you be allowed to stay in your seat."

"I don't need a note from my parents to exercise what you've taught is a basic right," the student said firmly.

"You do have that right," the teacher noted. "But I have a responsibility to keep order in the room, too."

The right <u>not</u> to speak

"Sorry, Mr. Resnick, but I refuse to say the Pledge or get a note from my parents," the student insisted. "We've learned the right of free speech means we have the right <u>not</u> to speak, too."

"Then, Dane, I'm going to have to discipline you for violating classroom rules," the teacher said.

The student's parents sued over the Pledge policy.

The school argued that the policy was designed to maintain students' rights while keeping order in the classroom.

Did the court's decision side with the school?

No. A federal court said –

- No one had the authority to compel the student to participate in any part of the ceremony
- The student's refusal didn't require parental consent, and
- The student's silent refusal didn't threaten classroom order.

Based on those standards, the must-stand policy was deemed illegal and unenforceable.

Cite: *Frazier v. Alexandre et al.*

Student: 'I don't pledge allegiance to the flag' – and his parents sue when he's disciplined for it

They say he has a right to protest; the school calls it a 'disruption'

Robert Ailes raised a clenched fist almost as soon as the students began reciting the Pledge of Allegiance.

All heads turned toward him, but teacher Tasha Hernandez waited until the Pledge was finished to speak to Robert, rather than calling attention to the action.

With Robert at her desk, she spoke in a calm voice: "You understand why we say the Pledge at the beginning of each day, don't you, Robert?"

"To show loyalty and respect for our country," he answered quickly. "That's why I refuse to recite it, and that's why my fist is clenched.

"I have no loyalty or respect for our government. We're waging an illegal war, and I'm opposed to it."

Surprised at first, Tasha composed herself and said, "You have a right to your opinions, but I'm going to have to ask you to keep them to yourself during the Pledge. Reciting it is mandatory in this school district and part of learning about our system of government. Plus, you're distracting the others.

"Please don't behave that way again," she continued. "If you do, I'll have to discipline you for it."

The next day ...

The following morning, Tasha stationed herself at the back of the room and kept an eye on Robert during the Pledge. Again, he raised a fist.

As promised, Tasha sent him to the principal's office, where he got three days' detention for disrupting a class activity. Robert's parents sued the school for violating the student's right of expression.

Did the school win?

Decision: No. A judge said the silent protest wasn't a "disruption." Rather, it was a protected – even if unpopular – expression of opposition to patriotism.

Key: Had the student shouted or been involved in truly disruptive behavior, the school might have been able to present a stronger case. However, as the judge noted, the right of free speech includes the freedom from being compelled to speak.

Cite: *Holloman v. Harland.*

Parents say school is culturally insensitive and excluding their child

Small town didn't realize new family would object to holiday songs

"Thanks for coming to my office so quickly," said Principal Meg Lestro as teacher Kellie Meer sat down.

"What's up?" asked Kellie.

"It's bad news. Our lawyer just called to say Ann's parents are suing the district – and you and me personally."

"But why?" asked Kellie.

"They say we made Ann feel left out at school and that's why they decided to home school her."

"But Ann had lots of friends," said Kellie, "and she wasn't shy in class."

"It's not about friends, it's about religion," said Meg. "They're Jewish and they say our holiday show made Ann feel like she didn't belong here."

"But why are they suing me?"

"Because the song you taught her class for the show mentioned Christmas."

"But the other parents loved the show," said Kellie. "It never even occurred to me anybody could find that song offensive."

"I know," said Meg. "We're a tight little community; the same people living here, generation after generation. I went to this school, myself," said Meg.

"So did my husband," said Kellie.

"I know," said Meg. "We're used to doing things the way we always have. But Ann's parents are suing over other things we've been doing for years. Like the parents' prayer group that meets here."

The district's lawyer asked the judge to dismiss the case. Did she agree?

Decision: No, a trial was needed.

The school may have violated the religious rights of Ann and her parents.

Public schools can't take any position on religion or promote religious groups, like a parents' prayer group – even if that's a long-standing community tradition.

Key: Teachers can't always be experts on diversity, but they need to remember religious holidays don't belong in class – except in lessons about culture or history. And one of the main reasons for this is so other-faith students won't feel excluded.

Cite: *Doe v. Wilson County School System.*

Students put teacher on hot seat over carol-free holiday concert

Event sparks holiday jeer – and lawsuit – from parent

Teacher Paul Yee got to school extra early, hoping to get a jump on the lesson-plan problem he was having. But no.

Turning a corner, he saw two boys tussling. "Hey," called Paul, rushing over to them. "Break it up, guys."

He grabbed the boys' shoulders and pushed them apart. "Juan, Daryn. What's this about?"

"It's about Juan's dad being a -" began Daryn angrily. Juan interrupted Daryn by lunging at him.

Paul grabbed Juan's shirt and hauled him back. "Cut it out," said Paul. "No more insults or punching. I want to hear about this one at a time. You go first, Juan."

Dad didn't like the holiday show

"You know how there wasn't any Christmas music in the Christmas show this year?" asked Juan.

"Holiday show," Paul corrected him. "But yeah. That was new this year. And you understand why – right?"

"To be anti-Christian?" asked Juan.

"You see?" Daryn burst out angrily. "And he called me a -"

"Shush," said Paul to Daryn. "You'll get your turn. We're doing this one at a time."

"Well, that's what my dad says," said Juan stubbornly. "He says this proves the school is anti-Christian. He also says that anybody who played in the band for it, like Daryn did, is a -"

"How can I be a pagan?" roared Daryn. "I go to your church!"

Calm down

"Look," said Paul, "I know you're mad, but if the shouting doesn't stop, we're going to the office to see Mr. Yancy."

Mr. Yancy was scary, and the boys backed away from each other as Paul had hoped.

"OK," said Paul. "It's your turn now, Daryn. What did Juan say?"

"That no real Christian would play in the band of a school that took the 'Christ' out of Christmas."

Was concert anti-religious?

"Thanks," said Paul as the boys scowled at each other. "I think I get the picture now.

"Juan, I'm sorry your dad was unhappy there weren't carols. But it wasn't anti-Christian. We also didn't have any Chanukah songs this year. The school decided to have no religious music at all."

"Oh, I know," said Juan. "It was more than just anti-Christian, it was anti-religious. That's what my dad said – that this school is just like Soviet Russia: anti-American."

Teacher explains the new rule

"Actually," said Paul, "this is very American. The new holiday concert policy is based on our Constitution. Our law respects families' religious rights so much that schools have to stay out of it completely and leave it to the parents. That's why I have to steer clear of religion in class, too."

Daryn seemed satisfied by this. Paul wasn't sure about Juan, but he let it go when Juan agreed to apologize and shake hands.

Paul sent Mr. Yancy an e-mail about what had happened, then forgot about it until he heard Juan's father had sued the school.

Juan's father said the holiday concert policy was illegal because it was hostile toward religion.

Did the judge agree?

Decision: No, the school won.

Legally, schools can't endorse or condemn religion. But by steering clear of religious music, this school was being neutral – not hostile.

Key: Students often echo their parents' strongest concerns and even fight their battles at school – which may be the first indication a school has of a coming lawsuit. That's another reason why it's so important for teachers to report every student fight to the office – even if they think they've dealt with the problem.

Cite: *Stratechuk v. Board of Educ., South Orange-Maplewood School Dist.*

Discussion points for teachers and principals:

Holiday concerts have become a real flash point at schools.

- Some educators believe it's misleading and educationally dishonest to ban religious songs – because most December holidays are religious.

- Others think selections like "Winter Wonderland" are a better option because they don't leave anyone in the audience feeling excluded.

Sharpen Your Judgment

Did outside speaker promote religion in class?

The tone of the phone call caught teacher Rick Shinkov off guard for a moment.

"I want to know why you're promoting religion in my daughter's class," demanded the angry parent, George Macon.

The teacher thought for a moment before responding: "Can you be more specific, Mr. Macon? When did I promote religion?"

"My daughter told me a representative from the Boy Scouts spoke to the class," the parent shot back. "Don't you know the Boy Scout oath, 'To do my duty to God and my country'? That's clear support for religion."

"I'm aware of the oath and that there's been some controversy about it," the teacher replied. "But the rep's visit was just part of our program for learning about community-service organizations. He never brought up the religious aspect."

"Just having him there was enough," the parent fumed. "You can't do that."

The parent eventually sued the teacher and the school for endorsing religion. The school countered that there was no endorsement because no mention of religion took place.

Did the school and the teacher win?

Sharpen Your Judgment – The Decision

Yes. A court ruled the teacher hadn't endorsed religion by bringing in a speaker from the Boy Scouts.

Allowing an organization's representative to visit a classroom does in a sense endorse the organization's mission and goals, the judge noted.

However, it would be a stretch to say the teacher "promoted religion" just because one part of the creed mentioned God.

Besides, as the teacher noted, the organization's views on God and religion – in a positive or negative way – weren't part of the school presentation.

Given all those factors, the teacher couldn't be fairly charged with allowing the promotion of religion in his classroom.

Analysis: Following common practice

Courts usually try to give schools and teachers some leeway in the choice of outside speakers who aid the learning process. But this case shows:

- It pays to follow the common practice of reviewing a speaker's presentation before the class hears it.
- You do have to tread carefully when inviting an organization that might have a motive of promoting religion.

Cite: *Scalise v. Boy Scouts of America.*

Secular item or religious symbol: Was teacher's choice of class material OK?

Mom sues, claiming teacher endorsed Christian views to Muslim student

Teacher Stephanie Hunt was decorating the bulletin board when Nyla Khan's mom walked into the classroom. "Hello, Ms. Hunt," she said. "We need to talk."

"Sure," Stephanie said. "Have a seat."

"Thanks to you, children make fun of Nyla," Ms. Khan said. "They laugh because we're Muslim and wear hijabs."

"If other students are teasing Nyla, I'll certainly address that," Stephanie said. "But why do you think it's my fault?"

Was teacher to blame?

"Because the bullying started during the holidays," Ms. Khan said. "Remember the books about 9/11 and different religions?

"Nyla said your book sounded like 9/11 was a war between Christians and Muslims," she continued. "And what about that candy cane story?"

"I never said 9/11 was a war between Christians and Muslims," Stephanie said calmly. "And candy canes are a secular image, not a religious symbol."

"The book said candy canes have a 'J' hook to remind people about Jesus," she said. "You owe Nyla a public apology!"

After discussing the issue with Ms. Khan, the principal said an apology wasn't necessary because Stephanie didn't do anything wrong.

That's when Ms. Khan sued, claiming the teacher endorsed Christianity over Nyla's religion.

The school asked the court to dismiss the claim. Did the court agree?

Decision: No, the court determined a trial was needed.

Key: The judge noted that candy canes can be a secular – rather than religious – symbol. However, the reading paired the candy cane with Christian messages, such as "remember the message of the candy maker: Jesus is the Christ!"

A reasonable jury could find that the teacher read books endorsing Christianity over other religions, so the claim must move forward, the court explained.

Cite: *Doe v. Cape Henlopen School Dist.*

Religious symbolism during the holidays: How far is too far?

Angry mom causes fundraising headache for teacher

Teacher Diane Price noticed a light snow had started falling. *At least it waited until the end of the day*, she thought.

"Class isn't over," Diane said as students loudly whispered about their snowball fight plans. "We still have one more thing to do – the fundraiser paperwork!"

"Here's what I need," she continued as the chit-chat faded. "If you're placing an order for holiday cards, I need the artwork that will be on the cards, the order forms and the payment envelope. After you turn it in, you can go."

Diane gathered the forms as students filed out of the classroom quickly.

As soon as the students walked out, a parent walked in. "We need to talk," Tara Smith's mother said.

Questions about the fundraiser

"Sure, Ms. Smith," Diane said, trying not to appear rushed. "Have a seat."

"I'm not clear about this holiday card fundraiser," Tara's mother said. "Can we go over the order form?"

"Sure," Diane agreed. "You can create and order customized holiday cards. Just choose one of Tara's drawings for the outside of the card. And then pick one of the verses from the vendor's list for the inside of the card."

"I picked this for the artwork," she said, holding up a picture Tara drew last week. "But the Bible verse I want is crossed out."

"Here are Christmas options. Do you like any of these?" Diane asked, pointing at the list.

"No," Tara's mother said insistently. "And I want to know why this one's marked out!"

"I'm sorry," Diane said. "That's a religious message, so we crossed it out."

Holiday cards

"But these are *holiday* cards!" Tara's mother said. "I don't understand what the problem is."

"This particular verse names Jesus – a specific belief," Diane tried to explain. "Schools can't show a preference for one religious belief over another."

"It's not as if you're teaching about Jesus – this is a fundraiser for the school," Tara's mother argued.

Diane sighed, wishing religious issues didn't pop up during the holidays. But they always did.

From experience, Diane knew she needed to get the principal involved. "I think we should go see Ms. Marks. She'll help us figure this out," Diane suggested.

The principal explained that the school couldn't do anything that might show a preference for one religion over another – and that's why teachers marked out the option that mentioned Jesus and quoted a verse from the Bible.

Mom's not happy

But Tara's mother wasn't satisfied. She sued, claiming school officials violated her speech rights by limiting her choice on the cards' verses.

The school argued that it *had* to remove the Bible verse from the order forms, because leaving it would've violated the Establishment Clause. It asked the court to dismiss the claims. Did it?

Decision: No, the court ruled in favor of Tara's mother.

Key: In this case, the order form was distributed *by* the school *from* a third-party vendor in the fundraising process, the court explained.

This meant the religious verse wasn't government speech, so it couldn't violate the Establishment Clause, the court ruled.

The court also pointed out: Because parents placed fundraiser orders in their own homes, the option of a Bible verse wasn't likely to cause a disruption at school.

Bottom line: Even though the school tried to make the right call, blocking the religious message violated parents' speech rights.

Cite: *Pounds v. Katy Independent School Dist.*

Discussion points for teachers and principals:

Answer these three questions to help you handle religious issues correctly during the holidays:

■ Is this message really the school's speech?

■ Is this message likely to cause a school disruption?

■ Is the school offering a variety of choices – or is the only option a religious one?

Invitations have a religious tone: Should teacher take action?

Six points to consider when students test the limits

"Hi, there," Teacher Olivia Gray said as student Matt Hunt walked into the classroom. "Why aren't you at lunch?"

"I have to put these in everyone's cubby hole first," he said.

"Well, what do you have there?" Olivia asked him.

"Invitations," Matt said. "They're for the spring break camp at my church."

"Invitations to a church camp?" Olivia repeated, buying herself time to think of the best response.

"Yep," Matt told her. "It's a lot of fun, and I want my friends to go this year."

"That's very thoughtful, Matt," Olivia said. "But we have to ask the principal before we pass those out. Put them back in your bookbag for now."

"OK," Matt agreed. "But can we go to the office right now?"

Are invitations 'religious' material?

Principal Heather Marks looked at Matt's invitations and decided that he couldn't pass them out during school.

"I understand that camp is fun," Principal Marks said. "But we have rules about passing things out at school. Maybe we can talk to your mom about this."

"OK," Matt said. "I'll ask my Mom if she can come in after school today."

Later that afternoon

After students were dismissed, Principal Marks and Olivia were in the office when Matt's mom arrived.

"Matt said you wouldn't let him pass out the camp invitations," she said. "This is ridiculous!"

"Religious materials can't be distributed at school," Principal Marks said.

"Matt tried to pass them out during lunch, right?" Matt's mom asked Olivia.

"Yes, that's right," Olivia said.

"Then he wasn't bothering anyone during class," his mom said.

Because the invitations were for a church camp, passing them out at school wasn't appropriate, Principal Marks tried to explain.

"I'm not letting you get away with this. I'm calling a lawyer!" she said as she left.

The next day, teachers sent out a letter, notifying parents that students were no longer allowed to distribute any student-to-student materials at school.

Matt's mom sued, claiming the school violated her son's speech rights. She also asked for a court order that would allow Matt to pass out the invitations. Did the judge grant her request?

Decision: Yes, the judge ordered the school to let Matt pass out the invitations.

Key: Courts look at four factors when considering whether a preliminary injunction is needed. In this instance, they were whether:

- Matt's mom was likely to prove her claim
- Matt would suffer irreparable injury without the court order
- the school would suffer if the court order was granted, and
- the public interest would be served with the preliminary injunction.

The court ruled that:

- Matt's mom was likely to win in court, as the school's blanket "no distribution" policy wasn't reasonable
- Matt would suffer if his request was denied
- the school wouldn't suffer, as Matt didn't cause a disruption when passing out the flyers during lunch, and
- the public interest would be served, as the injunction would protect students' speech rights.

The order was needed to protect Matt's rights, the court explained.

Cite: *J.S. v. Holly Area Schools.*

Discussion points for teachers and principals:

Consider the following questions to determine whether speech is acceptable at school.

■ Is it likely to cause a disruption?

■ Is it threatening?

■ Is it obscene?

■ Does it violate school rules?

■ Does it tout illegal drug use?

■ Does it violate someone else's privacy?

Sharpen Your Judgment

Is longstanding tradition OK? Parent says 'No!'

"I'll never get up to speed on the times," Teacher Diane Price said to fellow teacher Jennifer Wentz.

"Why?" Jennifer laughed.

"I take it you haven't heard about the school board's new Gideon Bible policy."

Parents not happy with 'compromise'

"Well, you know that group of parents who complained about the Gideons passing out Bibles in school?" Diane asked Jennifer. "I just don't understand all the hoopla. They've been distributing them for years – and it's not like we make students take them or even read them in class."

"Yeah, I know. It's different now. We taught children of former students for generations. Now we have a lot of new families coming in," Jennifer sighed. "Why? What's the latest?"

"Well, the board compromised and wrote an updated policy which allows the Gideons to pass out the Bibles to fifth-grade classrooms only, and students can pick them up. But a lot of parents still sued – and we lost!"

The district appealed the decision.

Did the court overturn the ruling?

Sharpen Your Judgment – The Decision

No, the district lost when the judge upheld the lower court's ruling.

The school district argued that it compromised with parents. The school agreed to limit the distribution of Bibles to older students who weren't as impressionable as the school's younger students. It argued that students weren't required to take a Bible or read it in school.

But parents argued the school promoted Christianity over other religions by distributing the Gideon Bibles in school. Parents maintained that school officials are not allowed to influence young, impressionable children's religious beliefs at school.

The court agreed with the students' parents, saying the policy allowing Gideons to distribute Bibles in school violates the Establishment Clause. Reason: The policy's main objective promotes Christianity by endorsing its message in school.

Analysis: Religion isn't a gray area

As this case shows, the Establishment Clause trumps even longstanding traditions.

The courts consistently rule that schools can't endorse one religion over another.

Cite: *Roark v. South Iron R-1 School Dist.*

Sharpen Your Judgment

Defining the limits on mixing school and religion

As she held up a sheet of paper, teacher Jan Millsap said, "I need to discuss something with you."

Principal Larry Azinger studied the paper and said, "About this?"

"Sort of," the teacher answered. "It's a proposed announcement for an after-school prayer meeting. I got it from one of my students, Renee McKeon."

"She's handing them out in the school?" Larry asked.

"She wants to," Jan explained. "And she wants to hold the prayer meeting in the building but after hours. What do you think?"

"My first reaction is to say no to handing them out in class," the principal said. "That sounds like a violation of policy.

"The meeting's a little trickier," Larry said. "This is a public school where nonreligious community groups hold meetings after hours. But I'm not sure about religious groups. I'll check with the district."

The district's attorney denied the group's request to hand out announcements and hold the meeting, leading to a lawsuit by the group.

Did the district win?

Sharpen Your Judgment – The Decision

Yes and no.

A federal court ruled that schools can refuse students' requests to distribute religious material in a public school during normal school hours.

The court said that allowing the distribution of such material would make it appear that the school was supporting and promoting a religious function – and would be a violation of the separation of church and state.

However, the court also ruled that the prayer group could hold meetings on school property after hours.

Reason: If other community groups have access to school property, so should a religious group, so long as it follows the rules and policies for conducting meetings at the school.

Further, students and even teachers and administrators are free to attend and participate in such meetings on their own time without restriction.

Analysis: One key limitation

The court's rulings were clear, but be aware of one limitation on school personnel attending such meetings: Those attending can't appear to be there in an official function as a representative of the school or district.

Cite: *Wigg v. Sioux Falls School Dist.*

Student's 'Jesus pencil' gifts put teacher on the spot: Now what?

Innocent Christmas gift or legal land mine?

Teacher Stephanie Hunt watched as students filed out of the cafeteria and dawdled down the hallway. She understood it wasn't easy for them to get excited about lessons when the holiday break was right around the corner.

Stephanie stood at her classroom door and coaxed students inside. While they settled into their seats, she passed out the exams she'd graded the night before.

She held student Danny Palmer's test patiently as he dug through his bookbag for a pencil.

After a minute, Danny called across the room to a classmate. "Hey, Tina. I need a couple of those Jesus pencils you were giving away in the lunchroom."

"OK, one minute," Tina called back.

But Stephanie didn't wait. She walked over to Tina's desk and said, "I need to speak to you in the hall, please."

Jesus pencil?

"Yes, Ms. Hunt?" Tina asked politely as they walked out of the classroom.

"What was Danny talking about in there?" Stephanie asked. "You passed out Jesus pencils in the lunchroom? What exactly is a Jesus pencil?"

"Oh, here," Tina said as she offered Stephanie a handful.

"I got them from my church," she continued. "You can have as many as you want – you know, for a Christmas present."

Stephanie glanced at the red and green pencils. Christmas messages were etched on them, such as:

- "Jesus is the reason for the season," and
- "Jesus loves me this I know, for the Bible tells me so."

"So you passed these out during lunch?" she asked.

"Yeah, aren't they the cutest little Christmas gifts?" Tina said, smiling. "And they were free – so I didn't go broke buying presents for my friends."

Let's just double-check ...

"It's really sweet of you to think of your friends," Stephanie said, easing into her concern. "You need to run this by the principal before you pass out any more though."

"Why?" Tina asked.

"Well, the pencils have a religious message on them, so you should get approval," Stephanie told her. "You don't want to get into trouble over this, right?"

"Of course they have a religious message: They are Christmas presents," Tina pointed out. "And besides, everyone likes them. I've been passing them out before and after school, too."

"You're right – it is the holiday season," Stephanie emphasized. "That's why we need to make sure these pencils are OK. We don't want to offend anyone."

The principal's take

The principal agreed with Stephanie and told Tina not to distribute the pencils.

Tina's parents sued, claiming the school violated her speech rights.

School officials said they couldn't allow students to distribute pencils with religious messages during the holiday season. They said some non-Christian students might perceive the school to be endorsing Christianity over other religions. They asked the court to dismiss the charges. Did it?

Decision: No, the court refused to dismiss the charges.

Keys: The court recognized that schools can restrict student speech if school officials have a reasonable belief that the speech is likely to cause a substantial disruption.

That wasn't the case here. First, distributing pencils, especially after school, wasn't likely to cause a substantial disruption. Further, the message wasn't lewd and did not promote illegal activity. And finally, students weren't required to accept the holiday gift.

Cite: *Morgan v. Plano Independent School Dist.*

Discussion points for teachers and principals:

Sometimes students can get pretty emotional about free speech rules – especially during the holiday season!

Here are three tips:

■ Remain calm – it isn't personal.

■ Show empathy – understanding may calm down students.

■ Diffuse anger – look for ways to solve the problem together.

How far do you have to go to keep religion out of school now?

Prayer at school events puts teacher on the hot seat

"What's holding up kickoff?" asked parent Alec Dulcy, sitting in the bleachers. He took his eyes off the empty sidelines to check his watch.

"Our team's probably still praying in the locker room," said parent Jon Kinski dryly.

"Oh, don't get me started," sighed Alec.

"It sounds like you're fed up with 'the praying coach,' too," said Jon.

"It's the team that's praying," disagreed Alec. "And what an overreaction – the school board saying they have to think it over before they decide if the coach can even bow his head or kneel during the prayer."

"Come on," said Jon. "We both know coach has been pushing that pregame prayer since he got here. He still is – and after everything the school board's told him about staying out of student prayer."

"But he is staying out of it," said Alec. "The board told him to stop leading the prayer. He did. He just wants to bow his head out of respect while the students pray."

Jon shook his head. "The students may lead the prayer now, but I think he's still the one secretly pulling the strings."

"You should run for school board," said Alec. "Oh, come on, Jon. Didn't you read the story in last night's paper? The team held a vote on whether to keep the pregame prayer – and they voted to keep it."

"But taking a vote on it wasn't their idea," said Jon. "The coach told them to take the vote."

"So what?" said Alec. "He didn't tell them how to vote, did he?"

"Maybe not in so many words," said Jon. "But he's the coach. He forced the issue, and they knew the result he wanted."

Just team 'spirit'?

"Everybody makes this sound like he's pushing religion," said Alec. "He keeps trying to explain that the real point of a pregame prayer is to motivate the team."

"But there must be other ways to do that," said Jon, "ways that don't put kids of different faiths on the spot if they want to be on the team. Look, the school board told him to leave student prayers to students. That was his cue to back off."

"Fine!" said Alec. "Let's ban him from the locker room, too. For crying out loud, all he wants to do is bow his head or kneel. What do you want him to do instead – plug his ears and sing?"

Jon opened his mouth to reply, but just then a cheer from the crowd made them look around. The team was running onto the field.

The week following the game, the school board met and turned down the coach's request to kneel or bow his head at team prayers.

The coach sued. He argued the school board violated his right to academic freedom as a coach and a teacher by stopping him from giving "character education" by modeling respect for prayer.

The school board disagreed. It told the court it needed to stop the coach from violating the constitution by endorsing religion at school-sponsored games.

Which side did the judge agree with?

Decision: The school board won.

The coach's right to academic freedom wasn't violated. The school board – not him – had the job of deciding what to teach students and how.

It also had a real need to stop the coach from breaking the law by endorsing religion at school. Given his past history of insisting on team prayers, it was clear he was still trying to participate in – not just show respect for – the team prayer.

Key: It's understandable why so many teachers struggle with the need to keep their religion out of class lectures and school-sponsored events. It's a big part of who they are, and they want to share it.

But the bottom line is: Courts consistently rule that students' religious instruction belongs to their parents.

Cite: *Borden v. School Dist. of Township of East Brunswick.*

Discussion points for teachers and principals:

What about a moment of silence instead of a prayer?

■ Some think this is a healthy break in a busy day for people to stop and recharge – there's nothing religious about it.

■ Others think so many groups have tried to smuggle prayer into school by calling it "a moment of silence" that other group activities are preferable – singing the school song, maybe.

Sharpen Your Judgment

Teacher protected students' faith ... Didn't she?

The phone beside Talya Mannix's stack of ungraded tests rang. She picked it up.

"Ms. Mannix speaking."

"Hello," said a man's voice. "This is Ruth Schwarz's dad."

"Hi, Mr. Schwarz. What can I do for you?"

"Ruth came home with a Bible yesterday."

"Right," said Talya. "The Gideons were here. They come by every year to pass out Bibles in the hall. But only to students who want them, Mr. Schwarz. We make sure the kids understand that's a purely personal choice. I made an announcement in class about that."

"Yes, Ruth told me," said Mr. Schwarz. "But your announcement wasn't enough to keep my Jewish daughter from being pressured into accepting a Christian Bible at school."

"What?" asked Talya. "What do you mean?"

"Ruth's classmates told her she'd be a 'heathen devil-worshipper' if she didn't come get a Bible. The only 'personal choice' she got to make was either accept something that goes against her faith or get harassed."

Mr. Schwarz sued, claiming the school had violated Ruth's religious rights. Did he win?

Sharpen Your Judgment – The Decision

Yes, Mr. Schwarz won.

Under the First Amendment, a government institution – such as a public school – can't endorse religion. It also can't pressure people concerning matters of faith.

This school did both by allowing a religious group to pass out Bibles on school property.

Analysis: Don't bring faith into school

So much about school is mandatory – the hours, the homework, the dress code. Because of that, even a mild suggestion from a teacher or principal can feel like an order to a student.

On top of that, adolescents are particularly vulnerable to peer pressure.

When those forces converge – and religion's in the mix – students can feel helpless to stand up for their own beliefs.

This pressure is an important reason behind the First Amendment's religious rules to keep people free of government interference with their faith. And that's why courts are so strict about keeping religion out of schools.

It's not the teachers' call which groups to allow on campus – but teachers can make sure they don't bring up their own religion in front of students, in the classroom or out.

Cite: *Roe v. Tangipahoa Parish School Board.*

3 Freedom of Speech and Association

TOPICS

I. STUDENTS 97

II. EMPLOYEES 111

III. ACADEMIC FREEDOM 116

IV. PARENTAL SPEECH AND ASSOCIATION RIGHTS 118

V. USE OF SCHOOL FACILITIES 121

VI. TEACHER SCENARIOS 125

CHAPTER THREE
Freedom of Speech and Association

I. STUDENTS

Overview

For over 40 years, courts have analyzed student speech cases under Tinker v. Des Moines Independent Community School Dist., *393 U.S. 503 (1969).* Tinker *was the first U.S. Supreme Court case to recognize student speech rights in schools. In it, the Court held that in order to regulate student speech, school officials must show "the student's activities would materially and substantially disrupt the work and discipline of the school."* Tinker *remains the starting point for student speech rights cases, but as the U.S. Court of Appeals, Fifth Circuit, recently observed, "since* Tinker, *every Supreme Court decision looking at speech has expanded the kinds of speech schools can regulate."*

The Supreme Court declined to apply Tinker *in its most recent student speech rights case,* Morse v. Frederick, *551 U.S. 393 (2007), noting "the constitutional rights of students in public school are not automatically coextensive with the rights of adults in other settings."*

Court Decisions

◆ A Mississippi student asked school administrators if she could attend her high school prom in a tuxedo with her same-sex partner. She was told that only boys were allowed to wear tuxedos to the prom and that girls would be required to wear dresses and could not slow dance together. After the student contacted the ACLU and threatened a lawsuit, the school board met and decided not to host a prom. In a federal district court action, the court found the board's claim that it only "withdrew its sponsorship" from the prom was "nothing more than semantics." The board had effectively cancelled the prom. The court found support for the student's First Amendment claim based on her identity and affiliation with a unique social group. **Government entities "cannot set-out homosexuals for special treatment."** In *Fricke v. Lynch*, 491 F.Supp. 381 (D.R.I. 1980), the court held a male student's desire to take a same-sex date to his prom "had significant expressive content which brought it within the ambit of the First Amendment." Additional support for the student's position came from a state circuit court in Alabama which held in 2008 that a school board could not legally cancel a prom to prevent a same-sex couple from attending.

Based on clearly established case law, the court found the board violated the student's rights by denying her request to bring her girlfriend as her date to the prom. Since she had been openly gay since eighth grade, the court held her wish to wear a tuxedo and attend the prom with a girl represented an intent to communicate a message that was protected by the First Amendment. While the student established a substantial likelihood of success on the merits of her First Amendment claim, she did not convince the court that the order she was requesting would be in the public interest. A parent-sponsored prom had been offered, and school officials represented that she would be welcome there. Relief was denied as against the public interest. *McMillen v. Itawamba County School Dist.*, 702 F.Supp.2d 699 (N.D. Miss. 2010).

◆ An 18-year-old Alaska high school student observed an Olympic Torch Relay that passed in front of his school. The school principal deemed the relay a school-approved social event or class trip. As torchbearers and camera crews passed, the student and his friends unfurled a 14-foot banner bearing the phrase "Bong Hits 4 Jesus." The principal instructed them to take down the banner, but the student refused to comply. She confiscated the banner and suspended him for 10 days. The district superintendent reduced the suspension to eight days. He found the principal had based the discipline on the banner's advocacy of illegal drug use, and not on any disagreement with the message. The school board also affirmed the suspension, and its decision was upheld by a federal district court.

Appeal reached the U.S. Supreme Court, which held the case involved "school speech." The relay was held during school hours and was sanctioned by the principal as "an approved social event or class trip." The board's rules were universally applied to school social events and class trips. The banner was directed to the school and was plainly visible to most students. **The principal reasonably determined that the banner would be interpreted by viewers as promoting illegal drug use.** While the message might be regarded as cryptic, offensive, amusing or nonsense, the Court agreed with the principal that it might advocate the use of illegal drugs. Supreme Court decisions on drug testing of student extracurricular programs have recognized that deterring drug use is an important and perhaps compelling interest. School officials in this case were dealing with a "far more serious and palpable" danger than that faced in *Tinker v. Des Moines Independent Community School Dist.*, below. The Court held that to allow the banner would have sent a powerful message to students that the school was not serious about its anti-drug message and the dangers of illegal drug use. *Morse v. Frederick*, 551 U.S. 393 (2007).

◆ In 1965, a group of Iowa adults and high school students publicized their objections to the hostilities in Vietnam by wearing black armbands during the holiday season. Three students and their parents had previously engaged in similar activities, and they decided to participate in this program. The principals of Des Moines schools became aware of the plan and adopted a policy that **any student wearing an armband to school would be asked to remove it or face suspension**. The three students wore their armbands and were all suspended until they agreed to come back without the armbands. The students did not return to their school until the planned protest period had ended.

The students sued the school district for First Amendment violations under 42 U.S.C. § 1983, seeking to prevent school officials from disciplining them, plus their nominal damages. A federal district court dismissed the complaint and the Eighth Circuit summarily affirmed the decision. On appeal, the Supreme Court stated neither students nor teachers shed their constitutional rights to freedom of speech or expression at the schoolhouse gate. **In order for school officials to justify prohibition of a particular expression of opinion, they must show something more than a mere desire to avoid the discomfort and unpleasantness associated with unpopular viewpoints.** Where there was no evidence that student expression would materially interfere with the requirements of appropriate discipline in the operation of the school, or collide with the rights of others, the prohibition was improper. The expressive act of wearing black armbands did not interrupt school activities or intrude in school affairs. The Court reversed the lower court decisions. *Tinker v. Des Moines Independent Community School Dist.*, 393 U.S. 503, 89 S.Ct. 733, 21 L.Ed.2d 733 (1969).

◆ A Washington high school student gave a speech nominating a classmate for a student election before an assembly of over 600 peers. All students were required to attend the assembly as part of the school's self-government program. **In his nominating speech, the student referred to his candidate in terms of an elaborate, explicit sexual metaphor, despite having been warned in advance by teachers not to do so.** Student reactions to the speech included laughter, graphic sexual gestures, hooting, bewilderment and embarrassment. When the student admitted he had deliberately used sexual innuendo in his speech, he was informed that he would be suspended for three days and that his name would be removed from the list of candidates for student speaker at graduation. The student sued the school district in a federal district court, claiming his First Amendment right to freedom of speech had been violated.

The court agreed and awarded him damages and attorneys' fees. It also ordered the school district to allow the student to speak at graduation. The decision was affirmed by the Ninth Circuit, under the authority of *Tinker*. On appeal, the Supreme Court reversed the decision, holding that **while public school students have the right to advocate unpopular and controversial views in school, that right must be balanced against the school interest in teaching socially appropriate behavior.** The Constitution does not protect obscene language, and a public school, as an instrument of the state, may legitimately establish standards of civil and mature conduct. *Bethel School Dist. No. 403 v. Fraser*, 478 U.S. 675, 106 S.Ct. 3159, 92 L.Ed.2d 549 (1986).

A. Protected Speech

1. Disciplinary Cases

Teacher Scenarios

Student plays ugly prank at talent show: What's teacher's best move? 125

Students embarrass school in public: What's the punishment? 126

Badmouthing the principal: What students can – and can't – say 126

Did teacher go too far when silencing foul-mouthed student? 127

Determining the difference between free speech and hate speech 128

Where to draw the line when students speak their minds 129

Court Decisions

◆ A California student and three others walked out of their middle school with the intent of participating in protests against pending immigration reform measures. The middle school vice principal allegedly threatened them harshly with discipline upon their return, calling them "dumb, dumb and dumber" and warning them of the possible legal consequences of their truancy. He also allegedly threatened them with a $250 fine and juvenile sentencing, but this did not occur. After returning home on the day of the discipline, the student committed suicide, leaving a note that stated "I killed myself because I have too many problems. ... Tell my teachers they're the best and tell [the vice principal] he is a mother f#@(-)ker." The student's estate sued the school district, vice principal and others for constitutional and state law violations. The case reached the U.S. Court of Appeals, Ninth Circuit, which found that **no First Amendment retaliation claim could be based on threats of discipline if it was based on a lawful consequence that was never administered**.

The policy of disciplining truancy violated no First Amendment rights, even if the students sought to leave for expressive purposes. Further, the vice principal's words were not a form of corporal punishment, and nothing indicated that he had a retaliatory or discriminatory motive. Finally, since the suicide was not foreseeable, the estate failed to show negligence. The court affirmed the judgment. *Corales v. Bennett*, 567 F.3d 554 (9th Cir. 2009).

◆ Tennessee students claimed that their varsity football coach humiliated and degraded players, used inappropriate language and required them to participate in a year-round conditioning program that violated school rules. He also apparently hit a player in the helmet and threw away college recruiting letters sent to "disfavored players." One student typed a petition to remove the coach, which eighteen players signed. When the coach learned of this, he summoned players into his office one by one to interview them. Players who signed the petition were allowed to stay on the team if they apologized and said they wanted to play for him. Four players who did not apologize were taken off the team. These students sued the coach, school board and others for First Amendment violations.

The case reached the U.S. Court of Appeals, Sixth Circuit, which noted that the players did not dispute their insubordinate actions during a team meeting. "Student athletes are subject to more restrictions than the student body at large." **The petition was a direct challenge to the coach's authority.** Therefore, it was not protected speech and there was no First Amendment violation. *Lowery v. Euverard*, 497 F.3d 584 (6th Cir. 2007).

◆ About 300 Hispanic students walked out of a Texas school to protest immigration reforms pending in Congress. Many wore T-shirts stating "We Are Not Criminals." The school principal, himself Hispanic, learned that some students planned to walk out of school the next day. Other faculty members believed some Caucasian and African-American students planned to wear T-shirts reading "Border Patrol" to antagonize them. The principal announced that any students who wore unauthorized shirts would be sent to the office, but about 130 students walked out of school. These students were suspended for three days. School administrators called most of their parents, but some students did not learn of the suspensions until they reported to school the next day. Many angry parents came to school, demanding to meet with the principal. After some parents refused to leave the building, school security asked them to leave.

Several families sued the district and superintendent in a federal district court for First Amendment violations. The court held **the principal acted to prevent disruption of the educational process**. Students were warned not to wear unauthorized T-shirts on the second day to prevent a possible race riot. "Where school administrators reasonably believe the students' uncontrolled exercise of expression would materially and substantially interfere with the work of the school or impinge upon the rights of other students, they may forbid such expression." The principal did not violate the First Amendment. *Doe v. Grove Public School Dist.*, 510 F.Supp.2d 425 (S.D. Tex. 2007).

◆ Most members of the boys varsity basketball team at an Oregon high school claimed that their head coach used abusive tactics, intimidated them, yelled incessantly and used profanity. After a game, the coach told them he would resign if they wanted it. The players drafted a petition requesting his resignation, and all but two players signed it. After the coach brought the petition to his principal, the school's athletic director and principal met with the team and told them they would have to board the team bus for a game that evening or forfeit their privilege to play in the game. Eight of them did not board the bus. The principal permanently suspended players who refused to board the bus from the team. They sued the coach, principal, and school district for speech rights violations. A federal court upheld the discipline, finding the students' speech and conduct were not constitutionally protected.

The students appealed to the Ninth Circuit, which found that the petition and grievances against the coach were "a form of pure speech." The students could not be disciplined unless there was a reasonable forecast of substantial disruption or material interference. The First Amendment protected the petition and the complaints to school administrators. However, the boycott of the game substantially disrupted and materially interfered with a school activity. **If students decide not to participate in an extracurricular activity on the day it is scheduled to take place, "their conduct will inevitably disrupt or interfere with the activity."** This was true even if the event was not cancelled. The case was remanded for further proceedings. *Pinard v. Clatskanie School Dist. 6J*, 446 F.3d 964 (9th Cir. 2006).

2. Threats and Bullying

In Boim v. Fulton County School Board, *this chapter, the U.S. Court of Appeals, Eleventh Circuit, compared threatening speech to falsely yelling 'fire' in a crowded theater. The court cited* Schenck v. U.S., *249 U.S. 47 (1919), the Supreme Court decision in which Justice Oliver Wendell Holmes stated the famous "yelling fire in a movie house" rule.*

Teacher Scenarios

Verbal threat or free speech: What's teacher's best move? 130

When students use their 'rights' to bully: Did T-shirt cross the line? 131

Freedom of expression or threat? When a school should take action 132

Was student expelled for a good reason – or just for 'being a kid'? 133

Was the school wrong when it expelled him for a 'harmless' threat? 134

Student willingly confesses to teacher: So why are parents suing? 134

Did teasing of overweight student go too far? 135

Teased student loses temper and threatens to 'pull a Columbine' 135

Court Decisions

◆ Death threats and insults based on sexual orientation were posted to the website of a California private school student. After some classmates were implicated in the postings, the student's father called the police. Based on a recommendation by the police, the family moved. The private school newspaper reported the postings and revealed the family's new address. The student filed a state court action against the school for negligence, violation of state hate crime laws and related claims. The case was dismissed and arbitrated under an agreement in the private school contract. An arbitrator held the school was not liable for the student postings, even though some of them were made from school computers. Under the arbitration agreement, the prevailing party was entitled to its costs and legal fees. The state court of appeal reversed an award of fees and costs of more than $521,000 which the arbitrator had made to the school.

The student filed a separate action in a California court, asserting violation of state hate crimes laws, defamation and infliction of emotional distress. The classmate asserted his comments were of public interest and protected by the First Amendment. He also said he intended the message as "jocular humor." The court denied the classmate's motion to strike the claims under a state strategic lawsuit against public participation (anti-SLAPP) statute. The classmate appealed to the Court of Appeal of California, which held he did not show the student's complaint was subject to the anti-SLAPP statute. **The classmate did not show the message was protected speech.** Even if the message was a teenage joke, the court found it did not concern a public issue. *D.C. v. R.R.*, 182 Cal.App.4th 1190, 106 Cal.Rptr.3d 399 (Cal. Ct. App. 2010).

◆ A New York student was accused of making an insulting remark after a Hispanic student died in a motorcycle accident. The student said he was only repeating a remark he heard elsewhere, but Hispanic students confronted him at school and the police were called. He was escorted from school for his own protection. In the next few days, the principal denied requests by the student and his mother to read a letter declaring his innocence or to distribute copies of it. Meanwhile, the threats continued, and police were assigned to protect his house. At a hearing, the superintendent found the student should be expelled for the final weeks of the school year. But the state commissioner of education found insufficient evidence that the student made an offensive remark. As a result, the expulsion was annulled and his record was cleared. After more off-campus threats, the student was sent out of state for his own protection.

A federal district court suit was filed against the school district, board members and administrators for constitutional rights violations. After the court held for the district and officials, appeal reached the U.S. Court of Appeals, Second Circuit. It held the officials had qualified immunity from any liability. Even if the student had a right to return to school to address his classmates, the court found it was reasonable for the officials to believe they were acting within constitutional and statutory bounds. There was no question to the court that the student's "mere presence in the school, with or without his speech, would likely result in violence or the threat of violence." **The question was not whether there had been actual disruption, but whether it could be forecast.** It was reasonable for officials to forecast disruption if they readmitted the student. Since their conduct was objectively reasonable, the lower court correctly awarded them qualified immunity. The court affirmed the judgment. *DeFabio v. East Hampton Union Free School Dist.*, 623 F.3d 71 (2d Cir. 2010).

◆ A New York fifth-grade student turned in an assignment with the words "blow up the school with all the teachers in it." He was suspended from school for five days, with a day of in-school suspension. His parents sued the school district for First Amendment violations. A federal court dismissed the case, explaining that the student's writing created a foreseeable risk of substantial disruption. On appeal, the Second Circuit held that a reasonable jury might find a speech rights violation. **At the time of the incident, the student was in fifth grade. His "threat" was a crayon drawing in response to an assignment, and it was not shared with classmates.** No other discipline suggested the student was violent, and further proceedings were required to decide if there was a foreseeable risk of a material and substantial disruption. The case was returned to the lower court. *Cuff v. Valley Cent. School Dist.*, 341 Fed.Appx. 692 (2d Cir. 2009).

After further consideration, the district court found the student had a record of discipline for misbehavior on the school bus, during recess, in the hallway and in the cafeteria. School staff had found his assignment to be "disturbing." Before turning in the assignment, the student had drawn a person shooting bullets at a group of people and written a story about a squirrel who stalked other squirrels before killing them. There was evidence that the assignment had frightened a child and alarmed the teacher. The court found the student could have acted on his threat. **It held the district did not have to show a substantial disruption was inevitable. Officials only had to show a likelihood of substantial disruption.** Requiring schools to wait until actual disruption occurred before investigating would "cripple the officials' ability to maintain order" and would be "disastrous public policy." Whether the student had the capacity to blow up the school or not was not a deciding factor. Instead, the court held the objective reasonableness of the administration's response was relevant. Based on the facts, the school could have reasonably viewed the student's assignment as an indication of violent intentions. *Cuff v. Valley Cent. School Dist.*, 714 F.Supp.2d 462 (S.D.N.Y. 2010).

◆ A Minnesota student wrote an essay "detailing a fantasy murder-suicide inspired by the school shooting that took place at Columbine High School." He placed the essay in his folder, and his teacher read it a few weeks later. After the teacher reported the disturbing and graphic content of the essay, a child protection worker obtained an order to place the student in protective custody. The student was taken to a youth mental health facility, where he underwent a psychiatric evaluation. He was found not a threat to himself or others, and he was released after a total of 72 hours in custody. The family sued the school district, teacher, principal, and county law enforcement and child protection officials in a federal court for constitutional rights violations. Claims against the school district, teacher and principal were dismissed, but the family proceeded with speech and Fourth Amendment claims against law enforcement and child protection officials. The case reached the U.S. Court of Appeals, Eighth Circuit, which held **the student's essay was unprotected by the First Amendment, which does not protect a "true threat."**

The essay was a serious threat, describing the student's "obsession with weapons and gore, a hatred for his English teacher," an attack at a high school, details of his teacher's murder and the narrator's suicide. *Riehm v. Engelking*, 538 F.3d 952 (8th Cir. 2008).

◆ A Texas student's notebook described a pseudo-Nazi group and a plan to commit a Columbine-style school shooting or a "coordinated shooting" at all schools in the district. The entries were reported to an assistant principal, who issued a three-day suspension for making terroristic threats. The student was then assigned to an alternative school. His parents sued the school district for First Amendment violations. The case reached the U.S. Court of Appeals, Fifth Circuit, which noted that the school environment made it possible for a single armed student to cause massive harm with little forewarning. Recent history demonstrated that threats against schools and students must be taken seriously. **Since school administrators could prohibit student speech that advocated illegal drug use, the same rule should apply to speech that threatens violence and massive death to a school population.** As student threats against a student body were not protected, the court found no constitutional violation. *Ponce v. Socorro Independent School Dist.*, 508 F.3d 765 (5th Cir. 2007).

◆ A Georgia high school student wrote a passage in her notebook labeled "Dream." It described, in first person, an account of a student's feelings while taking a gun to school, shooting her math teacher and being chased by the police. The student showed the notebook to a classmate. Her art teacher obtained the notebook and read the passage, then spoke with the school liaison officer and principal about it. The officer believed it was "planning in disguise as a dream," and the student was removed from class the next day.

At a meeting of school officials, the student and her parent, the student dismissed the narrative as creative fiction. The principal suspended the student for 10 days and recommended expelling her for threats of bodily harm, disregard of school rules and disrespectful conduct. The school board voted not to expel her, but it affirmed the suspension and retained a record of it. The student sued the school board for violation of her First Amendment rights. A federal district court held for the school board, and the student appealed to the U.S. Court of Appeals, Eleventh Circuit. It held that writing the narrative and showing it to a classmate was reasonably likely to cause material and substantial disruption. In the climate of increasing school violence and government oversight, **the school had a compelling interest in acting quickly to prevent violence on school property**. The court found no First Amendment violation. *Boim v. Fulton County School Dist.*, 494 F.3d 978 (11th Cir. 2007).

◆ A South Carolina teacher claimed a student disrupted her classroom for over two hours and took a swing at her. Officials filed a juvenile delinquency petition against him for violating a state statute "by willingly, unlawfully, and unnecessarily interfering with and disturbing the students and teachers." The student argued the law was unconstitutionally vague and overbroad in violation of the First Amendment. A state court upheld the statute and committed the student to the juvenile justice department. The student appealed to the state supreme court, arguing the law was overly broad because it punished protected speech and was so vague that persons of common intelligence would have to guess at its meaning. The court held **the statute did not prohibit any speech that was protected by the First Amendment**. By its terms, it criminalized "conduct that 'disturbs' or 'interferes' with schools, or is 'obnoxious.'" The statute was not a substantial threat to free speech, and dealt with school disturbances, not public forums. The state had a legitimate interest in preserving discipline and could prohibit conduct interfering with the state's legitimate objectives. *In re Amir X.S.*, 371 S.C. 380, 639 S.E.2d 144 (S.C. 2006).

◆ The U.S. Court of Appeals, Third Circuit, held **"a school's authority to control student speech in an elementary school is undoubtedly greater than in a high school setting."** Accordingly, a New Jersey elementary student who was suspended for saying "I'm going to shoot you" during recess did not show any speech rights violation. Her principal was entitled to discretion in finding threats of violence and simulated firearms use unacceptable. Officials need not provide students the same latitude afforded to adults and need not tolerate speech that is inconsistent with a school's basic educational mission. *S.G., as Guardian of A.G. v. Sayreville Board of Educ.*, 333 F.3d 417 (3d Cir. 2003).

3. Internet and Technology Cases

In Doninger v. Niehoff, *527 F.3d 41 (2d Cir. 2008), the U.S. Court of Appeals, Second Circuit, found the courts are in "complete disarray" about student cyber-speech. It held school administrators were due immunity for disciplining a student who called them "douchebags," finding "it is certainly unreasonable to expect school administrators ... to predict where the line between on- and off-campus speech will be drawn in this new digital era."*

Teacher Scenarios

Handling parents who want to 'make a deal' for special treatment..136

Student blog causes big problems for school – Can they discipline?...137

Did student really harass principal by writing about her on MySpace?.......................................138

Student suspended for fake online 'profile' of principal..138

Court Decisions

◆ A California student made a video off campus that showed some of her friends "ranting" about a classmate. The video was then posted on YouTube. An assistant principal viewed the video and told the student to take it off YouTube. Administrators suspended the student for two days, and she filed a federal district court action against the school district. In a 57-page order, the court found no Supreme Court case involving school regulation of off-campus student speech. **Several lower courts have held off-campus student speech that "makes its way onto campus" can be regulated, if the speech is reasonably likely to materially and substantially disrupt school.** The court found *Tinker v. Des Moines Independent Community School Dist.*, this chapter, relevant. It noted the U.S. Court of Appeals, Ninth Circuit, has applied *Tinker* "without regard to the location where the speech originated (off campus or on campus)."

Other courts have found "geographic boundaries generally carry little weight." Where a foreseeable risk of substantial disruption is established, "discipline for such speech is permissible." Applying *Tinker*, the court held school officials need more than undifferentiated fear or apprehension of a disturbance to overcome free expression. At most, the school had to address the concerns of an upset parent, and five students missed some class. *Tinker* did not support suspending the student based on the classmate's "hurt feelings," which "did not cause any type of school disruption." Finding no reasonable jury would believe the video disrupted the school, the court held for the student. Despite the speech rights violation, administrators had qualified immunity, as **the contours of student rights to make "a potentially defamatory and degrading video about a classmate" were not clearly established**. *J.C. v. Beverly Hills Unified School Dist.*, No. 2:08-cv-03824-SVW-CW (C.D. Cal. 11/16/09).

In a separate order, the court held school administrators also violated the student's due process rights. A school discipline manual and student handbook did not put her on notice that she could be punished for speech originating off campus. No language in the state Education Code placed students on notice that off-campus speech could lead to discipline. *J.C. v. Beverly Hills Unified School Dist.*, No. 2:08-cv-03824-SVW-CW (C.D. Cal. 12/8/09).

◆ A Pennsylvania middle school student used a home computer to make a fake profile of her school principal on MySpace.com. The profile said the principal was a "married, bisexual man whose interests include 'fucking in his office' and 'hitting on' students and their parents." The principal suspended the student for 10 days, and the student sued the school district and alleged a violation of her constitutional right to free speech. A Third Circuit panel ruled for the district on the free speech claim. It held school authorities need not wait until a substantial disruption actually occurs to curb the offending speech. The panel reasoned that the insinuations about the principal struck at the heart of his fitness to serve in the position. However, on further review the full Third Circuit later reversed the panel's decision. It held that the school district's actions violated the student's free speech rights because the speech "indisputably caused no substantial disruption in school and ... could not reasonably have led school officials to forecast substantial disruption in school[.]" *J.S. v. Blue Mountain School Dist.*, No. 08-4138, 2011 WL 2305973 (3d Cir. 6/13/11).

◆ A Pennsylvania high school student made a MySpace.com parody of his principal at his grandmother's house, using her computer during non-school hours. He used a photo of the principal from the school website and created bogus answers to survey questions on the site which indicated that the principal was a drug user whose "interests" were "transgender, appreciators of alcoholic beverages." The student accessed his web page at school and showed it to others. Student use of computer labs was limited for a week due to the school's response to the web profile. After the principal identified the student as the parody's creator, he suspended him for 10 days, placed him in an alternative program, banned him from extracurricular programs and denied his participation in graduation ceremonies. The case reached the U.S. Court of Appeals, Third Circuit, which held **school officials did not establish a sufficient nexus between the student's communication and substantial disruption of the school environment**. While the school district attempted to characterize the web page as "on-campus speech" under various theories, the court was not persuaded. The court found the relationship between the student's conduct and the school "attenuated." Schools may punish off-campus speech in only limited circumstances, so the judgment was affirmed. *Layshock v. Hermitage School Dist.*, 593 F.3d 249 (3d Cir. 2010).

◆ A dispute arose between Connecticut high school administrators and some student council members over the postponement of a battle-of-the-bands event called "Jamfest." Council members sent a mass email from a school computer urging recipients to contact the district superintendent. A student officer later posted an Internet blog stating that "jamfest is cancelled due to douchebags in central office." She wrote that the email had "pissed off" the superintendent and caused her to cancel the event, and suggested others "write something or call her to piss her off more." Several students added blog comments, including one that referred to the superintendent as "a dirty whore." The superintendent and principal continued to receive calls and emails about Jamfest. The principal barred the student from class office and from giving a campaign speech.

The student's mother sued the school district for speech rights violations. Appeal reached the U.S. Court of Appeals, Second Circuit. It held that **off-campus conduct could create a foreseeable risk of substantial school disruption. The off-campus character of the speech did not insulate the student from discipline.** The posting was designed to reach the school, and it "foreseeably created a risk of substantial disruption within the school environment." As the student threatened to disrupt efforts to resolve the Jamfest dispute, and she frustrated student government operations, the court affirmed the judgment. *Doninger v. Niehoff*, 527 F.3d 41 (2d Cir. 2008).

After the student graduated, the district court considered her monetary damage claim. It held administrators could bar her from office based on vulgar, offensive off-campus speech that was likely to be heard at school. But the officials were not entitled to immunity for prohibiting students from wearing T-shirts to support her. *Doninger v. Niehoff*, 594 F.Supp.2d 211 (D. Conn. 2009).

♦ A Missouri high school student sent instant messages to another student, saying he was depressed and wanted to take guns to school, kill other students, then kill himself. The school principal learned of the electronic conversation and called police. Juvenile proceedings were brought against the student, and an assistant principal suspended him. The superintendent extended the suspension to cover the rest of the school year, and the school board affirmed this. When the student attained majority, he sued, seeking the expungement of discipline from his record. A court found that the case required a trial. The record did not show that the student substantially disrupted the school. But as he had received a hearing and opportunity to be heard, his due process rights were satisfied. All claims against the superintendent were dismissed. *Mardis v. Hannibal Public School Dist. #60*, No. 2:08CV63 JCH, 2009 WL 1140037 (E.D. Mo. 4/28/09).

The court later found that **the student's instant messages were "true threats" that were not due First Amendment protection**. He should have reasonably known his messages would reach other students. The student's state of mind and access to weapons made his threats believable. He expressed the wish to kill at least five classmates, and told the confidante that he had a .357 magnum pistol. Since a reasonable person would take these messages as "true threats," officials "acted entirely within their permissible authority in imposing sanctions." There was no merit to the student's claim that his speech did not disrupt the school. Complaints by parents who were scared to send their children to school indicated substantial disruption. *Mardis v. Hannibal Public School Dist. #60*, 684 F.Supp.2d 1114 (E.D. Mo. 2010).

♦ A New York student sent his friends instant messages with a small, crude icon depicting a pistol firing a bullet at a person's head, with dots representing blood. Beneath the drawing were the words "Kill [my English teacher]." The student used his parents' computer and did not send the instant message icon to the teacher or any other school official. However, a classmate told the English teacher about the icon, and the report was forwarded to school officials and the police. The student admitted making the icon, and the school suspended him for five days. A police investigator determined the icon was a joke and criminal proceedings were ended. But a school hearing officer found the icon threatened the health, safety and welfare of others and disrupted the school environment.

The student was suspended for a year, and his parents sued the school district for speech rights violations and retaliation. A federal court found the icon was a "true threat" that was unprotected by the First Amendment. The parents appealed to the U.S. Court of Appeals, Second Circuit, which found a reasonably foreseeable risk that the icon would come to the attention of school authorities, and that it would materially and substantially disrupt school work and discipline. Because of the risk of disruption caused by the icon, the student enjoyed no speech protection. The fact that he created it off school property did not insulate him from school discipline. **Off-campus conduct can create a foreseeable risk of substantial disruption in school.** *Wisniewski v. Board of Educ. of Weedsport Cent. School Dist.*, 494 F.3d 34 (2d Cir. 2007).

♦ An 14-year-old Indiana student posted profanity on a fake MySpace.com page about her principal. The state brought delinquency proceedings against the student, including the offense of harassment under the Indiana Criminal Code. A juvenile court found that the student committed an act of harassment which, if done by an adult, would have constituted a crime. It then adjudicated the student delinquent. Appeal reached the Supreme Court of Indiana. It noted that in juvenile delinquency cases, the state must prove every element of the offense "beyond a reasonable doubt." The postings were in a "private profile" site on MySpace.com, where they could not be seen by the general public. The court found no evidence that the student expected the principal would see or learn about the private profile. There was no evidence or reasonable inference to show that the student had a subjective expectation that her conduct would be likely to come to the principal's attention. **In order to commit the offense of harassment, a person must "have the intent to harass, annoy, or alarm another person but with no intent of legitimate communication."** The evidence did not prove beyond a reasonable doubt that the student had the requisite intent to harass, annoy or alarm the principal when she made the posting. *A.B. v. State of Indiana*, 885 N.E.2d 1223 (Ind. 2008).

4. Confederate Flags

Recent federal appellate court decisions regarding Confederate flag displays at school have interpreted Tinker v. Des Moines Independent Community School Dist. *as not requiring disruption to have actually occurred for officials to regulate student speech. Officials may bar Confederate flag displays based on a **forecast** of substantial disruption or material interference.*

Teacher Scenarios

Managing tricky dress code issues: What teachers can and can't do *139*

Court Decisions

♦ A Texas high school responded to race-related problems by prohibiting Confederate flag displays on school grounds. The number of reported race incidents decreased over the next three years, but racial graffiti remained common in a boys' lavatory. A home-made Confederate flag was raised on the school flagpole on

Martin Luther King, Jr. day in 2006. When two students carried purses to school bearing large images of a Confederate flag, they were sent to the office. They were allowed to either go home or have a parent retrieve the purses. They chose to go home, but were not disciplined. They nevertheless sued the principal and school board for violating their constitutional rights.

A court awarded pretrial judgment to the school officials, and the girls appealed. Before the U.S. Court of Appeals, Fifth Circuit, the students argued they did not cause disruption, and that the flag symbolized their ancestry and Christian faith. They claimed that other ethnic groups were not prohibited from displaying Mexican flags, Malcolm X shirts and similar items. The court held that **school officials reasonably banned displays of the Confederate flag at school to prevent substantial and material disruption**. The decision was based on the history of racial hostility at the school, some of which involved Confederate flag displays. School officials reasonably anticipated that the flag would cause substantial disruption or material interference, based on evidence of racial hostility and tension. For this reason, the lower court had properly held for the school officials. *A.M. v. Cash*, 585 F.3d 214 (5th Cir. 2009).

◆ A Missouri high school community endured racially charged incidents and violence, leading to the withdrawal of three of the high school's 15-20 African-American students from school. A fight occurred at a high school basketball game after white players used racial slurs during the game. A Confederate flag was displayed near the locker rooms during the game. As a result of these and other incidents, the district superintendent banned students from displaying the Confederate flag on their clothing. Students who wore Confederate items to school were told to change their clothes. They later sued the school district, asserting First Amendment violations. A court found that no constitutional violation, as there was sufficient evidence of school disruption if the flag was allowed. The students appealed. The U.S. Court of Appeals, Eighth Circuit, held that the numerous racial events at the school made the school's actions constitutionally permissible. The court held *Tinker* **and cases interpreting it "allow a school to 'forecast' a disruption and take necessary precautions before racial tensions escalate out of hand."** As a result of the race-related incidents both in and out of school, the administration had reasonably banned in-school Confederate flag displays. The court affirmed the judgment for school officials. *B.W.A. v. Farmington R-7 School Dist.*, 554 F.3d 734 (8th Cir. 2009).

◆ A Tennessee school experienced racial fighting, and civil rights complaints and a lawsuit were filed against the school system. There were "multiple racially motivated threats and physical altercations," resulting in suspensions. Law enforcement officers maintained a presence at the school, and Confederate flag depictions were banned. Two students wore shirts depicting Confederate flags at school. After being told to either turn their shirts inside out or remove them, they filed a federal district court action. Appeal reached the U.S. Court of Appeals, Sixth Circuit, which held **school officials need not tolerate student speech that is inconsistent with their educational mission**. Schools may ban speech that would "materially and substantially interfere" with appropriate school discipline. But *Tinker v. Des Moines Independent Community School Dist.*, "does not require disruption to have actually occurred" for schools to regulate student speech. And *Tinker* did not require the expression itself to have been the source of past disruption. The graffiti was violent, and racial tensions had caused absenteeism, which the court found "the epitome of disruption in the educational process." As school officials had reasonably forecast disruption, they were entitled to judgment. *Barr v. LaFon*, 538 F.3d 554 (6th Cir. 2008).

B. Student Publications and Expression

Student publications are not "public forums," so school administrators may exercise editorial control over them if a reasonable basis exists for the belief that a publication would materially disrupt class work, involve substantial disorder or violate the rights of others.

Teacher Scenarios

Student club claims school had no right to censor its poster 140

Religious freedom: Setting limits on what students can say in class 141

Students feel threatened by his fictional story: Can he be punished? 142

When can school 'censor' student newspaper? 142

Court Decisions

◆ A Missouri high school principal objected to two articles prepared for publication in the school newspaper. Because the principal believed there was no time to edit the articles before the publication deadline, he deleted the two pages on which the articles appeared. Former students who were members of the newspaper staff sued, alleging that their First Amendment rights were violated when the pages were removed from the newspaper before publication.

A federal district court ruled in favor of the school district. The Eighth Circuit reversed, holding that the newspaper was a public forum "intended to be and operated as a conduit for student viewpoint." The U.S. Supreme Court agreed to hear the case and noted that school facilities, including school-sponsored newspapers, become public forums only if school authorities have intentionally opened those facilities for indiscriminate use by either the general public "or by some segment of the public, such as student organizations." The Court determined that since the district allowed a large amount of control by the journalism teacher and the principal, it had not intentionally opened the newspaper as a public forum for indiscriminate student speech. **School officials can exercise "editorial control over the style and content of student speech in school-sponsored expressive activities so long as their actions are reasonably related to legitimate pedagogical concerns."** Because the decision to delete two pages from the newspaper was reasonable, the Court found no violation of the First Amendment. *Hazelwood School Dist. v. Kuhlmeier*, 484 U.S. 260, 108 S.Ct. 562, 98 L.Ed.2d 592 (1988).

◆ A California high school student editor wrote an editorial for the school paper called "Immigration." He suggested all non-English speakers were illegal aliens. The principal allowed the publication of "Immigration," and Latino parents complained. After the superintendent instructed the principal to retract remaining copies of the paper, the principal apologized to students and parents for her "misinterpretation and misapplication of board policy in the publication of 'Immigration.'" Administrators wrote a letter to parents expressing regret over their decision to allow the publication. The student wrote another editorial entitled "Reverse Racism," which made provocative statements about race relations. The principal approved it for publication, but delayed publication until a counter-viewpoint editorial could be presented in the same issue.

The student sued in a state court for speech rights violations. The Court of Appeal of California held California Education Code Section 48907 protected student expression in school publications but prohibited "material which so incites students as to create a clear and present danger of the commission of unlawful acts on school premises or the violation of lawful school regulations." The editorial "Immigration" would not incite students to commit unlawful acts on school grounds, violate school rules, or pose a risk of substantially disrupting school operations. **Schools may only prohibit speech that incites disruption by specifically calling for a disturbance** or because the manner of expression "is so inflammatory that the speech itself provokes the disturbance." While the student was not disciplined, his rights were violated by the principal's statement that "Immigration" had been improperly published. *Smith v. Novato Unified School Dist.*, 150 Cal.App.4th 1439, 59 Cal.Rptr.3d 508 (Cal. Ct. App. 2007).

◆ The newly selected principal of a Washington high school threatened to sue her new school and the school newspaper's faculty advisor after the newspaper featured an article indicating that she was the student committee's "third choice" for principal. Student journalists claimed that after the new principal assumed her duties, she undertook many acts of retaliation based on the article. They claimed she objected to language for a new masthead for the newspaper declaring the paper was not subject to prior review. The current masthead stated that editorial decisions were student-made protected speech.

The students sued the school district in a federal court, which found that the newspaper was part of the curriculum, as students received grades and academic credit. A school policy provided for the review of all copy by the principal prior to publication. The court explained that "prior restraint" prohibited future speech, as opposed to punishing past speech. **The principal's "prior review" of the newspaper regulated only the time and manner of publication, and was not "prior restraint."** However, the court refused to dismiss their First Amendment challenge to the deletion of the proposed masthead. The newspaper was described as a school club in a student handbook and at freshman orientation. Students worked for long hours outside the school day to edit and produce each issue, and to sell advertising. The advisors had little control over the publication. The court also refused to dismiss the retaliation claims against the principal. *Lueneburg v. Everett School Dist. No. 2*, No. C05-2070RSM, 2007 WL 2069859 (W.D. Wash. 7/13/07).

◆ New Hampshire school yearbook editors considered publishing a picture of a student holding a shotgun and dressed in trap-shooting attire. The yearbook faculty advisor and the school principal encouraged the editors to make their own decision. The staff voted 8-2 not to publish the student's photograph in the senior portrait section of the yearbook. After the student's parents complained, the staff offered to publish the picture in the community sports section of the yearbook. The school board adopted a new publications policy banning the use of "props" in senior portraits. The student sued the board in a federal court for an order requiring the publication of the picture as his senior portrait. The court observed that the student editors were not coerced, unduly influenced or pressured by school officials to reject the student's picture. The editors believed that the display of a firearm would be inappropriate in a school publication, given school policies and recent tragedies such as Columbine. **The editorial judgment exercised by students was sufficiently independent from the school administration to avoid attribution to the school.** Thus, the student could not establish "state action." And while the revised board policy was state action, it was content neutral and viewpoint neutral. *Douglas v. Londonderry School Board*, 413 F.Supp.2d 1 (D.N.H. 2005).

C. Non-School Publications

Teacher Scenarios

Where to draw the line when your students speak their minds 143

When teachers can – and can't – limit what their students say 144

Court Decisions

◆ A Michigan eighth-grader came to school with red tape over his mouth and wrists, a sweatshirt reading "Pray to End Abortion" and leaflets containing abortion statistics.

After a teacher sent him to the office for causing a disruption, a guidance counselor told him to remove the tape and change his shirt or hide the message. The student returned to class but attempted to put his sweatshirt back on. The principal then repeated the directive not to wear it. As the student did not have approval to distribute the leaflets, the principal stated he could not hand them out. The principal had to pick up leaflets found in hallways. Although no discipline was imposed on the student, his parents sued the principal, school district and school officials in a federal district court. The parties agreed that the student could not come to school with tape on his mouth or wrists, but could wear the sweatshirt saying "Pray to End Abortion."

The court issued an order for the student, and the case reached the U.S. Court of Appeals, Sixth Circuit. It held **school hallways are "nonpublic forums" that do not possess the attributes of streets, parks and other places that are considered public forums**. School facilities may be deemed "public forums" only if authorities open them for indiscriminate use by the general public. Public forums are not created by government inaction. The school offered the student opportunities to post his leaflets on bulletin boards and to hand them out in the cafeteria during lunch. The court held regulation of his speech was "eminently reasonable." There was no indication of a desire to suppress his anti-abortion viewpoint. **It was reasonable for the school to require prior approval before permitting students to distribute literature at school.** The court reversed the judgment, holding the school policy on distribution of literature was not unconstitutional, as it was intended to prevent hallway clutter and congestion. *M.A.L. v. Kinsland*, 543 F.3d 841(6th Cir. 2008).

◆ Texas students and parents claimed an elementary school prevented speech about Christian religious beliefs and disallowed distributing religious items or literature at school. They filed a federal district court action against the school district, asserting First Amendment claims. The court held the "disruption" standard from *Tinker v. Des Moines Independent Community School Dist.*, this chapter, did not apply because the provisions being analyzed were content- and viewpoint-neutral. **The policy was not targeted at nonschool materials based on their content or viewpoint.** The power of the principal to review materials was limited in time and scope and there was provision for an appeal.

The policy's numerical limit of 10 copies was not arbitrary, as the families urged. Instead, the court found a limit appropriately balanced the school's need to conserve resources with the interest in normal student interactions. The school district had a substantial interest in limiting time, place and manner restrictions to distributions of over 10 copies of an item. A provision delegating power to school principals to determine time, place and manner of distributions of over 10 documents had clear guidelines for principals and did not offer them excessive discretion. The court awarded pretrial judgment to the school district. *Pounds v. Katy Independent School Dist.*, 517 F.Supp.2d 901 (S.D. Tex. 2007).

D. Personal Appearance and Dress Codes

1. Dress Codes

Clothing with expressive content may be protected as "speech" under the First Amendment and is subject to the balancing of interests test from Tinker v. Des Moines Independent Community School Dist. *But courts have rejected some claims that items such as T-shirts, jeans and body piercings are expressive at all. Officials may bar messages that materially disrupt school, involve substantial disorder or violate the rights of others. Dress codes implicate the Due Process Clause and must be specific enough to notify students of what speech is unacceptable, while not so broad as to prohibit protected expression.*

Teacher Scenarios

Student ignores dress code and gets ISS: Mom says teacher's to blame 144

When free speech and school traditions collide: What wins out? 145

Student writes nasty message on hand: Should teacher take action? 146

Offensive T-shirt or personal pride? Managing tricky free speech issues 147

When students' rights cause trouble: What you can and can't do 148

Student insists gun on shirt stands for patriotism – now what? 149

Teacher acts to prevent disruption: Where to draw the line – legally 150

When student's 'rights' create a disruption: What's the limit? 151

T-shirt says, 'I must shoot him' – can a teacher take action? 152

Enforcing dress codes in class: What you can and can't do 153

Student protests school policy with Nazi pin – What should teacher do? 154

Student won't heed warnings about T-shirt: What's next? 154

Mom says prom dress code's unfair: What should teacher say next? 155

Court Decisions

◆ A New Jersey school board adopted a uniform policy with significant input from the school community. Students could opt out of the policy for religious and medical reasons. A student tried to opt-out of the requirement based on "Constitutional Rights, Fundamental Freedom, Individual personal choice and Philosophical Beliefs." Upon being denied this request, he refused to comply, and after undergoing progressive discipline, he was suspended. When he entered high school, he again sought to opt out of the dress code, but was again denied his request. His family sued the board and several school officials. Appeal reached a New Jersey Appellate Division Court, where the parents claimed that a law authorizing education boards to adopt uniform dress codes violated the child's speech rights, as well as their own parental rights.

The court said parents have a fundamental right to decide whether to send their children to a public school, but do not have a fundamental right generally to direct how a public school teaches their children. The purpose of the law at issue was to assist in controlling the school environment and to keep the focus on learning. As these purposes were rationally related to the legitimate interest in quality education, the court found no constitutional violation. **Dressing as one chose was not expressive conduct that was due constitutional protection.** Here, the student "simply did not want to be told what to wear." The court also rejected the parents' claim based upon an asserted right to direct and control every aspect of their child's education, and the judgment was affirmed. *Dempsey v. Alston*, 405 N.J. Super. 499, 966 A.2d 1 (N.J. Super. Ct. App. Div. 2009).

◆ A Texas student wore a shirt to his school with "San Diego" printed on it. After an assistant principal told him this was a dress code violation, his parents brought him a "John Edwards for President '08" T-shirt to wear instead. But as the second shirt had a printed message, it also violated the dress code. Months later, the student sued the school district. By the time a hearing was held, a new dress code was in place. The court dismissed the case but asked to review the new dress code, which extended the ban on messages to polo shirts, and shirts with pro and university team logos or messages. Logos under two square inches, school spirit shirts, pins, buttons, wristbands, bumper stickers, and "principal-approved" messages of sponsored school clubs and teams were allowed. Each of the three shirts the student submitted to school administrators was disapproved. The court denied his request for an order to prevent enforcement of the dress code. He appealed to the U.S. Court of Appeals, Fifth Circuit.

The court rejected his argument that schools could only regulate specific kinds of speech. By allowing school logos and school-sponsored shirts, the school district did not suppress unpopular viewpoints. Instead, it provided students with more clothing options. As the code was content-neutral, it could be justified if it furthered an important government interest that was unrelated to expression. Among the reasons for adopting the dress code were improving student performance and attendance, instilling self-confidence, decreasing disciplinary referrals and lowering the drop-out rate. All these reasons furthered important government interests. Another valid goal was to promote professional and responsible dress for students preparing for the workforce. **"Federal courts should defer to school boards to decide what constitutes appropriate behavior and dress in public school."** The judgment was affirmed. *Palmer v. Waxahachie Independent School Dist.*, 579 F.3d 502 (5th Cir. 2009).

◆ A California school with a history of conflict over sexual orientation let a Gay-Straight Alliance group hold a "Day of Silence" to "teach tolerance." The 2003 event was accompanied by student fights. A group of students held an informal "Straight-Pride Day" and wore T-shirts with anti-gay slogans. Some students were asked to remove these shirts. Others were suspended for fighting. When the school allowed another "Day of Silence" in 2004, one student wore a T-shirt to school stating "I will not accept what God has condemned." The reverse of the shirt stated "homosexuality is shameful 'Romans 1:27.'" The student was detained in a school conference room for refusing to remove the shirt. Although he was not further disciplined, and no record of the incident was placed in his file, he sued the district and school officials for violating his speech and religious free exercise rights. The case reached the Ninth Circuit.

The court noted that *Tinker v. Des Moines Independent Community School Dist.* (this chapter) allows schools to **"prohibit speech that intrudes upon the rights of other students," or collides with the rights of others to be secure and to be let alone**. The T-shirt collided with other students' rights in the most fundamental way. Speech attacking minority students injured and intimidated them, damaged their sense of security and harmed their learning opportunities. Schools had a right to teach civic responsibility and tolerance, and did not have to permit hateful and injurious speech that ran counter to that message. *Harper v. Poway Unified School Dist.*, 445 F.3d 1166 (9th Cir. 2006).

After graduating, the students tried to pursue their claim for monetary damages. The case returned to the Ninth Circuit which held that the case was moot and that school officials had immunity from any damage claims. *Harper v. Poway Unified School Dist.*, 318 Fed.Appx. 540 (9th Cir. 2009).

◆ A Florida student had piercings and wore jewelry on her body, tongue, nasal septum, lip, navel and chest. She claimed her piercings were a way to express her "non-conformity and wild side" and expressed her individuality. An administrator told the student that her body jewelry violated the school dress code. The student refused to remove the jewelry and was assigned to lunch detention for four days for violating the dress code. She sued. A court ruled against her, and she appealed. The U.S. Court of Appeals, Eleventh Circuit, affirmed. It noted that students enjoy some speech rights at school, "but those constitutional rights are circumscribed by the special characteristics of the school environment." **While the First Amendment protects "symbolic speech," the Supreme**

Court has held that it does not apply unless "an intent to convey a particularized message was present." The court questioned whether a jewelry ban implicated the First Amendment. Here, the student did not show that the First Amendment protected her right to express individuality at school by wearing body-piercing jewelry. Her conduct had insufficient communication to earn such protection. The board had enforced the dress code in a viewpoint-neutral manner and the rule was narrowly tailored to support the school interest in education. *Bar-Navon v. Brevard County School Board*, 290 Fed.Appx. 273 (11th Cir. 2008).

◆ Arkansas students wore black armbands to protest a mandatory uniform policy for grades seven through 12. After a few students wore armbands over their uniforms, the school disciplined them. One of the students handed out a flyer criticizing the uniform policy without first obtaining the principal's approval. This violated a district "literature review policy" requiring advance approval by the principal. The students sued the school district and school officials for constitutional violations. A court held that the uniform policy did not violate any constitutional provision, and that school board members were entitled to qualified immunity. On the other hand, the district superintendent and a junior high school principal were denied immunity in their individual capacities for imposing discipline to suppress a particular viewpoint. *Tinker v. Des Moines Independent Community School Dist.*, this chapter, established student rights to wear armbands in a non-disruptive way. After a jury found the students suffered no damages, the court awarded nominal damages. The district appealed to the U.S. Court of Appeals, Eighth Circuit, which found ***Tinker* was so similar in all relevant aspects that it required a judgment for the students**. *Lowry v. Watson Chapel School Dist.*, 540 F.3d 752 (8th Cir. 2008).

◆ An Illinois student who opposed a student "Day of Silence" wore a T-shirt stating: "Be Happy, Not Gay" and "My Day of Silence, Straight Alliance." A school official made him ink out the phrase "Not Gay," and to avoid discipline he did not wear the shirt. The student sued school officials, arguing that the First Amendment permitted his expression. A court refused to issue an order allowing him to wear the T-shirt, and he appealed. The U.S. Court of Appeals, Seventh Circuit, found the school banned "Be Happy, Not Gay" under a rule forbidding derogatory comments about race, ethnicity, religion, gender, sexual orientation or disability. But the slogan was a play on words that was not derogatory. The message was not targeted and "only tepidly negative." It was highly speculative that the T-shirt would provoke harassment of homosexuals. **While the student failed to qualify for an order suspending the school rule pending the outcome of his lawsuit, he could wear the shirt on a preliminary basis.** *Nuxoll v. Indian Prairie School Dist. #204*, 523 F.3d 668 (7th Cir. 2008).

◆ A Los Angeles middle school adopted a uniform policy for faculty and students after it was declared one of California's lowest-performing schools. The policy was expected to help students by reducing any distractions caused by clothing, allow easy identification of non-students, prevent students from leaving campus, and help prevent gang-related incidents. The school reported significant improvements in attendance and test scores, and a decrease in behavior problems after adopting the policy. The policy had a parental opt-out feature, but if students came to school out of uniform, their parents were called.

A student who opted out of the policy claimed that administrators, security guards and staff confronted her for appearing out of uniform. She said she was barred from a Valentine's Day dance and other activities. She sued, and a state court held for the district on most of her civil rights and speech claims. On appeal, the Court of Appeal of California explained that conduct "is protected by the First Amendment only if it 'is inherently expressive.'" **"Personal expression in clothing or hair style, without more, is not protected speech."** The student's "generalized desire to express her middle-school individuality" was an "unfocused message of personal expression" that was unprotected. The court affirmed the judgment. *Land v. Los Angeles Unified School Dist.*, No. B189287, 2007 WL 1413227 (Cal. Ct. App. 5/15/07, review denied, 8/15/07).

◆ Eighth-graders attended a gifted education program in a Chicago school. The school held annual contests to design a class T-shirt. The gifted students voted for a shirt depicting a boy with an enormous head, misshapen teeth, a dilated pupil and a missing hand. The reverse of the shirt had the word "Gifties," a reference to the gifted program. The "Gifties" shirt lost the school election, and the students were prevented from wearing the shirts at school. They said the shirts poked fun at themselves and had "irony." However, the principal stated that they mocked disabled people and threatened school safety. Many gifted students wore the shirts to school. Those who did so were confined to their homerooms. Although the school eventually permitted students to resume wearing the shirt, they sued the school board. A federal district court held that the T-shirt design did not contain a statement or symbolic message.

On appeal, the U.S. Court of Appeals, Seventh Circuit, held **the school did not violate the First Amendment by acting to exclude the shirts, because the images on them did not express an idea or opinion**. Schools may prohibit clothing with inappropriate words or slogans. As the principal acted reasonably and did not abuse his discretion, the court affirmed the judgment for the board. *Brandt v. Board of Educ. of City of Chicago*, 480 F.3d 460 (7th Cir. 2007).

◆ A New Jersey school district's mandatory uniform policy prompted two fifth-graders to wear buttons with the phrase "No School Uniforms," and a slashed red circle. The printing overlaid a photograph depicting hundreds of boys in uniform. While the photograph was identified as portraying Hitler Youth, no swastikas were visible. The school district sent letters to the students' parents stating that the background images on the buttons were "objectionable," and threatening the students with suspension if they wore the buttons to school again. The parents sued the school board for First Amendment violations. A court found it likely that some might find the button offensive, or in poor taste. On the other hand, the image was "a rather innocuous photograph – rows and rows of young men," with no visible swastikas. The image was not obscene, and "the young men might easily be mistaken for a historical photograph of the Boy Scouts." The court found that to prevent students from wearing the buttons, the board would have to show that they would "substantially interfere with the work of the school or impinge upon the rights of other students." **As the buttons did not cause disruption, and the board did not demonstrate a specific and significant fear of disruption, the censorship was unwarranted.** *DePinto v. Bayonne Board of Educ.*, 514 F.Supp.2d 633 (D.N.J. 2007).

◆ A Vermont high school student wore a T-shirt to school that read "George W. Bush, Chicken-Hawk-In-Chief." Surrounding a caricature of the president's face superimposed on a chicken's body were images of oil rigs, dollar symbols, cocaine, a razor blade and a martini glass. A parent complained about the shirt to a staff member, who decided that it violated a dress code provision barring images of drugs and alcohol. The student refused to turn the shirt inside-out or cover images of drugs and alcohol and the word "cocaine." He left school, but wore the shirt to school the next two days. He wrote the word "Censored" on duct tape and placed it on the shirt over the word "cocaine." The school disciplined the student and sent him home for wearing the shirt.

The student sued school officials, and a federal court found a speech rights violation. The parties appealed to the U.S. Court of Appeals, Second Circuit, which found that the student's T-shirt did not contain expression that was "vulgar, lewd, indecent or plainly offensive." **"Tinker established a protective standard" under which student speech cannot be suppressed based on its content, but only if it is substantially disruptive.** The "plainly offensive" standard of *Bethel School Dist. No. 403 v. Fraser*, this chapter, was not triggered whenever a school decided a student's message conflicted with its educational mission. The student was entitled to an order permitting him to wear the shirt and clearing his record. *Guiles v. Marineau*, 461 F.3d 320 (2d Cir. 2006).

◆ A Kentucky middle school adopted a policy generally requiring students to wear solid-colored clothing and restricting tight, baggy, revealing, form-fitting or "distressed" clothing, as well as clothing that was "too long" or not of appropriate size and fit. A parent sued the school district, stating that his daughter wanted to "be able to wear clothes that look nice on her, that she feels good in and that express her individuality." After the case was filed, the council modified the code to prohibit blue jeans. The court held for the school district, and the parent appealed. The U.S. Court of Appeals, Sixth Circuit, held that the school district could enforce a dress code regulating pants and tops where the student did not seek to convey any particular message through her clothing. The First Amendment does not apply unless there is a "particularized message." The student here had no message, wanting only to "wear clothes she feels good in." Her First Amendment claim failed, as she only stated "a generalized and vague desire to express her middle-school individuality." A person's choice of clothing "does not possess the communicative elements necessary to be considered speech-like conduct." The dress code also did not interfere with the parent's rights, as **parents have no fundamental right generally to direct how public schools teach their children**. The court affirmed the judgment. *Blau v. Fort Thomas Public School Dist.*, 401 F.3d 381 (6th Cir. 2005).

2. Hair Length and Appearance

In Karr v. Schmidt, *460 F.2d 609 (5th Cir. 1972), the Fifth Circuit held that "there is no constitutional right to wear one's hair in a public high school in the length and style that suits the wearer."* Karr *created a* per se *rule that hair and grooming regulations are constitutional, so long as they are not arbitrary*

Teacher Scenarios

Tough call: How to handle gray areas in the dress code...156

Court Decisions

◆ An African-American male student was told to remove braids from his hair, even though no policy prohibited them. The school board revised its dress code to require all students to "wear their hair in a standard, acceptable style." All students were required to wear uniforms. Any hairstyle detrimental to student performance or school activities was prohibited. Male students could not wear their hair in braids, spiked, or in a style distracting to other students. However, females could wear braids. The student claimed that the policy had a disparate impact on African-American males and violated his equal protection, free exercise and speech rights. He sued the school board. A federal district court rejected his claim that he had been denied a hairstyle favored by African-American males in violation of the First Amendment. There was also no violation of his equal protection rights. A school committee had revised the dress code in conjunction with a school safety policy. The court held the dress code should be upheld under *Karr v. Schmidt*, above. **According to the court, the board's policy advanced legitimate concerns for discipline, avoiding disruption and fostering respect for authority.** *Fenceroy v. Morehouse Parish School Board*, No. Civ.A. 05-0480, 2006 WL 39255 (W.D. La. 2006).

◆ A Texas school board adopted a student grooming policy prohibiting boys from wearing their hair below the shirt collar. An elementary school principal observed a third-grade boy with a ponytail and advised him and his mother that he was in violation of the grooming policy. The school board suspended the student for three days for refusing to comply, and it placed him on in-school suspension. The student's mother removed him from school and sued the board for violating the Texas Constitution and state law. A state court permanently enjoined the board from enforcing the policy. But the Supreme Court of Texas held **the grooming policy did not deprive males of equal educational opportunities or impose other improper barriers**. The regulation of hair length and other grooming or dress requirements was not discriminatory on the basis of sex, and the court reversed the judgment. *Board of Trustees of Bastrop Independent School Dist. v. Toungate*, 958 S.W.2d 365 (Tex. 1997).

◆ A fourth-grade Indiana boy wore an earring to school, even after the school board revised its handbook to bar the wearing of jewelry by male students. After a five-day suspension, a hearing examiner recommended transferring the student to another school that did not have similar policies. The board adopted the recommendations, but the student refused to transfer. The family sued the school district in the state court system for a declaration and order prohibiting enforcement of the policy. The Court of Appeals of Indiana rejected an argument that the policy violated equal protection of the law because girls were permitted to wear earrings. Enforcement of a strict dress code was a factor in improving student attitudes. **The policy served the valid educational purpose of instilling discipline and creating a positive educational environment.** *Hines v. Caston School Corp.*, 651 N.E.2d 330 (Ind. Ct. App. 1995).

3. Gang Affiliation

A federal district court held in Brown v. Cabell County Board of Educ., *below, that schools may ban gang-related clothing if there is evidence of a potentially disruptive gang presence at school and gang-related disturbances. Borrowing language from recent Confederate flag cases, the court held the* **"test is not whether a student's statement has led to a disturbance or disruption, but whether it could reasonably be expected to lead to one."**

Court Decisions

◆ Gang activities at a West Virginia high school escalated when a gang leader was arrested for shooting a police officer. Gang members verbally assaulted the faculty and staff at school, and fights and disturbances became prevalent. The principal advised staff members that the slogan "Free A-Train" was banned. A student wrote "Free A-Train" on his hands several times and was suspended for 10 days. He sued the school board in a federal district court for speech rights violations. The court held schools may ban gang-related clothing if evidence indicates a potentially disruptive gang presence and gang-related disturbances.

Recent federal cases suggest schools may regulate expression if they can reasonably forecast material and substantial disruption at school. This defeated the student's claim that speech must lead to an actual disruption before school administrators may suppress it. As students and parents had expressed fear over the use of the slogan, administrators could reasonably forecast that allowing the student to keep displaying it may have exacerbated the tensions and increased these fears. The court held the "distraction from classes or intimidation from passive displays of support may serve as the basis of a disruption," and found no speech rights violation. *Brown v. Cabell County Board of Educ.*, 714 F.Supp.2d 587 (S.D. W.Va. 2010).

◆ An Illinois school disciplinary code defined "gang activity" as "prohibited student conduct." Gang activity included any act in furtherance of a gang, and use or possession of gang symbols, such as drawings, hand signs and attire. The code stated that gangs and their activities substantially disrupted school by their very nature. A student was suspended three times for drawing gang-related symbols, including an inverted pitchfork and crowns with five points. Each time, the student was informed about the code prohibition on gang symbols and warned of its disciplinary implications. After the third incident, the superintendent notified the student's mother of a proposed expulsion, the date of a hearing and the right of the student to counsel.

A school resource officer testified at the hearing that the pitchfork and crowns were gang-related signs. She said drawing them could be dangerous if misconstrued as a sign of disrespect by another gang. The school board voted to expel the student for the second half of the school year, and his mother sued. **A federal district court held that the student code sufficiently defined the term "gang symbol," using specific examples of prohibited conduct.** The court rejected all of the student's First Amendment arguments. And his due process claim failed because the board gave him three chances to conform his behavior to the code. Both he and his mother had been warned that his conduct was a violation before he was expelled. The decision to expel the student after documented violations of the student code was not contrary to the evidence or in conflict with board policy, and judgment was awarded to the school board. *Kelly v. Board of Educ. of McHenry Community High School Dist. 156*, No. 06 C 1512, 2007 WL 114300 (N.D. Ill. 1/10/07).

◆ A Kentucky board of education devised a student dress code based on the need to address a school gang problem, promote safety, prevent violence and disputes over clothing, and enable the identification of non-students and intruders on campus. The dress code limited the clothing available to students as well as the way it could be worn. It prohibited logos, shorts, cargo pants, jeans, the wearing of certain jewelry outside clothes and other specified items. Some students who were disciplined for dress code violations sued the school board, and the case reached the U.S. Court of Appeals, Sixth Circuit. It held that **school officials had an important and substantial interest in creating an appropriate learning environment by preventing the gang presence and limiting fights**. The regulation of student expression furthered an important government interest without suppressing free speech. The board believed the dress code would help reduce gang activity, ease tension among students who fought over attire and otherwise enhance student safety. The dress code addressed those issues in a manner that was unrelated to the expressive nature of student dress. School officials may control student speech or expression that is inconsistent with a school's educational mission. *Long v. Board of Educ. of Jefferson County, Kentucky*, 21 Fed.Appx. 252 (6th Cir. 2001).

II. EMPLOYEES

Overview

In Garcetti v. Ceballos, *547 U.S. 410 (2006), the Supreme Court held its public employee speech cases reflected "the common sense realization that government offices could not function if every employment decision became a constitutional matter."* **A public employee's speech pursuant to official duties is not protected by the First Amendment.** *Under* Garcetti, *courts must first determine if an employee's speech was made pursuant to official duties. If the speech was not made pursuant to official duties, the test from* Pickering v. Board of Educ., *391 U.S. 563 (1968), and* Connick v. Myers, *461 U.S. 138 (1983), applies. Under* Pickering *and* Connick, *employees have First Amendment protection (1) if they speak on matters of public concern and (2) their interest in public comment outweighs the government interest in efficient public service.*

A. Protected Speech

Teacher Scenarios

Parents really don't like controversial lesson plans: Is teacher out of line? 155

Court Decisions

◆ *Garcetti* involved a deputy district attorney in California who examined a search warrant affidavit presented by a defense attorney. He determined that it contained serious misrepresentations and recommended dismissing the case. At a subsequent meeting, a heated discussion ensued. The DA's office decided to proceed with the prosecution, and the deputy district attorney was reassigned, then transferred to another courthouse and denied a promotion. He sued county officials under 42 U.S.C. § 1983, claiming First Amendment violations. On appeal, **the U.S. Supreme Court held that "when public employees make statements pursuant to their official duties, the employees are not speaking as citizens for First Amendment purposes."** It was part of the deputy district attorney's job to advise his supervisors about the affidavit, and if his supervisors thought his speech was inflammatory or misguided, they had the authority to take corrective action against him. *Garcetti v. Ceballos*, 547 U.S. 410 (2006).

◆ A New York City teacher filed a grievance because school administrators failed to discipline a student who twice threw books at him. He understood that a student assault of a teacher violated a citywide policy. After the teacher told other teachers of his grievance, he claimed administrators retaliated against him by issuing bad performance reviews and a false report of sexually abusing a student. The board discharged the teacher, and he filed a federal district court case for speech rights violations. Applying *Garcetti v. Ceballos*, above, the court held the grievance was an aspect of the teacher's core duties of maintaining class discipline. But it held conversations with other teachers were not within the scope of his employment duties. The teacher appealed to the U.S. Court of Appeals, Second Circuit, regarding the grievance issue.

In addition to finding officials need wide latitude in managing government offices, *Garcetti* held that the First Amendment does not "constitutionalize the employee grievance." Statements made pursuant to official duties are not protected speech. According to the court, when the teacher filed a grievance to complain about his supervisor's failure to issue discipline to a student, he was "speaking pursuant to his official duties and thus not as a citizen." For this reason, the filing of the grievance was unprotected. In reaching this result, the court agreed with other federal circuits which have held that **under *Garcetti*, official duties need not be required by (or included in) an employee's job description**. Ability to maintain classroom discipline is "an indispensable prerequisite to effective teaching and classroom learning." As a grievance over the decision not to discipline the student was a means to fulfill a primary employment duty, the court held for the school board. *Weintraub v. Board of Educ. of City School Dist. of City of New York*, 593 F.3d 196 (2d Cir. 2010).

◆ A probationary California first-grade teacher complained about a student in her class who had severe behavior issues, and she told her principal she felt he should be evaluated for emotional disturbance. She had a poor relationship with the district's special education director, who eventually refused to speak to her without a witness. One of their encounters involved placement of the teacher's own disabled child. Other teachers complained that the teacher used her cell phone during classes and arrived late every day. Just prior to her discharge, the teacher left campus during lunch without permission. After the school board voted not to renew the teacher's contract, she sued the school district and several administrators in a state court under Section 44113 of the state Education Code.

The case reached the Court of Appeal of California, which explained that Section 44113 makes government employees liable for using official authority to interfere with a teacher's right to disclose improper governmental activities. The special education director and other non-supervisors of the teacher were exempt from Section 44113 liability. And the district was exempt from Section 44113 liability, since it was not an employee. But the principal, superintendent and a supervisory assistant superintendent were not exempt under the provision, as they had acted as "supervisory employees." Despite this finding, the court affirmed the decision for the school administrators, because the matters the teacher sought to disclose were not "improper governmental activities." **Her activities on behalf of special needs children were not considered a "protected disclosure" under Section 44113.** The teacher's complaints about unruly students and a failure to perform a timely special education assessment of her own child were unprotected, because they were made in a context of internal personnel or administrative matters. *Conn v. Western Placer Unified School Dist.*, 186 Cal.App.4th 1163, 113 Cal.Rptr.3d 116 (Cal. Ct. App. 2010).

◆ A Washington school employee made comments about her co-workers on an Internet blog. She was then transferred from a curriculum specialist position to a classroom teaching job. She claimed this was retaliation for her posting of blogs on the Internet that included "several highly personal and vituperative comments about her employers, union representatives and fellow teachers." In a federal district court action against the school district's human resources specialist, the employee claimed First Amendment protection for her postings.

The court held for the human resources specialist, and the employee appealed to the Ninth Circuit. The court found the employee's former position required her to enter into trusting mentor relationships with less experienced teachers, to whom she was to give honest, critical and private feedback. Her public blog resulted in complaints from co-workers, and one of them had refused to work with her, even though she had been assigned as her instructional coach. The transfer followed because **the blog fatally undermined her ability to enter into trusting relationships as an instructional coach**. The court found the blog had a harmful effect on the employee's working relationships, and common sense indicated that few teachers would expect to enter into a confidential and trusting relationship with her after reading her blog. Since the lower court properly found the employee's interest in speech did not outweigh the school district's interest in fulfilling its responsibilities, the court affirmed the judgment. *Richerson v. Beckon*, 337 Fed.Appx. 637 (9th Cir. 2009).

◆ A Nebraska school technical support coordinator claimed he was fired for telling staff members about pay irregularities, invalid contracts and funding discrepancies. He filed a federal district court action against the school district for speech rights violations. The case reached the U.S. Court of Appeals, Eighth Circuit, which found the coordinator admitted each instance of speech involved his job duties. **Since speech relating to a public employee's job duties is unprotected by the First Amendment, there was no constitutional violation.** *Anderson v. Douglas County School Dist.*, 342 Fed.Appx. 223 (8th Cir. 2009).

◆ An Idaho security employee advised a high school principal of student drug and weapons violations. He also expressed concern over school safety and emergency policies, which he felt were inadequate. Near this time, the principal took away some of the employee's job duties. The employee wrote a letter to district administrators complaining about the principal's handling of his reports. He criticized unresponsiveness to safety problems, inadequate staff training, concealment and insufficient documentation of safety violations, ineffective enforcement of truancy and sexual harassment policies, and inadequate fire safety planning. The employee substantiated his concerns with specific examples of students bringing weapons to school, harassing others and coming to school intoxicated. School officials later met with the employee at his home and outside school hours to discuss the concerns. At the end of the school year, his responsibilities were combined with those of three other positions in a new position. Another applicant was hired for this job and the employee sued the school district for retaliation in violation of state law and the First Amendment.

A federal court awarded pretrial judgment to the school district. On appeal, the Ninth Circuit explained that *Garcetti v. Ceballos*, this chapter, required it to determine whether the employee was speaking as a public employee or as a private citizen. However, the precise nature of the employee's duties was unclear. There was room for debate regarding whether he wrote the letter as part of his official duties. According to the Ninth Circuit, **the *Garcetti* inquiry was not a purely legal question over which a federal court could award pretrial judgment**. Speech rights present a mixed question of law and fact. There remained questions regarding the nature of the employee's duties, so the court reversed the judgment and returned the case to the lower court. *Posey v. Lake Pend Oreille School Dist. No. 84*, 546 F.3d 1121 (9th Cir. 2008).

◆ An Indiana teacher/coach had a history of addressing his opinions to the school board and other community members without first addressing them to his immediate supervisor, as required by a district "chain of command" policy. He allegedly provided an athletic club with information that encouraged a Title IX complaint against the school district, and also emailed the superintendent to ask how to file a Title IX suit. After the coach got into a fight with an assistant, 70 families presented the board with a petition requesting the coach's removal.

The school board voted to terminate the coach's contract, and he filed a federal court lawsuit for speech rights violations. The court held the chain of command policy was not an unconstitutional "prior restraint" on speech, and the U.S. Court of Appeals, Seventh Circuit, affirmed the judgment. Under *Garcetti v. Ceballos*, this chapter, the First Amendment does not protect employees while they make statements pursuant to their official duties. **The chain of command policy was not a "prior restraint" on speech.** It did not restrict any speech protected by the First Amendment, as it only implicated job responsibilities. The court found this did not limit speech rights, but only ensured that a speaker's views were not attributed to the board. There was no evidence that the board was motivated by retaliation when it voted to terminate the coach's contract. Instead, the record reflected that he lost his coaching job because of the troubled program he ran. *Samuelson v. LaPorte Community School Corp.*, 526 F.3d 1046 (7th Cir. 2008).

◆ A probationary Indiana teacher was in her first year of work for an elementary school. In response to a student's question, she stated that she had honked her car horn to show support for anti-war demonstrators who held a "Honk for Peace" sign denouncing military involvement in Iraq. Parents complained to the school principal, who told all teachers not to take sides in any political controversy. The teacher was not rehired, which she believed was based on her answer in the current events class. She sued the school system in a federal district court for violating the First Amendment. A court awarded pretrial judgment to the school system, and the teacher appealed to the Seventh Circuit. Although she admitted she made the comment while performing her official duties, she claimed she was still protected by academic freedom.

The court rejected her argument. Public school teachers "must hew to the approach prescribed by principals" and other school administrators. The court stated that "the school system does not 'regulate' teachers' speech as much as it hires that speech." **Teachers have to "stick to the prescribed curriculum" and have no constitutional right to interject their own views on curricular subject matter.** Teachers could not use their classes as platforms to voice their own perspectives. Students in public schools are a captive audience and they "ought not be subject to teachers' idiosyncratic perspectives." The teacher had been told she could teach the controversy about policy toward Iraq, so long as she kept her opinions to herself. As teachers could not advocate viewpoints that departed from the curriculum, the court held for the school system. *Mayer v. Monroe County Community School Corp.*, 474 F.3d 477 (7th Cir. 2007).

◆ Colorado charter school teachers were hired by a K-8 charter school under contracts indicating that the school board welcomed "constructive criticism" to enhance the school's program. Each teacher received satisfactory evaluations, and their contracts were renewed. The next year, the teachers and a paraprofessional grew concerned about the school's operations, management and mission. They held off-campus meetings to discuss school matters. Parents and others also attended. The teachers expressed their concerns to the board, which invited grievances "without fear of retaliation." However, the teachers contended that their grievances were ignored, and that the principal gave them less favorable job evaluations. Each teacher submitted a resignation letter effective well before the end of the school year. The board discussed the letters during a meeting at which the principal also submitted her resignation. After the principal resigned, the teachers unsuccessfully tried to rescind their own resignations.

The teachers claimed that the board then "blacklisted them from future employment," and they sued the charter school and its chartering school district. A court issued an order for the school and the district. On appeal, the U.S. Court of Appeals, Tenth Circuit, held that **the vast majority of the speech at issue involved personal job duties, and not the public concern**. However, the statements regarding official impropriety, as well as political speech, were matters of public concern. And the teachers' comments about their freedom of speech and expression related to the public concern, so they were constitutionally protected. Their discussions about the future of the school and upcoming board elections were also protected. The case was returned to the lower court for it to determine if the teachers' discussions on these subjects outweighed the school's interest in avoiding disruption. *Brammer-Holter v. Twin Peaks Charter Academy*, 492 F.3d 1192 (10th Cir. 2007).

◆ A Texas high school employee was athletic director and head football coach of a Dallas high school. He repeatedly asked the school's office manager for information about athletic activity funds. The coach wrote memorandums to the office manager and school principal, protesting the lack of information and seeking immediate funding for a tournament entry fee for one of the school's teams. Four days after receiving the memo, the principal stripped the coach of his athletic director duties. The district then voted against renewing his coaching contract. The district placed the office manager and principal on administrative leave pending an investigation into school financial matters.

The coach sued the district and school officials in a federal district court, asserting that he was retaliated against for engaging in protected speech. Appeal reached the U.S. Court of Appeals, Fifth Circuit. **The Fifth Circuit held that public employee speech cases use a "balancing test" between the speaker's expression and the employer's interests.** However, *Garcetti* "added a threshold layer" to the rules set by cases like *Pickering v. Board of Educ*. "Even if the speech is of great social importance, it is not protected by the First Amendment so long as it was made pursuant to the worker's official duties." The coach claimed that he wrote his memos as a taxpayer and a father, but the court disagreed, ruling that the memos focused on daily operations. The coach admitted he needed the information so he could operate the athletic department. As his speech was made in the course of performing his job, it was unprotected by the First Amendment. *Williams v. Dallas Independent School Dist.*, No. 05-11486, 2007 WL 504992 (5th Cir. 2/13/07).

◆ A Florida principal's school received a D grade on the Florida Comprehensive Assessment Test. The score improved to a C the next year, but the principal learned that the school would not receive additional staff or funding. He held a faculty vote to obtain teacher support for conversion to a charter school, as permitted by state law. The vote failed, but the principal continued his conversion efforts and advocacy. Although he had received a "high quality performance" rating four days earlier, the principal's contract was not renewed. He filed a complaint with the state education department, but an investigation found no direct correlation between non-renewal and his efforts to convert the school. The principal sued the district for First Amendment violations. A court held that the speech was unprotected, and the principal appealed to the Eleventh Circuit, which found that his efforts to convert the school were "part and parcel of his official duties."

In light of *Garcetti v. Ceballos*, this chapter, the principal's conduct was unprotected. Under *Garcetti*, **a public employee must speak both on a matter of public concern and as a citizen in order to gain First**

114 FREEDOM OF SPEECH AND ASSOCIATION

Amendment protection. The Supreme Court held in *Garcetti* that public employee speech on official duties is not insulated from employer discipline. The principal sought to convert his school in his capacity as a public employee, and not as a citizen. As the lower court had properly entered judgment for the school board, the judgment was affirmed. *D'Angelo v. School Board of Polk County, Florida*, 497 F.3d 1203 (11th Cir. 2007).

◆ A New Mexico school district hired a new director for its noncompliant Head Start program. Within six months, the program substantially complied with federal requirements. The director then told the district superintendent that up to 50% of the families enrolled in Head Start had misstated their incomes or family sizes and were ineligible for the program. The superintendent repeatedly raised the Head Start issue to the school board and others, but was put off each time. She instructed the director to report to federal authorities. The U.S. government investigated, found improprieties and ordered the repayment of over $500,000 in federal aid. The superintendent filed a complaint with the state attorney general stating that the board had made decisions in executive session without proper notice. After the attorney general ordered corrective action, the board demoted the superintendent and decided not to renew her contract for the next school year. She sued the district, its new superintendent and school board members for retaliation. A federal court denied motions for pretrial judgment.

On appeal, the U.S. Court of Appeals, Tenth Circuit, **commented that *Garcetti v. Ceballos* "profoundly alters how courts review First Amendment retaliation claims."** The *Garcetti* standard defeated a First Amendment claim based on reporting Head Start program deficiencies, since the reports were part of the superintendent's official duties. But the reporting of open meetings act violations to the New Mexico attorney general was outside the scope of her official job duties. That part of the lawsuit required a trial. *Casey v. West Las Vegas Independent School Dist.*, 473 F.3d 1323 (10th Cir. 2007).

◆ A Pennsylvania special education teacher who was admonished for trying to arrange counseling sessions for a student with suicidal feelings enjoyed no First Amendment protection in a federal lawsuit against her school district. The student's individualized education program (IEP) did not include psychological services. However, the teacher arranged for sessions and transported the student to them. She claimed the district then retaliated against her for trying to help the student. The Third Circuit held **the scheduling of therapy sessions and other assistance was not "expression," and had no First Amendment protection**. *Montanye v. Wissahickon School Dist.*, 218 Fed.Appx. 126 (3d Cir. 2007).

B. Personal Appearance and Dress Codes

School officials have considerable authority to regulate employee speech that could be perceived by the public as representing an official school view.

Court Decisions

◆ New York City Board of Education (BOE) regulations required school employees to maintain neutrality regarding political candidates while on duty or with students and precluded the distribution, posting or display of materials supporting any political candidate or organizations in BOE buildings or staff mailboxes. BOE teachers claimed that the regulations violated employee speech rights. They sought an order from a federal district court to prohibit enforcement of them. The court held school officials may impose reasonable restrictions on the speech of teachers, unless an open forum has been intentionally opened for indiscriminate use by the general public. **Schools have more authority to regulate teacher speech when there is a risk that the public would view it as bearing the school's imprimatur than when regulating personal expression.** As the regulation was neutral and left teachers ample alternatives for expression, the court upheld a ban on political button-wearing by teachers at school. There was no risk of attribution of political views to the BOE when political materials were posted in areas not accessible to students, so the BOE was ordered to allow posting of political items on bulletin boards and teacher mailboxes. *Weingarten v. Board of Educ. of City School Dist. of City of New York*, 591 F.Supp.2d 511 (S.D.N.Y. 2008).

Months later, the court considered motions by both parties for a permanent order. Only the issue of political buttons remained in dispute. The court noted the Supreme Court has allowed schools to regulate teacher speech in classrooms for legitimate pedagogical reasons (see *Hazelwood School Dist. v. Kuhlmeier*, this chapter). **So long as the school acted in good faith and banned buttons for legitimate pedagogical concerns, the regulation was constitutional.** The board's findings relating to button-wearing by teachers was entitled to deference. Students were a captive audience in their classes, and the board found teacher displays of political partisanship were inconsistent with the school's mission. As the teachers could not undermine the deference due the board to exercise its judgment in good faith, the court held for the board. *Weingarten v. Board of Educ. of City School Dist. of City of New York*, 680 F.Supp.2d 595 (S.D.N.Y. 2010).

◆ A California school district and the association representing its teachers could not reach a new agreement as their contract neared expiration. The association called for teachers to wear buttons supporting its bargaining position. Most of the teachers taught in self-contained classrooms in which only teachers and students were present. The district superintendent advised teachers of a district policy preventing them from engaging in any political activity during work time. Teachers complied with the directive, but the association filed an unfair practice charge against the district. The state Public Employee Relations Board (PERB) found that the wearing of buttons was not political activity and held that the district had interfered with the teachers' rights. The district appealed to the state court of appeal, which held that **button-wearing was "political activity" that could be barred under the state Education Code**. It was reasonable to prohibit public school teachers from political advocacy during instructional activities. The wearing of union buttons during instructional time was "inherently political." The court held that keeping the labor relations dispute from spilling into the classroom was a proper restriction of political activity and reversed the PERB's decision. *Turlock Joint Elementary School Dist. v. PERB*, 5 Cal.Rptr.3d 308 (Cal. Ct. App. 2003).

◆ *Turlock Joint Elementary School Dist. v. PERB*, above, is limited to instructional time. **A ban on political advocacy could not be enforced in noninstructional settings.** Another California district prohibited employees from distributing partisan election materials on school grounds and from campaigning during work hours. The teachers association objected to the policy and demanded its rescission so that teachers could wear buttons expressing their opposition to a state education finance voter initiative. A state superior court held the policy violated the First Amendment speech rights of teachers.

The Court of Appeal of California held state law allows schools to restrict the political speech of teachers during work hours. Because public school teachers have considerable power and influence in classroom situations and their speech may be reasonably interpreted as reflecting the official view of their school districts, it was reasonable to prohibit them from wearing political buttons in classrooms. This restriction did not violate the First Amendment or the state constitution, as school authorities must have the power to disassociate themselves from political controversy and the appearance of approval of political messages. **But it was unreasonable for the school district to restrict political speech by teachers outside their classrooms.** The court modified the decision so that teachers were prohibited from wearing political buttons only in the classroom. *California Teachers Ass'n v. Governing Board of San Diego Unified School Dist.*, 53 Cal.Rptr.2d 474 (Cal. Ct. App. 1996).

C. Association Rights

The following cases involve claims by or on behalf of individual rights to free association.

Court Decisions

◆ A California teachers' association placed political endorsements for two school board candidates in school district employee mailboxes. While the association was authorized to communicate with its members through their mailboxes, an administrator advised the association that California Education Code Section 7054 prohibited the use of school mail facilities to distribute materials containing political endorsements. The association filed an unfair practice charge with the California Public Employee Relations Board (PERB).

The action was dismissed, but appeal later reached the Supreme Court of California. The court found Section 7054 prohibited school districts and community colleges from using funds, services, supplies or equipment to urge support for (or the defeat of) any ballot measure or candidate, including board candidates. **California law stated that "the government may not 'take sides' in election contests or bestow an unfair advantage on one of several competing factions."** The Legislature found the use of public funds in elections would be inappropriate. The court found Section 7054 was "designed to avoid the use of public resources to perpetuate an incumbent candidate or his or her chosen successor, or to promote self-serving ballot initiatives" that would compromise the integrity of elections. Since "equipment" was intended to include mailboxes such as those used by the school district, Section 7054 applied. Permitting the district to restrict political speech did not run afoul of Government Code Section 3543.1, which permits employee organizations to use school bulletin boards, mailboxes and other means "subject to reasonable regulation." The ban on political endorsements was upheld as reasonable. Under established First Amendment law, school mailboxes were considered nonpublic forums. This meant the district could impose viewpoint-neutral regulations on the content of items placed there. Since the district had an important government interest, it was entitled to judgment. *San Leandro Teachers Ass'n v. San Leandro Unified School Dist.*, 209 P.3d 73, 95 Cal.Rptr.3d 164 (Cal. 2009).

◆ The Colorado Education Association (CEA) and an affiliate recruited members for walks to support a state senate candidate. Two individuals claimed this violated Article XXVIII of the Colorado Constitution. They also asserted that payments for union staff salaries, office supplies and materials were unconstitutional "expenditures" or "contributions." The individuals challenged the union activity with the Colorado Secretary of State, seeking to impose a $170,000 civil penalty. An administrative law judge (ALJ) rejected the claim that the unions had "coordinated" activities with the candidate and found no evidence of any "expenditure." The ALJ found the unions did not communicate beyond their own membership, complying with a state constitutional exception that permits communications among union members. The case reached the Supreme Court of Colorado, which held that **unions were expressly permitted to establish political committees and engage in other campaign activities among their members. The court found that campaign spending is a form of speech.**

The First Amendment protects political association, and limitations on political expenditures place a substantial restraint on speech and association. The state constitution's broad membership communication exception protects employee free speech and association rights. There was no evidence that the unions made unlawful expenditures or campaign contributions. The union communicated with members, not voters or the general public. Any indirect benefit to the candidate was also permitted by the state constitution's membership communication exception. As the ALJ had properly found the unions acted for the benefit of their own members, the court upheld her judgment. *Colorado Educ. Ass'n v. Rutt*, 184 P.3d 65 (Colo. 2008).

◆ A newspaper incorrectly reported that a Tennessee school superintendent would speak at a convention sponsored by a congregation that was primarily gay and lesbian. He submitted statements to two newspapers, informing them that he had declined the speaking invitations, and declared "that he did not endorse, uphold or understand homosexuality, but that he would not refuse to associate with gay people or refuse the opportunity to share with them his beliefs." Several board members believed the article called his judgment into question, undermined public confidence in him, and impaired his functioning. The board did not hire the superintendent to become the director of schools.

When the superintendent sued, a federal court held for the board and board members. The U.S. Court of Appeals, Sixth Circuit, held that the superintendent's intended prayer or speech touched on the public concern. The speech concerned religion and perhaps homosexuality, and would occur on his own time. **The superintendent sought to share his religious beliefs with the congregation and the community. This conduct was protected.** "It would contravene the intent of the First Amendment to permit the Board effectively to terminate [the superintendent] for his speech and religious beliefs in this way." The court reversed the judgment for three school board members who had apparently changed their view of the superintendent on the basis of his intended speech. The superintendent also stated claims under the Equal Protection Clause. The board members were not entitled to qualified immunity, as he had a clearly established right to express his religious beliefs. The case was returned to the lower court for further proceedings. *Scarbrough v. Morgan County Board of Educ.*, 470 F.3d 250 (6th Cir. 2006).

III. ACADEMIC FREEDOM

Overview

Schools have broad discretion in curricular matters and courts do not closely scrutinize reasonable school board decisions in this area. But once a decision has been made to place a particular book in a school library, the same level of discretion does not apply. In ACLU of Florida v. Miami-Dade County School Board, *below, a federal appeals court held a Florida school board had the authority to determine what books were to appear on school library shelves*

A. Library Materials

In Board of Educ. v. Pico, *below, the Supreme Court held the removal of books from a school library would be unconstitutional if it was motivated by an intent to deny students access to ideas with which school officials disagreed.*

Court Decisions

◆ A Miami parent was outraged to find a copy of "Vamos a Cuba" on the shelves of his daughter's public school library. As a former political prisoner from Cuba, he claimed the book was untruthful. After the book was removed from library shelves, the school board chairman said that the book offended the Cuban community. Another board member noted that the board was rejecting its school staff's recommendation due to political pressure. Still another board member suggested that if the board did not vote to remove the book from school libraries, they might find bombs under their cars. A different parent and two organizations sued the board for First Amendment and Due Process violations.

A federal district court prevented the board from removing the book, and the board appealed. On appeal, the U.S. Court of Appeals, Eleventh Circuit, noted the board found the book was inaccurate and had factual omissions. The board voted to replace the series with updated books. Here, the lower court improperly prevented the board from removing the book from school libraries. "Whatever else it prohibits, the First Amendment does not forbid a school board from removing a book because it contains factual inaccuracies, whether they be of commission or omission. **There is no constitutional right to have books containing mis-statements of objective facts shelved in a school library.**" Rather than banning the book, the school board was "removing" it from its library shelves. As the board had the sole authority to determine what books were to appear on school library shelves, the court held in its favor. *ACLU of Florida v. Miami-Dade County School Board*, 557 F.3d 1177 (11th Cir. 2009).

◆ The U.S. Supreme Court held that the right to receive information and ideas is "an inherent corollary of the rights of free speech and press" embodied in the First Amendment. The case arose when a New York school board rejected the recommendations of a committee of parents and school staff it had appointed and ordered that certain books be removed from school libraries. The board characterized the books as "anti-American, anti-Christian, anti-Semitic, and just plain filthy." Students sued the board and its individual members, alleging the board's actions violated their rights under the First Amendment. The Supreme Court noted that while school boards have broad discretion in the management of curriculum, they do not have absolute discretion to censor libraries and are required to comply with the First Amendment. **A decision to remove books from a school library is unconstitutional if it is motivated by an intent to deny students access to ideas with which school officials disagree.** *Board of Educ. v. Pico*, 457 U.S. 853, 102 S.Ct. 2799, 73 L.Ed.2d 435 (1982).

◆ The Children's Internet Protection Act (CIPA) requires public schools and libraries receiving federal technology grants or e-rate discounts to install filtering systems on computers used by children 17 or younger. Local school boards or agencies can decide what software to install and what to block. Two complaints filed in federal courts alleged that the CIPA violated the First and Fifth Amendments and sought to permanently bar the Federal Communications Commission from implementing the law. A three-judge federal panel found the law unconstitutional because a library patron might wish to remain anonymous or might be too embarrassed to ask for the filters to be removed to view sensitive materials. On appeal, the U.S. Supreme Court held Internet access in public libraries is not a public forum. For this reason, **libraries have discretion to choose what parts of the Internet they will offer patrons, in the same way they choose which books to put on the shelves.** "A public library does not acquire Internet terminals in order to create a public forum for Web publishers to express themselves, any more than it collects books in order to provide a public forum for the authors of books to speak." The Court found any concerns about innocuous websites being wrongly blocked were addressed by CIPA provisions allowing librarians to disable filters when asked by adult patrons.

The Court rejected the contention that people seeking medical, sexual or other sensitive information would be reluctant to ask for unblocking. It concluded "the Constitution does not guarantee the right to acquire information at a public library without any risk of embarrassment." *U.S. v. American Library Ass'n Inc.*, 539 U.S. 194, 123 S.Ct. 2297, 156 L.E.2d 221 (2003).

◆ A gay and lesbian organization donated books with homosexual themes to a Kansas school district. One of the books was already on library shelves, but no one had ever checked it out. The media publicized the donation and opponents burned copies of the book on school property. The superintendent recommended removing copies from the libraries and rejecting the donation. The school board voted to remove the books and refuse the donation, and a teacher and some students sued. A federal district court found the book had no vulgarity or explicit language and had won many literary awards. The district had failed to abide by its own rules in rejecting the donation and removing copies from its shelves. Board members indicated that they disapproved of the book's subject matter and had voted to remove it because of their disagreement with it. The failure of the board to follow its own procedures for library procurement affirmed the court's belief that **board members had been motivated to remove the book based on their personal disagreement with ideas expressed in it.** Removal of the book violated the constitutional rights of students attending district schools. The court issued an order requiring school officials to return copies to district libraries. *Case v. Unified School Dist. No. 233*, 908 F.Supp. 864 (D. Kan. 1995).

B. Textbook Selection

In Chiras v. Miller, *below, the Fifth Circuit held students have no constitutional right to compel the selection of classroom materials.*

Court Decisions

◆ A Texas student and the author of an environmental textbook had no constitutional right to compel the state board of education to select a particular textbook, according to the U.S. Court of Appeals, Fifth Circuit. Government can, without violating the constitution, selectively fund programs to encourage activities it believes are in the public interest, and may discriminate on the basis of viewpoint by choosing to fund one activity over another. Schools can thus promote policies and values of their own choosing, free from the forum analysis and the viewpoint-neutrality requirement. Devising the curriculum and selecting textbooks were core functions of the board, which needed to keep editorial judgment over the content of instructional materials for public school classrooms. The court agreed with the board that its selection of curricular materials was government speech. **Students have no constitutional right to compel the selection of classroom materials of their choosing.** *Chiras v. Miller*, 432 F.3d 606 (5th Cir. 2005).

◆ A group of parents whose children attended grade school in an Illinois school district sued for an order to prevent use of the Impressions Reading Series as the main supplemental reading program for grades kindergarten through five. The parents alleged that the series "foster[ed] a religious belief in the existence of superior beings exercising power over human beings" and focused on "supernatural beings" including "wizards, sorcerers, giants and unspecified creatures with supernatural powers." The court dismissed the lawsuit, and the parents appealed to the Seventh Circuit.

The court found the parents' argument (that use of the textbook series established a religion) speculative. Although the series contained some stories involving fantasy and make-believe, their presence in the series did not establish a coherent religion. The intent of the series was to stimulate imagination and improve reading skills by using the works of C.S. Lewis, A.A. Milne, Dr. Suess and other fiction writers. **The primary effect of using the series was not to endorse any religion, but to improve reading skills.** Use of the series did not impermissibly endorse religion under the Establishment Clause or the Free Exercise Clause. The court ruled for the school. *Fleischfresser v. Directors of School Dist. 200*, 15 F.3d 680 (7th Cir. 1994).

◆ A teacher in a Michigan public school taught a life science course using a textbook approved by the district's school board. He showed films to his class regarding human reproduction (*From Boy to Man* and *From Girl to Woman*) after obtaining approval from his principal. The films were shown to his seventh-grade classes with girls and boys in separate rooms, and only students with parental permission slips were allowed to attend. Both films had traditionally been shown to seventh-grade students in the school.

But after a board meeting where community residents demanded that the teacher be tarred and feathered for showing the films, the superintendent suspended the teacher with pay pending "administrative evaluation." The board approved this action. The teacher then sued the district for violating his First Amendment and other civil rights. A jury awarded the teacher $321,000 in compensatory and punitive damages. The U.S. Supreme Court reversed the decision and remanded the case. According to the Supreme Court, **an award of money** damages may be made only to compensate a person for actual injuries caused by deprivation of a constitutional right. Awards for abstract violations of the U.S. Constitution were not allowed. *Memphis Community School Dist. v. Stachura*, 477 U.S. 299, 106 S.Ct. 2537, 91 L.Ed.2d 249 (1986).

C. School Productions

In Boring v. Buncombe County Board of Educ., *below, a federal appeals court held the selection of a school play was part of the curriculum, not a matter of public concern for which a teacher could claim constitutional protection.*

Court Decisions

◆ A Nevada high school student selected a W.H. Auden poem containing the words "hell" and "damn" for recital at a statewide poetry reading competition. He practiced the poem twice a day for over two months. When the student recited the poem at a competition in the school, the dean of students emailed the English chair that it was objectionable due to inappropriate language. The student recited the poem again at a districtwide competition held off campus.

An administrator reprimanded English department members for allowing the recitation. The student learned he would have to choose a new poem for the state competition, as the Auden poem had profanity. He petitioned a federal district court for a temporary restraining order to prevent the school from interfering with his recitation. The court found the recitation of the Auden poem could not be considered vulgar, lewd, obscene or offensive. **Off-campus poetry recitation at a state competition sponsored by national organizations was not school-sponsored speech and was not a part of the curriculum or any regular classroom activity.** Where there was no showing that student speech would materially and substantially interfere with appropriate discipline, the court could not uphold speech restraint by school officials. A poem by a recognized poet, recited at an off-campus student competition authorized by the school, did not present even a remote risk of disruption. *Behymer-Smith v. Coral Academy of Science*, 427 F.Supp.2d 969 (D. Nev. 2006).

◆ A North Carolina high school English and drama instructor won numerous awards for directing and producing student plays. She selected a play for a state competition that depicted a divorced mother with a lesbian daughter and a daughter who was pregnant with an illegitimate child. Her advanced acting class won 17 of 21 possible awards at a regional competition for performing the play. But a parent objected to a scene from the play and the principal forbade students from performing it at the state finals. He later allowed the performance with the deletion of certain scenes. The school board approved a transfer of the teacher to a middle school for violating the district's controversial materials policy. She sued the board and school officials for retaliatory discharge.

After removal to a federal district court, the case was dismissed. A three-judge panel of the U.S. Court of Appeals, Fourth Circuit, rejected the board's argument that the First Amendment protects only original expression and not the selection of a play. The panel held that due to the important role that teachers play in society, the First Amendment extended to the selection of plays for high school drama classes. The full court reheard the case and vacated the panel decision, upholding the transfer. **The selection of a school play was part of a public school curriculum, and did not constitute a matter of public concern for which a teacher could claim constitutional protection.** *Boring v. Buncombe County Board of Educ.*, 136 F.3d 364 (4th Cir. 1998).

IV. PARENTAL SPEECH AND ASSOCIATION RIGHTS

Overview

The Supreme Court has recognized a fundamental right of parents to direct and control the upbringing of their children. This does not include a parental right to direct and control public school curriculums or enter school campuses without restriction. Courts have approved state actions that intrude on parental liberty, such as sex and health education programs, community service and attendance requirements, uniform policies, and condom distribution programs.

A. Access to School Campuses

Teacher Scenarios

Teacher's stuck in the middle when custody agreement is violated 157

Custody battle spills over into the classroom: What should teacher do? 157

Teacher caught up in the middle when divorced parents fight over child's education 158

Dad's banned from school – but teacher sees him walk in the door 158

Court Decisions

◆ A New Jersey student said her varsity basketball coach routinely criticized her, singled her out due to her weight and went on "profanity-laced tirades" about her and some teammates. Her parent complained to school administrators and appeared at board meetings at least four times to urge action against the coach and to discuss the need to address civility in coaching. At one of the meetings, he spoke against reappointing the coach. Five others spoke in favor of the coaching staff, and the coach was reappointed. Months later, the parent was cut off about 30 seconds into an address to the board at a meeting to consider a policy against behavior diminishing individual dignity and safety. Other speakers were allowed to exceed a five-minute limit on remarks. The parent filed a state court action against the school board for retaliation and also raised other claims. A jury found the board and school officials liable for negligent supervision, but the court dismissed the daughter's claims.

The court refused to reverse a $100,000 verdict for the parent for emotional distress. Appeal reached the Supreme Court of New Jersey, which held there was enough evidence for a jury to find the board president had silenced the parent for his viewpoints. The public comment period of a school board meeting is a public forum that can be limited only if justified without reference to the content of speech. **Once the board opened the floor for discussion, it could not deny the forum to those wishing to express less-favored or controversial views.** The court held the jury was free to find the warning by the president revealed impatience and antagonism toward a view he did not want to hear. Since the president's motive was not content neutral, the court held the parent established a First Amendment violation. But the court found the evidence of emotional distress was limited to transient embarrassment and humiliation. The case was returned to the trial court to reduce the damage award or to hold a new trial on damages. *Besler v. Board of Educ. of West Windsor-Plainsboro Regional School Dist.*, 201 N.J. 544, 993 A.2d 805 (N.J. 2010).

◆ Four Tennessee high school football players were dismissed from the team after signing a petition stating they hated their head coach and did not want to play for him. They filed an unsuccessful lawsuit against the school board in a federal court. Parents of the same students filed a new federal court action on their own behalf against the school board and two school officials. A jury held for the board and school officials, and the court ordered the parents to pay the board attorneys' fees and costs of over $87,000 as a sanction for bringing claims that were frivolous and intended to harass school officials. On appeal, the U.S. Court of Appeals, Sixth Circuit, found **a school board meeting was a "designated and limited public forum."**

The forum in this case was "limited," because people did not have to be allowed to engage in every type of speech there. **In a designated public forum, the government may regulate the time, place and manner of speech in a content-neutral fashion.** In this case, the board's content-neutral justifications for the policy had nothing to do with an individual's proposed speech. The court held the policy served a significant government interest in avoiding unstructured, chaotic school board meetings. There was no merit to the parents' claims that the policy was unconstitutionally vague and that the trial court had given the jury improper instructions. As the policy amounted to a content-neutral time, place and manner regulation, the court affirmed the judgment. But since the parents' claims were not frivolous, the court reversed the award of attorneys' fees for the board and school officials. *Lowery v. Jefferson County Board of Educ.*, 586 F.3d 427 (6th Cir. 2009).

◆ An Oklahoma parent agreed to check on another parent's daughter while volunteering at school. After obtaining approval to enter the classroom, the parent checked on the child, then spoke to a paraprofessional and other children for a few minutes. She then went to perform her volunteer duties and was again approached by the other parent to check on her daughter. The parent again looked in on the classroom. A school official sent her a letter banning her from school for five weeks for violating an Oklahoma law regarding "Interfering with Peaceful Conduct of Activities." After a hearing, the school reduced the time the parent was excluded from school, but she sued the district in federal district court for constitutional violations, including an interest in the care, custody and control of her children. The court held school officials were well within their bounds in limiting access, as "parents simply do not have a constitutional right to control each and every aspect of their children's education and oust the state's authority over that subject." **Public education is committed to the control of school authorities.** Federal courts in Kansas, Virginia, New Jersey, Texas and Michigan have held parents have no constitutional right to be on school grounds. *Mayberry v. Independent School Dist. No. 1 of Tulsa County, Oklahoma*, No. 08-CV-416-GKF-PJC, 2008 WL 5070703 (N.D. Okla. 11/21/08).

◆ South Carolina legislators considered a bill to offer parents tax credits for private and home school expenses. A local school board believed the bill would undermine public school education, and it resolved to express opposition to the bill. The board instructed its director of community relations to communicate its position, and she did so on the district's website. The site was linked to other websites operated by bill opponents. The director emailed school employees and circulated fact sheets and opinions expressing the district's position. A parent sought to use the same channels to voice his support for the bill. The superintendent denied the request, and the parent sued the school district in a federal district court. The case reached the U.S. Court of Appeals, Fourth Circuit. It held government speech is exempt from First Amendment scrutiny.

The Supreme Court has stated that "the government may advocate in support of its policies with speech that is not supported by all." Generally, the government may support valid programs and policies and advocate particular positions. The district had approved a message of opposition to the bill and could deny access to its channels of communications. The district did not create a limited public forum, and the parent's speech rights were not implicated. *Page v. Lexington County School Dist. One*, 531 F.3d 275 (4th Cir. 2008).

◆ A Texas principal instructed students not to wear controversial T-shirts the day after about 300 Hispanic students walked out of school as part of nationwide demonstrations to protest pending immigration reform legislation in Congress. The principal issued about 130 suspensions for disobeying his order not to wear protest T-shirts the day after the nationwide demonstration. Many angry parents came to protest the suspension of their children. After some parents refused to leave the building, school security asked them to leave the campus. Several families sued, asserting First Amendment violations. A court upheld the principal's action, noting that he was responding to threats of violence at a school with a history of high racial tension. The court also rejected a claim by parents that they had been excluded from campus in violation of their rights. **A school can prevent parental access to the premises when necessary to maintain order and prevent disruptions to the education environment.** *Doe v. Grove Public School Dist.*, 510 F.Supp.2d 425 (S.D. Tex. 2007).

♦ An Illinois parent was convicted of a crime which defined him as a child sex offender. However, he was not required to register under the Illinois Sex Offender Registration Act. He brought his children to school activities, games and practices, and picked them up for medical appointments and emergencies. A 2005 law prohibited child sex offenders from being on or within 500 feet of school grounds when children were present, unless the offender was a parent or guardian of a student attending the school, and was there to meet or confer with school staff about the child's performance and adjustment in school. The law further required a child sex offender to notify the school principal of his or her presence at a school. School officials denied the parent's requests to come to school for his own children's activities. The parent sued the school district for an order to allow him to attend school events, concerts and games with his family. He also sought to proceed under the fictitious name "John Doe." The court found the parent's interests in privacy did not outweigh the public interest in the open nature of court proceedings, and it ordered him to proceed under his true name. **The court denied his motion for permission to attend school events during the litigation.** *Doe v. Paris Union School Dist. No. 95*, No. 05-2249, 2006 WL 44304 (C.D. Ill. 2006).

♦ An Illinois mother had sole custody of her two children, but her divorce decree specified that the children's father had joint, equal access rights to school records. The parents were required to cooperate to ensure authorities sent them dual notices of their children's school progress and activities. The father criticized a school principal at public meetings, complained that nothing was done when his son was bullied, and claimed the school did not provide him notices, records, correspondence and other documents sent to custodial parents. He wrote letters to the principal about these matters, then stated that the principal excluded him from the playground when he sought to observe his son during recess, and turned him down as a volunteer playground monitor.

The father sued the principal and school district for constitutional and state law violations. A federal court dismissed the case, and he appealed. The U.S. Court of Appeals, Seventh Circuit, noted the difficulty for schools to accommodate demands by divorced parents. The father's rights concerning his children's records were no greater than the school's interest in keeping as free as possible from divorce matters. **The only constitutional right concerning the education of one's child was the right to choose the child's school.** This was not a right to participate in the school's management. Schools also have a valid interest in limiting a parent's presence on campus. While most of the father's criticisms of administrators were "personal," he also was critical of them in public meetings and questioned their inadequate responses to bullying. The district and the principal prevailed on the father's due process claims, but the equal protection and speech rights claims were remanded to the lower court for further consideration. *Crowley v. McKinney*, 400 F.3d 965 (7th Cir. 2005).

B. Curriculum

Courts have repeatedly rejected parental attempts to direct school curriculums through lawsuits. School boards have broad powers to direct and control curriculums. Parental rights to direct and control the education of children do not extend to the selection of the curriculum.

Teacher Scenarios

Can teacher poll students about attitudes toward sex? Parents' suit says 'No!' 159

Parent wants 'friend' to take part in conference 159

Is school discriminating against non-minorities? 160

Drawing the line when parents demand too much of your time 160

Court Decisions

♦ A New Hampshire taxpayer organization accused a school board of using public resources to engage in one-sided advocacy regarding election matters. The organization sued the board and town in state court, seeking an order to halt the board from sending any mailings on election issues. The court denied relief, finding "the government may use public funds to endorse its own measures." A final judgment for the board and town was affirmed by the state supreme court. The organization and its chairman then filed an action against the town and board in a federal district court, adding new claims and new taxpayers as parties. One claim alleged the town did not permit the organization to link its website to the town website while others were allowed to do so.

The court noted that most of the claims had (or could have) been raised in the state court case. It applied doctrines of *res judicata* and collateral estoppel, which bar claims between the same parties that have already been considered. On appeal, the U.S. Court of Appeals, First Circuit, held the addition of three new taxpayers did not change the outcome. Federal courts must give state court judgments the same effect they have under state law. **The court held the government may "speak for itself" and may use other parties to say its message.** For that reason, the town's decision to disallow the taxpayers from linking to their website was permissible. No similar group was allowed to link to the website. The town did not turn its website into a designated public forum by linking to a community event site. As the lower court had correctly held the remaining claims were barred, the judgment was affirmed. *Sutliffe v. Epping School Dist.*, 584 F.3d 314 (1st Cir. 2009).

◆ Pennsylvania parents who participated in elementary school curricular activities were subject to the same restriction on promotion of messages in class as their children. **So a parent could be barred from reading a religious text to kindergartners.** *Busch v. Marple Newton School Dist.*, 567 F.3d 89 (3d Cir. 2008).

◆ An Anabaptist Mennonite parent protested Pledge of Allegiance recitations at his children's school by handing out flyers on a sidewalk near a district high school. The district rejected as inappropriate the parent's submission for an advertisement for "www.CivilReligionSucks.com" in the school yearbook purporting to offer "flag desecration products." His request to distribute flyers at an elementary school was also denied. After the district rejected the parent's request to place an advertisement in a school newspaper, he sued.

A federal court explained that while parents have a due process right to bring up their own children, states may condition that right. The parent's rights did not vest him with the authority to intervene and modify the school curriculum. The Pledge was being administered in a constitutional way. Students were allowed to remain quietly seated during recitations. Nothing required school officials to actively notify students of their rights to object. **The parent did not have the right to "dictate school curriculum to suit his own religious point of view."** And educators may exercise control over school publications, which are considered curricular. *Myers v. Loudoun County School Board*, 500 F.Supp.2d 539 (E.D. Va. 2007).

◆ A California volunteer mental health counselor developed a psychological assessment questionnaire as part of her master's degree program in psychology. The district agreed to survey first-, third- and fifth-graders and use the results for an intervention program to help children reduce barriers to learning created by anxiety, depression, aggression and verbal abuse. The counselor sought the consent of parents in a letter stating the nature and purpose of the questionnaire. She did not mention that 10 of the 79 questions involved sexual topics. After the survey was administered, parents learned of the survey questions about sex.

Students were asked if they felt they touched their private parts too much, could not stop thinking about sex, thought of touching others' private parts, had "sex feelings in my body," or washed themselves because of feeling "dirty on the inside." **Parents claimed they would not have consented to the survey had they known of these questions.** They sued the school district for constitutional privacy rights violations, and included a state law negligence claim. A federal district court dismissed the case, and the parents appealed. The U.S. Court of Appeals, Ninth Circuit, rejected the parents' claim to a fundamental right to control the upbringing of their children by "introducing them to matters of and relating to sex in accordance with their personal religious values and beliefs," and to exclusively determine when and how their children were exposed to sexually explicit subjects. Parents have a limited fundamental liberty interest to make decisions about the care, custody and control of their children. As they could not dictate the curriculum, the judgment was affirmed. *Fields v. Palmdale School Dist.*, 427 F.3d 1197 (9th Cir. 2005).

V. USE OF SCHOOL FACILITIES

Overview

Schools may establish reasonable rules governing the time, place and manner of speech on school property. As in religious speech cases, the reasonableness of these rules depends upon the type of forum established by the school. A "limited public forum" exists on property that is generally open for use by the public. Time, manner and place regulations regarding a limited public forum must be content-neutral and narrowly tailored to serve a significant governmental interest. They must also provide for ample alternative channels of communication.

A. Student Organizations and Demonstrations

Student First Amendment rights are not coextensive with those of adults. School demonstrations may be enjoined if they are materially disruptive or invade the rights of others. Many student group access cases interpret the federal Equal Access Act (EAA), 20 U.S.C. §§ 4071-4074.

The U.S. Supreme Court relied on K-12 school law precedents in holding that a state-affiliated California law college could deny official recognition to a Christian student organization because the group only accepted members who shared the organization's beliefs about religion and sexual orientation.

Teacher Scenarios

Does student have a right to use PA system?....161

Court Decisions

◆ Hastings College of Law allowed officially recognized Registered Student Organizations (RSOs) to use college communications channels, office space and email accounts. RSO events were subsidized by student fees. To gain RSO status, groups had to be non-commercial and comply with school policies, including a nondiscrimination policy. The Christian Legal Society (CLS) did not accept students whose religious convictions differed from its Statement of Faith, which affirmed belief in Christian tenets. The group also believed sexual activity should not take place outside marriage between a man and a woman. The CLS sought an exemption from the nondiscrimination policy, but Hastings found the group excluded students from membership based on their religion and sexual orientation. Hastings denied the request to recognize CLS as an RSO for noncompliance with its nondiscrimination policy. In a federal district court action against Hastings, the CLS asserted speech, religious free exercise and due process violations. The court upheld Hastings' policy. After the Ninth Circuit affirmed the judgment, the U.S. Supreme Court heard the case.

The Court held some restrictions on access to limited public forums are allowed. Regulations on speech are allowed only if they serve a compelling state interest. According to the Court, the CLS faced only indirect pressure to modify its policies. The group could still exclude any person for any reason if it decided to forgo the benefits of RSO recognition. Hastings' policy applied to "all comers." **Among the Court's findings was that an all-comers policy ensured a student was not forced to fund any group that might exclude her.** An all-comers requirement helped Hastings "police" its policy without inquiring into the reasons for restricting RSO membership. The Court found Hastings reasonably believed its policy encouraged tolerance, cooperation and learning among its students. While the CLS could not take advantage of RSO benefits, electronic media and social networking sites reduced the importance of RSO channels. As for the CLS's argument that Hastings had no legitimate interest in regulating its membership, the Court held Hastings could "reasonably draw a line in the sand permitting all organizations to express what they wish but no group to discriminate in membership." The policy did not distinguish among groups based on viewpoint, and the Court held it was "textbook viewpoint neutral." *Christian Legal Society Chapter of the Univ. of California, Hastings College of Law v. Martinez*, 130 S.Ct. 2971 (U.S. 2010).

◆ A group of Florida students sought official recognition of a gay-straight alliance club. They claimed their purpose was to promote tolerance and equality among students, regardless of sexual orientation or gender identity. They sought to create a safe, respectful learning environment for all students and to work with the school administration and other clubs to end prejudice and harassment. The principal denied approval of official recognition as a school club with access to school facilities on the same basis as other student clubs. The club sued, asserting that the school board had violated the EAA. A court explained that the EAA prohibits schools from denying equal access and fair opportunities on the basis of religious, political, philosophical or other content of speech that may be expected at meetings of student groups in limited open forums. The school board claimed the club was "sex-based" and that its speech presented a threat to school order. The court held that **the board did not offer any evidence to refute the club's assertion that it did not discuss sex**, let alone promote sexual activity. The court also rejected the board's claim that the club would interfere with its abstinence-based sex education curriculum. The court ordered the board to recognize the club and grant the privileges given to other student clubs. *Gay-Straight Alliance of Okeechobee High School v. School Board of Okeechobee County*, 483 F.Supp.2d 1224 (S.D. Fla. 2007).

In later activity, the court held the club had a tolerance-based message that did not materially or substantially interfere with discipline in school operations. To justify its refusal to recognize the club as a school organization, the school board had to show more than mere discomfort and unpleasantness associated with an unpopular viewpoint. Despite prevailing, the club did not demonstrate compensable injury, and it was awarded only $1 in nominal damages. *Gonzalez v. School Board of Okeechobee County*, 571 F.Supp.2d 1257 (S.D. Fla. 2008).

◆ An 18-year-old Virginia student distributed small anti-abortion flyers at school in his sophomore and junior years as part of a "Pro-Life Day of Silent Solidarity." No disruption was reported. As a high school senior, the student again handed out anti-abortion literature in school hallways and the cafeteria during non-instructional times. The principal called the student to his office to tell him he could only distribute the flyers before or after school. The student contacted a lawyer, and within a month, the district devised a rule for students who were not associated with approved student organizations or curricular programs. It gave them no option for distributing non-school materials during the school day. The student sued the school district for an order to prohibit the enforcement of the ban on distribution of his materials.

The court found that the rule virtually banned the circulation of all written communication during the instructional day. It held the district had to show that the student's speech presented a reasonable fear of materially disrupting class work, creating substantial disorder, or invading the rights of others. **There was no evidence that the student's anti-abortion literature would cause disruption in the school.** The district had acted with a remote apprehension of disturbance rather than a specific and significant fear of disruption. The student had distributed similar literature the two previous school years without disruption. The rule was unreasonable. The court granted the student's request for a preliminary order preventing the board from enforcing the rule. *Raker v. Frederick County Public Schools*, 470 F.Supp.2d 634 (W.D. Va. 2007).

◆ A Texas school board adopted a policy allowing non-curriculum-related student clubs to meet and use school bulletin boards and public address systems. It also had an "abstinence-only policy" banning all speech about sexual activity. A gay/straight club sought permission to post notices about its meetings and to distribute flyers at school and use the school's PA system. Club members addressed the board and stated that their goals were to educate and help the community, improve relations between heterosexuals and homosexuals, and "educate willing youth about safe sex, AIDS, hatred, etc."

The board did not act on the club's request, and the club was not allowed to post advertisements in school. Administrators turned down further requests to use school facilities, and club members sued for First Amendment and

Equal Access Act (EAA) violations. A federal district court held that **the district had a compelling interest in protecting student health and well-being and preventing recognition of groups based on sexual activity**. There was obscene material on the club's website. As club members failed to show that any other groups intended to discuss sexual content, they could not show discrimination against their viewpoint. The district was entitled to pretrial judgment on the First Amendment and EAA claims. The EAA does not limit a school's authority to maintain order and discipline on school grounds. The club's stated goals contradicted the district curriculum, and the superintendent was entitled to qualified immunity. *Caudillo v. Lubbock Independent School Dist.*, 311 F.Supp.2d 550 (N.D. Tex. 2004).

♦ A Kentucky high school's site-based decision-making council approved a proposal for a gay straight alliance (GSA) club. Students who opposed the GSA club protested, and many parents threatened to remove their children from the school system. The school board then voted to ban all non-curricular clubs. The principal let the GSA club use school facilities as an outside organization, but did not allow the club to meet in homerooms or before school in a classroom. Four other non-curriculum-related student organizations retained access to school facilities during this time. The GSA club and its members sued for an order requiring the board to afford it the same opportunity to use school facilities as other student clubs enjoyed. A federal district court rejected the board's argument that the other organizations were "curriculum related."

A school opens up a "limited open forum" if it allows even one non-curriculum-related student group to use its facilities. A club cannot be denied permission to meet at school during noninstructional time if others may do so. When a limited open forum has been created, a school may prohibit only meetings that materially and substantially interfere with school activities. Here, the school's treatment of the GSA club was a content-based restriction that was forbidden by the EAA. The board could not deny access to its facilities based on the uproar caused by recognition of the GSA club. *Boyd County High School Gay Straight Alliance v. Board of Educ. of Boyd County*, 258 F.Supp.2d 667 (E.D. Ky. 2003).

B. Non-Student Groups

Court Decisions

♦ Over time, Utah municipal officials accepted at least 11 monuments for display from private groups or individuals, including a wishing well, fire station, a September 11 monument, and a Ten Commandments monument. A Gnostic Christian organization called "Summum" sought to build a monument on public grounds containing its "Seven Aphorisms," or principles of creation. The organization stated that the Aphorisms had been handed down from God to Moses with the Ten Commandments, but withheld because the people were not ready to receive them. When the city declined Summum's request, the group sought a federal court order directing the city to permit its project.

The court denied the request, but the U.S. Court of Appeals, Tenth Circuit, held that the city had to allow the monument, as parks are traditionally considered public forums for speech. Appeal reached the U.S. Supreme Court, which held that **the First Amendment restricts government regulation of private speech, but does not regulate government speech**. The Court declared that government entities may "speak for themselves." Government entities may exercise the freedom to express their own views when receiving assistance from private sources when they deliver a "government-controlled message." Government speech must comply with constitutional provisions, such as the Establishment Clause, and the government was accountable to the electorate and the political process for its advocacy. When private speech was allowed in a public forum, the government could not place content-based restrictions upon private speech. In this case, the permanent monuments on display were "government speech" that the city could control. A "forum analysis" did not apply to the installation of permanent monuments on public property. The Court reversed the judgment. *Pleasant Grove City, Utah v. Summum*, 129 S.Ct. 1125 (U.S. 2009).

♦ Anti-abortion activists drove a truck around a California middle school, displaying enlarged, graphic images of early-term aborted fetuses. An assistant principal observed that some students became upset and felt that the pictures on the truck created a traffic hazard, so he contacted the sheriff's department. Two deputies arrived, detained the activists for about 75 minutes and searched their vehicles. Deputies talked with their supervisors about the legality of stopping the display. The assistant principal and a deputy instructed the activists to leave, after reading California Penal Code Section 626.8 to them. Section 626.8 prohibited a person from coming into school buildings or grounds where the person's "presence or acts interfere with the peaceful conduct of the activities of the school or disrupt the school or its pupils or school activities." The activists sued the deputies, the sheriff's department and assistant principal for violating their speech rights and for an unreasonable search and seizure.

A federal district court dismissed the case, and the activists appealed to the U.S. Court of Appeals, Ninth Circuit. The court agreed with the activists that the deputies and assistant principal applied section 626.8 unconstitutionally. **Peaceful public expressions of ideas cannot be prohibited because they may be offensive to others, or simply because bystanders may object.** Any disruption caused by the graphic display was a result of student reaction and discussion. Section 626.8 applied only to interference or disruption caused by the manner of a person's expressive conduct. The law could not be used to infringe upon the lawful exercise of protected speech. Thus, the judgment on the speech rights claim was reversed. While the deputies and assistant principal had violated the activists' speech rights, they were entitled to qualified immunity, since they made a reasonable mistake in believing that Section 626.8 applied. However, the deputies were denied immunity for the long detention of the activists. The investigation should not have taken more than the few minutes needed to check for outstanding warrants. *Center for Bio-Ethical Reform v. Los Angeles County Sheriff Dep't*, 533 F.3d 780 (9th Cir. 2008).

♦ A Montana speaker received $1,000 from a ministerial association to serve as the master of ceremonies at a religious rally held the evening after a school assembly. He claimed that the board reversed a decision to allow him to speak at the assembly in violation of the First Amendment. The U.S. Court of Appeals, Ninth Circuit, held that **the speaker had no protected interest in addressing a public school assembly**. He was not being paid by the board, and was thus not deprived of any valuable government benefit. The speaker later gave his speech off school grounds, and was paid by the ministerial association. No other federal circuit court had found that permission to speak at a school assembly was a valuable government benefit. *Carpenter v. Dillon Elementary School Dist. 10*, 149 Fed.Appx. 645 (9th Cir. 2005).

♦ The No Child Left Behind Act requires each local educational agency that receives assistance under the Act to provide military recruiters access to secondary student names, addresses and telephone numbers. The section, 20 U.S.C. § 7908, has a parental notice requirement. The Solomon Amendment, applicable to higher education institutions, has no such provision. In 2006, the Supreme Court held that law schools had to provide the military the same access granted to all other employment recruiters under the Solomon Act. It held that the broad and sweeping power of Congress to provide for defense included the authority to require campus access for military recruiters. **Congress was free to attach reasonable conditions to federal funding, and the Solomon Amendment regulated conduct, not speech.** *Rumsfeld v. Forum for Academic and Institutional Rights*, 547 U.S. 47 (2006).

VI. TEACHER SCENARIOS

Student plays ugly prank at talent show: What's teacher's best move?

Was cell phone joke funny – or offensive?

Teacher Kay Harris smiled as she watched her students perform in the school talent show.

"Hey! What are you guys up to?" she whispered to the boys who were laughing beside her. "Come on! Get ready, you're up next for the final act!"

Her students had done a fabulous job on the program. *Pulled it off without a hitch*, Kay thought as one of her best students, Brad Lane, walked to center stage.

He was a natural, delivering his monologue with a touch of humor.

In the audience, parents and students laughed at Brad's dramatic flair as he said the last line. "I just have one final message for you," he said, raising his hand up over his head.

Seemingly out of nowhere, a girl's voice gushed loudly, "Oh my gosh! I'm so horny!"

For a split second, the audience was silent, and Kay froze.

Damage control

Screeching laughter from students in the audience jolted Kay back to reality, and she jumped into action. She pulled the cord quickly, and the curtain fell.

When Kay stepped out from behind the curtain, her mind was racing. "I'd like to apologize to everyone in the audience," she said with as much grace as possible.

"Clearly, that was not the intended last thought our final performer wanted to leave you with."

"Again, I'd like to offer my apologies, and I hope you enjoyed most of our show," she said as she stepped behind the curtain.

Find the source

Kay went backstage, determined to find the girl who ruined the program.

Instead, she ran into Brad and his friends, who were laughing.

"No! Shut up, man," Brad hissed at one of the boys, glancing at Kay with a guilty look on his face.

"Brad," Kay said knowingly. "Why did you tell everyone to be quiet just now when I walked up?"

"I don't know," he said, shoving his hand into his hoodie pocket.

"What's in your hand?" she asked him.

Brad pulled his cell phone out of his pocket, and the other boys snickered again.

"I'm not letting this go, so you may as well tell me what's going on," Kay said.

Brad sighed, pushing a button on the phone.

Kay heard the crude girl again.

Another cell phone problem

"Let me get this straight," Kay said as her eyes narrowed. "That's a recording on your phone? You played that clip instead of saying the last line?"

Kay took Brad and his phone to the principal's office.

Brad was suspended.

Brad's parents sued, claiming his speech rights were violated. They said Brad's recording wasn't plainly offensive, and it didn't disrupt class time.

The teacher said she couldn't allow students to play offensive recordings during performances.

She asked the court to dismiss the claim.

Did it?

Decision: Yes, the court dismissed the claim.

Key: Even though Brad's recorded message wasn't played during class time, it was still played during a school program, the court pointed out.

The judge ruled the school correctly limited Brad's speech because the recording stored on his phone may have been offensive to parents and female students who attended the program.

Cite: *Walters v. Dobbins.*

Discussion points for teachers and principals:

It seems as if cell phones are causing more and more trouble as technology advances.

This teacher handled the situation correctly by:

■ Asking the student why the phone was funny instead of searching it, and

■ Sending the student (and his phone) to the principal's office.

Students embarrass school in public: What's the punishment?

But, they argue, 'We weren't in class at the time'

Principal Renee Rossi scanned the folder as she spoke: "Let's go back over this, just to be sure we have the facts."

"OK," teacher Jean Alston said. "As we agreed, I let my class out early to watch the Olympic Torch Relay in front of the school."

"You tied that to a history unit you were teaching, right?" the principal noted.

"Right," the teacher quickly confirmed. "I told them I'd be there, so they'd know I wanted them to attend and not just take off."

"And it was during the relay that the two students unfurled the banner?"

"Yes, they obviously had it planned well beforehand," the teacher noted. "It must have taken them a while to make that banner."

Recommends punishment

Looking once more at the file, the principal read from it: "'Bong Hits 4 Jesus.' That's what the banner said?"

"You can imagine my reaction," the teacher responded. "Everyone stopped to look at the banner. So I went over and grabbed it. Then I told the two of them that I was recommending punishment."

"Well, the parents are saying the kids had a right to display the banner," the principal said. "In fact, they may sue over it."

The parents did sue. Did the school win the case?

Decision: Yes. The school won when the U.S. Supreme Court said that allowing the banner would have sent the message that the school was not serious about its anti-drug message and the dangers of illegal drug use.

The school argued that the students were attending the parade as part of a school function and that the banner put the school in a bad light in the community.

The Court said the principal of the school reasonably determined that the banner would be interpreted by viewers as promoting illegal drug use.

The Court also rejected the students' claim that the case did not involve school speech. The relay was held during school hours, and it was sanctioned by the school principal as "an approved social event or class trip," the Court said. Also, the banner was directed toward the school, and it was plainly visible to most of the school's students.

Key: Deterring drug use is an important interest of schools.

Cite: *Morse v. Frederick.*

Sharpen Your Judgment

Badmouthing the principal: What students can – and can't – say

Ellen Holmes did a double-take when she read the sheet of paper the laser printer churned out.

"Everyone knows Principal Dobbs bought a boat with the money he stole from our activities fund."

Just as the teacher moved to pluck the sheet of paper from the printer, student Gary Oxford reached for the paper, too.

"That's mine, Ms. Holmes," he said. "It's part of what I'm doing for my personal-journal assignment."

The teacher placed the paper in her desk drawer and said, "Hold on, Gary. This may be for your personal journal, but that doesn't give you the right to libel Principal Dobbs, especially when you're using a school computer. Besides, what you've written isn't true. He doesn't even own a boat."

"That doesn't matter," the student insisted. "A personal journal is personal, and so is what I write in it."

The teacher ended up disciplining the student for using school resources to libel a staff member. But the student's parents fought the discipline in court, arguing invasion of privacy.

Did the discipline hold up in court?

Sharpen Your Judgment – The Decision

Yes. A court ruled the teacher could legally seize the paper and discipline the student for writing the message.

Students do retain their <u>reasonable</u> privacy rights in school, as well as protection from unwarranted search and seizure, the court explained. But the key here is the word "reasonable."

What's not reasonable? A student can't expect privacy when doing a legitimate school assignment, on school property and involving the use of school resources.

The court said, under those circumstances, no student could expect privacy or protection from search and seizure, particularly when the message produced tarnishes the reputation of a staff member and threatens to disrupt order and respect in the school.

The lesson of rights vs. limits

Of course, part of what you do as a teacher is inform students about rights and the limitations on rights.

This case illustrates one of those limitations. The right of free speech isn't absolute, though some students and parents may think it is.

Students should be made aware that no one is free to say and do whatever pops into their heads.

Cite: *Matos v. Clinton School.*

Did teacher go too far when silencing foul-mouthed student?

Balancing 'freedom of expression' with maintaining order

After the other students had left the classroom, Nicole Wiredale walked to the teacher's desk and said, "You wanted to talk to me."

Teacher Missie Ames nodded as she spoke: "Yes, Nicole. It's about your language in class."

"My language?"

"Several times now you've used obscene words and curses, and I've warned you about it," the teacher noted.

The girl replied, "Well, sometimes the other girls bother me ... "

"I understand," the teacher said. "That still doesn't give you the right to use that kind of language here. So I'm giving you a final warning. One more incident, and I'm going to recommend three days of internal suspension and a penalty on your grade."

The student responded with a sullen "OK" and left.

She ignores warning

Two days later, in the middle of a lesson, the teacher heard Nicole's unmistakable voice shout:

"You better get the %#&! away from me or I'm going to kick your %#&! into the middle of next week!"

The teacher took a deep breath and walked toward Nicole's seat to make sure the situation didn't get worse.

"That's enough now, Nicole," the teacher said calmly. "See me after class."

Then she continued with the day's lesson.

Parents' reply

"And now I think you'll understand why Nicole is being punished," the teacher wrapped up her explanation two days later in a meeting with the girl's parents.

The father spoke first: "You're a teacher, so you understand free-speech rights. I'm not condoning what Nicole said. I'm just asking if this doesn't strike you as a violation of her rights."

"Well, what would you suggest I do if all the students started talking that way in class?" the teacher asked. "How could I possibly maintain control?"

"First of all, it wasn't all the students who spoke out, just one," the father noted. "And I would think as a teacher you should be able to maintain control without violating the students' rights."

The teacher sensed she was being drawn into a debate that would never get to the goal of preventing Nicole from using obscene language in the classroom.

"I've spoken with our principal about this, and she agrees that we're taking the right steps here and that we're not violating anyone's rights," the teacher said.

"The punishment is going to have to stand so Nicole learns it's not OK to talk that way in class."

"Maybe it's not quite as simple as that," the girl's mother spoke up. "We're prepared to fight this legally if we have to."

The decision

Eventually, the parents filed a lawsuit insisting that the teacher had no right to silence their child.

The school argued in court that the need to maintain order superseded any free-speech rights of the student.

To overrule the punishment would result in chaos, the school insisted.

Did the court's decision side with the school?

Decision: Yes. A federal district court agreed the teacher had a duty to punish and stop the use of obscenity in the classroom.

The court said free speech is of course important, but in schools, it applies to political opinions or ideas about current events. To stifle or punish opinions would be a violation of free speech.

But random, angry obscenities in the classroom don't meet the standards of opinions and ideas, and aren't protected.

Cite: *Anderson v. Milbank School Dist.*

Discussion points for teachers and principals:

Courts have established a line in the classroom between what's protected speech and what can be curbed and disciplined:

■ Protected speech generally falls into the category of opinions and ideas, even when they're controversial or unpopular.

■ Not protected would be speech aimed at simply inflaming or at disrupting the education process.

Determining the difference between free speech and hate speech

What limits can a teacher set in the classroom?

After class, teacher Philip Offerman leafed through the sheets of paper his students had submitted containing topic choices for their oral essays on diversity.

One got his attention immediately: "Why Homosexuality is a Sin."

The teacher made a note to speak to Mara Hughes, the student who had submitted the topic.

'It's wrong'

"Mara, let's talk about your oral-essay assignment on diversity," the teacher began the next-day meeting. "Can you give me some idea of what you're going to say?"

"Sure, Mr. Offerman," the student nodded. "Basically, I'm going to say that homosexuals choose their lifestyle, that it can hurt them and others, and that God is going to punish them."

"What we're looking for in this assignment is some fact-based information about diversity," the teacher explained.

"For instance, you might pick out a person from history and explain how diversity affected that person."

"I think I understand," Mara replied. "But that's not what I want to do. I'd like to stick with the topic I gave you."

"Then I'm going to have to insist that you pick another topic," the teacher said. "I'll give you a little extra time to choose a new one and prepare your essay."

Mara frowned but said nothing as she stood up and walked away.

And the teacher was less than surprised when, a few days letter, Mara handed him a note from her parents: *"We'd like to talk to you about Mara's oral essay on diversity."*

The meeting

After everyone shook hands and exchanged greetings, Mara's father began:

"Our religious beliefs tell us that homosexuality is wrong, and that's what we've taught Mara."

The teacher nodded and said, "Of course I respect your beliefs, but here in school, we're obligated to place some limits on what students say about their beliefs."

"Why?" the mother asked.

"Well, what if a student said all Christians should be beaten up?" the teacher explained. "We certainly wouldn't allow that."

"All right, I understand," the father said.

"But our daughter isn't advocating violence or saying people don't have rights. She's just describing our beliefs about a certain type of behavior."

The mother added: "We've discussed this, and if you won't give in, we're prepared to go to court to protect our beliefs."

The decision

Arguing that the teacher and the school were attempting to deny their child's First Amendment rights, the parents sued to allow the girl to deliver the oral essay.

The school's lawyer said the assignment wasn't supposed to be opinion-based, and that the essay could offend some students.

Did the court's decision side with the school?

Decision: No.

A federal judge ordered the school to allow the student to present the oral essay, with some stipulations.

The guidance the judge offered:

- As long as the essay fell under the broad topic of "diversity," it fulfilled the requirements of the assignment. In a sense, the student was simply proposing that she did not believe all diversity was beneficial.

- Presentation of the essay should proceed so long as its content didn't advocate violence against or denial of rights to a particular group. To allow such expression could be illegal and disrupt the education process.

So, if the parents agreed with the judge's stipulations, the student could go ahead and make her presentation to the class.

Cite: *Hansen v. Ann Arbor Public Schools.*

Discussion points for teachers and principals:

Courts recognize that maintaining order and education sometimes means limiting what students say in the classroom. But most courts insist the limitation:

■ must have a clear, defined purpose that furthers rights and education goals, and

■ not be put in place just because someone might be offended; the limitation should involve protecting rights and safety.

Where to draw the line when students speak their minds

What are the limits on free speech in the classroom?

Teacher Diane Mallard had a packed class schedule that day, and couldn't afford any interruptions.

Unfortunately, that's exactly what she got as she was about to start the reading lesson – an interruption.

Diane noticed several students gathered around Sydney's desk. She walked over to check out what was going on.

"OK, everybody – back to your seats please," directed Diane as she moved closer to Sydney's desk.

"What's that?" Diane whispered to Sydney, pointing to a sheet of signatures.

"I'm protesting the circus trip we're going on next Friday. I think it's cruel to make animals do those circus tricks – so I'm asking everyone to sign my petition against the trip," answered Sydney.

"Sydney, please put that away now. I'll talk to you about it later," said Diane.

"Why? I'm just asking them to sign," Sydney said.

"I said we'll discuss this later, not now. Please put it away and get your book out so you can begin your quiet reading time," Diane instructed her in a firm voice. "We have a lot to get done today."

Sydney let out a sigh. Then she plopped the open book down on the desk and began reading.

At the end of the day, Diane spoke with Sydney privately.

"It's fine that you have an opinion, but you have to express it at the appropriate time."

Conduct OK

About three weeks later, Diane found a message in her mailbox from Principal Vicky Kanter asking her to stop by her office as soon as possible.

When her students went to gym class, Diane walked down to Vicky's office. The door was open.

"Hi, Vicky. Is this a good time?" asked Diane.

"Sure. Just give me a minute to wrap up what I'm doing," said Vicky.

Diane sat down. Vicky grabbed a manila folder on her desk and looked up at Diane.

'We have a problem'

"We have a problem. Sydney's parents are suing you and the school for what happened in your class a few weeks ago," said Vicky. "They don't think you had a right to stop Sydney from passing around her petition."

Diane thought for a moment and then spoke: "She wanted to pass it around during class time, and I told her that she couldn't."

"And what did Sydney do?" asked Vicky.

"She got a little huffy but then cooperated," said Diane. "Later, I sat down with her and explained why I stopped her from passing around the petition at that time."

The parents said the teacher and the school violated the student's right to free speech.

The school said the teacher had a good reason to stop Sydney from passing around the petition since it interrupted the class routine and the learning environment.

Was the teacher right?

Decision: Yes. The student had no right to circulate a petition during what was to be a quiet reading period.

Teachers may restrict a student's speech rights if there are legitimate reasons. In this case, the teacher needed to maintain order and move on with the planned activity.

Key: Diane took two important steps that protected her and the school from the charge of violating free-speech rights. She:

- controlled the classroom situation appropriately to minimize the disruption, and
- set the ground rules for a student's right to express her opinion – a right that has strict limits.

Cite: *Walker-Serrano v. Leonard.*

Discussion points for teachers and principals:

Students' free-speech rights vary depending on their grade level and the classroom circumstances.

To help you determine the extent of students' speech rights, consider:

■ the classroom situation and how allowing the student to express an opinion will affect the education process, and

■ the age and maturity of the student.

Verbal threat or free speech: What's teacher's best move?

4 need-to-know steps for teachers

Here comes another long week, teacher Kay Brown thought as the dismissal bell rang. She walked into the classroom where detention students were waiting.

"Happy Monday afternoon," Kay said to the students. "Put your phones and iPods away. It's time to get to work."

After a minute, the room was quiet and students were working on their homework.

That's what Kay thought anyway. But she was wrong.

When Kay looked up, she saw Miles Scott, a student, tapping the keys on his cell phone. "Miles, what are you doing?" Kay asked him patiently.

Miles didn't respond.

"OK, put your phone away," Kay said.

Texting continues

"No," Miles said as he tapped out his text message.

"Miles, you're not making this easy on either of us," Kay said. "Put the phone away right now, or I'm calling the SRO."

"Call him. I don't care," Miles said. Then in a whisper he muttered, "Bitch."

Kay called the SRO on duty, who confiscated the cell phone and took Miles to the office.

Later that week

Is there a full moon? We have a full house in detention today, Kay thought as she took a quick head count of students. "Happy Friday!"

"I'm going to the other detention room," Miles said loudly.

"Fine," Kay said. "But you have to wait for the SRO to walk you over. I'll call him now."

"That's stupid," Miles argued half-heartedly as he fiddled with his cell phone.

"No phones, Miles. You still have to follow the rules while you're in here," Kay said.

Miles stood up and yelled at Kay, "This is fucking bullshit."

He walked to the door, stopped to glare at Kay and said, "You're a fucking bitch."

The other students stared at the scene unfolding between Miles and Kay. She tried to stay calm. "Miles, do not leave. Wait for the SRO."

But as Miles walked out, he yelled at Kay, "Get away from me, you stupid fucking bitch!"

That afternoon, the principal suspended Miles for 10 days.

He was also convicted of two counts of abuse of a teacher.

Miles appealed, arguing his speech was protected by the First Amendment. A long legal battle ensued and went all the way to the state supreme court.

Was the conviction overturned?

The high court's take

Decision: The state supreme court reversed the finding that Miles was delinquent.

Key: In order to be found guilty of verbally abusing a teacher, Miles had to use "fighting words." That means his language would have to be likely to provoke "the average person" to retaliate for the verbal attack, the court noted.

The court acknowledged that Miles was very disrespectful, but muttering profanity isn't likely to make someone angry enough to retaliate, the court ruled.

The court also agreed that Miles showed disrespect to his teacher with his challenging stance and repeated cursing. But even that behavior isn't likely to make the average teacher "beat the student," the court explained.

The court pointed to the teacher's professionalism during the incident, which showed she wasn't motivated to retaliate against the student.

Lesson learned: The school's suspension was sufficient discipline for the reprehensible behavior – but legal action was not appropriate because Miles' speech didn't rise to the level of "fighting words," the court explained.

Cite: *In re Nickolas.*

Discussion points for teachers and principals:

When her student's behavior crossed the line, this teacher took the right steps. She:

■ remained calm

■ attempted to reason with the student

■ called the SRO when safety became a concern, and

■ referred the student to the office for discipline.

When students use their 'rights' to bully: Did T-shirt cross the line?

4 dress code takeaways for teachers

Teacher Beth Lee put her whiteboard in edit mode to add some last-minute notes to the lesson as her students walked into the classroom. "Have a seat, everyone," she said without looking up.

Students took their seats, but their loud chatter continued.

Wow, spring fever is in the air, Beth thought as she put the infrared pen into the bracket and turned around.

That's when Beth saw Claire Smith's T-shirt. "Be Happy, Not Gay" was written on the back.

"Claire, I'd like to talk to you in the hall, please," Beth said quietly.

"Sure, Ms. Lee," Claire agreed and followed Beth into the hallway.

Beth closed the classroom door and said, "We need to talk about your T-shirt."

'Can't I express my opinion, too?'

"Do you like it?" Claire asked.

Beth couldn't believe her ears. "Claire, you can't wear that T-shirt at school."

Claire looked surprised. "But why not?" she asked innocently.

"Claire, the message on your T-shirt might offend some of your classmates," Beth said. "You need to turn it inside out."

"You're worried about me offending them?" Claire asked. "Nobody cared yesterday when that gay club wore 'Be Who You Are' T-shirts. That offended me!"

"Claire, this is different," Beth tried to explain, choosing her words carefully. "Your shirt implies that being homosexual is a bad thing."

"It's supposed to," Claire said. "Gay people need to read the Bible and ask for forgiveness for their sins."

Clever – not OK

"Wait a – " Beth started to say, but Claire interrupted her.

"And besides, it's also a play on words. See? A long time ago, gay used to mean happy," Claire explained. "Get it?"

"I get it," Beth said, "but I don't think it's appropriate for school."

"Come on, Ms. Lee," Claire argued. "You're an English teacher. You should, like, give me extra credit for expressing myself in such a clever way."

"Are you serious? Or are you just being sassy?" Beth asked.

Without waiting for an answer, Beth said, "Go to the bathroom and fix your shirt."

"No," Claire said quietly. "I have the right to express my opinion just like the others did yesterday."

"If you don't change, we're going to get the principal's opinion on your T-shirt," Beth said.

"Fine!" Claire said as she whirled around on her heels and walked toward the office.

The principal's take

The principal agreed with Beth and said Claire's T-shirt wasn't appropriate to wear at school.

Claire refused to change, so the principal called her parents. They sued, claiming a violation of Claire's free speech rights.

Did they win?

Decision: A district court dismissed the claim, but on appeal, that decision was overturned.

Key: The appellate court disagreed with the school's assertion that the slogan "Be Happy, Not Gay" written on the T-shirt amounted to "fighting words."

To reach the level of fighting words, speech has to be so perverse that it's likely to cause the average person to want to retaliate, the court explained.

This speech commented on a controversial subject without promoting violence, the court ruled.

For this reason, the court concluded that this speech was "only tepidly negative" and did not amount to fighting words.

Cite: *Zamecnik v. Indian Prairie School Dist.*

Discussion points for teachers and principals:

Students don't give up speech rights at the school doors. Student speech is generally OK unless it:

- causes – or is likely to cause – a substantial disruption
- interferes with education or violates school rules
- constitutes privacy violations or is obscene, or
- promotes illegal drug use.

Freedom of expression or threat? When a school should take action

Parent argues teacher should have called him – not the police

Ellen Tidball nodded to her administrative assistant, took a breath and then answered the phone.

"Good morning, Mr. Langs," she said in an even voice. "This is Principal Tidball. What can I do for you?"

"Maybe you'll want to start by telling me why you got my son arrested over some silly drawings," Edward Langs muttered.

"We didn't consider them silly," the principal explained. "They're drawings of a student throwing a bomb at the school and shooting other students. As soon as one of the teachers saw them, she had to take action, Mr. Langs."

"We're aware our son has some problems and we're dealing with them," the parent went on in a calmer voice. "But did you really have to call the police?"

"That wasn't just about the drawings," she answered. "When the teacher searched his book bag, we found drug paraphernalia and a knife."

'Out of bounds'?

The parent's voice rose: "Let's talk about that for a minute. My son does those drawings at home, a friend of his brings them into the school and shows them to a teacher, and the next thing that happened is the teacher searches my boy and you call the cops."

"That's reasonably accurate," she noted.

"Then you realize you were way out of bounds, right?" he snapped back at her.

3 mistakes

Without waiting for her response, he continued.

"No. 1, he can draw anything he wants at home. We still have freedom of expression in this country.

"No. 2, you and the teacher performed an illegal search, since my son never brought those drawings into school.

"You can't just search him over some drawings someone else took into the school.

"And No. 3, you call the cops and have him arrested over this. That's ridiculous."

Mandated action

The principal waited a moment before replying, just to make certain he was done speaking.

"The fact that your son didn't bring the drawings in has no bearing on the problem. Once we became aware of them, we had to take steps to …"

"Why didn't you just call me?" he interrupted.

"The policy mandates that we search the student immediately to prevent violence," she explained. "And if we uncover anything suspicious, we're obligated to call the police."

What's the Constitution say?

"I find it amazing that you have a school full of teachers there, and not one of you has ever heard of the United States Constitution," he changed course.

"In our home, our son can draw anything he wants to, and that's protected expression.

"And then you and your teacher compound the problem by conducting an illegal search.

"A lawyer's going to have a field day with this one."

Eventually, the parent sued the school, arguing his son's rights were violated.

The district lawyer argued the principal and teacher were forced to take quick action to ensure no one in the school was hurt.

Were the principal and teacher right in this instance?

Decision: Yes. A court ruled they made the right decision by searching the student to prevent any possibility of violence.

In this case, the court noted, the safety of the school trumps the First Amendment – in the same oft-noted way that freedom of speech doesn't allow someone to yell "fire!" in a crowded theater.

Cite: *Porter v. Ascension Parish School Board.*

Discussion points for teachers and principals:

Normally, what a student writes, says and does at home can be considered under the protection of constitutional rights. There are exceptions, however, when the material:

■ finds its way into the school, no matter how it gets there, and

■ is of the type that appears to pose a threat to safety.

In those instances, searches by school staff and law-enforcement involvement are justified.

Was student expelled for a good reason – or just for being 'a kid'?

"Why can't you listen to sense?" Kai Simond's father asked the principal. "I thought the school board made me mad, but that was before I agreed to come talk to you and Kai's teacher."

"We understand Kai's expulsion is a blow, Jack," said Principal Alice Lee, glancing across her desk at teacher Julie Gunther. "But we want to make sure you understand why Julie did the right thing."

"Well, I don't!" said Jack. "The whole reason I'm this angry is because I don't think she handled it right at all."

Jack turned to Julie to ask, "What were you thinking when you dragged the resource officer into this? It was dumb of Kai to aim that pellet gun at Gail. But that's all it was – just dumb, not mean. You know it went off by accident."

"What Kai intended to do isn't really the problem here," said the principal.

"I disagree!" said Jack. "How can you punish him for an accident? Kai's friend asked him how the pellet gun worked and Kai was dumb enough to show him by aiming it at his own girlfriend's leg. Then it went off by mistake."

"But Jack," said Julie, "the real problem here is that Kai had a weapon at school."

"That's something a teacher has to report," added the principal.

"Weapon!" scoffed Jack. "Have you ever tried to do any damage with a dinky little air gun? It didn't do much more than startle Gail. That tiny welt on her leg was gone in two days. She's not even mad. And you know her dad testified at Kai's hearing to say what a great kid he is. Gail and her folks don't have a problem with it, but you dragged in the police!"

"It's our school resource officer's job to deal with things like this," said the principal. "Julie was right to alert him. And the only reason this happened at all was because Kai brought his air gun to school. He knew it was against the weapons policy."

Weapon or toy?

"How can a toy be against the weapons policy?" fumed Jack. "Nobody in their right mind would consider that pellet gun a weapon. Heck, Kai could have hurt Gail just about as bad with a rubber band.

"I know Kai acts without thinking sometimes," said Jack, "but he doesn't deserve this. He's high spirited. He's a kid."

Jack turned furiously to Julie. "Kai said he told you it was an accident! He said he was sorry and it wouldn't happen again. You're his teacher. You see him every day, and you know he's not a troublemaker. So, why on earth couldn't you cut him some slack? Haven't you ever made a mistake?"

Not waiting for an answer, Jack stood up. "This is just completely unfair and I am not going to put up with it."

Kai and his father sued, arguing the school couldn't expel Kai for having a weapon at school because his pellet gun wasn't a weapon.

They argued that if Kai was expelled simply because he had an object that could be used to hurt someone, other students had to be expelled for having pencils.

Did the court find for them?

Decision: No, the court affirmed Kai's expulsion.

The judge agreed Kai may not have meant to hurt his girlfriend, but also found the school board was right to decide a pellet gun is a weapon.

A pellet gun shoots plastic capsules at high velocity. This can cause serious injury. Some people have even been killed by a plastic pellet striking them in the eye.

Key: It's natural to have sympathy for parents whose kids have made a mistake that calls for serious discipline. And it can be hard to get blamed by parents who disagree with the school's policies. But as a teacher, it's your job to follow them – and to keep the safety of the students in mind.

Cite: *Picone v. Bangor Area School Dist.*

Discussion points for teachers and principals:

It can seem like things are out of hand when a third-grader is expelled for having scissors and a school play needs written permission from the district just to carry bows and arrows onstage.

But one school recently found a loaded handgun in a fourth-grader's backpack. Another just found a teen's gun because of its new rule – aimed at preventing concealed weapons – that forbids kids to wear coats indoors.

Was the school wrong when it expelled him for a 'harmless' threat?

Teacher shocked by lyrics in student's song

Sophia Litton tugged at her maternity blouse and kept control of her emotions as she spoke to parents Ann and Jack Markum.

"As John's teacher, I have to take all threats seriously. And what he recorded on this CD seems like a threat to me."

Jack shifted in his seat and replied: "Look, I agree that some of John's music is a little 'out there,' but he'd never hurt anyone. He has no record of violence."

"I don't want you to think this is personal, that the problem is just because John wrote lyrics that said, 'Kill Litton's baby,' Sophia winced. "I'd be bringing this up even if I weren't pregnant or been mentioned. Our policy says flatly we have to deal with all threats of violence."

'Overreaction'?

"Of course, we're embarrassed about this," the mother said. "And the idea that John would hand out copies of that stuff to everyone at school is terrible.

"But I agree with my husband that it's pretty much a harmless threat – that John would never hurt anyone. And are you sure you aren't overreacting just because you're named in the CD?"

Sophia kept her composure and said firmly: "I report the facts and make recommendations, but a decision about John won't be up to me. It's a matter of district policy on how to treat threats."

"Sure, but what you say and do will carry a lot of weight," the father argued. "And you have to agree, you're not impartial about this. That alone is enough for us to contest any discipline."

After a hearing, the school board expelled John, supporting the recommendation of the principal and the teacher. His parents hired a lawyer to reinstate the student. Did the school district and the teacher win?

Decision: Yes they did. The court said the teacher and the school acted properly by following policy and not making a judgment about whether the threat was "serious."

Key: The first reaction to any threat is to treat it as a possible first step to violence. Remember to follow policy, even if you're personally involved.

Cite: *Wilson ex rel. Geiger v. Hinsdale Elementary School Dist.*

Sharpen Your Judgment

Student willingly confesses to teacher: So why are parents suing?

Student Leah Raines burst into the classroom waving a note and shouting, "Miss Macon, Miss Macon, look what I found in the girls room."

Teacher Robin Macon examined the note scrawled in purple ink: *"A bomb will go off in this school tomorrow morning."*

Acting quickly, the teacher told the other students to keep working and then took Leah aside. "You found this in the girls room when you went there?" the teacher asked. "And did you see anyone else go in or out?"

"No, no one," the girl answered.

Then the teacher noticed a purple pen sticking out of the student's pocket, and asked, "Can I take a look at that pen?"

The teacher made a few doodles with the pen and saw that they matched the ink on the bomb note. Then she posed a question: "Leah, did you write that note? That's a crime, you know."

"OK, OK, I did and I was just kidding," the blushing student blurted.

When the student's confession led to an expulsion, the parents sued, arguing that a "questionable" confession and matching ink weren't enough to substantiate the punishment.

Did the school win the case?

Sharpen Your Judgment – The Decision

Yes, ultimately the school won.

An appeals court ruled the teacher had properly questioned the student, and the evidence was strong enough to support the punishment.

Initially, a lower court ruled the punishment couldn't be supported by the evidence and rescinded the expulsion.

But the appeals court noted:

- appropriate circumstantial evidence often was enough to prove guilt in criminal court, so
- the same standard held for making judgments on whether to discipline students.

To demand that the school follow a higher standard than do criminal courts was unfair, the court noted.

No 'iron-clad' standard

This ruling is good news for educators.

Courts generally recognize that teachers and administrators have to act on reasonable suspicions and less-than-conclusive evidence.

To rule otherwise, the court said, would tie their hands in almost any disciplinary situation.

Cite: *A.B. v. Slippery Rock Area School Dist.*

Did teasing of overweight student go too far?

Teacher had to make tough call on the spot

"You've gotta help me," said student Sam Niobe, pulling teacher Cal Bentzen to one side of the busy hallway.

"What's wrong?" asked Cal.

"I know I've got a weight problem. But ... But ..."

"Take a deep breath, Sam."

"This time they've gone too far. You won't believe what they wrote about me on the cafeteria wall."

"What?" asked Cal. "Show me!"

Sam led Cal to the empty cafeteria. One wall was covered with bright red letters, "How much do you think Sam weighs: More or less than two tons?"

A fast solution

"That's awful," said Cal. Just then the bell rang to signal the start of class. "Oh no. My T.A.'s not here today so I have to get to class. Quick, Sam, come here."

Opening a supply closet, Cal said, "It looks like it's written in lipstick. This cleaner and paper towels should take it off."

"Are you serious?" asked Sam. "The graffiti is bad enough – now I have to clean it up myself?"

"Lunch is next period, and I'm sure you want this off before then," reasoned Cal. "Listen, swing by my room when you're done and I'll write you a pass. Then we can talk to Vice Principal Hubert about this during lunch."

Sam removed the graffiti, but he sued the school for emotional distress. He said the school should have done the cleaning – not him.

Did he win?

Decision: No. Under these circumstances, it was OK to ask Sam to clean the wall.

The judge said the teacher took reasonable steps to remove the graffiti once he saw it.

Sam claimed the teacher knew that making him clean off the graffiti would deeply upset him.

But the judge said the only predictable way the teacher could have intentionally hurt Sam would have been if he left the graffiti on the wall.

Key: Teachers aren't expected to be perfect, they just need to act reasonably under the circumstances – and Cal did here.

He was in a tight spot because he couldn't leave his class unsupervised but knew the graffiti had to come down fast – before other students had a chance to read it and add to Sam's shame.

Asking Sam to clean the graffiti was a reasonable way out of this bind.

Cite: *Dawson v. Grove Public School Dist.*

Teased student loses temper and threatens to 'pull a Columbine'

Teachers know student was arrested for guns. What should they do?

"Wasn't yesterday's presentation great?" teacher Millie Gant asked teacher Lucy Alvarez as they monitored the library during lunch.

"Yes," said Lucy. "The speaker really got his tolerance message across. And he was so funny with the student volunteers."

Millie chuckled. "Especially that skit where he had Kathy play Britney Spears and Jody play Osama bin Laden."

Lucy frowned. "But you know what? Everybody was calling Jody 'Osama' before class today – and he looked like he was getting really fed up."

Enough is enough!

Just then, they heard a student call, "Hey, everybody! It's Osama!"

The teachers looked up to see Jody stop and scowl at a table of students.

"Give it a rest already," said Jody.

"Can't take a joke – huh, Osama?"

"Stop it!" roared Jody. "Stop calling me Osama – or I'll pull a Columbine!"

The students at the table froze. Lucy started toward Jody, but Millie grabbed her arm. "Be careful," she whispered.

Teachers make the safe choice

"I've known Jody for years," said Lucy. "I'll talk to him. He'll listen to me."

"No," said Millie. "You'd better take this seriously. Don't you remember Jody was arrested for having a gun last year? I think we should call the office instead."

They did, and administrators talked to Jody. As his school record was clean and he was graduating soon, they suspended him instead of expelling him. But Jody sued, claiming this violated free speech. Did it?

Decision: No, Jody made a threat that the school had a duty to take seriously.

Key: After tragedies like Columbine, it's important to make sure you're on top of the emergency procedures you need to follow – such as who to call if you feel it's not safe to approach a student.

Cite: *Johnson v. New Brighton Area School Dist.*

Handling parents who want to 'make a deal' for special treatment

What happens when they insist, 'You made a promise'?

"You're no cop," parent Ross Geiger shouted on the other end of the phone. "Who are you to question my son like some criminal?"

"Let me explain the circumstances," teacher Ben Alvarez said in an even voice. "Someone stole an iPod from another student's backpack. Your son Alex was one of only three students in the room at the time. I simply asked him if he knew anything about who took the iPod."

"He said he didn't do it, right?"

"That's what he said," the teacher replied. "And we really can't say for sure what happened to the iPod ..."

"Let me tell you something," the parent interrupted. "Anything like this comes up again, you let me know before you question Alex so I can consult with my lawyer. Understood?"

"I understand, but ..." the teacher said just before the parent hung up.

Another problem

A week later, a student approached the teacher and said, "Mr. Alvarez, someone stole my lunch money. I'm pretty sure it was Alex Geiger. And he wouldn't give it back to me when I asked him for it. He said, 'I'm keeping the iPod, and I'm keeping your money, too.'"

"How much money was it?" the teacher asked.

"A five-dollar bill," the student said in a low voice.

With that, the teacher approached Alex Geiger and said, "Alex, we have a problem with some missing money, and I'd like to talk to you about it."

The boy got a panicked look as he blurted out, "I was only playing. I wasn't going to keep the money."

He then dug into a pocket and pulled out a five-dollar bill while whispering a hoarse "here."

Parent's reply

The next day, at a tense meeting in the assistant principal's office, Ross Geiger thrust a finger at Ben Alvarez and said, "You did exactly what we agreed you wouldn't do. You lied to me on the phone."

"Lied to you?" the teacher said.

"That's right, lied," the parent raised his voice. "You said you'd contact me if there was ever an incident and my son was suspected.

"Instead, you went right ahead and questioned him. And now you're recommending he be punished for theft?"

Assistant principal Maria Macon spoke up: "Your son did admit to stealing the money. We don't have much choice about punishing him. Our policies are clear about that."

"That's not the point," the parent responded. "Your teacher agreed he wouldn't interrogate Alex without contacting me, so my lawyer could get involved."

"I'm not trying to split hairs here, but I never agreed to that," the teacher maintained. "You may have made that request. That doesn't mean I said OK."

"You think you can get away with weasel-wording?" the parent said as he stood up. "Now my lawyer is going to get involved."

The decision

The parent sued the teacher and the school for (a) questioning the student without informing him of his rights and (b) reneging on an agreement to contact the parent.

The school argued that the teacher had a duty to question the student and that even if there had been an agreement, it didn't represent a contract between the school and the parent.

Did the school win?

Decision: Yes. A judge said the teacher was well within his authority to speak to a student suspected of theft.

The judge also noted that the existence of an agreement between the parent and the teacher was in doubt.

But even if an agreement had existed, it didn't relieve the teacher of his duty to act on what was clear suspicion.

Cite: *T.M.M. ex rel. D.L.M. v. Lake Oswego School Dist.*

Discussion points for teachers and principals:

Some parents believe they can cut informal, even unstated, "side deals" about treatment of students. To discourage the perception:

■ Keep parents aware of the school's rules and policies, and that fair treatment obligates you to follow them.

■ In language that's as clear as possible, inform parents that there can be no binding agreements that exempt children from the rules.

Student blog causes big problems for school – Can they discipline?

School may have violated student's free speech in blogosphere

Student council sponsor Pat Fentiss looked around the library table at the council members' tense expressions.

"I know you're upset we've had to postpone the Battle of the Bands," said Pat. "But Mr. Green can't be in charge of the tech side this year with his broken arm."

"Let's hire a pro," urged student Emma Bent. "Then we can still have it as planned."

"That's not how it works," said Pat. "There are procedures the principal has to follow."

"Great," moaned Emma. "Bureaucracy. So it'll take forever and all the bands will cancel. But maybe that's the point."

"What do you mean?" asked Pat.

"The principal *hates* rap. So why not just drag out the paperwork until the whole nasty 'noise fest' disappears?"

"That's a creative conspiracy theory," said Pat dryly, "but it's not what's actually going on. The principal was here until midnight last night, trying to get band night back on track.

"The problem is she's been flooded with calls and e-mails ever since we announced the postponement. That's making it hard for her to even get to the real problem. So, she wants me to tell you we need your help to calm things down. As student leaders, we know you'll set a good example."

"Set a good example?" echoed Emma. "That sounds like a code. What's the real message – 'Shut up and do what you're told'?"

"It's no code," said Pat. "You've known all along that supporting the school goes with class office.

"And right now we need your help in letting other students know we're moving as fast as we can to set a new date."

Emma blogs

That night at home, Emma uploaded this message to her blog:

"They CLAIM they cancelled Battle of the Bands because the only cool teacher in this sorry district busted his arm. Like nobody else could do the tech stuff! What a LAME excuse to postpone all that awful 'noise' ... indefinitely. Let the principal know YOU'RE ON TO HER. Here's her e-mail and phone number. Let your voice be heard!"

Principal lets her voice be heard

The next day, the calls and e-mails to the principal doubled. After several people said they were letting their voices be heard as Emma Bent suggested, the principal had a look online. Later, she called Emma to the office.

"Hi, Emma," she said, raising her voice to be heard over the phones ringing in the outer office.

"Last night, an English teacher at the middle school agreed to be our techie for band night. It'll be held on the 20th – in case you want to announce that on your blog."

"You read my blog?"

"Yes. So did Ms. Fentiss. We've talked. Instead of helping us cool things down, you spread lies and encouraged people to take me on.

"That's not behavior we can put up with from student council members. We've decided you can't run for reelection."

Emma sues

Emma and her mother sued, saying the school violated Emma's rights by disciplining her for off-campus speech. Did it?

Decision: No.

Since Emma's blog created such a foreseeable risk of disruption to work and discipline at school, it didn't matter where she created it.

Also, being on the student council is a privilege. The school can take it away if students don't comply with the obligations that go with it.

Key: This teacher was direct in explaining council members' duties. There are limits even on protected speech, and this teacher was doing her job when she pointed out an important one to her students.

Cite: *Doninger v. Niehoff.*

Discussion points for teachers and principals:

Educators disagree about how much "dissidence" student leaders should be allowed to voice.

■ Some believe openly criticizing the administration is disloyalty that hurts discipline and spirit.

■ Others point out that the First Amendment was enacted to keep the establishment from becoming oppressive. They think open criticism teaches students to be engaged citizens.

Did student really harass principal by writing about her on MySpace?

Student has to go to delinquency hearing for criticizing school online

"You had no right to read my posts on Erin's MySpace page," said student Jamie Dease. "You're not on her 'friends' list!"

"No," said Principal Britta Bay, "but a 'friend' gave a print-out to Ms. Gonzalez." She nodded at the teacher sitting by Jamie. "And anyhow, Jamie, this is supposedly 'Principal Butt-a Bay's' page – not Erin's."

"It was just a joke," said Jamie. "I know I wrote mean stuff and used bad language, but you shouldn't have seen it!"

"But what about your group page, Jamie?" asked teacher Reya Gonzales softly. "It's not private. Anyone can see it."

"I know," said Jamie. "And that's why it's so different from what I wrote on the 'Butt-a …' I mean, on Erin's page."

The principal sighed and picked up a print-out from her desk. She read aloud: "'Erin got the whole 'blanking' book thrown at her for a harmless joke! She's expelled, grounded, her mom took her laptop and now she has to go to court. This whole 'blanking' school is full of over-reacting 'blanking' idiots!'"

"Oh," said Jamie. "Well. Sorry about the swearing, but that is what I think."

"Jamie, this isn't acceptable and I'm afraid there are going to be consequences."

A prosecutor brought delinquency charges against Jamie, and a judge found she'd broken the law: intentionally harassing the principal by "transmitting indecent or profane words" that weren't "legitimate communication."

The case went all the way up to the state supreme court. What did it decide?

Decision: Jamie wasn't delinquent.

Jamie didn't intend the principal to read the first post. It was "friends only," so she thought the principal would never see it. And despite the swearing, her second post was a "legitimate communication" about what Jamie saw as an unfair punishment.

Key: Students often show other students' posts to teachers first. If it's a threat or likely to disrupt school, teachers need to pass them along to the office ASAP.

Cite: *A.B. v. State of Indiana.*

Student suspended for fake online 'profile' of principal

He claims discipline for posting violated his free speech rights

"Bad news, Barb," said teacher Vince Dugliosi, coming into the vice principal's office.

"Now what?" she asked.

"Another fake MySpace profile of Principal Chao," said Vince.

"No!" she cried. "That makes three!"

"Yup," said Vince grimly. "When I came into the computer lab, the kids were all huddled around a screen, giggling. I got there before they could shut it down. And when I saw it, I really saw red."

"Is it worse than the others?" asked Barb apprehensively.

"It's just as disrespectful!" said Vince angrily. "Just as insulting."

"I am going to hate ruining his day with this," said Barb, shaking her head. "What did you do when you saw it, Vince?"

"Somehow, I kept my cool. Even when Bill let it slip that Elyan posted it."

"Oh, not Elyan again!" moaned Barb. "Did he use a lab computer?"

"No," said Vince. "I just checked the logs. But it turns out kids have looked at all three fake profiles from the lab."

"Did you have any trouble getting them back to their seats?" asked Barb.

"No," scowled Vince. "They acted like nothing had even happened!"

"They don't care," said Barb. "But I think it's time to let them know we do."

Elyan was suspended for posting insulting remarks online about the principal. His parents sued, saying this violated his free speech rights. Did it?

Decision: Yes. To justify a suspension, the fake profile had to cause a serious disruption at school. It didn't. The school hadn't even realized students had been looking at the profile on school computers.

It also mattered that Elyan didn't create it at school. Schools have much less authority over off-campus speech.

Key: It's understandable to want to come down hard on disrespect for a colleague. But you can't suppress student speech just because you find it offensive.

Cite: *Layshock v. Hermitage School Dist.*

Managing tricky dress code issues: What teachers can and can't do

Court rules on whether accessories are included in dress code

Teacher Olivia Gray watched as students dawdled down the hallway.

She understood that it wasn't easy for students to get excited about lessons when the holiday break was right around the corner.

Olivia stood at her classroom door and coaxed students inside. While they settled into their seats, she passed out the tests she had graded the night before.

She held Lisa Mead's test patiently, waiting as the student dug through her purse looking for a pencil.

When Lisa found the pencil and hung her purse on the back of her chair, Olivia noticed the Confederate flag embroidered on the denim bag.

Really? Not today, Olivia thought.

She leaned down and whispered, "Lisa, I'd like to speak to you in the hall."

Purse violates dress code

"Yes, Ms. Gray?" Lisa asked politely as they stepped into the hall.

"Lisa, your purse violates the dress code," Olivia said. "Go to the office."

"I don't get it. I'm not wearing my purse," Lisa pointed out. "I don't see how it violates the dress code."

"Well, that's a technicality," Olivia said. "The Confederate flag is banned in the dress code – and I'm sure accessories are included."

"This is ridiculous," Lisa argued. "What's wrong with my purse?"

"Many people think the Confederate flag is a racist symbol," Olivia explained.

"I don't think it's racist," Lisa countered. "My ancestors fought in the Civil War. This flag is a symbol of my heritage."

"I see your point," Olivia began, choosing her words carefully in an attempt to resolve the situation without a headache.

"But we've had fights in school over the Confederate flag and race," she continued. "And we don't want to offend anyone or cause any fights, right?"

Why are other symbols OK?

"I don't care about hurting everyone's feelings. What about me?" Lisa shot back as her voice rose an octave. "I'm offended!"

"I'm forced to look at Malcolm X and 'Rainbow-pride' T-shirts," she continued. "I've even seen a Mexican flag! So what about my rights? Where do I fit in?"

Olivia knew Lisa was getting very upset. "I think we should go to the office and figure this out."

The principal explained that the Confederate flag had caused serious disruptions at school.

The options

Lisa had two choices: She could leave her purse in the office until the end of the day – or her parents could pick it up right away.

Lisa refused both options, and the principal said the alternative was to be sent home for the day. She chose to be sent home.

Lisa's parents sued, claiming the school violated her speech rights and her right to equal protection.

They said Lisa was disciplined for violating the dress code while other students were allowed to wear clothing with "equally inappropriate" symbols.

The school asked the court to dismiss the charges. Did it?

Decision: Yes, the court dismissed Lisa's claim.

Key: Two key factors swayed the judge. First, school officials can limit students' speech if they have a reasonable belief that the speech will cause a disruption. Here, they pointed to previous fights.

And second, although Lisa's parents claimed other students wore "inappropriate" symbols without being punished, they couldn't show that those symbols caused a disruption at school.

Cite: *A.M. ex. rel. McAllum v. Cash.*

Discussion points for teachers and principals:

Dress codes are getting trickier than ever. It's a good idea to have a specific plan ready when issues pop up. Try this three-step plan:

- Explain why rules are in place.

- Suggest ways to "fix" the problem, such as removing the item from sight.

- When in doubt, send the student to the office for a second opinion.

Student club claims school had no right to censor its poster

On her way out of the vice principal's office, teacher Pam Felder's feet were dragging. She headed down the hall toward a meeting of the club she sponsored.

Usually she looked forward to these meetings. But today she had to explain to the kids why the vice principal was about to take their Conservative Club's poster down from the lobby.

"Hello," she said, trying to sound cheerful as she walked into the classroom. "Why don't we settle down and get started, because I have something to -"

Just then, Joe burst into the room. "What's the deal?" he asked. "Mr. Kanto's taking down our poster!"

"What's going on now?" yelled a student in the back.

"Relax," said Pam. "Quiet down and I'll explain. I just talked to Mr. Kanto about this and -"

"Don't even bother me with his excuses," blazed Joe. "I'm sure he fed you some kind of 'fair' reason for this. But you know the real reason is because we believe in staying the course in Iraq. Not a popular opinion at this school! You know this is just Kanto's way of shutting us up."

"I know nothing of the kind," said Pam calmly. "But I will agree you kids have stirred up controversy with some of your views, and I know that hasn't always been easy."

"Right," said Joe angrily. "Like the French teacher calling us hatemongers." The other students gave a rumble of agreement. "Or the coach saying we were a bunch of intolerant little -"

"OK, Joe," said Pam. "No point getting us all worked up over that again. Here's our chance to prove how tolerant and understanding we are. I know you'll get why the poster had to come down once I explain."

"Oh, let's hear it," sighed Joe.

"It's because our sponsor club's national Web site is on the poster. The problem is one of the links from that site."

"That link goes to a site that has films of terrorists executing hostages in Iraq."

"What!" cried Joe. "They can't even stand to face the reality of what terrorists are really like? Why we have to fight this war, have to -"

"Joe, please," said Pam. "Your classmates' parents don't want them exposed to that kind of violence. And neither do I," she added.

"But they show violent liberal films at school all the time!" cried Joe. "*Fahrenheit 9/11*! *Schindler's List*, for gosh sakes. But of course those films support a liberal agenda, so naturally they allow them in school."

"Joe," said Pam patiently, "there's a huge difference between a Hollywood movie and real footage of murders."

"Oh, it's always different when Mr. Kanto gets to decide," Joe muttered.

Joe sued the school, arguing its objection to violent film content was only an excuse to censor his political speech. Joe also claimed the school only allowed liberal views.

Did the judge agree to the school's request to dismiss the case?

Decision: No, a trial was needed.

Joe's evidence suggested his club's poster might have been taken down for political reasons.

First, several students told the judge teachers were openly hostile to the Conservative Club's views. Second, the school had shown liberal films despite their violent content – such as *Schindler's List* and *Fahrenheit 9/11*.

Key: More and more schools are wrestling with difficult problems posed by controversial student clubs. You might find yourself the sponsor of an unpopular club – or on the other side, arguing: "A club like this doesn't belong at school."

But no matter whether you approve or disapprove of a club's mission, each club the school allows has to be treated the same. As this scenario demonstrates, even an appearance of unfairness can lead to a lawsuit.

Cite: *Bowler v. Town of Hudson.*

Discussion points for teachers and principals:

Encouraging students to express themselves is important – and you can help them learn to communicate well by suggesting they:

■ research the issues first

■ come up with convincing arguments

■ listen to opponents' points before responding, and

■ keep the debate focused on issues, not personalities.

Religious freedom: Setting limits on what students can say in class

Parents insist teacher went too far in rejecting child's work

Before school started, Addie Gopal divided the students' construction-paper signs into two stacks on the office table.

"OK, I'll bite," fellow teacher Cam Wilson laughed as she walked in. "Why two stacks of signs?"

Addie explained: "On the right are the ones I'm allowing the students to hang in the classroom as part of our 'brightening up' project. On the left are the ones that won't get hung.

"Some of them are just inappropriate for school."

"For instance?" Cam asked.

"Some borderline obscenity, objectionable song lyrics," Addie answered, "plus religious themes – quotes from Scripture and that kind of stuff. I expect my decisions won't be popular with the students, but I'm going to give the rejected ones a chance to do new signs."

A week later she found herself explaining one of those decisions in the office of principal Leah Kemp.

The confrontation

"OK, Addie," the principal began, "tell me about the conversation with Sophia Clark over the signs she put together for the classroom."

"I guess it began when I looked at the content of the signs. I have them here," Addie said as she held them up for Leah to see.

Do unto others as you would have them do to you.
Luke 6:31

A house divided against itself cannot stand.
Mark 3:25

"I told Sophia I was sorry we couldn't use her signs because of their religious content," Addie said as she put the signs down.

"She said that wasn't fair, that I was picking on her because of her religious beliefs."

Others treated the same

The principal made a few notes and then spoke as she looked up: "But Sophia's signs weren't the only ones you rejected, right?"

"That's right," the teacher nodded. "There were several others that I rejected because I thought they were inappropriate for the classroom. I told each of the children why and, as with Sophia, I gave them a chance to do the project over."

The principal asked: "But none of the other rejected ones had religious themes?"

"Correct," Addie replied.

"And Sophia was the only one who refused to re-do her sign?"

"That's correct, too," Addie said. "She was very firm about refusing. And since it was an extracurricular project, I didn't press the issue."

"I guess you know by now that her parents *are* pressing the issue," the principal said. "Their lawyer contacted the district and said they're filing suit for denial of religious freedom and First Amendment rights.

"It looks as if we're going to fight this one in court."

The decision

Were the principal and the teacher right in this instance?

Decision: Yes. A court ruled in favor of the school because:

- Teachers need control over what's in the classroom to maintain an atmosphere that doesn't distract from learning, and
- A classroom wall is considered a "nonpublic forum" that doesn't fall under the First Amendment.

Be aware that the second part of the ruling – the nonpublic forum – was the key to victory in this case.

In other cases of this type, rulings have gone against the schools because the site of the writing or other expressions was considered a public one.

For instance, a sidewalk outside the school could be a public area open to expression in the form of signs or speech.

Cite: *Bannon v. School District of Palm Beach County.*

Discussion points for teachers and principals:

Teachers can decide which views can be expressed by students in the classroom, no matter if those views are spoken, written or in drawings. Just double-check to be sure:

■ All students receive the same opportunities to express themselves, and

■ Students understand what types of expression are considered inappropriate for the classroom.

Students feel threatened by his fictional story: Can he be punished?

Writing assignment becomes source of controversy

The words on the page jumped out at teacher Mitch Laska.

"Then Jake took out his knife and stabbed Cynthia and Jeremy."

Student Cynthia Abrams interrupted, "Jake gave copies of that paper to Jeremy and me, and it really creeped us out."

Naming names

Later that day, Mitch Laska began: "Jake, let's discuss your creative-writing assignment for my class."

"Sure, Mr. Laska," Jake replied. "What about it?"

"It contains some violent images, which bother me a little, but there's something else that bothers me more."

"Like what?" the student asked.

"All of the first names in the story are the same as those of students in this class, including you."

"Well, maybe I wasn't so creative when it came to that," Jake explained. "I just couldn't come up with other names."

"OK, but it's no secret you don't get along with Cynthia and Jeremy," the teacher noted. "So it seems more than coincidental that you have a character with your name stabbing two other characters named 'Cynthia' and 'Jeremy.'"

The boy's voice took a harder edge: "I told you I just stuck some names in there."

"Maybe so," the teacher said, "but I think I'm going to have to refer this to the principal for a decision about taking disciplinary action. Other students feel threatened by it."

When the school brought disciplinary action against Jake, his parents sued for violation of First Amendment rights.

Did the school win?

Decision: Yes. A judge said the school was obligated to take action when a student made an obvious threat.

Key: A threat of violence is almost always legal motivation for investigation and action, but especially so when the threat seems aimed at specific people.

Cite: *D.F. ex rel. Finkle v. Board of Educ. of Syosset Cent. School Dist.*

Sharpen Your Judgment

When can school 'censor' student newspaper?

Principal Jerome Procter handed the sheets of paper to the parent while saying, "This certainly wasn't what we had in mind when we started the student newspaper."

"Maybe not," parent Heidi Flagler replied as she took them. "But when you encourage students like my daughter to be 'journalists,' you have to live with the consequences. Besides, what did she do that was so awful?"

"Open criticism of the board, taking sides in a lawsuit against the district," he replied.

"This story your daughter wrote goes over the line in my opinion and in the opinion of the paper's faculty adviser."

"That's just it – a matter of opinion," she countered. "With your permission, this paper gets distributed to the community. And they've covered controversial subjects concerning the town before."

"As administrators, it's up to us to make the call on this," he explained. "We can't let it go."

"Then I guess I'll have to see what my lawyer says," she announced as she got up.

The student's parents sued the district for censorship. The district argued it had final approval of the content. Did the district win?

Sharpen Your Judgment – The Decision

No, the district lost when a judge ruled the administrators didn't have the authority to kill the story in the student newspaper.

Normally, the judge explained, a student newspaper isn't considered a public forum and operates under the authority of administrators and faculty.

The difference in this case? By allowing and encouraging public circulation of the newspaper – beyond the borders of the school – and coverage of controversial subjects, school officials:

- placed the paper in the public forum, and
- lost the authority to control content.

Administrators can modify stories to ensure accuracy and avoid libel, but out-and-out censorship in such cases won't fly.

Consider two rules

This case sends a clear warning about student newspapers. In summary, the school retains control of the content if:

- the paper has limited circulation mainly within the school and among the student population, and
- it covers stories mainly about in-school topics and is part of the education process.

Cite: *Dean v. Utica Community Schools.*

Where to draw the line when your students speak their minds

How should teacher handle student's in-class protest?

Teacher Katya Prinski wanted to get to school extra early – so naturally hit every red light on the way. Her lesson plan was derailed the previous day by a lively debate on abortion. She needed to jump right in today and make up for the lost time.

But when she got to class, the students were smirking and pointing to student Marc Ferrier. A strip of red duct tape was over his mouth and he wore a red shirt that said: "Pray to End Abortion."

More potential disruption

It looks like we're dealing with more of this today, thought Katya. Out loud, she said, "Good morning" and walked over to put her bag by her desk. "Ted and Mahalia, please put your answers to yesterday's questions on the board while I talk to Marc in the hall."

"It'll be a one-sided chat," joked one student. The others laughed.

"Settle down," said Katya. "I'll be back in five minutes and expect to see answers on the board and everybody ready to discuss them."

Student claims right to protest

In the hall, Katya asked, "Could you take the tape off your mouth and tell me what all this is about, Marc?"

Marc peeled off the tape and said, "It's a protest. Kids all over the country are doing it today. There's a Web site with information about the protest. According to the Web site, we students have a right to do this."

Student explains

"A right to do what, exactly?" asked Katya.

"Tape our mouths to remind people abortion silences babies. And wear the sweatshirt and hand out flyers. But teachers can make us take off the tape to answer questions in class and stuff."

"Whoa," said Katya. "Back up, Marc. Leaflets? You have leaflets?"

"Yeah. I handed out a bunch already. I'll hand out more later."

But there's a rule about leaflets

"Did you clear that with the principal?" asked Katya.

"Of course not!" said Marc. "He's not my minister. He can't say a thing to me about my religion."

"No," agreed Katya. "But it's a school rule that he needs to OK leaflets in advance. He has to make sure they're not obscene or illegal or likely to start fights. I'll write you a pass. You can go talk to him now."

But the principal refused to OK Marc's leaflets on the spot. He needed more time to consider them. Because of this, Marc couldn't pass out any more for that day's protest.

Can school set limits?

When the next protest was coming up, Marc's parents sued. They asked the judge to order the principal to allow Marc's leaflets.

The principal said Marc could only pass out leaflets in the cafeteria, not the halls. But the court found that violated Marc's rights because his leaflets weren't likely to disrupt the school.

The principal appealed. Did the court agree Marc's rights were violated?

Decision: No. The lower court used the wrong legal standard. Instead of disruption, it should have looked at whether the school's time, place and manner rules about handing out leaflets were reasonable – and they were.

Key: The Web has made it easier to "rally the troops" for student protests on sensitive issues, like abortion and gay rights. The Web sites provide online instructions, flyers to print out and clothing with slogans for students to order.

Aided by the power of the Internet, organizers of protests like the one described in the above case are able to reach almost all students – including yours. These protests are regularly scheduled during the year. If you haven't done so already, talk to your administrators about how you would respond to such a protest at school.

Cite: *M.A.L. v. Kinsland.*

Discussion points for teachers and principals:

Students participating in national protests are urged to inform the school about it in advance and ask for cooperation.

■ Some educators think schools should help all they can – students are exercising their rights and debate's educational.

■ Others think sensitive issues are too divisive, so schools should do everything legally permitted to discourage a protest at school.

Sharpen Your Judgment

When teachers can – and can't – limit what their students say

Terrance Pruitt waited for the other students to leave the room and then approached teacher Lori Sutherlin: "You wanted to see me?"

"Yes, Terrance," she said as she held and studied a sheet of paper. "I was looking at your choice for the Chamber of Commerce's poetry-recitation contest."

"Right," the student nodded. "Auden's 'The More Loving One.' I think it's cool."

"It's a classic," the teacher agreed. "But there's a problem." With that, she held up a copy of the poem and pointed to two words: hell and damn. "You know our classroom policy about using obscenity, even when it's part of another's written work," the teacher reminded him.

"I do know the policy," the student replied. "But I'm not going to recite it in the classroom or even in school. I'll be at the Chamber of Commerce building."

"Sorry," the teacher said. "I still can't approve this as part of our participation in the contest. The policy is meant to uphold a set of standards for everyone."

The boy's parents sued to allow the reading. They argued the poem was an established work and the reading wasn't subject to classroom rules.

Did the school and the teacher win?

Sharpen Your Judgment – The Decision

No. A court ruled in favor of the parents and against the school, based on two factors:

1. The words in the poem were in the context of an established work.
2. The teacher might have been within her authority to bar the reading if it had taken place in the classroom. In this instance, however, the reading wouldn't be part of the in-class learning process and presented no disruption to that process.

This ruling doesn't detract from a teacher's authority in the classroom or a school's responsibility for maintaining order. Instead, the ruling sets limits on what schools can bar or allow in activities that are unconnected or loosely connected with school functions.

And the ruling provides a good two-part guide for making a determination in such cases. Will the student's conduct or performance:

- cause a disruption in the learning process, or
- interfere with order in the school?

In this instance, the judge said the answer was "no" to both. And so the ruling went in favor of the parents.

Cite: *Behymer-Smith v. Coral Academy of Science.*

Student ignores dress code and gets ISS: Mom says teacher's to blame

Student refuses to follow dress code rules for religious exemption

Teacher Diane Price was straightening her desk, getting ready to leave for the day, when she heard a familiar voice.

"I hope you're happy," Matt Werth's mother said, walking into the classroom. "Why did you send Matt to the office? You know his hair isn't a problem."

"Ms. Werth, please have a seat," Diane said, pointing to a chair.

"Thanks to you, Matt's in ISS," Mrs. Werth shot back as she sat down.

Dress code exceptions

"That's not true," Diane said, taking a deep breath. "I warned Matt several times. He knows that he's supposed to wear his braid tucked into the back of his shirt. But he refused."

"Of course he refused to hide his hair," Ms. Werth said. "It's never been cut. It's part of our religion and culture."

"I appreciate that," Diane said. "And the school board does, too. That's why Matt was granted a dress-code exception. But he's not honoring that exception.

"The school board decided Matt didn't have to cut his hair, but he's supposed to keep his braid tucked in his T-shirt," Diane explained for the umpteenth time.

"This is ridiculous," Ms. Werth said as she stood up. "Making Matt hide his hair is discrimination." She sued the school, claiming the dress code violated Matt's religious freedom. Did the court agree?

Decision: Yes, the court ruled that the dress code violated Matt's right to free exercise of religion.

Key: The judge noted that the teacher followed the policy. In most instances, that's enough to keep the school out of legal trouble.

But in this case, the policy wasn't fair to Matt, the judge said.

The school board granted a religious exception that put Matt under "constant threat of punishment should his hair ... escape his shirt. This threat is real," the court explained.

Cite: *A.A. v. Needville Independent School Dist.*

When free speech and school tradition collide: What wins out?

Student says 'no' to cap and gown

Teacher Amy Keller unlocked her classroom door as she tried to balance a box in one hand. Just then a student came around the corner. "Thanks, Dakota," Amy said as he held the door.

"What's in the box?" Dakota asked as he watched Amy heave it onto her desk.

"It's for the graduating seniors," Amy told him. "As this year's class sponsor, I'm in charge of handing out caps and gowns.

"Voila," she continued, holding up one of the tassels for inspection. "What do you think of the colors?"

"Well," Dakota sighed. "I don't know."

"Very funny," Amy said and laughed, thinking Dakota was kidding around.

"I hope you didn't order one for me," Dakota told her. "That's a white man's graduation wardrobe."

Tradition or tribal customs?

"You're kidding, right?" Amy asked him, suddenly concerned. "I thought you were just joking."

"No, I'm not," Dakota told her. "When you started helping the student council with graduation plans, I told you that I wanted to wear my tribal regalia and clothing at graduation."

"Oh," Amy said, sighing with relief. "I know. Several members of the class are in your tribe – that's why we planned the feather and plume ceremonies.

"These are for students to wear when diplomas are awarded," she continued.

"I don't think so," Dakota said.

"But Dakota," Amy asked him, "won't you at least wear your cap and gown during the traditional ceremony?"

"You don't understand," Dakota said. "I need to stand up in front of my family as a man of my tribe."

"That's why we incorporated tribal customs into the traditional ceremony," Amy said. "You're a man of your tribe and a graduating senior at this school. Does one role have to override the other?"

"How can I be an honorable warrior if I'm wearing a white man's gown instead of my tribe's regalia?" Dakota asked.

"I don't know, Dakota," she said. "Let's talk to the principal."

The principal's take

The principal stood firm on the rules: If Dakota refused to wear the cap and gown during the traditional part of the ceremony, he wouldn't be allowed to participate at all.

Dakota sued, claiming the rule violated his speech rights.

The school insisted it had the authority to require students to wear a cap and gown at its graduation – a school-sponsored event. It asked the court to dismiss the claim. Did it?

Decision: Yes, the court dismissed Dakota's claim.

Key: Educators have more discretion to regulate student speech during school-sponsored events, the court explained.

Graduation rituals celebrate:
• students' achievements as individuals and as a group
• the school's status as an institution of learning, and
• teachers' achievements as educators.

Schools invest both time and resources in graduation ceremonies to create an atmosphere of celebration for everyone involved, the court explained.

Commencement is a school-sponsored event, the court said.

When students sit together as a class in caps and gowns, that tradition celebrates their "journey together through years of learning at school," the court pointed out.

Because caps and gowns are universal symbols of achievement, the school's policy is reasonable, and it doesn't violate students' speech rights, the court ruled.

Cite: *Bear v. Fleming.*

Discussion points for teachers and principals:

Under the *Hazelwood* test, speech can be regulated at school-sponsored events to ensure the:

■ participants learn the lesson the activity is designed to teach

■ audience isn't exposed to material that is inappropriate for their level of maturity, and

■ views of an individual aren't erroneously attributed to the school or district.

Student writes nasty message on hand: Should teacher take action?

The blurry line between speech 'rights' and disruptions

Teacher Stephanie Hunt wasn't exactly fond of cafeteria duty. And considering the heightened potential for trouble, she was really on edge.

The trouble started last week when a group of students started wearing T-shirts with "Free Fuller" written on them – in support of a classmate who was arrested.

The rumor mill churned with whispers about gang-related activity – which scared the students who weren't wearing the T-shirts. The school quickly banned the slogan on the T-shirts. Since then, the student body remained divided.

Today, Stephanie's eyes darted back and forth – on the lookout for the next sign of trouble. She spotted it quickly.

Several students were huddled up. From experience, Stephanie knew something was going on over there.

More trouble ahead

"OK, gang," she said as she walked up, "what's so fascinating that it's holding up the lunch line?"

Student Dan Willis was the center of attention. "Uh, nothing really," he answered as he reached for a tray. The group snickered.

Stephanie saw the cause of the commotion: Dan had written "Free Fuller" on his hands with a marker.

"Dan, you know that slogan's banned at school. I want you to go wash your hands," Stephanie urged him, "before you get in trouble."

Dan left the lunchroom and washed his hands.

Take two

Later that afternoon, Stephanie saw Dan fumbling with the lock on his locker. He had re-written "Free Fuller" on his hands.

"Dan," she sighed, "come with me."

"It's not fair," he said, following her into the empty classroom.

"You know we banned that slogan for a reason, Dan."

"But I don't get it – this is stupid. The rule is that we can't wear our 'Free Fuller' T-shirts," Dan complained. "I can write what I want to on my own hands, can't I?"

"You know Fuller was arrested for shooting someone. That scared a lot of students – and made them afraid of possible gangs at school. That's why we banned the slogan."

"That doesn't mean he did it," Dan argued, "and you know I'm not in a gang."

"Dan, if you refuse to wash your hands, I'm going to send you to the principal's office."

Dan's eyes widened. "Why would you want to turn me in?"

"I don't want to report you, but I have to report broken rules," she told him. "Last chance: Go wash your hands."

Dan shook his head silently.

"OK, let's go."

Principal's take

The principal agreed with Stephanie and told Dan to wash his hands. When Dan refused, he was suspended for 10 days.

Dan's parents sued, claiming the school violated Dan's free speech rights.

The school said the slogan caused a serious disruption.

It asked the court to dismiss the lawsuit. Did the judge agree?

Decision: No, the judge ruled a trial was needed to see if the school violated Dan's speech rights.

Clearly, the slogan on the T-shirts caused a substantial disruption, but the judge wasn't convinced the slogan written on Dan's hand caused an equal disruption.

Key: School officials can limit students' speech if it causes a major problem at school. In this instance, the school's decision to ban T-shirts displaying the slogan was justified.

But prohibiting the phrase altogether may have crossed the line and violated Dan's speech rights.

Cite: *Brown v. Cabell County Board of Educ.*

Discussion points for teachers and principals:

Even though the judge ruled a trial was needed, this teacher made the right calls, including:

- asking the student to wash his hands
- explaining the situation the first time he refused, and
- turning the matter over to the principal when her explanation didn't convince the student to respect the ban.

Offensive T-shirt or personal pride? Managing tricky free speech issues

What you can – and can't – do in class

Teacher Connie Mays wrote instructions on the board while students filed into her class. She turned around just in time to see David Stevens walk in, sporting a T-shirt with the Confederate flag.

Connie sighed and walked over to David's desk. "I'd like to speak to you in the hall, please."

David had a self-satisfied smirk as the two walked out of the classroom. "What's up, Ms. Mays?" he asked.

"Now, David," she forced a smile as she continued, "you know very well 'what's up.' So why don't we talk about that T-shirt you're wearing?"

"What?" he asked, feigning innocence.

"You know that the Confederate flag has been banned since that group of students hung a huge Stars-and-Bars flag in the hallway."

"But I didn't hang it up," David insisted.

Flag caused racial tension

"I didn't say you did. Regardless, you remember the mess caused by the flag. Now, fix your shirt. We don't need another commotion."

David stared at Connie for a long moment, then said, "Fine."

Two days later, David walked into Connie's class wearing another T-shirt with a Confederate flag. This time, she stopped him before he took his seat. "Let's talk."

In the hallway, David blurted out, "I know you think my shirt is racist, but it's not! This shirt represents my southern pride, and I should be proud of who I am and where I'm from."

Dress code bans flag

"This isn't about what I think," Connie sighed. "We've had racial problems here because of that flag. The dress code bans the flag – end of story. Now, turn your shirt inside out."

"No," he argued. "What about me? Don't I have the right to show my pride, too?"

Connie tried to find just a little more patience. "Fix your shirt, or I will send you to the office. You don't want that, do you?"

"Send me," he said, remaining incorrigible. "I don't care."

Connie sent David to the office, and the principal repeated the instructions: Turn the T-shirt inside out. David refused again and was sent home for the day.

Two weeks later, David showed up for Connie's class donning a belt buckle with a Confederate flag.

"We've been over this," Connie said. "Take it off, David."

"I have the right to show my southern heritage," David said. "And it doesn't mean I'm a racist."

"I didn't call you a racist," Connie pointed out, and she sent him to the office.

In the principal's office

The principal suspended David for insubordination. His parents filed a lawsuit, claiming the school violated David's free speech rights.

School officials said the ban was enforced because the Confederate flag had caused problems at school. They asked the court to dismiss the lawsuit. Did the judge agree?

Decision: Yes, the judge agreed the school had a reasonable belief that lifting the ban on the Confederate flag would cause a disruption at school.

Of course David has the right to be proud of his southern roots, explained the court. But speech rights are limited at school, especially when speech is likely to cause disruptions, ruled the court.

Key: School officials were able to point to specific examples of prior school disruptions caused by the Confederate flag. Being able to show an actual history of problems rather than just the potential for problems swayed the judge to the school's side in this case.

Cite: *Defoe v. Sid Spiva.*

Discussion points for teachers and principals:

Students can be adamant – especially when it comes to clothes and individuality. But it's always a good idea to enforce rules consistently:

- Talk to the student
- Offer the student a chance to fix the problem (removing the banned clothing), and
- Send uncooperative students to the office.

When students' rights cause trouble: What you can and can't do

Dad expected special treatment – but teacher set limits

It had been a rough week for teacher Lara Bart and she'd capped it off by staying late on Friday to grade papers. As she picked up her bag to go home, she was glad this week was finally over. But just then, student Tina Feiffer's father walked into her classroom.

"Hi, Mr. Feiffer," said Lara. "What can I do for you?"

"We need to talk about Tina," Mr. Feiffer said.

"Well, I know you can't have a problem with her grades," said Lara. "She's in the top of her class."

"This isn't about grades," said Mr. Feiffer. "Tina's a great kid who should be in a good position for college. But you've wrecked her chance of a scholarship."

"What?" asked Lara.

Teacher reported dress code violations

"You've been the first teacher to see Tina every morning since the new dress code started," said Mr. Feiffer. "When you saw she wasn't wearing her uniform, you got to decide what happened next. But instead of being reasonable about it, you just kept shipping her off to the office. So thanks to you, my straight-arrow daughter has a discipline record that makes her look like Al Capone."

Didn't just 'ship' student to office

"That's not what happened," said Lara, forcing herself to stay calm. "I talked to Tina privately to ask why she was wearing a Christian T-shirt instead of the polo shirt of her new uniform."

"And did she tell you?" asked Mr. Feiffer. "She thinks it's morally wrong that the dress code stops her from wearing shirts that express her faith."

"Yes," agreed Lara. "But not wearing the uniform is still against the rules."

Teacher tried to solve the problem

"I couldn't just let her break a rule that everyone has to follow," said Lara. "So I told her I'd have to send her to the office if she didn't change into her polo in the girls' room. And I warned her it could go on her permanent record if she was disciplined for it."

"You warned her? But kids don't get long-term consequences! You're the adult. Why didn't you run interference for her – send her home sick, or something?"

"Every day?" asked Lara. "Mr. Feiffer, it's not like this happened only once."

"You still could have done more. Or maybe you don't care that Tina has to apply for college next year – with a school record that makes her look like a hoodlum!"

"I understand your frustration, Mr. Feiffer. And I'd be happy to write Tina a letter of reference to go with her college applications. I could explain she's a good person who did this because of strong beliefs – not just to cause trouble or break rules."

"Thanks," said Mr. Feiffer as he stalked out. "But I think you've done enough already."

Dad sues

The school refused to clear Tina's record, so her father sued, saying the dress code violated her religious rights.

Tina's dad asked the judge to declare the policy illegal and order the school to clear Tina's record. Did the judge agree?

Decision: No. It was legal.

The policy was OK because it didn't target religion, applied to every student the same way and had the valid purpose of eliminating clothing-related distractions.

Key: Sometimes "troublemakers" are students trying to do the right thing. That's no free pass to break rules, but does alert teachers it might be a good idea to explain to idealists (and their parents) about the harsh consequences they might not see coming – like discipline that could hurt scholarship and college chances.

Cite: *Jacobs v. Clark County School Dist.*

Discussion points for teachers and principals:

T-shirts at school can be legal battlegrounds. So should schools just ban them like this one did?

■ Some say yes because almost any message can be "fighting words" – or even bullying – to those who disagree with it.

■ Some say no because such disputes give schools a chance to help students learn how to handle other people's opposing viewpoints with civility.

Student insists gun on his shirt stands for patriotism – now what?

Teacher asks student not to wear 'offensive shirt'

Student Joe Silva was scowling at teacher Dayle Myron as they faced each other in the quiet hall outside class. She was trying to explain why his T-shirt wasn't appropriate for school – but it wasn't going well.

"My uncle gave me this shirt," said Joe. "He's risking his life for us in Iraq right this very minute. And he got this for me at a PX stateside just before he went away."

Dayle looked at the shirt again. It had a huge image of a handgun over the words: "Lifetime U.S. Terrorist Hunting Permit – No Bag Limit." She sighed and tried again.

"Listen, Joe. I can imagine how much it must mean to you to know he was thinking of you at a time like that. I can understand why that shirt's so important to you."

"Yeah," said Joe gruffly. "It is."

What the T-shirt's really saying?

"But will you try to see your classmates' point of view? They don't know your uncle or the sacrifice he's making for his country. They just see a message suggesting it's OK to hunt and kill human beings. And that's not a message we can allow at school."

Joe scowled at Dayle again.

"Look," she sighed. "It's really upsetting some of your classmates. That's why they asked me to talk to you about it."

"So what if it upsets them!" said Joe. "Their liberal views upset me all the time. Maybe it's their turn to put up with my views for a change, the way I always have to put up with theirs."

"That can be frustrating," said Dayle. "But I keep trying to explain this isn't about politics. It's the gun on your shirt. It's making other kids nervous."

"But why?"

"It makes them think about school shootings."

"But that's crazy," said Joe. "A picture can't shoot them. If I was walking around with a real gun, even I'd be nervous. But this is a picture."

"Yes," said Dayle. "But some pictures aren't OK at school – especially not with text that says it's OK to shoot people. That's why they say it's scaring them and making it hard to concentrate."

"Well!" muttered Joe. "I'd love to see how they function outside of school. Plenty of worse shirts than this out there!"

"Point taken," sighed Dayle. "But this is a school, and we have special rules. And that's true outside school, too. You can't wear just anything you like to work, either."

Dayle glanced at her watch. "We need to get back to class now. That 15 minutes I gave them to read the chapter is up. I'll talk to the principal about this after class, OK? We'll see what she has to say."

Joe shook his head as they headed back to class. "If she says I can't wear this shirt, my folks will have a big, bad problem with it."

Patriotic – or violent – message?

The principal said Joe couldn't wear the shirt to school again – and his parents sued.

They argued this was a ban on political speech. They said the shirt expressed support for the troops and – since it hadn't caused a school disruption – Joe had a right to wear it at school.

Did the judge agree with them?

Decision: No, the judge said it was OK for administrators to ban the shirt at school.

This wasn't protected political speech. While Joe and his family associated patriotism with the shirt, the message it actually delivered promoted violence and lawlessness: hunting and killing people. This is a message schools can forbid.

Key: As teachers, it's natural to sympathize with students, even when they break rules – especially if you know the particulars about their personalities and home lives that explain why they don't think they're doing anything wrong. But your best bet is to understand the rules and apply them fairly to everyone.

Cite: *Miller v. Penn Manor School Dist.*

Discussion points for teachers and principals:

Do violent images or messages ever have a place in school?

■ Some say no, arguing that events like Columbine show how important it is to keep schools a violence-free zone.

■ Others say yes, saying that the extraordinary level of violence in movies, TV and games make it a duty for schools to teach students how to responsibly deal with violent images.

Teacher acts to prevent disruption: Where to draw the line – legally

What happens when 'free expression' could lead to a fight?

That whole week at school had been a tense one for Ron Berquist and the other teachers.

"I'll bet I've broken up three fights since that Gay Pride march in front of the school," he said to a colleague. "The kids are really on edge about this, and everyone seems to be taking sides."

The next day brought more problems as the students filed into Berquist's class, and one of them, David Gargan, wore a T-shirt that said: *"Homosexuality is shameful – Romans 1:27."*

After the class, the teacher tapped the boy on the shoulder and said, "I'd like to talk to you for a moment."

The student said nothing as he followed the teacher to the desk at the front of the room.

He refuses

"David, I'm not going to tap dance with this one," the teacher said firmly.

"I want you to take off the T-shirt right here and then wear it inside-out so that no one can see the message. And don't wear it in my class again."

The student looked down at the floor and said "no" in a quiet but clear voice. "I can express my opinion and my religious beliefs."

"Last chance, David," the teacher warned. "Wear it inside-out or we head to the principal's office to deal with this."

The boy's voice grew louder: "Go for it. I'm not taking off the T-shirt."

A day later ...

The next day, Ron Berquist sat in a strained meeting with David Gargan's parents.

"What were you thinking when you threatened and disciplined our son over a passage in the Bible?" the father asked while leaning forward.

"I wouldn't characterize what I said as a threat," the teacher explained. "I gave him a choice, and I acted in what I thought were his best interests, and the school's."

"His best interests?" the mother exclaimed. "You're going to have to explain that one to me."

"Well, consider what's happened here in the last week," the teacher answered. "We've had several fights over this homosexuality issue, and I didn't want to let slide something that could result in an attack on your son."

That led to a brief pause. Then the father spoke again.

"We appreciate your concern for David's safety, but we've taught him to stand up for his beliefs. Your actions go against that."

The teacher took a breath and said calmly, "Mr. and Mrs. Gargan, all I can tell you is that I acted in everyone's best interests, and there was no attempt to deprive David of the right to religious beliefs."

"Maybe not," the father countered. "But that's what resulted, and we intend to do something about it."

The decision

The parents filed a lawsuit charging the teacher and the school with violating the student's right to religion.

In court, the school contended that circumstances, a threat of violence, and the intimidation of a minority group of students canceled out that right.

Did the court's decision side with the school?

Decision: Yes. A federal court agreed that, given the volatile circumstances, the teacher and the school had a duty to prevent the student from wearing the T-shirt.

Note: The decision in this case differs from a ruling in a similar case in which a court OK'd a student wearing a shirt with a message protesting abortion.

Difference: The court said the abortion message was protected opinion and not meant to intimidate minority students.

Cite: *Harper v. Poway Unified School Dist.*

Discussion points for teachers and principals:

Of course, students don't give up their rights at the schoolhouse door. However, you can limit those rights if exercising them:

■ Presents a danger to anyone, including the student who insists on the right, and

■ Is amid circumstances in which a reasonable person might believe that exercising the right could lead to disruption in the school.

When student's 'rights' create a disruption: What's the limit?

He advocates strong stance

"Just when you think you've seen everything," teacher Brian Hillerich said to himself as he walked into his sixth-grade classroom to start the day.

"I thought most of these kids were too young for this."

The "this" involved the attire of student Will O'Dell. In large block letters, "ABORTION =" covered nearly the entire right leg of Will's well-worn jeans. The other leg sported the word "MURDER" in the same-size letters.

"Will, let's talk for a minute," the teacher said as he took the student aside while the others settled in before the bell. Already, however, the teacher noted several of the students were giggling about the jeans.

'Not about me'

"Is this about the message on my jeans?" Will asked immediately.

"It is," the teacher confirmed.

"You're pro-abortion?" Will countered.

"This has nothing to do with my feelings about abortion," Brian said. "I'm interested only in making sure no one's distracted from doing what they're supposed to be doing in this classroom today.

"So," he continued, "let me ask you: Do your parents know what you wore to school today?"

"Do they know?" the student said in mock surprise. "Not only do they know – they approve."

"All right," the teacher said. "I'll discuss this with your parents, but until then, please don't wear those jeans into my classroom again."

"And if I do?"

"I'll ask the principal to suspend you for being a disruption," the teacher said.

The next morning, the teacher checked his mailbox at school and he spotted a note: "Call Frank O'Dell," accompanied by a phone number.

That afternoon

"Mr. O'Dell, Brian Hillerich – Will's teacher – returning your call. How are you?"

"Fine," Frank O'Dell replied. "But what's the problem with my son's opposition to abortion?"

"As I told Will," he began, "this isn't about abortion. I'm trying to keep him from creating a disruption in school."

"You mean every time someone wears a jersey or a jacket with a message on it, that causes a disruption?" the parent asked.

"I wouldn't go that far," the teacher replied. "But I can tell you that just last week we suspended a student who refused to take off a jacket that said, 'Drugs and sex: the more, the better.' So we have banned other messages."

Not the same thing?

"I don't think that's the same thing," the parent said. "Will isn't advocating sex or drug use. He's opposing abortion, and I agree with him."

"I'm not disputing your beliefs or Will's," the teacher explained. "I'm just asking that he keep it out of the classroom, for the sake of learning."

"And I'm refusing your request," the parent said flatly.

Ultimately, the family sued over the ban on the jeans and the message, saying it was the student's right to wear them.

The school countered by noting that decisions to ban disruptive messages about sex and drugs had been upheld. Did the school win?

Decision: No. A judge ruled the student could wear the jeans. And the judge outlined the difference between messages about abortion and about sex and drugs:

One message – abortion – is protected expression about a valid issue; the other message advocates behavior that's counter to what the school is trying to teach. Plus, the "disruption" wasn't severe enough to overrule protected expression.

Cite: *Nixon v. Northern Local School Dist. Board of Educ.*

Discussion points for teachers and principals:

Just being "controversial" isn't always a measure of whether certain messages or types of expressions can be banned in a school setting. Banning requires that the message:

■ advocates behavior that's harmful to learning – such as drug use, and

■ presents a real and persistent disruption, to the point that it interferes with the mission of the school.

T-shirt says, 'I must shoot him' – can a teacher take action?

Drawing the line on a dress code violation

George Costello had gotten used to seeing his students in mock military outfits, but this seemed over the top.

That's why he stopped student Brian Gentry and said, "Let me take a better look at that T-shirt you're wearing."

Large block letters on the front of the olive-drab-green jersey spelled out "My Rifle." In smaller script on the back: "I must shoot straighter than my enemy who is trying to kill me. I must shoot him before he shoots me."

The teacher said, "Brian, let's talk."

"You have a problem with my T-shirt?" the student asked. "It's part of the U.S. Marine Creed."

"I'm as patriotic as the next person," the teacher said. "But the message could be misinterpreted. You know what's going on these days and the reaction to that stuff."

"So what do you want me to do about it?" the student said.

"Please don't wear it again," the teacher said firmly.

George thought the matter was finished – until a week later, when Brian walked into the classroom wearing the same T-shirt and a defiant smile to go along with it.

The teacher considered the situation for a moment and then again took the student aside.

"I thought we had an agreement," George began.

"I talked to my parents about the T-shirt, and they agreed with me that it was OK to wear it," Brian said loudly.

"OK, then, I guess I'm going to have to send you to the principal's office for discipline," the teacher announced.

Reasonable approach?

The next day, George took the phone call he'd been expecting. It was Brian Gentry's father.

"What's the idea behind disciplining my son for wearing a Marine T-shirt and then barring him from wearing it again?"

"Mr. Gentry, I explained that to Brian, and I think you'll understand my reasoning," George replied.

"This isn't about the Marines or patriotism. When kids wear clothing in school that makes statements about shooting people, we have to take action. You understand what the climate is about these things."

"Did someone complain about the T-shirt?" the father asked.

"Not that I know of," the teacher said. "The thing is, though, if we wait for someone to complain, people will get the idea that we're not concerned about violence, and then if something does happen, they want to know why we weren't paying attention.

"You see the position we're in."

One more question

"Let me ask another question," the father continued. "Has Brian ever given you trouble or shown violent behavior?"

"No," the teacher replied quickly. "But you have to see that this isn't about Brian. It's about our policy to discourage signs of violence in school."

"I think you went overboard," the father said. "As a Marine veteran, I'm not going to stand for it."

Who wins?

The family sued, citing violation of the student's free-speech rights. The school countered that it had a responsibility to discourage violence.

Did the teacher and the school win in this case?

Decision: No. A judge ruled the T-shirt was a statement about the Marine Creed and not a statement about violence.

The judge noted that the school might have had a stronger case had the wearing of the T-shirt created an obvious disruption to education or if others had complained about the shirt or expressed fear.

Ruling: It's OK to wear a shirt depicting the Marine Creed.

Cite: *Griggs v. Ft. Wayne School Board.*

Discussion points for teachers and principals:

In today's climate regarding violence in schools, educators of course have a responsibility to clamp down on threatening expression or behavior. Just try to remember, however:

■ Blanket bans on military-related expression can be tough to justify, and

■ Courts often side with students and parents who can show no one felt threatened by the message.

Enforcing dress codes in class: What you can and can't do

'It's just a joke' – but does it go over the line?

After a couple of weeks, teacher Renee Alston decided everything was going fairly well with new student Katie Dutch.

Renee remembered the meeting with Katie's mother, who said, "We recognize that Katie has a physical disability, in that she can't walk like other children, but she's tough and we encourage her to handle herself with other children."

Indeed, despite Katie's need for leg braces and a pair of walking canes, she managed to keep up with the others, and most of the students seemed sensitive to the situation.

Most – but not all.

Renee noticed that a group of three or four students in the class had taken to kidding Katie with comments like, "Hey, how about a race?"

She always managed a laugh and a retort like, "Bet I could beat you."

That day, however, their actions went way past a kidding comment.

As the students settled in for class, the small group that had made the comments removed their jackets to reveal identical T-shirts that read "The Cripple Crusaders" and a caricature of a child who looked a lot like Katie.

Renee stifled a gasp and stole a quick look at Katie, who had a hurt expression.

The teacher ordered the T-shirt wearers to her desk.

She spoke in a low, firm voice: "For today, I want each of you to either remove those T-shirts or turn them inside out. And don't wear them ever again in this school."

One student, Michael Winston, protested in a whisper:

"C'mon, Ms. Alston. We had these made up at the mall just to joke with Katie and make her feel like part of the group. What's wrong with that?"

Renee quickly replied: "We have a dress code here that bans clothing with a design that ridicules or demeans anyone. And we're going to follow it. Anyone who doesn't will be punished."

She later reported the incident to Principal Andre Geary, and hoped it would end there.

It didn't.

More than a joke?

Three days later, Michael Winston marched into the classroom wearing the "Cripple Crusaders" T-shirt again.

Again, Renee took him aside and spoke in a controlled voice.

"Michael, you recall our conversation a few days ago?"

"I do," he replied sharply. "But I told you the T-shirt was a joke and we didn't mean any harm."

Renee decided to take a few minutes to explain to Michael how hurtful the T-shirt could be to Katie, hoping he'd understand the reasons for her insisting he take it off.

He wouldn't budge.

"It's not obscene or anything like that, so I'm going to wear it," he said angrily.

The call on discipline

"I'm sorry to hear that, Michael," Renee said. "You give me no choice but to recommend an internal suspension and detention every day you wear that shirt."

When Michael's parents heard about the punishment, they sued the teacher and the school for overstepping their authority over what students may or may not wear.

The teacher insisted she enforced the dress code to keep order and a civil atmosphere in the school.

Was the teacher right?

Decision: Yes. A court ruled the teacher and the school were right to enforce the dress code banning clothing that demeans or ridicules.

It's within a district's authority to ban clothing that could hinder learning or send harmful messages aimed at individuals or groups.

Cite: *Walker-Serrano v. Leonard.*

Discussion points for teachers and principals:

Often, as you know, enforcing dress codes isn't black-and-white.

Fortunately, though, courts do give teachers and schools some leeway in making the decision because:

■ The classroom isn't considered a "public forum," where students can use dress to protest or ridicule, and

■ The level of disruption, if any, is a determining factor in how the situation should be handled.

Sharpen Your Judgment

Student protests school policy with Nazi pin – What should teacher do?

Teacher Rich Wayle saw the button on student Kathy Huff's collar – but not clearly.

As she passed him after class he asked, "What does your pin say?"

She came over to show him and he saw "New Dress Code" Xed out in bright red.

"They're forcing us to look exactly alike," she said.

He squinted at the button, trying to see the photo under the caption. "Are those boy scouts?" he asked.

"No," said Kathy. "Hitler Youth boys."

Wow! thought Rich. Staying calm, he said, "That could really offend people."

"I don't mean it to. I used this picture because these boys are all exactly alike."

"OK, but that doesn't mean it won't upset people and lead to trouble. We'd better run this one past the principal."

"Great," she fumed. "I can't even complain."

Told she'd be suspended if she wore the pin to school again, Kathy sued. She asked the judge to order the school to let her wear it until her free speech case was decided – because she was likely to win.

Did the judge agree?

Sharpen Your Judgment – The Decision

Yes, the judge agreed Kathy was likely to win, so the school had to let her wear the button until the trial.

Denying someone a constitutional right – even for only a few months until a trial is held – is so serious that this protection is needed.

The judge decided Kathy would probably win because her button hadn't caused disruption at school and he didn't think it was likely to.

The school could have banned a profane or suggestive button, but there was nothing obviously forbidden about this one.

The judge decided the photo wasn't likely to lead to high emotions or fights. While Nazi images might, the boys in this photo looked like Boy Scouts. They weren't giving the Hitler salute and there were no swastikas.

Analysis: Inform even if in doubt

This ruling may have gone against the school, but the teacher was right to bring Kathy's protest button to the principal's attention.

Teachers aren't expected to solve First Amendment cases. Even courts struggle with that. But it's a big help if teachers can spot potential problems – and hopefully help avert them – by letting the office know what's going on in the halls.

Cite: *DePinto v. Bayonne Board of Educ.*

Student won't heed warnings about T-shirt: What's next?

Parents back her on message others find 'disturbing'

Teacher Cole Carver considered the best approach to take concerning Allison Walkins and her T-shirt.

"Allison," he began, "I've received some complaints from other students about the message on the T-shirt you've worn a few times. We may have to take some action."

"You mean the pro-life T-shirt?" the student asked.

"Well, yes," he nodded. "We're talking about the one that says 'abortion is murder' on the front."

"Are those students in favor of abortion?" she replied. "Are you?"

"How I feel about the issue isn't important," he replied. "And to tell you the truth, I don't know how the students feel. All they've said is they find the message disturbing and that it's distracting to them in class."

'Not my problem'

"Why is the distraction my problem?" the student suddenly bristled. "No one's forcing them to look at it."

"I understand what you're saying," the teacher said calmly. "But my responsibility is to run a classroom where students feel comfortable and able to learn. So I'm going to ask for your cooperation. I'm asking that you not wear the T-shirt in this class," he said.

"And if I refuse?" she asked.

"Then you'll force me to discipline you for being a disruption," he answered.

"Then go ahead," she shot back. "But I'm going to continue to wear the T-shirt."

High standard for disruption

With her parents' backing, Allison wore the shirt in class again, and the teacher followed through on the discipline.

As a result, the parents sued, saying their child's freedom of expression had been denied. The school contested the suit in court.

Did the school win the suit?

Decision: No. A judge ruled that the fact that a few students said they were "distracted" didn't have enough weight to justify the claim of a disruption or for barring a form of expression.

Key: The standard is high for barring political or controversial expression by students.

You'll have to show a clear link between the message and how it disrupts the educational process.

Cite: *K.D. v. Fillmore Cent. School Dist.*

Mom says prom dress code's unfair: What should teacher say next?

Teacher hands out prom dress code rules, but mom doesn't like them

"Can I talk to you for a minute?" a woman said as she walked into teacher Amy Hill's classroom.

"Sure," Amy said. "I'm sorry, but I don't recognize you. Have we met?"

"I'm Sue Clark's mother," she said. "And I want to know why my daughter can't wear a tux to the prom!"

"I didn't know she wanted to," Amy stammered, taken aback.

'You knew what she wanted'

"Well, it's not a secret that Sue has a girlfriend," Ms. Clark shot back. "She was upset when you gave her that handbook that says girls have to wear dresses."

"I didn't put two-and-two together, Ms. Clark," Amy told her. "Sue didn't ask me about wearing a tux.

"But I would suggest you and she speak to the principal," Amy suggested. "Perhaps ... "

"Perhaps what?" Ms. Clark demanded, interrupting Amy.

"I'm not sure," Amy admitted, "but I think talking to the principal would be a good place to start."

Ms. Clark picked up her purse. "You haven't heard the last of this. I promise!"

When the principal refused to make an exception to the dress code, Ms. Clark sued, claiming the school violated Sue's speech rights. Did the court agree?

Decision: Yes, the court ruled that the school's prom dress code violated Sue's rights under the First Amendment.

Key: The judge noted the teacher and the school were following policy, but in this case, the policy was flawed.

This school's policy required female students to wear dresses to the prom. But schools don't have the authority to require female students to "wear clothing that has traditionally been deemed as female" attire, the court explained.

By requiring Sue to conform to traditional clothing, the school violated her speech rights, the court ruled.

Cite: *McMillen v. Itawamba School Dist.*

Parents really don't like controversial lesson plans: Is teacher out of line?

Teacher claims censorship violated her speech rights

Teacher Mia Knight sighed, playing with her food in the teachers' lounge.

"What's wrong?" fellow teacher Chase Ford asked. "You seem down today."

"No, I'm mad," Mia said quietly. "I just found out that my contract isn't going to be renewed after this year."

"What happened?" Chase asked her.

Controversial lessons ...

"My students held a debate on censorship," Mia said. "We used the '100 most controversial books' list."

"Some parents didn't like that – and Principal Marks told me to let her know about any controversial themes that might be discussed – before the classes," she continued. "I even told her the school purchased those books for our libraries."

"Hmmm," Chase said, stirring his coffee. "How'd that go?"

"She didn't like that," Mia admitted. "All of a sudden, my judgment was being questioned. Honestly, I think my contract isn't being renewed because of the 'bad press' from parents being angry."

"What are you going to do?" Chase asked her.

"I don't know," Mia said. Eventually, she filed suit, claiming the district retaliated against her because of the controversial lesson. She said the district violated her speech rights.

Did the judge agree?

Decision: No, the judge ruled that Mia's speech rights weren't violated.

Key: Teachers are public employees.

In order to prove a First Amendment retaliation claim, public employees have to show that their speech wasn't made "pursuant to official duties," the court ruled. That wasn't the case here – Mia claimed her speech rights were violated in the course of teaching, the court explained.

Teachers must follow district rules on in-class curricular decisions – if they don't, they can't claim speech rights violations.

Cite: *Evans-Marshall v. Board of Educ. of the Tipp City Exempt Village School Dist.*

Tough call: How to handle gray areas in the dress code

'My body art's who I am,' says student to teacher

Joe was at school early to get a jump on grading papers. When he got up for a second cup of coffee, he was surprised to see student Tracy Kerr in the hall – but she didn't see him.

He watched her sneak past the office and then speed up and take off around the corner.

Joe sighed, thinking: Just when I was finally starting a day off right. I hope this isn't about her body piercings again.

Joe followed Tracy. When he turned the corner, he saw her standing in front of the mirror in her open locker. She was working a stud into her nose.

Joe must have made a noise because Tracy suddenly looked around. Seeing him, she froze.

Wishing he'd managed to get his coffee first, Joe walked down the hall to her. "Hi, Tracy," he said. "I'd tell you that jewelry violates the dress code, but you already know that. And I see you've got all your other metal studs ready to put in, too," he added with a sigh, spotting them on her locker shelf.

"Why are you still doing this when Principal Smith gave you permission to wear clear plastic studs? She really worked with you and your dad to find a way to let you keep your piercings without violating the dress policy."

"It's archaic to only let us have pierced ears," said Tracy angrily. "Is this 1958?"

"We've been through this," said Joe. "Everyone has to follow the rules and dress appropriately for school. Do you think I like wearing a tie every day?"

"But I want my friends to see the real me," said Tracy. "I think my body art is awesome and so do my friends. It's who we are."

"I understand," said Joe. "But can you understand this? The real me sings with an opera group. That doesn't mean I can belt out 'Figaro, Figaro' at school. It would distract everybody, just like your metal studs distract people. That's why you can only wear the clear ones."

"Those plastic studs give me infections," said Tracy.

"I'm sorry to hear that," said Joe, "but that doesn't give you a pass on a rule that everybody else has to follow."

Tracy stared down at the floor.

"So," said Joe quietly, "will you please take out the nose stud and leave all that jewelry in your locker while you're at school?"

"No," snapped Tracy. "That stupid policy doesn't have the right to decide who I can and can't be. I hear what you're saying, Mr. Grell, but it doesn't change my mind. And if you send me to the vice principal again, I'll tell her the same thing."

The vice principal gave Tracy five days of lunch detention, and Tracy and her father sued the school.

They said the dress code stopped Tracy from displaying her individuality, and this violated her right to free expression.

Did the judge agree it did?

Decision: No, the dress code was legal and it left many other ways for Tracy to express her individuality while at school.

Schools can limit some student expression as long as there are still plenty of ways left for a student to get the same message across.

Key: You can't handle everything on your own, obviously. But the hard part is trying to figure out when to get the administrators involved.

If it's a dress code violation easily solved by removing jewelry (as here) or turning a T-shirt inside out to hide an offensive message or symbol, it's probably safe to tackle it on your own.

But there are times when you need to turn the situation over to the office. And the people in charge of discipline where you teach can tell you where that line is drawn at your school.

Cite: *Bar-Navon v. School Board of Brevard County.*

Discussion points for teachers and principals:

Dress code supporters say dress codes:

- promote safety by eliminating gang-wear and ID'ing intruders, and
- help students focus on learning instead of on revealing clothes and designer labels.

Opponents say dress codes:

- push mindless conformity, and
- can't solve discipline problems.

What's the thinking behind your school's policy on student attire?

Teacher's stuck in the middle when custody agreement is violated

Non-custodial mom sues the school over dad's decision

Teacher Beth Lee handed Principal Heather Marks the printed e-mail from Tom Smith's mom.

"So she's mad because we didn't call her after we suspended Tom for fighting?" Heather asked, scanning the e-mail. "OK, run it by me again – from the beginning."

Divorced parents battle it out

"Tom's mother put her name down as a contact. But Tom's dad has custody, and he told us not to contact her," Beth said.

"Ugh! We don't need to get caught up in custody issues," Heather said. "I know that she's upset, but we have to respect custodial parents' wishes. That's policy."

"That's what I said," Beth agreed. "But then she told me about this court order– "

"Court order?" Heather interrupted.

"Apparently, their custody ruling says both parents have to be notified by the school in an emergency," Beth sighed.

"And to make matters worse," she continued, "the court order says if one parent can't be reached, then the other parent is the first point of contact.

"But I didn't know about the court order, and now his mom's threatening to sue," Beth said.

"This hardly qualifies as an emergency. Maybe we can help them figure this out," Heather said.

But Tom's mother sued the school, claiming it deprived her right to parent her son. Did the court agree?

Decision: No, the court granted summary judgment for the school.

Key: To prove her claim, Tom's mother had to show school officials overstepped their bounds by making a decision about Tom's education or upbringing. That didn't happen here.

In this case, school officials suspended Tom for violating the rules and released him to the custodial parent. Expecting school officials to notify Tom's mother every time he's released to his father is unreasonable, the court explained.

Cite: *Vendouri v. Gaylord.*

Custody battle spills over into the classroom: What should teacher do?

Non-custodial mom accuses teacher of violating her right to parent

Teacher Amy Keller looked up when she heard a knock on the door. "Continue reading silently, please," she said.

When Amy opened the door, a woman said, "I need to see my son, Dave Reid."

Oh no! I don't have time for the custody fight today, Amy thought. She stepped into the hall, closing the door behind her. "Hi, Wendy. Do you have a visitor's pass from the office?"

"What do you mean?" Wendy asked loudly, getting visibly upset. "It's my son's birthday – and I want to see him now!"

Dad doesn't want Mom visiting school

"I know it's Dave's birthday," Amy said. "But we have to follow the rules. School visitors have to sign in at the main office."

Hoping to avoid a scene that her students might overhear, Amy purposely didn't ask Wendy if Dave's dad had given her permission to visit today.

Wendy changed her strategy. "You know I don't like signing in at the office," she said, smiling sweetly. "They always want a lot of paperwork and custody nonsense. I just want to see my son."

Amy looked at Wendy with kindness, but spoke with as much firmness as she could manage. "Wendy, I can't allow anyone to come into the classroom without a visitor pass from the office."

"You can't keep me away from my son," she shouted as she stormed away.

Wendy sued, claiming the school violated her constitutional rights by refusing to allow her to see her child.

Did the court agree?

Decision: No, the court dismissed Wendy's claim.

Key: School employees didn't violate Wendy's right to parent her child, as a previous court order had granted custody to her ex-husband, the court ruled. As per district policy, teachers must obey court orders pertaining to custody agreements – which meant the teacher couldn't allow Wendy to visit Dave without his father's prior permission, the court explained.

Cite: *Schmidt v. Des Moines Public Schools.*

Teacher caught up in the middle when divorced parents fight over child's education

Does noncustodial parent have a right to 'more involvement'?

Arthur McCann began the phone call with a blunt question: "Where were you when my son was beaten up while on the school playground?"

Teacher Joyce Wardlow replied quickly, "First, he wasn't 'beaten up.' He was involved in a fight."

"And I was right there as a monitor. I broke it up as soon as I spotted it."

He volunteers to 'help'

The parent changed topics: "This isn't the first time my son's been in a fight there, and my ex-wife is unwilling to do anything about it. So that's why I want to get more involved."

"More involved?" the teacher asked.

"That's right," he answered. "I told my ex-wife she should be a parent-monitor to protect our son, but she doesn't care. Since that's the case, I want to come in and be a volunteer parent-monitor."

Joyce considered the request and then gave her answer: "That's something you'll have to run by our principal, but I can tell you the idea wouldn't get my recommendation. We already have all the monitors we need, and I talked about the situation repeatedly with your ex-wife."

"Oh, I get it," he shot back. "I'm divorced and she has custody, so you're shutting me out in favor of my ex-wife."

"My understanding is that she's the custodial parent," the teacher noted. "That's why we contact her."

"Well, I'm tired of being treated like a second-class citizen," he said as he hung up.

He sued the school and the teacher for discriminating against a noncustodial parent. The teacher and the school argued they were following policies for dealing with children of divorced parents.

Did the school win?

Decision: Yes. A court said teachers shouldn't have to play referee in choosing involvement of divorced parents.

Key: The teacher did keep the custodial parent informed of all issues concerning the child, in line with the policies of the district.

Cite: *Crowley v. McKinney.*

Dad's banned from school – but teacher sees him walk in the door

What's her best next move?

Teacher Feliz Novarro looked around the cafeteria, enjoying the sight of her students having lunch with their parents.

With everybody's jobs so hectic these days, Feliz thought it was great so many parents managed to accept the school's invitation to join their child for lunch.

Of course, Feliz realized, unusual events like this could also mean unexpected problems. She reminded herself to keep her guard up and her eyes open, just in case.

Here comes trouble

Almost as soon as Feliz had the thought, she saw a man walk into the cafeteria. If this was a parent, he was very late for the lunch. Feliz automatically took her cell phone from her pocket as she squinted at the man, trying to recognize him.

Suddenly she did. It was Mr. Cooper. And he'd been banned from school for being loud and abusive to staff.

Feliz immediately pushed the button that dialed the principal's cell and saw him answer his phone on the other side of the cafeteria. "Hello?" she heard him say.

"Hi, it's Feliz. I just saw Mr. Cooper walk in by the east entrance."

"Uh-oh," he said. "OK. Thanks. I'm on my way."

Dad refuses to leave

When the principal tried to quietly remind Mr. Cooper he wasn't allowed at school any more, Mr. Cooper started to shout and swear at him.

To minimize the disruption, the principal stepped aside to let Mr. Cooper join his daughter – then called the police.

When an officer arrived, the father screamed at him, too. The officer arrested Mr. Cooper for disorderly conduct. He was convicted, but appealed.

Decision: Conviction affirmed.

Key: Teachers can't stop some parents from causing big problems at school. But teachers can make sure they know who the real troublemakers are – and the correct drill to follow if they see them break a rule.

Cite: *Yowler v. State.*

Can teacher poll students about attitudes toward sex? Parents' suit says 'No!'

They object to voluntary survey that's key part of the lesson

As soon as science teacher Ed Levinson answered the phone, he heard the full blast of the voice of Albert Lewis.

"Have you people lost your minds over at that school?" the parent growled.

And without waiting for the teacher to respond, Lewis continued: "How can you survey your seventh-grade students – my daughter included – on their views about sex without even running the questionnaire past the parents?"

3 valid points

"Mr. Lewis, let me explain three things," the teacher replied in an even voice.

"One, we did the poll to get some baseline information on our students' knowledge of the subject. It wasn't meant to pry.

"Two, we explained to the students that taking the poll was voluntary. No student was required to take it, and there was no penalty for refusing.

"Three, we told the students not to put their names on the responses. It was done totally anonymously."

The parent was silent for a moment, but then spoke: "My daughter said she felt pressured to take the poll and felt you'd know whose answers belonged to who.

"And I can tell you, a couple of other parents are upset about this, too," he added. "Don't be surprised if we sue."

The parents did sue, arguing that the teacher and the school had circumvented the parental authority.

Did the teacher and the school win?

Decision: Yes. An appeals court upheld the use of the voluntary survey as a tool for educating the students.

Key: The teacher showed that the survey had a direct link to the lesson and indeed provided information that enhanced the effectiveness of the lesson. And the fact that the poll was anonymous and voluntary helped the school's case.

Note: The U.S. House of Representatives is considering legislation that reverses the decision, but for now the court's ruling still stands.

Cite: *C.N. v. Ridgewood Board of Educ.*

Sharpen Your Judgment
Parent wants 'friend' to take part in conference

Teacher Anna Jacobi checked her paperwork before the meeting with the parent of one of her students, Lisa Settler. Then, in walked Lisa's mother – and a man Anna hadn't met.

"Hi, Ms. Jacobi," the parent smiled. "I'm ready to discuss how we're going to deal with Lisa's learning disability. By the way, thanks for recommending that we have her tested."

"Glad I could help," the teacher replied and then turned to the man while extending her hand. "I'm Anna Jacobi. Have we met?"

Before he could speak, the parent said through an embarrassed smile, "Oh, sorry. Let me introduce my fiance, Andrew Oldham."

"Nice to meet you," the teacher said as they shook hands. "But I'm sorry, you'll have to leave the room while we talk about Lisa. I can talk only to a parent."

He spoke for the first time: "We're going to be married next year, and I plan to adopt Lisa. So, obviously, I insist on being in on any discussions about her future."

The teacher refused, and the parent and the fiance sued the school for denial of access to information about the child.

Did the school win?

Sharpen Your Judgment – The Decision

Yes, the school won.

The parent insisted that denying the fiance access to information interfered with the disabled child's receiving the required "free and appropriate" public education.

But the school cited the parts of the Individuals with Disabilities Act (IDEA) that protect student privacy and restrict access to student records.

The IDEA rules, the school argued, designate only parents and legal guardians as authorized to have access to the information.

The court agreed with the school.

No matter what the relationship – or potential relationship – between an adult and student, only parents or guardians can have access to records, make decisions and discuss courses of action for disabled students.

(Of course, in legal proceedings, an attorney can have access to information.)

Setting the record straight – first

You can avoid confusion and friction by making sure parents understand the policies regarding access to disabled students' info. Some parents believe they're empowered to designate another to take part in conferences. But in most states, they cannot.

Cite: *D.L. v. Unified School Dist. No. 497.*

Sharpen Your Judgment

Is school discriminating against non-minorities?

"And this book!" raged student Wendy Tempesti's mother. She slammed it down on Principal Jan Adler's desk. "This is what Wendy's expected to read for class!"

"Yes," agreed Jan calmly, recognizing the cover. "It's about -"

"I know what it's about!" cried Mrs. Tempesti. "It's about poisoning my child's mind with trash that makes illegal immigrants seem OK by making you feel sorry for them! But this is just par for the course around here."

"What do you mean?" asked Jan.

"All this 'diversity,'" said Mrs. Tempesti. "I notice Wendy and I are left out of that. We're only white, Christian Americans. Everybody has special rights but us."

"Not special rights," disagreed Jan quietly, "just the same rights."

"But that's all we want," said Mrs. Tempesti, "the same respect for our heritage."

Mrs. Tempesti sued, arguing the school violated her parental rights by not giving mainstream families' values and beliefs equal importance.

Did the judge dismiss her lawsuit or did it go to trial?

Sharpen Your Judgment – The Decision

The judge dismissed her lawsuit.

Mrs. Tempesti has a fundamental constitutional right to make parental decisions for her own child – but not to dictate what a public school teaches all its students.

The mother claimed the school violated her rights by not giving her values and beliefs the same time and attention it put into promoting diversity – but this didn't violate her rights.

Mrs. Tempesti's parental rights include deciding whether to send Wendy to public or private school. They don't include making the decisions about Wendy's school's curriculum.

If parents had this right, schools would be in the impossible situation of having to cater to multiple standards – and parents could restrict the flow of information at school.

Analysis: Encourage parents' speech, too

Parents seem to object to everything these days – especially books that express attitudes they disapprove of. But it's a school's mission, and a teacher's job, to expose students to a wealth of information. When education bumps up against parents' beliefs, some teachers suggest parents take advantage of the moment by sitting down with their child to explain exactly where they stand on the issue.

Cite: *Preskar v. U.S.*

Sharpen Your Judgment

Drawing the line when parents demand too much of your time

Teacher Cam Balek picked up the phone, but her eyes were still focused on her packed e-mail inbox. An angry voice blasted from the earpiece.

"Where have you been?"

It was Amy's mother again. Cam took a deep breath then said, "Hi, Mrs. Smith."

"I've been leaving you messages all morning!" she yelled. "And e-mailing! Where have you been?"

"Teaching," said Cam calmly. "My free period only just started."

"But I need to know what'll be on Amy's next math test. And if you think a letter from the school's lawyer will scare me away from making sure she's prepared for it, you're wrong!"

"We both care about her work," said Cam quietly. "But we're trying to make sure you understand that we can't take all your calls or drop everything to get right back to you."

"That's ridiculous!" said Mrs. Smith. "If I have to fight you people in court, I will."

Mrs. Smith sued, claiming school staff's refusal to communicate with her was violating her right to be in charge of Amy's education and upbringing.

Did Mrs. Smith win?

Sharpen Your Judgment – The Decision

No, Mrs. Smith didn't win.

Mrs. Smith argued Cam and the principal violated her parental rights because they wouldn't communicate with her on her terms – but the court agreed with the school that it wasn't for Mrs. Smith to set the terms.

Being in charge of a child's upbringing doesn't give any parent the right to overwhelm school staff with constant e-mails and phone calls, demand immediate responses, or behave in a loud and angry way.

The lawyer's letter had explained to Mrs. Smith, "Essentially, your conduct interferes with school district staff's ability to perform their jobs."

Analysis: Share important info

When you encounter "high maintenance" parents, it's important to keep your principal in the loop.

Principals don't usually have to enlist the school attorney to help with a demanding parent – but they always need to know if something unusual is going on.

Luckily, you don't usually have to take this step because most parents respond to reason. Potential lawsuits are nipped in the bud all the time by teachers' tact and common sense.

Cite: *Gaines-Hanna v. Farmington Public School Dist.*

Sharpen Your Judgment

Does student have a right to use PA system?

"What?" Teacher Rich Wells asked Principal Heather Marks. "Kevin Bales' parents say we violated his speech rights?"

"I know," Heather said. "I can't believe Kevin actually wanted to use the PA system to tell people he didn't make that racial remark."

"I know! And we traced the comment back to him," Rich agreed. "Talk about making a bad situation even worse."

"Kevin must've known that would anger some of our Hispanic students," Heather said.

"It sure did," Rich said. "I brought Kevin to the office because a group was planning to jump him. I never wanted any of this lawsuit stuff to happen."

"Trust me," Heather said. "Talking about it on the PA system will only fan the flames. We're just looking out for Kevin's safety."

"So that's why his parents think we violated his speech rights – because we didn't let Kevin discuss it on the PA system?" he asked.

Heather nodded and said, "We'll see what happens in court."

Kevin's parents sued, claiming the school violated his speech rights.

Did the judge agree?

Sharpen Your Judgment – The Decision

No, the judge ruled in favor of the school.

Kevin's parents claimed the school violated his speech rights because it wouldn't let him make a public statement denying a racist remark on the school's PA system.

But school officials argued it couldn't allow Kevin to address the student body over the PA system. They insisted the speech would be likely to make an already-tense situation even worse. School officials pointed to threats made by students who were offended by Kevin's remarks.

The judge agreed with school officials. If Kevin made a speech denouncing the remark, it was reasonable to believe that it would likely cause more tension, the court ruled.

Students have limited speech rights at school, the court explained. If officials reasonably believe speech will cause a disruption, they have the authority to impose limits on student speech.

Analysis: Safety trumps speech rights

As this case shows, school officials are well within the parameters of the law when refusing to allow speech that is likely to cause a disruption or a safety risk.

Cite: *Defabio v. East Hampton School Dist.*

4 Harassment and Discrimination

TOPICS

I. SEXUAL HARASSMENT 165

II. RACE AND NATIONAL ORIGIN DISCRIMINATION 172

III. RELIGIOUS DISCRIMINATION 174

IV. TEACHER SCENARIOS 175

CHAPTER FOUR
Harassment and Discrimination

I. SEXUAL HARASSMENT

Overview

Title IX of the Education Amendments of 1972 prohibits sex discrimination by all recipients of federal funding. In Davis v. Monroe County Board of Educ., *this chapter, the Supreme Court held school districts may be held liable under Title IX for student-on-student harassment. To establish liability under* Davis, *students must show (1) sexual harassment by peers; (2) deliberate indifference by school officials with actual knowledge of harassment; and (3) harassment so severe, pervasive and objectively offensive it deprived the student of access to educational opportunities. A teacher's knowledge of peer harassment is sufficient to create "actual knowledge" that may trigger liability for a district.*

In Fitzgerald v. Barnstable School Committee, *the U.S. Supreme Court held Title IX does not bar Equal Protection claims under 42 U.S.C. § 1983. Section 1983 is a federal statute that creates no rights itself, but enforces rights created by federal laws and the Constitution. Section 1983 imposes liability on a school district that has a policy or custom of violating constitutional rights.*

A. Texting, Sexting and Electronic Harassment

Facebook, texting and other electronic communication forms have created new concerns about inappropriate contacts among students, and between school employees and students. The relatively high liability standards under both Title IX and Section 1983 have been criticized as not preventing the sexual abuse of students. One response by school attorneys has been to urge school districts to enforce strict boundaries between students and school employees.

Court Decisions

◆ Parents began complaining about text messages from an Arkansas coach to female students. He agreed to stop the texting, but he also told one student that "her mother could stay with him" when the team had an out-of-town game. Another student told the superintendent that her ninth-grade cousin "might have a crush" on the coach. She said the ninth-grader often left classes to visit him in the gym. The student went to the ninth-grader's house to inform her mother of her suspicions. The coach denied anything was going on. The mother later approached the principal during a school board meeting to discuss rumors about a relationship between the coach and her daughter. The cousin tearfully volunteered more information and allegedly identified staff members who knew of inappropriate conduct. According to the ninth-grader's parent, the principal said she would investigate further, but she failed to do so before going on maternity leave. While she was on leave, the coach was accused of texting a student "OMG you look good today." After the principal returned from her leave, she received two new reports of misconduct by the coach. Based on these and other concerns, the district made preparations to non-renew his contract.

When students reported details of sexual contact between the coach and ninth-grader, the coach was arrested. He was eventually prosecuted and sentenced to 10 years in prison. The ninth-grader's parents filed a Title IX case against the school district, principal and other school officials. They added constitutional claims under 42 U.S.C. § 1983. A federal district court dismissed the claims against the school district and most of the claims against the officials, but the principal was denied immunity. On appeal, the U.S. Court of Appeals, Eighth Circuit, found the principal could be held liable for constitutional violations if she was deliberately indifferent to a pattern of unconstitutional acts by the coach. This required proof that she knew of his conduct but failed to take remedial action in a manner that caused the ninth-grader's injury. **The court held the coach's text messages did not provide the principal "actual notice of sexual abuse." Inappropriate comments alone did not alert her to a possible sexual relationship.** Even the most suggestive text message – "OMG you look good today" – did not indicate sexual conduct or abuse. The principal and superintendent investigated each report they received, and during the relevant time there was no evidence of improper contact. The court held "a student's familiar behavior with a teacher or even an 'excessive amount of time' spent with a teacher, without more, does not automatically give rise to a reasonable inference of sexual abuse." As a result, the lower court's denial of qualified immunity to the principal was reversed. Nor was the school district liable under Title IX. *Doe v. Flaherty*, 623 F.3d 577 (8th Cir. 2010).

◆ A New York student received three emails from a male classmate's school email account. One was profane and disparaged her appearance, and the others sought sexual relations. Although the student promptly reported the emails to the school administration, the classmate denied sending them and claimed other students had his email password. The classmate's account was later disabled, but the sender of the emails was never conclusively identified. Believing that the school district's investigation was inadequate, the student sued the school district in a federal district court for violating Title IX and other federal laws. The court held that no reasonable jury could find the student met the liability standard under Title IX for peer sexual harassment established in *Davis v. Monroe County School Board*, this chapter. The student appealed to the U.S. Court of Appeals, Second Circuit, which explained the *Davis* standard.

To prevail on a Title IX claim, the student had to show the school district acted with deliberate indifference that was so severe, pervasive, and objectively offensive that it barred her access to an educational opportunity or benefit. As the district court held, the student did not meet these requirements. While the emails were offensive, they fell well short of the kind of conduct necessary to create liability under Title IX. Since three offensive emails in a 10-day time period did not demonstrate "severe and pervasive harassment," the Title IX claim had been properly resolved in favor of the school district. The student's equal protection claim based on the district's allegedly more aggressive investigation and pursuit of a prior incident of race-based misconduct did not persuade the court, and the judgment was affirmed. *R.S. v. Board of Educ. of the Hastings-on-Hudson Union Free School Dist.*, 371 Fed.Appx. 231 (2d Cir. 2010).

◆ A Michigan high school soccer coach addressed players with obscenities, engaged them in "flirtatious conversations," and made suggestive remarks. He called players and sent them emails at unusual hours. He told one student on the team that he had "a special interest" in a particular teammate. The student said that when she discouraged the coach from pursuing the teammate, he threatened the entire team with consequences. The assistant principal, principal and athletic director met with him to address complaints by parents about his late-evening communications. The administrators composed a memo prohibiting him from late calls and from emailing players unless he copied the assistant principal. The coach was prohibited from counseling players about personal matters, conducting activities off-campus without parents present, and from inappropriate relationships. The teammate later informed the student she had broken off her relationship with the coach. According to the student, the coach blamed her for this and threatened to "break her nose and take out her knees so she would never play soccer again." The coach then threatened suicide. Police arrived at his residence, recovered a pistol, and took him to a hospital.

The coach resigned and was prohibited from entering school property. The student transferred to a different school and sued the district, coach and school officials. The case reached the U.S. Court of Appeals, Sixth Circuit, which held that **the coach's threats to harm the student did not involve any sexual communication**. While the threats were an abuse of authority, they did not pertain to sex. Verbal or physical conduct or communications that are not sexual in nature cannot be considered sexual harassment. The court noted that liability can be imposed for creating hostile environment harassment only if there is reasonable notice and failure to take action by officials. Here, the extent of the coach's misconduct did not become known until he resigned. *Henderson v. Walled Lake Consolidated Schools*, 469 F.3d 479 (6th Cir. 2006).

B. Sexual Harassment by Students

Teacher Scenarios

Teacher ignored student-on-student sexual harassment, mom claims 175

Did teacher do enough to protect bullied student? 175

Did school do enough after harassment complaint? 176

Court Decisions

◆ An Illinois student told her mother that a Junior Reserve Officer Training Corps (JROTC) instructor had improperly touched her at school and at JROTC stations. After the instructor admitted wrongdoing, he was charged criminally and resigned from his position. According to the student's stepfather, the JROTC supervisor told him "this incident has happened before, and it just in time goes away." After the charges against the instructor were published, two other female students came forward and reported that he abused them as well.

In a federal district court sexual harassment action, the student included an equal protection claim under 42 U.S.C. § 1983 against the district and the JROTC supervisor. She also brought a claim under Title IX against the district. The court found the Title IX claim precluded any Section 1983 claim based on supervisory liability. Judgment was entered for the school district, and the student appealed. The U.S. Court of Appeals, Seventh Circuit, found the dismissal of the Section 1983 claim for equal protection violations was based on a theory of supervisory liability. It noted the U.S. Supreme Court held Title IX did not bar Section 1983 claims against school officials in *Fitzgerald v. Barnstable School Committee*, below. But as the Section 1983 claim was based on supervisory liability, the court held **the lack of any knowledge of the instructor's misconduct by either the school district or the JROTC supervisor was fatal to the claim**. No school official knew of any sexual abuse of the student until the day she reported it. The court found remarks attributed to the JROTC supervisor were insufficient to pursue the Section 1983 claims. As a result, they had been properly dismissed. In urging Title IX liability, the student said that after she reported the abuse by the JROTC instructor, other students taunted her, put gum in her hair and threatened her. But the court refused to consider this as a form of "student-on-student harassment" that might create Title IX liability for the school district. As there was no legal support for the student's Title IX theory, the judgment for the district and supervisor was affirmed. *Trentadue v. Redmon*, 619 F.3d 648 (7th Cir. 2010).

◆ A Massachusetts kindergarten student told her parents that a third-grader on her school bus bullied her into lifting her skirt. The parents reported this to the principal, but the third-grader repeatedly denied the report, and the school could not corroborate the student's account. After she said the boy made her pull down her underpants and spread her legs, the school called the police, who found insufficient evidence for criminal charges. Finding insufficient evidence for school discipline, the principal suggested transferring the kindergartner to a different bus or leaving rows of empty seats between students of different ages.

The parents suggested moving the third-grader instead, or placing a monitor on the bus. The superintendent denied the requests. After the parents reported that the student had experienced more encounters with the third-grader at school, she began staying home. The family sued the school committee under 42 U.S.C. § 1983, claiming a violation of Title IX. A federal court and the First Circuit held that Title IX's private remedy precluded using 42 U.S.C. § 1983 to advance Title IX claims. The U.S. Supreme Court reversed the judgment. It held that Title IX was not meant to be the exclusive mechanism for addressing gender discrimination in the schools. Nor was it meant to be a substitute for parallel Section 1983 lawsuits as a means of enforcing constitutional rights. According to the Supreme Court, **Section 1983 was available as a remedy to enforce Equal Protection claims for gender discrimination in schools**. *Fitzgerald v. Barnstable School Committee*, 129 S.Ct. 788 (U.S. 2009).

◆ A Texas cheerleader claimed an African-American player on her high school's basketball team sexually assaulted her at a party. She stated that the player and another African-American were arrested for the assault, but that due to racial division in the grand jury, there was no indictment against them. At a school basketball game, the cheerleader cheered for the team but refused to cheer for the African-American player. School officials required her to either cheer when others cheered or go home. After the cheerleader left, she was removed from the squad for the school year. In a federal district court action against the school district and several officials, she asserted constitutional rights violations.

The court dismissed the case, and appeal went to the U.S. Court of Appeals, Fifth Circuit. It reviewed the cheerleader's claim that school officials deprived her of a due process right to be free from bodily injury and stigmatization. There was no allegation of a violation of bodily integrity. The court found that psychological injury alone was not a violation of a due process right to bodily integrity. As the Supreme Court of Texas has held, "students do not possess a constitutionally protected interest in their participation in extracurricular activities." The lower court correctly dismissed the case under the terms of the cheerleading contract, since failure to cheer was a valid ground for removal. **There was no basis for an equal protection claim, as the cheerleader did not show she was treated differently from others or show that gender had motivated any actions by officials.** There was no merit to her claims for First Amendment violations based on her refusal to cheer. Since the lower court judgment was not reached in error, the court affirmed it. *Doe v. Silsbee Independent School Dist.*, No. 09-41075, 2010 WL 3736233 (5th Cir. 9/16/10).

◆ An Ohio school bus monitor reported that a 12-year-old student performed oral sex on a 17-year-old high school student in the back of their school bus. Police and child protection authorities were called, and both students were suspended from school for 10 days. When the student returned from her suspension, she was required to sit at the front of the bus. The high school student was assigned to another bus. The student claimed others on the bus called her a "whore" and a "slut." After her stepfather called the school to complain, the taunting stopped. Although the student's mother said she reported the taunting and spoke to the principal three times, he later denied this. A few days after the student returned to school from her suspension, she was suspended again for 10 days for stealing an iPod and for lying. An expulsion was proposed based on theft, lying and earlier rules violations. After a board hearing, the student was expelled for theft, disruption and lying. Her mother sued the school district in a federal district court for failure to respond to sexual harassment in violation of Title IX.

According to the court, **federal funding recipients may be held liable for student-on-student harassment if the recipient is deliberately indifferent to harassment that is so severe, pervasive and objectively offensive that it deprives a victim of access to educational opportunities**. The board was not liable for the assault, as no prior incidents gave it reason to suspect the high school student would force the student to engage in oral sex on the bus. After the incident, the high school student was immediately disciplined and assigned to another bus. Damages are unavailable for insults, banter, teasing, shoving and pushing, even if it is gender-specific. As the verbal harassment did not deny the student equal access to educational opportunities, the board and principal were entitled to pretrial judgment on the harassment claims. But the court found enough evidence to allow the student's retaliation claims to proceed. The proximity in time between the complaints of harassment and the referral for expulsion created an inference that the family's complaints may have motivated the discipline. The Title IX retaliation claim and a related First Amendment claim were not dismissed. *Marcum v. Board of Educ. of Bloom-Carroll Local School Dist.*, 727 F.Supp.2d 657 (S.D. Ohio 2010).

◆ A Georgia fifth-grader complained to her teacher of sexual harassment by a male student. The teacher did not immediately notify the principal about it. Although the harasser was eventually charged with sexual battery, school officials took no action against him. The fifth-grader sued the school board for Title IX violations. A federal district court dismissed the case, and the U.S. Court of Appeals, Eleventh Circuit, affirmed. The U.S. Supreme Court reversed the judgment, holding that **school districts may be held liable under Title IX for deliberate indifference to known acts of peer sexual harassment, where the school's response is clearly unreasonable under the circumstances**.

A recipient of federal funds may be liable for student-on-student sexual harassment, where the recipient is deliberately indifferent to known sexual harassment and the harasser is under the recipient's disciplinary authority. To create Title IX liability, the harassment must be so severe, pervasive and objectively offensive that it deprives the victim of access to educational opportunities or benefits. The Court held the harassment alleged by the student in this case was sufficiently severe enough to avoid pretrial dismissal. The judgment was reversed and the case was returned to the lower courts. *Davis v. Monroe County Board of Educ.*, 526 U.S. 629 (1999).

◆ An Illinois kindergartner reported that a male classmate jumped on her back during a recess period near the start of the school year. He continued to exhibit inappropriate behavior, including repeatedly unzipping his pants. He also jumped on and kissed other female students. The principal suspended the classmate for two days and reassigned him to a new classroom, lunch and recess period. However, the classmate and kindergartner were later returned to the same lunch and recess periods, and the classmate's behavior apparently continued. A counselor diagnosed the kindergartner as having acute stress disorder and separation anxiety, and she received therapy. The school district granted the parents' request to transfer her to a different school for first grade, and they sued the district for sexual harassment.

The case reached the U.S. Court of Appeals, Seventh Circuit, which held that kindergartners could not engage in sexual harassment. Young students are still learning how to act appropriately, and they "regularly interact in a manner that would be unacceptable among adults." For this reason, **"simple acts of teasing and name-calling among children" do not create Title IX liability**. The kindergartner was unable to report conduct other than "vague and unspecific" allegations that the classmate "bothered her by doing nasty stuff." This did not provide the court with necessary details to evaluate its severity and pervasiveness. The kindergartner was not denied access to an education, as neither her grades nor her attendance suffered. As the district's response to the harassment was not clearly unreasonable and did not amount to deliberate indifference, the court held for the district. *Gabrielle M. v. Park Forest-Chicago Heights School Dist. 163*, 315 F.3d 817 (7th Cir. 2003).

◆ Two female second-graders claimed a boy repeatedly chased, touched and grabbed them and often made sexual remarks and gestures, but they did not communicate the sexual nature of his actions, and no adult saw him engage in overtly sexual behavior. Near the end of the school year, a third girl began attending the school and promptly complained to her teacher that the boy had told her to "suck his dick." The third girl's mother contacted the principal and teacher and was told that the school was working with the boy's parents to resolve his problems. After meeting with the third girl's mother, the principal suspended the boy. The principal instructed the teacher to keep him away from the third girl. When the girls' attorney notified the principal that the boy's misconduct was continuing, the school suspended him for the rest of the school year. The families sued the school board under Title IX.

The case reached the Eleventh Circuit, which stated that **damages are not available for "simple acts of teasing and mere name-calling"** among children even when comments target differences in gender. Although the conduct alleged by the first two girls persisted for months and was sexually explicit and vulgar, it was not so severe, pervasive or offensive that it denied them access to their education. They suffered no physical exclusion from school facilities. While the third girl's complaints were more explicit, the school responded to them and it was not deliberately indifferent. The court ruled for the school board. *Hawkins v. Sarasota County School Board*, 322 F.3d 1279 (11th Cir. 2003).

C. Sexual Harassment by Staff

◆ In 1998, the U.S. Supreme Court examined the liability of school districts for sexual harassment of students by teachers and other staff under Title IX. The case involved a Texas student who had a sexual relationship with a teacher. The Court rejected the liability standard advocated by the student and by the U.S. government, which resembled *respondeat superior* (vicarious) liability under Title VII. Title IX contains an administrative enforcement mechanism that assumes actual notice has been provided to officials prior to the imposition of enforcement remedies. **An award of damages would be inappropriate in a Title IX case unless an official with the authority to address the discrimination failed to act despite actual knowledge of it, in a manner amounting to deliberate indifference** to discrimination. Here, there was insufficient evidence that a school official should have known about the relationship to impose Title IX liability. Accordingly, the district could not be held liable for the teacher's misconduct. *Gebser v. Lago Vista Independent School Dist.*, 524 U.S. 274, 118 S.Ct. 1989, 141 L.Ed.2d 277 (1998).

◆ An Alabama personnel director investigated a teacher's misconduct three times, and each time the teacher denied the charge. After the third incident, the school board transferred him from a high school to an elementary school. There, a female student complained that he made an inappropriate comment. The principal told him that additional reports would result in discharge. Later in the same school year, female students complained about the way the teacher told them to do push-ups. The principal "ordered him not to place himself in such a questionable situation." An 11-year-old disabled student sought to transfer from his class, stating that classmates teased her about her disabilities. Over a year later, she told a school counselor that the teacher had raped her. The counselor promptly notified the student's parents and school officials.

The personnel director immediately placed the teacher on administrative leave and began investigating. The teacher retired, and the parents sued the school board and personnel director, asserting that the district was deliberately indifferent to the risk of harm to their child. The case reached the Supreme Court of Alabama, which held that the board was not an arm of the state for purposes of Eleventh Amendment immunity. However, the director was entitled to qualified immunity. **His failure to recommend the teacher's termination did not amount to deliberate indifference to the student's constitutional rights.** *Madison County Board of Educ. v. Reaves*, 1 So.3d 980 (Ala. 2008).

◆ An Idaho teacher had sexual relations with an 18-year-old student. When this was revealed, the teacher resigned. The student sued the teacher, school district and school officials, including claims for negligent supervision and violation of Title IX. She presented evidence of post-traumatic stress disorder (PTSD), but offered no medical records or damage estimates. The school district offered testimony from a psychologist who stated that her emotional problems were triggered by the lawsuit itself, not the sexual relationship. The jury found the district liable for negligent supervision. However, it found that the student did not prove any damages, and it awarded her none. On appeal, the Supreme Court of Idaho held a reasonable jury could have found the student proved no damages. **Her own experts disagreed as to her condition, with one finding she did not have PTSD.** The district's expert had found the student had no significant psychological difficulties until after the lawsuit was filed. The court upheld the jury's findings. *Hei v. Holzer*, 181 P.3d 489 (Idaho 2008).

◆ A Virginia gym teacher was accused of improperly touching two girls. The school principal responded to the complaints, investigated them and reported her findings to her supervisor. Her investigation set into motion police and child protection investigations, which found both complaints unfounded. A school investigator found that the teacher's actions were unintentional. Four years after the incidents, the teacher was fired for unprofessional conduct and insubordination. An adult former student learned of his misconduct and claimed he had improperly touched her when she was an elementary school student. She sued the school district and principal for sexual harassment, but a federal district court found no deliberate indifference by the principal.

The former student appealed to the U.S. Court of Appeals, Fourth Circuit, which noted that the standard of "deliberate indifference" is a high one. **Supervisory officials may be held liable for a subordinate's constitutional violations, but only if they have knowledge of the misconduct.** It must be demonstrated that the supervisor's response was so inadequate as to show deliberate indifference or "tacit authorization of the alleged offensive practices," and a link to the injury. To show "deliberate indifference" by the principal, the adult former student would have to show "continued inaction in the face of documented widespread abuses." The principal had responded reasonably to the risk that the gym teacher was sexually abusing students. As there was no evidence that closer supervision would have made any difference in this case, the lower court had properly held for the principal. *Sanders v. Brown*, 257 Fed.Appx. 666 (4th Cir. 2007).

◆ An assistant school superintendent in Georgia received an anonymous email during the school year, accusing a teacher of having inappropriate relationships with a list of students who had graduated or dropped out of school. She learned of a similar complaint against the teacher three years earlier, but the student involved in that incident vehemently denied anything inappropriate. The teacher denied both the report and the email accusation. The assistant superintendent warned her, both orally and in writing, to avoid any appearance of impropriety with students and situations where she would be alone with male students. Vehicles owned by the teacher and the troubled student were later seen parked together in some woods. The superintendent promptly notified the school board and the police, and asked the state Professional Standards Commission (PSC) to investigate the incident. She told the principal to monitor the two, prevent unnecessary contact between them and to report suspicious behavior to her. The teacher resigned and surrendered her teaching certificate after a substitute teacher discovered a note written by the student that threatened to expose their relationship if she did not comply with certain demands. The parents sued the district for Title IX and civil rights violations under 42 U.S.C. § 1983. The court held for the school district, and the parents appealed.

The U.S. Court of Appeals, Eleventh Circuit, held that the parents failed to show that school officials acted with deliberate indifference. They responded to each report of misconduct by investigating the charges and interviewing relevant persons. The officials consistently monitored the teacher and warned her about her interaction with students. They requested a PSC investigation after they received the first report specifically linking the teacher and student, monitored her and confronted her when the explicit note was discovered. In light of the many corrective measures taken by district officials, they were not deliberately indifferent. **A district is not deliberately indifferent because the measures it takes are ultimately ineffective in stopping the harassment.** The court affirmed the judgment for the district. *Sauls v. Pierce County School Dist.*, 399 F.3d 1279 (11th Cir. 2005).

D. Sexual Orientation

In the following case, the Court of Appeal of California observed that school administrators are better situated to address peer sexual harassment than are courts. Administrators can take affirmative steps to combat racism, sexism and other forms of bias which the courts cannot. And administrative actions are typically resolved far more quickly than private lawsuits.

Teacher Scenarios

Student harassment: 'But they didn't hurt him' 176

A boy can't wear a dress to the prom – can he? 177

Gay-Lesbian student group claims discrimination 177

Court Decisions

◆ Two California students claimed they were subjected to so much severe verbal and physical anti-gay harassment that they had to leave school. They kept logs of anti-gay peer harassment and gave them to school administrators. After getting little response, the students completed their high school careers in home study programs. They sued the school district, principal, assistant principal and district superintendent. A jury found that the district violated the Education Code and that the principal and assistant principal violated the male student's rights under the Equal Protection Clause. According to the jury, the principal violated the female student's equal protection rights. The verdict awarded the male student $175,000 in damages and the female student $125,000. They also received attorneys' fees of over $427,000. The Court of Appeal of California found the students had made out a successful claim for "deliberate indifference" to known anti-gay harassment. This satisfied the stringent Title IX standard.

In finding for the students on their equal protection claims, the jury had found that **administrators had actual notice of harassment but were deliberately indifferent to it**. As the principal was an appropriate person to act on behalf of the school district to address peer sexual orientation harassment, and there was evidence that the administrators took no meaningful action to stop the harassment, the judgment was upheld. *Donovan v. Poway Unified School Dist.*, 167 Cal.App.4th 567, 84 Cal.Rptr.3d 285 (Cal. Ct. App. 2008).

♦ A New Jersey student claimed he was repeatedly and severely taunted by classmates who directed homosexual epithets at him beginning in grade four. He endured slurs in the halls and was struck while in the school cafeteria, when 10 to 15 students surrounded and taunted him. The assistant principal did not punish or reprimand the students. During the student's eighth-grade year, his mother claimed a school guidance counselor simply urged her son to "toughen up and turn the other cheek." The principal later agreed to let the student leave classes to report problems directly to him, and the school began to discipline perpetrators. Verbal abuse persisted, but to a lesser degree. When the student entered high school, the harassment resurfaced. To avoid derision on school buses, he decided to walk home from school. He reported being followed by others as he walked home. Other students punched him and knocked him down, and he had to miss school. The students were suspended for 10 days and one pled guilty to assault charges. The student never returned to the high school, and his mother filed a harassment complaint with the state Division on Civil Rights. The student won $50,000 in emotional distress damages, and his mother won $10,000 for emotional distress. The district was fined $10,000 and ordered to pay attorneys' fees. A state appellate division court affirmed the $50,000 award for the student, but it reversed the award for his mother. On appeal, the Supreme Court of New Jersey **recognized a cause of action against school districts for student-on-student harassment based on perceived sexual orientation**. Liability would be imposed for peer harassment only if a district failed to reasonably address harassment and the district knew or should have known about it. The case was returned to the lower courts. *L.W. v. Toms River Regional Schools Board of Educ.*, 189 N.J. 381, 915 A.2d 535 (N.J. 2007).

♦ An Iowa student claimed that he endured years of severe harassment at school due to a perception that he was homosexual. He stated that school administrators failed to provide a safe environment after dozens of incidents of vandalization and physical assault. The school resource officer advised him to either ignore a harassing classmate or confront him. When the student confronted the classmate, the two got into a fight. The school suspended both students, and they were arrested for disorderly conduct. The student sued the district and several school and police officials for civil rights violations. A court upheld the school's anti-fighting policy as content and viewpoint neutral. The school had a strong interest in maintaining order to promote its learning environment, and the anti-fighting policy helped promote this interest. **The district could not be held liable for "negligent" failure to stop harassment.** The student showed a likelihood of success on his Title IX claim by alleging repeated harassment resulting in a hostile environment that forced him to leave school. He also claimed administrators knew of the harassment but were deliberately indifferent to it. Despite the student's strong showing on his Title IX claim, he was not entitled to a preliminary order preventing his suspension. *Doe v. Perry Community School Dist.*, 316 F.Supp.2d 809 (S.D. Iowa 2004).

♦ A group of California students who were (or were perceived by peers to be) gay, lesbian or bisexual claimed harassment by classmates over a seven-year period. The students stated that school officials took little or no action to protect them, and they sued the school district, its board and several school administrators. A federal district court held that the students presented evidence of official failure to remedy peer harassment and that this failure was based on sexual orientation. As the students' right to be free from sexual orientation discrimination was clearly established, the officials were not entitled to immunity. The officials appealed to the Ninth Circuit, which found evidence of years of harassment during which school administrators failed to enforce policies to protect the students. **There was evidence that school administrators were motivated by intentional discrimination or acted with deliberate indifference, despite many complaints.** This included failure to respond or inadequate response to at least two assault incidents, as well as repeated verbal harassment and pornography given to the students or placed in lockers. The district court had properly denied immunity to the administrators. *Flores v. Morgan Hill Unified School Dist.*, 324 F.3d 1130 (9th Cir. 2003).

♦ A lesbian student was allowed to proceed with discrimination claims against California school administrators who barred her from taking a physical education class based on her sexual orientation. She sued the school district and officials for violations of the Equal Protection Clause through 42 U.S.C. § 1983, also asserting state law claims. A court denied the school officials' motion for pretrial judgment based on Eleventh Amendment immunity. **Sexual orientation discrimination gives rise to an equal protection claim.** *Massey v. Banning Unified School Dist.*, 256 F.Supp.2d 1090 (C.D. Cal. 2003).

E. Students with Disabilities

Teacher Scenarios

Did school provide enough lunchtime supervision? 179

Court Decisions

◆ A Philadelphia special education student had difficulty speaking and asking for help, and she had significantly below-average communications skills. When she was 16 and in tenth grade, another special education student approached her sexually. As a result, her parent sought one-on-one supervision for her. Some time later, the student was led away from the school cafeteria by a male student to an auditorium balcony. Students were not permitted there, but they could and did manipulate the doors to gain entry without permission. In the balcony area, five male students sexually assaulted the student. In a lawsuit against the school district, school officials, the student perpetrators and their parents, the student's parent claimed school officials knew that the balcony created a hazard.

A federal district court considered evidence that the high school had been identified as a "persistently dangerous school" under the No Child Left Behind Act. A school safety advocate stated that the school district had under-reported violent incidents in prior years and that the district had a policy of not expelling students, even if they committed serious offenses involving assault or weapons. The court held that to establish municipal liability, a party must show that a constitutional violation occurred as the result of a custom or policy. It had to be shown that a school decisionmaker was deliberately indifferent to a risk of a constitutional violation, despite notice of harm. According to the court, **the Due Process Clause is a limitation on state power and not "a guarantee of certain minimal levels of safety and security."** There was no state obligation to prevent harm by a private person. Assurances of protection could not form the basis of a due process violation claim. Alleged failure by the school to keep the balcony area sealed and failure to report and properly discipline students could not be construed as "affirmative acts." An argument based on allowing violent students to persist in unlawful behavior due to failure to discipline them did not support a claim for a "state-created danger." *Brown v. School Dist. of Philadelphia*, Civil Action No. 08-2787, 2010 WL 2991741 (E.D. Pa. 7/28/10).

◆ A Michigan student endured harassment and bullying by classmates for years. When he reported harassment, an administrator allegedly said "kids will be kids, it's middle school." The harassment escalated during seventh grade, and a teacher even teased him in front of a full class, after which he became withdrawn and said he wanted to quit school. His grades fell, and he hid during lunch to avoid taunting. When he entered grade eight, he was found eligible for special education. An individualized education program (IEP) placed him in a resource room where the teacher helped him cope with peers. After a good eighth-grade experience, the student advanced to grade nine, where the high school principal refused to let him use the old resource room, even though it was in the same building. When the student was a junior, a baseball team member sexually assaulted him in the locker room as another student prevented his escape. While the assaulting student was expelled for eight days, the other student was only verbally reprimanded. The student refused to return to the high school, and his family sued the school district for violating Title IX.

A court found no deliberate indifference by the district under Title IX. On appeal, the U.S. Court of Appeals, Sixth Circuit, noted that each time the family reported an incident and the school knew who the perpetrators were, the district responded. This was not "deliberate indifference." However, **refusing to let the student use the old resource room might be deliberate indifference, opening the door for Title IX liability**. The court returned the case to the lower court. *Patterson v. Hudson Area Schools*, 551 F.3d 438 (9th Cir. 2008).

When the case returned to the district court, the school district sought to dismiss it for failure to first request a due process hearing under the Individuals with Disabilities Education Act (IDEA). The district also sought to exclude from evidence any testimony of a non-sexual nature. The court held that even though the student had an IEP, the case arose under Title IX of the Education Amendments of 1972, not the IDEA or other laws protecting disabled persons. The court found Title IX intends to protect students from sex discrimination, not general bullying. While damages are available in a Title IX action for harassment that is so severe, pervasive and objectively offensive that it denied equal access to education, they are not available for simple acts of teasing and name-calling. Some evidence that the school district sought to exclude had sexual overtones and might be more than just teasing or bullying. But the court held materials relating to any time after the student stopped going to school could be excluded. *Patterson v. Hudson Area Schools*, No. 05-74439, 2010 WL 455410 (E.D. Mich. 2/3/10).

◆ A 16-year-old Texas special education student with mental retardation and a speech impairment functioned at the approximate level of a second-grader. According to her family, she was sexually assaulted at her middle school by a male special needs student with a previous disciplinary record of violence and displaying pornographic material. Despite this history, the students were left unattended in a classroom for 15-20 minutes. The student reported to an aide that the male student exposed himself to her, grabbed her, kissed her and raised up her dress. Although the aide separated the two immediately, she did not report the incident until the next day. The principal called the school district police, and police officers questioned the male student and a teacher. No police action was taken against the male student, but the school separated the students and assigned an escort to the female student between all her classes. After he shouted intimidating profanities at her, he was sent to another school.

The student's family sued the school district for sexual harassment under Title IX. A federal district court dismissed the case, and the U.S. Court of Appeals, Fifth Circuit, affirmed the judgment. It held that to establish school liability under Title IX, there must be sexual harassment so severe, pervasive and objectively offensive that it deprives the victim of access to educational opportunities or benefits. In addition, **a school district must have actual knowledge of harassment, yet act with**

deliberate indifference to it. According to the court, the student did not prove the requirements for Title IX liability. The actions in this case were not "so severe, pervasive and objectively offensive" as to deprive the student of access to education. And the school district took several remedial actions designed to prevent future incidents. *Watkins v. La Marque Independent. School Dist.*, 308 Fed.Appx. 781 (5th Cir. 2009).

II. RACE AND NATIONAL ORIGIN DISCRIMINATION

Title VI of the Civil Rights Act of 1964 prohibits race discrimination in any program that receives federal funds. Title VI is based on equal protection principles, and many discrimination complaints allege violations of Title VI, the Equal Protection Clause, and analogous state law provisions. **Courts require proof of intentional discrimination in Title VI cases.** *School officials may be held liable under Title VI if they are deliberately indifferent to clearly established student rights. This occurs where a pattern or practice of civil rights violations is shown that is attributable to policy-making employees.*

Teacher Scenarios

Parents call discipline racist – did teacher take the right steps? 178

Court Decisions

◆ A Minnesota special school district opened an alternative school to serve immigrant students with limited English skills and little or no formal education. Thirteen students claimed that the placement provided little educational benefit and effectively guaranteed that they would not graduate. They claimed that the school warehoused them and had no coherent curriculum. Several failed to pass a state test required for high school graduation. A report by the state education department found that the school improperly refused to test students at the school for special education eligibility until they had at least three years of English Language Learner instruction. Although some of the students had graduated, they filed a federal district court action against the school and the district for violating the Equal Educational Opportunities Act (EEOA), Title VI of the Civil Rights Act of 1964, and the Minnesota Human Rights Act (MHRA).

After the court ruled for the school district, the students appealed. The U.S. Court of Appeals, Eighth Circuit, held **Title VI prohibits only intentional discrimination**. There was no strong evidence of discrimination in this case based on the statements by school personal. Significantly, **the students did not identify students who were treated more favorably by the school district to whom they could be compared**. Eleven of the students presented no evidence of injury from the policy of not testing ELL students for special education needs until they took three years of ELL classes. As for the remaining two, the district stated it did not believe they could be reliably assessed for special services until they had been in the country long enough to learn English. The court found this was a legitimate, nondiscriminatory reason. No school or district policy singled out foreign-born students. The testing policy applied to ELL students, not those born outside the U.S. According to the court, "language and national origin are not interchangeable." A policy treating ELL students differently than others in the district was not one that discriminated on the basis of national origin. Review of the legislative history of the EEOA revealed that the act did not offer monetary damage awards. The MHRA was interpreted similarly to the EEOA, and as all the claims failed, the court affirmed the judgment. *Mumid v. Abraham Lincoln High School*, 618 F.3d 789 (8th Cir. 2010).

◆ Nine North Carolina students sued the Durham Public School System, asserting a "wholesale challenge" to its disciplinary process. They claimed that they were disciplined more severely than white students for less serious offenses. In addition, the students claimed that the board's anti-gang policy was unconstitutionally vague. A state trial court dismissed the action, and the students appealed. The Court of Appeals of North Carolina held that most of the claims had been properly dismissed, as each individual student failed to allege a claim for relief against each individual official. But the lower court would have to reconsider a due process claim brought on behalf of a now-deceased student who had been suspended for 13 days. His mother claimed that the superintendent of schools misled her and backdated correspondence to make a long-term suspension appear to be a short-term suspension. The trial court was also to reconsider a challenge to the school board's anti-gang policy. On appeal, the Supreme Court of North Carolina held the student had an adequate remedy under state law. So he could not sue the board for due process violations. Here, **two North Carolina statutes allowed any student who was suspended in excess of 10 school days to appeal to the education board, and then to a state court**. The court did not consider the gang policy issue, which was to return to the trial court. *Copper v. Denlinger*, 688 S.E.2d 426 (N.C. 2010).

◆ New Jersey school officials called the police after discovering an African-American student had a knife at school. He petitioned the state department of education to reverse his 10-day suspension. According to the student and his father, white students were only suspended three to five days for similar conduct. After the suspension was upheld, the student's father, who served as the student's attorney, filed a state court action against the school district for civil rights violations. He also filed a series of requests for public records and court actions seeking statistics about violent incidents in the district to support his discrimination claim. These requests were made under the state Open Public Records Act (OPRA). When the district provided copies of disciplinary records, the father made an OPRA request for additional records that he believed were in the district's possession. When this request did not yield the information being sought, he filed another state court action. This time, he sought the names of the police departments and officers who responded to 47 weapons-related incidents in district schools from 2001 to 2007. The school district disputed that there were 47 weapons incidents and provided records for a lower number.

A state trial court eventually resolved the three OPRA actions in favor of the district. It held there had been a sufficient response under the OPRA, and it found that 249 Violence, Vandalism and Substance Abuse Incident reports sought by the father did not exist. The district was not required to research, analyze records and report "incident details" as the father sought. In the civil rights case, the court held for the district and denied a request for extension of the pretrial discovery period. Appeal went before a New Jersey Appellate Division Court, which consolidated the three OPRA cases with the civil rights action. It held there was no denial of access to records under the OPRA or common law. The court found the father had received all the records he was due. The OPRA and common law claims for access to documents "kept the parties in a continuous, multi-faceted battle" and complicated the litigation. As for the civil rights claim, **the court found the student did not show any discrimination in his discipline or the report to the police. A 10-day suspension was not significantly different from the suspensions imposed on white students.** Since there was no statistically or legally significant basis to support a finding of discrimination based on the suspension or the call to police, the court affirmed the judgment. *O.R. v. Kniewel*, Nos. L-2293, L-2380-07, L-2686-06, L-2316-06, 2010 WL 1191088 (N.J. Super. Ct. App. Div. 3/17/10).

◆ Georgia school administrators received a report that an African-American student stole an MP3 player from another student's locker and tried to sell it. A white male stated that he and the African-American student stole the player together after going locker to locker. He accused the African-American student of selling the MP3 player for $40. The assistant principal interviewed the African-American student, who denied the allegations. She then searched his locker and found a dead cell phone that was later determined to be stolen from a middle school in the district. Investigators questioned the African-American student a second time about the stolen MP3 player. He admitted trying to sell it to a friend but claimed he did not steal it and was not aware that it had been stolen. After school officials suspended him for eight days, he sued them.

A federal district court held that the search and seizure claims did not state a Fourth Amendment or due process violation. As for the equal protection claims, they failed because the student did not show that he was "similarly situated" to his white classmate. On appeal, the U.S. Court of Appeals, Eleventh Circuit, affirmed, noting that in cases involving short-term suspensions of 10 days or less, **"once school administrators tell a student what they heard or saw, ask why they heard or saw it, and allow a brief response, a student has received all the process that the Fourteenth Amendment demands."** *Roy v. Fulton County School Dist.*, 288 Fed.Appx. 686 (11th Cir. 2008).

◆ A Kansas student claimed that the principal and teachers at his alternative school repeatedly forbade students of Hispanic origin from speaking Spanish. According to the student, the principal suspended him after telling him "he was not in Mexico" and that "he should speak only English on school premises." The student's father brought the suspension notice to the superintendent, who overturned the suspension. The family sued the superintendent, principal, teachers, school board and district, and members of the school board. The complaint alleged race and national origin discrimination in violation of Title VI and the Equal Protection Clause.

The court noted that the EEOC has stated that rigid English-only workplace rules may violate Title VII of the Civil Rights Act. **By claiming that school officials singled out students of Hispanic origin and targeted them for attributes based upon race or national origin, the student made out a valid equal protection claim.** But the principal and teacher were entitled to qualified immunity from liability because no case had established a right to speak a foreign language at a public school. However, the school district could still be held liable for the principal's acts, because she had authority to take corrective action to end the discrimination. *Rubio v. Turner Unified School Dist.*, 453 F.Supp.2d 1295 (D. Kan. 2006).

◆ An Oklahoma school district maintained a "fight policy" subjecting second-time offenders to expulsion for a semester. After the district expelled two African-American students for violating the fight policy, they alleged that white students were not expelled despite similar conduct. They claimed that the principal tolerated racial slurs and epithets by white students and allowed swastikas and the letters "KKK" to be inscribed in desks and placed in the lockers or notebooks of African-American students. The students sued the district for violating Title VI. A court awarded pretrial judgment to the district, and the students appealed to the Tenth Circuit.

The court noted that since the students could not disprove the school's legitimate reasons for discipline, pretrial judgment was appropriate on the intentional discrimination claim. However, the students were entitled to an opportunity to prove their assertions of the principal's inaction in the face of a racist environment. **School administrators could be liable under Title VI for remaining "deliberately indifferent" to known acts of "student-on-student harassment."** The hostile race environment claim was remanded to the district court, with instructions to apply the standard of liability for peer sexual harassment claims from *Davis v. Monroe County Board of Educ.*, this chapter. The hostile race environment claim was returned to the district court so it could determine if the harassment was so severe, pervasive and objectively offensive that it deprived the victims of access to educational benefits or opportunities. *Bryant v. Independent School Dist. No. I-38, Garvin County, Oklahoma*, 334 F.3d 928 (10th Cir. 2003).

III. RELIGIOUS DISCRIMINATION

Cases involving religion and public schools typically arise under the Establishment and Free Exercise Clauses of the First Amendment.

◆ A Delaware fourth-grade student from a Muslim family said her teacher isolated her by reading Christmas books and telling a candy cane story that was supposed to symbolize Christian beliefs. She said her teacher's classroom discussions deviated from a textbook and framed the events of 9/11 "as a war of Christians versus Muslims." But the student was afraid to complain about the teacher. She said that her classmates teased her. When the student finally complained to her mother that she was upset by the Christian books and Christmas discussions in her classroom, the mother asked school officials for an apology and a statement to the class that she had done nothing wrong. The mother's suggestions were rejected, but after the ACLU became involved, the teacher agreed to let the student make a presentation to the class. A transfer of the student then followed, but her friends shunned and taunted her.

In a federal district court action, the student filed claims under Article I, Section One of the Delaware Constitution, which the court found analogous to the Establishment and Free Exercise Clauses of the First Amendment. As the Supreme Court has held, **the government cannot promote or affiliate itself with any religious doctrine or organization, nor is it permitted to discriminate on grounds of religious belief or practice**. Although school officials claimed the student was not coerced in violation of her Free Exercise rights, the court allowed the claim to proceed. There were fact issues about whether the teacher violated the student's rights under the state constitution's Preference Clause. A reasonable jury might find that phrases from the teacher's candy cane story, such as "Jesus is the pure Lamb of God," and "Jesus is the Christ," lacked any secular purpose and endorsed Christianity. As a result, pretrial judgment was denied regarding discussions about Christian readings and the candy cane story. But the court found the 9/11 textbook portrayed historic events evenhandedly and served a secular educational purpose that neither enhanced nor inhibited religion. A claim alleging retaliation for protected speech required further consideration. The court found a reasonable jury might agree with the student that her transfer to another classroom was an adverse action. An equal protection claim also required further consideration, since the court found the teacher read Christmas books to the class every day for about one month but did not recognize other religious holidays. *Doe v. Cape Henlopen School Dist.*, Civ. No. 05-424-SLR, 2011 WL 64073 (D. Del. 1/7/11).

◆ A New York parent claimed a charter school principal forced her child to eat during a fast. Without the help of an attorney, the parent sued the charter school and principal in a federal district court for religious discrimination. She claimed the principal defied her instructions, isolated the child in the cafeteria and presented her with food. The complaint asserted only that this "violated her freedom of religion." The court found the complaint legally deficient. There was no direct claim that the school or the principal were "acting under color of state law," which was necessary to find a constitutional rights violation under 42 U.S.C. § 1983. It was unclear whether charter schools were "state actors" subject to liability under 42 U.S.C. § 1983. Even if the charter school was a state actor, the parent did not allege misconduct that resulted from an official policy or custom, which is a prerequisite for Section 1983 liability.

While the Free Exercise Clause is "an unflinching pledge to allow our citizenry to explore religious beliefs in accordance with the dictates of their conscience," the court held "not every belief put forward as 'religious' is elevated to constitutional status." **To survive dismissal, the court found there had to be a reasonable possibility that the parent had sincerely held convictions with theological, rather than secular grounds.** She also had to show the school put a substantial burden upon her and interfered with a central religious doctrine. In this case, the parent did not assert religious beliefs that were genuine and sincerely held. She stated no facts concerning her religious beliefs or their importance. Even if the parent's view was believed, the court found a general reference to "familial religious practice," without explanation of the importance of fasting, was insufficient to allege a sincerely held religious belief. As a result, the religious free exercise challenge failed. Regarding the Equal Protection Clause claim, the court held the parent had to show intentional discrimination based on a protected classification, such as religious belief. But she did not allege that the school and principal knew what her religion was or even offer any facts concerning the family's religion. As filed, the complaint was deficient. However, the court offered the parent a second chance to file a complaint so she could include facts supporting her claims. *Meadows v. Lesh*, No. 10-CV-00223(M), 2010 WL 3730105 (W.D.N.Y. 9/17/10).

IV. TEACHER SCENARIOS

Teacher ignored student-on-student sexual harassment, Mom claims

Mom sues school after second incident in restroom

Teacher Beth Lee sighed as she re-read the email from Terry Brown's mother. She knew their meeting wasn't going to be an easy one. Just then, Ms. Brown walked into the classroom.

"Hi, have a seat," Beth said, pulling up a chair for Terry's mother.

"How could you let this happen again?" Ms. Brown asked.

"Last month this Billy kid touched my son's genitals in the bathroom," she continued. "And today Terry came home complaining about another problem with the same kid!"

"I'm very sorry, Ms. Brown," Beth said. "After the incident last month, we moved the desks so Billy and Terry don't sit together, and we haven't let them use the restroom at the same time."

Mom says response didn't work ...

"So? It didn't help!" Ms. Brown shot back. "Terry told me Billy tried to 'bump on his behind' again."

"Yes, that's what Terry told me, too," Beth confirmed. "I am so sorry this happened, and we're going to talk to Billy's parents again."

"Oh, you're going to talk to his parents again?" Ms. Brown asked, her voice dripping with sarcasm.

"Clearly, you weren't watching the kids," she continued. "You'll be hearing from my lawyer!"

Ms. Brown sued, claiming the school was indifferent to student-on-student sexual harassment.

The school asked the court to dismiss the claim. Did it?

Decision: Yes, the court dismissed Ms. Brown's claim.

Key: Although school officials' response failed to prevent a second incident, they did take action, the court noted.

The teacher moved the students' seats and refused to let the boys go to the restroom together – so she wasn't indifferent, the court explained.

Cite: *Brooks v. City of Philadelphia.*

Sharpen Your Judgment

Did teacher do enough to protect bullied student?

"Bad news," Principal Ellen Kinsey told teacher Jean Hamlin, "Ted was attacked at school today. Again."

"Oh, no. By the same boys as last time?"

"It's always new ones," sighed Ellen. "Kids leave Ted alone once we punish them. But it was the same old stuff: the gay jokes, the obscene pictures, the dirty remarks."

Teacher wonders what would help

"I try to keep an eye on Ted and break up anything that seems suspicious," said Jean. "Can I do anything else?"

"Probably not. Ted's mom says the only thing that worked was Ted's hour a day in the reference room with Mr. Felt. They want that reinstated, but Ted's outside the age limit for that program now. It's a shame. Mr. Felt helped Ted fend off attacks better. Now it's all getting out of control again."

A few weeks later, as a "joke," Ted was sexually assaulted in the locker room.

His parents sued, saying the school had mishandled the fact that other students were sexually harassing Ted. The school disagreed, saying it properly disciplined all harassers – and asked the court to dismiss the case. Did it?

Sharpen Your Judgment – The Decision

No, the judge didn't dismiss the case.

Ted's parents claimed the school was "deliberately indifferent" to student-on-student sexual harassment. This violates Title IX.

Schools can usually avoid this claim by responding to reports quickly: talking to involved students and disciplining harassers.

This school did that repeatedly. But the judge decided a trial was needed because it wasn't stopping the harassment.

Analysis: Doing what works

The judge was concerned that the school had a tactic it knew reduced the harassment – but didn't use it. Giving Ted an hour a day with a resource room counselor had helped him deal better with other students so that he could keep attacks from turning even uglier.

Teachers don't set school policy – but because they're in the front lines with students and parents, they may know sooner than administrators when an otherwise sensible school policy just isn't getting the job done.

Sharing this info with the office can make a big difference – not only in meeting students' needs but in helping your school avoid a lawsuit.

Cite: *Patterson v. Hudson Area Schools.*

Sharpen Your Judgment

Did school do enough after harassment complaint?

Teacher Ron Samuels knocked lightly on the door of Principal Heather Marks. "I got your message that you wanted to see me," Samuels said. "What's up?"

"It's about Tricia Johansen," Marks said.

"Oh, I still get chills when I think about what happened to her in one of our classrooms," Samuels said.

"Well, to make matters worse, her parents are suing us," Marks replied.

"Suing us? It's awful what happened to Tricia. But I don't understand how it's our fault," Samuels said.

School took several steps

"I know," Marks said. "We could never have predicted what happened."

"And as soon as we heard that Bobby grabbed Tricia and tried to kiss her after class – and then exposed himself to her when she resisted – we took action right away," Marks claimed.

"We did our best to separate them after that," Marks continued. "We even assigned Tricia an escort between classes right away."

"You got the police involved, too," Samuels said. "And then Bobby was moved to a different school. We did everything we could."

"Tricia's parents don't think so," Marks said. "They say we should have done more, especially since Bobby had a disciplinary history."

Did the district win the case?

Sharpen Your Judgment – The Decision

Yes, an appeals court affirmed a ruling which held the school district was not liable.

The parents of the girl said the district should be held liable for sexual harassment because the boy had a prior disciplinary record. They claimed the district should have known better than to leave him alone with their daughter.

The district claimed it wasn't liable. It pointed out that it separated the two students right away and initiated a police investigation. Also, when the boy shouted profanities at the girl, he was sent to another school.

The court agreed with the district. To prove sexual harassment, the parents had to show the district knew about severe harassment and let it go unchecked. The parents didn't meet this high standard, the court said.

Analysis: Quick response is key

To win, parents who raise sexual harassment cases like these have to show schools were "deliberately indifferent" to harassment. This is a tough standard to meet, and it's especially tough to prove harassment when the school reacts quickly and is responsive.

In this case, the school took several steps in response to the report, and it wasn't liable.

Cite: *Watkins v. La Marque Independent School Dist.*

Sharpen Your Judgment

Student harassment: 'But they didn't hurt him'

The student timidly slid the note toward the teacher while saying, "Here's another one."

Teacher Lon Barber silently read the scrawled words: *"Hey Frank the Fag. Got a new boyfriend yet?"*

"That makes three notes like this in the last month, right?" the teacher asked.

"Right," Frank Arnold nodded. "Always from people in your fourth-period class. They're the same people who purposely bump into me and make jokes about me because I'm gay."

"Frank, I've talked to the students you've identified and told them I disapprove of how they're treating you," the teacher explained. "They always say they're just joking and have never really hurt you physically. Is that correct?"

"It's pretty much true," the student said. "No one's ever hit me or anything like that."

"Then I don't think there's much else we can do about it," the teacher said.

The student and his parents said the school wasn't doing enough to prevent the harassment, and decided to sue.

The school argued its options were limited because no one had actually attacked Frank physically. Did the school win the case?

Sharpen Your Judgment – The Decision

No. The school lost when a judge decided that teachers and officials hadn't done enough to stop the harassment.

The judge explained that harassment doesn't have to involve physical harm before a school must take action.

Crude jokes, "innocent" pushing and shoving, insulting notes and other behaviors all reach the level of harassment that must be acted upon and stopped.

Analysis: New problem – same standards

The area of student gay harassment is one that's fairly new to schools and the courts.

Until recently, most types of complaints fell into the cases involving sexual, religious or racial harassment. In those cases, harassment has to be dealt with and stopped.

And that's the standard many courts are using when it comes to gay harassment.

Most judges have issued the same warning that came out of this case: As with any type of harassment, gay harassment can take many forms.

Whatever forms it takes, schools must stop it and punish the offenders.

Cite: *Ramelli v. Poway Unified School Dist.*

Sharpen Your Judgment

A boy can't wear a dress to the prom – can he?

"I'm really sorry, Bill," said teacher Sophie Glazer, blocking the student's way in to the prom. "The principal told us not to let you in if you're wearing a dress. And you are."

"Unbelievable!" said Bill. "Someone needs to explain to her what transgendered means."

Principal tried to find a compromise

"That's enough, Bill," said Sophie mildly. "I understand you're upset. But you know our dress code doesn't allow clothes that broadcast sexual orientation. And you also know how hard the principal's been working to bend that rule for you without breaking it. She said she offered you a compromise for tonight, too: wearing a women's pant suit instead of a tux."

"Ms. Glazer," said Bill, "would you have been willing to wear a pants suit to your prom?"

"I really am sorry, Bill," said Sophie. "But your dress definitely violates the dress code. We can't just ignore that. But if you want to go change into a pants suit, I'll wait for you here and escort you in personally when you come back."

Instead, Bill left the prom. He sued, calling the dress code illegal and saying the school had violated his Title IX and free speech rights.

Did the judge dismiss Bill's lawsuit?

Sharpen Your Judgment

Gay-Lesbian student club claims discrimination

"Hey, Janie," yelled student Phil Tobin down the noisy hallway. "Wait up!"

Student Janie Washington stopped to watch Phil make his way to her through the crowd. "What?" she asked when he got there.

"How come you didn't read that notice I gave you about my club's car wash on this morning's announcements?"

"Mr. Drew didn't approve it. He said I can't make announcements for noncurricular clubs."

"Noncurr-WHAT-ular?" asked Phil.

"You know. Clubs not tied to a class taught here. The French Club gets announcements. Your Gay-Lesbian Awareness Club doesn't. Oh. He said you can't have a car wash here, either."

"What? Then how come the cheerleaders got one? And why did the Chess Club get an announcement this morning? Since when does the school offer chess and cheerleading classes?"

"I don't know, Phil. Talk to Mr. Drew."

Phil did, saying other noncurricular clubs got more benefits. When the school refused to provide them to his club, too, Phil sued, claiming this violated his rights.

Did the judge agree?

Sharpen Your Judgment – The Decision

No, the judge didn't dismiss Bill's lawsuit.

More info was needed before the court could determine if:

- Bill had a free speech right to wear the prom dress – because doing so sent a message others would understand, or
- the dress code violated Title IX – which can prohibit stereotypes based on gender.

Analysis: Proceed with caution

There's no definite yes or no yet on whether schools have to let students "cross dress" at the prom. But since courts are taking the question seriously, you should, too.

Is this a trend? This judge didn't simply uphold the dress code. And another school, facing an almost identical lawsuit, backed down and changed its dress code.

The good news is: Teacher-chaperones are likely to have warning about nontraditional promwear. In both lawsuits, the students told a principal what they planned to wear.

And since other schools are facing this, it also gives you a heads up on finding out how the office wants you to deal with it if you wind up facing a boy in a dress or a girl in a tux.

Cite: *Logan v. Gary Community School Corp.*

Sharpen Your Judgment – The Decision

Yes, the judge agreed that denying one noncurricular club the same benefits the others got violated the Equal Access Act.

This federal law prevents discrimination against student groups that adults may be uncomfortable with – such as: religious clubs or Gay-Straight Alliance groups.

But it is OK for schools to provide more benefits to clubs that tie in to classes taught in the curriculum.

For example: A school can legally provide a field trip to a math club, but deny one to a prayer club.

What isn't OK is if a school gives some of its noncurricular clubs more benefits than others. Like here, where a chess club got a morning announcement but a Gay-Lesbian club didn't.

And keep in mind that courts will scrutinize claims of unequal treatment even more closely if they're made by a controversial club.

Analysis: Same groups get same benefits

Sometimes, protecting a student club falls to the faculty sponsor. If you're the one working with the office to make sure a club is treated fairly, keep the curricular-noncurricular distinction in mind.

Cite: *Straights and Gays for Equality v. Osseo Area Schools-Dist. No. 279.*

Parents call discipline racist – did teacher take the right steps?

Student victim took the law into her own hands

Teacher Joy Lewis looked up at the hall clock as she was finally leaving for the day. She'd been focusing so hard on her grading that she hadn't realized it was 5 p.m. already.

No wonder the halls were so empty! But as Joy turned a corner, she saw student Tiffany Jones reaching into an open locker.

"Hi, Tiffany," said Joy. Tiffany jumped at the sound of Joy's voice and then quickly pulled her hand out of the locker.

"Sorry," laughed Joy. "I didn't mean to scare you. Hey, wait a minute," she added, "Isn't your locker downstairs? Don't I pass you there every morning?"

"Uh ... Yeah. This is ... I'm just getting something for a friend. She's sick."

The student is obviously lying

Joy glanced down into the open bag by Tiffany's feet. "So, you're bringing your friend three iPods? And a BlackBerry in one of those custom-made covers with 'Sheri' spelled in sequins? Is Sheri your sick friend's name?"

"Fine!" said Tiffany angrily. "All right already. I get it. You know."

"Know what?" asked Joy quietly.

"That I ... took this stuff. I jimmied the locker doors open with this, OK?" added Tiffany, pulling a screwdriver out of her back pocket and handing it to Joy.

This is serious

"Did you bring this screwdriver with you from home?" asked Joy.

"Yes. Why?"

"I guess you really thought this out beforehand."

"Yeah, I did," said Tiffany. "So what? You know why I did this!"

"No, I don't," said Joy.

"Oh, come on! Sheri? Because of what Sheri and her whole mean group of white girls did to me."

Student suffered racial attack

"Sheri and her mean group of ... Oh," said Joy, realizing what Tiffany meant.

"Pretending I was their slave," said Tiffany tightly.

"That was awful," agreed Joy. "We don't put up with anything like that at this school. That's why their parents got called in and the girls had to apologize to you in the office and then got suspended."

"And that's why I'm paying them back by taking things they care about while they're at choir practice," said Tiffany.

"What?" said Joy. "No, Tiffany. You just lost me. Pick up the bag, OK? We need to go see if Officer Garcia's still in his office."

"You're turning me in?" asked Tiffany, shocked. "After what I just told you? Hey, no. I'll put the stuff back. Just cut me some slack."

"I can't," said Joy. "Tiffany, I'm sorry you had such a terrible experience. But I still have to report anybody who breaks the rules."

"Exactly what I'd expect a white teacher to say," muttered Tiffany, grabbing her bag and following Joy.

Discrimination?

Tiffany was suspended for stealing, and her parents sued under Title VI, calling it racial discrimination.

At trial, their psychologist testified Tiffany's stealing was clearly connected to a racial attack.

Did the judge agree the suspension was discriminatory?

Decision: No, this wasn't racially biased discipline.

The Supreme Court has held Title VI doesn't require schools to try to make it up to victims of peer racial harassment. Instead, schools only have to respond to harassment reports in a reasonable way. This school did.

Key: Like everyone else, teachers need to be careful to avoid even the appearance of discrimination. The best way? Basic fairness. Apply the same rules the same way with every student you deal with.

Cite: *D.T. v. Somers Cent. School Dist.*

Discussion points for teachers and principals:

Serious behavior problems can follow mistreatment. But what's the best response when students act out after suffering abuse?

- Some educators think discipline should slide here – it's more important to show these kids empathy and kindness exist, too.

- But others think the rules matter even more because they can teach students that everyone's accountable for his/her actions.

Sharpen Your Judgment

Did school provide enough lunchtime supervision?

"Nice suit!" assistant principal Ron Davis said to Principal Mary Salinger. "Is it a special occasion?"

"Not exactly," Mary replied. "I'm meeting with the school's lawyers today on that Jerry Kenney case."

"It's terrible how that student sexually assaulted a classmate at recess, especially since she's a special needs student," Ron said.

"I know," Mary said. "But now the girl's parents are saying we weren't watching the kids closely enough."

"I never did like that alcove where the attack happened," Mary continued. "But we had it marked off with those yellow chains, and we told all the students to stay away from it."

"We had plenty of people out there supervising," Ron said. "And we knew that spot had been a problem, so it was checked about every five minutes."

"I don't know what else we could have done," Ron added.

"The girl's parents are saying we needed to provide more supervision because of her mental disability," Mary said. "I just hope the court doesn't find us responsible."

The victim's parents sued the school district for negligent supervision. A trial court issued a ruling for the district, but the parents filed an appeal.

Did the appeals court find that the lower court made the right call?

Sharpen Your Judgment – The Decision

No, the appeals court reversed the trial court's ruling for the district and reinstated the parents' claims.

The girl's parents claimed the district did not provide enough supervision during the recess period. They said a special needs child like their daughter needed extra supervision. The school should have known she couldn't take care of herself, they claimed.

The district said it did all it could. The area around the alcove was marked by a yellow chain, and students were told it was off limits during lunch break.

The appeals court agreed with the parents. The key question was whether the harm to the child was foreseeable. Because the school allowed a hidden area to be maintained on its campus – an area it knew was a problem – an attack on a special needs student was foreseeable, it ruled.

Analysis: Heightened duty for vulnerable students

There are two key lessons from this case. First, if you know you have a problem area, you have to make sure it's inaccessible to students. And second, your duty to supervise is heightened when it comes to more vulnerable students, such as those with mental disabilities.

Cite: *Jennifer C. v. Los Angeles Unified School Dist.*

5 Student Discipline

TOPICS

I. EXPULSIONS AND SUSPENSIONS 183

II. STUDENT SEARCH AND SEIZURE 197

III. CORPORAL PUNISHMENT 210

IV. TEACHER SCENARIOS 215

CHAPTER FIVE
Student Discipline

I. EXPULSIONS AND SUSPENSIONS

Overview

The Due Process Clause of the Fourteenth Amendment prohibits the states from depriving any person of life, liberty or property without due process of law. "Due process" requires school districts to provide students all the notices and procedural protections to which they are entitled under state law or school policies when they are faced with school discipline.

The U.S. Supreme Court first recognized due process rights in a student disciplinary case in Goss v. Lopez, *below. Students facing short-term suspensions and other minor school discipline have minimal due process rights. An informal discussion between the student and administrator typically satisfies due process for suspensions of up to 10 days. The student must be advised of the charges supporting the suspension and receive an opportunity to tell his or her side of the story. When a suspension is for a longer term, greater procedural protections apply, which may include a formal hearing.*

The Supreme Court's decision in Mathews v. Eldridge, *424 U.S. 319 (1976), indicated that* Goss *is merely a starting point for a due process analysis in longer term suspension and expulsion cases.* Mathews *explained that "due process is flexible, and calls for such procedural protections as the particular situation demands." State laws typically explain the specific procedures that are required, and afford greater protections for long-term discipline.*

A. Due Process

Court Decisions

♦ In *Goss v. Lopez*, the U.S. Supreme Court recognized a due process right to receive notice and a hearing in student disciplinary actions. In *Goss*, Ohio students had been suspended from school for up to 10 days for participating in demonstrations and other school disturbances. Their suspensions were handed down without a hearing either before or after the school board's ruling. The Supreme Court held that students facing temporary suspensions from a public school have property and liberty interests in their education that are protected by the Due Process Clause of the Fourteenth Amendment. **Students faced with suspension or expulsion must be given oral or written notice of the charges against them along with some opportunity to present their version of what happened.** Recognizing that situations often do not allow time to follow adequate procedures prior to the suspensions, such as in cases where there is a danger to students or property, the Court stated that, at the very least, **proper notice and a hearing should be given as soon after the suspension as is practicable.** The Court also stated that if a student is threatened with a suspension longer than 10 days, more elaborate procedural safeguards may be necessary. *Goss v. Lopez*, 419 U.S. 565, 95 S.Ct. 729, 42 L.Ed.2d 725 (1975).

1. Notice and Procedural Protections

Teacher Scenarios

Mom claims hearing was a 'sham' because teacher's mind was made up..............................215

Handling parents who want to 'make a deal' for special treatment..216

Parents sue school for $800,000 – did teacher have the right to take cell phone?......................217

Court Decisions

♦ A Minnesota student hit another student over the head with a hard plastic tray, disrupting the school cafeteria. The student believed she would be expelled for violating a disciplinary policy against assault and fighting, and she waived her right to a hearing before the school board. The board then expelled her for a full calendar year. Her case reached the Court of Appeals of Minnesota, which found the board did not explain its decision as required by the state Pupil Fair Dismissal Act. When the case returned to the board, it made a new resolution explaining its decision and finding the student committed two offenses: "assault with the lunch tray (used as a weapon)," and attempting to break away when being escorted from the cafeteria in order to harm the other student. In its initial notices to the student and her family, the board did not specify that it considered the lunch tray a "weapon." As other students had been expelled for a full calendar year for assault incidents, the board felt it had to do so in this case.

On appeal, the state commissioner of education found the board violated the student's due process rights. The case came before the court of appeals a second time. It noted the board did not refer to the weapons policy until after the student had waived her right to a hearing. While the board had removed references to the weapons policy after the commissioner's decision, the court found this did not absolve it from its previous reliance upon an improper consideration. The board failed to explain in sufficient detail why the student's conduct warranted a full calendar year expulsion. At no time prior to the hearing did the school board indicate that it viewed the use of a lunch tray as a weapons policy violation. **Education is a fundamental right under the state constitution and is protected by the Due Process Clause of the Fourteenth Amendment, and the board could not deny a student's due process rights.** As the board reached its decision in violation of the student's due process rights, the court affirmed the commissioner's decision in her favor. *Matter* *of Expulsion of N.Y.B.*, No. A09-670, 2010 WL 1541260 (Minn. Ct. App. 4/20/10).

◆ A Washington student who was accused of off-campus marijuana smoking received a new chance to avoid a 55-day suspension. Reversing a lower court decision, the U.S. Court of Appeals, Ninth Circuit, noted the suspension was based on hearsay statements by people having no affiliation with the school. In issuing the suspension, **the school district did not question or produce the witnesses and did not reveal the substance of their statements**. The case was sent back to a federal district court to determine if the student had a due process interest in state regulations permitting students to question and confront witnesses in certain cases. It also had to be determined whether the student had asked for a chance to question the witnesses. *T.T. v. Bellevue School Dist.*, 376 Fed.Appx. 769 (9th Cir. 2010).

◆ South Carolina brothers were approached by other students as they walked through the school parking lot to a football practice. After a heated exchange, a coach intervened, but was unable to stop a fight. One student inadvertently hit the coach. As a result, the students were immediately suspended from school. The brothers pursued hearings and appeared before a school panel. But the panel voted to expel them, and the decision was upheld by the school board. Instead of appealing to a state court, the brothers sued the board for negligence, due process violations and other constitutional claims. The district sought dismissal of all claims. The case reached the Court of Appeals of South Carolina, where the brothers argued a direct appeal from the expulsion order would have been futile because the school year in question would have ended by the time of a court hearing. State law permitted a civil action for damages in lieu of a direct appeal from a school board expulsion, relieving them of any administrative exhaustion requirement. **Since a direct appeal from the board order would not have provided immediate relief, the court refused to dismiss the due process issue** and let the case proceed. *Stinney v. Sumter School Dist. 17*, 382 S.C. 352, 675 S.E.2d 760 (S.C. Ct. App. 2009).

◆ A Nevada student took a knife on a school-sponsored choir trip. He was suspended for 10 days pending expulsion. The next school day, a vice principal drafted a letter explaining the district's weapons policy and detailing the violation. A school disciplinary panel held a hearing at which the charges against the student were read, and a police liaison officer testified. The student claimed he had brought the knife to school accidentally, and his parents verified this. After the hearing, the panel recommended expulsion for the remaining weeks of the school year. The school board met with the assistant superintendent in a closed session, and accepted his expulsion recommendation. The family was excluded from the session, and a federal district court action followed. The court noted that **some form of hearing is required before a student can be deprived of a property interest in public school attendance**.

In long-term disciplinary cases, the Ninth Circuit has required procedural protections such as representation by counsel, the opportunity to present witnesses and the ability to cross-examine adverse witnesses. In this case, the disciplinary panel hearing met the heightened requirements for expulsions. The student was provided with the relevant regulations before a hearing where he could present evidence, call and cross-examine witnesses and have counsel. There was nothing improper about the assistant superintendent's presence at the board meeting. A school administrator involved with initiating disciplinary charges may participate in the deliberations. The court held for the district. *Hardie v. Churchill County School Dist.*, No. 3:07-CV-310-RAM, 2009 WL 875486 (D. Nev. 3/30/09).

◆ North Carolina students accused school officials of disciplining them in a discriminatory manner and sued them for due process and equal protection violations. They also alleged that the school board's anti-gang policy was unconstitutional. A state court dismissed the case, and the Court of Appeals of North Carolina, held that most of the due process claims were legally insufficient as they failed to allege a claim for relief on behalf of each individual student against each individual official. An exception was a due process claim asserting that the superintendent wrote a misleading letter to a student's mother that was "designed to cut off" his appeal rights. Punitive damages would be available if the claim was successful. The right to a notice and opportunity to be heard was clearly established by the Supreme Court. For that reason, the superintendent could not claim immunity. The trial court would have to reconsider a challenge to the school board policy on gangs and gang-related activity. *Copper v. Denlinger*, 667 S.E.2d 470 (N.C. Ct. App. 2008).

On appeal, the Supreme Court of North Carolina explained that to bring a direct state constitutional claim against an education board, it must be alleged that no adequate state law remedy existed. Two North Carolina statutes allowed any student who was suspended in excess of 10 school days to appeal to the education board, and then to a state court. **As there was a statutory right to appeal, an adequate state law remedy existed, and any constitutional claim was barred.** For similar reasons, federal due process claims against the superintendent failed. The gang policy issue was returned to the trial court for further proceedings. *Copper v. Denlinger*, 688 S.E.2d 426 (N.C. 2010).

◆ An Illinois security guard wrote up a student for "posturing" with a group of students who were flashing gang signs in the school cafeteria. A police officer became involved, and the school suspended the student for 10 days pending an expulsion hearing. A school hearing officer wrote the student a letter that expulsion for "subversive organizations" was being recommended. At the hearing, the hearing officer charged the student with another offense for "Fighting/Mob Action." The student admitted lending support to Latin Kings gang members. The security guard and police officer did not attend the hearing, at which the student's father made several remarks in English. After the hearing, the school board voted to expel the student. He sued the school district and officials in a federal district court for due process violations, including the district's failure to provide his parents with a Spanish-language interpreter.

After the court held for the school district, the U.S. Court of Appeals, Seventh Circuit, affirmed the judgment. It noted that the student had admitted wrongdoing, and he received notice and a meaningful opportunity to be heard. **Due process does not require schools to offer the trial-type safeguards of a delinquency proceeding.** Under *Goss v. Lopez*, this chapter, no delay is necessary between the time notice is given and the time of the discussion with the student. While a two-semester expulsion was a harsh punishment, the due process claim could not succeed. *Coronado v. Valleyview Public School Dist. 365-U*, 537 F.3d 791 (7th Cir. 2008).

◆ Parents of an Iowa student who was arrested and detained in a juvenile detention center could not claim any monetary damages in a civil action against her school district. The state court of appeals affirmed a trial court ruling that the district had no duty to notify the parents that their daughter had been arrested. **There was no deprivation of any parental rights, and the parents had no standing to assert a claim based on their child's due process rights.** School officials made many attempts to contact them after the student was detained. *Simmons v. Sioux City Community School Dist.*, 743 N.W.2d 872 (Table) (Iowa Ct. App. 2007).

◆ A California student was suspended for placing liquid white board cleaner in a teacher's water bottle. After investigating, the principal sent the student a "notice of extension of suspension," stating that his presence at school would threaten the instructional process. The student was charged with participating in the placement of the cleaner in the water bottle, and puncturing the cleaner's container with a knife he brought to school. The student's parents submitted written apologies on his behalf and sought his return to school. They rejected alternative placement offers. After weeks of negotiations, a school district placement counselor notified the parents of an "administrative placement" of their son at a different middle school. An appeal panel upheld the transfer.

The case reached the Court of Appeal of California, which noted that the state **Education Code allowed an initial student suspension of five days.** The principal was only authorized to extend the suspension until the school board made a decision. Here, the student had been suspended for over 60 days, and his involuntary transfer was part of an expulsion process. The district had filed documents indicating that he committed an expellable offense. However, it never provided a school board hearing, and placed the student in a regular middle school. The district did not provide the student with an expulsion hearing, and the administrative appeal did not comply with the Education Code. *Gliane v. Long Beach Unified School Dist.*, No. B193345, 2007 WL 2111045 (Cal. Ct. App. 7/24/07).

◆ **A Mississippi school board did not deprive a student of due process by failing to provide him with a list of witnesses in advance of his expulsion hearing** for selling drugs at school. The state court of appeals rejected his claim that he was not informed of the charges against him because a key witness had changed his story. The witness had only changed the date of one alleged drug purchase. As the charges were based on continuous incidents, this change was insignificant. *T.B. v. Board of Trustees of Vicksburg Warren School Dist.*, 931 So.2d 634 (Miss. Ct. App. 2006).

◆ A Louisiana school board expelled a student for 12 months during her eighth-grade year. Near the end of the school year, her parents petitioned a trial court for an order requiring the board to evaluate her for placement in ninth grade. The court denied the request, as the 12-month expulsion period was not yet complete. The court of appeal directed the board to answer seven questions, then granted the family's request. The Louisiana Supreme Court vacated the court of appeal's decision. It held that **appellate courts are prohibited from receiving new evidence**. The case was returned to the trial court for an expedited hearing to consider whether the board was obligated to provide the student with any alternative education. *B.W.S. v. Livingston Parish School Board*, 936 So.2d 181 (La. 2006).

◆ The Wyoming Supreme Court held that a school board's appeal from a lower court decision reversing a student suspension was moot, as the student had already graduated. The board had expelled the student for violating a state law prohibiting the possession, use, transfer, carrying or selling of a deadly weapon on school property or grounds. The expulsion was modified to a 10-day in-school suspension and the student was required to abide by a behavior contract. **The student appealed to a state court, which held that the board violated the notice and hearing requirements of Wyoming law.** The court also found insufficient evidence to support the discipline. The appeal to the supreme court was moot, as the student had already served his suspension and graduated. *Board of Trustees of Fremont County School Dist. #25 v. BM*, 129 P.3d 317 (Wyo. 2006).

◆ The Supreme Court of Colorado affirmed a lower court decision vacating a student expulsion order, because **the student's school board refused to allow her to call witnesses to provide evidence of her good character at her expulsion hearing**. The district expelled the student for fighting, but it denied her request to present statements from her teachers at her hearing. The supreme court agreed with the trial court that the school district violated her due process rights and made it "as difficult as possible" to present evidence in her favor. *Nichols v. DeStefano*, 84 P.3d 496 (Colo. 2004).

◆ Several South Carolina seniors vandalized a high school they did not attend. After they were suspended, a state trial court granted their request for a temporary injunction, but the South Carolina Court of Appeals held that the trial court had no jurisdiction to hear any case involving a short-term student suspension. The students appealed to the state supreme court, which noted that **state law did not permit judicial review of student suspensions of 10 days or less.**

Otherwise, students and parents might burden the court system and strain school resources with a flood of appeals from short-term suspensions. The students received notice, an explanation and an opportunity to respond, which was all the process they were due under *Goss v. Lopez*. The court affirmed the appellate court's decision. *Floyd v. Horry County School Dist.*, 569 S.E.2d 343 (S.C. 2002).

2. Alternative Placements

Court Decisions

◆ A North Carolina student was suspended for the second semester of her sophomore year for fighting. She was not offered alternative education. After a hearing, a school panel upheld the superintendent's decision to suspend her without services. In a state court lawsuit, the student asserted violation of her right to a sound basic education under the North Carolina constitution. A state trial court dismissed the case, and appeal reached the Supreme Court of North Carolina. It held state law vested school administrators with authority to issue long-term suspensions to students who willfully violated school conduct policies. But the law required education boards to establish alternative learning programs and to adopt guidelines for assigning students to long-term discipline.

According to the court, state law provided a comprehensive scheme that granted students a right to an alternative education "when feasible and appropriate" during long-term suspensions. **There was no constitutional right to an alternative education, but there was a constitutional right for a suspended student to know the reason for exclusion from school.** In reaching this conclusion, the court accepted the student's claim that prior rulings on state educational funding applied to her case. The funding cases established that "equal access to participation in our public school system is a fundamental right, guaranteed by our state constitution and protected by considerations of procedural due process." While students had a right to a sound basic education under the state constitution, the court held school administrators had to articulate an important or significant reason for denying a student access to an alternative education. In this case, administrators did not articulate a reason for denying the student access to alternative education. Since she had a right to education guaranteed by the North Carolina Constitution, the court reversed the judgment and returned the case to the lower courts so the education board could have an opportunity to explain why alternative education had been denied. *King v. Beaufort County Board of Educ.*, 364 S.E.2d 368 (N.C. 2010).

◆ A Texas student was assigned to an alternative school for being involved in a brawl in his high school hallway. A school assistant principal allegedly reported that the student was arrested after striking an officer. Part of the fight was videotaped, and the assistant principal observed the student's behavior. At an informal hearing among the assistant principal, student and parents, the family was notified of a three-day suspension followed by a 45-day assignment to an alternative education program. A district administrator heard an appeal by the family but upheld the decision. In response, the student sued the school district and several officials in a federal district court for civil rights violations. **The court held placement in alternative education programs did not implicate due process rights.** Instead, they were considered transfers from one school program to another "with stricter discipline." Since the student had an opportunity to explain his version of the facts in the meeting with the assistant principal, due process was satisfied. Many courts, including the Supreme Court in *Goss v. Lopez*, this chapter, have recognized that **sometimes a school disciplinarian may be a witness to the conduct forming the basis for discipline.** Nothing indicated the assistant principal or a police officer in this case had any preexisting bias toward the student. Finding no due process violation, the court held for the school district. *Salas v. United Independent School Dist.*, Civ. No. L-08-22, 2009 WL 1035068 (S.D. Tex. 4/17/09).

◆ A Texas school security officer opened a purse found on school property to help determine who owned it. A cheerleader's school athletic pass and what was later identified as a hydrocodone pill were found inside the purse. The school district held a hearing to consider expelling the cheerleader for violating its zero-tolerance anti-drug policy. A school hearing officer determined that the pill most likely belonged to the parent of another student and not the cheerleader. The district placed the cheerleader in an alternative education program for 36 days and excluded her from the cheerleading squad for the 2005-06 school year, as specified by the school's "cheerleader constitution." The school board upheld the decision, and the cheerleader completed the alternative assignment. She later obtained a court order reinstating her to the cheerleading squad, and the school district appealed. The Court of Appeals of Texas held that **a board's decision regarding an alternative education program was final and unappealable.** The court upheld the placement and the district's decision to keep incident records. *Flour Bluff Independent School Dist. v. R.S.*, No. 13-05-623-CV, 2006 WL 949968 (Tex. Ct. App. 2006).

◆ A Michigan student dropped out of high school but was admitted to an alternative education program called "Skills Quest." Enrollment in the program was discretionary with the district superintendent and required students to comply with its attendance policy and the district's student code of conduct. The student was charged with murder and jailed in an adult correctional facility. A state court ordered the county sheriff to segregate him from adult prisoners as required by state law. The student expressed suicidal thoughts and was placed on "suicide watch." He was later released from jail after a preliminary hearing, based on lack of admissible evidence. The superintendent rejected his request to reenter Skills Quest, but reversed himself after another individual confessed to the murder. The student re-enrolled in Skills Quest but dropped out after only a month. He then sued state, county and school officials in a federal district court for civil rights violations. The district court granted pretrial judgment to the sheriff and district but denied it to the superintendent.

The parties appealed.

The U.S. Court of Appeals, Sixth Circuit, noted that the student chose to forgo his right to a free public education when he dropped out of school. **Neither the Michigan Constitution nor state law mandated alternative education programs.** The student could not show a legitimate claim to participate in Skills Quest, since participation was "entirely at the discretion of the superintendent and continues only so long as the participant abides by the program's rules and policies." As the student had no right to an alternative education, he could not show a due process violation. The court ruled for the sheriff, school district and superintendent. *Daniels v. Woodside*, 396 F.3d 730 (6th Cir. 2005).

◆ A Wyoming school district expelled three students for marijuana violations. One was enrolled in special education programs and continued receiving the educational services described in his individualized education program. The others were adjudicated delinquent in juvenile court proceedings. The court held that the Wyoming Constitution imposed a duty on the school district to provide the students a free appropriate education during their expulsion periods.

The Supreme Court of Wyoming held that while education is a fundamental right under the Wyoming Constitution, the state interest in student safety and welfare was compelling enough to temporarily interfere with this right. It noted with approval *Fowler v. Williamson*, 39 N.C. App. 715, 251 S.E.2d 889 (N.C. Ct. App. 1979), a North Carolina case recognizing that educational services are contingent upon appropriate conduct. The school district had offered students an education system that conformed to its constitutional obligation to provide an equal opportunity for a quality education. **Reasonable suspension rules did not deny the right to an education; they only denied students an opportunity to misbehave.** Students could be temporarily denied educational services if their conduct threatened the safety and welfare of others. School districts were in the best position to judge student actions, and the district was not required to provide lawfully expelled students with an alternate education under the circumstances of this case. The court rejected the claim that the expulsions violated the non-disabled students' equal protection rights. Special education students must receive services under federal law, even after discipline is imposed. *In re R.M.*, 102 P.3d 868 (Wyo. 2004).

3. Zero-Tolerance Policies

Teacher Scenarios

Disciplining difficult students: When zero-tolerance policies hold up 218

Court Decisions

◆ Texas school officials found a small amount of alcohol in a vehicle parked on school property. Under the school district's zero-tolerance policy, the student who had driven the vehicle to school had to be placed in an alternative school. After several hearings, an alternative school assignment was upheld. According to the district superintendent, the student would have been allowed to avoid the placement had he presented evidence to support his claim that he did not know there was any alcohol in his vehicle. The student sued the school district and officials in the state court system for due process violations. The court held for the district, and he appealed to the Court of Appeals of Texas, arguing the district's disciplinary procedures did not meet minimal due process standards.

According to the student, the school district's policy subjected students to punishment even if they did not knowingly or consciously possess alcohol. The court held he did not show the zero-tolerance policy was unconstitutional as it was applied to him. It noted that zero-tolerance policies "have promoted consistency over rationality." **Strict adherence to a zero-tolerance policy, without consideration of a student's state of mind, "would appear to run afoul of substantive due process notions."** But there was no due process violation in this case, because the superintendent offered the student a chance to show he did not know about the alcohol. As the district provided him "an escape mechanism in lieu of strict application of the zero-tolerance policy," his due process challenge failed. *Hinterlong v. Arlington Independent School Dist.*, No. 2-09-050-CV, 2010 WL 522641 (Tex. Ct. App. 2/11/10).

◆ The Fifth Circuit affirmed the assignment of a Mississippi honor student to an alternative school after a cup of beer was found in a car she had parked in a school lot. Her parent had left the beer in the car, and she said she did not know about it. She appealed the transfer decision to the school board and a federal court, without success. She withdrew from school and obtained a GED. The Fifth Circuit held that however misguided the school district might have been for applying its zero-tolerance policy, the case had to be dismissed. The Supreme Court has observed that public education relies upon the discretion and judgment of school administrators and board members. **An alternative school assignment implicated no constitutional rights.** *Langley v. Monroe County School Dist.*, 264 Fed.Appx. 366 (5th Cir. 2008).

◆ A Florida student who was suspended for violating a school's zero-tolerance policy against weapons possession had no right to appeal the school board decision to the state court system. The Court of Appeal of Florida held the case was properly dismissed because **the Florida Administrative Procedure Act does not permit court review of a suspension order**. The court rejected the student's assertion that he could appeal his suspension because he faced a possible expulsion. Instead, only a hearing that results in an actual expulsion is available for court review. *D.K. v. Dist. School Board of Indian River County*, 981 So.2d 667 (Fla. Dist. Ct. App. 2008).

◆ A drug dog alerted on an honor student's truck during a routine check of a Texas school parking lot. The student consented to a search by the police, who found brass knuckles in the glove box. The brass knuckles belonged to a friend, and the student didn't know they were there. But school board policy held students responsible for the contents of their vehicles. A hearing officer ruled that the Texas Education Code required expulsion. The board voted to expel the student for one day and to assign him to an alternative school for the rest of the school year. After a state court granted the student's request for a preliminary order halting the expulsion, the school board appealed. The Court of Appeals of Texas found the Texas Education Code required school districts to specify whether they considered intent or lack of intent as a factor in student expulsions.

School districts could choose between adopting zero-tolerance policies, or allowing alternatives for involuntary possession of prohibited weapons. In this case, the district policy allowed it to consider intent, and it could decline to expel the student if possession of a weapon was involuntary. The hearing officer incorrectly interpreted the Education Code as requiring expulsion, even if possession of a prohibited weapon was unknowing. The trial court did not abuse its discretion in issuing a temporary injunction to halt the expulsion. *Tarkington Independent School Dist. v. Ellis*, 200 S.W.3d 794 (Tex. Ct. App. 2006).

◆ A California school district regulation required an immediate suspension with a recommended expulsion for three or more fighting incidents in a year. A 12-year-old student was involved in three fights in one school year. A hearing panel upheld the principal's recommendation for expulsion, and the student was placed in an alternative program. The student was suspended there for physically confronting a staff member. The school district placed her in a community school, where she claimed older male students sexually harassed and physically assaulted her. She sued the district in a state court, which dismissed her personal injury claim. But the court held the district's policy requiring the principal to recommend expulsion violated state law and the Due Process Clause. On appeal, the Court of Appeal of California noted that state law permitted an impartial hearing panel to hold expulsion hearings. **The court found the district's zero-tolerance provision consistent with the education code.** The policy did not require expulsion for specified offenses. It only put these cases before an impartial hearing panel. The elimination of a principal's discretion to refrain from referring a case to a hearing did not deprive students of due process. The court reversed the judgment. *T.H. v. San Diego Unified School Dist.*, 122 Cal.App.4th 1267, 19 Cal.Rptr.3d 532 (Cal. Ct. App. 2004).

B. Misconduct

1. Sexual Harassment

Court Decisions

◆ South Carolina school officials charged a 14-year-old girl with a "sexual offense" for entering a boys' lavatory. A video camera recorded her following a male student into the lavatory, where she remained for about a minute. The student claimed she went into the lavatory to retrieve a comb that the male had taken from her. But the school suspended her for 10 days and recommended an expulsion for the rest of the year, based on a sexual offense. Earlier in the school year, she had been suspended for two days for a verbal altercation with a classmate. Prior to an expulsion hearing, a school administrator and a hearing officer watched the videotape of the student entering the lavatory. But the tape was recorded over before the student was allowed to view it. The hearing officer found the student committed a sexual offense and expelled her for the rest of the school year. A state court reversed the decision, finding no substantial evidence of a sexual offense. It also found a violation of due process rights.

On appeal, the Court of Appeals of South Carolina noted that the school district did not present any additional evidence to support the charge of sexual offense beyond the videotape. Any prior acts of disruption by the student had no bearing on the case. The school district had chosen not to expel her for her prior conduct. **The only evidence of a sexual offense was the student's voluntary entry into the boys' lavatory for about one minute in pursuit of another student.** Since there was no evidence of sexual activity by the student or the male, and no male student indicated that anything sexual had occurred, there was no substantial evidence in support of the expulsion. The judgment for the student was affirmed. *Doe v. Richland County School Dist. Two*, 382 S.C. 656, 677 S.E.2d 610 (S.C. Ct. App. 2009).

◆ A Michigan school counselor made a presentation to a language arts class. She saw a student place his fingers in his mouth and believed he was making a sexual gesture about her. The school suspended the student and he appealed to the district superintendent, who interviewed the counselor, student and a classmate who saw the gesture. The students asserted that the gesture simply indicated boredom. The superintendent found the counselor more reliable and upheld the suspension for "indecency," as defined in the high school's student handbook. A trial court affirmed the discipline, and the student appealed.

The Court of Appeals of Michigan held that courts are bound by school administrators' findings when there is any evidence in the record to support them. **A student must be guilty of some willful or malicious act of detriment to a school before being suspended or expelled.** This is "something more than a petty or trivial offense" against school rules. The court found the student's gesture qualified as "gross misbehavior and misconduct," as it was both willful and malicious. The school complied with due process requirements for a short-term suspension by giving him oral notice of the general nature of the charges and a chance to be heard. Allowing him to go unpunished for embarrassing a school employee would welcome more disrespect. *Kloberdanz v. Swan Valley School Dist.*, No. 256208, 2006 WL 234880 (Mich. Ct. App. 2006).

◆ A California student was accused of sexually related misconduct, including grabbing a girl by the buttocks, groping other boys, making inappropriate comments or gestures, and simulating masturbation or sex. He denied most of the allegations, explaining that he had accidentally touched the girl. The student's father, an attorney, attended a meeting to consider discipline. The school principal said that he had interviewed several credible witnesses and issued a five-day suspension. The student served his suspension, then graduated. He sued the school district under 42 U.S.C. § 1983. A court held that the district violated his due process rights and awarded him general damages of $45,000, punitive damages of $50,000 and attorneys' fees of $72,268.

The school district appealed to the California Court of Appeal, which found **the principal had complied with the "notice and opportunity to respond" requirements of** *Goss v. Lopez* (this chapter). He had adequately explained the reasons for the suspension and was not required to give the student any further procedural protections to comply with *Goss*. The student was not entitled to learn the identities of his accusers, and had the principal done so, the school district might be exposed to further lawsuits. The district had issued a proper suspension, and the court reversed the judgment. *Granowitz v. Redlands Unified School Dist.*, 129 Cal.Rptr.2d 410 (Cal. Ct. App. 2003).

◆ A Massachusetts high school student sodomized a six-year-old and was charged with various felonies. His principal obtained a police report in which the student described the incident as "a joke." The principal suspended the student, finding he posed a threat to the safety, security and welfare of students at the high school. After a hearing, the superintendent upheld the suspension, but a court later reversed the suspension, finding the superintendent's action was an abuse of discretion. On appeal, the Massachusetts Supreme Judicial Court observed that a felony charge against a student, by itself, is an insufficient basis for suspension. There must be a finding that the student's continued presence in school would have a substantial detrimental effect on the general welfare of the school.

A suspension may be overturned only if it is so arbitrary and capricious that it constitutes an abuse of discretion and lacks any rational explanation. **Here, the superintendent's decision was within his discretion because it was fully supported by the evidence.** The principal was permitted to draw inferences from the nature of the crime and the student's lack of remorse. Given the seriousness of the charges, the principal reasonably concluded there was a danger the student would attempt similar behavior at school. The court reversed and remanded the case. *Doe v. Superintendent of Schools of Stoughton*, 437 Mass. 1, 767 N.E.2d 1054 (Mass. 2002).

2. Drugs, Alcohol and Weapons Possession

In a case involving off-campus alcohol consumption by an Arkansas student, the U.S. Supreme Court limited the role of federal courts to construe school regulations differently than a school board. An Arkansas school board had a rule requiring the mandatory suspension of students who were "under the influence of" or in possession of narcotics, hallucinogenics, drugs or controlled substances. The Supreme Court held the board had authority to expel a student for drinking alcohol off campus and returning to school. Board of Educ. v. McCluskey, *458 U.S. 966, 102 S.Ct. 3469, 73 L.Ed.2d 1273 (1982). But in the following case, an Alabama school board improperly disciplined a student for being under the influence of alcohol at a school prom under a rule that only addressed the "use" of alcohol while on school property or at a school function.*

Teacher Scenarios

Parents sue after teacher's inquiry takes an unexpected turn 215

Was student expelled for a good reason – or just for being 'a kid'? 219

Court Decisions

◆ Alabama high school staff members noticed a student smelled of alcohol at a school prom. A Breathalyzer test showed his blood-alcohol level was between .001 and .006. A disciplinary committee held a hearing and found no evidence of alcohol possession at the prom. The student was also not "under the influence of alcohol to the extent that he would have been guilty of ... criminal offenses." Based on findings that he drank alcohol on the day of the prom, the board suspended him and sent him to an alternative school. The reason stated was being under the influence of alcohol at the prom in violation of a school handbook provision. In a juvenile court hearing, the court found the term "use" from the school policy meant "to ingest alcohol while on school property or at any other school function." As there was no evidence that the student had "used" alcohol on school property or at a school function, the court held he did not violate the policy. In addition to reinstating the student, the court found the school's alcohol policy did not address punishment and the discipline imposed was unreasonable. Appeal reached the Court of Civil Appeals of Alabama.

The court noted a 1985 decision by the state supreme court held that "a board of education must comply with the policies it adopts." Rules and regulations governing student conduct had to be sufficiently definite to provide them reasonable notice that they must conform their conduct to the expected requirements. In this case, the school had applied a student handbook provision to students who used alcohol shortly before going to the prom. **A policy that did not notify the student of possible consequences for arriving at the prom after drinking alcohol deprived him of due process.** The court affirmed the juvenile court's decision reinstating him to school. *Monroe County Board of Educ. v. K.B.*, No. 2090746, 2010 WL 3611918 (Ala. Civ. Ct. App. 9/17/10).

◆ After a Mississippi student reportedly sold drugs on campus, the school principal searched his backpack and found an item described as either a nail file or a knife. A school district appeals committee voted to expel the student after a hearing, and the school board met to review the case.

At his hearing, the student was permitted to argue that the item was a nail file. But since the item was unavailable for inspection, the board assigned to the superintendent the decision of determining whether it was a prohibited item. He decided it was a knife. The board upheld the expulsion, and the student was placed in an alternative school. Within weeks, he was accused of possessing marijuana.

Another appeals committee hearing was scheduled to review a new expulsion recommendation. A notice to the student described his offense and the charges. In addition, the notice offered the student a right to have counsel present and to cross-examine witnesses. After the student spoke at the hearing, the committee accepted the expulsion recommendation. The student appealed, and the Supreme Court of Mississippi found **a reasonable basis for the board to find that the item was a knife and not a nail file**. The Mississippi Code did not require the school board to physically examine the weapon. As the student was permitted to speak on his own behalf before the appeals committee, due process was satisfied. The court reinstated the board's decision. *Hinds County School Dist. Board of Trustees v. D.L.B.*, 10 So.3d 387 (Miss. 2008).

♦ A Wisconsin high school student admitted writing a note that a bomb was in a school locker, resulting in the school being evacuated and students being moved off-campus. The school lost over four hours of instructional time. A state court placed the student on probation after he pled no contest to making a bomb scare under a state criminal statute. In addition to ordering him to perform 100 hours of community service, the court ordered him to pay the school district restitution of over $18,000. The student appealed the order to pay restitution. The Court of Appeals of Wisconsin noted that most of the amount represented salaries and benefits of teachers and staff who had been working but had to evacuate the school due to his note. According to the student, the district did not suffer a true financial loss. But the court held that a determination of restitution is within a court's discretion. **Pay for teachers and staff who had to vacate the building amounted to "special damages" that could form the basis of an order for restitution.** As deprivation of employee productivity was a "loss in itself," restitution was reasonable. *State of Wisconsin v. Vanbeek*, 316 Wis.2d 527, 765 N.W.2d 834, 2009 WI App 37 (Wis. Ct. App. 2009).

♦ A Pennsylvania student said another student told him he had vodka in a bottle of iced tea he brought to lunch. He admitted taking a drink from the bottle, "because he didn't believe him." The student said he knew a third student had also taken a drink prior to lunch. School administrators suspended the student and brought expulsion proceedings against him. The school board expelled him for 18 days, based on his admission and the results of Breathalyzer testing administered in school. The student appealed to a state court. Meanwhile, he completed his expulsion period and performed community service that was imposed as a prerequisite for his return to school. The court affirmed the school board's order, and the student appealed.

The Commonwealth Court of Pennsylvania observed that school administrators had not required the student to give a statement. Instead, they merely provided him with an opportunity to voluntarily do so. The board drew a reasonable inference that there was alcohol in the bottle of iced tea based on the student's statement and Breathalyzer testing. The student argued that a school district policy (based on a federal law) had been violated. The policy (and the law) prohibited surveys, analysis or evaluations revealing illegal, antisocial, self-incriminating and demeaning behavior by minors, without prior consent by parents. The court rejected this argument, noting that the provision did not apply to interviews conducted by school administrators for student disciplinary purposes. **School officials "have a substantial interest in maintaining a safe and educational environment on school grounds."** The court affirmed the judgment. *Haas v. West Shore School Dist.*, 915 A.2d 1254 (Pa. Commw. Ct. 2007).

♦ A Missouri high school student brought toy guns to school twice. The toys shot small pieces of plastic. On the first occasion, the student shot at another student who was standing outside their school. On the second, two toy guns were found locked in his car on school property. The school superintendent issued an immediate 10-day suspension for the incidents, finding the student in possession of a "weapon" which he had used on school property. The school board voted in a closed session to exclude the student from school for one year. The student was provided a hearing where he was represented by an attorney, allowed to present evidence and to call and cross-examine witnesses.

The board voted to uphold the 180-day suspension. The student appealed, arguing that the school handbook definition of "weapon" did not include toys and other look-alike items. The Court of Appeals of Missouri **found that superintendents may modify expulsion requirements on a case-by-case basis to comply with requirements of federal laws,** including the Individuals with Disabilities Education Act. The school board had adopted a weapons guide separate from the student handbook several years earlier. The guide's definition of "weapon" included any object designed to look like or imitate a dangerous weapon. While the guidelines were not personally handed to each student or parent, they were accessible through a school district website and upon request. The guidelines were properly applied to the student. The toy guns were "dangerous instruments" because they could cause an eye injury. The court upheld the suspension. *Moore v. Appleton City R-II School Dist.*, 232 S.W.3d 642 (Mo. Ct. App. 2007).

♦ A New York student talked with other students about a gun while they were in the school cafeteria. Police decided to lockdown the school, and guns were found off school grounds. The student was suspended for the rest of the school year. The state education commissioner affirmed the suspension, but a New York court held the hearing officer denied the student a fair hearing and vacated the discipline. The student sued the board and hearing officer for civil rights violations. A state court dismissed the student's due process claim, since he had already received notice and a hearing to consider his suspension. This was all the process to which he was entitled. The state court had vacated the discipline, curing any procedural defects. The court held that talking with students about handguns was a material and substantial disruption of the educational process. The suspension did not violate the student's substantive due process rights.

The court agreed with the board that public school students may be disciplined for conduct off school grounds, if there is a connection between the behavior and the school. Misconduct occurring off campus may adversely affect the educational process or endanger students. However, the court refused to dismiss the student's speech rights claim. He raised a valid equal protection claim by asserting that the other students implicated in the conversation were only suspended for three weeks, while he was suspended for the rest of the school year. The court refused to dismiss the equal protection claims against the board and hearing officer, and held they were not entitled to qualified immunity. *Cohn v. New Paltz Cent. School Dist.*, 363 F.Supp.2d 421 (N.D. N.Y. 2005). The Second Circuit affirmed the decision in a brief memorandum. *Cohn v. New Paltz Cent. School Dist.*, 171 Fed.Appx. 877 (2d Cir. 2006).

◆ A Kentucky high school received a bomb threat. A private company under contract with the district to provide canine detection services found no explosives, but a dog alerted to a car parked in the school parking lot. The principal called the student from his class but did not accompany him to the parking lot, despite a board policy requiring principals or their designees to be present when any student search was conducted. A dog handler went with the student to the car and found marijuana inside it. The student was suspended pending an expulsion hearing, then expelled by the board.

When the student sued, the Court of Appeals of Kentucky held that **the board's policy mandated that the school principal or designee be present during any student search**. Because the evidence for the expulsion was obtained in violation of the board's own policy, the decision to expel the student was arbitrarily based on incompetent evidence. The board had to comply with its own policy. Since the only evidence used against the student was inadmissible, the expulsion was in error. *M.K.J. v. Bourbon County Board of Educ.*, No.2003-CA-0003520MN, 2004 WL 1948461 (Ky. Ct. App. 2004).

◆ A Pennsylvania court held that **a school district had no power to expel an honor student for using drugs on a school playground after school hours, when no school activity was taking place.** A trial court properly found that the student was not under school supervision at the time of the incident and had exceeded its statutory powers by expelling him. The school board had voluntarily reinstated the student to school prior to the trial court decision, and the court's order required it to expunge the expulsion from his record. *D.O.F. v. Lewisburg Area School Dist.*, 868 A.2d 28 (Pa. Commw. Ct. 2004).

◆ A New Mexico school security guard noticed a car parked in a faculty lot without a required permit. He contacted a law enforcement agency to check its registration and then observed a knife in plain view between the passenger seat and console. The guard called the student who had driven the car from his class and had him open the car. He found a sheathed hunting knife, handgun, ammunition and drug paraphernalia. The student claimed he did not know the items were in the car, which belonged to his brother. He was then suspended pending a hearing. A hearing officer held that the student should be suspended for a year. The school board upheld the decision, and the student sued for civil rights violations. A court found that the board could not suspend a student who unknowingly brought drugs or weapons to school. It granted the student a preliminary injunction that allowed him to return to school and graduate.

Appeal reached the U.S. Court of Appeals, Tenth Circuit, which held that a school suspension decision is to be upheld unless it is arbitrary, lacking a rational basis or shocking to the conscience. Here, the board did not suspend the student for "unknowingly" bringing a knife to school. Instead, it found that he should have known he was in possession of a knife, since it was in plain view to persons standing outside the car. He also should have known that he was responsible for the vehicle and its contents. **The possession of weapons on school property threatened the board's interest in school safety, and there was a rational basis for the one-year suspension.** The suspension did not violate the student's civil rights. *Butler v. Rio Rancho Public Schools Board of Educ.*, 341 F.3d 1197 (10th Cir. 2003).

◆ An Indiana middle school student gave caffeine pills to eight classmates. One classmate was taken to the emergency room for a rapid heartbeat and other symptoms. An assistant principal confiscated the pills from the student's locker. The school suspended the student for five days, pending expulsion. At the expulsion hearing, the assistant principal read into the record statements by six students who took pills. The hearing officer upheld the expulsion and ordered the student to complete a substance abuse assessment, enroll in counseling and perform 15 hours of community service. Students who accepted pills were barred from extracurricular activities and field trips for the semester. The student sued the school system in a federal district court, which found she admitted distributing the pills. **A reasonably intelligent 13-year-old would understand that the distribution of caffeine pills at school was improper.**

The presentation of student testimony through the assistant principal did not violate the student's due process rights. She had no constitutional right to cross-examine these students. The district was relieved of more formal procedures because the need to protect student witnesses greatly outweighed the slight value of providing the student their names. Also, the student's equal protection claims failed, despite her claim that the expulsion was "grossly unfair" in comparison with the discipline imposed on other students. The court awarded judgment to the district and officials. *Wagner v. Fort Wayne Community Schools*, 255 F.Supp.2d 915 (N.D. Ind. 2003).

◆ An Idaho student left a pellet gun in a car parked on school grounds. Another student took the gun and superficially wounded a third student with it. The first two students admitted possessing the gun, and the principal suspended them. The superintendent and principal met with the students and their parents to discuss the suspensions and inform them of a hearing. Letters from the principal and superintendent confirmed the hearing. The board suspended both students for 13 days after their hearing, then voted to expel them for over three months. The students were notified of their expulsions for violating Idaho law.

At a second hearing, the board again voted for expulsion. A state trial court found that the board had acted arbitrarily and abused its discretion, but the Idaho Supreme Court reversed this decision. It stated that while procedural errors during a suspension may justify judicial relief, there were none in this case. By the time the students had requested a court order, their suspensions had been over for two months. **State procedures for student discipline are not as strict as criminal or juvenile protections.** In school disciplinary cases, notice of the incidents giving rise to discipline is generally sufficient. The board reasonably found their presence detrimental to others at the school. *Rogers v. Gooding Public Joint School Dist. No. 231*, 20 P.3d 16 (Idaho 2001).

3. Extracurricular and Co-Curricular Events

Teacher Scenarios

Student insults teacher – at the shopping mall 220

Court Decisions

◆ A group of Ohio students attended a school-sponsored student exchange program in Germany. Before the trip, a teacher explained to students that they would stay with a "host family" for two weeks. While in Germany, a number of students consumed alcoholic beverages at biergartens with their "host parents." They were of legal drinking age in Germany and believed they were permitted to drink without supervision. Upon returning home, the school suspended the students for three to five days for violating student code prohibitions on consuming or possessing alcohol while in the school's control and custody.

The students asked for a hearing before the school board, arguing that the teacher had "verbally created an exception to the school's code of conduct regarding the consumption of alcohol." The board overturned the suspensions but required the students to perform community service. An Ohio trial court vacated the discipline, and the Court of Appeals of Ohio affirmed. **Here, the teacher had "engrafted an exception on the disciplinary code's provisions concerning alcohol consumption."** The students and their parents had all stated that their understanding of the policy allowed parents and host parents to determine the circumstances for alcohol consumption by students. *Brosch v. Mariemont City School Dist. Board of Educ.*, No. C-050283, 2006 WL 250947, 2006-Ohio-453 (Ohio Ct. App. 2006).

◆ Missouri cheerleading squad members reported that two cheerleaders were drinking alcohol before a school football jamboree. An investigation by the squad's faculty advisor was inconclusive. The principal later began a new investigation, but the parents of the cheerleaders did not cooperate, and one of them removed her daughter from school. The parents then sued the school district and school officials. The principal continued his investigation and obtained statements from several students who said they had seen the two cheerleaders drinking alcohol. The principal suspended both cheerleaders for 10 days for being under the influence of alcohol at a school event. He advised the parents of the decision, and the district sent them written confirmations of the suspensions, informing them of the reason for the action and their right to school board review. The parents did not respond. The court held for the district and officials, and the parents appealed.

The U.S. Court of Appeals, Eighth Circuit, noted evidence that the cheerleaders knew drinking alcohol before a school event violated the school disciplinary code. The court rejected the parents' claim that the district "patently failed to train" its employees. The district provided coaches with triennial training sessions for responding to student misconduct. **To establish school liability for failing to train staff, the parents would have to prove that the district showed deliberate indifference to student rights.** The court found no deliberate indifference by the district in this case. The cheerleaders received proper notice that they were being charged with a violation of the school code. Although the parents complained that the district had deprived their daughters of due process, they themselves had terminated contact with the principal. The students had the opportunity to present their side of the story, satisfying due process requirements. As the suspensions were based on violations of a longstanding, published policy, the judgment was affirmed. *Jennings v. Wentzville R-IV School Dist.*, 397 F.3d 1118 (8th Cir. 2005).

◆ An Indiana wrestling coach confiscated some negatives from a student who was a member of the school wrestling team. A school administrator instructed the coach to develop the negatives, which revealed the student and three other wrestlers naked in the boys' shower room. The school principal recommended expelling the student for "possessing or distributing pornographic material." The student's attorney argued at an expulsion hearing that the district code did not specify this offense. The hearing officer upheld the recommendation for expulsion, but the decision was reversed after a school administrative review.

The student returned to school after six weeks and made up his work. A federal district court reviewed his complaint and held that the principal and hearing officer were entitled to qualified immunity in the case. The student appealed to the U.S. Court of Appeals, Seventh Circuit, which held that the conduct of the principal and hearing officer did not meet the high threshold for proving a substantive due process violation. **School officials are entitled to qualified immunity for federal civil rights violations, unless the unlawfulness of their conduct is apparent in light of preexisting law.** While the school administrators had "exercised questionable judgment," they were entitled to qualified immunity. *Tun v. Whitticker*, 398 F.3d 899 (7th Cir. 2005).

4. Fighting and Violence

Michigan's highest court held a group of teachers and their employee association could pursue an action against their school board to enforce a state law requiring the expulsion of students who assaulted employees.

Teacher Scenarios

'But he was just being a kid,' parents insist 220

Protecting students from a bully: How far should a teacher go?..221

Was student being creative – or making a threat? 222

Bullies torment classmate – what more could teacher have done?..222

Court Decisions

♦ Section 380.1311a(1) of Michigan Compiled Laws requires the permanent expulsion of a student in grade six or above for a physical assault at school against a school employee, volunteer or contractor. If an assault is reported to the school, the school board is required by law to "expel the pupil from the school district permanently." Four teachers claimed that pupils in grade six or higher physically assaulted them in their classrooms and that the assaults were reported to a school administrator. Instead of expelling the students, the school district only suspended them. The teachers and their association filed an action in the state court system against the school board under Section 380.1311a(1).

The court held it had no authority to supervise a school district's exercise of discretion, and the state court of appeals affirmed the decision. Appeal reached the Supreme Court of Michigan, which first held the teachers had legal standing to pursue the case. They were likely to suffer an injury that other members of the public did not face. The lower court decisions denying standing to the teachers would "slam the courthouse door" on numerous controversies, and the court reversed the judgment. **The legislative history of Section 380.1311 revealed an intent to create a safe school environment and a more effective workplace for teachers.** As a result, the lower court decisions for the board were reversed. The court of appeals would have to rule on the remaining issues that had not been considered. *Lansing Schools Educ. Ass'n MEA/NEA v. Lansing Board of Educ.*, 487 Mich. 387, 792 N.W.2d 686 (Mich. 2010).

♦ North Carolina school staff members tried to break up a fight between two students in the cafeteria. One of the students admitted hitting a teacher about 20 seconds after being separated from the other student. An assistant principal interviewed the students, staff members and witnesses. Police also conducted an investigation. The student was charged as a juvenile with assault on a school employee and disorderly conduct, and the other student was charged as an adult with a misdemeanor. The school board suspended the student for 10 days for violating four school board policies, including one providing for a long-term suspension for assaulting a school employee. After the suspension was imposed under North Carolina law, the student received a hearing where he was represented by an attorney and had the opportunity to present evidence, call witnesses and make arguments. A hearing panel voted to affirm a recommendation to place him in an alternative setting. The panel decision was affirmed by a discipline review committee, and the superintendent approved it.

Another hearing was held before the school board, where the student was again represented by counsel. Again, the long-term suspension was upheld. A state superior court affirmed the decision, and appeal reached the Court of Appeals of North Carolina. It appeared to the court that the student had an opportunity to learn the nature of his offense and respond to the charges. He received two hearings, which included an "exhaustive fact-finding inquiry" by the school board. **While the student asserted self-defense, he had admitted a delay of 20 seconds from the end of the fight to the time he hit the teacher.** No witnesses supported his claim of self-defense. **State law required imposing a long-term suspension for violating the policy against assaulting school employees.** Protecting school employees is a goal of school discipline, so the court upheld a long-term suspension. There was no showing that an alternative placement was inadequate to provide a sound, basic education. Federal privacy laws prevented the student from obtaining the educational records of his fight opponent. The court affirmed the judgment. *Watson-Green v. Wake County Board of Educ.*, 700 S.E.2d 249 (N.C. Ct. App. 2010).

♦ A Washington student threatened his older sisters at home with scissors and a knife. The girls barricaded themselves in a room and called their father. He called 911, and police took the student into custody, then informed school administrators of the incident. The principal told the student's mother that the student could not remain at school, and the district superintendent expelled the student on an emergency basis, advising the parents that he would have to undergo a violence risk assessment by a district-approved mental health professional as a condition for re-entering school. After he missed 10 days of school, a therapist found he was not a danger to himself or others. The student returned to school and later sued the district and superintendent. A court held that the district did not violate his due process rights, and that where a student poses a continuing danger, the school need not provide prior notice of discipline.

The student appealed to the U.S. Court of Appeals, Ninth Circuit, which held that the student and his mother had met with a district representative, who gave them oral notice of the exclusion pending a meeting with the superintendent. The superintendent later met with them for several hours to discuss the incident and his pending expulsion. Accordingly, the student received adequate notice of the charge and a hearing under *Goss*. **The expulsion did not violate the student's due process rights.** *Doe v. Mercer Island School Dist. No. 400*, 288 Fed.Appx. 426 (9th Cir. 2008).

◆ Two North Carolina students transferred into a new school system, where they were bullied by other students. In their first semester there, one of them became involved in a fight with another student at a school basketball game. Both children were removed from the attendance roll for the next semester, based on the family's out-of-district residency and one student's violation of the student code. Before the education board issued a final decision, the parent sued it for breach of contract, violation of board policy and constitutional violations. The court dismissed the case, and the Court of Appeals of North Carolina affirmed. State law provided for appeal to a local education board following a final administrative decision for the discipline of a student, violations of law, school board rules and policies, and policies regarding grade retention of students. **The parent was first required to obtain a final decision of the board before proceeding to court.** Here, the board had not issued a final decision at the time she filed her state court action. *Hentz v. Asheville City Board of Educ.*, 658 S.E.2d 520 (N.C. Ct. App. 2008).

◆ An Arkansas student shouted at a classmate near their school cafeteria and approached her until a teacher intervened. The principal received a handwritten note from the student in which she threatened the classmate's life and described her plan to initiate a fight. The principal suspended the student pending a recommended expulsion, and the school board expelled her. She obtained a court order allowing her to return to school a few days later, and the district appealed. The Arkansas Court of Appeals agreed with the district that the county court had ignored its proper role by substituting its judgment for that of the school board. **The Arkansas Code requires school boards to hold students strictly accountable for disorderly conduct in school**, and there is a general policy against court intervention in matters that are properly before school authorities. The county court had no power to substitute its judgment for that of the school board, and the appeals court reversed its judgment. *Cross County School Dist. v. Spencer*, 58 S.W.3d 406 (Ark. Ct. App. 2001).

5. Cell Phones and Electronic Devices

Off-campus student electronic communications often have a negative impact on school grounds, forcing educators to consider discipline for events that take place off-campus. In such cases, schools may seek the involvement of law enforcement officials and look to criminal laws to justify school discipline.

Teacher Scenarios

Texting in class: How far can teacher go
to maintain order? 223

Innocent joke or real threat? The best steps
a teacher can take 224

Court Decisions

◆ An Arkansas teacher confiscated a student's cell phone as he was using it in violation of a school rule. Although his parents demanded the return of the phone, it remained in the school office for two weeks, as required by a district policy. It was then returned, but the family sued the teacher and principal in a state court for trespass and taking property without due process of law. The court held for the district, and appeal reached the Supreme Court of Arkansas.

On appeal, the parents claimed Section 6-18-502 of the Arkansas Code did not authorize the confiscation. They argued that Americans have Fourth Amendment rights to be secure in their persons and property and to be free from unreasonable searches and seizures without due process. The court explained that Section 6-18-502 pertained only to the suspension or dismissal of students from public schools. It was insufficient to simply claim that no law authorized the confiscation. In prior decisions, the court made clear that a party's argument will not be considered unless it is convincing or supported by authority. **Section 6-18-502 declared that school policies were to "prescribe minimum and maximum penalties, including students' suspension or dismissal from school."** Arkansas school boards have broad discretion to direct school operations, and "courts have no power to interfere with such boards in the exercise of that discretion unless there is a clear abuse of it." The court refused to interfere with the board's decision about the best way to enforce its policy. The family did not cite any authority defining a property right to have a cell phone at school. As a result, the judgment for school officials was affirmed. *Koch v. Adams*, No. 09-829, 2010 WL 986775 (Ark. 3/18/10).

◆ An investigation of "sexting" among high school students was begun when Tunkhannock, Pennsylvania school officials found photos of nude and semi-nude female students on cell phones. Officials learned that male students traded the images over their cell phones. The district attorney investigated and made a public statement to the media that possession of inappropriate images of minors could justify criminal prosecution for possession or distribution of child pornography. The district attorney presented teens suspected of sexting with a choice of either attending an education program or facing child pornography charges. As part of the education program, female students would have to write a report detailing "why you are here," "what you did," and "why it was wrong."

Three parents brought a federal court action to halt the proceeding, arguing the threatened prosecution came in retaliation for refusal to attend the education program. The court granted them preliminary relief. An appeal was made to the U.S. Court of Appeals, Third Circuit. While the appeal was pending, the district attorney dropped charges against two students. The other student and her parent pursued the appeal. The court stated that parents have a Fourteenth Amendment Due Process right to raise their children without undue state interference. The court found the parent objected to the lessons in morality, and held **the government cannot coerce parents to accept official ideas of morality and gender roles**. While the district attorney could offer a voluntary education program, he could not coerce attendance by threatening prosecution. The parent showed a reasonable likelihood of prevailing on both her claim that the district attorney violated her right to parental autonomy and her daughter's right to be free from compelled speech. Government action requiring an individual to state a particular message is coercive and violates the First Amendment. As it appeared the district attorney made a retaliatory threat of prosecution, the court upheld the preliminary order. *Miller v. Mitchell*, 598 F.3d 139 (3d Cir. 2010).

◆ A Mississippi school faculty member confiscated a student's cell phone in his class. Pictures on the phone showed the student dancing at home and a classmate holding a BB gun at the student's house. Deeming the items "gang pictures," the principal suspended the student under a school discipline rule prohibiting students from wearing or displaying clothing, accessories, drawings or messages associated with gangs or crime. At a school disciplinary hearing, a municipal police sergeant said he recognized gang signs in the pictures, and the principal said the student "was a threat to school safety." The hearing officer recommended expelling the student for the rest of the school year, and the board of education affirmed the order. **A federal district court held the search of the cell phone did not violate the Fourth Amendment. The city was entitled to dismissal of the claim, and city and school officials had immunity.** A crucial factor was that the student was using his phone in violation of a school rule.

The court said that once the staff member saw the student improperly using the phone, it was reasonable for him to find out why he was using it. The student might have been using the phone to cheat or talk to another student. But the court found no explanation for finding the student was a threat to the school. The sergeant did not state a basis for believing the pictures had gang signs. The court was "troubled" that the student "somehow found himself expelled for an entire school year when the only offense he committed was the minor offense of bringing a phone on school grounds." It was clear to the court that he did not violate the anti-gang policy. The pictures were taken at the student's home, and it appeared that the district misapplied its anti-gang policy. As the most likely reason for expulsion was the principal's testimony that the student was "a threat to school safety," the court found it possible that the expulsion was based on subjective beliefs and not conduct. In a footnote, the court advised the district to consider a settlement. *J.W. v. Desoto County School Dist.*, Civil Action No. 2:09-cv-00155-MPM-DAS, 2010 WL 4394059 (N.D. Miss. 11/1/10).

◆ At a school event called Class Day, an Arkansas student played an audio clip from his cell phone of a female student saying "oh my gosh, I'm horny!" A school official confiscated the phone, suspended him for three days and barred him from graduation ceremonies. The family sued the school district and officials in a state court for violating the state Civil Rights Act and the student's speech and due process rights. It was asserted that the discipline was retaliatory because the female in the clip was the stepdaughter of a school board member who happened to be in attendance at the assembly. A state circuit court held for the district, since the student was immediately advised of his improper conduct and his parents received written notification of the discipline and an opportunity to meet with the superintendent. As the district provided the due process required by *Goss v. Lopez*, 419 U.S. 565 (1975), the court found no violation.

Regarding the speech rights claim, the court cited *Bethel School Dist. No. 403 v. Fraser*, 478 U.S. 675 (1986), for the proposition that schools may determine what constitutes lewd, indecent or offensive speech. Since the court found no speech rights violation and no violation of the Arkansas Civil Rights Act, it held for the school district. On appeal, the Supreme Court of Arkansas found the student had to assert a deprivation of a right, privilege or immunity secured by the Arkansas Constitution to prevail. **Since the family did not show why federal decisions should be applied to find a violation of the state Civil Rights Act, the court refused to develop an argument on his behalf.** Instead, it held the circuit court judgment for the district and officials should be affirmed. *Walters v. Dobbins*, No. 09-1004, 2010 WL 2131869 (Ark. 5/27/10).

◆ New York City school rules forbade students from bringing cell phones into public schools without authorization from principals. A state court held that any enforcement system focusing on the use, rather than possession, of cell phones would require teachers to observe and enforce the ban. Teachers would become involved in confronting students and punishment decisions. For that reason, the board had a rational basis for a complete ban. The involvement of teachers in enforcing the cell phone ban would take time from their teaching mission and increase the perception of teachers as adversaries to students. Each principal could address specific situations by allowing students to carry cell phones when there was a special need for it. The court refused to recognize a "constitutional right to bear cell phones," and it rejected claims by parents who asserted a right to be able to communicate with their children at school.

On appeal, the New York Supreme Court, Appellate Division, upheld the cell phone policy, finding it beyond court review. It was not unreasonable for the school system to ban cell phones, which by their nature could be used surreptitiously and in violation of school rules. Significantly, the court held that "the department has a rational interest in having its teachers and staff devote their time to educating students and not waging a 'war' against cell phones." **The use of cell phones for cheating, sexual harassment, prank calls and intimidation was a threat to order in the schools.** The judgment was affirmed. *Price v. New York City Board of Educ.*, 51 A.D.3d 277, 855 N.Y.S.2d 530 (N.Y. App. Div. 2008).

◆ A student with a record of computer-related misconduct admitted helping another student hack into a Pennsylvania school district computer system. He admitted supplying the other student user names and passwords to allow him to install software and manipulate the district's database. The student was suspended pending an expulsion hearing for violating the school's computer use policy. The policy allowed discipline for violating local, state or federal law. After a school board hearing, the board found the student had violated the computer use policy as well as the state school code and felony provisions of the state crimes code. The board expelled him for the rest of the school year. The student's attorney noted that the school computer use policy did not specify that a violation of the policy could lead to expulsion, but a state common pleas court affirmed the board's decision. On appeal, the Commonwealth Court of Pennsylvania, held **"[g]iven his history, a 10-day suspension was not likely to get his attention because he did not learn from his prior suspension for computer misconduct."** Since the student's conduct would be a felony under the state crimes code, "an expulsion was entirely appropriate." The board had properly exercised its discretion to expel him, and the judgment was affirmed. *M.T. v. Cent. York School Dist.*, 937 A.2d 538 (Pa. Commw. Ct. 2007).

◆ A Tennessee eighth-grade teacher seized a student's cell phone when it began to ring in a classroom. A student code provision prohibited cell phones and other devices on school property during school hours. Violations were to be reported to the principal, and the phone or device was to be confiscated for 30 days. The code of conduct imposed a one-day, in-school suspension for first offenses and required minimal due process. The student's parent went to the school to retrieve the phone, but the principal refused to return it. The vice principal then assigned the student a day of in-school suspension. The parents sued the school board, principal and vice principal in a federal district court for constitutional rights violations. The court dismissed the father's due process claim for retention of the phone, but not the student's due process claim.

The school board appealed to the U.S. Court of Appeals, Sixth Circuit. The court reviewed *Goss v. Lopez*, this chapter, and held an in-school suspension could deprive a student of educational opportunities in the same way an out-of-school suspension would. However, the in-school suspension in this case did not resemble the suspensions issued in *Goss*. The student was allowed to do her school work. Her attendance was recorded in the same manner as if she had attended regular classes by state law. The court found other courts have held **in-school suspensions do not implicate a student's property interest in public education**. In *Wise v. Pea Ridge School Dist.*, 855 F.2d 560 (8th Cir. 1988), a special education student was suspended for three days in a special classroom due to tardiness. The *Wise* court refused to apply *Goss* to a temporary, in-school suspension. The court agreed with *Wise*, as **"in-school suspension does not exclude the student from school and consequently a student's property interest in public education is not implicated."** A one-day in-school suspension, during which the student was recorded as in attendance and was allowed to do her schoolwork did not deprive her of any due process rights, and the court reversed the judgment. *Laney v. Farley*, 501 F.3d 577 (6th Cir. 2007).

◆ A Delaware student used his cell phone at a school assembly, in violation of the school code of conduct. He refused to surrender his phone to a staff member, and the principal asked him four times to hand it over. The principal told the student he would have to come with him to the office. The student still refused to move, and the principal tried to escort him from the assembly by the elbow. The student struggled, pushed the principal and stepped on his foot. After being removed from the assembly, he continued to use his cell phone. The student remained disruptive in the school office and told the principal "you can't touch me," and "just wait till I call my mom. She'll sue you." He also threatened other students and teachers. The police arrived at the school and took the student into custody. The school board expelled the student for the rest of the school year and assigned him to an alternative school. The state board of education affirmed the action, and the student appealed to a state superior court.

The court held the state board could overturn a local board decision only if it was contrary to state law or state regulations, was not supported by substantial evidence, or was arbitrary and capricious. The court found sufficient evidence that the student had pushed the principal and stepped on his foot. **The student had intentionally and offensively touched the principal in violation of the school code.** Expulsion with referral to an alternative program was not disproportionate to the misconduct. *Jordan v. Smyrna School Dist. Board of Educ.*, No. 05A-02-004, 2006 WL 1149149 (Del. Super. Ct. 2006).

C. Academic Expulsions or Suspensions

Court Decisions

◆ An Ohio student and his parents were Chinese citizens in the U.S. on visas. In addition to earning straight As, the student was a master violinist. After being questioned about a recent high grade on a biology test, the student admitted obtaining a biology test bank via the Internet by guessing the teacher's password and accessing a school computer. The assistant principal completed a notice of removal and/or intended suspension form that indicated a five-day suspension. It also stated that expulsion was possible. The assistant principal notified the family he was recommending expulsion for violating Ohio laws against computer break-ins. Due to the student's visa status and pending criminal charges, he faced possible deportation. A board hearing officer limited the hearing's duration to one hour because "it was a busy day." After the hearing, the hearing officer notified the family that the suspension should be upheld. However, no conclusions of fact were sent to the family as required by Ohio statute. A state court affirmed the suspension. On appeal, the Court of Appeals of Ohio agreed with the family that there should have been a hearing in the trial court under the statute to supplement the deficient administrative record.

As the hearing transcript did not record all the statements, and the hearing officer did not file any conclusions of law, the parents were entitled to submit additional evidence at another hearing. In the absence of a record, the court was unable to tell what rules the student may have violated, or the evidence upon which the board relied. **While the student's behavior was not to be condoned, he deserved an opportunity to present additional evidence under the circumstances.** *Huang v. Kent City School Dist. Board of Educ.*, No. 2008-P-0038, 2008 WL 4901779 (Ohio Ct. App. 11/14/08).

◆ An Oregon student had Attention Deficit Hyperactivity Disorder. With the help of the school football team's quarterback, he created counterfeit money. Both students were caught passing counterfeit bills at the student store. The student was charged with forgery and suspended for ongoing disciplinary issues, including a minor-in-possession charge, two harassment and misconduct complaints, and at least one athletic code violation. The school informed the student that since he intended to finish his course load outside of the classroom, the district was recommending expulsion for the rest of the year. The actual proceedings would be stayed if certain conditions were met. The quarterback received an in-school suspension for four days, and a three-week suspension from athletic activity and community service/grounds work at the high school.

In a federal district court action, the student asserted the greater punishment assigned to him was based on his learning disabilities. The court noted that **as long as there was a rational basis for the difference in the way the students were treated, the district was entitled to judgment**. This was because disabled students are not a "protected class" under the Equal Protection Clause. The court noted the student's prior disciplinary record and the fact that the quarterback had no disciplinary history. This distinction permitted disciplining the learning disabled student differently. *Schneider v. Corvallis School Dist. 509J*, No. CIV 05-6375-TC, 2006 WL 3827457 (D. Or. 2006).

◆ A student enrolled in the University of Michigan's "Inteflex" program – a special six-year course of study leading to both an undergraduate and medical degree. He struggled with the curriculum and failed the NBME Part I, receiving the lowest score in the brief history of the Inteflex program. The university's medical school executive board reviewed the student's academic career and decided to drop him from registration in the program. It denied his request to retake the NBME Part I. The student sued the university in a federal court, claiming due process violations. The evidence showed that the university had a practice of allowing students who had failed the NBME Part I to retake the test up to four times. The student was the only person ever refused permission to retake the test. Nonetheless, the court held that his dismissal did not violate the Due Process Clause. The U.S. Supreme Court agreed. The **Due Process Clause was not offended because "the University's liberal retesting custom gave rise to no state law entitlement to retake NBME Part I."** *Regents of Univ. of Michigan v. Ewing*, 474 U.S. 214, 106 S.Ct. 507, 88 L.Ed.2d 523 (1985).

II. STUDENT SEARCH AND SEIZURE

Overview

In New Jersey v. T.L.O., *below, the Supreme Court held the warrant and probable cause requirement of the Fourth Amendment does not apply to school officials who search students suspected of violating a law or school rules. Instead, the legality of a student search depends upon the reasonableness of the search in light of all the circumstances. A search performed by school officials must be "reasonable at its inception" and "not overly intrusive under all the circumstances." A student's age and sex are relevant considerations when evaluating the intrusiveness of a search. The Supreme Court revisited* T.L.O. *in* Safford Unified School Dist. #1 v. Redding. *The Supreme Court clarified that "justified at its inception" means reasonable grounds for suspecting that a search will turn up evidence of a rules violation.*

A. Fourth Amendment "Reasonable Suspicion"

1. Searches Based on Individualized Suspicion

Teacher Scenarios

Teacher and assistant principal's search crossed the line, Dad claims 224

Possible drug possession: Did search go too far? 225

Did student's suspicious behavior justify a search? 225

Student refuses to submit to search: What's teacher's next move? 226

Student's 'slang' in class tipped off teacher to search his jacket 227

198 STUDENT DISCIPLINE

Random searches: Parents say 'no way' 227

Educators have good hunches – but is that enough to search a student? 228

Court Decisions

◆ A teacher at a New Jersey high school found two girls smoking in a school lavatory in violation of school rules. She brought them to the assistant vice principal's office, where one of the girls admitted to smoking in the lavatory. However, the other girl denied even being a smoker. The assistant vice principal then asked the latter girl to come to his private office, where he opened her purse and found a pack of cigarettes. As he reached for them, he noticed rolling papers and decided to thoroughly search the entire purse. He found marijuana, a pipe, empty plastic bags, a substantial number of one dollar bills and a list of "people who owe me money." The matter was then turned over to the police. A juvenile court hearing was held, and the girl was adjudicated delinquent. She appealed the juvenile court's determination, contending that her constitutional rights had been violated by the search of her purse. She argued that the evidence against her should have been excluded from the juvenile court proceeding.

The U.S. Supreme Court held the search did not violate the Fourth Amendment. It said: "The legality of a search of a student should depend simply on the reasonableness, under all the circumstances, of the search." Two considerations are relevant in determining the reasonableness of a search. First, **the search must be justified initially by reasonable suspicion of a violation**. Second, **the scope and conduct of the search must be reasonably related to the circumstances which gave rise to the search, and school officials must take into account the student's age, sex and the nature of the offense**. The Court upheld the search of the student in this case because the initial search for cigarettes was supported by reasonable suspicion. The discovery of rolling papers then justified the further searching of the purse, since such papers are commonly used to roll marijuana cigarettes. The Court affirmed the delinquency adjudication, ruling the "reasonableness" standard was met by school officials in these circumstances and the evidence was properly obtained. *New Jersey v. T.L.O.*, 469 U.S. 325, 105 S.Ct. 733, 83 L.Ed.2d 720 (1985).

◆ A New York middle school teacher reported that her classroom was being disturbed by a musical noise from a cell phone. The dean of the school arrived to investigate and enforce the school's rule prohibiting cell phone use in class. After a student realized the dean intended to search each student in the room for the source of the noise, he removed a hunting knife with a six-inch blade from his pocket and handed it over to the dean. As he was 15 years old, he was charged in a state family court with the delinquent act of weapons possession. The student moved to suppress evidence of his knife possession, claiming it was unlawfully obtained in violation of the state and federal constitutions. The court denied the motion and adjudicated him delinquent. On appeal, the New York Supreme Court, Appellate Division, held **the dean did not perform a "search" of the student, because he was holding the knife and it was in plain view**.

Even if there was a search, the dean's actions were justified. Asking students to empty their pockets was a non-intrusive, practical means of finding an unauthorized cell phone. The dean had a reasonable basis to believe a student in the class was violating school rules, and that the sound was disruptive. The family court had properly found the dean was trying to restore order, "which is not a law enforcement interest." Accordingly, he required neither probable cause nor reasonable suspicion to justify asking the students to empty their pockets. The appellate court upheld the family court's finding of delinquency. *In re Elvin G.*, 47 A.D.3d 527, 851 N.Y.S.2d 129 (N.Y. App. Div. 2008).

◆ A California elementary school prohibited personal articles and clothing suggesting tobacco, drug or alcohol use, sexual promiscuity, profanity, vulgarity and other inappropriate subjects. A seventh-grader wore a shirt with pro-life messages and images of fetuses to school. She claimed the images were "similar to images of unborn infants regularly contained in health and science textbooks." She claimed that a school clerk stopped her from eating her breakfast, subjected her to ridicule, and led her to the school office. There she was ordered to remove the shirt, which was confiscated for the school day.

According to the student, other students were allowed to wear clothes to school with personal messages. She brought multiple claims against the school district and officials, including one that school officials had confiscated her shirt without legal justification. **The court held that seizures of a student or personal items are subject to a reasonableness standard.** Since the student raised issues of possible arbitrary, capricious or unreasonable conduct, the court denied the district's motion for dismissal of the Fourth Amendment claim. *T.A. v. McSwain Union Elementary School Dist.*, No. CV-F-08-1986, 2009 WL 1748793 (E.D. Cal. 6/18/09).

◆ A student informant identified an 18-year-old adult student as one of several students who might be involved in drug dealing at an Ohio high school. The assistant principal summoned the adult student to the office, where he agreed to a pat-down search. Several hundred dollars were found in his wallet, which he claimed was pay from his job. Administrators asked to search his car, and he told them they would only find cigarettes. A search confirmed that the student possessed cigarettes and lighters, and he was suspended for three days.

The school board rejected the student's appeal, and an Ohio common pleas court upheld the suspension. On appeal to the Court of Appeals of Ohio, the student argued the informant's report was an insufficient reason for a search or questioning. Moreover, he admitted having the cigarettes, making a search unnecessary. **The court found a student search is justified at its inception when there are reasonable grounds for suspecting it will turn up evidence of a violation of school rules or a law.** The assistant principal believed the informant was trustworthy, making the search justified at its inception. The search was reasonable in scope because the student admitted contraband would be found in his car. A school policy called for only a warning to adult school district employees who possessed tobacco, while students were subject to suspension. Since students were distinguishable from district employees and could be treated differently, the court found no equal protection violation and upheld the discipline. *Mayeux v. Board of Educ. of Painesville Township School Dist.*, No. 2007-L-099, 2008 WL 754979 (Ohio Ct. App. 3/21/08).

◆ A Florida student felt dizzy at school and lost consciousness in a lavatory. He then told a school monitor he did not feel well. The monitor escorted the student to a school office. The assistant principal later said that the student was quiet, subdued and a little pale. She ordered the student to empty out his pockets and bookbag. After noticing a plastic baggie that appeared to contain marijuana, she called the police. The contents of the bag tested positive for marijuana. The student was arrested and charged with marijuana possession. A Florida court denied his motion to suppress the evidence and adjudicated him delinquent. The student appealed to a Florida District Court of Appeal. The court explained that school officials must have reasonable grounds to suspect that a search will result in evidence that the student has violated the law or school rules. Here, the search was premised upon the student's lavatory incident and his appearance. **The student's pale or quiet appearance alone was "entirely consistent with non-criminal behavior such as illness."** The court reversed the adjudication of delinquency. *C.G. v. State of Florida*, 941 So.2d 503 (Fla. Dist. Ct. App. 2007).

◆ A California school security employee saw three teenagers sitting on the front lawn of a high school during school hours. Because the employee did not recognize any of them as students, he called a police officer. The officer approached the intruders and asked them for identification. One of them produced identification from another school. The officer decided to escort the three intruders to the office to verify their identities. For his own safety, he decided to pat them down. The officer discovered a knife with a locking blade on one intruder and confiscated it. The intruder was charged with unlawful possession of the knife on school property. A state superior court denied his motion to exclude the knife as evidence, and he appealed.

The Court of Appeal of California held that the special need for schools to maintain a safe and orderly learning environment required different search and seizure rules than those for the general public. **Searches of students are justified if there is reasonable suspicion of a violation of a law, school rule or regulation.** Students may be detained without any particularized suspicion, so long as the detention is not arbitrary, capricious or for the purpose of harassment. Here, the intruder did not attend the school. He had a lesser right of privacy than students who were properly on school grounds. The officer had ample cause to believe the intruder did not belong on campus. The state's interest in preventing violence on a high school campus outweighed the minimal invasion to the intruder's privacy rights. As the pat-down search was proper, the court affirmed the judgment. *In re Jose Y.*, 141 Cal.App.4th 748, 46 Cal.Rptr.3d 268 (Cal. Ct. App. 2006).

◆ A Pennsylvania student had his cell phone on, in violation of a school policy. When a teacher confiscated the phone, a text message appeared on its screen from another student requesting marijuana. The teacher and an assistant principal then called nine students listed in the cell phone's directory to see if their phones were turned on in violation of school policy. They accessed the student's text messages and voice mail and used the phone's instant messaging feature. The student stated the district superintendent later told the press that the student was a drug user or peddler, and the family sued the teacher, assistant principal, superintendent and school district in a federal district court. It held the superintendent could not assert absolute immunity for his statements to the press. The teacher and assistant principal also had no immunity for the invasion of privacy claims. **The court agreed with the family that accessing the phone directory, voice mail and text messages, and use of the phone to call persons listed in the directory amounted to a "search or seizure" under the Fourth Amendment.** The court found no basis for the "search," as it was not done to find evidence of wrongdoing by the student, but instead to obtain evidence of possible misconduct by others. The Fourth Amendment claims would proceed. *Klump v. Nazareth Area School Dist.*, 425 F.Supp.2d 622 (E.D. Pa. 2006).

◆ An Atlanta high school resource officer was instructed by another officer to stop a car with some possible truant students in it. When the officer stopped the car, the front seat passenger tried to jump out. He removed marijuana from his pocket when the officer approached. The officer handcuffed all four of the car's occupants. An assistant principal arrived and instructed the officer to search the others for marijuana. A search of one student revealed car keys and $500. The officer and assistant principal searched this student's car and found a handgun in it. A K-9 unit arrived and found 15 bags of marijuana in the car. A county superior court held the search "bore no relation to the stated reason for the stop." It was based on the discovery of a key, some money, rumors and suspicion. Such actions were "whimsical, tyrannical and unreasonable" under *State v. Young*, 234 Ga. 488, 216 S.E.2d 586 (Ga. 1975).

On appeal, the Court of Appeals of Georgia noted that **searches by school officials are "subject only to the most minimal restraints necessary to insure that students are not whimsically stripped of personal privacy and subjected to petty tyranny."** The state supreme court gave great leeway to school officials in *Young*, but distinguished between searches conducted by school officials and those involving police. *Young* was inapplicable if a school official directed a search by the police. The court held a police resource officer should be considered a law enforcement officer and not a school official. The student's first contact with the police came when the car was stopped. *Young* did not apply, and the search was governed by the Fourth Amendment. The court rejected the state's assertion that the stop was valid on the basis of suspected truancy. As the stop was not justified, and the student's consent to search was obtained illegally, the court upheld his motion to suppress evidence seized from his car. *State v. Scott*, 279 Ga.App. 52, 630 S.E.2d 563 (Ga. Ct. App. 2006).

♦ A Pennsylvania assistant principal detained a student for nearly four hours while investigating a classmate's claim that the student touched her in a sexual manner without her consent. The student denied unwanted touching. The assistant principal told him to remain in a conference room while he interviewed witnesses. The student remained there and did school work for several hours. The principal later suspended him for four days for inappropriate conduct. The student sued the school district, board and administrators in a federal district court for constitutional rights violations. The court held for the district, and he appealed. On appeal, the U.S. Court of Appeals, Third Circuit, held confinement in a conference room for nearly four hours was a "seizure."

Public school searches are governed by the "reasonableness standard" of *New Jersey v. T.L.O.*, above. **What is reasonable depends on the context of the search. In school cases, the courts balance the need for a search against the personal invasion which the search entails.** The court noted the detention was to investigate the incident, and to determine appropriate punishment. **In light of the serious nature of the charge, it was reasonable for the school to detain the student.** The court rejected his due process claim, as the assistant principal allowed him to present his side of the story before discipline was administered. *Shuman v. Penn Manor School Dist.*, 422 F.3d 141 (3d Cir. 2005).

♦ A Massachusetts school administrator saw three students in a parking lot when they should have been in class. A search of one student yielded a small bag of marijuana. A juvenile court denied his motion to suppress the marijuana evidence and found him delinquent. On appeal, the Supreme Judicial Court of Massachusetts explained that **reasonable suspicion is not a hunch or "unparticularized suspicion," but instead requires common-sense conclusions about human behavior.** In this case, the student had recently been truant and failed to bring his mother to a meeting to discuss it. School officials had no evidence he possessed contraband or had violated a law or school rule. The court rejected the argument that the search was appropriate based on the student's truancy. A violation of school rules, standing alone, would not provide reasonable grounds for a search unless the specific facts of the violation created a reasonable suspicion of a violation. As there was no information of an individualized nature that the student might have contraband, any search was unreasonable at its inception and the court vacated the juvenile court order. *Comwlth. of Massachusetts v. Damian D.*, 752 N.E.2d 679 (Mass. 2001).

♦ A California high school security officer observed a student in an area that was off limits to students. When she approached him, she noticed he became "very paranoid and nervous." After the student entered a classroom, the officer and a colleague summoned him to the hallway and performed a pat-down search that yielded a knife. The state filed charges against the student and placed him on probation. On appeal, the Supreme Court of California explained that schools may enact disciplinary rules and regulations and enforce them through police or security officers. The school environment calls for immediate, effective action, and school officials are allowed to exercise the same degree of physical control over students as parents are privileged to exercise.

Students are deprived of liberty while at school, and detention by a school official for questioning does not increase the limitations already in effect by being in school. Student may be stopped, told to remain in or leave a classroom, sent to the office and held after school. Individualized suspicion is usually needed to perform a search or seizure, but special needs exist at schools that relax this requirement. Detentions on school grounds did not violate the Constitution, so long as they were not arbitrary, capricious or for the purposes of harassment. Since the student did not allege the officer acted arbitrarily, capriciously or in a harassing manner, the court affirmed the judgment. *In re Randy G.*, 26 Cal. 4th 556, 110 Cal. Rptr. 2d 516, 28 P.3d 239 (Cal. 2001).

2. Off-Campus Searches

Teacher Scenarios

Off-site search leads to controversy 228

Court Decisions

♦ Minnesota students attending an auto shop class were bused to a body shop for class instruction. En route, the teacher observed a student holding a knife that was passed to him from a classmate. When the bus arrived at the body shop, the teacher called a school coordinator to report the knife. The coordinator and principal decided each student should be searched, and the principal called a school liaison officer. Before the search began, the classmate voluntarily handed over the knife. The liaison officer found a collapsible baton in the student's pocket, and he was charged with violating a state law prohibiting possession of a dangerous weapon on school property. The district brought an expulsion proceeding against the student for violating its ban on weapons and look-alikes.

The student pursued civil rights claims against the liaison officer and his municipality. The case reached the Eighth Circuit, which noted that while law officers are normally required to have probable cause of wrongdoing to support a search or seizure of persons or property, the more lenient standard of "reasonable suspicion" applies to searches and seizures in the context of public schools. School officials may conduct a search that is "justified at its inception" and reasonable in scope. The court held that **the *New Jersey v. T.L.O.* standard applies to law enforcement officers who conduct student searches**

away from traditional school grounds. School administrators initiated the search, and one of them played a substantial role in it. The fact that the search took place off school grounds did not call for imposing the stricter probable cause standard. The liaison officer's conduct was reasonable, as he did not know whether other students might also have weapons. As the search was justified and reasonable in scope, the officer was entitled to immunity. *Shade v. City of Farmington, Minnesota*, 309 F.3d 1054 (8th Cir. 2002).

◆ Before leaving for a school-sponsored trip, New York students were informed that drugs and alcohol were banned and that participants would be subject to room searches. Each student signed a pledge to avoid alcohol and drugs. The pledge recited that a violation would result in disqualification from senior activities and graduation ceremonies. During the trip, the school principal smelled marijuana where many of the students had congregated in the hallway of their motel. He then obtained a hotel security pass key and searched most of their rooms. The principal found marijuana in the safe of one room. He sent two students home early and suspended them from school for three days.

The students sued the principal and school district. A court held that students under supervision in school activities, including field trips, are subject to the reasonable suspicion standard for student searches first announced by the U.S. Supreme Court in *New Jersey v. T.L.O.*, not the more stringent Fourth Amendment probable cause standard. **The students had no legitimate reason to expect complete privacy in their hotel rooms, and it was reasonable for the principal to search the rooms** based on his detection of marijuana smoke and the gathering of students. This was true even though he was without individualized suspicion that any one student possessed drugs. The court upheld the search. *Rhodes v. Guarricino*, 54 F.Supp.2d 186 (S.D.N.Y. 1999).

3. Locker Searches

Teacher Scenarios

Drugs found in locker after student confides in teacher..229

Court Decisions

◆ A Maryland student attended a school for students with emotional, learning and behavioral difficulties. The school system's search and seizure policy allowed administrators to search students or their lockers if there was probable cause to believe that a student had items whose possession would constitute a Maryland criminal offense, including weapons, drugs and drug paraphernalia, alcohol or pagers. The principal pursued an anonymous tip that there were drugs or weapons at the middle school and authorized a search of all middle school lockers. A school security officer opened the student's locker in the student's absence and found a book bag containing a folding knife and pager.

In juvenile court proceedings, the student admitted possessing the items but moved to suppress them as evidence, claiming the school policy created a reasonable expectation of privacy in his locker. The juvenile court disagreed, and appeal reached the state's highest court. The Court of Appeals of Maryland held state law, not school policy, defined and controlled the authority of school officials to conduct locker searches. The only evidence indicating the student had a privacy expectation in his locker was the school policy. **Maryland Education Article Section 7-308 permitted reasonable searches of students based on a reasonable belief that a student possessed an item whose possession would create a criminal offense.** School lockers are designated school property and subject to search by school officials. Accordingly, the school policy was invalid and could not serve as the basis for a reasonable privacy expectation. *In re Patrick Y.*, 358 Md. 50, 746 A.2d 405 (Md. 2000).

4. Strip Searches

In Safford Unified School Dist. #1 v. Redding, *below, the Supreme Court discussed the distinction between the "probable cause" standard for police searches and the "reasonable suspicion" standard for school searches. It held "probable cause" requires evidence that raises "a fair probability" or a "substantial chance of discovering evidence of criminal activity."* **By contrast, the Court held "the standard for school searches could as readily be described as a moderate chance of finding evidence of wrongdoing."**

Teacher Scenarios

School strip-searches student over iPod: Went way too far, Mom says 229

Court Decisions

◆ An Arizona assistant middle school principal questioned a 13-year-old student about knives, lighters and a cigarette found in her planner. When the student denied owning any of the contraband, the assistant principal questioned her about prescription-strength ibuprofen pills and an over-the-counter painkiller. After the student denied knowing about the pills, the assistant principal told her he had received a report from a male student that she was giving pills to others at school. She denied this and allowed the assistant principal to search her belongings. He found no contraband there but told female staff members to further search the student in the nurse's office. An administrative assistant and school nurse asked the student to remove her jacket, socks, shoes, pants and T-shirt. They then instructed her to pull her bra to the side and shake it. Finally, the two staff members told the student to pull out the elastic of her underpants.

No pills were found in the search. The student's mother filed a federal district court action against the school district and school officials for Fourth Amendment violations. The case reached the U.S. Supreme Court, which noted that *New Jersey v. T.L.O.*, this chapter, used "a standard of reasonableness that stops short of probable cause." In this case, the male student's report created suspicion enough to justify the search of the student's backpack and outer clothing. But asking her to pull away her underwear and expose her breasts and pelvic area made the search **"categorically distinct, requiring distinct elements of justification on the part of school authorities for going beyond a search of outer clothing and belongings."** The Court cited a psychology journal study that found a strip search can cause serious emotional damage. Some schools find strip searches are never reasonable. While the indignity of a search did not necessarily outlaw it, the Court found "the suspicion failed to match the degree of intrusion." The assistant principal had no reason to suspect the student was hiding drugs or painkillers in her underwear. The Court stated "the *T.L.O.* concern to limit a school search to reasonable scope requires the support of reasonable suspicion of danger or of resort to underwear for hiding evidence of wrongdoing before a search can reasonably make the quantum leap from outer clothes and backpacks to exposure of intimate parts." Despite the constitutional violation, the law regarding student searches was not so well established as to deprive school officials of qualified immunity from liability. The case was returned to the district court for further consideration. *Safford Unified School Dist. #1 v. Redding*, 129 S.Ct. 2633 (U.S. 2009).

◆ Two students in an Ohio high school nursing class reported missing cash, a credit card and gift cards. The other 15 or 16 students in the class were taken to the first aid room, where their purses, books, shoes, socks and pockets were searched. After a search of each student's locker, staff members received a report that an unidentified student was hiding the missing items in her bra. The school director then instructed a female instructor to search the students in the lavatory. Eleven students sued the school district, instructors and other school officials in a federal district court for violating their Fourth Amendment rights. The court denied the officials' request for qualified immunity. On appeal, the U.S. Court of Appeals, Sixth Circuit, affirmed the judgment, and the officials appealed to the U.S. Supreme Court. It returned the case to the Sixth Circuit in view of its decision in *Safford Unified School Dist. #1 v. Redding*, above.

The Sixth Circuit held there must be "reasonable grounds for suspecting that the search will turn up evidence that the student has violated or is violating either the law or the rules of the school." **A student handbook policy did not create mutual consent to conduct the strip searches, as the district argued.** There was no waiver of privacy expectations, as some students did not even know about the policy. Repeating its finding in *Beard v. Whitmore Lake School Dist.*, this chapter, the court held "students have a significant privacy interest in their unclothed bodies." The severity of the school's need in this case was held "slight." A search for money served a much less important interest than a search for drugs or weapons. Any interest in searching for the missing items was "diluted considerably" when the entire class was searched. The court found the search was unlikely to uncover any evidence and violated the students' rights. As a result, the court again denied the officials' claim to immunity. *Knisley v. Pike County Joint Vocational School Dist.*, 604 F.3d 977 (6th Cir. 2010).

◆ A federal district court held Illinois charter school officials were immune to claims filed by a student who was strip-searched by a security guard and police officer. Prior to a trial, the school principal and dean sought to dismiss the federal law claims on the basis of qualified immunity. In *Safford Unified School Dist. v. Redding*, this chapter, the Supreme Court held that a school official searching a student may claim qualified immunity where no clearly established law reveals a constitutional violation. In this case, the student could not show the law regarding school strip searches was "clearly established" at the time of the search. Although the *Redding* case found Arizona school officials violated a middle school student's rights by conducting an overly intrusive search, the decision was not released until after the search in this case. As for the other claims, the court rejected the student's argument that school and municipal officials placed her in a position of danger by allowing the search to go forward.

There was no allegation of an official policy or practice of civil rights violations, requiring dismissal of the claims against the school and its board. The court found the student did not allege any other incident of failure to train employees. **A single, isolated incident of wrongdoing by a non-policymaker was insufficient to establish municipal liability.** Rejecting other state law claims such as intentional infliction of emotional distress and false arrest, the court disposed of many of the student's claims prior to any trial. *S.J. v. Perspectives Charter School*, 685 F.Supp.2d 847 (N.D. Ill. 2010).

◆ A Georgia high school student violated a ban on electronic communication devices by bringing an iPod and cell phone to class. After confiscating the iPod and putting it in a drawer, the teacher left the room, and a classmate took it from the drawer. When the teacher returned, he found the iPod missing and asked who had taken it. After no student admitted having the iPod, all of them were told to open their book bags, turn out their pockets and untuck their shirts. A classmate later confided the identity of the iPod taker to the assistant principal. He avoided confronting the iPod taker to protect the identity of the informer, and told the school discipline secretary to take each of the girls to a closet where they were to shake out their blouses and roll down their waistbands.

Although the identity of the iPod taker was already known, the secretary told a student to remove her pants and underwear. The student sued the teacher, district and others in a federal district court. It held student searches must be "justified at its inception." **This meant reasonable grounds for suspecting that the search will turn up evidence of a violation of rules must be present.** In *Thomas v. Roberts*, 261 F.3d 1160 (11th Cir. 2001), the Eleventh Circuit considered a strip search of Georgia fifth-graders for $26 in missing cash. *Roberts* put schools on notice that a strip search for non-dangerous contraband violates the Fourth Amendment. Officials lacked individualized suspicion that the student had the iPod, and the assistant principal acknowledged the search was to protect the informant. As the search was not based on individualized suspicion that the student had an iPod, a jury could find a Fourth Amendment violation if she was searched as she claimed. But as the assistant principal was not a "final policymaker" for the district, there could be no district liability on the federal claims. *Foster v. Raspberry*, 652 F.Supp.2d 1342 (M.D. Ga. 2009).

◆ An Alabama seventh-grade teacher reported her $450 makeup bag and $12 in cash were missing. The principal, an assistant principal and a counselor told students to empty their book bags and purses and take off their shoes and socks. Students were told to pull out their pants pockets, and the assistant principal and counselor patted down a few of them. The assistant principal stuck her hand into a student's pockets. The counselor reached into the pockets of male students and ran her hand down one student's thigh. The principal took some boys into the hallway for questioning. He then found the makeup bag in a trash can. The $12 was not in the bag, but the teacher said she was no longer concerned about it. Despite this response, the principal took the boys to the boys' lavatory, where he told them to drop their pants and raise their shirts. The counselor took the girls to the lavatory and asked most of them to do the same. A few were also told to pull up their bras. Parents of the students sued the school board, principal, assistant principal, and counselor for Fourth Amendment violations.

A federal district court noted the school handbook warned school officials to avoid group searches where individualized suspicion was lacking. School officials were to call the police and parents if a more intrusive search was required. The policy forbade strip searching. The court found that the officials did not have any individualized suspicion that any student took the makeup bag. The classroom searches which did not involve the touching of students were justified, but **a strip search for the possible theft of $12 was unreasonable. The strip searches were intrusive and violated the district's own policy.** As the search was beyond the school officials' authority, they were not entitled to qualified immunity from the Fourth Amendment violation claims. *H.Y. v. Russell County Board of Educ.*, 490 F.Supp.2d 1174 (M.D. Ala. 2007).

◆ Connecticut school officials held a security search prior to the boarding of buses to a senior class picnic. A student was found with a pack of cigarettes, but no action was taken against her. A classmate then reported to a teacher that the student said she planned to hide marijuana in her pants after the security check. The principal instructed the nurse to search the student's underpants. The nurse expressed apprehension, and the student's mother was called. While waiting for her, the principal searched the student's purse and found cigarettes and a lighter inside it. The mother arrived and agreed to help with the search after being told the police would be called otherwise. The nurse and mother then performed the search behind a curtain. The student was required to raise her shirt, pull down her bra and skirt, and pull her underpants away from her body. The search revealed no marijuana, and she was allowed to attend the picnic. She later sued the principal and other officials for constitutional violations. A federal district court upheld the search under *New Jersey v. T.L.O.*, (this chapter).

The U.S. Court of Appeals, Second Circuit, considered the case and reviewed *Cornfield v. Consolidated High School Dist.*, 991 F.2d 1316 (7th Cir. 1993), an Illinois case that found an intrusive strip search required such a high level of suspicion that it approached probable cause. Here, the factors relied on by the school officials were insufficient to create reasonable suspicion for a strip search. While the teacher may have been entitled to rely on the classmate as a reliable informant, the principal was not. After receiving the tip, the principal did not investigate or try to corroborate the classmate's account. **A student's history of drug use could be a factor justifying a school search. However, the student in this case was not previously disciplined for any drug offense.** The "discovery" of cigarettes and a lighter had only a tenuous connection to the report of marijuana possession. School officials had already seen this contraband during the security check and did not confiscate any items or express concern. *Phaneuf v. Fraikin*, 448 F.3d 591 (2d Cir. 2006).

◆ A Michigan student told her gym teacher that money had been stolen from her during class. A teacher who was acting principal called the police. The gym teacher searched backpacks of male students in the class, without success. A male teacher searched the boys in their locker room, instructing them to lower their pants and underwear and remove their shirts. A police officer arrived and told the teacher to continue searching, and said the girls should be checked in the same way as the boys "to prevent any claims of gender discrimination." The acting principal and a female teacher then searched the girls in their locker room, requiring them to pull up their shirts and pull down their pants. About 25 students were searched, but the stolen money was not discovered. The students sued the school district, teachers and police officer in a federal district court.

The case reached the U.S. Court of Appeals, Sixth Circuit, which stated that a **search for missing money served a less important governmental interest than a search for drugs or weapons**. This interest was further diluted when a school searched over 20 students with no reason to suspect any one in particular. The search was unlikely to succeed and was unlawful. But as *New Jersey v. T.L.O.* and relevant Sixth Circuit cases did not discuss strip searches, the law was sufficiently unclear that the teachers and officer were entitled to qualified immunity. *Beard v. Whitmore Lake School Dist.*, 402 F.3d 598 (6th Cir. 2005).

After the district court dismissed other claims, the students brought a second appeal to the Sixth Circuit. The court held that to hold the school district liable for not sufficiently training its teachers and maintaining a custom or policy of tolerating unconstitutional searches the students had to show "deliberate indifference" by the district. But the district had a two-page policy governing student searches and seizures, plus five pages of guidelines. The teachers had disregarded these policies when performing the search. It was unclear that the search was unconstitutional at the time it was performed, and the need for further training was not so obvious that the school district could be found "deliberately indifferent" to student constitutional rights. The court rejected the students' additional arguments and affirmed the judgment. *Beard v. Whitmore Lake School Dist.*, 244 Fed.Appx. 607 (6th Cir. 2007).

5. State Constitutional Cases

In In re P.E.A., *754 P.2d 382 (Col. 1988), the Colorado Supreme Court held the search of a student's car for contraband was justified at its inception. The Supreme Court of New Jersey looked to the Colorado decision in* State v. Best, *below, to support the application of a reasonableness standard to the search of vehicles parked on school property. Officials took action that was reasonably related to the objectives of the search and not excessively intrusive.*

Court Decisions

◆ A New Jersey assistant principal (AP) received a report that a high school student was under the influence of drugs. After being taken to the AP's office and interviewed, the student denied any wrongdoing. A search of the student's pockets yielded three white capsules. The AP then searched the student's car and denied his request to call his father. The car search yielded contraband, including a bag containing what appeared to be illegal drugs. A school resource officer arrested the student, who waived his right to remain silent and admitted that the contraband belonged to him. In juvenile proceedings, the student moved to suppress evidence seized from his car as a violation of his right to be free from unreasonable searches and seizures. Based on a finding that the AP's search of the car was reasonably related to a suspicion that the student had drugs and posed a danger to the school, the trial court denied the student's motion.

A state appellate division court affirmed the judgment, and the student appealed to the Supreme Court of New Jersey. On appeal, the court explained that under *New Jersey v. T.L.O.*, this chapter, the school setting required some easing of police search standards in view of the need to maintain school discipline and safety. **The court found no reason to avoid the *T.L.O.* standard in vehicle cases, as "the school setting calls for protections geared toward the safety of students."** The court was not convinced by the student's claim to a greater expectation of privacy in his car than he might have in a locker or purse. A reasonable grounds standard applied to the search of a student's car on school property by school authorities. Based on a classmate's statements and his apparent drug use, and the student's statements and possession of pills, it was reasonable for the AP to extend the search to the student's car. The court affirmed the judgment. *State v. Best*, 201 N.J. 100, 987 A.2d 605 (N.J. 2010).

Oregon's highest court held a "reasonable suspicion" standard from federal law could apply to student searches in cases decided under the state constitution. But the court limited the standard to serious threats of harm.

◆ An Oregon assistant high school principal learned a student had been seen trying to sell marijuana near the school. The student was called to the office and told that an anonymous witness saw him trying to sell drugs. After speaking to his mother, the student agreed to turn his pockets inside out. Marijuana, plastic bags and a pipe were found, and he admitted he had tried to sell marijuana. In juvenile court proceedings, the student claimed any evidence seized by school officials should be excluded from trial because there was no probable cause for a search. Finding probable cause was unnecessary, the juvenile court utilized the "reasonable suspicion" standard used by federal courts in deciding public school students' Fourth Amendment claims. Applying this standard, the court held the search was lawful. It also concluded that the student was delinquent.

Appeal reached the Supreme Court of Oregon. It discussed Article I, Section 9, of the Oregon Constitution, which prohibits unreasonable searches or seizures. The court held school searches are different from law enforcement searches. **But only searches involving safety concerns justify a departure from the warrant and probable cause requirements.** When school officials perceive an immediate threat to safety, they need the ability to take prompt, reasonable steps. School officials have wide latitude to take safety precautions. This latitude applies when officials have reasonable suspicion based on specific and articulable facts that an individual poses a threat to safety or possesses an item posing such a threat. Reasonable suspicion applies to searches for drugs on school property. Important limits apply to searches under the new rule. School officials cannot rely on generalizations about suspected drug use or use information that is not specific or current. Since officials reasonably suspected that the student had illegal drugs at the time of the search and that he intended to sell them at school, the judgment was affirmed. *State ex rel. Juvenile Dep't of Clackamas County v. M.A.D.*, 348 Or. 381, 233 P.3d 437 (Or. 2010).

◆ Several people told a Florida middle school principal that a student had been drinking alcohol with her friend at home the day before. Upon interviewing the student, the principal learned that the two girls drank alcohol before school. A sibling of the student then took them to school. A child study committee met and found the student was under the influence of alcohol at school. A school board hearing was held to consider expulsion for attending school after drinking alcohol and disrupting the orderly conduct of the school.

A final school board order expelled the student for substantially disrupting the orderly conduct of the school and for gross misconduct in violation of a school policy against drinking alcohol. On appeal, a Florida District Court of Appeal found **Section 1006.07 of Florida Statutes and the own school's policy limited the board's power to punish students to conduct occurring on school grounds or during school-provided transportation.** In this case, the consumption of alcohol occurred at the student's residence about 45 minutes before school began. As she argued, the board could not punish her for drinking alcohol at home. There was no evidence that the student was under the influence of alcohol at school or that she behaved in an impaired manner. Since the court found no evidence that the student disrupted the learning environment despite her ingestion of alcohol, she could not be expelled under the school policy. As a result, the court vacated the school board's decision. *A.B.E. v. School Board of Brevard County*, 33 So.3d 795 (Fla. Dist. Ct. App. 2010).

B. Random Testing Policies

The U.S. Supreme Court has upheld random testing programs for students seeking to participate in extracurricular activities and use school parking facilities. According to the Court, students participating in extracurricular programs have a reduced expectation of privacy when compared to the general student population, justifying random testing. See Chapter Eight for more cases concerning random searches of students in interscholastic athletics.

Court Decisions

◆ An Oregon school district responded to increased student drug use by instituting a random drug-testing policy for all students wishing to participate in varsity athletics. A student who wanted to play football refused to sign the drug-testing consent form and was suspended from sports for the season. His parents sued the district in a federal district court. The court upheld the policy, but the Ninth Circuit held it violated the U.S. and Oregon Constitutions. On appeal, the Supreme Court noted **students have a lesser expectation of privacy than the general populace, and that student-athletes had an even lower expectation of privacy in the locker room**. The Supreme Court held the invasion of privacy in this case was no worse than what was typically encountered in public restrooms. Positive test results were disclosed to only a limited number of school employees. **The insignificant invasion of student privacy was outweighed by the district's important interest in addressing drug use by students who risked physical harm while playing sports.** The Court vacated the judgment and remanded the case. *Vernonia School Dist. 47J v. Acton*, 515 U.S. 646, 115 S.Ct. 2386, 132 L.Ed.2d 564 (1995).

◆ An Oklahoma school district adopted a policy requiring all students who sought to participate in extracurricular activities to submit to random drug testing. A student challenged the policy in a federal district court, which awarded summary judgment to the board. On appeal, the Tenth Circuit held student drug use in the Oklahoma district was far from epidemic or an immediate crisis and reversed the judgment. The board appealed to the U.S. Supreme Court, which noted the testing policy was adopted to protect students.

The Court found no reason to limit drug testing to student-athletes, extending *Vernonia* to cover all extracurricular activities participants. Participants in these activities had limited privacy rights, as they voluntarily subjected themselves to certain intrusions on their privacy. They also agreed to abide by extracurricular club rules and requirements that did not apply to the student body at large. The policy's intrusion on student privacy was minimal. Test results could have no impact on student discipline or academics, but could only lead to the limitation of extracurricular activities participation. By contrast, the district and board had an important interest in preventing student drug use. The Court found sufficient evidence of drug use by students to justify the policy. **It deemed the policy a reasonably effective means of addressing legitimate concerns in preventing, deterring and detecting student drug use.** *Board of Educ. of Independent School Dist. 92, Pottawatomie County v. Earls*, 536 U.S. 822, 122 S.Ct. 2559, 153 L.Ed.2d 735 (2002).

◆ A federal district court held that daily searches of disabled students at segregated facilities operated by a public school special education cooperative violated the Fourth Amendment prohibition on unreasonable searches and seizures. **The court found the cooperative's programs were educational and not punitive in nature.** This distinguished the case from *C.N.H. v. Florida*, 927 So.2d 1 (Fla. Dist. Ct. App. 2006), where a court approved of daily pat-down searches at an alternative school where students attended by court order and in lieu of confinement. In this case, the students did not attend school in lieu of detention. **A policy of daily, suspicionless searches was unconstitutional.** A jury would have to decide whether daily searches over a course of years was "highly offensive" under state law principles. *Hough v. Shakopee Public Schools*, 608 F.Supp.2d 1087 (D. Minn. 2009).

◆ An Arkansas district handbook permitted random searches of book bags, backpacks, purses and other containers at all times on school property. A staff member found some marijuana in a student's purse after all the students in her classroom were ordered to wait in the hall during a search. The student sued the district for constitutional rights violations. A court awarded pretrial judgment to the district, and the student appealed. The Eighth Circuit held that students have a legitimate, though limited, privacy expectation in their personal belongings while in school. Subjecting them to full-scale searches without any suspicion of wrongdoing virtually eliminated their privacy interests. There was no evidence of any special circumstances that would justify the intrusiveness of the district policy. **Searches involving "people rummaging through personal belongings" were much more intrusive than searches involving metal detectors or police dogs.** As the policy was highly intrusive and not justified by any significant school interest, the court held that it violated the Fourth Amendment. *Doe v. Little Rock School Dist.*, 380 F.3d 349 (8th Cir. 2004).

◆ A Pennsylvania school district required students who sought to participate in extracurricular activities or obtain a school parking permit to agree to random urinalysis testing. The policy was intended to deter drug use, prevent physical harm and require students to serve as role models for their peers. Two students sued the district for violating Article I, Section 8 of the Pennsylvania Constitution, which prohibits unreasonable searches and seizures. The court held for the district, but the Commonwealth Court of Pennsylvania reversed.

On appeal, the Supreme Court of Pennsylvania said Article I, Section 8 recognized stronger privacy interests than those recognized by the Fourth Amendment. And here, the policy was not a trivial incursion on student privacy. Students had a reasonable expectation that their excretory functions would only be modestly diminished at school. The district suggested no specialized need to test students for drugs and alcohol based on an existing problem, and there was no showing the group targeted for testing presented a drug problem. The policy unconstitutionally authorized a direct invasion on student privacy, with no suspicion that targeted students used drugs or alcohol in greater numbers than those who were exempt. The court held that **random testing of all students in extracurricular activities was unreasonable**, and it affirmed the judgment. *Theodore v. Delaware Valley School Dist.*, 575 Pa. 321, 836 A.2d 76 (Pa. 2003).

◆ A New Jersey school district implemented a series of policies to deter students from using drugs and alcohol, and to refer those with abuse problems into counseling. The school board implemented a random drug-and-alcohol-testing program for all interscholastic sports participants. It later accepted a task force recommendation to expand the testing to all extracurricular participants and those who held school parking permits. Test results were confidential and those who tested positive for drug or alcohol use did not face other school penalties or criminal prosecution. Parents sued the board and superintendent for violating Article I, Paragraph 7 of the New Jersey Constitution.

The case reached the Supreme Court of New Jersey, which commented that Article I, Paragraph 7 was nearly identical to the Fourth Amendment. The court employed the *Vernonia* factors for evaluating the constitutionality of testing programs for interscholastic sports participants. It embraced U.S. Supreme Court language approving of the use of minimally obtrusive drug testing to address the nationwide drug epidemic. The testing program was justified by the special need to maintain school order and safety. **Extracurricular activities participants and those seeking parking privileges subjected themselves to additional regulation that did not apply to all students.** The collection process afforded privacy and protected personal dignity. The court rejected the parents' invitation to interpret the state constitution as providing greater protection of individual rights than the Fourth Amendment. It affirmed the decision, cautioning other districts not to interpret its holding as "an automatic green light" to replicate the district's program. *Joye v. Hunterdon Cent. Regional High School Board of Educ.*, 176 N.J. 568, 826 A.2d 624 (N.J. 2003).

◆ An Indiana district adopted a random drug-testing policy for students in grades 7-12 who participated in school athletics, extracurricular and co-curricular activities, and those who wished to park vehicles on campus. Positive tests did not result in academic penalties, were not documented and were not disclosed to legal authorities. Those who submitted negative retests had their privileges reinstated, but those who submitted positive retests could be retested and barred from returning to activities for up to a year. Two students who participated in extracurricular activities sued the district for violations of the Indiana Constitution. A state court held for the district, and the case reached the Supreme Court of Indiana. It rejected the students' claim that the policy should be analyzed under the "individualized suspicion standard" applicable to police.

School searches were substantively different from law enforcement searches because the relationship between school officials and students was not adversarial. School officials did not offer test results to law enforcement agencies or use them for school discipline, undercutting the rationale for use of an individualized suspicion standard. Students enjoy less privacy at school than do adults in comparable situations. The voluntary decision to submit to drug testing further decreased student privacy expectations. The policy only deprived students of participation in the extracurricular part of an activity and was upheld. *Linke v. Northwestern School Corp.*, 763 N.E.2d 972 (Ind. 2002).

C. Police Involvement

School officials are not agents of the police, as they act to ensure student safety and maintain school order, not combat crime. For this reason, the courts have held school officials do not need to advise students of their Fifth Amendment rights or have probable cause to conduct student searches. However, the presence of municipal police during a school search may complicate the correct constitutional standard to apply.

1. *Miranda* Warnings

*When people are taken into police custody, they must be advised of their Fifth and Sixth Amendment rights. Otherwise, any statement may not be used in juvenile or criminal proceedings. The advisory includes the right to remain silent, to know that any statement can be used against the person in court, and the right to have assistance of counsel. This is known as a "*Miranda *warning," based on* Miranda v. Arizona, 384 U.S. 436 (1966).

Courts in Texas, Rhode Island, New Jersey, Massachusetts, Florida and California have held school liaison officers need not issue Miranda *warnings when questioning students about school rules violations, but the Supreme Court of Pennsylvania has held they must. The Oregon Court of Appeals refused to apply the* Miranda *requirement in a civil action to reverse a school expulsion..*

Teacher Scenarios

Teacher had the right to question student – but did she go too far?......................................*230*

Parents sue over teacher's meeting
with students 231

Court Decisions

◆ An anonymous informant told Wisconsin school officials that a student had drugs at school. He consented to the search of his person, book bag and locker by a school liaison officer and a municipal police officer. When no drugs were found, an assistant principal searched the student's car and found marijuana, a pipe, Oxycontin and cash. She turned over these items to the police, who arrested the student and took him to the police station, where he received his criminal rights warnings, known as "*Miranda* rights." Prior to trial, the student sought to exclude evidence seized from his car and any statements he made during the investigation. He claimed he was "in custody" of the police at the time he was questioned in the parking lot. If this was the case, it was necessary to read him his *Miranda* rights at that time. The court denied the student's motions to suppress his statements and the evidence seized from his car.

On appeal, the Court of Appeals of Wisconsin found ***Miranda* warnings are only required when a person is in police "custody."** Whether a person is in custody depends upon the circumstances. Formal arrest, restraint on freedom of movement, or interrogation that is likely to elicit an incriminating response are examples of "custody" for *Miranda* purposes. Here, while the student was "escorted" to his car by police, an assistant principal was still in control of the investigation, up to and including the search of the car. Moreover, the student was not cuffed, and he was not detained for more than 15 minutes. Finding that a reasonable person would not have considered himself to be in "custody" at the time, the student was not entitled to have his *Miranda* rights read to him in the parking lot. The court also found the search reasonable under the circumstances. *State of Wisconsin v. Schloegel*, 769 N.W.2d 130 (Wis. Ct. App. 2009).

◆ A Tennessee student told a school resource officer that marijuana found in his truck belonged to him. As they returned to the school building, the student also admitted he had left school to smoke marijuana with a friend that morning. The resource officer took the student to juvenile court and charged him. The student later moved to suppress his statements on grounds that she did not inform him of his *Miranda* rights prior to questioning. The juvenile court denied the student's motion, finding the student was not in police custody at the time.

On appeal, the Supreme Court of Tennessee held that **the student was not confined for questioning, and he was not in police "custody."** Thus, his incriminating statements had been properly admitted into evidence. However, since *T.L.O.* was decided, there has been an increased presence of law enforcement officers in public schools. Municipalities have "blended" the traditional duties of school officials and law officers to protect the safety of students and teachers. Based on the resource officer's duties, a new trial would be held to find whether the search required probable cause or reasonable suspicion. *R.D.S. v. State of Tennessee*, 245 S.W.3d 356 (Tenn. 2008).

◆ A Boston middle school student showed a clear plastic bag containing over 50 bullets to other students. The school resource officer confiscated the bullets, and later conducted a pat-down search that yielded no further evidence. The officer then read the student his *Miranda* warnings and asked him to disclose the location of his gun. The student said he did not have a gun. His mother and grandmother arrived at school, and the officer continued questioning the student without informing the adults of the student's *Miranda* rights. After an expulsion hearing the same day, the student led the officer to the gun, which he had hidden in a yard in a residential area. In juvenile delinquency proceedings, the judge found the resource officer had unlawfully failed to provide the student *Miranda* warnings in the presence of an interested adult, as required by state law.

The case reached the Supreme Judicial Court of Massachusetts, which noted that the juvenile court judge refused to apply the "limited public safety exception" to *Miranda* established by the U.S. Supreme Court in *New York v. Quarles*, 467 U.S. 649 (1984). Here, the student was only 13 years old. **Juvenile suspects under 14 may not waive their *Miranda* rights in the absence of an interested adult, such as a parent.** But the resource officer here was faced with an emergency situation that required him to protect 890 middle school students as well as area residents. Under the circumstances, he reasonably concluded that there was an immediate need to question the student. The student's possession of 50 bullets was enough to support the inference that a gun was in close proximity. This was valid reason to invoke the public safety exception to *Miranda*. Accordingly, the court reversed the juvenile court order. *Comwlth. v. Dillon D.*, 448 Mass. 793, 863 N.E.2d 1287 (Mass. 2007).

◆ Several Virginia elementary school students reported to their teacher that a 10-year-old student brought a gun to school. An assistant principal questioned the student repeatedly in her office and searched her book bag and desk. After no weapon was found, the assistant principal allowed the student to leave. The following Monday, the assistant principal and principal interviewed some of the student witnesses. One of them said the student had thrown a handgun into the woods adjoining the school. School officials called police and brought the student to the office. They resumed the interrogation, despite her complaints of illness and requests to see her mother. The police continued interrogating the student, with school administrators present. The student repeatedly asked for her mother, but officials denied her requests. She claimed they detained her for over one hour and refused to let her go to the lavatory. The officers found no weapon and did not call the student's mother until after they left. The student and her mother sued school and police officials for due process and Fourth Amendment violations. But a federal district court dismissed the case.

The student appealed to the U.S. Court of Appeals, Fourth Circuit, which refused to adopt a general rule requiring school administrators to notify parents during school investigations, or to forbid student detentions of a particular length. Virginia law and school board rules required a principal to make reasonable efforts to contact parents or guardians before police interrogations. The Constitution imposed no parental notification duty while a student was detained. When school officials seize a student in a constitutional manner and tell police the basis for their suspicion, the detention is justified at its inception. **When a student detention justifies police involvement, no Fourth Amendment violation occurs.** The officers detained the student only until they determined that no guns were on school grounds. The court found no fault with the efforts of the school officials to protect school safety, and it affirmed the judgment. *Wofford v. Evans*, 390 F.3d 318 (4th Cir. 2004).

◆ An Oregon student was suspended from school and subjected to a juvenile court adjudication. A vice principal called the student's mother several weeks later, and told her the student was again in the school office. The mother told the vice principal she was very uncomfortable with him talking to her son without her lawyer present. The next month, school officials questioned the student for two hours after a teacher smelled marijuana smoke coming from a restroom while the student and a classmate were there. The student first denied using marijuana, but later admitted it to the vice principal and other officials. As required by school policy, they reported this admission to municipal police.

After the school board voted for expulsion, the student appealed to an Oregon trial court, claiming he was entitled to *Miranda* warnings when he was questioned by school officials. The court dismissed the case because no police officers were involved and the matter was not a criminal prosecution. The student appealed to the Court of Appeals of Oregon, which **found no authority for suppressing evidence in a school disciplinary hearing on grounds of failure to administer *Miranda* warnings.** A school expulsion did not resemble the deprivation of liberty present in criminal cases. The differences between a school expulsion and a juvenile proceeding required affirming the judgment for the school officials. *T.M.M. v. Lake Oswego School Dist.*, 198 Or.App. 572, 108 P.3d 1211 (Or. Ct. App. 2005).

2. Police-Assisted Searches

Court Decisions

◆ A Texas school parking lot attendant told the principal that three students were smoking in a car parked in a school lot. The principal encountered the students and directed them to her office. She noted that one of them wore baggy shorts and believed he might have a concealed weapon. The student refused her request to empty his pockets and she obtained the assistance of a municipal police officer assigned to the high school. **The officer patted down the student and found him in possession of marijuana.** The state prosecuted the student in juvenile court for possession of marijuana in a drug-free zone. The court denied the student's pretrial motion to suppress the marijuana. He pleaded no contest to drug possession and was fined and placed under community supervision for one year. The student appealed to the Texas Court of Appeals.

On appeal, the student claimed the officer lacked reasonable suspicion to pat him down. The court held that **where school officials initiate a search, or police involvement is minimal, the "reasonable suspicion" test applies**, not the more exacting "probable cause" standard applicable to traditional law enforcement searches. Because the student was smoking in the parking lot, wore baggy shorts and refused to empty his pockets, reasonable grounds existed for suspecting a search would turn up evidence of a rules violation. The search was reasonably related to the objectives of the search and not excessively intrusive in view of the student's age and sex. So it did not violate the Fourth Amendment. *Russell v. State of Texas*, 74 S.W.3d 887 (Tex. Ct. App. 2002).

◆ A resource officer was assigned to work at a New Hampshire school by the municipal police department. Due to the many searches there, administrators agreed to investigate less serious matters, including drug possession, and refer those involving weapons or a threat to school safety to the officer. If the officer felt he lacked probable cause for an arrest, he would deem the case a "school issue" and let administrators handle it. A science teacher observed a student passing tinfoil to a classmate and reported it to the resource officer. The officer referred the student to an assistant principal. The assistant principal and another administrator questioned the student and asked if they could search him. He agreed and they discovered tinfoil that the student admitted "might be LSD." The administrators contacted the resource officer and returned the case to him.

A state court granted the student's motion to suppress evidence found by the administrators, finding they acted as agents of the police and had to provide him the safeguards afforded to criminal suspects. The state appealed to the New Hampshire Supreme Court, which noted that **school officials may take on the mantle of criminal investigators if they assume police duties. That is what occurred in this case**, as there was an understanding between the resource officer and school officials on how violations would be investigated. The court cautioned school administrators to "be vigilant not to assume responsibilities beyond the scope of their administrative duties" when establishing working relationships with police. Because an agency relationship existed between the police and school officials, the court affirmed the order for the student. *State of New Hampshire v. Heirtzler*, 789 A.2d 634 (N.H. 2001).

3. Drug-Sniffing Dogs

In Burbank v. Canton Board of Educ., *below, a Connecticut court applied a "public smell doctrine" to a search of school lockers and parking lots using police dogs. The court relied on a 1982 Texas case which reasoned that the* **use of dogs to sniff for contraband in unattended lockers and cars is not a Fourth Amendment "search" at all.** *Odors emanating from a person or property are* *"considered exposed to the public 'view' and, therefore, unprotected."* Horton v. Goose Creek Independent School Dist., *690 F.2d 470 (5th Cir. 1982).*

Court Decisions

◆ A Connecticut school board regulation authorized drug searches by dogs of school property to which students had access during the school day, including lockers, classrooms and parking areas. Dogs were not allowed to sniff persons and were not used in occupied classrooms. During the first period of a school day, the principals of a middle and high school announced a dog sweep search, and alerted students and faculty that they were to "stay put" in their classrooms, unless an emergency occurred. A dog alerted on one car in a school parking lot, and a student was arrested for a small amount of marijuana found there.

Students had to remain in their first period classes for about one hour and 50 minutes, and missed at least one full class period. Several parents asked a state court for a permanent order to either prohibit warrantless dog-sniff sweep searches, or require notice to parents at least 48 hours in advance of any search. The court stated that **dog-sniff searches of cars or unattended lockers were not even a "search" under the Fourth Amendment**. Requiring students to stay in their classrooms for over an hour was not a "seizure," as the families claimed. Here, the students would have normally been in class at the time of the search anyway. And the parents had no right to receive advance notice of dog-sniff searches, as they claimed. The court denied the parents' request for an order to halt the dog sweeps or to receive advance notice of future sweep searches. *Burbank v. Canton Board of Educ.*, No. CV 094043192S, 2009 WL 3366272 (Conn. Ct. Super. 9/14/09).

◆ An Alabama county sheriff's department conducted a drug-sweep search using drug-sniffing dogs at a school. A small package of drugs was found under a table where a student had been sitting. Law officers patted him down and asked him to empty his pockets. After a classmate said that the drugs belonged to the student, two male officers took him to a teachers' lounge, where a strip search yielded no further drugs. A second student was asked to empty his pockets onto a table in the cafeteria where all vocational students had been taken. The officers then led their dogs through the cafeteria and patted down students, even though no dogs alerted. A third student was called to the school parking lot when dogs alerted on his car. He then attempted to swallow a small package, and officers tried to make him spit it out. The third student admitted the package contained marijuana seeds, and the officers made him strip to his underwear while in the parking lot. The students sued the school board, school officials and law enforcement officers for violating their constitutional rights.

The court found the search of the first student was reasonable. Drugs were found at his table, and a classmate said he had placed them there. The police therefore had "individualized suspicion" of a violation. The second student did not show any constitutional violation occurred when he was required to empty his pockets. **A search may be conducted without individualized suspicion when student privacy interests are minimal and important governmental interests exist.** As the search was reasonably related to the objective of finding illegal drugs, it met the *T.L.O.* reasonableness standard. The search of the third student was supported by individualized suspicion, as sniffing dogs had alerted to his car. However, the search was excessively intrusive because the police officers required him to strip to his underwear while in a public parking lot. The school officials were entitled to judgment, however, as there was no evidence that they participated in any constitutional rights violation. *Rudolph v. Lowndes County Board of Educ.*, 242 F.Supp.2d 1107 (M.D. Ala. 2003).

4. Liability Issues

In Chavez v. Martinez, *538 U.S. 760 (2003), the U.S. Supreme Court held courts cannot award damages against police investigators who wrongly induce suspects to provide incriminating information unless it is actually used in a criminal prosecution. Until compelled statements are used in a criminal case, there is no potential violation of the Fifth Amendment self-incrimination clause.*

Court Decisions

◆ A Miami-area high school student was spotted walking away from the campus of a school he did not attend at 7:25 a.m. Police had warned him not to enter the school's safety zone on two prior occasions, and they arrested him. State prosecutors filed a delinquency petition against the student, and he was charged with trespass in a school safety zone and resisting arrest. The student moved to dismiss the petition, arguing that the law unconstitutionally restricted peaceful conduct and communication.

The case reached the Florida District Court of Appeal, Third District, which observed that a Florida statute makes it unlawful for any person to enter a "school safety zone" without legitimate business or other authorization at the school from one hour prior to the start of school until one hour after the end of school. The statute allowed those with proper authorization or legitimate business at a school to remain in a school zone. The student did not show that persons seeking to engage in constitutionally protected speech or assemblies could not receive "authorization" to do so. He did not show that persons who had received notices barring them from school safety zones have First Amendment rights to return to a school safety zone to express themselves. **The law was clearly intended to protect children, which is a compelling government interest.** The court affirmed the order declaring the student a juvenile delinquent. *J.L.S. v. State*, 947 So.2d 641 (Fla. Dist. Ct. App. 2007).

◆ An Idaho high school custodian discovered a stack of flyers in a school parking lot alleging sexual activities by a local judge's daughter. The principal investigated the incident and learned who made the documents. She also found that the documents were not produced at school. About two months later, the judge came to the school and sought to interview some students about a note he had received concerning his daughter's conduct. The principal allowed the judge and a staff member to interview three students without notice to their parents. This violated a school policy. The three students sued the principal and school district, asserting civil rights and tort claims. A federal district court held that there was no "search" under the Fourth Amendment. However, it was possible that the students were "seized" and underwent due process violations.

The students said they did not feel free to leave the office, and were aware of the judge's position. It appeared he had threatened at least one student with prosecution for failing to answer a question. Some of the questions had nothing to do with the note and might have been beyond the scope of the school's interest or authority. At the time of the interview, the principal already knew who had written the note. The court denied her request for qualified immunity, as she allowed the interviews without first contacting parents, in violation of district policies and due process guidelines. **There was no reasonable educational interest in asking students about their off-campus sexual activities or their interpersonal relationships.** A trial was required. *Howard v. Yakovac*, No. CV 04-202-S-ELJ, 2006 WL 1207615 (D. Idaho 2006).

◆ An Idaho student was developmentally disabled and had a form of autism. His school called a police officer to his class twice to observe his aggressive behavior with school staff. During one episode, the student hit the officer while she was trying to calm him. On another day, the student continuously tapped on his desk and was "verbally aggressive" toward teachers. School staff called the officer, who attempted to block the student from exiting, then took him to the floor, handcuffed him and hobbled his legs. After being restrained, the student was sent to hospital on "mental hold," while he struggled against confinement and remained verbally aggressive. The student later sued the school district and the police officer, claiming the district was negligent and the officer used excessive force in violation of the Fourth Amendment. A court held that the district and officer were immune. The student appealed to the U.S. Court of Appeals, Ninth Circuit, arguing that the district breached a duty to protect him by calling the police officer, creating an unreasonable risk of harm.

The court observed that the district did not employ the officer and had no real or apparent authority over her. **The district did not breach an asserted duty to intervene in her handling of the incident.** The student did not show that the district could have foreseen the officer would harm or endanger him. She knew of non-invasive techniques and had been able to calm him during past episodes. The type and amount of force the officer used was excessive. However, she was entitled to qualified immunity. There was no clearly established right to be free of the kind of force used in this case. *Hayenga v. Nampa School Dist. No. 131*, 123 Fed.Appx. 783 (9th Cir. 2005).

◆ A New York school employee told a middle school principal that two high school students regularly sold marijuana at their school. The principal accompanied the employee to the high school principal's office to report this. The employee learned from students that the high school students were planning to bring marijuana to school. She reported this to a state police officer, who came to the school and asked the principal to search the students. The principal agreed, and the students were searched separately by the principal, school dean and officer. They were asked to empty their pockets and book bags, to raise pants legs to expose their socks, and finally to drop their pants and turn around. Neither student was touched at any time, and no drugs were found.

One of the students alleged that other students saw him through the window of the principal's office in only his underwear. His father sued the district, principal and officer for civil rights violations. A court noted that *New Jersey v. T.L.O.* does not explain the legal standard to apply when police and school officials combine to conduct a school search. The court held for the district, principal and officer. A state appellate division court held that officials who perform discretionary functions are entitled to qualified immunity if their conduct does not violate clearly established rights of which a reasonable person would have known. The court acknowledged the ambiguous state of the law in mixed police/school searches. Given this ambiguity, **police officers of reasonable competence could have disagreed about whether probable cause was required for a search conducted by school officials**. The complaint against the officer had been correctly dismissed. *Doyle v. Rondout Valley Cent. School Dist.*, 770 N.Y.S.2d 480 (N.Y. App. Div. 2004).

III. CORPORAL PUNISHMENT

Overview

The U.S. Supreme Court held in Ingraham v. Wright, *below, that the infliction of corporal punishment implicates student liberty interests under the Due Process Clause of the Fourteenth Amendment. However, as corporal punishment was authorized by common law, the Court refused to create any procedural safeguards for students beyond those offered by state law. Corporal punishment is distinguishable from "reasonable physical force" to restrain unruly students, maintain order and prevent injury, as permitted by state law.*

In 2009, Florida legislators amended state law to limit the use of zero-tolerance policies and require school boards that permit corporal punishment as a form of discipline to review such policies every three years.

Court Decisions

◆ The U.S. Supreme Court held that the use of corporal punishment is a matter of state law. Two Florida students were paddled by school administrators. One was beaten so severely he missed 11 days of school. The other suffered a hematoma and lost the use of his arm for a week. The parents sued school authorities, alleging cruel and unusual punishment and due process violations. **The Supreme**

Court held that the Eighth Amendment prohibition against cruel and unusual punishment did not apply to corporal punishment in schools. The Court's reasoning for this decision lay in the relative openness of the school system and its surveillance by the community. The Eighth Amendment was intended to protect the rights of incarcerated persons, not students. State civil and criminal penalties restrained school employees from issuing unreasonable punishment. While corporal punishment implicated the Due Process Clause, state law vested the decision to issue it with school officials. The Court found corporal punishment served important educational interests. There was no requirement for notice and a hearing prior to imposing corporal punishment as the practice was authorized and limited by state law. *Ingraham v. Wright*, 430 U.S. 651, 97 S.Ct. 1401, 51 L.Ed.2d 711 (1977).

A. Student Due Process Rights

Court Decisions

◆ A Florida student with autism became aggressive and had trouble obeying rules and completing schoolwork. He pushed and bit others, growled, cursed, scratched himself and threatened to blow up his school. According to the student, the teacher used profanity daily and called him names. The teacher was placed on leave after two aides reported she had held down another child in the student's class until his eyes swelled and his lips turned blue. Reports were made to the state child abuse hotline, and the teacher was suspended and barred from school grounds. She was eventually convicted of one out of four counts of child abuse. A federal district court action was filed against the teacher on behalf of the student. In pretrial activity, two teaching aides stated that the teacher, who weighed almost 300 pounds, had straddled the student or pinned him against an object and pulled his arms behind his back. One aide testified that the teacher had used restraints in a way that could cause asphyxiation.

The court dismissed claims under the Due Process Clause of the Fourteenth Amendment and Section 504 of the Rehabilitation Act. On appeal, the Eleventh Circuit affirmed the judgment. It held only the most egregious official conduct violates the Constitution. **Corporal punishment has been held actionable by courts only when it is arbitrary, egregious and shocks the conscience.** A tripping incident was not corporal punishment. As for the other incidents, it appeared to the court that the teacher was attempting to restore order, maintain discipline or protect the student from harming himself. In each case, the student refused to go to his "cool down room," called the teacher names or threatened her. The court found no evidence that the teacher provoked the student into misbehaving. Evidence established that the teacher used restraints only until the student calmed down or agreed to comply with her instructions. Each incident lasted only a few minutes. There was also no evidence that the punishment of the student was based on his disability, defeating any discrimination claim. *T.W. v. School Board of Seminole County, Florida*, 610 F.3d 588 (11th Cir. 2010).

◆ A Tennessee student claimed two basketball coaches routinely paddled him for missing basketball practice, being late or other misconduct. He claimed one of the coaches punched him in the chest and paddled him for missing a car wash. The student said coaches sometimes paddled him for getting poor grades or misconduct. The student transferred schools in his eleventh-grade year and sued the coaches, school principal, the Memphis City Schools and its superintendent in a federal district court. After dismissing some of the claims, the court held a jury trial. A jury returned a verdict for the school system and officials on the remaining claims, and the student appealed.

On appeal, the U.S. Court of Appeals, Sixth Circuit, reviewed evidence that neither the student nor his parent ever complained about the paddlings to the principal or other officials. He never sought medical treatment and admitted he was not seriously harmed. One of the coaches stated that he might have paddled the student two or three times in all. The other coach stated he had paddled the student about 10 times over a three-year period. The Sixth Circuit noted that **Section 49-6-4103 of the Tennessee Code permits teachers and principals to use corporal punishment** "in a reasonable manner against any pupil for good cause in order to maintain discipline and order within the public schools." A school policy also permitted paddling. A 1944 state supreme court decision held that **"if corporal punishment is moderate and is inflicted with a proper instrument the teacher is as a rule, not liable civilly for assault and battery."** As only excessive punishment will subject a teacher to civil liability, the state law assault and battery claims failed. As for the constitutional claims, the court explained that there is a due process liberty interest in freedom from bodily injury. But the standard for a violation is high, and to prevail, the student had to show force so severe and so disproportionate to the need and "so inspired by malice or sadism" as to literally be "shocking to the conscience." He admitted he was not seriously injured, and the judgment was affirmed. *Nolan v. Memphis City Schools*, 589 F.3d 257 (6th Cir. 2009).

◆ A Georgia eighth-grade student was assigned to a remedial reading class. He arrived late to class, then talked to a classmate. The teacher told the classmate to leave the room, and the student tried to leave with him, refusing to return to his seat when she instructed him to do so. The teacher yelled and shook her finger at him. As the student moved to the door, she blocked it, and he initiated some physical contact with her. The teacher then grabbed the student by the neck. He claimed she squeezed his neck until he could not breathe. The teacher said she was afraid the student was preparing to hit her and put her hands on him to protect herself. The district placed her on administrative leave, and she soon resigned. The student sued the teacher, principal, district superintendent and school district. A federal court awarded pretrial judgment to the school officials, and the student appealed.

The U.S. Court of Appeals, Eleventh Circuit, held that regardless of whether the teacher acted in self-defense or imposed corporal punishment, there was no constitutional violation. **School officials violate substantive due process** rights under the Fourteenth Amendment only when their conduct is considered arbitrary or "shocking to the conscience." Neither party disputed that the teacher was acting within the scope of her discretionary authority. The force she used was not "obviously excessive," and she acted only after he repeatedly disobeyed her. She was entitled to official immunity. *Peterson v. Baker*, 504 F.3d 1331(11th Cir. 2007).

◆ An 18-year-old Texas student attended a public charter school during the 2003-04 school year. The principal disciplined her for leaving campus during a school day. He attempted to administer corporal punishment with a wooden paddle. The student resisted and received temporary, minor injuries to her hand by trying to block the paddle. She sued the school and principal. The case reached the U.S. Court of Appeals, Fifth Circuit, which held that **corporal punishment of public school students deprives them of substantive due process rights only when "arbitrary, capricious or wholly unrelated to the legitimate state goal of maintaining an atmosphere conducive to learning."** Corporal punishment is not arbitrary so long as the state affords local remedies. Texas law afforded adequate remedies for excessive corporal punishment claims. For this reason, the student's due process claims failed. There was no merit to her claim that adult status increased her rights. While the student did not have to attend school past the age of 18, she had voluntarily chosen to do so. Having agreed to attend school, she was not free to disregard school rules. *Serafin v. School of Excellence in Educ.*, 252 Fed.Appx. 684 (5th Cir. 2007).

◆ The U.S. Court of Appeals, Eleventh Circuit, upheld a federal court order denying qualified immunity to an Alabama principal accused of beating a student. The student claimed the principal called him into his office for disciplinary reasons and hit him in the head, ribs and back with a metal cane. His mother sued the district and principal for violating his federal civil rights. The principal sought pretrial judgment, asserting qualified immunity. He alleged that the student had previously been disciplined for bringing a weapon to school, justifying his use of force. The court denied the request for immunity, and the principal appealed to the Eleventh Circuit. The court held that repeatedly striking a 13-year-old with a metal cane was an obvious constitutional violation. It rejected the principal's assertion that any prior incident involving weapons possession allowed him to beat the student. *Ingraham v. Wright* held that the deliberate infliction of physical pain by school authorities as punishment implicated student due process rights. The Alabama Supreme Court has held that **corporal punishment deprives students of their substantive due process rights when it is arbitrary, capricious or unrelated to the legitimate goal of maintaining an atmosphere conducive to learning.** The principal was not entitled to qualified immunity. The case required a trial. *Kirkland v. Greene County Board of Educ.*, 347 F.3d 903 (11th Cir. 2003).

◆ A Hawaii elementary school teacher sent a student to the office for fighting. Once there, the student refused to stand still against a wall for time-out punishment. The vice principal warned the student that he would take him outside and tape him to a tree if he did not stand still. He then made good on his threat by taping the student to the tree with masking tape. After about five minutes, a fifth-grade student told the vice principal that "she did not think he should be doing that." The vice principal allowed her to remove the tape from the student. The student's family sued the state education department and vice principal for constitutional rights violations. A court denied the vice principal's motion for pretrial judgment. He appealed to the Ninth Circuit, which held that school seizures violated the Fourth Amendment if they were objectively unreasonable under the circumstances. There was no suggestion in this case that the student was a danger to others. **Taping an eight-year-old to a tree was objectively unreasonable conduct.** The court affirmed the judgment. *Doe v. State of Hawaii*, 334 F.3d 906 (9th Cir. 2003).

◆ When a teacher observed an Arkansas ninth-grader violently kicking a vending machine, she attempted to stop him. The student initially ignored the teacher, but stopped kicking the machine when she began to shake him by the arms. The principal of the adjacent high school grabbed the student's neck and shirt collar, led him from the school and "threw" him on a bench, where he landed on his shoulder. The principal instructed the school's resource officer to handcuff the student, and he was taken to the county jail. The student's mother then took him to an emergency room, where he was diagnosed with a strained neck and treated. The student's mother sued the principal, and a federal court awarded pretrial judgment to the principal. On appeal, the Eighth Circuit stated that the principal's conduct could not be considered shocking to the conscience unless it was malicious and sadistic. There was no evidence that he disliked the student or had even met him before. **School administrators are entitled to substantial deference in their efforts to maintain order and discipline.** The principal responded quickly and decisively to an incident of serious student misbehavior, and the court affirmed the judgment in his favor. *Golden ex rel. Balch v. Anders*, 324 F.3d 650 (8th Cir. 2003).

B. Teacher Liability Protection

Subpart Five of the No Child Left Behind (NCLB) Act (20 U.S.C. §§ 6731-38) is the Paul D. Coverdell Teacher Protection Act. This NCLB Act provision protects school staff from liability if they act on behalf of the school, within the scope of their employment, in conformity with law and "in furtherance of efforts to control, discipline, expel, or suspend a student or maintain order or control in the classroom or school;" ... and there is no willful or criminal misconduct, gross negligence or reckless misconduct or flagrant disregard for rights. The Coverdell Act provision parallels state law provisions protecting school employees from liability when they restrain students in order to preserve order in the school or to prevent injury. For example, Oklahoma law prohibits any liability from the use of necessary and reasonable force to control and discipline a student, or from taking good faith actions to suspend a student.

The NCLB provision also prohibits punitive damage awards against teachers unless there is "clear and convincing evidence that the harm was proximately caused by an act or omission of such teacher that constitutes willful or criminal misconduct" or flagrant indifference to rights.

Teacher Scenarios

*Teacher's and student's stories conflict –
will court have to decide?* 231

*How far can a teacher go to maintain
class discipline?* 232

*Was teacher keeping order –
or blowing her stack?* 233

Court Decisions

◆ A Nevada teacher was accused of grabbing and choking a student who was trying to push open a door where entry was not allowed. Although the teacher denied choking the student, he admitted touching his chest and admonishing him. After the incident, the student visited a doctor and an uncertified counselor for "emotional and psychological treatments." In an arbitration proceeding, the student won past medical expenses for his family practitioner and a physical therapist. However, the arbitrator did not award costs for the counselor due to his inadequate credentials. The student then sued the teacher and school district in a state court for negligence. On the first day of trial, the teacher and district moved for immunity. They cited the Paul D. Coverdell Teacher Protection Act, described in the paragraphs above. The court found the teacher's conduct was unreasonable and outside the act's protections.

The court awarded general damages and expenses of $27,270, an amount that was slightly lower than the arbitration award. This included the $5,700 charged by the counselor that had not been allowed in arbitration. Appeal reached the Supreme Court of Nevada, where the student claimed a Coverdell Act defense could not be raised at the beginning of a trial. Instead, he argued the act created an "affirmative defense" that had to be raised at the time of the initial response to a complaint. The court agreed that **the Coverdell Act defense was an affirmative defense which had to be asserted in the response to the complaint**. It then found the counselor's fees were excessive and unreasonable. When the state legislature enacted laws regulating psychologists, it intended to prevent laypersons from practicing the profession. As a result, the award of $5,700 for the counselor's services was found "illegal and not recoverable." *Webb v. Clark County School Dist.*, 145 Nev. 47, 218 P.3d 1239 (Nev. 2009).

◆ An Ohio student's mother claimed that a teacher grabbed, choked and shoved her son in front of the rest of his first-grade class, causing serious physical injury. She sued the school system, its board, and the teacher for negligence and intentional conduct. A court awarded pretrial judgment to the school board but denied it to the teacher. The Court of Appeals of Ohio explained that the trial court had properly awarded judgment to the school system. It then considered the teacher's claim to state law immunity and noted that **the family's assertion that she willfully, wantonly and recklessly grabbed, choked and shoved the student was sufficient to deny immunity**. The case against her would proceed. *Rogers v. Akron City School System*, No. CV 2006-05-2869, 2008 WL 2439674 (Ohio Ct. App. 6/18/08).

◆ An Ohio school district banned corporal punishment in its schools in 1987. Substitute teachers had to undergo training on the subject before becoming eligible for hire. During orientation, they were informed of the district policy prohibiting corporal punishment and told how to handle student misconduct. Substitutes had to seek assistance from the principal or assistant principal if a student disciplinary situation occurred. One substitute worked for the school district for four years when a third grader claimed that the substitute "slammed her into a chalkboard, threw her on the ground, and choked her" for a minute because she did not have a pencil with her. Her parent sued the school district.

The case reached the U.S. Court of Appeals, Sixth Circuit, which rejected the parent's claim that the state Tort Liability Act violated the Ohio Constitution. To show corporal punishment violates the Constitution, a student must show the force applied caused injury so severe, was so disproportionate to the need presented, and was so inspired by malice or sadism that it amounted to a brutal and inhumane abuse of official power that was shocking to the conscience. In this case, **the student did not show that the district was deliberately indifferent to student abuse by substitute teachers**. There had been only two incidents in a two-year period in a school district with 127 schools serving over 69,000 students. This did not create "notice" of constitutional problems. The court affirmed the judgment for the school district. *Ellis v. Cleveland Municipal School Dist.*, 455 F.3d 690 (6th Cir. 2006).

◆ In a case involving a student with attention deficit hyperactivity disorder, the Louisiana Court of Appeal ruled that a school properly applied corporal punishment, which was expressly allowed in Louisiana. The rules governing its use allowed corporal punishment only after other methods had failed. The court found the rules protected student due process rights, required a staff witness, and specified the paddle and the number of strokes to be used. An assistant principal testified that he paddled the student because of the severity of the misconduct and only after other methods failed. He complied with board rules and felt the student needed immediate negative reinforcement. The student had a pattern of misbehavior, including fighting, kicking, cursing, biting and taking things. His parents complained of other methods and refused counseling. **The law did not require advance parental consent.** *Setliff v. Rapides Parish School Board*, 888 So.2d 1156 (La. Ct. App. 2004).

◆ A Colorado school custodian broke up a fight between two students in a school hallway. He "head-butted" the student he perceived to be the **aggressor** and told him "there's always someone bigger than you. Now get out of here." The district investigated the incident and proposed discharging the custodian for inappropriate contact with a student. After a hearing before the superintendent under the collective bargaining agreement, discharge for deliberate or inappropriate conduct was recommended, and the school board approved this. In a state court action, the court held the discharge was unlawful, and it ordered the district to reinstate the custodian to his job with back wages. In doing so, the court conducted a new hearing, described by courts as "*de novo* review." But the Supreme Court of Colorado held the trial court should not have conducted a separate review. Instead, it should have relied on the school board hearing. The district provided the custodian a hearing as required by the collective bargaining agreement. School boards, not courts, retained discretion over employees and the enforcement of their own conduct and discipline codes. *Widder v. Durango School Dist. No. 9-R*, 85 P.3d 518 (Colo. 2004).

◆ A Florida teacher called school security to escort a student from class for disruptive behavior. A security officer brought the student to a detention room. The two "got into a disagreement," and the student claimed the officer began to beat him. Two more security officers then arrived at the room and allegedly kicked and punched the student. The student and his family sued the school board and officers for constitutional rights violations and battery. The Florida District Court of Appeal noted that **in general, state subdivisions were not liable for the acts or omissions of employees who acted outside the scope of their employment**. However, the security officers here acted within the scope of their authority when escorting the student from class and restraining him. Thus, a trial court would have to consider whether their actions were within the scope of a state statute on immunity. The court remanded the case to determine whether the board had immunity under that statute. *Carestio v. School Board of Broward County*, 866 So.2d 754 (Fla. Dist. Ct. App. 2004).

IV. TEACHER SCENARIOS

Mom claims hearing was a 'sham' because teacher's mind was made up

Student put pills in teacher's drink: Will discipline stand?

Teacher Jacob Hinson was grading an essay when the classroom door flew open – and hit the wall with a loud thud.

Dana Cot's mother shook a piece of paper in Jacob's face. "I hope you have a good explanation for this," she said.

"I am guessing that's the letter about Dana's one-day suspension," Jacob said.

'Punishment doesn't fit the crime'

"You just couldn't give Dana a break at the hearing," Ms. Cot said snarkily.

"I'm sorry if you're upset," Jacob said, "but Dana did put pills in my soda can."

"She told you she was going to throw it away," Ms. Cot argued. "She apologized."

Jacob took a deep breath. "With all due respect, that doesn't make me feel better. Dana shouldn't have pills at school, and she shouldn't put medicine in people's drinks. If someone had – "

Ms. Cot interrupted him. "She found those pills on your desk. She was going to throw the pills and the can away. But you accused her of trying to poison you."

"I heard what Dana said at the hearing," Jacob said.

"That hearing was a joke. Everyone's mind was made up before it even started. I'll see you in court over this," she said, waving the letter around again.

Ms. Cot sued, claiming the school violated Dana's due process rights. She said the hearing was a farce because school officials already had their minds made up.

School officials argued that Dana was given a fair hearing – and noted she was suspended for just one day. They asked the court to uphold the suspension. Did it?

Decision: Yes, the court upheld Dana's one-day suspension.

Key: The judge said if the court accepted this argument, all disciplinary actions could be overturned with an "it wasn't fair" plea.

Due process violations occur when students aren't given the opportunity to speak, explained the judge.

Cite: *Schomburg v. Johnson.*

Parents sue after teacher's inquiry takes an unexpected turn

He uncovers evidence of another violation of school rules

The loud laughter and distinct smell of marijuana coming from the boys room caught the attention of teacher Darren Haygood.

"Stop right there," he ordered the three students as they walked out. "I want all of you to empty your pockets on that table."

Two of the students said little and complied. Nothing suspicious showed up.

The third student, Jesse Lindt, wasn't so agreeable.

"You can't search me," he shouted. "I haven't done anything, and you haven't seen me do anything."

The choice

"We can do this one of two ways," the teacher countered. "You can empty your pockets, or I can have the principal call the police and have them search you. It's your choice."

"OK," the student grumbled as he fished into his pockets and began placing the contents on the table.

The teacher examined the pile: no drug paraphernalia, but there was a cigarette lighter, a few dollars, some change – and a large knife with a locking blade.

"Every student, including you, has been warned about the rules on weapons in school," the teacher said as he confiscated the knife. "You're looking at a suspension, plus the principal's going to have to notify the police."

When the school suspended the student, his parents filed a lawsuit arguing:

- The search was done without cause and was illegal, and
- Any evidence of wrongdoing uncovered by the search couldn't be used as a justification for the suspension.

Did the school win?

Decision: Yes. A court ruled the search was conducted legally because of the teacher's suspicion about drug use.

Key: The teacher was able to explain his reason for the search – a specific concern about drug use in school – meaning the search wasn't random and was legal.

Cite: *In re Mario C.*

Handling parents who want to 'make a deal' for special treatment

What happens when they insist, 'You made a promise'?

"You're no cop," parent Ross Geiger shouted on the other end of the phone. "Who are you to question my son like some criminal?"

"Let me explain the circumstances," teacher Ben Alvarez said in an even voice. "Someone stole an iPod from another student's backpack. Your son Alex was one of only three students in the room at the time. I simply asked him if he knew anything about who took the iPod."

"He said he didn't do it, right?"

"That's what he said," the teacher replied. "And we really can't say for sure what happened to the iPod ..."

"Let me tell you something," the parent interrupted. "Anything like this comes up again, you let me know before you question Alex so I can consult with my lawyer. Understood?"

"I understand, but ..." the teacher said just before the parent hung up.

Another problem

A week later, a student approached the teacher and said, "Mr. Alvarez, someone stole my lunch money. I'm pretty sure it was Alex Geiger. And he wouldn't give it back to me when I asked him for it. He said, 'I'm keeping the iPod, and I'm keeping your money, too.'"

"How much money was it?" the teacher asked.

"A five-dollar bill," the student said in a low voice.

With that, the teacher approached Alex Geiger and said, "Alex, we have a problem with some missing money, and I'd like to talk to you about it."

The boy got a panicked look as he blurted out, "I was only playing. I wasn't going to keep the money."

He then dug into a pocket and pulled out a five-dollar bill while whispering a hoarse "here."

Parent's reply

The next day, at a tense meeting in the assistant principal's office, Ross Geiger thrust a finger at Ben Alvarez and said, "You did exactly what we agreed you wouldn't do. You lied to me on the phone."

"Lied to you?" the teacher said.

"That's right, lied," the parent raised his voice. "You said you'd contact me if there was ever an incident and my son was suspected.

"Instead, you went right ahead and questioned him. And now you're recommending he be punished for theft?"

Assistant principal Maria Macon spoke up: "Your son did admit to stealing the money. We don't have much choice about punishing him. Our policies are clear about that."

"That's not the point," the parent responded. "Your teacher agreed he wouldn't interrogate Alex without contacting me, so my lawyer could get involved."

"I'm not trying to split hairs here, but I never agreed to that," the teacher maintained. "You may have made that request. That doesn't mean I said OK."

"You think you can get away with weasel-wording?" the parent said as he stood up. "Now my lawyer is going to get involved."

The decision

The parent sued the teacher and the school for (a) questioning the student without informing him of his rights and (b) reneging on an agreement to contact the parent.

The school argued that the teacher had a duty to question the student and that even if there had been an agreement, it didn't represent a contract between the school and the parent.

Did the school win?

Decision: Yes. A judge said the teacher was well within his authority to speak to a student suspected of theft.

The judge also noted that the existence of an agreement between the parent and the teacher was in doubt.

But even if an agreement had existed, it didn't relieve the teacher of his duty to act on what was clear suspicion.

Cite: *T.M.M. ex rel. D.L.M. v. Lake Oswego School Dist.*

Discussion points for teachers and principals:

Some parents believe they can cut informal, even unstated, "side deals" about treatment of students. To discourage the perception:

■ Keep parents aware of the school's rules and policies, and that fair treatment obligates you to follow them.

■ In language that's as clear as possible, inform parents that there can be no binding agreements that exempt children from the rules.

Parents sue school for $800,000 – did teacher have the right to take cell phone?

"Good point," said history teacher Pilar Garcia, very pleased.

She dreamed of classes like this. All the students were paying attention today and Mona Haust, who usually only slumped and doodled in the back row, had raised her hand to make a comment.

"That's right, Mona," said Pilar. "The Medici were bankers. Could you explain to the class why that's so -"

But before Pilar could finish her sentence, she was interrupted by a cell phone ringtone that she didn't recognize – but the students did.

No longer focused on Florence of the 1500s, some kids whooped, others giggled, and several of them began to sing the words of the song.

"All right," said Pilar loudly to the class as she strode down an aisle toward the jingling music. "Settle down, please!"

Pilar stopped in front of a boy who was fumbling inside his backpack. The ringtone stopped. He looked up to see Pilar holding out her hand.

"No way," objected student Bryan Metson, clutching the phone protectively to his chest.

"You know the new rule," Pilar reminded him. "You're not even allowed to have that phone at school. And you know I have to take it away and bring you to the principal for this."

"And then I don't get my phone back for 30 days," snapped Bryan. "Well, that policy's ridiculous."

"Please gather your things quietly," said Pilar. "We have to go to the office."

"And," Bryan continued, "I get a suspension on top of that. For the vile, heinous crime of -"

"Please pack your things," said Pilar. "And I still need the phone."

She held out her hand again. Bryan hesitated and then gave it to her.

"Great," he complained, shoving his history textbook into his backpack. "Now I can't reach my parents if I need them. I just hope nothing bad happens to me in the next 30 days. Because if it does -"

"Enough," said Pilar. "You can tell your concerns to the principal."

"Why would they even make a rule like this?" asked Bryan angrily, zipping his backpack and standing up. "Just to push us around? Just to crack the whip?"

Actually, thought Pilar, leading the way to the door, the rule exists to prevent class disruptions like the one your phone just caused.

Pilar gestured to her teacher's aide to watch the class for her.

The school confiscated Bryan's phone for 30 days and suspended him for one day by having him do homework in the office instead of attending classes.

Did suspension violate rights?

Bryan's parents sued, requesting $800,000 in damages. They claimed the school violated Bryan's right to due process.

Did it?

Decision: No. There's no constitutional right to a cell phone.

Also, this one-day, in-school suspension didn't deprive Bryan of his right to public education.

It only lasted one day, which Bryan spent doing homework. Also, he was recorded as present at school.

Key: The last thing teachers need are more class disruptions, and cell phones can be a major source of distraction at school.

The good news is that courts have been supporting educators' attempts to keep them out of the classroom by upholding cell phone policies against parents' challenges.

Some parents have tried to turn cell phones into a safety issue of constitutional significance. But courts have focused more on the need for order in school.

Cite: *Laney v. Farley.*

Discussion points for teachers and principals:

Virtually all schools forbid cell phone use in class, but some approaches are strict (to eliminate cheating and disruption) while others are more lenient (to ensure family contact).

New York City doesn't allow them in the building, and some Texas districts impose a $15 fine for using a cell phone at school.

Miami and Detroit allow students to have, but not use, them at school. Maryland high school students have this privilege, too, and it's been extended to include middle school students.

Disciplining difficult students: When zero-tolerance policies hold up

Can behavior 'contract' contain a firm commitment?

As the students crowded together to head to lunch, teacher Luke Adrian saw the fight break out.

"Oh, not Ronald Mayfield again," the teacher said under his breath as he quickly moved to break up the shoving match between Ronald and another boy, Reed Hayes.

"Reed, you're going to pay a visit to the principal's office," the teacher said over the boy's protests.

"And, Ronald, we'll discuss your punishment later."

"But it was his fault," Ronald wailed.

"I saw what happened," the teacher said. "You cut in front of Reed and elbowed him. We'll talk about this later – with your parents."

Not the first time

Later that week, the teacher sat in the small office along with Ronald's parents. It wasn't the first time they'd met.

"Your son has been involved in three fights this year," the teacher noted.

"We've been lucky that no one has been seriously hurt, but the time has come to take some further action on this, before someone does get hurt."

"'Further action'?" the father repeated. "Like what?"

The teacher reached for a file folder, pulled out a slip of paper and slid it across the desk while replying, "I thought we'd try something like this."

The boy's mother picked up the paper and read the heading aloud: "Agreement to Zero-Tolerance Policy for Fighting."

"Let me explain," the teacher added. "I'm asking the both of you and Ronald to sign this. As you'll see when you read it fully, it's an agreement that Ronald will not fight again."

"And if he does, all concerned agree he'll be expelled."

What's the point?

"What good does this do?" the father asked.

"Well, it establishes the punishment for another incident," the teacher answered. "And it puts everyone, including Ronald, on notice that we won't tolerate any more fighting."

"All right," the father said as the mother nodded in agreement. "We'll try it."

The next day, Ronald handed the teacher the agreement, which bore the signatures of the boy and both parents.

And two days later, Ronald started another fight in class.

The decision

When the teacher sought to enforce the zero-tolerance agreement, the district concurred and in a hearing, expelled the student. The parents sued, saying the agreement wasn't a legal contract and couldn't be enforced.

In court, the parents contended that the use of a zero-tolerance agreement involving violence meant that the teacher violated the student's and parents' constitutional rights to due process.

The school insisted the agreement only resulted after other attempts to stop the fighting, and that the expulsion hearing met the due-process requirement.

Did the court's decision side with the school?

Decision: Yes. A judge held that a zero-tolerance agreement signed by parents and students is enforceable and doesn't violate any due process right so long as other standard procedures are followed, such as a hearing.

The combination of the repeated offenses, the signed agreement plus the hearing added up to a legal and binding procedure that honored the student's rights.

Cite: *T.H. v. San Diego Unified School Dist.*

Discussion points for teachers and principals:

Informal agreements, or "contracts," with students can be used as a basis for discipline. Just try to be sure:

■ the agreement serves as part of the process but doesn't make up the whole process; it can't substitute for formal hearings and procedures, and

■ the agreement doesn't commit the student to giving up a constitutional right.

Was student expelled for a good reason – or just for being 'a kid'?

"Why can't you listen to sense?" Kai Simond's father asked the principal. "I thought the school board made me mad, but that was before I agreed to come talk to you and Kai's teacher."

"We understand Kai's expulsion is a blow, Jack," said Principal Alice Lee, glancing across her desk at teacher Julie Gunther. "But we want to make sure you understand why Julie did the right thing."

"Well, I don't!" said Jack. "The whole reason I'm this angry is because I don't think she handled it right at all."

Jack turned to Julie to ask, "What were you thinking when you dragged the resource officer into this? It was dumb of Kai to aim that pellet gun at Gail. But that's all it was – just dumb, not mean. You know it went off by accident."

"What Kai intended to do isn't really the problem here," said the principal.

"I disagree!" said Jack. "How can you punish him for an accident? Kai's friend asked him how the pellet gun worked, and Kai was dumb enough to show him by aiming it at his own girlfriend's leg. Then it went off by mistake."

"But Jack," said Julie, "the real problem here is that Kai had a weapon at school."

"That's something a teacher has to report," added the principal.

"Weapon!" scoffed Jack. "Have you ever tried to do any damage with a dinky little air gun? It didn't do much more than startle Gail. That tiny welt on her leg was gone in two days. She's not even mad. And you know her dad testified at Kai's hearing to say what a great kid he is. Gail and her folks don't have a problem with it, but you dragged in the police!"

"It's our school resource officer's job to deal with things like this," said the principal. "Julie was right to alert him. And the only reason this happened at all was because Kai brought his air gun to school. He knew it was against the weapons policy."

Weapon or toy?

"How can a toy be against the weapons policy?" fumed Jack. "Nobody in their right mind would consider that pellet gun a weapon. Heck, Kai could have hurt Gail just about as bad with a rubber band.

"I know Kai acts without thinking sometimes," said Jack, "but he doesn't deserve this. He's high spirited. He's a kid."

Jack turned furiously to Julie. "Kai said he told you it was an accident! He said he was sorry and it wouldn't happen again. You're his teacher. You see him every day, and you know he's not a troublemaker. So, why on earth couldn't you cut him some slack? Haven't you ever made a mistake?"

Not waiting for an answer, Jack stood up. "This is just completely unfair, and I am not going to put up with it."

Kai and his father sued, arguing the school couldn't expel Kai for having a weapon at school because his pellet gun wasn't a weapon.

They argued that if Kai was expelled simply because he had an object that could be used to hurt someone, other students had to be expelled for having pencils.

Did the court find for them?

Decision: No, the court affirmed Kai's expulsion.

The judge agreed Kai may not have meant to hurt his girlfriend, but also found the school board was right to decide a pellet gun is a weapon.

A pellet gun shoots plastic capsules at high velocity. This can cause serious injury. Some people have even been killed by a plastic pellet striking them in the eye.

Key: It's natural to have sympathy for parents whose kids have made a mistake that calls for serious discipline. And it can be hard to get blamed by parents who disagree with the school's policies. But as a teacher, it's your job to follow them – and to keep the safety of the students in mind.

Cite: *Picone v. Bangor Area School Dist.*

Discussion points for teachers and principals:

It can seem like things are out of hand when a third-grader is expelled for having scissors and a school play needs written permission from the district just to carry bows and arrows onstage.

But one school found a loaded handgun in a fourth-grader's backpack. Another found a teen's gun because of its new rule – aimed at preventing concealed weapons – that forbids kids to wear coats indoors.

Sharpen Your Judgment

Student insults teacher – at the shopping mall

As soon as she sat down, the parent began speaking: "Tell me again why you recommended disciplining my son."

Teacher Lawrence Alvarez responded: "Last Sunday, when I was at the mall with my wife, we ran into your son Carl and his friends. I said hello, and he said to his friends, 'Here's that dumb spic that's my teacher.'"

The boy's mother shifted in her seat and said, "Obviously, I disapprove of that, but I want to question Carl myself. If he did that, I'll punish him. But I don't see why you're recommending in-school punishment."

"It's not about me personally," the teacher explained. "We need to be sure the students show respect for all teachers. And the punishment only involves detention for a few days and being barred from a one-day class trip."

"But Carl was looking forward to that trip, and the detention interferes with some of his after-school activities, like sports," the parent said.

"Sorry," the teacher replied, "but the punishment is supposed to hurt a little."

The parent refused to agree and sued the teacher and the school for unfair retaliation.

Did the school win?

Sharpen Your Judgment – The Decision

Yes. The school won when a federal judge ruled the punishment was reasonable and fit the situation, and furthered the school's goal of maintaining respect for teachers.

The parent tried to argue that incidents that take place outside the school come solely under a parent's authority so long as no laws are broken.

The judge conceded that in-school punishment for a confrontation that took place outside a school indeed was a borderline call. But two factors weighed heavily in the school's favor:

- As part of the learning process, a school has a responsibility to ensure that students show reasonable respect for teachers, even outside school.
- The school meted out reasonable discipline for the offense, and the student's education wasn't harmed. In other words, the punishment fit the crime.

Analysis: Avoiding appearance of revenge

This case shows that teachers and schools have some authority to deal with incidents that take place off school grounds.

Remember the judge's decision, however: The punishment must be reasonable and not appear to be revenge or retaliation.

Cite: *Fenton v. Spear.*

Sharpen Your Judgment

'But he was just being a kid,' parents insist

"I'm afraid our legal troubles with Evan Wilson's parents aren't over yet," Principal Heather Marks told teacher Gina Richards.

"I know they sued for speech violations," Gina said. "But I heard the case was dismissed."

"It was," Heather explained. "But now Evan's parents are appealing the ruling."

"I got chills when Evan handed his paper in and I saw what he wrote. It said he wants to blow up the school with the teachers in it," Gina said. "I had to send him to the office. What did his parents expect me to do?"

"Well, now his parents are saying he doesn't have a record of discipline problems, and we should've seen that he was just being a kid," Heather told her.

"Have his parents ever watched the news?" Gina asked, fuming. "Are we supposed to wait around and let a Columbine incident happen here? Because I couldn't live with myself if that happened, and I didn't at least try to stop it."

"I understand where you're coming from," Heather said, reassuring Gina. "We'll just have to let it play out in court again."

Evan's parents appealed the ruling and asked the court to hear their son's case.

Did the judge agree?

Sharpen Your Judgment – The Decision

Yes, the court overturned the ruling and sent the case back to the lower court for further proceedings.

The judge noted that Evan wrote a threatening message on a class assignment. And clearly, the teacher took the threat seriously. As a result, the school suspended Evan according to its policy.

But the judge also pointed out: At the time of the suspension, Evan was a 10-year-old, fifth-grade student who didn't have a history of discipline problems.

Even more important, Evan handed the assignment in to his teacher, rather than showing it to classmates – so the court wasn't sure that Evan's assignment caused a disruption at school. Based on the information available, Evan's speech rights may have been violated, the court ruled. So the case was sent back to the lower court for further review.

Analysis: The tricky balance ...

Keeping schools safe while protecting students' rights requires a delicate balance.

As this case shows, it's always a good idea to review circumstances on a case-by-case basis first – and then make disciplinary decisions.

Cite: *Cuff v. Valley Cent. School Dist.*

Protecting students from a bully: How far should a teacher go?

Classroom outburst leads to questions about 'control'

Her fellow teachers had already warned Laura Hernandez about Dwight Abramson at the start of the school year.

"Out of the blue, he'll start a fight," the assistant principal had added to the warnings on the first day of school. "We've seen it happen several times, so try to keep an eye on him."

She did, and for a week, he seemed OK.

On Monday morning ...

"Here's what happens to people who walk in front of me in the cafeteria!" Laura heard Dwight shout while she was at another student's desk checking an assignment. She turned to see Dwight choking another student.

Laura squeezed between the two and managed to pry Dwight's hands off the student's throat.

"Sit right there, Dwight," she gestured toward the nearest empty seat, and then checked the other student, Aaron Wilcox.

"You OK?" she asked.

"Uh, uh, I guess so," Aaron rasped while trying to catch his breath.

Keeping a cautious eye on Dwight, the teacher backed up toward the telephone and called the principal's office for assistance.

"There's been a fight here, and I need medical attention for one student and the other student taken to the principal's office," she said in a calm voice.

An irate call

The next day, Laura got a message to call the mother of the student who'd been attacked.

"Mrs. Wilcox, this is Laura Hernandez. I hope Aaron is OK and that ..."

"OK?" The parent broke in. "That maniac nearly killed my son, and no one prevented it."

"Unfortunately, things like that happen in school," the teacher explained. "You can't anticipate everything a student will do."

"Look, I know all about Dwight Abramson," the parent said. "He lives just down the street, so I know he's been disciplined for fighting in school before. You must have known about it, too."

Lack of 'control'?

"I'm not going to discuss Dwight's disciplinary record," Laura noted. "But I'm sure our principal will do whatever's appropriate with him."

"Hasn't someone figured out that discipline doesn't work with that kid?" the parent asked. "The problem doesn't seem to be one of discipline – it's a question of controlling him in the classroom."

"We do everything we can," the teacher responded in an even voice.

"Well, my son can hardly speak because of the attack, and he's worried about returning to school and what's going to happen with Dwight."

"That's understandable," Laura affirmed. "We'll help him."

"Like you 'helped' him before?" the parent remarked. "No thanks. I'll leave that to my lawyer."

She sues

The parent of the boy who was attacked ended up suing the teacher and the district for failing to provide a safe learning environment for her son.

The parent argued in court that the teacher knew about the student's violent past and should have been more cautious about preventing further violence.

Did the teacher take appropriate action in this instance?

Decision: Yes. A judge ruled the teacher had been properly supervising the class, and couldn't have taken any more reasonable steps to prevent the attack.

The court noted that the teacher was aware of the student's history of violence and had been wary, but couldn't be expected to control his every movement and impulse.

Cite: *Smith v. Half Hollow Hills Cent. School Dist.*

Discussion points for teachers and principals:

No one has a crystal ball that can predict when violence will erupt in the classroom.

Courts recognize that but expect teachers to:

■ keep aware of students with violent pasts

■ watch for incidents that might spark a violent confrontation, and

■ take immediate action to stop violence and ensure safety.

Was student being creative – or making a threat?

Parents claim student had the right to create violent story

"What's with the notebook, Allie?" asked art teacher Tod Welks. "How many times do I have to tell you to put that away and work on your drawing?"

Student Allie Fiore froze and then just stared up at him.

"All right," he said firmly, "if it's that much of a distraction, you'd better just give it to me."

Instead, she dropped it to her lap and sang, "Say please!" He raised his eyebrows at this.

"All right, all right," she muttered. She fumbled under the art table and then pulled out a different notebook.

"That's not the same one," said Tod. "Come on, Allie. Stop wasting class time. You know I want the one you've been using to ignore your drawing all period."

She took it out from under the table and thrust it at him, writing-side up. The words blood, gun, shoot jumped off the page at him.

A threat?

An hour later, Tod sat across the desk from Vice Principal Carter.

"Wow," said the vice principal, looking up from Allie's notebook.

"But it's just her imagination, right?" asked Tod. "Just a story about shooting a teacher?"

"It's a little too close to reality for my liking," said the vice principal, "especially after the shooting last month in the next district over. Plus she's describing Mr. Jones, her math teacher. What if she's serious?"

Only a story?

The school suspended Allie for making a threat, but Allie's parents argued it was just creative writing.

They sued, saying that disciplining her for writing a short story violated her right to free speech.

Did they win?

Decision: No.

This writing wasn't protected by the First Amendment because the school could reasonably interpret it as a threat.

Having the writing at school made it more likely to be read there, and it was likely to cause a serious school disruption if it was.

This was especially true given the national climate of increasing school violence plus a recent gun-related incident at a local school.

Key: Courts uphold discipline for potential school violence. This court wrote that it's "imperative" schools have the authority to deal with this effectively.

Cite: *Boim v. Fulton County School Dist.*

Sharpen Your Judgment

Bullies torment classmate – what more could teacher have done?

Principal Felice Boren stepped out of her office when she heard teacher Joy Diego's voice.

"Joy! Welcome back from maternity leave! Could I see you a minute?"

"Sure," said Joy, coming inside.

"Sorry to throw this at you first thing in the morning on your first day back," said Felice. "But I wanted to let you know Bailey's mother is suing."

But we did everything right!

"Why?" asked Joy. "Did those boys pick on Bailey again?"

"Yes. You know I phoned her mom as soon as she e-mailed me about the nasty names Ed and Ari called Bailey. Then I disciplined the boys and called their parents in."

"Right," said Joy. "And I moved Bailey's seat across the room. Then I called her mom, too. What did we miss?"

"Telling the substitute," sighed Felice. "While you were on leave, she used an old seating chart. She moved Bailey back to her old seat. Bailey didn't object. Then the boys said something even worse."

Bailey's parents sued, saying the school didn't do enough to stop the harassment.

Did the school win?

Sharpen Your Judgment – The Decision

Yes, the school won.

The judge dismissed the case, finding the school did enough to deal with the harassment.

This was because the school responded each time it learned the boys had made harassing remarks, and its response wasn't "clearly unreasonable."

The school:

- disciplined the harassers
- physically separated them from their victim, and
- communicated with the parents of all involved students.

A "reasonable" response always depends on the circumstances, but this approach seemed to work – until a substitute teacher unwittingly moved the harassers back near their victim.

Analysis: Leave clear instructions

Subs can usually be counted on not to tinker with things like seating. But, as this case illustrates, unexpected things come up that you can't control.

That's why you should always leave clear and complete instructions for subs. Here, for example: "Don't let Ed and Ari sit near Bailey."

Cite: *Lewis ex rel. Miller v. Booneville School Dist.*

Texting in class: How far can teachers go to maintain order?

Teacher followed cell phone policy – so why's Mom suing?

Teacher Ellie Aims was working on the usual beginning-of-the-school-year housekeeping tasks as her students filed into class.

As usual, Ellie was pressed for time because of the extra work. She looked forward to establishing a regular routine with her students.

"Good morning, everyone," Ellie said. "I've arranged the seating chart, so look carefully for your name. Once you sit down, please get started on the assignment that's on the board."

So far, so good, Ellie thought, resuming her lesson plan as students settled in and started working on the assignment.

But a few minutes later, Ellie looked up and saw a student texting on his cell phone. "Max," she said, "put it away. You know you're not allowed to text in class."

Max put the phone in his pocket without arguing.

Cell phone interrupts group work

After the class finished the assignment, Ellie divided students into groups to go over the answers.

The classroom came to life as students debated the correct responses.

As Ellie circled the room, she noticed one group was huddled together quietly. "How's it going over here?" she asked.

When she spoke, Ellie noticed the entire group flinched – and that's when she saw the distraction: Max's cell phone.

Confiscating the phone

"Give me the cell phone," Ellie said, taking it from him.

"Why?" Max asked her.

"You know why," Ellie said, refusing to be dragged into a debate. She walked to her desk and slid the phone into a manila envelope.

"Wait!" Max said. "I need to take my SIM card out first."

"Why?" Ellie asked him. "I've already sealed the envelope."

"But I really need my SIM card," Max insisted. "All of my private info is stored on that card."

"You should have thought about that before you broke the rules," Ellie said. "If you really want that SIM card, you can ask the principal about getting it back."

"Come on, Ms. Aims," Max argued. "It's not fair."

"We just went over the phone policy," Ellie said. "Remember the responsibility contract you and your parents signed?"

Max continued to argue, so Ellie sent him to the office.

The principal's take

The principal agreed with Ellie and refused to return Max's card. His parents could pick up the phone in two weeks, as per school policy, the principal explained.

Max sued, claiming the school wrongfully took his property. He said keeping his phone for two weeks amounted to trespass to chattels. He claimed they should've returned the SIM card to ensure his personal info wasn't viewed.

But school officials argued they followed the discipline policy – and they didn't search Max's phone. They asked the court to dismiss the claim.

Did it?

Decision: Yes, the court dismissed Max's claim.

Key: Schools have the authority to prevent distractions at school. That was the case here.

The court noted all that the teacher did correctly. She:

- followed the school's policy
- shared the policy with the student and his parents, and
- made sure to collect signed responsibility contracts.

And because Max's phone wasn't searched, his trespass to chattels claim failed, the court explained.

Cite: *Koch v. Adams.*

Discussion points for teachers and principals:

No doubt about it: Handling cell phone issues is tricky business. Three best practices to remember when confiscating cell phones are:

■ <u>Do not search</u> students' phones.

■ Place the student's confiscated phone in a manila envelope immediately, seal the envelope and sign across the seal.

■ Turn the envelope over to the principal for storage/return.

Sharpen Your Judgment

Innocent joke or real threat? The best steps a teacher can take

Teacher Lori Pisa heard a giggle. She looked up to see student Jen Mack holding up her assigned class calculator. "BOMB IN GYM" was on its screen.

"That's not funny," said Lori.

"This appeared when I turned it on," Jen said.

"But why are you giggling?"

"It struck me as funny. It's ridiculous."

"Funny? It's a threat!"

"No," said Jen. "Kids type jokes into the calculators all the time."

"But what if it's not a joke this time? We'd better tell the principal," said Lori.

"No! What's she going to do – call in the bomb squad? Come on. It's a joke."

The principal did report the threat, and the bomb squad found no explosives.

Based on Lori's calculator assignment sheet, the principal decided another student, Casey, most likely made the threat. Also, two of her friends said Casey did it to get out of school for the day.

A judge found Casey made the bomb threat, but Casey appealed, arguing the evidence against her wasn't good enough.

Did the judge agree?

Sharpen Your Judgment – The Decision

No, the judge didn't agree. There was plenty of evidence to show Casey made the bomb threat.

When adults are accused, the crime must be proved beyond a reasonable doubt. But this was a juvenile court matter. In this case, the judge was supposed to consider the evidence in the way most favorable to the school.

Casey argued they couldn't prove she made the threat because no one saw her type in the words.

But it was enough that the calculator assignment sheet showed Casey was the last student who used the calculator before Jen, and that two of Casey's friends said she'd admitted she did it.

Analysis: Take threats seriously

Luckily, this turned out to be a false alarm, but the teacher was right to report it immediately – even though she probably had lingering doubts it might only be a prank, and no one wants to make the school look bad.

But weighed against the harm if it turns out to be real, every threat has to be reported.

This is true even if the "threat" turns out to be a hoax – because you can't know until it's checked out.

Cite: *In re B.D.N.*

Teacher and assistant principal's search crossed the line, Dad claims

Dad sues school after cell phone search

When teacher Chase Ford walked into his office, assistant principal Rich Wells closed his email. "Have a seat."

"Let me guess: You want to talk about Luke and the cell phone incident," Chase said as he sat down. "Right?"

"Yep," Rich said. "His father's mad that we suspended Luke for those gang pictures stored on his phone. Fill me in."

'Not a reason to search'

"I was handing out a pop quiz when Luke started texting," Chase said. "I told him to put the phone away, but he didn't, so I took it."

"That's it?" Rich asked.

"Pretty much," Chase told him. "Luke argued a little bit. He claimed he wasn't texting but reading a text from his dad.

"But for all I knew, Luke could've been cheating on the quiz," Chase continued. "Texting is against class rules. More and more students are using their phones to cheat. I can't just turn a blind eye to it."

"And when we looked at the phone we didn't find evidence of cheating, but we did find the gang photos," Rich said.

"Right," Chase confirmed.

"Luke's father is threatening to sue. He claims we shouldn't have looked through Luke's cell phone," Rich said.

Luke's father did sue, claiming the cell phone search was unreasonable. The school asked the court to dismiss the claim. Did it?

Decision: Yes, the court dismissed the claim that the search was unreasonable.

Key: Although the search didn't reveal any evidence of cheating, the teacher had a reasonable suspicion of wrongdoing, the court noted.

The court pointed out that Luke broke cell phone rules during class, and he refused to comply with the rules after a verbal warning. His actions showed he was doing something wrong, the court explained.

Cite: *J.W. v. DeSoto School Dist.*

Sharpen Your Judgment

Possible drug possession: Did search go too far?

Teachers Sandy Snead and Lisa Hanes met up in the lounge for some coffee. Sandy asked, "Got a second?"

"Of course," Lisa said. "What's up?"

"Remember the other day, when a student accused Amy of sharing pills at school?"

"Yeah," Lisa said. "You passed the info on to the office."

"I reported it, but now I'm not sure I made the right choice," Sandy sighed. "To make a long story short: Amy was searched, and they didn't find any pills. Her mom's furious."

"I get her frustration, but the school had to investigate, right?" Lisa asked.

"Turns out, the search included more than Amy's bag. They had her strip down to her underwear – and she felt, um, pretty exposed," Sandy sighed. "I shouldn't have said a word."

"Wait a minute," Lisa told her. "You had to contact the office. I know you didn't want this to happen – but after you make a report, it's out of your hands."

"I just feel terrible about what happened."

Amy's mom sued, claiming the school took the search too far.

Did the court agree?

Sharpen Your Judgment – The Decision

Yes, the court agreed that the school took the search too far.

The court noted that school officials had a reason to be suspicious: Someone reported Amy may have had drugs. But a strip search wasn't justified. A reasonable search would've stopped after Amy's belongings were searched, the court said.

In spite of the violation, school officials were entitled to qualified immunity because the law regarding strip searches was not clearly established at the time of the search.

Looking forward, school officials should consider applicable factors, the court ruled.

In this case, relevant factors included:

- the student's age and sex, and
- prior awareness that the suspected drugs didn't pose a huge threat to student safety.

Analysis: Do what you can ...

Teachers have to report concerns, and schools have to investigate. As this case shows, balancing students' safety while respecting rights can be tricky business. Best practices: Review circumstances on a case-by-case basis to determine the best course of action.

Cite: *Safford Unified School Dist. #1 v. Redding.*

Did student's suspicious behavior justify a search?

Money was missing from teacher's desk drawer

"Can you believe last year's World Series hero is here to talk about the danger of steroids?" asked teacher's aide Mariah Girard.

I was there the day he pitched that no-hitter," teacher Dru Zabinsky told her.

But just as the speech began, Dru saw student Ted Klesker loping up the aisle and out of the auditorium.

Suspicious?

When Ted hadn't returned in 15 minutes, Dru went to her classroom. Her purse was missing $20.

When she got back to the auditorium, Ted still wasn't there. When he finally strolled up, she told him they were going to see School Resource Officer Licata.

Ted waited outside while Dru finished telling the officer the story. " ... and Ted asked if I lock the drawer where we keep our purses," she added, remembering one last thing. "Not thinking, I said, 'No.'"

When Ted came in, Licata smiled then said, "Money's missing from Ms. Zabinsky's desk. Do you know anything about it?"

"No," said Ted quickly.

"But I hear you left assembly?"

"I had to use the john."

"But you were gone so long. Are you sick? Do you need the nurse?"

"Yes," said Ted. "I mean, no."

The search

"Will you empty your pockets?"

"Sure," agreed Ted, relaxing.

Seeing Ted's sneaker was untied, Licata asked, "And take off your shoes?"

Ted froze.

The missing money was in his shoe. Ted admitted he took it from his teacher's desk.

Ted was charged with petty theft. His parents sued, claiming the teacher and officer didn't have justifiable reasons to search him.

Did the court agree?

Decision: No. The teacher and officer had reasonable suspicion to search Ted. They could clearly explain why they suspected he stole the money. Also, the search was OK because it wasn't too intrusive given Ted's age, gender and the nature of his misconduct.

Key: Before you suggest a search, make sure you have good reasons to suspect a rule was broken and that a search could prove it was.

Cite: *In Re Welfare of T.J.R.*

Student refuses to submit to search: What's teacher's next move?

She needs to protect others from possible violence

Heidi Jamison did a double-take when, out of the corner of her eye, she spotted what looked like a knife in the hand of Aaron West, one of the boys in her fifth-grade classroom.

Just as quickly, though, Aaron appeared to slip it into his pocket.

The teacher was almost certain it was a metallic object, but was it really a knife? She decided to keep an eye on Aaron to see if she could confirm her suspicions.

A little later that day, just as lunch period was beginning, she started to realize her instincts had been correct.

"Miss Jamison," student Alisha Robinson spoke in a whisper as she approached the teacher. "Aaron West told me he was going to stab me if I didn't shut up.

"He said it to Marvis Hernandez, too."

Immediate action

That was enough evidence to act on, the teacher decided. And she had to do so immediately, before a student or staff member got hurt.

"Aaron," she called to him, "please step over here for a minute."

The boy hesitated, thrust his hands into his pockets and slowly walked toward the teacher.

"What's up, Miss Jamison?"

As she spoke, the teacher kept a steady eye on the student. She felt she had to act immediately or risk injury to a student or staff member. "I want you to empty your pockets onto my desk and then stand back."

"Why?" the boy protested. "I haven't done anything."

"Then you should have no reason to disobey me. Please do as I say and empty your pockets."

"No!" he shouted. "You can't search me. I told you, I haven't done anything."

He refuses

The boy still kept his hands in his pockets as the teacher sized up whether he posed a threat.

"All right, Aaron," the teacher said in a firm voice. "You can empty your pockets onto my desk.

"Or, if you don't, I can call down to the principal's office and recommend that we call your parents and have you suspended for refusing to do as I ask."

The student responded with a cold stare and silence. He refused to speak or empty his pockets, as several seconds passed.

Without speaking to the boy again, she called the principal's office and briefly explained the situation.

What else could be done?

Two weeks later, Heidi Jamison and her principal sat in a small conference room with the district's lawyer, Elaine Hoover.

"You understand that after Aaron was suspended for refusing your order, his parents filed a lawsuit?" the lawyer began.

"They say you violated his Fourth Amendment rights against search and seizure."

"I'm not sure what else I could have done," the teacher replied.

"Had you considered calling the office sooner or maybe the police?"

"I felt like I had to take some sort of action right away to avoid an incident," the teacher explained.

"Sounds reasonable," the lawyer said. "Let's see what happens."

Was the teacher's action confirmed by the court?

Decision: Yes. An appeals court ruled the teacher and the school had not violated the Fourth Amendment's ban on illegal search and seizure.

The court noted the teacher had reason to believe that the student posed a threat to others in the school and took appropriate action and followed policy in ordering the boy to empty his pockets.

Cite: *Maimonis v. Urbanski.*

Discussion points for teachers and principals:

Students, like adults, have constitutional rights against illegal searches. But most courts recognize that teachers and administrators often need to act quickly. Judges do warn that:

■ There must be reasonable cause to believe the student is concealing an illegal or dangerous object, and

■ The search should be initiated to maintain safety or order in the school.

Student's 'slang' in class tipped off teacher to search his jacket

But was it OK for teacher to also search every jacket in the room?

Teacher Jon Shute tapped on the principal's office door. "Hi, Anne," he said. "You wanted to see me?"

"Yes. It's about the day you searched Kyle Winter's jacket," said Anne.

"Again? I thought the hearing settled that. The judge decided Kyle stole the 17 credit cards I found in his pocket."

"Yes. But now Kyle's appealing. So I just wanted to hear again about what made you decide the search was needed."

The whole thing smelled bad

"Kyle was 45 minutes late – already fishy. Then he told me he'd missed his bus. But I heard him whispering to Phil that he'd gone 'shopping' and gotten a 'stack,'" said Jon.

"So that told you he'd really been at a store, stealing a stack of credit cards?"

"Oh, no," said Jon. "I had no idea what that meant. But I figured it must be slang for something bad – probably illegal."

"So you went through Kyle's jacket while the kids were out of the room?"

"Not just Kyle's. I searched all the jackets hanging at the back of the room. I didn't know which was whose. But when I found the credit cards, I figured that jacket was Kyle's. And I was right, wasn't I?"

"Yes," sighed Anne. "But now Kyle's lawyer says your search can't stand up – that it was just a fishing expedition."

Was there a valid reason to search?

Kyle's lawyer argued Kyle's conviction had to be overturned. Did the judge agree?

Decision: Yes. This search was illegal.

The teacher didn't know what Kyle's slang meant. He only had a hunch a search would show Kyle had broken a school rule or the law. A hunch isn't enough. The search was also illegal because it wasn't confined to the suspected student only.

Key: Even searches by experts like the police get challenged in court. That's why your school may want you to stick to only passing along any suspicions you have about students – not acting on them yourself.

Cite: *D.M. v. State.*

Sharpen Your Judgment
Random searches: Parents say 'no way'

Kelly Michaels spoke as she sat down to eat lunch with fellow teacher Barb Nichols: "Let me ask you a question about the random student searches we've been doing."

"What about them?" asked Barb.

"We may be going too far. I mean, take the other day, when the police found marijuana in Joan Bilko's purse," said Kelly. "Don't misunderstand me – she shouldn't be bringing drugs into school – it's just that they're searching students' personal belongings without any real cause."

"I thought the district policy allowed appropriate staff and police to do searches like that," said Barb. "In our meeting on it, we were told it was to keep drugs and other contraband out of the school."

"But we've never had an obvious problem here that might prompt a search like that," Kelly noted.

"I'm concerned that going through students' personal belongings takes the policy over the line."

The parents of the student who was found with marijuana had the same concerns. They ended up suing the district for invading the student's privacy by conducting an illegal search.

Did the district win the case?

Sharpen Your Judgment – The Decision

No. The district lost.

The court said the district policy permitting random student searches had been abused. The only time a school may search a student's belongings is when it must do so for cause, such as to address a specific problem that's been identified in school.

If the school had reasonable suspicion about a problem – such as credible information that a student was bringing drugs into the school – the search might have been justified.

Avoiding a lawsuit

The court agreed with the parents that the district violated the student's right to privacy by rummaging through her purse. Students have a legitimate – although limited – expectation of privacy in their personal belongings in school.

With that in mind, this case illustrates how difficult it can be to balance a school's concern for maintaining safety and order with a student's right to privacy.

While it's not a teacher's job to oversee everything that happens in school or make a judgment about polices and the law, you can play a part in avoiding a lawsuit by alerting the principal to conduct you think is questionable.

Cite: *Doe v. Little Rock School Dist.*

Educators have good hunches – but is that enough to search a student?

Student says: Only guilty of being in wrong place at wrong time

Teacher Jen Hicks valued her tutoring sessions with student Dee Pilcher, but there were always too many interruptions. Like now. Glancing up, Jen saw student Hayley Kaz in front of her desk.

"I need to give Dee something."

"Dee and I are working now," said Jen.

"But ..." said Hayley, staring at Dee.

"Come on, Hayley," sighed Jen. She stood and led the way to the door. But when she turned around, Hayley was still in front of the desk. "Hayley!" Jen called. Then, for good measure, Jen walked Hayley all the way down the hall.

When Jen got back to the classroom, she smelled marijuana smoke and saw that Dee's eyes were very bloodshot.

Both girls are searched

Jen took Dee to the assistant principal, Mr. Kern. After Jen told him the story, he called Hayley to the office, too. When she got there, Mr. Kern explained why he wanted Hayley to empty her pockets.

"You mean you're searching me because I was in the general area just before Dee got busted for doing something really stupid?"

"Let's go, Hayley," said Mr. Kern.

"Fine!" she fumed, putting coins, keys and her wallet on his desk.

"What's in the wallet?" he asked. She frowned at him. "Hayley, if you have anything you shouldn't, just hand it over."

She hesitated but then pulled a small bag of marijuana out of her wallet.

Hayley was charged as a delinquent, but appealed, arguing the search violated her Fourth Amendment rights. Did it?

Decision: Yes. Schools have to give specific reasons why a search is likely to provide evidence the student broke a school rule or the law. There wasn't enough to connect Hayley to Dee's wrongdoing.

Key: This search wasn't OK, but the judge made a point of writing that these are hard calls – and that teachers need to report all the details they know.

Cite: *C.A. v. State.*

Sharpen Your Judgment
Off-site search leads to controversy

With the plastic toy pistol on the table between them, Principal Avery Buddin spoke with teacher Marsha Chapel.

"You're right," the principal nodded. "It does look like a real gun."

"That's what I thought when I saw it sticking out of Alex Walston's book bag while we were at the museum field trip," the teacher said.

"Just let me make sure I understand what happened," the principal said as he made notes. "You saw what you thought was a gun. So you immediately snatched the bag from Alex and pulled out what turned out to be the toy pistol. Do I have that right?"

"That's about it," the teacher answered. "I considered that it might be a toy, but with our policy banning look-alike weapons, I decided to act right away."

"Alex's parents don't agree with us," the principal said. "They say that since you weren't on school grounds, you should have called a cop, who would have done a legal search. They're talking about suing."

The parents did sue, saying the teacher didn't follow legal procedure.

Did the school and the teacher win?

Sharpen Your Judgment – The Decision

Yes. A court found in favor of the school and the teacher.

The decision rested on two factors:

1. While an off-campus search might have been better conducted by a police officer, the risk involved in waiting compelled the teacher to act quickly.
2. Even when off-campus, students can't expect to receive immunity from standard school procedures. So, if a search would have been considered "normal" in school, it likewise would be classified that way off-campus during a school function.

The reasonable suspicion that a weapon was present and the need to ensure safety for all students were enough to tilt the case in the school's favor.

Analysis: A lesser requirement

In several similar cases, courts have drawn a clear line between the "probable cause" required for search by a police officer and the lesser requirement of "reasonable suspicion" that governs searches by school staff.

If you can show a direct reason for conducting a search, you're on pretty safe ground. And if the venue is an off-campus school function, that generally doesn't raise the legal bar in favor of student rights.

Cite: *Shade v. City of Farmington.*

Drugs found in locker after student confides in teacher

Anonymous tip is OK because teacher vouched for it

Just before lunch, teacher Julie Winn was grading essays in her empty classroom during her only free period. She heard student Stu Jackson's voice and looked up.

"Ms. Winn? C-c-could I ask you a question about, you know, what I told you yesterday?"

"Sure, Stu. And don't be nervous. It's just us."

"Did you talk to Vice Principal Wentz yet?"

"Yes," said Julie. "I told him a student told me Jason had a hash pipe at school."

"But not that it was me who told you?"

"Right," she said. "And he told me he'd look into it."

Risks a beating

"Thanks," said Stu. "Those guys really mess up snitches. But Jason keeps taunting me he's going to get my little sister high. I have to do something. She's only 13 and thinks he's cute.

"But you know what? Jason doesn't always have that pipe with him. I know he has it today because he was flashing it around on the bus. Could you tell Mr. Wentz that? Right now?"

Julie was already pushing back her chair – even though it probably meant she'd be staying late to finish grading the essays. "Sure," she told Stu. "I'll go talk to him."

Julie went to the office and told Vice Principal Wentz what Stu had told her, identifying Stu only as "one of my best students."

Legal basis for locker search?

Because of what Julie told him, Mr. Wentz searched Jason's locker. In it, he found not only the pipe but also a cube of hashish in foil.

A judge found Jason delinquent, but Jason's lawyer appealed, claiming the search was illegal because the anonymous tip wasn't reliable.

Was the locker search legal?

Decision: Yes. Mr. Wentz could rely on the tip because he could rely on Julie.

Since the vice principal knew and trusted the teacher, the judge decided the vice principal could assume the teacher:

- vouched for the tipster's reliability, and
- would tell him if anything made her doubt it.

Key: There can be good reasons to protect a student's identity. But not all schools allow teachers to honor that confidentiality under all circumstances. So it's wise to check your school's policy before making any promises to keep your students' secrets.

Cite: *In re Juvenile 2006-406.*

School strip-searches student over iPod: Went way too far, Mom says

Classmate steals student's confiscated iPod from teacher's desk

"What happened in here today?" Kara Dean's mother demanded. "Kara told me she had to take off her clothes because you people were looking for an iPod – and she wasn't even the one who had it!"

"Ms. Dean, I know you're upset. Let me explain," Teacher Jacob Hinson said.

Student broke the rules

"Kara brought her iPod to class today. She let one of her friends use it."

"Yeah? Well, I'm still wondering why my daughter had to take her clothes off in a closet," Ms. Dean snapped at him.

"To make a long story short, I confiscated the iPod and put it in my desk. I stepped into the hall for a moment, and someone took Kara's iPod out of my desk," Jacob continued, "I asked, but no one gave it back – or would say who took it. So I asked the assistant principal to come in."

"Kara said her friend Dina told the assistant principal which boy took it," Ms. Dean replied.

"Yes, the assistant principal wanted to protect Dina's identity. That's why all of the girls were searched privately first."

"Do you hear what you're saying? That doesn't even make sense!"

"But we straightened everything out."

"After my daughter removed her clothing!" Ms. Dean said pointedly. "You can all expect to hear from my lawyer!" Ms. Dean sued, claiming the search violated Kara's rights. Did it?

Decision: Yes, the school's search violated Kara's rights, the court ruled.

Key: The search was overly intrusive because the threat level didn't match the level of the intrusiveness. Put simply, iPods may disrupt class, but they aren't dangerous, the court explained.

School officials who were directly involved in the search weren't entitled to qualified immunity because the law clearly established that this search crossed the line.

Cite: *Foster v. Raspberry.*

Teacher had the right to question student – but did she go too far?

Court makes ruling after parent complains about treatment

A week after the theft at the school, teacher Lucia Granholm got a call from the parent of one of the students she'd questioned.

"Did you question my son Michael about that?" the parent, Norman Rakes, asked at the beginning of the call.

"I did, since he was in the room at the time the money was stolen from a student's backpack," the teacher explained. "He answered my questions, and as far as I could tell, he had nothing to do with it."

"Well, I'm a little uncomfortable with your questioning him without me or a lawyer there," the parent said. "After all, we're talking about criminal activity, and I don't want my son questioned without having some kind of representation."

"I understand," the teacher replied.

Two weeks later ...

Lucia walked past the boys' restroom and noticed the distinct odor of marijuana.

And out walked Michael Rakes.

"Michael, stop right there," she ordered.

Grinning and glassy-eyed, he said, "Why? What did I do?"

"That's what I want to know," the teacher said. "For starters, I think you were smoking marijuana in there. Were you?"

Still grinning, he said, "Uh, no, I wasn't."

Then the boy broke into laughter as he said, "Well, maybe just a little toke, Ms. Granholm."

With that, the teacher walked the student to the principal's office, where she described the exchange she'd had with Michael.

Eventually, he was suspended, and that led to another call from the boy's father.

The 'promise'

"You lied to me," an angry Norman Rakes shouted.

"Lied?" the teacher responded. "When did I ..."

"When you promised me you wouldn't question my son without me or a lawyer present," he shot back.

"Then you went right ahead and interrogated him. Because of that, he got suspended."

"He got suspended for smoking marijuana in the boys' restroom," she said. "All I did was ask him if that's what he was doing.

"And as far as I can remember, I never promised you anything about how or whether I would question Michael about breaking school rules."

"Oh, sure, start backpedaling and weasel-wording," he grumbled. "You agreed that you wouldn't question Michael."

Rights trampled

"I'm not going to argue about that with you," she said. "But you have to understand that when a teacher suspects a student of drug use in school, we have to take action. It's our responsibility."

"It's not your responsibility to play cop," the parent declared. "Haven't you ever heard of something called '*Miranda* rights'? Or do you think you can just trample all over them because you're a teacher?

"Well, you can't, and my lawyer's going to prove it."

He sues

Eventually, the parent sued the teacher and the school for questioning the student without informing him of his rights.

Did the teacher take appropriate action in this instance?

Decision: Yes. A judge said on-the-spot disciplinary actions in school aren't the same as criminal proceedings. Teachers have leeway to ask questions as a means of maintaining order and discipline.

The parent was right about one thing: Teachers aren't police officers. But that only served to refute the idea that teachers have to explain *Miranda* rights to students. That's the responsibility of police officers, not teachers.

Cite: *T.M.M. v. Lake Oswego School Dist.*

Discussion points for teachers and principals:

Courts have affirmed the right of educators to question students about suspected rule-breaking and criminal activity in school.

Remember, however, that right is limited generally to:

■ anything done on school grounds or during official school-related activities, and

■ times when you reasonably suspect that the student is involved or has relevant information.

Sharpen Your Judgment

Parents sue over teacher's meeting with students

"Mornin', Miss Chan," student Beth Mero greeted the teacher who doubled as an academic coach of the school's science team.

"Hi, Beth," Tina Chan responded. "Nice effort at Friday's district science competition."

"Thanks," Beth sighed. "It's frustrating, though, to work so hard and then have the team do so poorly. And we all know it was because Rob and Jeremy were so awful."

"Don't be so hard on them," the teacher said. "We all have bad days."

"But are we all drunk on our bad days?" Beth muttered sarcastically.

"What? Are you saying Rob and Jeremy were drunk at the competition?"

"Everyone on the team knew it," Beth huffed. "They told all of us."

That day, the teacher confronted the two students about the charge, and they admitted to drinking before the competition.

When the school principal told the parents their boys were being punished, the parents filed a lawsuit saying the teacher's meeting with the students violated their *Miranda* rights.

Did the school win the suit?

Sharpen Your Judgment – The Decision

Yes. The school won the case.

The judge noted that, while students do have rights during investigations involving breaking school rules – such as being drunk at a school function – those rights aren't the same as the ones in a criminal proceeding.

So, the teacher didn't violate the student's rights by speaking to them about a possible violation and asking them questions.

In fact, at the meeting the students were free to refuse to answer the charge.

The judge did note that the teacher might have been better off not meeting with the students and taking the complaint directly to the school administration.

The matter could have been handled at that level with little or no risk about charges of violations of rights.

The safer route

In this instance, the teacher took reasonable steps to find out if the rules had been broken. And she held the meeting with the students to give them a fair chance to give their side of the story.

That's admirable, but as the judge noted, an investigation at the administrative level is the safer, better way to go.

Cite: *Jennings & Schwaigert v. Wentzville School Dist.*

Teacher's and student's stories conflict – will court have to decide?

Was teacher using excessive force or just controlling his classroom?

"I need to hear again about that day in your classroom," principal Ann Lowe told teacher Steve Gale as he sat down in front of her desk. "The day you walked in and the five boys were running around bouncing the little ball off the walls."

"OK," said Steve. " Well, I said, 'Knock it off!' A classroom isn't the place for that. And those little balls can be dangerous."

"Right," agreed Ann.

"But the boys were too loud and riled up to hear me. Luckily, just then the ball got away from them and rolled over to me. I crouched down to catch it. But just as I did, Pat put his foot on my fingers.

"I said, 'That's my hand.' And Pat said, 'That's my SuperBall.' Then he stepped down harder. So I used my free hand to reach behind his knee. I gave his leg a yank to get his foot off of me."

Is that the real story?

"OK," said Ann. "But I just had Pat and his parents in my office. "They claim you didn't grab Pat's leg, but his crotch.'

"What?" said Steve. "But you know there are witnesses."

"That's another problem," said Ann. "I know they're Pat's best friends, but two of the boys are backing up his story now. And Pat says you gave him a groin injury."

"But I was at Friday's football game," said Steve. "Pat played linebacker. How'd he do that if he's injured?"

"Good question," said Ann. "The other boys still say it happened just the way you say it did. But Pat's parents are very upset. They're threatening to sue you, Steve."

Pat's parents did sue. They claimed the teacher used excessive force against a student. Did they win?

Decision: No. The evidence pointed to the teacher having used only reasonable force to maintain order – which was legal.

Key: Judges usually give teachers the benefit of the doubt when their story conflicts with a student's – especially if class control's part of the equation and the principal's investigation bears that out.

Cite: *Wolf v. Snyder.*

How far can a teacher go to maintain class discipline?

Angry girl was about to strike a classmate

If there was one thing Teresa Barnum dreaded about teaching, it was the prospect of breaking up a fight between two students.

"I love my job," she had told a friend. "But I wonder if I'd remember all the district's training and procedures if I actually had to face a violent situation."

She was about to find out.

A simple answer, then ...

"All right, class, let's see how you did on your math assignment," Teresa began on a Thursday morning. "Now, who can give me the answer to No. 1?"

She took a moment to scan the upraised hands before pointing to one.

"Julie?"

"The answer's 456."

"Close, but not correct," the teacher said. "Anyone else?" She called on Sarah.

"465."

"That's right, Sarah." Teresa nodded. "Now let's talk about how you arrived at that ..."

Before she could finish, Julie jumped out of her seat, ran over to Sarah's desk with a fist cocked. "That's the third time this week you showed me up," screamed Julie.

The teacher dashed from the front of the room to Sarah's desk in the fourth row and wedged herself between the two students.

As Julie struggled to get around Teresa, the teacher used her hands to deflect Julie's attempt to swing at the other student.

"Julie, come with me," Teresa said firmly as she nudged the girl toward the front of the room.

The teacher then made a quick call to the office to arrange for someone to escort Julie to see the principal.

Angry mother

The next day, Julie was absent from class. And at lunchtime, Teresa spotted a note in her mailbox. It was from the school principal, Ginny Angelos.

"See me as soon as you can. Ginny."

"What's up?" Teresa said as she walked into the office.

"We have a problem," the principal announced. "Julie's mother was here this morning. She says you bruised Julie's wrist. I think the term she used was you 'physically abused' her daughter."

Teresa replied: "You read my report of the whole thing, didn't you? Nothing like that happened."

"Right," Ginny nodded. "And the children I talked to confirmed your story. What's more, I told Julie's mother that the nurse checked her daughter and found no physical harm."

"But I want to make sure I have the story straight. The details are important because Julie's mother demanded you be fired, or else she's going to sue the district for allowing her child to be injured."

'She was ready to strike'

Teresa slowly went back over the details of the scuffle as Ginny took notes.

"So you never put a hand on Julie other than to stop her from hitting Sarah," Ginny summarized.

"That's right," Teresa said.

"I followed the district policy. I didn't touch her until it looked like she was ready to strike."

"OK," Ginny said. "It looks like we're going to have a meeting to determine if your action yesterday was justified."

Did the teacher act correctly to stop the fight?

Decision: Yes. The district backed Teresa and said she used appropriate measures needed to stop the fight. Then Julie's mother brought a lawsuit.

The judge threw out the case. Based on the district's policies on when teachers were allowed to use force and how the teacher followed those policies, the proper steps were taken in this situation.

Cite: *Widder v. Durango School Dist. No. 9-R.*

Discussion points for teachers and principals:

While many new education initiatives place more and more responsibilities on teachers, the No Child Left Behind Act also gives you expanded:

■ authority to undertake reasonable actions to maintain order, including force, and

■ protection from liability if you're acting to further efforts to control, discipline or expel a student.

Sharpen Your Judgment

Was teacher keeping order – or blowing her stack?

"You're late," said teacher Krista Drucker as students Jim and Jamal strolled into her class. As usual, they were laughing hard at some private joke, so she spoke up. "The bell rang 10 minutes ago. Do you have passes?"

Jim turned to wave his hands at her, as if she was hysterical and he was trying to calm her down. This made Jamal double over with laughter. The rest of the class snickered.

"Hilarious," said Krista coolly. "I'll talk to you first, Jamal. Please come into the hall. Jim, take your seat for now."

"I'm coming, too," said Jim in a deep voice, sticking out his arms to walk like Frankenstein as he tried to follow them. The class laughed.

Krista barred the doorway with her arm. "You heard me, Jim. Sit down."

Jim tried to slap Krista's arm out of his way and then pinched it hard. Krista turned and grabbed him by the scruff of his neck. She gave him a push. "Sit down," she said firmly.

"Ow!" he howled. "You hurt me!"

Jim and his mother sued Krista for battery, but Krista asked the court to rule in her favor.

Did it?

Sharpen Your Judgment – The Decision

Yes, the court ruled in the teacher's favor.

Jim's mother couldn't sue Krista for battery unless she could prove Krista touched Jim with the malicious intent of causing him pain.

Jim's mother argued Krista did so – that Krista was mad at Jim for clowning around and meant to hurt him when she grabbed him.

But even if this was true, it wasn't enough. This teacher was clearly trying to regain control of a student who'd defied and pinched her – not trying to hurt him.

Analysis: Only protect yourself

Most state laws take it into account that unexpected things can happen in the classroom that a teacher will have to deal with on her feet.

Many school districts have policies that they require their teachers to follow if they're attacked by students.

But things don't always happen in the predictable way that school policies anticipate. So you should also know that, generally, you're allowed to defend yourself if attacked. But if you ever have to do so in class, only use just enough force to keep the student from hurting you or anyone else.

Cite: *Peterson v. Baker.*

Academic Practices

TOPICS

I. REFORM LEGISLATION	237
II. CURRICULUM AND GRADING	245
III. STUDENT RECORDS	249
IV. TESTING	256
V. EDUCATIONAL MALPRACTICE	257
VI. ADMISSIONS AND ATTENDANCE	258
VII. COMPULSORY ATTENDANCE	262
VIII. TEACHER SCENARIOS	266

CHAPTER SIX
Academic Practices

I. REFORM LEGISLATION

Overview

The No Child Left Behind (NCLB) Act of 2001 reauthorized the Elementary and Secondary Education Act (ESEA) of 1965. It requires the states to use academic assessments to annually review school progress and determine if "adequate yearly progress" (AYP) has been made under state standards. The AYP requirement is a condition for the receipt of Title I funds under the ESEA.

Schools that fail to achieve AYP for two consecutive years are designated for "school improvement." If a school does not make AYP after two years of improvement status, it is subject to "corrective action." This may entail replacing teachers or an entirely new curriculum. A school failing to make AYP after a year of corrective action must be "restructured." This involves replacing staff, converting to charter school status or surrendering direct control to state officials. NCLB Act notice and transfer provisions are triggered when schools are identified for improvement, corrective action or restructuring.

A federal regulation defining "highly qualified teacher" under the No Child Left Behind (NCLB) Act was declared in violation of Congressional intent because it permitted some California teachers to become highly qualified without obtaining full state certification.

A. The No Child Left Behind Act of 2001

Court Decisions

◆ Under the NCLB Act, alternative-route teachers meet the "highly qualified teacher" designation only by obtaining "full state certification." But a federal regulation, 34 C.F.R. Part 200.56(a)(1)(i), permitted an alternative-route teacher to gain "highly qualified" status without first obtaining "full state certification." Students, parents and two nonprofit organizations claimed the regulation and a parallel California state education regulation allowed a disproportionate number of intern teachers to teach in minority and low-income California schools. The challengers said California intern teachers lacked "full state certification," which is part of the definition of a highly qualified teacher under the NCLB Act.

A federal district court heard evidence that the state's intern teachers were concentrated in schools that served low-income and minority students. But the court upheld the regulation. On appeal, the U.S. Court of Appeals, Ninth Circuit, held **the federal regulation impermissibly expanded the highly qualified teacher definition of 20 U.S.C. § 7801(23) to include alternative-route teachers in the process of obtaining full certification.** Since 34 C.F.R. Part 200.56(a)(2)(ii) was inconsistent with congressional intent, the court invalidated it. The state and federal regulations permitted California and its school districts to ignore the disproportionate number of interns teaching in schools in minority and low-income areas, and the court held the challengers could pursue the case. States could define full certification as they chose, but the NCLB Act required them to take steps to ensure fully certified teachers were proportionately represented in the teaching staffs of minority and low-income schools. The court reversed the judgment and returned the case to the lower court. *Renee v. Duncan*, 623 F.3d 787 (9th Cir. 2010).

◆ A federal appeals court refused to review Connecticut's challenge to federal interpretations of the No Child Left Behind Act. According to Connecticut officials, the NCLB Act's "unfunded mandates provision" required the state to be fully funded for any costs of complying with the NCLB Act. It stated it was currently spending $41.6 million of its own funds to comply with the act. The court ruled against the state, which appealed. The U.S. Court of Appeals, Second Circuit, held arguments regarding the unfunded mandates provision were not ready for judicial review. This claim could be decided once there was an administrative record. The district court was entitled to find the disposition of the proposed plan amendments and request for waivers was not arbitrary or capricious. An NCLB Act provision stated that approval of a state plan should not be declined before a hearing. **But the pending legal issue was the meaning of the unfunded mandates provision, which was not yet ripe for review.** Since the court held that claim was not ready for review, it found no reason to order a hearing on the plan amendments before arguments about the unfunded mandates provision were heard. *Connecticut v. Duncan*, 612 F.3d 107 (2d Cir. 2010).

As a federal court recently noted, every court to have considered a private claim for relief under the NCLB Act has found the Act does not allow one.

◆ The number of Newark, New Jersey schools "in need of improvement" under the NCLB Act increased from 37 in 2003-04 to 51 in 2006-07. An audit revealed that the district did not meet its NCLB Act obligation to notify parents of their rights to obtain transfers and supplemental educational services (SES) for their children. A group of Newark parents filed a class action suit against the school system, asserting NCLB Act violations. A federal court held that the Act did not create individually enforceable rights and dismissed the complaint. On appeal, the U.S. Court of Appeals, Third Circuit, explained that the NCLB Act was enacted by Congress under its Spending Clause powers. As with other Spending Clause legislation, the NCLB Act offered federal money to the states in return for an agreement by the states to perform specific actions. **Unlike federal civil rights legislation, the NCLB Act's "penalties" section did not offer any remedy in the event of noncompliance.** Instead, states that failed to meet the Act's requirements were subject to withholding of funds by the Secretary of the U.S. Department of Education. Thus, the parents lacked a private right of action to enforce

◆ The NCLB Act's "Unfunded Mandates Provision" prevents the Act from being construed to authorize an officer or employee of the federal government to mandate that a state or state subdivision spend funds or incur costs not paid for under the Act. School districts from Michigan, Texas and Vermont joined the National Education Association (NEA) and NEA affiliates in a federal action against the Secretary of the U.S. Department of Education, seeking a federal court declaration that she was misinterpreting the Unfunded Mandates Provision. They argued that states need not comply with NCLB Act requirements where federal funding did not cover the increased costs of NCLB Act compliance. A federal court refused to interpret the NCLB Act to excuse states from complying with requirements of the Act that imposed additional costs on states. **The states had to comply with the NCLB Act regardless of any federal funding shortfall.** On appeal, the U.S. Court of Appeals, Sixth Circuit, reached a tie vote, meaning that the lower court's decision stood. As a result, the judgment for the Secretary was affirmed. *School Dist. of City of Pontiac v. Secretary of U.S. Dep't of Educ.*, 584 F.3d 253 (6th Cir. 2009).

◆ Two Illinois school districts and a group of parents sued the U.S. Department of Education in a federal court, arguing that certain NCLB Act requirements were in conflict with those of the Individuals with Disabilities Education Act (IDEA). The court held that the districts and parents lacked legal standing to bring the lawsuit. It also held that the IDEA and the NCLB Act established voluntary programs and that school districts could solve any problem created by the laws by simply turning down federal funds. The districts and parents appealed to the U.S. Court of Appeals, Seventh Circuit.

The court held that the districts and parents had standing to proceed with the lawsuit because they had no option but to follow the state's lead. Both federal laws required states to opt in or opt out for a year or more at a time. Once a district accepted a grant it had to comply with all program requirements. This condition was sufficient to establish standing. However, the claim of the districts and parents was too weak to pursue any further. **The IDEA had to give way to the NCLB Act if there was truly any conflict between the laws.** The 2004 IDEA amendments were designed in part to conform the IDEA with the NCLB Act, not to displace it. If there was any conflict between the 2001 NCLB Act and IDEA enactments from between 1970 and 1990, NCLB would prevail. The court dismissed the case. *Board of Educ. of Ottawa Township High School Dist. 140 v. Spellings*, 517 F.3d 922 (7th Cir. 2008).

◆ The state of Michigan approved a provider to contract for supplemental educational services (SES) such as tutoring. After the provider served about 1,000 Detroit students during the 2005-06 school year, the Detroit Public School District (DPS) terminated the contract for failing to provide services and not paying its employees. The provider sued DPS in a federal court, asserting state and federal claims. It claimed that the DPS terminated the contract without cause and in retaliation for exercising First Amendment rights.

The court noted that the DPS had taken the action based on failure to provide services and failure to pay its employees. The NCLB Act does not create a private claim for relief. **NCLB simply required districts that fail to make adequate yearly progress to pay for tutoring of low-income students by contracting with SES providers.** The act did not unambiguously create a right for SES providers to enforce claims against a district. The law focused on the rights of children rather than SES providers. The court dismissed the provider's $1 million claim for due process violations. The DPS's decision to remove the provider's name from its approved list did not prevent it from doing business. Being named on a provider list did not amount to a protected property interest. The court dismissed the case. *Alliance For Children, Inc. v. City of Detroit Public Schools*, 475 F.Supp.2d 655 (E.D. Mich. 2007).

◆ Pennsylvania's education secretary identified 13 schools in the Reading School District as failing to achieve AYP. NCLB requires districts to report the test scores of four subgroups when the number of students in the subgroup exceeds a state-designated number. The secretary had established this "N" number at 40, based on several computer studies. The district claimed that the secretary arbitrarily set the N number and did not provide adequate assistance. The district sued the secretary. The Commonwealth Court of Pennsylvania found no evidence to contradict the secretary's selection of the number 40 as appropriate. Plus the secretary provided the district with adequate technical assistance. **The state was not required to provide all the assistance specified in the NCLB Act at the moment a school was identified for improvement.** The secretary did not abuse her discretion. *Reading School Dist. v. Dep't of Educ.*, 855 A.2d 166 (Pa. Commw. Ct. 2004).

The school district then sent the department its plans to bring six schools into compliance. It submitted a cost estimate for the plan in excess of $26 million for 2003-2004. The district estimated it would receive about $8 million in federal funding, and it asked the state education department for the shortfall. The department did not respond to the request for funds, but found six schools and the district as a whole failed to achieve AYP for 2003-2004 and would be placed on level-one or level-two sanctions for 2004-2005. The district appealed, asserting that the department did not provide federal funds to implement the act, mandatory technical assistance to sanctioned schools, or Spanish language testing on a required statewide assessment. The state education secretary dismissed the district's appeal. The district appealed again to the commonwealth court, which held that the department violated the district's due process rights by limiting the grounds for appeal in its policy. *Reading School Dist. v. Dep't of Educ.*, 875 A.2d 1218 (Pa. Commw. Ct. 2005).

B. State Reform Acts

Before the No Child Left Behind Act of 2001, state legislatures were addressing public school accountability in reform legislation designed to improve student performance. In 2002, the Sixth Circuit upheld the Michigan School Reform Act, which replaced Detroit's elected school board with an appointed one. The Equal Protection Clause did not prevent the legislature from enacting experimental reforms where no suspect class or fundamental right was involved. Moore v. Detroit School Reform Board, *239 F.3d 352 (6th Cir. 2002).*

The Pennsylvania Educational Empowerment Act (EEA) was enacted to "fix broken school districts" in urban areas. It placed districts with a history of low test scores on a state list. Although the Pennsylvania Supreme Court struck down the EEA as special legislation in Harrisburg School Dist. v. Hickock, *563 Pa. 391, 761 A.2d 1132 (Pa. 2000), it upheld amended legislation that expanded the class of cities for which placement on the empowerment district could be waived in* Harrisburg School Dist. v. Zogby, *574 Pa. 121, 828 A.2d 1079 (Pa. 2003). In 2010, the Pennsylvania Supreme Court held a law concerning a financially distressed, poor-performing school district was unconstitutional because it was worded to apply only to that district.*

Court Decisions

◆ Due to a history of low test scores, the Duquesne City School District was placed on Pennsylvania's education empowerment list in 2000. It was declared a financially distressed school district, and its management and operations were placed under a special board of control. In 2007, the special board of control eliminated the district's only high school. After the state department of education approved the action, the board laid off 18 district employees. No agreements to enroll high school students were made with neighboring school districts. Six weeks after the school closure, the General Assembly enacted Act 45 of 2007, which gave the state education secretary authority to designate two or more districts to accept high school students from a distressed district. Act 45 required that employees who were furloughed by the closure of a high school be hired on a preferential basis by a district within three miles of the distressed district. Employees of districts located within three miles of Duquesne City School District noted only Duquesne met all of Act 45's requirements. They claimed Act 45 was a "special law" that violated the state constitution.

After the Commonwealth Court held Act 45 was not special legislation, appeal reached the Supreme Court of Pennsylvania. **It held Article III, Section 32 of the state constitution prohibits local or special laws regulating school districts.** Duquesne was the only member of the initial class of districts described by Act 45, and no other district could meet Act 45's criteria unless "a highly improbable convergence of events" transpired. The court held the class of districts created by Act 45 was substantially closed to new members. The practical effect of the law was to assure that affected Duquesne staff members would be given preferential hiring treatment. As parts of Act 45 were "special legislation" prohibited by the state constitution, the court reversed the judgment. West Mifflin Area School Dist. v. Zahorchak, 4 A.3d 1042 (Pa. 2010).

◆ In 1998, the Missouri legislature passed SB 781 as part of a settlement in a long-running federal lawsuit to desegregate St. Louis public schools. SB 781 created the Transitional School District (TSD) to handle the transition from federal court supervision to local control. SB 781 further provided that if the St. Louis school district lost its accreditation after the restoration of control to the city board, the general authority over the school district transferred back to the TSD. This provision was carried forward into law as Section 162.1100 of the Revised Statutes of Missouri. The St. Louis school district's performance was at or below minimally acceptable levels after 1994, and in 2006, the state board reestablished the TSD. When the district lost its accreditation, it sued the state board. Meanwhile, a special administrative board took control of St. Louis public schools. After a trial, the state board prevailed. The district appealed to the Supreme Court of Missouri, arguing that Section 162.110 was special legislation that violated the state constitution. The court disagreed. While Section 162.1100 created a classification that was characteristic of special legislation, the state constitution was not violated. Board of Educ. of City of St. Louis v. Missouri State Board of Educ., 271 S.W.3d 1 (Mo. 2008).

◆ The Kentucky Education Reform Act (KERA) created site-based councils to provide greater accountability and decentralize school management. A KERA provision, KRS § 160.345(2)(h), required site-based councils to select principals from applicants recommended by the district superintendent. A superintendent fired a high school principal for poor performance. He received nine applications for the resulting vacancy, including one from the former principal. The superintendent forwarded only three applications to the site-based council. The council asked for the others, but the superintendent refused and appointed one of his three candidates as interim principal. A state court ordered the superintendent to forward all nine applications, and the council then recommended rehiring the former principal. The state supreme court consolidated the case with that of an assistant principal who claimed she was passed over for a vacancy due to gender. It held neither superintendent had the authority to limit the pool of "qualified applicants" under Section 160.345(2)(h). **Site-based councils were created in direct response to widespread mismanagement caused by an overly centralized system of school governance.** Superintendents had to send site-based councils the applications of all applicants who met state law requirements, including the assistant principal and the fired principal. Young v. Hammond, 139 S.W.3d 895 (Ky. 2004).

◆ In 1993, Maryland's state education board adopted school performance standards that mandated reporting requirements and improvement plans for each public school. Schools that did not meet the standards were placed under the direct control of the local school board. If they failed to improve under local reconstitution, they were designated for "state reconstitution." By 2000, the state board had placed 97 Maryland schools under local reconstitution, 83 of which were in Baltimore. The state board reconstituted three low-performing Baltimore schools, but their performance remained stagnant after three years.

The state board hired a private company to provide the schools curriculum, instructional services, support personnel, teaching tools, special education and related services, educational services for limited and non-English-proficient students and other services. The company hired and managed the professional staff for the three schools. The collective bargaining agent (CBA) for school employees sued the state education board in a state court, arguing the board could not adopt regulations creating student performance standards and reconstitution. The court held the board was statutorily authorized to contract with the company. On appeal, the Court of Appeals of Maryland rejected the CBA's claim that state law did not authorize the state reconstitution regulations. Even if the board initially lacked such authority, the general assembly enacted legislation in 1997, 1999 and 2000 showing its awareness and approval for the board to contract with private vendors under the reconstitution regulations. The 1997, 1999 and 2000 laws also recognized that **under state reconstitution, public school teachers might be employed by private entities**. It could be inferred that the legislature approved of and ratified the reconstitution regulations. The court affirmed the judgment. *Baltimore Teachers Union v. Maryland State Board of Educ.*, 379 Md. 192, 840 A.2d 728 (Md. 2004).

C. Charter Schools

1. Legislation

Charter school laws were among the first of the educational reforms of the 1990s to be tested in the courts. They have survived numerous legal challenges asserting violations of state and federal constitutional provisions. But a Florida law shifting the power to authorize charter schools from local boards to a state commission violated a provision of the Florida Constitution.

Court Decisions

◆ In 2006, Florida Statutes Section 1002.335 established the state Schools of Excellence Commission as an independent state entity with power to authorize charter schools throughout the state. Local boards lost their former authority to charter schools. At least 31 local school boards filed resolutions with the state board, seeking to retain their former authority to authorize charter schools. The state board permitted only three local boards to retain this authority. Several boards then appealed. According to a state district court of appeal, article IX section 4 of the Florida Constitution requires school boards to operate, control and supervise all free public schools within their districts. The court held **Section 1002.335 "permits and encourages the creation of a parallel system of free public education escaping the operation and control of local elected school boards."** It vested a commission of state board appointees with the powers of operation, control and supervision that were reserved to local boards. Rejecting the state board's arguments that the new law furthered the goals of systemic uniformity and efficiency, the court found Section 1002.335 in "total and fatal conflict" with article IX, section 4 of the Florida Constitution, and held the act unconstitutional. *Duval County School Board v. State Board of Educ.*, 998 So.2d 641 (Fla. Ct. App. 2008).

◆ An Illinois education association petitioned the state Educational Labor Relations Board to represent charter school employees. The school district that was the governing body of the charter school argued that the labor relations board lacked authority, as the Illinois Education Labor Act (IELA) did not apply to charter schools. The district claimed it was not an "educational employer" as defined by the Act. The board found that charter schools were not exempt from IELA coverage. On appeal, the Appellate Court of Illinois found that **the Charter Schools Law exempted charter schools from "all other state laws and regulations in the School Code governing public schools and local board policies,"** with the exception of seven specific statutes. Among the seven exemptions were laws relating to employee background checks, student discipline, government tort immunity, nonprofit indemnification, abused and neglected children reporting, student record care and report card standards.

Significantly, the Charter School Law did not specify an exemption for the IELA. This indicated the absence of the IELA from the list of Charter School Law exceptions meant the IELA did not apply to charter schools. As the board had incorrectly found that the Education Labor Act applied to charter schools, the decision was reversed. A 2009 amendment to the charter law specified that the governing body of a charter school is an "educational employer." As of January 1, 2010, charter schools must comply with the IELA, but the change did not apply to this case. *Northern Kane Educ. Corp. v. Cambridge Lakes Educ. Ass'n, IEA-NEA*, 394 Ill.App.3d 755, 914 N.E.2d 1286 (Ill. App. Ct. 2009).

◆ A South Carolina academy applied to a school district to open as a charter school for the 2004-05 school year. The district's board gave the academy conditional approval, contingent upon finding a site in the district prior to August 2003. The academy notified the board that it had located a site in the district, and the board paid it over $87,000. But the academy obtained another site, and the state education department approved it. The academy was not ready to open when public schools opened for the 2004-05 school year. It tried to open in a temporary location, but when the school district reported this to the education department, the department directed the academy's closure. The academy obtained a conditional certificate to hold classes in an alternate facility. The school board held a hearing and ruled that the academy had not met four conditions for approval and that it had no contract with the district. The conditions of approval related to space, facility, equipment and personnel.

Although the academy did not meet the conditions, it appealed to the state board of education, which affirmed the local board's decision. On appeal, the Supreme Court of South Carolina reviewed the state Charter School Act and held that **a conditional charter did not confer due process rights on a charter applicant**. Even if there was a lack of due process, the local board had remedied this by holding a hearing. The academy was required to meet the terms of its application. *James Academy of Excellence v. Dorchester County School Dist. Two*, 376 S.C. 293, 657 S.E.2d 469 (S.C. 2008).

◆ A Pennsylvania resident requested an auditor's report and financial statements from a charter school. He also sought information about the written arrangement between the school and a private management entity. The school claimed it was not an agency of the commonwealth and that the state Right-to-Know Act did not apply to it. The management entity denied the resident's request for records on grounds that it was a private company. The resident sued the school for disclosure. A state common pleas court held for the resident and ordered the school to provide copies of the requested records.

On appeal, the Supreme Court of Pennsylvania held that the Right-to-Know Act required "agencies" to make public records accessible for inspection and duplication. Among the agencies required to disclose records were the offices, departments, boards or commissions of the executive branch. **School districts were similar to the entities explicitly listed in the Right-to-Know Act and they qualified as "agencies."** Charter schools were independent public schools created for the essential governmental service of education. As organizations performing essential governmental functions, charter schools were "agencies" covered by the Right-to-Know Act. The court affirmed the judgment. *Zager v. Chester Community Charter School*, 594 Pa. 166, 934 A.2d 1227 (Pa. 2007).

◆ A Wisconsin "virtual academy" was established as a charter school to provide curriculum by Internet and mail to students statewide. Parents had the primary day-to-day responsibility for implementing education. The academy's administrative offices were within the district that established it. The Wisconsin Education Association Council sued the establishing school district, state superintendent of instruction and others, claiming that the school violated state charter school, open enrollment and teacher certification statutes. A court held for the district and state superintendent. On appeal, the state court of appeals found academy students studied and completed assignments under the direction of their parents, who were not licensed. This violated the law. Academy teachers worked from their homes across the state, not just in the district. This also violated the law because **the charter school law prohibited a school board from establishing a charter school located outside the district**. While the academy's offices remained in the district, the statutory term "school" could not be construed to exclude the teachers and students making up the academy. The court also reversed the trial court's decision on the open enrollment issue. As operation of the academy violated three Wisconsin laws, the court reversed the judgment. *Johnson v. Burmaster*, 307 Wis.2d 213, 744 N.W.2d 900 (Wis. Ct. App. 2007), review denied, 749 N.W.2d 662 (Wis. 2008).

◆ Massachusetts law authorized "Commonwealth" and "Horace Mann" charter schools. Horace Mann charter schools were subject to approval by local school committees, but Commonwealth schools were independent of a school committee. The law charged the board of education with the final determination on granting charters and allowed the board to revoke charters. A school committee that served four towns approved an application for a Commonwealth charter school focusing on advanced learning in math and science. The school committees of three towns sued the board, and the case reached the Supreme Judicial Court of Massachusetts. It held the board had the final decision to grant a charter. **No state law or regulation permitted appeals from a board decision.** The trial court had correctly held it lacked authority to review the board's decisions. Public hearings are legislative, not adversary in nature. The legislature did not intend school committees to obtain judicial review in Commonwealth charter school cases. Local school committees could make the process unworkable and unwieldy and played a limited role in the application process. *School Committee of Hudson v. Board of Educ.*, 448 Mass. 565, 863 N.E.2d 22 (Mass. 2007).

◆ The Ohio Federation of Teachers, Ohio Congress of Parents and Teachers, and the Ohio School Boards Association challenged the state's program of community schools, known elsewhere as charter schools. The challengers sought a declaration that community schools violated the Ohio Constitution and sought restoration of funds "diverted" from school districts. The case reached the Supreme Court of Ohio, which found the General Assembly's authority to set educational standards and requirements for common schools allowed it to set different standards for community schools. The General Assembly complied with the constitution by adding flexible, deregulated education opportunities to the school system. Community schools had to administer the standardized tests given in traditional public schools and were monitored by the state education department. The court rejected the claim by community school opponents that the state's funding method diverted funds from school districts. The General Assembly had exclusive authority to spend tax revenues to further a statewide system of schools. There was no violation of state constitutional provisions for local control of city school boards and local tax revenue. **The General Assembly did not intrude upon local powers by creating additional schools that were not part of a school district.** *Ohio Congress of Parents and Teachers v. State Board of Educ.*, 111 Ohio St.3d 568, 857 N.E.2d 1148 (Ohio 2006).

2. Applications

Court Decisions

◆ An Ohio church sought to sponsor community schools (known elsewhere as charter schools). But the state education department found it ineligible, since neither the church nor its parent, Presbyterian Church USA, was an "education-oriented" entity as required by Section 3314.02(C) of the revised state code. An appeal under Section 119.12 of the state code to a county common pleas court was dismissed, and the state court of appeals then affirmed the judgment.

On appeal, the Supreme Court of Ohio noted Section 3314.015(B) of the state code made "final" a department determination regarding an entity's status as "education-oriented." But as the church argued, another state code provision declared that any decision by the department to disapprove an entity for sponsorship of a community school "may be appealed." Section 3314.015(B)(3) made a department determination regarding "education-oriented" status appealable under state code Section 119.12. Community school provisions did not say department decisions were "not appealable." They only stated that they were "final." **A key to review by appellate courts is that there is a "final" order from which a party may appeal.** "Final" meant the opposite of "not appealable." Since the community school provisions did not prohibit an appeal by the church, the court reversed the judgment and returned the case to the lower courts for further activity. *Brookwood Presbyterian Church v. Ohio Dep't of Educ.*, 127 Ohio St.3d 469, 940 N.E.2d 1256 (Ohio 2010).

◆ A Maryland school board charter review committee rejected a charter application as incomplete. In a 10-page letter, the committee described the deficiencies and sought clarification from the applicant in 50 areas. After the application was resubmitted, the committee found only eight of its concerns had been satisfied. Charter school representatives met with the committee to discuss the school application. Using a county public school "analytical scoring rubric," the board assigned the application only 189 of 530 possible points. After the board voted down the application, it sent the applicants a breakdown of its evaluation criteria, the scoring rubric and the score. Charter school applicants appealed to the Maryland State Board of Education (MSBE), which held the process had been fair. Appeal reached the Court of Special Appeals of Maryland.

The court found **the Maryland Public Charter School Program vested county education boards with primary chartering authority and that the MSBE had broad authority over the administration of public schools**. Prior MSBE rulings permitted local boards to withhold charter application scoring rubrics, so long as the process was otherwise explained. As the MSBE found, the committee explained the deficiencies in a 10-page letter and held four meetings to discuss its action. The court found the MSBE's review of the local decision was consistent with its prior cases. An argument that the local board was "generally opposed to granting a charter" did not show local bias made the board unable to make a fair and impartial decision. As the court found nothing illegal, arbitrary or capricious about the denial of the application, it held for the board. *Board of Educ. of Somerset County v. Somerset Advocates for Educ.*, 189 Md.App. 385, 984 A.2d 405 (Md. Ct. Spec. App. 2009).

◆ A Florida charter school application stated that students who scored at or above the 25th percentile in norm-referenced tests would be considered as having demonstrated acceptable student performance standards. The local board denied the application, finding that this measure would render the school unaccountable and that the 25th percentile was lower than its own standards. Moreover, the academy did not make reasonable enrollment projections and had overestimated its capital budget by $1 million. The academy appealed to the state Charter School Appeals Commission, where it asserted the 25th percentile had been a typographical error and should have been the 51st percentile.

The commission found no requirement that a school grade be a part of a charter application, and no substantial evidence of a deficiency. The state board then granted the application. On appeal, the District Court of Appeal of Florida found the application was not deficient. **There was no state law requirement for a school "A" goal.** The academy offered to correct its typographical error, and the application was sufficient with respect to student assessment and accountability. The academy overcame any reason for denying the application regarding budget and class size. **The state charter school law did not permit the state board to open charter schools.** Once a charter application was granted, the school board had control over the process. The board had authority to revoke a charter, and it still operated, controlled and supervised all free public schools in the district. Rejecting the local board's argument that the state board order violated its authority to control and supervise public schools, the court affirmed the state board's decision. *School Board of Volusia County v. Academies of Excellence*, 974 So.2d 1186 (Fla. Dist. Ct. App. 2008).

◆ South Carolina applicants submitted a charter school application and met with a state Charter School Advisory Committee to review compliance with the state Charter Schools Act. The committee voted to certify the application, but the board for the school district in which the charter school was to be located voted to deny it at a public hearing. The board found the application deficient in at least seven areas; thus, it would adversely affect other students in the district. The state board of education reversed the decision, holding that the local board's factual findings and legal conclusions were not based on substantial evidence. A state court affirmed, and the case reached the Supreme Court of South Carolina, which explained that courts may not substitute their judgment for that of a state agency on the weight of evidence. However, they may reverse or modify decisions that are clearly erroneous.

The Charter School Act permitted the denial of applications that did not meet the specific requirements of S.C. Code Sections 59-40-50 or 59-40-60, that failed to meet the spirit or intent of the act, or that adversely affected the other students in the district. Instead of providing a written explanation of the reasons for denial of the application, and citing specific standards, the local board had only spoken in generalized terms. **The local board had clearly failed to meet the act's requirements.** The judgment for the applicants was affirmed. *Lee County School Dist. Board of Trustees v. MLD Charter School Academy Planning Committee*, 371 S.C. 561, 641 S.E.2d 24 (S.C. 2007).

◆ A Florida charter school concentrated on serving poor children, many of whom had failed at other schools. Its operator applied for two new charters. The board denied the application under a policy that required applicants already having charters from the board to demonstrate a record of success in operating an exemplary charter school for the past two fiscal years. "An exemplary charter school" was one with at least a "B" grade or significant annual learning gains. The school board found the existing charter school to be non-exemplary based on its financial and academic performance. The school received a "D" grade for 2003-04 and was projected for a D or F in 2004-05.

The Florida District Court of Appeal upheld the decision to deny the application. The Charter School Law required applicants to demonstrate how their schools would use "guiding principles" and meet a state-defined purpose. Among other things, charter applicants had to provide a detailed curriculum plan showing how students would be provided with services to meet state standards. The local board's policy of requiring "exemplary performance" was a practical and reasonable approach to testing an applicant's academic and financial abilities. **Competent, substantial evidence indicated that the application was fiscally and academically noncompliant**, and there was good cause to deny it. *Imhotep-Nguzo Saba Charter School v. Dep't of Educ.*, 947 So.2d 1279 (Fla. Dist. Ct. App. 2007).

◆ Illinois charter school applicants submitted a proposal for a school that would offer unemployed high school drop-outs opportunities to earn a diploma while acquiring vocational skills. Participants would divide time between school and work at low-income housing sites. The state board noted that the district had a $32.65 million deficit and faced additional budget cuts if it lost a pending voter referendum. It found the proposal not economically sound. A state court affirmed, as did the Appellate Court of Illinois. The applicants appealed to the Supreme Court of Illinois.

The applicants argued that the state board could not deny a charter school proposal solely because of a school district's financial condition. They asserted that their proposal met 14 of the 15 statutory requirements. Reducing the statutory inquiry into a single question of finance would defeat the purpose of the charter schools law, which was to create educational choice and competition. The supreme court disagreed, explaining that the charter schools law made a district's finances a "legitimate concern." The applicants in this case had refused to accept anything but 100% per capita funding. **The court found that the terms of a proposed charter, including funding issues, must permit both the school and the district to be financially secure.** It agreed with the state board's interpretation of the law as requiring proposals to meet all 15 statutory requirements. As the proposal was not in the best interests of students in the district, the court affirmed the board's decision. *Comprehensive Community Solutions v. Rockford School Dist. No. 205*, 216 Ill.2d 455, 297 Ill.Dec. 221, 837 N.E.2d 1 (Ill. 2005).

3. Operations and Finance

Florida's highest court held a school board could immediately terminate the charters of two schools based on financial emergency without affording them protections under the state Administrative Procedure Act. Ohio's Supreme Court held community schools seeking to appeal from a sponsor's termination decision are bound to comply with state law procedures. New York's highest court held charter school construction and renovation projects are not public works, meaning the state's prevailing wage provisions are inapplicable to them.

Court Decisions

◆ In 2000, the New York Department of Labor decided that charter schools were generally not considered to be public entities. Thus, a state prevailing wage law for those working on public projects did not apply. But in 2007, the department issued an opinion letter declaring the prevailing wage law should apply to charter school projects. Soon, the state commissioner of labor notified the Charter Schools Institute and state education department that the prevailing wage laws would be enforced for new charter school projects after a specified date. Charter schools and supporting organizations filed a state court action for a declaration that the commissioner's new position exceeded her authority and an order declaring the prevailing wage laws inapplicable to charter schools.

A state trial court held a charter agreement was a public contract and that charter school construction and renovation projects were public works. An appellate division court reversed the judgment, and appeal reached the state's highest court. The New York Court of Appeals found the prevailing wage laws applied to public agency contracts for the employment of laborers, workmen or mechanics on "public works projects." According to the court, a charter agreement was not a contract for public work. **A charter was an authorizing agreement by which an agency determined a charter applicant was competent for state licensure.** While the court held New York charter schools bore some similarities to public entities, the prevailing wage law identified only four covered public entities. None were educational entities such as charter schools. Finding the prevailing wage law did not apply to charter schools, the court affirmed the appellate division's judgment. *New York Charter School Ass'n v. Smith*, 15 N.Y.3d 403, 940 N.E.2d 522, 914 N.Y.S.2d 696 (N.Y. 2010).

◆ A Cincinnati community school sponsor placed a school on probation, then suspended it from operating. The sponsor gave the school a statutory written notice of its right to request an informal hearing within 14 days, but the school sought a direct appeal to the state education department. Asserting the school waived its appeal rights, the sponsor advised the department that the contract was terminated. Unable to continue operating, the school appealed to the state supreme court, which found that the state code permitted a sponsor to terminate a community school contract upon 90 days' written notice. Notice must include reasons for the action and a statement that the school may request an informal hearing within 14 days. A school may appeal from an adverse decision to the state education board. **A community school contract was terminated upon the passage of 90 days after the date of a sponsor's notice.** As the sponsor complied with statutory requirements, the court held that the school was not entitled to relief. *State ex rel. Nation Building Technical Academy v. Ohio Dep't of Educ.*, 123 Ohio St.3d 35, 913 N.E.2d 977 (Ohio 2009).

◆ A 2005 New York Charter School Law amendment directed the state comptroller to audit all school districts and charter schools in the state. Several New York City charter schools filed a state court challenge to the comptroller's authority to do the audits. The case reached the Court of Appeals of New York, which found the legislature designated the state board of regents and chartering entities as the public agents authorized to supervise and oversee charter schools. **Charter school audits could not be construed as "incidental to the audits of school districts."** The state comptroller could not claim the power to conduct the audits on the basis of the receipt of state funds and the performance of a governmental function. Once paid to a charter school, public funds were no longer under state control. As a check on their accountability, charters had to be renewed each five years and could be lost if educational standards were not met. The court ruled for the charter schools. *In re New York Charter Schools Ass'n v. DiNapoli*, 13 N.Y.2d 120, 914 N.E.2d 991 (N.Y. 2009).

◆ A Florida school board voted to terminate two charter schools with long histories of financial mismanagement. The board indicated the action was for "good cause" under Florida law, based on the severity of recent audit findings. Although a charter provision permitted termination upon 24 hours' notice, the school operators claimed the procedural protections of the state Administrative Procedure Act (APA). The state board of education voted to uphold the immediate termination of both charters. Appeal reached the Supreme Court of Florida, which noted that **the law permits the immediate termination of charters for "good cause" shown**, or when the health, safety or welfare of the students is threatened. School boards did not have to follow the APA when there were emergency-type circumstances involving the health, safety or welfare of students, or where other good cause necessitated immediate action. *School Board of Palm Beach County, Florida v. Survivors Charter Schools*, 3 So.3d 1220 (Fla. 2009).

◆ A California nonprofit organization called Islamic Relief sponsored a charter school with two Minnesota campuses. For the 2008-09 school year, the academy expected to receive $3.8 million in funds from the state of Minnesota. A vast majority of the academy's students were Somali Muslims. The ACLU claimed that the academy violated the Establishment Clause by permitting prayer sessions during school hours in which parents, volunteers and teachers participated. The academy was accused of endorsing Islamic dress codes and dietary practices, and providing bus transportation only at the end of an after-school religious program. The ACLU asserted that the academy preferred "Muslim" religious practice. A federal court held that while Islamic Relief was not a state actor, it still had potential liability for an Establishment Clause violation due to its role in the traditional function of public education.

Minnesota charter schools are a part of the public school system under state law, and the state Charter School Law (CSL) required each school sponsor to assure compliance with nonsectarian requirements. Therefore, the case required a trial and the court refused to dismiss the lawsuit. For example, **religious entanglement created by the academy's dress code and the busing schedule required a factual inquiry**. The role played by Islamic Relief in the academy's operations also required further scrutiny. *American Civil Liberties Union of Minnesota v. Tarek Ibn Ziyad Academy*, Civil No. 09-138 (DWF/JJG), 2009 WL 2215072 (D. Minn. 7/21/09).

◆ A Texas charter school had a significant enrollment increase after converting a private school to an open enrollment charter school. The charter school board hired the subsidiary of a management company to run the school under a five-year management contract. The parent management company's president signed the contract, which assigned claims to the management company to collect fees owed to the subsidiary. Relations strained between the school operators, the management company and the subsidiary, and the contract was ended after only one year. The company sued for breach of contract, and a state court awarded it a directed verdict of $250,899 and attorneys' fees.

On appeal, the Court of Appeals of Texas affirmed the part of the judgment regarding breach of contract damages for management fees owed to the subsidiary. The court then considered a claim regarding unlawful "advances" by the parent company to the school. **State law prohibited the governing body of an open-enrollment charter school from accepting a loan from a management company under contract to manage a charter school.** By law, the "advances" were prohibited loans, voiding the contract. Even if that contract was valid, the parent company could not show a contract existed without proving its own illegal conduct. For this reason, the lower court should have granted the school operators a directed verdict on that claim. *Academy of Skills & Knowledge v. Charter Schools, USA*, 260 S.W.3d 529 (Tex. Ct. App. 2008).

◆ Baltimore's school board rejected applications for funding by three different charter schools. Appeals came before the state board of education (SBE), and then the Maryland Court of Appeals. The court found the SBE's calculation of an "average cost" included students who would receive Title I or special education funds or services. This would in turn require the charter schools to adjust their budgets. The SBE acted within its discretion by deciding the cases. Allowing local boards to decide "what funding is commensurate with the amounts disbursed to the other public schools" risked disparate local methods of implementing a uniform law and undercut the SBE's authority to interpret education law. The legislature must have envisioned that the SBE would have primary authority to interpret the law. **The law's "commensurate funding" language necessarily had a per-student basis, and there was no error in the SBE's use of an average per-student approach.** As a result, the SBE decisions were upheld. *Baltimore City Board of School Commissioners v. City Neighbors Charter School*, 400 Md. 324, 929 A.2d 113 (Md. 2007).

◆ A Texas corporation operated three "distance learning" charter schools in California. Families of students enrolled in the schools claimed the schools did not provide computers, instruction, assessment, review, curriculum, equipment, supplies or services, but collected over $20 million in state funding. The families asserted that the corporation aggressively recruited poor rural districts to approve charter schools. The districts then intentionally failed to perform their oversight duties. The families sued the corporation and chartering districts for breach of contract, misrepresentation, constitutional violations and misuse of taxpayer funds. They added a claim under the California False Claims Act (CFCA) for submission of fraudulent claims and an Unfair Competition Law (UCL) claim for unfair and deceptive business practices. A state court dismissed the CFCA, UCL and breach of contract claims as unrecognizable private claims for "educational malfeasance." The Supreme Court of California reversed. **Charter school operators were "persons" who could be held liable under the CFCA.** And UCL purposes were served by subjecting the school operators to deceptive business practices claims. The case was returned to a lower court for further proceedings. *Wells v. One2One Learning Foundation*, 39 Cal.4th 1164, 48 Cal.Rptr.3d 108, 141 P.2d 225 (Cal. 2006).

◆ The Individuals with Disabilities with Education Act (IDEA) and the Elementary and Secondary Education Act (ESEA) authorize state recipients of federal funds to distribute grant money to local educational agencies (LEAs). Public charter schools are within the definition of an LEA under both laws. A U.S. Department of Education audit of the Arizona Department of Education (ADE) concluded the ADE had improperly awarded ESEA and IDEA funds to for-profit entities that operated charter schools in the state. The Arizona State Board for Charter Schools and several for-profit charter school operators petitioned for review. A federal court held that the statutes expressed a congressional mandate that in order to receive federal funds, charter schools must be nonprofit. The state board and the schools appealed. The Ninth Circuit affirmed. **Only nonprofit institutional day or residential schools are eligible for federal funding under the ESEA and IDEA.** Congress clearly intended to "prohibit the funding of for-profit schools, charter or otherwise." *Arizona State Board for Charter Schools v. U.S. Dep't of Educ.*, 464 F.3d 1003 (9th Cir. 2006).

◆ A California charter school submitted a facilities request to a school district to serve 223 students in grades K-8. The district rejected the school's request to use a single site that was being used primarily for nonacademic purposes. The district's "final facilities offer" to the school included 9.5 classrooms at five different school sites a total of 65 miles apart. The school sued the district, asserting violation of the state Charter Schools Act. The Court of Appeal of California explained that the **Education Code required districts to allow charter schools to use any facility not currently used by a district**. Charter school facilities had to be "contiguous," and state education department regulations required districts to minimize the number of sites and consider student safety. A charter school should be housed at a single site, if one with sufficient capacity exists. The district had to provide the school with facilities that were both reasonably equivalent and contiguous. Providing five sites did not balance the needs of the charter school and district-run schools. The district's decision was reversed and remanded for an order requiring a new final offer of facilities. *Ridgecrest Charter School v. Sierra Sands Unified School Dist.*, 130 Cal.App.4th 986, 30 Cal.Rptr.3d 648 (Cal. Ct. App. 2005).

◆ The Court of Appeal of California held that state Education Code § 47614 required school districts to make facilities sufficient for a charter school to accommodate all the school's in-district students in a manner similar to other district schools. Charter schools had to provide districts with a reasonable projection of average daily classroom attendance of their in-district students. Section 47614 allowed districts to deny facilities requests for projections of less than 80 students for a year. **Section 47614 did not require charter schools to "demonstrate arithmetical precision" in their projections.** A charter school had to submit reasonable projections for in-district students to the school district by October 1 of the preceding fiscal year. In this case, a charter school had given an incomplete response to a school district's request for information such as student names, dates of birth, grade levels, home addresses and parent names. As a result, there was a rational reason for the district to deny the school's facilities request based on safety concerns. *Environmental Charter High School v. Centinela Valley Union High School Dist.*, 122 Cal.App. 4th 139, 18 Cal.Rptr.3d 417 (Cal. Ct. App. 2004).

II. CURRICULUM AND GRADING

Overview

Educators have considerable discretion in academic, curricular and grading matters. Courts do not subject official decisions in these areas to close judicial scrutiny. For religious challenges to curriculums, please see Chapter Two. Constitutional challenges on secular grounds appear in Chapter Three. Testing is considered in Section IV of this chapter. For cases involving students with disabilities, see Chapter Seven.

A. Curriculum

Teacher Scenarios

Mom accuses teacher of 'cutting' PE time.........266

Court Decisions

◆ A Washington fourth-grade student was part of his school district's highly capable program. At his parents' request, he was allowed to skip to grade six the next school year. In the next three years, the student completed grades six, seven and eight. His father then objected to a proposal to promote him to grade nine and suggested that he enroll in one eighth-grade class. He asked the school district to designate his son a ninth-grader for academic purposes, and an eighth-grader for athletic and estimated graduation date purposes. After the district denied the father's request, he sued the district in a state court. The court held for the school district, and appeal reached the Court of Appeals of Washington.

On appeal, the father stated the athletic issue had been resolved. His only concern was his son's academics and his wish for a 2013 graduation date. The court found the question was not "ripe" and thus inappropriate for a court order. Under the state constitution, the student had a right to be "amply provided with an education" through a general and uniform system of public schools. While state public schools were open to qualified individuals between ages five and 21, the court found this did not translate into a constitutional right to remain in the public school system until age 18 via grade retention. Graduation depended upon completion of required credits, and many events could affect a district's decision to graduate a student. **School boards were vested with the final responsibility for creating policies to ensure the quality of educational programs and providing student opportunities.** Promotion of the student to grade nine and assigning him an estimated graduation date of 2012 did not violate any constitutional rights. *McColl v. Sequim School Dist.*, 152 Wash.App. 1066 (Wash. Ct. App. 2009).

◆ A Kentucky school offered six weighted classes that were graded on a five-point scale rather than a four-point scale to reflect their difficulty. A student whose goal was to be class valedictorian took all six weighted offerings to improve her chances. Near the end of her senior year, she learned that she did not receive weighted credit for a course she had already completed called "Dual Credit History." A school policy limited the receipt of weighted credit to only five courses. Weighted credit could be obtained for either Political Science or Dual Credit History, but not both. The student argued that she should receive weighted credit for both courses, and she sued the school board, its members and other school officials in a state court. She claimed that the code of conduct created a contract with her, which the board had breached. She also asserted that she was given different advice than that given to other students and that she had been subjected to humiliation, embarrassment and ridicule. She said her lower class standing resulted in lost scholarships and caused emotional distress. The family sought a ruling that would retroactively declare the student valedictorian.

After a hearing, the court dismissed the case, and the family appealed to the Court of Appeals of Kentucky. It held that the lower court had based the judgment on an adequate record. **The interpretation of a written document was a matter of law for a court to decide, not for jurors to resolve.** The trial court had correctly interpreted a disputed phrase in the policy. As the lower court had properly dismissed the case, the judgment for the board was affirmed. *Carnes v. Russell County Board of Educ.*, No. 2007-CA-000273-MR, 2008 WL 4530887 (Ky. Ct. App. 9/17/08), review denied, 6/17/09).

◆ A Connecticut parent challenged the use of "the Responsive Classroom" model by a school her children had attended many years earlier. The Responsive Classroom model was designed to improve cooperation and communication among students and faculty. It involved meetings where students discussed concerns and teachers mediated arguments. The parent claimed the paradigm "encouraged, created and tolerated an atmosphere of chaos, disruptiveness and violence" at the school, interrupted the structure necessary for learning, and increased student tensions and confrontations. She waited until years after her children had left the school to sue school officials, and did not claim any actual violence against her children, but claimed they witnessed bullying of other students. The court found no evidence that others victimized any children, and no evidence of a "culture of violence or chaos," as the parent alleged. Teachers and other staff "described only the usual sorts of school-based problems with none of the dramatic upheaval" she alleged. **The principal had handled disciplinary problems and tried to foster an atmosphere of communication and cooperation.** Students suffered no emotional damage, and there was no extreme or outrageous conduct by school officials. Most of what the parent related in her testimony concerned her own emotional state, and not that of her children. She did not prove any part of her emotional distress claim against the school board and principal. *Bell v. West Haven Board of Educ.*, No. NNH-CV-970399597, 2005 WL 1971264 (Conn. Super. Ct. 2005).

◆ A Texas student was in first place in a race for school valedictorian. She claimed the school principal intentionally scheduled a Spanish III class at an inconvenient time for her that was calculated to assist a classmate's effort to become valedictorian. The student's parents demanded that Spanish III be deleted from the curriculum. When the principal refused, the parents were granted a hearing to discuss removing Spanish III from the curriculum, but they were not allowed to cross-examine witnesses or discuss additional grievances. The parents sued the board for constitutional rights violations. A federal court held that the parents were not entitled to cross-examine witnesses or discuss prior inconsistent decisions by the school administration. The student had no constitutionally protected interest to attend a course of her choosing at a particular time. **Although education is of "unquestioned importance," it has not been recognized as a fundamental right under either the U.S. or Texas Constitution.** The student had no protected property interest in becoming class valedictorian. The property interest recognized in education cases such as *Goss v. Lopez*, 419 U.S. 565 (1975), is the right to participate in the overall educational process, not in a particular course or individual component of the process. The court ruled for the board. *Jeffrey v. Board of Trustees of Bells Independent School Dist.*, 261 F.Supp.2d 719 (E.D. Tex. 2003).

B. Bilingual Education

In Lau v. Nichols, *414 U.S. 563 (1974), the U.S. Supreme Court held non-English-speaking students in San Francisco schools could claim protection under Title VI of the Civil Rights Act of 1964. Non-English speakers cannot be denied meaningful opportunities to participate in educational programs.*

Court Decisions

◆ As a result of claims by African-American students against nine Texas school districts in 1971, broad aspects of the Texas educational system were placed under federal court supervision. Mexican-American students intervened in the case in 1972, and the nine districts were required to provide them equal educational opportunities. The Texas Education Agency was ordered to study the needs of all minority students in the state. In 1981, the court ordered state officials to offer bilingual instruction to limited-English proficient students, based on "*de jure* discrimination" and violation of the Equal Educational Opportunities Act (EEOA). The U.S. Court of Appeals, Fifth Circuit, reversed the judgment in 1982, expressing concern that no school districts were parties.

In 2006, the Mexican-American intervenors reopened the case, and the court found violations of both the 1971 order and the EEOA. It ordered the state to create a new monitoring system and language programming to fulfill EEOA requirements. State officials appealed to the Fifth Circuit, which found a new monitoring system and secondary LEP language program for all the districts would require an extraordinary effort in a very short time. To prove a violation of the 1971 order, the intervenors would have to show the action flowed from a *de jure* segregated system. This was not shown, as **Texas at no time separated Anglo and Mexican-Americans by law**. Because *de jure* segregation of Mexican-American students was not shown, the 1971 order could not be enforced by the intervenors. As for an EEOA violation, the lower court had failed to address the instructions issued in 1982. At that time, the Fifth Circuit found little reason to resolve the case on a statewide basis. **Problems varied by district and would by necessity present local questions for each individual district.** Since the issues raised by the intervenors could not have been properly addressed in the absence of the individual school districts, the court returned the case to the district court. *U.S. v. State of Texas*, 601 F.3d 354 (5th Cir. 2010).

◆ Nine California school districts challenged a state board policy requiring English language testing of limited-English-proficient (LEP) students on state tests. According to the districts, English language testing of LEP students was not "valid and reliable" as required by the No Child Left Behind (NCLB) Act, and they faced sanctions for failing to meet adequate yearly progress. The Court of Appeal of California noted that **the NCLB Act did not require native language testing of LEP students**. Students had to be provided reasonable accommodations on assessments. To the extent practicable, assessments were to be "in the language and form most likely to yield accurate data on what such students know and can do in academic concern areas, until such students have achieved English language proficiency." In 1998, California voters had enacted Proposition 227 to require English instruction of public school students with very limited exceptions to promote the rapid development of English for LEP students. The NCLB Act "invites each state to make its own judgment call in fashioning a testing program for its LEP students" consistent with NCLB Act requirements. State board decisions were entitled to deference, and the board had engaged in a deliberative policymaking process to determine how LEP students would be tested. *Coachella Valley Unified School Dist. v. State of California*, 176 Cal.App.4th 93, 98 Cal.Rptr.3d 9 (Cal. Ct. App. 2009).

◆ After California enacted Proposition 227, LEP students brought a federal court action against state officials, asserting Proposition 227 violated the Equal Protection Clause. The court found no constitutional violation. On appeal, **the Ninth Circuit found nothing in the record indicating that Proposition 227 was race-motivated**. The state's bilingual education system did not operate to remedy identified patterns of racial discrimination but was instead intended to improve the educational system. The reallocation of political authority represented by Proposition 227 addressed educational, not racial issues, and the fact that most of California's LEP student population was Latino did not create a viable equal protection claim. The court affirmed the judgment. *Valeria v. Davis*, 307 F.3d 1036 (9th Cir. 2002).

◆ New Mexico enacted the Bilingual Multicultural Education Act (BMEA) to ensure equal educational opportunities for students by making local school districts eligible for bilingual instruction. To qualify for the program, districts had to provide for the educational needs of linguistically and culturally different students, including Native American students. The Albuquerque Public School District operated the Alternative Language Services (ALS) program pursuant to the BMEA, providing bilingual education for limited-English-proficient students. The U.S. Department of Education's Office for Civil Rights, which oversees Title VI compliance, reviewed the ALS program and entered into an agreement for corrective action with the district. The agreement established new procedures for identifying and serving limited-English-proficient students.

A group of Albuquerque students in the ALS program sued the district in a federal court, asserting the BMEA and ALS program were discriminatory, since they classified and placed students on the basis of race or national origin. The case reached the U.S. Court of Appeals, Tenth Circuit. It held **the BMEA did not violate the Equal Protection Clause or Title VI**. There was no evidence that the district violated the agreement with the Office for Civil Rights by forcing students to participate in the ALS program without notice or consent. The ALS program and the BMEA did not violate the federal Equal Education Opportunity Act's mandate to take appropriate action to overcome language barriers that impede equal participation by its students. *Carbajal v. Albuquerque Public School Dist.*, 43 Fed.Appx. 306 (10th Cir. 2002).

C. Grading

In Regents of Univ. of Michigan v. Ewing, *474 U.S. 214 (1985), the Supreme Court held courts may not override academic decisions unless there is "such a substantial departure from accepted academic norms as to demonstrate that the person or committee responsible did not actually exercise professional judgment." An Ohio school did not have to change a student's grades even though the teachers who assigned them deviated from a school policy.*

Teacher Scenarios

'I deserve a better grade for
my work' 266

Court Decisions

◆ An Ohio student just missed A grades in two advanced placement classes. She said her calculus teacher improperly averaged grades and claimed her writing teacher incorrectly weighted grades. This violated a general school board policy requiring that full-year grades be weighted and semester grades be averaged. After the teachers declined to change the grades, the student and her father met with the principal and later with the school superintendent, school board and counsel. The board heard the teachers' explanations for assigning the grades and then approved the grades. The state education department denied the student relief, and she filed a state court complaint. Before the court, the calculus teacher said he had used his grading method for years and had told the principal when he began to use it. The writing teacher also stated that she had obtained approval for her grading policy and had been using it for about 10 years.

A judgment was issued for the school district, and the student appealed. The Court of Appeals of Ohio held that to obtain relief, the student had to establish a "clear legal right." But she only cited state laws and rules requiring schools to keep records and issue diplomas. Under either version of the grading guidelines, **the court found teachers had discretion to create alternative grading systems and report them to the principal**. The board had followed its policies by discussing the matter with the family, and the principal and superintendent reviewed the case. Both teachers used the same grading method for all their students and did not treat the student differently from others. As she did not show her grades were unfair or arbitrary, her request for a court order had been properly dismissed. *Hingel v. Board of Educ. of Austintown Local School Dist.*, No. 08 MA 258, 2009 WL 4547721 (Ohio Ct. App. 11/23/09).

◆ An Arkansas middle school student participated in his school's accelerated reader program, in which students could win prizes or awards by reading books and taking tests based on them. He stated that he read four of five books in the *Harry Potter* series because of the high points assigned to the books. After the student scored 100% on each of the tests, his reading teacher accused him of cheating, stating it was impossible to read the books in one week. The student's classroom teacher agreed and confronted him about cheating. The student's mother sought reinstatement of the scores. The school principal permitted only one score to be reinstated, finding no obligation to reinstate the others under program incentive rules. The student sought a court order requiring the principal and teachers to reinstate the cancelled scores, apologize publicly and by letter, and prevent them from "further humiliating and using coercive tactics."

The court dismissed the case and awarded the school district $1,500 in attorneys' fees. The student appealed to the state supreme court, which held that **no law compelled school officials to reinstate scores in voluntary reading programs**. The court found "a general policy against intervention by the courts in matters best left to school authorities." Reinstatement of test scores was left to the discretion of school officials. As the student had no legal remedy available, the court affirmed the judgment, including the award of attorneys' fees. *T.J. v. Hargrove*, 362 Ark. 649, 210 S.W.3d 79 (Ark. 2005).

◆ A Michigan student ranked first in his class at the end of his junior year. He maintained dual enrollment in his high school during his senior year but took no classes there. The student worked as a paralegal in his mother's law office for an employer-based course taken through a county intermediate district. Although an "A" was the highest possible grade under the intermediate district policy, the student's high school district allowed A+ grades. The student's mother awarded him an A+ for the employer-based course, but his report card indicated an A. The high school district refused the mother's request to change the grade, and the student sued for due process violations. A state court held for the district. Before the state court of appeals, the student argued that a high school district policy allowing grades to be weighted or adjusted did not apply to intermediate district courses. The court stated that **a district's board of education had authority to implement a grading system under Michigan law**. The paralegal training course was administered by the intermediate school district, not the high school, so the highest possible grade was an A. The high school district's policy prevented weighting or adjustment of the grade. Since the student had no vested property interest in an A+ and no legal right to a particular grade, the court affirmed the judgment. *Delekta v.*

Memphis Community Schools, No. 249325, 2004 WL 2290462 (Mich. Ct. App. 2004).

◆ **An Ohio school district did not violate a student's rights by suspending her for excessive tardiness** under an attendance policy that assigned students failing grades for poor attendance. An Ohio appeals court upheld the policy as a constitutional means of promoting good attendance. According to the appeals court, under state law, school policies are generally left to the discretion of the school board. The board policy in this case promoted attendance for academic performance and provided sanctions for excessive unexcused absences. It distinguished between excused and unexcused absences and was neither unreasonable nor unconstitutional. *Smith v. Revere Local School Dist. Board of Educ.*, No. 20275, 2001 WL 489980 (Ohio Ct. App. 2001).

◆ A California middle school music teacher assigned three students conduct grades of "needs improvement" or "unsatisfactory." Parents complained about the poor conduct grades, which made the students ineligible for honor society and field trips. The principal then changed the grades to "satisfactory" without consulting the teacher. The teacher filed a grievance that was denied at all three levels, culminating with the school board. The teacher and his collective bargaining association sued the district and principal in the state court system. The California Court of Appeal noted that the state Education Code provides that **a grade assigned by a classroom teacher is final and can be changed only in limited circumstances such as clerical or mechanical mistake**, or where the assignment is characterized by bad faith or incompetency. The court rejected the district's argument that the code section did not apply to citizenship grades. Citizenship grades reflected a teacher's assessment of student performance for cooperation, attitude and effort, and there was no reason to believe the legislature meant to distinguish them from academic marks. Even if citizenship marks were not considered grades, the district had exceeded its authority in changing them. *Las Virgenes Educators Ass'n v. Las Virgenes Unified School Dist.*, 102 Cal.Rptr.2d 901 (Cal. Ct. App. 2000).

III. STUDENT RECORDS

Overview

Parents and eligible students have rights to access education records and protect their records from access by unauthorized persons under the Family Educational Rights and Privacy Act of 1974 (FERPA), 20 U.S.C. § 1232g. In Gonzaga Univ. v. Doe, 536 U.S. 273 (2002), this chapter, the U.S. Supreme Court held FERPA does not authorize private lawsuits. Analogous state laws protect student records and may create greater rights than under FERPA.

FERPA applies only to "education records," which are records "directly related to a student" and "maintained by an educational agency or institution or by a party acting for the agency or institution." Records that originate from a school, or are created by nonschool entities, may become education records if they are "maintained" by a school. Notes used only as a personal memory aid and kept in the sole possession of the maker are outside FERPA's coverage.

Federal regulations interpreting FERPA state when personally identifiable information may be disclosed without consent by a parent or eligible student. "Personal identifiers" may indirectly identify a student, and include date and place of birth, mother's maiden name, or "information that, alone or in combination," may allow identification by a reasonable person in the school community. A FERPA regulation at 34 C.F.R. Part 99.31(a)(1) requires **educational institutions to "use reasonable methods to ensure that school officials obtain access to only those education records in which they have legitimate educational interests."** *The regulation permits educational agencies to disclose education records without consent to another institution, even after a student has enrolled or transferred, for reasons related to enrollment or transfer.*

Under 34 C.F.R. Part 99.36 personally identifiable information from an education record may be disclosed to parents and other appropriate parties in connection with "health and safety emergencies." *A student's social security number or student identification number is personally identifiable information that may not be disclosed as directory information under 34 C.F.R. Part 99.3.*

The Health Insurance Portability and Accountability Act (HIPAA) was enacted to ensure continued health insurance for persons changing jobs, and to address the problem of health information confidentiality. Under federal regulations, records covered by FERPA are exempt from HIPAA. However, since schools typically provide services deemed to be within HIPAA definitions, schools may be considered "covered entities" under HIPAA in some situations.

Several federal court decisions have held HIPAA does not create a private right of action for individuals to bring lawsuits. These include Dominic J. v. Wyoming Valley West High School, *362 F.Supp.2d 560 (M.D. Pa. 2005),* Runkle v. Gonzales, *391 F.Supp.2d 210 (D.D.C. 2005), and* Swift v. Lake Park High School Dist. 108, *No. 03 C 5003, 2003 WL 22388878 (N.D. Ill. 2003).*

A. Student and Parental Rights

An Iowa school superintendent did not violate state law by discussing with school board members and staff a report by a parent about her daughter's involvement with a teacher, as the community already knew of the relationship.

Teacher Scenarios

Did teacher properly discard the student's
confidential paperwork? 267

Court Decisions

◆ A 21-year-old Iowa teaching assistant and coach exchanged text messages with a ninth-grader. The two had sexual contact, and the student told a friend. When her mother learned about the relationship, she met with the district superintendent. During their meeting, he took a full page of notes, which were later shown to a school attorney. The coach was placed on administrative leave and reported to the police, and a criminal investigation was begun. The mother claimed the superintendent identified the student in discussions with the school board, administrators and staff and that a board member spoke publicly about the incident. A lawsuit was filed against the school district for privacy rights violations. A state court held the superintendent's notes were not a "confidential public record" under Iowa Code Section 22.7. There was no violation of a state administrative rule on child abuse investigation procedures, and the school district was entitled to judgment. Appeal reached the Court of Appeals of Iowa.

The court explained that Iowa Code Chapter 22 establishes a right of access to governmental records and requires that certain categories of government records be kept confidential. Since the superintendent's notes were made as part of his official duties, they were school records. But the court noted he relied on his memory when speaking with the board and staff, not his notes. It held **Section 22.7 "is not a general privacy law that prohibits public officials from discussing information that is neither a record itself nor derived from a record."** Section 22.7(18) of the state code did not give the mother a cause of action. Her verbal report was not filed with a designated investigator. There was no merit to the claim that a state administrative provision governing child abuse reports by school employees was violated. As a result, the court affirmed the judgment for the school district. *V.II. v. Hampton-Dumont Community School Dist.*, No. 09-0364, 2009 WL 5126111 (Iowa Ct. App. 12/30/09).

◆ A divorced New Hampshire mother did not have physical custody of her child. In addition to claiming lack of appropriate notice when her son missed school, she claimed an individualized education program (IEP) team member violated her rights by exchanging confidential medical information with her son's physician against her wishes. In a federal district court action, the mother asserted due process violations. The court reviewed evidence that the child's father had primary residential responsibility for the child. A family court order directed the school to call both parents in an emergency. The mother had refused to sign a release for her son's medical records and told IEP team members not to contact medical providers. But the father had signed a release that would allow a physician to exchange medical records with the school.

The father had physical custody of the child through legal proceedings that provided full due process to the mother. **There was no constitutional right to notification from the school whenever the child was released to his father.** The mother did not claim interference with her custody rights or a transfer of custody of sufficient magnitude to trigger constitutional concerns. Even if such rights existed, the court held school officials would have immunity based on the absence of any clearly established law supporting the claims. There was no merit to a claim against the father. The court dismissed the case. *Vendouri v. Gaylord*, Civil No. 10-cv-277-SM, 2010 WL 3417921 (D.N.H. 8/27/10).

◆ An Illinois student's parent requested all test questions from honors biology exams. He was offered an opportunity to examine test booklets at school or at home and to hand-copy test questions, so long as they were returned the next day and no photo-copies were made. The parent sued the school district in the state court system, seeking a declaration that the booklet was a "student record" under the state School Records Act. A trial court held that the booklets did not come under the Act, as they were devoid of any student marks or other identifying information. The Appellate Court of Illinois affirmed the decision.

While the case was pending, the parent requested copies of his daughter's algebra exams. The district provided him the parts of exam booklets with the student's answers and calculations, but it blocked the test questions. The parent filed a new action. This time, the appellate court noted the student had written her name, and wrote answers and calculations on the test booklets. **As they contained student markings and other identifying information, the booklets were "student records."** The marked-on algebra test booklets were covered by the Act, so the parent had a right to inspect and copy them. Unlike federal law, the state act allowed parents to "copy" student records, not just "inspect and review" them. *Garlick v. Oak Park and River Forest High School Dist. #200*, 389 Ill.App.3d 306, 905 N.E.2d 930 (Ill. App. Ct. 2009).

◆ Texas school officials claimed that a couple made 2,274 record requests, representing 120,000 pages of documents and 551 open records determinations by the state attorney general's office. The district asserted that the couple's behavior was disruptive and harassing, and claimed it placed a "crippling burden on its office and personnel resources." The couple allegedly made duplicative requests for information, and 162 separate requests for information were "cancelled" after a great deal of time and effort had been spent responding to them. The school district sued the couple for public nuisance and abuse of governmental process under the Texas Public Information Act (PIA). Asserting the cost of prior records requests was $700,000, district officials sought to limit future record requests through a state court-ordered procedure.

The court held that it had no authority to hear the case because the PIA does not create a cause of action for enforcement by the courts. The Court of Appeals of Texas held that **the PIA prohibited a public agency such as a school district from suing a record requestor in a state court**. The only action authorized by the PIA for a governmental body or officer involving public information was an action brought to challenge a decision by the state attorney general's office. In order to bring a proper PIA suit, the school district had to first obtain an attorney general opinion as to whether the disclosures were required. The court rejected the district's argument that there should be an exception in this case because of the extreme burden placed on it by the couple's multiple records requests. The court affirmed the judgment. *Lake Travis Independent School Dist. v. Lovelace*, 243 S.W.3d 244 (Tex. Ct. App. 2007).

◆ A New York school district superintendent told staff members they had a duty to inform parents about student pregnancies. He said a student's disclosure of pregnancy to staff members was unprotected by any privilege and might trigger legal reporting obligations. Staff members who learned of a student's pregnancy "should immediately" report it to a school social worker, who should then "encourage" the student to disclose a pregnancy to her parents. If a student would not inform her parents, the memorandum stated that a social worker "should offer to meet with the parents and the student to help the student inform her parents" and/or offer to inform the student's parents in the student's absence. If a student continued refusing these prompts, the social worker "should inform the student that she/he will inform the parents." The district teachers' association sued the school board and superintendent on behalf of students. A federal court held the association lacked standing to file the action.

On appeal, the U.S. Court of Appeals, Second Circuit, held **the association did not establish any risk of civil liability or professional discipline**. The superintendent stated that he would not discipline staff members for their actions with respect to parental pregnancy notification. The memorandum was non-mandatory, and the court affirmed the judgment for the school board. *Port Washington Teachers' Ass'n v. Board of Educ. of Port Washington Union Free School Dist.*, 478 F.3d 494 (2d Cir. 2007).

◆ An Oklahoma student told his parents and a middle school counselor that he had sex with a high school student who was known to be HIV-positive. Soon, about half his eighth-grade class learned of this. The middle school counselor contacted the principal and the student's father. The student soon noticed graffiti at school stating that he had AIDS, and other students asked him about it. He came to the school principal's office and asked to use the phone "to call his attorney." The principal refused, stating that he could phone his parents. The student's mother then came to school. She said the principal did not cooperate and refused to address incidents of bullying and graffiti. The student did not return to school, but he passed his classes through a home-based program.

The parents sued the school district in a federal court for sexual harassment and other claims. The court held for the school district, finding the student was not targeted for abuse because of his gender. The district did not exclude him from school, as the home-based program was his mother's idea. While unpleasant, the graffiti and rumors were not so unbearable as to deprive the student of a quality public education. The family did not assert valid claims for defamation and negligence. **The complaint only asserted a possibility that school personnel could have spread the rumor of HIV positive status.** *Dawson v. The Grove Public School Dist.*, No. 06-CV-555-TCK FHM, 2007 WL 2874831 (N.D. Okla. 9/27/07).

◆ A Minnesota student told his mother other students had papers about him and were calling him names. She recognized the papers as copies of a report used to determine special education eligibility. The wind had blown the papers out of an open garbage bag at school and students found the report in a parking lot. The mother sued the school district for violating the Minnesota Government Data Practices Act (MGDPA). A jury found the district violated the MGDPA and awarded the student $60,000 in damages for pain, embarrassment and emotional distress, and $80,000 in future damages. On appeal, **the Court of Appeals of Minnesota held that the MGDPA required each school district to establish appropriate security safeguards for all records containing data on individuals**. Evidence indicated that the district did not establish appropriate safeguards. District manuals had no procedures for destroying documents, and employees were not properly trained. There was evidence that the incident would have a devastating effect on the student for a lifetime, and the court affirmed the judgment. *Scott v. Minneapolis Public Schools, Special Dist. No. 1*, No. A05-649, 2006 WL 997721 (Minn. Ct. App. 2006).

◆ New Jersey social service agencies assembled a community group to assess local youth needs. The town education board agreed to survey its students for the community group to understand youth needs, attitudes and behavior, and to better use town programs and resources. The survey sought information about drug and alcohol use, sexual activity, violence, suicide, racial attitudes and parent-child relationships. Some parents expressed concern that explicit questions about drug and alcohol use, sexual activity and suicide suggested "such activity was within normal adolescent experience." Objecting students and parents sued the board and school officials for violations of the FERPA and the U.S. Constitution. Appeal reached the Third Circuit, which found that all students in the district participated in the survey, indicating involuntariness. Parents were not told how they could avoid their child's participation. But the survey protected anonymity. **The constitutional right to prevent disclosure of intimate facts is not absolute, and is balanced against the public interest in health and safety.** Privacy rights did not extend to this survey, as disclosure of personal information occurred in the aggregate and personal data was safeguarded. *C.N. v. Ridgewood Board of Educ.*, 430 F.3d 159 (3d Cir. 2005).

◆ A Pennsylvania school district did not violate the state Right to Know Act by denying a citizen's request for copies of letters to and from the district superintendent. The Commonwealth Court of Pennsylvania held that the letters were not "public records" under the act. Also, **public agencies may charge a reasonable fee when copying public records**. The 25 cents per copy charged by the school district in this case was reasonable. *Weiss v. Williamsport Area School Dist.*, 872 A.2d 269 (Pa. Commw. Ct. 2005).

♦ A Florida superintendent made an 8,000-page investigation report on a school principal accused of misconduct. It referenced other faculty members and included confidential student information. The superintendent notified the principal and other faculty members that they could receive copies of the report with student information blocked to prevent disclosure of identifying material. Faculty members sued the superintendent to require the district to release the report with no restrictions. A state court directed the board to provide the faculty members the report with all student identifying information blocked. The faculty members appealed to the Florida Court of Appeal, arguing they were unable to respond to the report. The court held that **all student identifying information should be concealed in the report**. State law made all personally identifiable student records and reports confidential and exempt from disclosure. As rights of faculty members to respond to the report did not "trump" the right of students to keep the information confidential, the court reversed the judgment. *Johnson v. Deluz*, 875 So.2d 1 (Fla. Dist. Ct. App. 2004).

♦ A Washington private school student intended to teach in the state's public school system after his graduation. At the time, the state required new teachers to obtain an affidavit of good moral character from the dean of their college or university. When the university's teacher certification specialist overheard a conversation implicating the student in sexual misconduct with a classmate, she commenced an investigation of the student and reported the allegations against him to the state teacher certification agency. She later informed the student that the university would not provide him with the affidavit of good moral character he needed for certification as a Washington teacher. The student sued the university and the specialist under state law and 42 U.S.C. § 1983 for violating FERPA. A jury awarded him over $1 million in damages. The case reached the U.S. Supreme Court, which held that **FERPA creates no personal rights that can be enforced in a court under Section 1983**. Congress enacted FERPA to force schools to respect students' privacy with respect to education records. It did not confer enforceable rights upon students. The Court reversed and remanded the case to a state court for further proceedings. *Gonzaga Univ. v. Doe*, 536 U.S. 273, 122 S.Ct. 2268, 153 L.Ed.2d 309 (2002).

♦ An Oklahoma parent learned that teachers asked students to grade each other's assignments and then call out the results in class. She asserted that the policy was embarrassing to her children and sued the school district and school administrators for violations of FERPA and the Due Process Clause. A federal district court held the policy did not violate any constitutional privacy rights and that the practice of calling out grades did not involve "education records" within the meaning of FERPA. A federal appeals court reversed the judgment.

The U.S. Supreme Court accepted the district's petition to review the case. It observed that an "education record" under FERPA is one that is "maintained by an educational agency or institution or by a person acting for such agency or institution." According to the court, student papers are not "maintained" within the meaning of FERPA when students correct them or call out grades. **The word "maintain" suggested that FERPA records were kept in files or cabinets in a "records room at the school or on a permanent secure database."** The momentary handling of assignments by students did not conform to this definition. The appeals court committed error by deciding that a student acted for an educational institution under FERPA when assisting with grading. Because Congress did not intend to intervene in drastic fashion with traditional state functions by exercising minute control over teaching methods, the Court reversed and remanded the case. *Owasso Independent School Dist. No. I-011 v. Falvo*, 534 U.S. 426, 122 S.Ct. 934, 151 L.Ed.2d 896 (2002).

♦ A Massachusetts student disrupted his special education classroom and directed racial slurs at his teacher. He was suspected of writing racial graffiti on the blackboard in her room and in hallways. The graffiti was photographed and police were provided samples of the student's schoolwork to help determine whether it matched the graffiti. Massachusetts prosecuted the student for malicious destruction of property and violation of civil rights. A trial court held the handwriting samples had been obtained in violation of a state law requiring student or parental consent prior to the release of a "student record." But the Supreme Judicial Court of Massachusetts **rejected the student's argument that his handwriting samples were "student records"** within the meaning of state law. Homework, tests and other assignments were not a part of a student's transcript and were not typically "kept" by schools. The school had a clear obligation to use the student's papers only for educational purposes, but it also had an obligation to prevent racial harassment and property damage. *Comwlth. of Massachusetts v. Buccella*, 434 Mass. 473, 751 N.E.2d 373 (Mass. 2001).

B. Media Requests

FERPA's general definition of "education records" is: "those records, files, documents and other materials which – (i) contain information directly related to a student; and (ii) are maintained by an educational agency or institution or by a person acting for such agency or institution." This includes personally identifiable information that may reveal a student's identity. **Courts have held that records pertaining to a single student meet these criteria, but statistical compilations do not.** *Thus, compiled student disciplinary hearing information could be released to the media under FERPA and the state Open Records Act in* Hardin County Schools v. Foster, *40 S.W.3d 865 (Ky. 2001).*

Court Decisions

♦ A Washington student with a severe peanut allergy died on a school field trip after he ate a school lunch with peanut products. The district superintendent revealed that the district had provided the peanut products despite knowing of his severe allergy. The district and family entered into mediation and the family accepted $960,000 in return for a release of all claims. The parties made a joint press release and agreed that the district and staff would decline to comment to the press about the case. The district denied a newspaper publisher's request for 75 documents, including its investigation report, the settlement agreement and investigation notes by the investigator and school attorneys.

The school district, family and student's estate sought a state court order exempting the records from public disclosure. The case reached the Supreme Court of Washington, which held **the Washington Public Records Act requires agencies to make public records available for public inspection and copying, unless an exemption applies**. The documents sought were classified as "work product," prepared in anticipation of the lawsuit and were exempt from disclosure. Teachers and a volunteer nurse chaperone were "clients whose communications with the attorneys were privileged." Even if the documents were not protected from disclosure as "work product," they were protected by the attorney-client privilege. *Soter v. Cowles Publishing Co.*, 174 P.3d 69 (Wash. 2007).

◆ Montana students were disciplined for shooting others on school property with plastic BBs. The school board held a closed hearing to consider their discipline. The board opened the session after deciding on the discipline, then returned to closed session to take the action it discussed. A newspaper publisher noted that the board's previous practice had been to publicly reveal the nature of the student discipline while referencing students with an anonymous number. After the district superintendent refused a further request for information about the discipline, the publisher sued the school district in the state court system.

Appeal reached the Supreme Court of Montana, which found "student records" included student names and addresses, birth days, achievement levels and immunization records. Each school board must maintain a record of any discipline that is educationally related. **Courts in Ohio, Missouri and Georgia have held that disciplinary records are not "education records" as defined by FERPA.** Courts in Indiana and Wisconsin have held that once the names of students are blocked out, they are no longer "education records." The court decided that FERPA did not prevent the public release of student disciplinary records after student names were blocked. As there was no basis for refusing the publisher's request for information under FERPA or state law, the lower court decision was reversed. *Board of Trustees, Cut Bank Public Schools v. Cut Bank Pioneer Press*, 337 Mont. 229, 2007 MT 115, 160 P.3d 482 (Mont. 2007).

◆ The Massachusetts Education Department administered the Massachusetts Comprehensive Assessment System (MCAS) to over 220,000 students in three grades. It contracted with Harcourt Educational Measurement to score the tests. A *Boston Globe* reporter asked the department's commissioner for release of all 2000 MCAS scores, as soon as the department received them. Five days later, the department released statewide test results to the public, but did not include compiled test results for individual schools as they were not yet available. After receiving individual school testing information, the department announced an additional one-week delay in releasing results, to allow local school officials time to correct errors. The *Globe* sought a state court order to require the immediate release of 2000 MCAS test results, but the court denied the request.

The *Globe* appealed to the Massachusetts Supreme Judicial Court, which stated that the state public records law allows the custodian 10 days to comply with a records request. Here, the release of public records within 10 days was presumed reasonable and the department complied with the law by releasing the results in seven days. **As the department had an obligation to release accurate information, it did not unreasonably delay releasing the MCAS scores by allowing local districts to review the raw scores for errors.** The court affirmed the judgment for the department. *Globe Newspaper Co. v. Commissioner of Educ.*, 439 Mass. 124, 786 N.E.2d 328 (Mass. 2003).

◆ A *Chicago Tribune* reporter requested over a million records on current and former Chicago public school students. The request included personal data such as school, medical or special education status, attendance, race, transportation status, free or reduced-cost lunch status, class rank, grade average, bilingual education status, date of birth, and standardized test scores. The board of education denied the request as burdensome and as a high risk of disclosing personal information in violation of federal and state laws including the Freedom of Information Act (FOIA) and Student Records Act. The *Tribune* sued the board, and the case reached the Appellate Court of Illinois. It noted the FOIA required public bodies to comply with record requests unless an exemption applied. **FOIA's student records exemption was a *per se* rule that did not require a case-by-case balancing of the competing interests in public information and individual privacy**. The clear language of the FOIA created an exemption from disclosure for student files. Most of the data requested by the *Tribune* was considered private and confidential. Because the request was entitled to the *per se* exemption, the board had properly denied it. *Chicago Tribune Co. v. Board of Educ. of City of Chicago*, 332 Ill.App.3d 60, 773 N.E.2d 674 (Ill. App. Ct. 2002).

◆ A California school district denied requests to disclose student suspension and expulsion records based on student privacy rights. Statistical information on school discipline was offered instead. The record requestor sued the district, citing Education Code § 48918 and a state attorney general's opinion deeming student names and the reasons for expulsions "public information." The state court of appeal stated student records are generally unavailable to the public. But the Education Code treated expulsion records differently. Although students may opt for a private expulsion hearing, the formal action and expulsion records were public. Under federal law, student disciplinary records are protected from public disclosure as "education records." **Since FERPA conditions the receipt of federal funding on conformity with its provisions, the district risked the withdrawal of federal funds if it disclosed the requested**

student expulsion records. The court held it was impossible for the district to obey both laws, so FERPA preempted state law. *Rim of the World Unified School Dist. v. Superior Court*, 104 Cal.App.4th 1393, 129 Cal.Rptr.2d 11 (Cal. Ct. App. 2002).

C. Electronic and Video Records

A California school district did not violate state and federal education record requirements by providing parents only printed copies of emails in their child's permanent file, rather than any and all emails in their electronic format that personally identified him. Emails had a "fleeting nature" and were not "education records" unless they were placed in a student's permanent file.

Court Decisions

◆ A California child with autism received special education from a county special education agency. His parents asked for copies of "any and all electronic mail sent or received" by the agency concerning or personally identifying their child. They then clarified that they sought emails in their electronic format. The county sent the parents hard copies of emails that had been printed and placed in their child's permanent file, but it refused to provide electronically formatted emails. The parents complained to the state department of education (DOE) and asserted violations of federal law when the district "unilaterally purged the original electronic files." The DOE held hard copies of emails in the student's files were "pupil records" under state law that had to be provided to parents within five business days of a request. But the DOE held the county did not have to provide emails in an electronic format and found the county was not required to notify parents before purging emails, which were not "educational records."

In a federal district court suit asserting state and federal records violations, the court found the Individuals with Disabilities Education Act (IDEA) required the county to provide parents a child's "education records." IDEA regulations referred to FERPA's definition of "education records." The court held **the DOE correctly found only those emails that personally identified the child and were "maintained" by an educational agency were "education records" under the IDEA and FERPA.** DOE correctly found the county had produced the child's education records by providing hard copies of all the emails that personally identified him and were maintained in his permanent file. Only those emails that were both maintained by the county and which personally identified the student were considered to be "education records." The court held that emails in electronic format were not "maintained" by the county. **Emails had a "fleeting nature" and were not "education records" unless they were placed in a student's permanent file.** The county did not "unlawfully purge" emails without notice to the parents. *S.A. v. Tulare County Office of Educ.*, No. CV F 08-1215 LJO GSA, 2009 WL 3126322 (E.D. Cal. 9/24/09).

◆ A Pennsylvania student discovered webcam photos and screenshots of himself on a school laptop. The school district agreed to disable the security tracking software on the laptop, but the student and others pursued a federal district court case. The court prohibited the district and its agents from remotely activating webcams on laptop computers issued to students. Under the court order, the school district could not remotely capture screenshots of laptops, except for maintenance, repairs or trouble-shooting. **The district could use an alternate means to track lost, stolen or missing laptops.** A global positioning system or other anti-theft device that did not permit the activation of webcams or capture screenshots was permitted. The order prevented the district from accessing any student-created files on laptops, such as emails, instant messages, Internet use logs and web-browsing histories. Under the court order, the district was required to adopt official policies governing the use, distribution and maintenance of student laptops. It was further required to issue regulations for student privacy on laptops and to train staff on the oversight and enforcement of the policies. Under the order, the school district would have to provide students and their parents an opportunity to view images already taken from webcams. Such images were to be destroyed when the process was completed. *Robbins v. Lower Merion School Dist.*, No. 10-665, 2010 WL 1976869 (E.D. Pa. 5/14/10).

◆ Parents of students attending the Whitney E. Houston Academy (a performing arts school) signed a form consenting to the videotaping, photographing or sound recording of their children "in classroom, playground, auditorium activities or productions." Consent was given with knowledge that recordings might appear in the media or be used for school exhibits and public relations. The academy PTA presented a play and videotaped it. Copies of the videotape were later made available for sale through the PTA. A student who had a non-speaking role tripped during the show. Although her parent never saw a copy of the videotape, she claimed that it exploited her daughter and sued the PTA for invasion of her daughter's privacy rights. A state court found no evidence that the PTA had received a commercial benefit and that it had acted with a charitable purpose. On appeal, a state appellate court noted that since the PTA was a charitable organization, the parent would have had to show her child's likeness was used for financial or commercial benefit. **An invasion of privacy claim requires proof that a party has used the likeness of another person without consent for commercial benefit, and proof of damages.** It was not sufficient for the parent to simply claim that the recording of her daughter, by itself, established a claim for appropriation of her likeness. The lower court had correctly held for the PTA. *Jeffries v. Whitney E. Houston Academy P.T.A.*, No. L-1389-07, 2009 WL 2136174 (N.J. Super. Ct. App. Div. 7/20/09).

◆ A Tennessee school board approved of the installation of video surveillance cameras throughout a middle school building. There were no specific guidelines for the project. When the school year began, an assistant principal discovered that cameras had been placed to record areas of locker rooms where students dressed for sports activities. Four months later, a visiting girls' basketball coach complained to the school principal after her team members noticed a camera. The principal incorrectly assured the coach that the camera was not activated. The camera was on, and it recorded images of students changing their clothes.

Some of the students and their parents sued the school board, the director of schools, the principal and the assistant principal. The case reached the U.S. Court of Appeals, Sixth Circuit, which held there is a Fourth Amendment "right to shield one's naked body from view by members of the opposite sex." **Even in locker rooms, the students retained a significant privacy interest in their unclothed bodies.** Students using locker rooms had a reasonable expectation that no one would videotape them without their knowledge. Video surveillance is inherently intrusive. A reasonable school administrator would know that students had a privacy right against being surreptitiously videotaped while changing clothes. For this reason, the court held the principal and assistant principal were not entitled to qualified immunity from liability. *Brannum v. Overton County School Board*, 516 F.3d 489 (6th Cir. 2008).

◆ A surveillance video camera on a school bus videotaped a fight by two elementary students. The school district denied a request by the parents of one of the students for a copy of the tape. The district claimed the videotape was exempt from public disclosure under the Washington Public Disclosure Act (PDA). The parents sued, and a court agreed with the district's decision not to disclose the tape. The videotape contained information that would allow a viewer to identify a student, and the tape was "maintained" by the district for potential discipline. The Washington Court of Appeals affirmed.

On appeal, the Supreme Court of Washington explained that the videotape was a "public record" and that the district was an "agency" under the PDA. So the district had to disclose the videotape unless an exemption applied. The student file exemption contemplated the protection of materials in a public student's permanent file, such as student "grades, standardized test results, assessments, psychological or physical evaluations, class schedule, address, telephone number, social security number, and other similar records." Here, the surveillance camera was a means of maintaining security and safety on school buses. The videotape differed significantly from the type of records maintained in student personal files. Because **the videotape could not be legally withheld as a student file document**, the court reversed the judgment. *Lindeman v. Kelso School Dist. No. 458*, 162 Wash.2d 196, 172 P.3d 329 (Wash. 2007).

◆ A New York court held **a videotape of a student fighting with a teacher during school was not an education record under FERPA**. The school district had voluntarily disclosed it to the police. Under FERPA, education records are "records, files, documents and other material which contain information directly related to a student." FERPA is intended to protect records relating to a student's performance and does not apply to a videotape recorded to maintain the school's security and safety. The student's rights to appeal his suspension outweighed the district's interest in protecting the confidentiality of school records. While FERPA does not create a private right of action, the student was not suing the district. He was petitioning the court to have the videotape released so he could appeal the suspension. The court granted the student's request to release the videotape. *Rome City School Dist. Disciplinary Hearing v. Grifasi*, 10 Misc.3d 1034, 806 N.Y.S.2d 381 (N.Y. Sup. Ct. 2005).

◆ A Florida District Court of Appeal held that **videotapes of students on school buses were "records and reports" under the school code**. The court had previously used the definition of "personally identifiable information" from FERPA. But FERPA calls for the denial of eligibility for federal funds only if an educational agency violates federal privacy requirements. The Florida Code went beyond FERPA by protecting the privacy of students against the release of any personal information contained in records or reports permitting the personal identification of a student. The state code protected as confidential even those records or reports that were redacted of any personally identifying information. *WFTV, Inc. v. School Board of Seminole*, 874 So.2d 48 (Fla. Dist. Ct. App. 2004).

◆ A group of Kentucky special education students complained that their teacher mistreated them. The school installed cameras in her classroom to monitor her performance. The principal denied the teacher's request to view class videotapes under the state open records act, stating that they were "education records" under FERPA and its Kentucky counterpart, the KFERPA. The district superintendent claimed that both FERPA and KFERPA prohibited the release of the videotapes to the teacher, and the state attorney general upheld this ruling. A state court held for the district, and the teacher appealed.

The Court of Appeals of Kentucky found that the lower court failed to consider a state Open Records Act exception permitting teachers to inspect "education records." **A FERPA exception exists for school officials, including teachers, who have "legitimate educational interests" in a student from whom consent would otherwise be required.** The lower court erroneously found that the teacher did not qualify for FERPA and KFERPA exceptions. Although the videotapes were "education records" under FERPA and KFERPA, the teacher was not just a "member of the public." Instead, her request had to be judged in view of her position as a teacher who was present in the classroom when the videotapes were recorded. The only way to prevent the teacher from viewing the videotapes under FERPA or KFERPA would be to find that she lacked "a legitimate educational interest." As the board did not show this, the court reversed and remanded the case for a hearing. *Medley v. Board of Educ. of Shelby County*, No. 2003-CA-001515-MR, 2004 WL 2367229 (Ky. Ct. App. 2004).

IV. TESTING

Overview

Ohio teachers who questioned the validity of student progress examinations were denied access to copies of the exams, which cost the district over $800,000 and were entitled to protection under trade secret laws.

Teacher Scenarios

Teacher thinks a colleague may have 'helped' students with the state test 267

Court Decisions

◆ Cincinnati Public Schools (CPS) spent $809,000 to hire a testing agency to develop exams for students in grades nine through eleven. CPS kept the exams in a secure area at a central location prior to administration. Students and staff members were forbidden from copying exams, which were collected immediately after being administered. A CPS teacher grew concerned over the design, implementation and scoring of the exams. About 60 other CPS teachers signed a petition seeking copies of the ninth-grade exam. CPS denied the request, arguing that the exams had secure and copyrighted material. After mediation failed, the teacher sought a special order, called a "writ of mandamus," from the Supreme Court of Ohio. The court held that this remedy is available to compel compliance with the Ohio Public Records Act. Since the semester exams were created to fulfill CPS policy decisions, the Public Records Act applied. An exception to the Act applies to trade secrets and copyrighted materials.

The Ohio Uniform Trade Secrets Act defined "trade secret" to include any information with independent economic value as a result of not being generally known, or which was the subject of reasonable efforts to maintain its secrecy. CPS had spent a great amount of money in developing the exams, which would have little or no value if they were made public. It would cost a considerable sum to recreate the exams. CPS estimated that replacing just half the questions on the ninth- and tenth-grade exams would exceed $270,000. It was clear that CPS had taken steps to maintain the secrecy of the exams. Thus, the exams were trade secrets. As the exams were subject to a Public Records Act exception, CPS did not have to disclose them to the teacher. *State ex rel. Perrea v. Cincinnati Public Schools*, 123 Ohio St.3d 410, 916 N.E.2d 1049 (Ohio 2009).

◆ The NCLB Act requires assessment of limited English proficient (LEP) students in English once they have attended school in the U.S. for at least three consecutive years, unless a time extension is warranted. Assessments are to be in the language and form most likely to yield accurate data on student knowledge until English proficiency is attained. Arizona voters approved Proposition 203, which required all children in state public schools to be instructed in English. Proposition 203 specified a standardized, nationally normed written test of academic subject matter, administered in English at least annually. According to Arizona officials, a verbal agreement was reached between the state education department and the U.S. Department of Education (DOE) regarding the inclusion of LEP student scores in AYP calculations. State officials claimed the DOE agreed to permit appeals of AYP calculations on grounds that LEP student test scores could not be a valid, reliable indicator of academic proficiency due to language deficiencies. A DOE monitoring team found that Arizona improperly used the NCLB Act appeals process to remove LEP assessment scores from AYP calculations.

The DOE ordered the state to cease this use of appeals and to use practices minimizing language barriers to LEP students. The state education department sued the DOE in a federal court for breach of the oral agreement to permit appeals for LEP students. The court agreed with the DOE's argument that **a breach of contract claim could not be based on a claim that the DOE promised to interpret the NCLB Act a certain way**. However, the state could amend its complaint to add an Administrative Procedures Act claim regarding its state plan amendment under the NCLB Act. *Horne v. U.S. Dep't of Educ.*, No. CV-08-1141-PHX-MHM, 2009 WL 775432 (D. Ariz. 3/23/09).

◆ A New York student complained of excessive noise at a state Specialized High School Admissions Test administration site. He was later denied a state court order that would have permitted him to retake the test. A state appellate division court held that the New York City Board of Education's decision was vested with education officials and was not appropriate for review by a court. The case was moot because the test had already been administered. *Tessler v. Board of Educ. of City of New York*, 854 N.Y.S.2d 66 (N.Y. App. Div. 2008).

◆ In 2003, the California state board of education announced that all public school students graduating in spring 2006 would have to pass both the language arts and mathematics parts of the California High School Exit Exam to receive a diploma. Districts had to offer supplemental instruction to all students who did not demonstrate sufficient progress toward passing. The legislature appropriated $20 million in supplemental funding for districts with the highest percentage of students who had not yet passed the exam. The state superintendent of public instruction distributed supplemental funding only to districts in which 28% or more of the class of 2006 had yet to pass the exam.

A lawsuit was filed in Alameda County Superior Court on behalf of 47,000 students who had satisfied other diploma requirements for spring 2006, but had yet to pass at least one part of the exam. The case alleged equal protection and due process violations. The court found that students in poor communities were not provided equal opportunities to learn the materials tested on the exam. Some schools had not fully aligned curriculums to the exam, and the lack of preparation disproportionately affected English language learners. The court issued an order preventing the state from requiring students in the class of 2006 to pass the exam as a condition of graduation. The state court of appeal held that **the superintendent had authority to give priority to the schools with the highest numbers of students who failed both parts of the exam**. The court found nothing arbitrary in the allocation of a limited sum of money to benefit school districts that appeared to have the greatest need. Students failing the exam had nine publicly funded options to continue their education and obtain diplomas. Awarding diplomas without passing the exam would stigmatize these students, deprive them of remedial instruction available to pass the exam, and debase the value of a diploma. Cases holding that education is a fundamental right did not support the finding of a fundamental right to a diploma. *O'Connell v. Superior Court of Alameda County,* 47 Cal.Rptr.3d 147 (Cal. Ct. App. 2006).

◆ A Maryland principal intern was accused of misconduct when taking a Praxis Series School Leaders Licensure Assessment Test. When she took the test, a site administrator submitted irregularity reports citing her for misconduct. The reports were based on alleged failure to stop writing in her test booklet when time was called. The intern challenged the reports in writing, stating that she had conformed completely to the test standards described to her. The Educational Testing Service (ETS) then cancelled her scores and returned her fee. The intern sued the ETS and the site administrator for breach of contract and other claims. The judge awarded pretrial judgment to the ETS on the breach of contract claim and dismissed all of the intern's remaining claims. The intern appealed to the state court of special appeals, which noted that **the ETS reserved the right to cancel a test score for misconduct**. However, the court agreed with the intern that a jury should be allowed to determine if her test scores had been cancelled in bad faith. The court reversed the judgment and remanded the case to the trial court. The intern would have to "surmount a gigantic hurdle" unless she could show that the administrator had some motive to lie. *Hildebrant v. Educational Testing Service,* 171 Md.App. 23, 908 A.2d 657 (Md. Ct. Spec. App. 2006).

◆ A Florida district court of appeal upheld an administrative ruling **rejecting charges that a teacher provided inappropriate assistance to her students during the Florida Comprehensive Assessment Test**. The state education practices commission filed a complaint against the teacher for providing answers and other help to her students on the test. However, after a hearing, an administrative law judge found all of the commission's student witnesses not credible. The judge accepted the testimony of the lone student who testified for the teacher. The commission held another hearing and issued a final order suspending the teacher's certification. The court of appeal held that the commission had improperly modified the judge's findings. As substantial evidence supported the judge's decision, the complaint was dismissed. *Stinson v. Winn,* 938 So.2d 554 (Fla. Dist. Ct. App. 2006).

◆ The Massachusetts Education Reform Act of 1993 specified a comprehensive diagnostic assessment of students in the fourth, eighth and tenth grades, with satisfaction of the tenth-grade examination a high school graduation requirement. Although student failure rates were as high as 53% in some core areas on the first MCAS administration in 1998, the board made the English, math, science and social studies parts of the exam a graduation requirement for students in the class of 2003. The board planned to phase other subjects into the graduation requirement and to raise the threshold scaled score over time. By 2003, about 90% of the state's seniors passed the tenth-grade MCAS and became eligible to graduate. Students who did not pass could receive remediation after grade 12 and further opportunities to take the exam. A group of students from the class of 2003 sued, challenging the regulation requiring them to pass the MCAS exam as a graduation prerequisite. All but one of the students attended public schools, and some of them received special education. The court denied their request for an order prohibiting the state education board from enforcing the regulation.

The students appealed to the Supreme Judicial Court, which held that **the board had the authority to gradually incorporate core areas in the MCAS examination, and to test students in English and math before doing so in other areas**. The regulation largely accomplished the Reform Act goal of holding educators accountable through required academic standards, curriculum frameworks and competency determinations. The legislature twice ratified the MCAS exam appropriating substantial funds for remediation programs. This indicated acceptance of the board's phase-in approach. The court affirmed the lower court decision. *Student No. 9 v. Board of Educ.,* 440 Mass. 752, 802 N.E.2d 105 (Mass. 2004).

V. EDUCATIONAL MALPRACTICE

Overview

Claims of educational malpractice have, for the most part, failed. Courts have been reluctant to interfere with a school's internal operations.

Court Decisions

◆ A Florida family obtained an evaluation of their son after he experienced problems in school. He was found eligible for special education and provided with an individual education plan. The family then received information about the Celebration School. The family claimed that Osceola County School Board employees told them Celebration School provided "a quality education based upon a time-tested and successful curriculum known as 'best practices.'" After moving to the Town of Celebration, and enrolling their children in Celebration School, the parents became disenchanted with the school and placed their children in private schools. They sued the school board for misrepresentation. A court dismissed the action, and the parents appealed. A state court of appeal reinstated their claim based on a special education appeal that had been voluntarily dismissed in a federal court.

The court found that the claims for fraudulent inducement and negligent misrepresentation were not "educational malpractice claims," as the trial court had found. The trial court should have allowed the parents to amend their complaint to allege sufficient facts and attempt to prove each element of these claims. However, **the trial court had properly dismissed the family's claim under the Florida Constitution, which guarantees a high-quality free public education**. There was no benchmark for determining how to define a "high-quality education." This determination was for the legislature to make. *Simon v. Celebration Co.*, 883 So.2d 826 (Fla. Dist. Ct. App. 2004).

◆ A group of parents sued the Denver Public Schools and its superintendent for failing to provide students with a quality education. The complaint asserted that the school system failed to provide course books, failed to impose adequate discipline on students, improperly used credit waivers to inflate graduation rates, maintained a pattern of poorly performing schools, and used "dumbed-down" standards for measuring school performance. It also alleged damages for intellectual and emotional harm, diminution of educational and career opportunities, discrimination, and asserted that parents were forced to send their children to private or alternative schools. A court dismissed the case on grounds that the constitutional and statutory claims were not justiciable. It agreed with the board that the contract claim failed because no contractual relationship existed between public schools and their students.

The state court of appeals agreed to review the contract claim and distinguished it from contract claims against private schools. Contract claims attacking the general quality of public education have been rejected because they are not truly based in contract but instead seek damages for educational malpractice. **Public school students, unlike those attending private schools, have not individually contracted with their school systems for specific educational services and cannot assert breach of contract claims.** There was no legally enforceable promise to provide a curriculum, books or other educational services in this case. The court held the matter was political in nature and not within the power of the courts to decide. No court in the nation has recognized a breach of contract claim rooted in legislative policy. The court affirmed the judgment for the board and superintendent. *Denver Parents Ass'n v. Denver Board of Educ.*, 10 P.3d 662 (Colo. Ct. App. 2000).

VI. ADMISSIONS AND ATTENDANCE

Overview

The Equal Protection Clause of the Fourteenth Amendment requires government agencies to apply the law equally to all persons. Due to the history of official segregation prior to Brown v. Board of Educ.*, 347 U.S. 483 (1954), all government classifications based on race are subject to strict judicial scrutiny*

A. Race, Admission and School Assignment

Court Decisions

◆ Seattle never operated a dual system of racially segregated schools, but it used race as a tiebreaker in allocating ninth-grade slots for oversubscribed high schools. Jefferson County, Kentucky formerly operated a dual school system, but a federal court declared the system unitary in 2000 and freed it from federal court supervision. Both school districts voluntarily adopted student assignment plans that relied in part upon race. Jefferson County considered race when making some elementary school assignments and in ruling on transfer requests. It tried to assure that a school's racial balance was within a range reflecting the district's racial composition. Parents of students who were denied the school assignment of their choice sued the school systems. Federal circuit courts later upheld the student assignment plans used in both of the school systems.

Appeal reached the U.S. Supreme Court, which noted that the plans did not allow meaningful individual review of applicants but instead relied on racial classifications in a "non-individualized, mechanical way." The classifications would only shift a small number of students. By contrast, consideration of race was critical in tripling minority representation at Michigan Law School in *Grutter v. Bollinger*, below. The diversity interest approved by the Court in *Grutter* "was not focused on race alone but encompassed 'all factors that may contribute to student body diversity.'" The plans in this case "employ only a limited notion of diversity, viewing race exclusively in white/nonwhite terms in Seattle and black/'other' terms in Jefferson County." The Court found that enrolling students without regard to race would yield "a substantially diverse student body without any definition of diversity." **Allowing racial balancing was unconstitutional, and using it as a compelling end in itself would assure that race would always be relevant.** This could justify permanent racial classifications, promote notions of racial inferiority and lead to racial hostility. The Court reversed the judgments. *Parents Involved in Community Schools v. Seattle School Dist. No. 1*, 551 U.S. 701, 127 S.Ct. 2738 (2007).

◆ Parents of students attending school in Berkeley Unified School District (BUSD) had to rank the school program they preferred for their children. While BUSD attempted to assign students on the basis of parental preference, it made assignments in priority categories. BUSD used neighborhood demographics when assigning students to elementary schools and high school programs. Instead of considering individual student race, BUSD used neighborhood data based on 445 "planning areas" of four-to-eight city blocks. Students in these areas were assigned a score based on their area's demographics. Areas were evaluated by average neighborhood household income, average education level of adults residing in the neighborhood, and neighborhood racial composition.

Each student within an area was treated the same in assignments, regardless of his or her own race. A parent group charged BUSD with violating Proposition 209, which prohibits state and local government units (including school districts) from discriminating against, or granting preferential treatment to, any individual or group based on race, sex, color, ethnicity or national origin in public employment, education or contracting. The Court of Appeal of California held that the plan did not violate the state constitution, as it did "not show partiality, prejudice, or preference to any student on the basis of that student's race." **All students in an area were treated equally, regardless of individual race or personal characteristics.** To the extent that any preference was given, it was on the basis of the collective composition of a student's neighborhood. *American Civil Rights Foundation v. Berkeley Unified School Dist.*, 172 Cal.App.4th 207, 90 Cal.Rptr.3d 789 (Cal. Ct. App. 2009).

◆ Massachusetts state officials pressured the Lynn School Committee to stop approving transfers that had a segregative effect on its schools. Lynn officials amended the district school attendance plan to guarantee student attendance in neighborhood schools by **only allowing transfers that "improved the racial balance in either the neighborhood school or the destination school."** Objecting parents sued, raising Equal Protection Clause and related claims. After an 11-day trial, the court held that "since the implementation of the Plan the Lynn schools have become a success story." The court upheld the plan. The U.S. Court of Appeals, First Circuit, affirmed, and the U.S. Supreme Court denied review, apparently ending the case. However, when the U.S. Supreme Court struck down student assignment policies in *Parents Involved in Community Schools v. Seattle School Dist. No. 1*, this chapter, the Lynn parents took note of the similarities among the assignment policies in Seattle, Louisville and Lynn. They filed a complaint to overcome the 2005 First Circuit judgment. A federal court dismissed the case, and the First Circuit refused to reopen it. *Comfort v. Lynn School Committee*, 560 F.3d 22 (1st Cir. 2009).

◆ Los Angeles Unified School District (LAUSD) operated magnet programs under a desegregation order which ended 18 years of state court litigation. A state court entered a final order in 1981 that approved an integration plan relying in part on magnet schools and a Permit With Transportation (PWT) program. Both programs took student race or ethnicity into account in school applications and admissions. The case ended when the U.S. Supreme Court let stand LAUSD's magnet and PWT programs in *Crawford v. Board of Educ*, 458 U.S. 527 (1982). In 1996, California voters approved Proposition 209 to amend the state constitution to prohibit public education programs from discriminating against, or giving preferential treatment to any individual or group on the basis of race, ethnicity or national origin. LAUSD continued to assign students to magnet schools on a priority point system that relied in part on student racial and ethnic designations. In 2005, an organization sued LAUSD, claiming that it relied on racial classifications in violation of Proposition 209.

The case reached the California Court of Appeal, which agreed with LAUSD and its expert that desegregation orders do not terminate simply because court supervision of plan implementation has ended. Desegregation efforts were still under way in LAUSD schools in 1996. The 1981 court order had never been reversed, overruled, vacated, revoked, modified or withdrawn. **The Supreme Court has held that school districts may rely on the ongoing validity of a desegregation order.** The court mandate for LAUSD was to take reasonably feasible steps to desegregate its schools, and LAUSD remained subject to this constitutional duty. As the 1981 *Crawford* order was in existence when Proposition 209 took effect in 1996, the magnet and PWT programs were upheld. *American Civil Rights Foundation v. Los Angeles Unified School Dist.*, 169 Cal.App.4th 436, 86 Cal.Rptr.3d 754 (Cal. Ct. App. 2008).

◆ In two cases involving the University of Michigan, the Supreme Court considered the use of race in higher education admissions.

In the first case, the U.S. Court of Appeals, Sixth Circuit, upheld the University of Michigan Law School's admissions policy. The appeals court found that the law school had a compelling interest in achieving a diverse student body. The Supreme Court noted that any governmental distinction based on race must be examined under the strict scrutiny standard. Under this standard, the classification must be "narrowly tailored to further compelling governmental interests." The Court concluded, based on *Regents of the Univ. of California v. Bakke*, 438 U.S. 265 (1978), that the goal of having a diverse student body is a compelling governmental interest. **The law school admissions policy utilized a narrowly tailored method of achieving that interest through its consideration of race as a "plus" factor.** The Court held the policy was flexible, and it did not create an impermissible quota system. One of the most important factors supporting the decision was the individualized review of applicants that considered several race-neutral factors. *Grutter v. Bollinger,* 539 U.S. 306, 123 S.Ct. 2325, 156 L.E.2d 304 (2003).

The second Michigan case involved the undergraduate admissions policy for the university's College of Literature, Science and the Arts. During the course of the litigation, the policy was changed several times. The policy being considered by the Supreme Court awarded applicants from underrepresented minority groups 20 points. Applicants were awarded points for a variety of factors, and they needed at least 100 points for admission. The Court applied the strict scrutiny analysis to the policy and held that it was not narrowly tailored to achieve the compelling state interest in diversity declared by the university.

The policy impermissibly gave underrepresented minority students an advantage or preference by automatically awarding them 20 points. The policy was also deficient because it failed to require an individualized review of each applicant, which is essential when race is a consideration. *Gratz v. Bollinger,* 539 U.S. 244, 123 S.Ct. 2411, 156 L.Ed.2d 257 (2003).

◆ A Wisconsin school district had no formal policy or practice for elementary school class assignments, but a principal issued a memo to staff, urging the balancing of classes according to student gender, ethnicity, academic ability, special needs and parental input. The parents of an African-American student requested their daughter learn from a teacher with high expectations. They also expressed concerns about some negative incidents she had experienced with special education students. After the start of the school year, the student's teacher divided her class into five small groups and put two African-American students in each group, so that they sat together in pairs. She justified this because she believed "African-American students need a buddy, and sometimes it works well if they have someone else working with them because they view things in a global manner." She also seated Hispanic students in pairs.

The student's family sued the school district and school officials, alleging that the assignment and seating policies violated the Equal Protection Clause. The court awarded pretrial judgment to the district and officials, finding the decision to place the student was the result of race-neutral factors. It found no evidence that the teacher's seating policy resulted in different treatment of the student. The U.S. Court of Appeals, Seventh Circuit, affirmed the decision concerning the school assignment policy. The student's assignment took into consideration her parents' race-neutral concerns. But the lower court should not have awarded pretrial judgment to the teacher on the Equal Protection claim. **Even if the teacher believed she was acting in the best interests of minority students by seating them in pairs, her action was based purely on race.** Because the law in this area was well established, the teacher was not entitled to qualified immunity on the equal protection claim arising from the seating policy. The court reversed in part and remanded the case. *Billings v. Madison Metropolitan School Dist.*, 259 F.3d 807 (7th Cir. 2001).

B. Age and Residency Requirements

Federal law requires schools to provide homeless students with access to the same free, appropriate public education as other children receive. This includes transportation, special education, English learner, gifted and talented programs and school lunch programs for which students meet eligibility requirements. Under the McKinney-Vento Homeless Assistance Act, homeless children cannot be stigmatized or segregated from a "mainstream school environment on the basis of their being homeless." The No Child Left Behind (NCLB) Act reauthorized the McKinney-Vento Act.

If a homeless student's school enrollment is disputed, the Act requires school districts to immediately admit a student to the school in which enrollment is sought, pending resolution of the dispute.

Schools must notify the parents of homeless children about the NCLB Act's school choice provisions. Schools must continue the education of a homeless student in the student's "school of origin," or enroll the student in a public school that non-homeless students in the same attendance area are eligible to attend. NCLB section 722(g), codified at 42 U.S.C. § 11432, defines "school of origin" as the school a child attended when permanently housed or "the school in which the child or youth was last enrolled."

Court Decisions

◆ A five-year-old Texas student went to live with his aunt. His birth mother lived outside the school district. The aunt sought to pre-enroll the student in a kindergarten class, but the school registrar informed her that she could not enroll him without proof that she had the legal right to act as his guardian or parent. Later in the day, the registrar rejected a power of attorney document signed by the student's mother. The aunt obtained a legal aid attorney, who asserted that a power of attorney was sufficient to establish residency under a section of the Texas Education Code. The section requires non-resident persons under 18 years of age to establish that their presence in a school district is not for the primary purpose of participation in extracurricular activities. The school district maintained that the section did not create a basis for school enrollment. Instead of pursuing the board's grievance procedure, the aunt filed a lawsuit.

The district superintendent then decided to admit the student on the basis of the power of attorney. When the aunt tried to continue the lawsuit anyway, claiming that the district might again exclude the student, a federal district **court dismissed the case, finding the district had never denied the student admission.** The U.S. Court of Appeals, Fifth Circuit, affirmed. Had the aunt awaited a decision by the superintendent or filed a proper grievance, she would have forced the district's initial decisionmaker to take a definitive position. *Zepeda v. Boerne Independent School Dist.*, 294 Fed.Appx. 834 (5th Cir. 2008).

◆ Six New York families claimed that homeless children in Suffolk County missed significant amounts of school time due to a systematic failure to provide them with access to education and transportation. The families sued state education officials, who sought to dismiss the case. A federal court explained that the McKinney-Vento Act required states to assure that homeless children had access to a free and appropriate public education. The Act directed local education agencies to immediately enroll homeless students, even if they were unable to produce the records normally required for enrollment. **Enrolling schools must immediately contact the school last attended by a homeless student to obtain necessary records, and they must help parents of homeless students obtain necessary immunizations or medical records.** The court held that Congress intended to create a private right of action to enforce the McKinney-Vento Act. Thus, the families were appropriate representatives of homeless students in Suffolk County, and the court certified the case as a class action. *National Law Center on Homelessness and Poverty, R.I. v. State of New York*, 224 F.R.D. 314 (E.D.N.Y. 2004).

The New York Court of Appeals applied state law consistently with the No Child Left Behind Act in the following case, in which a homeless student's last permanent residence counted, not his brief stay in a homeless shelter.

◆ A New York family rented a house in Springs School District for parts of two school years. The family was evicted, and the children moved to temporary homes, including stays in motels and with relatives. The mother was jailed for part of this time, and the family moved into a homeless shelter in the Longwood School District. The county Department of Social Services (DSS) placed the children in foster care, and they then began attending Longwood schools. DSS forms indicated Springs as the "district of origin" for the children. Longwood filed a claim against Springs for tuition reimbursement for the children. When Springs refused, Longwood sued Springs. A state trial court held for Longwood, ruling the mother's last permanent home was in the Springs School District.

The New York Supreme Court, Appellate Division, reversed the judgment, holding that the mother's temporary stay in the homeless shelter obligated Longwood to pay for the children's education. The New York Court of Appeals noted that the school district in which a child resided at the time of a social services placement had to bear the child's instructional costs. The court agreed with Longwood that the family's last permanent residence was what counted, not a brief stay in a shelter. **Residence was established by physical presence as an inhabitant within the district, combined with an intent to remain.** Districts were required to provide tuition-free education only to students whose parents or guardians resided in the district. The "temporary stayovers" following the eviction, including time in the homeless shelter, did not change the family residence. As a result, the court reversed the judgment. *Longwood Cent. School Dist. v. Springs Union Free School Dist.*, 1 N.Y.3d 385, 774 N.Y.S.2d 857, 806 N.E.2d 970 (N.Y. 2004).

◆ A disabled Colorado student and her family moved out of her school district when she was in second grade. The district permitted her to stay in her school for the rest of the year. It readmitted her to the school for third and fourth grade under the state's school choice law. However, the district denied her application to re-enroll for grade five, stating that its special education program had exceeded its capacity. A special education due process hearing officer held for the district, and an administrative law judge affirmed. The parents moved back into the school district and re-enrolled their daughter in the school she had formerly attended. They sued the district for violating the state school choice law, among others. The court awarded pretrial judgment to the district.

On appeal, the state court of appeals held that the school choice law allowed elementary students who became district "nonresidents" during a school year or between school years to remain in their schools. This right extended only to the next school year and did not entitle a nonresident student to return for subsequent school years, as the parents argued. The district's special education programs exceeded nonresident enrollment limits. **The school choice statute authorized the district to deny re-enrollment based on nonresident status.** The district had a "potentially limitless" obligation to provide special education to disabled resident students, but this was distinct from any obligation to accept nonresidents under the school choice law. The court affirmed the judgment. *Bradshaw v. Cherry Creek School Dist. No. 5*, 98 P.3d 886 (Colo. Ct. App. 2003).

◆ A parent who lived in Chicago sent her daughter to North Carolina after the girl was threatened with assault. The student's uncle attempted to enroll her in a local school, but the district superintendent denied admission because she was not domiciled in a county school administrative unit. The family filed a state court action that reached the North Carolina Court of Appeals.

The court observed that **a child who is not domiciled in a local administrative unit may attend its schools without paying tuition if the child resides with an adult in the unit as the result of a parent or guardian's death, serious illness, incapacity or incarceration**. A non-domiciliary student may also enroll in school in another administrative unit in cases of abandonment, child abuse or natural disaster. In these cases, the student must present an affidavit including a statement that the claim to residency is not primarily related to attendance at a particular school and that an adult with whom the child resides accepts responsibility for the child's educational decisions. The court rejected the family's argument that the law violated due process and equal protection rights. In *Martinez v. Bynum* (this chapter), the U.S. Supreme Court upheld a Texas law conditioning public school enrollment on residency within a school district or proof that enrollment was not being sought for the sole purpose of attending school within the district. The North Carolina statute, like the Texas law, was a reasonable standard for determining the residential status of public school students. *Graham v. Mock*, 545 S.E.2d 263 (N.C. Ct. App. 2001).

◆ The Texas Education Code permitted school districts to deny free admission to minors who lived apart from a "parent, guardian, or the person having lawful control of him" if the minor's primary purpose in being in the district was to attend local public schools. A minor left his parent's home in Mexico to live with his sister in a Texas town for the purpose of attending school there. When the school district denied his application for tuition-free admission, his sister sued, alleging that the law was unconstitutional. A federal court held for the state, and the Fifth Circuit Court of Appeals affirmed.

The U.S. Supreme Court upheld the residency requirement. **A bona fide residence requirement, appropriately defined and uniformly applied, furthered a substantial state interest** in assuring that services provided for residents were enjoyed only by residents. Such a requirement with respect to attendance in public free schools did not violate the Equal Protection Clause. Residence generally requires both physical presence and intention to remain. As long as the child was not living in the district for the sole purpose of attending school, he satisfied the statutory test. The Court held that this was a bona fide residency requirement and that the Constitution permits a state to restrict eligibility for tuition-free education to its bona fide residents. *Martinez v. Bynum*, 461 U.S. 321, 103 S.Ct. 1838, 75 L.Ed.2d 879 (1983).

◆ In May 1975, the Texas legislature revised its education laws to withhold from school districts any state funds for the education of children who were not legally admitted into the U.S. It authorized school districts to deny enrollment to these children. A group filed a class action on behalf of school-age children of Mexican origin who could not establish they had been legally admitted into the U.S. The action complained of the exclusion of the children from public school. A federal court prevented the school district from denying a free education to the children, and the U.S. Court of Appeals, Fifth Circuit, upheld the decision. The legislation was also challenged by numerous other plaintiffs. The court held that the law violated the Equal Protection Clause, and the Fifth Circuit affirmed. The Supreme Court granted review. The state claimed that undocumented aliens were not "persons" within the jurisdiction of Texas, and so were not entitled to equal protection of its laws. The Court rejected this argument, stating that **whatever an alien's status under the immigration laws, an alien is a "person" in any sense of the term**.

The term "within its jurisdiction" was meant as a term of geographic location, and the Equal Protection Clause extended its protection to all persons within a state, whether citizen or stranger. The statute could not be upheld because it did not advance any substantial state interest. The Texas statute imposed a lifetime hardship on a discrete class of children not accountable for their disabling status. There was no evidence to show the exclusion of the children would improve the overall quality of education in the state. *Plyler v. Doe*, 457 U.S. 202, 102 S.Ct. 2382, 72 L.Ed.2d 786 (1982).

VII. COMPULSORY ATTENDANCE

Overview

States have a compelling interest in providing public education and may establish and enforce reasonable school attendance laws.

A. Compulsory Attendance and Truancy

Teacher Scenarios

The ultimate dilemma: Give good student a break or follow the policy?...268

Court Decisions

◆ A Maryland school attendance worker recorded a student as absent from school 74 days during the 2006-07 school year. State prosecutors filed an adult truancy petition against the student's parent for violating the state compulsory attendance act. The parent and student claimed that the student usually arrived at school on a regular basis. But the student admitted that once at school, she often cut her classes and was "hanging out" in school hallways. The parent asserted that after her child was at school, she was in the care and custody of school officials. The trial judge expressed disbelief at the parent for failing to ask her child about missing classes and found her "involved in" the child's truancy. After the court upheld the petition and placed the parent on probation, she appealed to the Court of Appeals of Maryland.

The lower court had found the parent's testimony both "incomprehensible" and incredible. As it was error for the trial court judge to make an inference that the opposite of her testimony must be true, the parent was entitled to a new trial. Once the daughter entered the school building, her custody shifted to the school. No language in the compulsory attendance law made it clear to a parent that criminal liability would be imposed on a parent whose child cut classes. **While children were being educated during the school day, their parents transferred to school officials the power to act as their guardians.** Evidence that the student was not in her homeroom when attendance was taken would be sufficient to establish that she did not attend school on that day. In order to find that the parent violated the compulsory attendance law at a new trial, there had to be "proof beyond a reasonable doubt" that her child did not attend school. *In re Gloria H.*, 410 Md. 562, 979 A.2d 710 (Md. 2009).

◆ A Kentucky middle school student accumulated 21 unexcused absences in a two-month period, and a family court complaint was filed against him. He argued that his school district should have determined if his truancy was a manifestation of a disability prior to filing the action. A school attendance coordinator testified that she made a home visit, mailed numerous letters and made many phone calls to gain compliance. Her intervention did not help and the student only complained that "he did not like school." After a hearing, the court found the student habitually truant. While he could remain at home, he was required to attend counseling and school, and cooperate with a state family services agency. On appeal, the Court of Appeals of Kentucky found that **prior to filing a truancy complaint, a school director of pupil personnel must determine the causes of a student's truancy, assess home conditions and conduct home visits**. All these requirements were met and ample evidence supported the finding of habitual truancy. And nothing in the Individuals with Disabilities Education Act (IDEA) required a manifestation determination to see if his truancy related to a disability. The court affirmed the judgment. *R.B.J. v. Comwlth. of Kentucky*, No. 2008-CA-001349-ME, 2009 WL 1349219 (Ky. Ct. App. 5/15/09).

◆ A New Mexico student of African American and Hispanic heritage received special education for a specific learning disability. In eighth grade, she stopped coming to school, due in part to family problems. The student was charged with aggravated battery and assault of her mother and brother with a deadly weapon. After serving time in juvenile facilities, she was placed in a residential treatment center. Upon returning to school, the student used drugs and alcohol at school and received numerous disciplinary referrals for truancy. She skipped school to provoke her mother's boyfriend into leaving their home.

The student became pregnant and was sent to a day shelter. She was then suspended for fighting at school. Her mother claimed the school district denied her access to a Wilson Reading System program and filed an unsuccessful special education due process action. The student transferred to another school district, where she enrolled in a Wilson class. She earned a 4.0 grade average for grade nine, then dropped out due to more family turmoil and drug use. The parent sued the residence school district for equal protection and Title VI violations. A court found no merit to the student's claim that she did not benefit from her education. On appeal, the U.S. Court of Appeals, Tenth Circuit, denied her claim under the Individuals with Disabilities Education Act. **She was seeking the very services she would have received by simply returning to school.** *Garcia v. Board of Educ. of Albuquerque Public Schools*, 520 F.3d 1116 (10th Cir. 2008).

♦ A St. Louis city ordinance made parents responsible for truancy by their minor children. Parents who knowingly allowed their children to miss school without excuse could be fined $25 for each day of school missed. A city municipal court judge directed a minor student who had an infant child to participate in therapy, attend school every day and refrain from using force against her own parents. The family was ordered to cooperate with the court or face contempt charges. The minor student's mother claimed the student assaulted her. The judge held the minor student in contempt of court and encouraged the mother to file criminal charges against her. She filed charges but dropped them within a few days. The judge later ordered the mother to be incarcerated for several days until her next appearance. The mother claimed that while she was incarcerated, state social workers took custody of her grandson.

The grandson, who was the truant minor student's son, was then adopted by a foster family. The mother sued the judge and city for civil rights violations. A court awarded judgment to the city and found the judge was entitled to immunity. The U.S. Court of Appeals, Eighth Circuit, found **a municipality is liable for federal civil rights violations only where an official with final policymaking responsibility makes a deliberate choice to violate constitutional rights**. The judge's order was a judicial decision for which the city could not be held responsible. As the order incarcerating the mother was not a final policy decision of the type creating municipal liability, the court affirmed the judgment. *Granda v. City of St. Louis*, 472 F.3d 565 (8th Cir. 2007).

♦ **Wisconsin's compulsory school attendance statute requires any person having control of a school-age child to "cause the child to attend school regularly. ..."** The statute cross-references other Wisconsin statutes detailing state procedures for truancy, including a statute that requires each school board to establish written attendance policies. The parent of a student who was absent without excuse eight times during a three-month period failed to respond to repeated notices from the school to meet with officials. The district attorney's office brought charges against the student's parent, resulting in a misdemeanor conviction. On appeal to the Court of Appeals of Wisconsin, the parent argued that the compulsory attendance statute was unconstitutionally vague because it did not define "regularly." The court found the statute sufficiently definite and understandable to a person of average intelligence. It sufficiently cross-referenced other statutes so that the full statutory scheme of mandatory attendance was clear. The court rejected the parent's defense that the student was uncontrollable, because evidence indicated she had a consistent pattern of unexcused absences dating from kindergarten. The court upheld the statute and affirmed the conviction. *State v. White*, 509 N.W.2d 434 (Wis. Ct. App. 1993).

♦ An 18-year-old West Virginia student missed five days of school without an excuse. He was warned that continued absences could result in criminal prosecution. After continuing unexcused absences, the county prosecutor's office filed a criminal complaint against the student. After he was convicted of violating a state compulsory attendance statute, he petitioned the Supreme Court of Appeals of West Virginia for review. The court observed that the compulsory attendance statute mandated school attendance for children between the ages of six and 16 and provided enforcement sanctions against parents, guardians or custodians, but not against individual students. **There was no possibility of liability under the statute for a non-attending student, regardless of age.** The court ruled for the student. *State ex rel. Estes v. Egnor*, 443 S.E.2d 193 (W. Va. 1994).

B. Home Study Programs

Court Decisions

♦ Pennsylvania law permitted home education programs. School districts reviewed home education programs for compliance with minimum hours of instruction, course requirements and student progress. Parents of children being homeschooled had to file affidavits every year indicating their compliance with compulsory attendance law requirements, and had to get annual written evaluations of each child's work. School superintendents were charged with ensuring that home-schooled children received an appropriate education. If a superintendent determined appropriate education was not taking place, there could be a request for more information and the possibility of a hearing. A hearing officer who found that an appropriate education was not taking place could order the student into a remedial program, or a public or private school.

A group of parents who homeschooled their children sought exemptions from the Religious Freedom Protection Act. The districts denied their requests. After truancy prosecutions were begun, the parents filed separate suits against the districts that were eventually consolidated before a federal district court. The cases reached the U.S. Court of Appeals, Third Circuit. It found that **in practice, school districts exercised a "limited level of oversight" over home education programs**. The court held the Free Exercise Clause does not relieve persons from a valid and neutral law of general applicability. A law was "neutral" if it did not target religiously motivated conduct. In this case, the act was a neutral law of general applicability. It did not target religious practices or selectively burden religiously motivated conduct. Nothing suggested school officials discriminated against religiously based home education programs. The act was rationally related to legitimate government objectives. As the right of parents to control the education of their children was "neither absolute nor unqualified," the court held for the school districts. *Combs v. Homer-Center School Dist.*, 540 F.3d 231 (3d Cir. 2008).

◆ A California family had a 20-year history of intervention by children and family services. The parents were subject to a dependency court proceeding for charges of physical abuse, neglect and failure to prevent sexual abuse. They were uncooperative with authorities, and the mother once attempted to hide the children from them. After two children were declared dependent due to the abuse and neglect of their siblings, their attorney sought an order requiring that they be sent to a public or private school, rather than educated at home. The request was made to allow the children to be in regular contact with mandatory reporters. A state superior court refused the request, finding "parents have an absolute constitutional right to home school their children."

On appeal, the state court of appeal found that state law does not expressly permit homeschooling. But recent provisions of law indicated that the legislature recognized homeschooling is taking place. The court explained that homeschooling arose as an issue in the case because one child, who had been homeschooled by the mother, wanted to attend public school. The children and families agency claimed the child was dependent on the additional basis that her parents' refusal to send her to public school placed her at risk of serious emotional damage. The superior court had incorrectly found there was an absolute parental right to homeschool children. Instead, **the constitutional liberty interest of parents to direct the education of their children had to yield to the state interest in child protection and safety**. The court noted this was a dependency case in which the children had been found dependent due to abuse and neglect of a sibling. "The parents in dependency have been judicially determined not to be fit," wrote the court. Without contact with mandated reporters at school, the court found child safety might not be guaranteed. By allowing the children to attend school, they could remain in their home, while educators would provide "an extra layer of protection." The court returned the case to the superior court for reconsideration. *Jonathan L. v. Superior Court*, 165 Cal.App.4th 1074, 81 Cal.Rptr.3d 517 (Cal. Ct. App. 2008).

◆ The Court of Appeals of Michigan upheld an order by a family court to exercise jurisdiction over a student with disabilities whose mother claimed she was homeschooling him. Evidence indicated that she was not even at home during most of the school day. The family court found that the student had missed 111 out of the 134 days of the current school year. The court noted the mother's reluctance to use negative consequences for improper conduct by the student. The court found that it was not in the student's best interests to be homeschooled, especially where this required him to be unsupervised for most of the day. **The court found the mother's home-schooling plan "painfully neglectful" of his educational needs.** Although this was not a severe case of educational neglect, it was proper for the trial court to assume jurisdiction over the student. *Manchester Public Schools v. Flint*, No. 240251, 2003 WL 22244692 (Mich. Ct. App. 2003).

◆ Two Massachusetts children were not enrolled in school and lacked approved home-schooling plans. The parents contended that school committee approval of their home-schooling activities would conflict with their learner-led approach to education, and that the Constitution prohibited infringement on their privacy and family rights. The school committee initiated a state district court proceeding for the care and protection of the children. The court found the parents had failed over a two-year period to show the children's educational needs were being met, effectively preventing any evaluation of their educational level and instructional methods. The parents did not comply with a court order to file educational plans, resulting in adjudication of the children as in need of care and protection. The court transferred legal custody of the children to the social services department, although they remained in their parents' physical custody. The parents appealed to the Appellate Court of Massachusetts.

The court noted that the trial court order had required the parents to submit a detailed home-schooling plan to the school committee to allow assessment of the program and the children's progress. **This was a legitimate educational condition that a school committee could impose on a home-school proposal without infringing on the constitutional rights of a family.** The U.S. Supreme Court has recognized a degree of parental autonomy to direct the education of children, but state laws effectively incorporated this requirement by allowing for flexibility in the evaluation of private instruction. The parents rejected accommodations proposed by the school committee, and the custody order was entered only after they had received a final opportunity to comply with the committee's requests. The court affirmed the order for temporary care and protection. *In re Ivan*, 717 N.E.2d 1020 (Mass. App. Ct. 1999).

C. Attendance Policies

Court Decisions

◆ The Court of Appeal of Louisiana denied relief to a student who was expelled in her eighth-grade year and sought to return the next year as a ninth-grader. She based her claim on her progress as a home-schooled student and her passing score on the state's LEAP test with mastery achievement levels. The parents had sought to have the school board evaluate the student since August 2006, but a state trial court denied their request and the case became mired in appeal procedures. The court of appeal chastised the school board and trial court for allowing the student to go without an evaluation until February 2007. Both the court of appeal and state supreme court had ordered such an evaluation. **The school board's decision to return the** student to grade eight appeared to be arbitrary. However, only 65 days remained in the school year, and it was now too late for her to meet the relevant attendance and lesson requirements. *B.W.S., Jr. v. Livingston Parish School Board*, 960 So.2d 997 (La. Ct. App. 2007).

◆ An Alabama high school handbook required the referral of tardy students first into parent conferences, then for discipline or alternative programs. After a student's third unexcused absence in a semester, the handbook provided for referral to an "early warning program" conducted by the county juvenile court system. After a student's tenth tardy in one semester, the school principal reported her to the school truant officer. The principal did not refer her to the early warning program or contact her parents, as specified in the school handbook. The truant officer filed a child in need of supervision petition in the juvenile court. After a trial, the court adjudicated the student a child in need of supervision and placed her on probation for the rest of the school year.

On appeal, the student asserted that the principal violated the Compulsory School Attendance Law and school policy by failing to investigate the causes of her tardiness before referring her to the truant officer. **The Alabama Court of Civil Appeals found nothing in state law requiring the principal to investigate the causes of a student's tardiness.** The principal did not violate the student's due process rights by failing to follow the student handbook's progressive discipline policies before submitting her name to the truant officer. The handbook placed a duty on students to provide a timely excuse for their absences. The student was unable to show that the school selectively enforced the prosecution of truancy cases. The court affirmed the judgment. *S.H. v. State of Alabama*, 868 So.2d 1110 (Ala. Civ. App. 2003).

◆ An Ohio school policy required the school to provide parents with written notification of state compulsory education laws upon a student's third unexcused absence. After the fifth absence, the school was required to hold an informal conference with the parents, student and a probation officer, and upon the tenth absence, a formal hearing was mandated. A student was absent without excuse approximately 20 days during a four-month period. On some occasions the parents explained there was a medical problem. The school accepted these explanations until the parents applied to the county educational service center for permission to home-school the student. But the school did not send them any notices concerning truancy proceedings. The service center advised the principal that the student's home school application was being denied, and the principal filed a complaint against the parents in an Ohio county court on charges of contributing to the delinquency of a minor.

The court conducted a jury trial and sentenced the parents to seven days in jail and fines of $250. They appealed to a state appeals court, which reversed the judgment. The state failed to meet its burden of proof to show that under local standards, the student was habitually truant. **Because truancy involved more than absenteeism, the court held the state was required to show a lack of excuse or permission as established by school policy.** In this case, the state failed to prove that it had sent the parents written notices that their daughter was absent without an excuse for three or more days. Without this proof, the state could not satisfy the essential element of habitual truancy. *State v. Smrekar*, No. 99 CO 35, 2000 Ohio App. Lexis 5381, 2000 WL 1726518 (Ohio Ct. App. 2000).

VIII. TEACHER SCENARIOS

Sharpen Your Judgment

Mom accuses teacher of 'cutting' PE time

"Coach, we have an angry mom," assistant principal Rich Wells said as Vinny Travo walked into his office. "Fill me in on the situation with Todd Smee's mother."

"She thinks Todd isn't getting his fair share of PE time," Vinny said.

"OK," Rich said. "What else can you tell me about it? Because she's threatening to sue."

"Todd's mom has been complaining about our schedule. She claims PE time falls short of the Education Code requirements," Vinny said.

"So she wants more PE time?" Rich asked.

"Yep," Vinny confirmed. "She says we short gym classes by 80 minutes over a 10-day span.

"I tried to explain that the Code offers guidelines and we have some discretion on how we carry things out," Vinny continued. "When I told her that I follow the district schedule, Todd's mom said she'd call you."

"OK," Rich said. "I'm going to call the district office to give a heads-up on this."

Todd's mother did sue, claiming the school violated the Education Code by cutting PE time.

Did the judge agree?

Sharpen Your Judgment – The Decision

Yes, the judge ruled that the school's PE schedule violated the Education Code.

The student and his mother claimed the school's PE schedule shorted students 80 minutes of physical activity every 10 days.

The school insisted that the Education Code was a guide, and individual schools have the authority to use discretion to determine how PE programs are administered at the school.

The judge looked at the Education Code and noted that the language specifically stated the minimum time allotted for PE, which the school failed to meet.

What about school officials' discretionary powers to carry out programs at their school?

Discretion gives school officials authority to decide how to fulfill requirements, but schools still have to provide the required minimum, the judge explained.

Analysis: How – not what

As this case shows, school officials who try to stretch their authority can get into trouble.

Bottom line: School officials' discretion is limited, and it doesn't override written rules.

Cite: *Doe v. Albany Unified School Dist.*

Sharpen Your Judgment

'I deserve a better grade for my work'

Cathy Charles hoped that confronting her student, Patrick Jackson, might resolve the issue before it got bigger.

"Patrick, I've looked at your completion list for extra-credit reading assignments, and there's a problem."

"A problem?" the student asked.

"Yes," the teacher nodded. "You say you read four 500-page books in two weeks. That seems impossible to me, given that you had other school work to do, too."

"Well, that's your opinion," the student stammered. "I read every one of those books, and that's supposed to be good enough to get me an 'A' in reading."

"Are you sure you want to stay with that story?" the teacher asked. "I think just about any teacher is going to agree that no student at your grade level could have done all that reading in such a short time."

"I don't care," the boy's voice rose. "I did the reading, and I want the grade."

When the teacher refused to give the student credit for the claim, the parents sued the teacher and the school.

Did the school win?

Sharpen Your Judgment – The Decision

Yes. The school won the case when the court OK'd denial of the demand for extra reading credit.

The parents based their argument on the fact that the teacher and the school had laid out the guidelines for extra credit, and the student had followed those guidelines.

The guidelines didn't include any provision for the teacher's assessment that the student wasn't being truthful.

The teacher and the school contended that there was no need for stated guidelines covering a teacher's judgment about the likelihood of a student telling the truth. That's understood, they insisted.

The court agreed with the teacher and the school. The basis of the ruling: Teachers have to have wide latitude in making justifiable judgment calls about a student's work.

One exception

It's worth noting in this case that the court did set out one scenario that could have changed the decision.

Had the student and his parents been able to show that the denial was unreasonable and part of a pattern of revenge against the student, the court might have made an opposite ruling.

Cite: *T.J. v. Hargrove.*

Did the teacher properly discard the student's confidential paperwork?

Procedures come under attack when test scores are revealed

The district's lawyer took notes as he spoke to the teacher and the principal.

"Jamie Harvey's parents filed suit charging you caused their son emotional distress and violated their privacy rights. So let's go over the sequence of events."

Teacher Roger Hajek nodded and began: "It started when I broke up a fight between Jamie and two other students. It was the second time that week Jamie had been involved in a fight, so I contacted his parents and talked with them about it."

"And that's when the mother said it was 'all your fault'?"

"Right," the teacher answered. "They said he got into the fights because some of the kids were calling him 'stupid' after they saw part of his assessment summary report that showed some of his test scores."

"And the kids picked the report out of the wastebasket in your room, right?" the lawyer asked.

"That's correct," the teacher said. "I had thrown out some old paperwork, and a page of the assessment summary was included in the trash."

Principal Deb Bowie spoke for the first time: "We're mandated to safeguard existing records, but there's no district policy on discarding student records."

"Well, the parents say the school wasn't careful enough with the records," the lawyer explained. "That's the basis of their lawsuit."

Defining the 'records-security process'

In court, the school argued that the teacher had disposed of the records in a standard way and hadn't left them out for students or others to see.

Did the school win the suit?

Decision: No. A judge ruled the disposal of records was part of the safeguarding process, and that the teacher and the school should have been more careful.

Key: The case shows that storing records securely meets only part of a school's obligation to maintain student privacy. Any action involving those records – including disposal – should be considered, too.

Cite: *Scott v. Minneapolis Public Schools.*

Teacher thinks a colleague may have 'helped' students with the state test

Now what should she do?

"Can I talk to you?" whispered Deena Welch, sitting down by fellow teacher Kelly Maws in the teacher's lounge.

"Sure," said Kelly. "But why are you whispering? We're alone in here."

"OK," said Deena, but still kept her voice low. "It's about the state test – and that practice worksheet Pat came up with to help students prepare for the math section."

"Pat and her corny jokes," said Kelly. "'*If Vice Principal Embry catches you with this worksheet, eat it!*'"

"But now we know why she said that."

"What do you mean?" asked Deena.

"You didn't notice when we did the math section yesterday? Pat's worksheet is just like the questions on the real test. It can't only be a coincidence."

Did practice test use real questions?

"*What?*" said Deena. "Are you accusing Pat of helping students cheat?"

"What other explanation is there?" asked Kelly. "And it explains her 'spy jokes,' too."

"But where would Pat even get the real test questions?"

"She's a proctor," said Deena. "Pat already had a book with the real questions when she passed out her worksheet."

"Should we report this?" asked Kelly.

Teacher said she only changed wording

Deena told administrators what she suspected, and the board of education gave Pat a hearing.

There, Pat admitted changing her practice questions after she saw the test – but only because she thought the test's wording was clearer. After comparing her worksheet to the test, the board suspended Pat from teaching for a year. She appealed.

Decision: Suspension was proper.

Key: Most teachers have strong feelings about the state test. But whether you're for or against it, so much is riding on the test that teachers need to be like Caesar's wife where it's concerned: above suspicion.

Cite: *Luscre-Miles v. Dep't of Educ.*

The ultimate dilemma: Give good student a break or follow the policy?

'But it's only ten minutes,' student pleads with teacher

Teacher Ellie Aims looked at the clock when a tardy student walked into class. "Sara, I need to see you in the hall."

"I'm sorry," Sara said as she walked out of the classroom.

"We've talked about this," Ellie said. "And you're ten minutes late today."

'Just one more chance'

"It won't happen again," she said.

"Sara, I know you're a good girl, but I've heard that promise before," Ellie said. "I have to send you to the office."

"No!" Sara argued. "You can't send me to the office. I've already had Saturday detention. I'll get in trouble. Just give me one more chance – please!"

"I just can't do that," Ellie said.

"Come on, Ms. A," she said. "I need a break on this. It wasn't my fault."

"I'm really sorry, Sara," Ellie said. "But this is your tenth tardy. Let's go."

The principal reported Sara to the truancy officer for her excessive tardies. At a hearing, Sara was found delinquent and put on probation. She appealed, saying school officials violated her due process rights.

She claimed they refused to listen to her reasons for being late before reporting her to the truancy officer. She asked the court to reverse the decision. Did it?

Decision: No, the court refused to overturn the ruling.

Key: The school did not violate Sara's due process rights, the court ruled. It explained two key factors in its decision:

- Sara was tardy on several occasions, and school officials disciplined Sara with steps (sending her to the office and Saturday detention) listed in its progressive discipline policy, and
- school policy and state law don't require school administrators to investigate reasons behind truancy before reporting students to truant officers.

The court said school officials handled Sara's truancy correctly.

Cite: *S.H. v. State of Alabama.*

7 Students with Disabilities

TOPICS

I. THE IDEA 271

II. DISCIPLINE OF STUDENTS WITH DISABILITIES 275

III. PLACEMENT OF STUDENTS WITH DISABILITIES 279

IV. RELATED SERVICES 288

V. TUITION REIMBURSEMENT..290

VI. TRANSITION AND GRADUATION..293

VII. SCHOOL LIABILITY 295

VIII. TEACHER SCENARIOS 302

CHAPTER SEVEN
Students with Disabilities

I. THE IDEA

Overview

Each of the states has enacted special education laws that parallel the Individuals with Disabilities Education Act (IDEA) in order to comply with federal standards and become eligible for funding. Unlike Section 504 of the Rehabilitation Act, the IDEA does not prohibit discrimination on the basis of disability. It imposes obligations on the states and requires compliance with IDEA procedures as a condition of receiving federal funds.

To receive IDEA funds, states must maintain a policy assuring that all children with disabilities have access to a free appropriate public education (FAPE). "FAPE" refers to special education and related services provided at public expense that meet state educational agency standards in conformity with an individualized education program (IEP). Local educational agencies (LEAs) receiving IDEA funds must make satisfactory assurances they are identifying and providing special education services to resident students with disabilities.

A. IDEA Substantive Requirements

In Board of Educ. v. Rowley, *the U.S. Supreme Court held the IDEA establishes only a basic floor of opportunity for students with disabilities, and imposes no requirement on school districts to maximize student potential.*

Rowley *limits a court's inquiry to two things – whether the district has complied with IDEA procedural protections, and whether the IEP was reasonably calculated to enable the student to receive educational benefits.* *If a school district satisfies this two-part inquiry, the court's analysis is at an end.*

In recent years, federal appeals courts have suggested a "meaningful benefit" standard. But in J.L. v. Mercer Island School Dist., *the Ninth Circuit demonstrated it did not intend to deviate from* Rowley. *In* Thompson R2-J School Dist. v. Luke P., *the Tenth Circuit reached a similar result.*

Court Decisions

♦ The parents of a Minnesota child sought to have accommodations provided for extracurricular activities in which she might wish to engage. However, they did not identify any specific activity at that time. The student later identified volleyball and after-school clubs as activities she was interested in. Her parents also sought accommodations so she could attend an off-campus fifth-grade graduation party. The district refused to provide accommodations relating to the party since it was a private event sponsored by the parent-teacher organization. In the lawsuit that followed, the state court of appeals held the school district did not have to provide accommodations for the child to attend a private party. But it did have to provide accommodations for the specific activities the student had identified – volleyball and after-school clubs. The case reached the Minnesota Supreme Court, which affirmed the decision in part. **The student did not have to prove that she would receive educational benefits from extracurricular and nonacademic activities in order to qualify for supplemental aides and services.** The IEP team would have to consider whether the extracurricular and nonacademic activities were appropriate. *Independent School Dist. No. 12, Centennial v. Minnesota Dep't of Educ.*, 788 N.W.2d 907 (Minn. 2010).

♦ A New Jersey high school student designated as "other health impaired" received special education and did well in his classes but tested poorly in standardized tests. His parents became concerned with his education and requested a due process hearing, where they noted that his reading skills were at a third-grade level. His teachers and other school employees testified that standardized test scores were unreliable and that academic progress was a better indicator of success, but an administrative law judge disagreed and ruled for the parents. A federal court reversed that decision, but **the Third Circuit held the student's good grades did not indicate that he was making educational progress**. In this case, the school district failed to incorporate necessary recommendations made by the parents' experts and by the student's teachers and evaluators. *D.S. v. Bayonne Board of Educ.*, 602 F.3d 553 (3d Cir. 2010).

♦ A Washington student with learning disabilities attended regular classes and progressed from grade to grade. Her parents became dissatisfied with her education and found an independent evaluator who suggested that no public school in the state could provide her an adequate education. The parents enrolled their daughter in a Massachusetts private school and sought tuition reimbursement from their school district. A federal court held an administrative law judge improperly relied on *Board of Educ. v. Rowley*. According to the court, *Rowley* was superseded by post-1982 IDEA amendments. **The case reached the Ninth Circuit, which held the *Rowley* standard is still appropriate for determining whether a child has received an appropriate education.** Congress never disapproved of *Rowley* in any of the amendments to the IDEA. *J.L. v. Mercer Island School Dist.*, 575 F.3d 1025 (9th Cir. 2009).

♦ A New York student with hearing impairments sought the provision of a sign-language interpreter from her school district. She had residual hearing and was an excellent lipreader, which allowed her to attain above-average grades and to advance through school easily. The student's parents requested the services of a sign-language interpreter at school district expense, arguing that the IDEA required the district to maximize her potential. A federal court held that the disparity between the student's achievement and her potential to perform as she would if not for her disability deprived her of a free appropriate public education. This decision was affirmed by the U.S. Court of Appeals,

Second Circuit, and the U.S. Supreme Court agreed to review the case.

The Court found no requirement in the IDEA that public schools maximize the potential of each student with a disability. The opportunities provided to each student by their school varied from student to student. The IDEA was primarily designed to guarantee access to students with disabilities to allow them to meaningfully benefit from public education. The IDEA protected the right to access education by means of its procedural protections, including the annual IEP meeting and review process. In IDEA cases, courts were to limit their inquiry to **whether the district had complied with IDEA procedural protections, and whether the IEP was reasonably calculated to enable the student to receive educational benefits**. If the district satisfied this two-part inquiry, the court's analysis was at an end and the district was entitled to judgment. *Board of Educ. v. Rowley*, 458 U.S. 176 (1982).

◆ Ohio parents disagreed with the IEP prepared for their autistic son and placed him in a private school. They filed a due process hearing request but lost at two administrative levels. Without an attorney, they appealed. A federal court held for the school district, and the Sixth Circuit later held they could not pursue the case without hiring an attorney. **The U.S. Supreme Court heard the parents' appeal, and held the IDEA accorded them independently enforceable rights.** As it would be inconsistent with the statutory scheme to bar them from continuing to assert these enforceable rights in federal court, the Court reversed the judgment, permitting them to pursue their case. *Winkelman v. Parma City School Dist.*, 550 U.S. 516 (2007).

◆ A Tennessee school board violated the rights of a student with autism by failing to consider Lovaas programming and improperly staffing his IEP team meetings. The Sixth Circuit held **"meaningful educational benefit" had to be gauged in relation to the student's potential**. The IDEA's legislative history supported exceeding the "meaningful educational benefits" standard where there was a "difference between self-sufficiency and a life of dependence" for a child. *Hamilton County Dep't of Educ. v. Deal*, 392 F.3d 840 (5th Cir. 2004).

The Sixth Circuit returned the case to a federal court, which held that the school district's proposals were substantively appropriate for the student. The court awarded the parents half of their request for reimbursement for Lovaas services, and they appealed. The Sixth Circuit affirmed the decision. As the district's IEPs were reasonably calculated to offer the student a meaningful educational benefit, the reduction in reimbursement was reasonable. *Deal v. Hamilton County Dep't of Educ.*, 258 Fed.Appx. 863 (6th Cir. 2008).

◆ Colorado parents claimed their school district did not address their autistic son's inability to generalize skills he learned at school to other settings. Despite his apparent progress toward IEP goals and objectives, his home behavior was characterized as "unevenly tempered." The child often displayed inappropriate and violent behavior at home and in public places. He had sleep problems, and he sometimes intentionally spread bowel movements around his bedroom. While the child was toilet-trained at school by grade one, he was unable to transfer this skill to his home and other settings. His parents placed him in the Boston Higashi School (BHS) and presented the IEP team with a list of goals from their private therapist's recommendations. After the IEP team proposed an IEP incorporating virtually all the goals sought by the parents, they declined the offer and filed a due process hearing request, seeking reimbursement for the BHS placement. The case reached the U.S. Court of Appeals, Tenth Circuit.

The court held the substantive IDEA standard for the provision of a free appropriate public education is not onerous. **Congress did not impose any greater substantive educational standard than would be necessary to make access to education "meaningful."** *Rowley* rejected "self-sufficiency" as a substantive IDEA standard. The IDEA was not designed to remedy a poor home setting or to make up for some other deficit not covered by the act. Generalization across settings was not required to show educational benefit. The school district did not have to do more than provide an IEP that enabled the child to make measurable and adequate gains in the classroom. *Thompson R2-J School Dist. v. Luke P.*, 540 F.3d 1143 (10th Cir. 2008).

B. Procedural Protections

1. IEPs and Team Meetings

The individualized education program (IEP) is the IDEA's most important procedural protection. The IDEA requires adequate notice to parents and opportunities for parental participation in the development of a student's IEP. A school district "must include the parents of a child with a disability in an IEP meeting unless they affirmatively refuse to attend."

Court Decisions

◆ The parents of a Vermont student with a disability asserted that their school district violated the IDEA because the student's applied media instructor, a regular education teacher, missed some IEP meetings. They claimed that his increased presence might have led to a different placement. After they began due process proceedings, the case reached the Second Circuit, which ruled against them. **The court held the absence of a regular educator at any given IEP meeting is not necessarily a procedural violation of the IDEA.** The instructor's participation in this case was held appropriate under the circumstances. He attended some meetings, and the parents decided to enroll their child in a particular applied media course without regard to the instructor's opinion. Thus, they suffered no harm. *K.L.A. v. Windham Southeast Supervisory Union*, 371 Fed.Appx. 151 (2d Cir. 2010).

◆ The parents of a New York student who had problems in large group settings attended committee on special education (CSE) meetings at which the student's IEP was changed from a classroom of 24 students to a 12:1:1 setting. The parents rejected the proposed IEP and placed the student in a private school and then sought tuition reimbursement. A federal court found the IEP procedurally deficient because the student's special education teacher did not attend the CSE meetings. However, the Second Circuit reversed, noting that **the IEP coordinator at the student's school had attended the CSE meetings along with the student's general education teacher** and that the IEP was reasonably calculated to provide educational benefits. No tuition was awarded. *A.H. v. Dep't of Educ. of City of New York*, 394 Fed.Appx. 718 (2d Cir. 2010).

◆ Parents of an autistic preschool child were denied a ruling that school officials "predetermined" a placement and failed to provide him intensive one-on-one therapy. The U.S. Court of Appeals, Fourth Circuit, affirmed a lower court order finding the school considered information from the parents at IEP meetings. A hearing officer found the parents "derailed the IEP process" by preventing thorough discussions, and many of their own suggestions were adopted in the IEP. **Use of a draft IEP did not show predetermination.** The court affirmed a judgment for school officials under several disability laws. *J.D. v. Kanawha County Board of Educ.*, 357 Fed.Appx. 515 (4th Cir. 2009).

◆ A California school district scheduled an IEP meeting without first checking the parents' availability. The parents had a history of not attending such meetings, and they did not return a signed copy of the IEP meeting notice. The mother asked the district to reschedule the meeting, but the district met in her absence. The parents filed an administrative action against the district for IDEA procedural violations. Eventually the case reached the Ninth Circuit, which held that regardless of the parents' history and the reason for their unavailability on the date in question, the district had an affirmative duty to comply with the IDEA. It held **a school district "must include the parents of a child with a disability in an IEP meeting unless they affirmatively refuse to attend."** By proceeding with the IEP meeting in the parents' absence, the district violated the IDEA. This justified a finding that the student was denied a free appropriate public education for an entire school year. *Drobnicki v. Poway Unified School Dist.*, 358 Fed.Appx. 788 (9th Cir. 2009).

◆ The parents of an autistic student in California claimed that their district violated the IDEA because no teacher from the student's private school attended IEP team meetings. The case reached the Ninth Circuit, which held the district provided a valid IEP. **The court held the exclusion of a private school teacher from IEP team meetings did not result in lost educational opportunities for the student.** However, the school district did have to continue to co-fund an in-home intervention program while the appeals process was completed. The stay-put provision of the IDEA required the district to maintain the student's current educational placement during the appeals process. *Joshua A. v. Rocklin Unified School Dist.*, 319 Fed.Appx. 692, 559 F.3d 1036 (9th Cir. 2009).

◆ The parents of an Ohio student had a contentious relationship with their school district, and they filed numerous administrative complaints. They sought to tape IEP meetings without prior consent and objected to the presence of a school attorney there. As a result of the disputes, the parties were unable to negotiate an IEP. The district filed a due process request and the case reached a federal court, which held that the district's attorney could be present at the IEP meetings. Further, **canceling IEP meetings because of conditions the parents imposed did not deprive them of any due process rights**. *Horen v. Board of Educ. of Toledo City School Dist.*, 594 F.Supp.2d 833 (N.D. Ohio 2009).

◆ A California school district convened an IEP team meeting that included a student's adaptive physical education (PE) teacher from three years earlier. Given the student's disabilities, adaptive PE was one of his most significant IEP components. The PE teacher had recently visited his school to evaluate his needs and was familiar with his current situation. His parents claimed an IDEA violation because his most current special education providers did not attend the meeting. The Ninth Circuit held **the IDEA does not require the most current teacher to attend an IEP meeting. Rather, it requires a special education teacher or provider who has actually taught the student.** Not all a student's special education teachers need to attend the IEP meeting. *A.G. v. Placentia-Yorba Linda Unified School Dist.*, 320 Fed.Appx. 519 (9th Cir. 2009).

◆ A Connecticut student with serious emotional disturbance had increasing behavioral problems as he entered middle school. He was transferred to a state-approved special education day school, where he achieved good grades. His parents sought a private school placement, fearing he was not being sufficiently challenged. After an evaluation, the school board adopted several of the parents' suggested changes to the IEP, and offered a placement in a regional school for students with emotional and behavioral difficulties. The parents rejected the IEP and challenged it in an IDEA due process proceeding. The case reached the Second Circuit, which held that schools comply with the IDEA when parents have adequate opportunities to participate in the development of the IEP. **Nothing in the IDEA requires that parents consent to an IEP.** Because the initial and revised IEPs were sufficient, the board had offered an appropriate IEP. *A.E. v. Westport Board of Educ.*, 251 Fed.Appx. 685 (2d Cir. 2007).

◆ A Virginia student with Asperger's syndrome and a nonverbal learning disability was subjected to teasing and assaults by other students. At the IEP meeting for his ninth-grade school year, the discussion focused on his levels of performance and goals and objectives. The team decided the student would be placed at an unspecified private day school even though the student's mother believed neither of two suggested schools was appropriate for him. The family sought placement in a residential school, and the Fourth Circuit ultimately agreed. **Failure to**

identify a particular school in the IEP was an IDEA violation. *A.K. v. Alexandria City School Board*, 484 F.3d 672 (4th Cir. 2007).

The case returned to the district court, which held that the district had to pay the parents over $135,000 in tuition and transportation costs. *A.K. v. Alexandria City School Board*, 544 F.Supp.2d 487 (E.D. Va. 2008).

♦ A California student with ADHD and reactive detachment disorder was expelled from three preschool programs for classroom misconduct. In first grade, the district declared her ineligible for special education under the IDEA, but eligible for accommodation under Section 504. She continued to have behavior problems in elementary school. Her mother placed her in a private residential facility in Montana, then sought tuition reimbursement. The school convened an IEP team meeting, but no representative from the facility attended. After the team again found the student ineligible for special education, the family initiated an IDEA proceeding. A federal court and the Ninth Circuit held **any procedural error by the district in failing to properly staff the IEP team meeting was harmless because the student failed to show that she had a qualifying disability under the IDEA.** *R.B. v. Napa Valley Unified School Dist.*, 496 F.3d 932 (9th Cir. 2007).

♦ An Ohio student began experiencing disciplinary problems in sixth grade and his IEP was then changed twice. His mother rejected his seventh-grade IEP on the grounds that it had been predetermined by the IEP team. She eventually sued, and the case reached the Sixth Circuit. The court of appeals held that predetermination is not the same as preparation and that the **IEP team members could prepare reports and come to meetings with pre-formed opinions about the best course of action for a student**. Here, the parties had met 16 times over a two-year period and had daily communications about homework. The school district's preparation work prior to the IEP meeting did not violate the IDEA. *Nack v. Orange City School Dist.*, 454 F.3d 604 (6th Cir. 2006).

2. Notice and Hearing Requirements

Local educational agencies must provide parents with notices of their procedural rights once a year, and upon an initial referral or evaluation for special education and related services, the filing of a due process complaint, or other parental request. Schools and school districts may place procedural safeguard notices on their websites. The reauthorized IDEA sets a two-year limitation period on the filing of IDEA complaints. A party appealing from an adverse due process hearing decision must appeal within 90 days from the date of the hearing officer's decision, unless the state has its own limitation period.

Court Decisions

♦ A Maryland student with learning disabilities and a speech impairment attended private schools for years. His parents then sought to place him through the Montgomery County Public Schools. The district evaluated him and drafted an IEP that would have placed him in one of two district middle schools. The parents rejected the offer, and requested a hearing. An administrative law judge (ALJ) found the evidence was close, and held the parents had the burden of persuasion in the case. As a result of this allocation of the burden, the district won. The case reached the U.S. Supreme Court, which explained that the party filing the lawsuit, who seeks to change the state of affairs, should be expected to bear the burden of proof. This was the case, for example, in cases arising under Title VII of the Civil Rights Act of 1964 and the Americans with Disabilities Act. Congress has repeatedly amended the IDEA to reduce its administrative and litigation costs. **The Court held parents who challenge their children's IEPs in special education due process hearings have the burden of proving the IEPs are inappropriate.** The Court affirmed the judgment, holding the burden of proof in an administrative hearing to challenge an IEP is on the party seeking relief. *Schaffer v. Weast*, 546 U.S. 49 (2005).

When the case returned to a federal district court, the parents challenged the student's eighth-grade IEP by presenting evidence of the changes made to his tenth-grade IEP. The school district countered with evidence that the student had graduated with a 3.4 grade point average. The court ruled for the school district, and the Fourth Circuit affirmed the judgment. **Using the tenth-grade IEP to challenge the eighth-grade IEP would promote a hindsight-based review that conflicted with the IDEA's structure and purpose.** *Schaffer v. Weast*, 554 F.3d 470 (4th Cir. 2009).

♦ While incarcerated, the father of a child with a disability attempted to challenge a decision that the student did not need additional special instruction. The board denied his request to review assessment materials and obtain an impartial due process hearing because he had no custodial rights over the child. A federal district court held that **non-custodial status did not automatically divest the father of all parental rights**. On appeal, the Second Circuit ruled that the lower court would have to decide whether the mother should be joined as a necessary party by examining state law and the divorce decree. *Fuentes v. Board of Educ. of City of New York*, 136 Fed.Appx. 448 (2d Cir. 2005).

The case was then returned to the district court, which again held the father lacked legal standing to pursue the case. He filed another appeal. The Second Circuit rejected the father's claim that the case should be resolved under the IDEA. **Amendments to the IDEA in 2004 did not create a presumption that biological parents have a right to sue under the IDEA,** so long as a custody or divorce decree did not restrict those rights. As state law would determine the answer to the parental rights questions, the court certified a question to the state's highest court. It asked: "[w]hether, under New York law, the biological and non-custodial parent of a child retains the right to participate in decisions pertaining to the education of the child where (1) the custodial parent is granted exclusive custody of the child and (2) the divorce decree and custody order are silent as to the right to control such decisions." *Fuentes v. Board of Educ. of City of New York*, 540 F.d 145 (2d Cir. 2008).

The New York Court of Appeals accepted the question from the Second Circuit. **It held that although a non-custodial parent has the right to participate in a child's education, that parent does not have the right to "control educational decisions" absent an express provision in the custody agreement.** Thus, the father could not challenge the district's provision of educational services to the student. *Fuentes v. Board of Educ. of City of New York*, 12 N.Y.3d 309, 907 N.E.2d 696 (N.Y. 2009).

C. Implementation of IEPs

In a Texas case, the U.S. Court of Appeals, Fifth Circuit, described a test for assessing whether a school district has adequately implemented an IEP. The court assessed whether education was being provided in a coordinated and collaborative manner by key stakeholders and whether the student was receiving positive academic and nonacademic benefits. **A student challenging the adequacy of an IEP must demonstrate that school authorities failed to implement substantial or significant IEP provisions.** Houston Independent School Dist. v. Bobby R., 200 F.3d 341 (5th Cir. 2000).

Teacher Scenarios

Is teacher required to 'handle' service dog? 302

Did teacher make right call with disabled student? 302

Parents say teacher crossed the line by restraining student who acted up 303

Mother says school has to permit deaf son's service dog 304

Court Decisions

◆ The mother of a Washington student with autism believed that the in-home ABA therapists provided by her district were not properly trained. She began taking him to a private therapist. The school district then began offering ABA therapy and discontinued paying for the private therapist. The mother refused to let her son attend an extended school year program because she believed the staff was improperly trained. She rejected another IEP offer and sought due process. The case reached the Washington Court of Appeals, which noted that the IEP offered a free appropriate public education even though the IEP team ultimately rejected the mother's position that she had been denied an adequate opportunity to participate in IEP meetings. She had attended the meetings with an advocate and an autism consultant and rejected several attempts to evaluate the student. **The IEP was flexible enough to allow the modifications offered by the district to address the mother's concerns after the IEP was adopted.** *Hensley v. Colville School Dist.*, 148 Wash.App. 1032 (Wash. Ct. App. 2009).

◆ A New Jersey student's IEP called for a personal aide for the full school day as well as 10 hours of at-home tutoring a week at school board expense. Aides were to be trained in Lovaas methodology, which is also known as applied behavioral analysis. When the school district could not find a Lovaas-trained aide, the student's mother did so and the district then hired him. The aide resigned, and it took the school district a while to replace him. During this time, the mother kept her son at home and hired another Lovaas-trained aide, whom the district also hired. She made extra payments to the aides the district provided, then sought reimbursement for those payments. However, a federal district court and later the U.S. Court of Appeals, Third Circuit, ruled for the school board. It found the school board had no idea she was making the payments. Further, the **delay in finding a replacement aide did not amount to a denial of a free appropriate public education**. *Fisher v. Stafford Township Board of Educ.*, 289 Fed.Appx. 520 (3d Cir. 2008).

◆ A severely autistic Oregon student transitioned from elementary to middle school, where his father claimed the school district failed to implement key parts of his IEP. He requested a due process hearing, and an administrative law judge held the district was adequately implementing the student's IEP, except for math instruction. She ordered the district to remedy that aspect of the IEP. A federal court affirmed her ruling, and the Ninth Circuit then largely upheld the decision in favor of the district. It noted that **minor failures in implementing an IEP are not automatic violations of the IDEA. Only a material failure to implement an IEP violates the IDEA.** "A material failure occurs when the services a school provides to a disabled child fall significantly short of the services required by the child's IEP." Because the district had remedied the math instruction deficiency, there were no substantive IDEA violations. *Van Duyn v. Baker School Dist. 5J*, 481 F.3d 770 (9th Cir. 2007).

II. DISCIPLINE OF STUDENTS WITH DISABILITIES

Overview

In Doe v. Todd County School Dist., *this chapter, the U.S. Court of Appeals, Eighth Circuit, held the change of a student's placement "is primarily an educational, not a disciplinary, decision." But the IDEA states that disciplinary removals of over 10 school days, or a pattern of removals that exceeds 10 days in a school year, may constitute a "change in placement." See 20 U.S.C. § 1415(k)(G). Students who violate a student code of conduct may be placed in an appropriate interim alternative setting. The IDEA allows schools to "consider any unique circumstances on a case-by-case basis when determining whether to order a change in placement" for a student with disabilities who violates a student code of conduct. See 20 U.S.C. § 1415(k). It specifies the "special circumstances" in which schools may remove a student to an interim alternative educational setting for up to 45 days, regardless of whether the behavior leading to discipline is a manifestation of a disability.*

The "special circumstances" are: weapons possession, the sale, use or possession of drugs; or infliction of serious bodily injury while at school, on school grounds, or at a school event. A hearing officer reviewing a disciplinary removal may return the child to his or her placement, or order a change in placement to an appropriate interim alternative setting for not more than 45 school days. To do so, the hearing officer must find maintaining the current placement is "substantially likely to result in injury."

In Honig v. Doe, *below, the U.S. Supreme Court held that while a school district cannot unilaterally change the placement of a disabled student it feels is be dangerous,* ***the district can use "its normal procedures for dealing with children who are endangering themselves or others," such as "time-outs, detention, the restriction of privileges," or suspension.***

Teacher Scenarios

Mom claims teacher was out of line: Students voted to remove classmate 304

Learning-disabled student acts up: Should punishment be less severe? 305

Dealing with difficult students: When to draw the line 306

Student excluded from field trip – for ADHD? 307

They commit same offense but don't get same punishment 307

A. Discipline as a Change in Placement

Court Decisions

◆ Two emotionally disturbed children in California were each suspended for five days for misbehavior that included destroying school property and assaulting and making sexual comments to other students. Pursuant to state law, the suspensions were continued indefinitely during the pendency of expulsion proceedings. The students sued the school district in U.S. district court contesting the extended suspensions on the ground that they violated the "stay-put" provision of the IDEA, which provides that a student must be kept in his or her "then-current" educational placement during the pendency of proceedings which contemplate a change in placement. The district court issued an injunction preventing the expulsion, and the school district appealed. The U.S. Court of Appeals, Ninth Circuit, held the indefinite suspensions constituted a prohibited "change in placement" without notice under the IDEA. There was no "dangerousness" exception to the IDEA's "stay-put" provision.

On appeal, the U.S. Supreme Court held the intended purpose of the "stay-put" provision was to prevent schools from changing a child's educational placement over parental objections until all IDEA proceedings were completed. While the IDEA provided for interim placements where parents and school officials were able to agree on one, there was no emergency exception for dangerous students. **Where a disabled student poses an immediate threat to the safety of others, school officials may temporarily suspend him or her for up to 10 school days.** The Court affirmed the court of appeals' decision that indefinite suspensions violated the "stay-put" provision of the IDEA. It modified the decision by holding that suspensions up to 10 rather than up to 30 days do not constitute a change in placement. Significantly, the Court held that **a school district can use "its normal procedures for dealing with children who are endangering themselves or others," such as "time-outs, detention, the restriction of privileges," or suspension**. The Court also upheld the court of appeals' ruling that states could be required to provide services directly to disabled students where a local school district fails to do so. *Honig v. Doe,* 484 U.S. 305, 108 S.Ct. 592, 98 L.Ed.2d 686 (1988).

B. Manifestation Determinations

A manifestation determination review is required when disciplinary action would result in a disabled child's removal from school for over 10 days in a school year. ***The student's IEP team must perform the review.*** *Parents and IEP team members are to determine "if the conduct in question was caused by, or had a direct and substantial relationship, to the child's disability." If so, the team must determine if the conduct was a direct result of failure to implement the IEP.* ***If the team finds the child's behavior is not a manifestation of a disability, the disciplinary procedures applied to non-disabled children may be applied to the child.*** *A student whose misconduct is not a manifestation of a disability is still entitled to regular disciplinary procedures. If the team finds the misconduct is related to the child's disability, it may still seek the parents' agreement to change the placement. A local education agency (LEA) that disciplines a student with disabilities must continue to provide the student with a free appropriate public education if a placement is changed. This is irrespective of whether the child's behavior is found to manifest a disability.*

Court Decisions

◆ A South Dakota student fought with another student and brought a knife to school. After being suspended, a manifestation determination meeting was held, and the IEP team found his misconduct was not a manifestation of his learning disability. After missing four days of school, he was placed in an alternative educational setting. His grandmother asked for a school board hearing but was informed that was not possible because the student was no longer suspended. In his alternative placement, the student received two hours of instruction four days a week instead of his usual 30 hours per week. In a federal court action, the court held the alternative placement amounted to a long-term suspension that exceeded 10 days. It held the student was entitled to a hearing before the school board, just like any other student facing similar discipline. On appeal, the U.S. Court of Appeals, Eighth Circuit, agreed with the school district that the student had only been suspended for four days. The assistant principal had explained the charges to the student and given him an opportunity to respond.

As suspensions of 10 days or less trigger only minimal due process protection, due process had been satisfied. The IEP team could have removed the student from school for up to 45 school days under a section of the IDEA allowing schools to place a student in an interim alternative educational setting. The team also had the option to place him in an alternative educational setting with parental consent. This is what had actually occurred, as the grandmother agreed to the change to obtain counseling and instructional services. **Federal law expressly provided that IEP teams must determine any interim alternative educational placement.** Once the IEP team changed the student's placement with the grandmother's consent, the team, and not the school board, "became the decision-maker authorized to change his placement" under 34 C.F.R. Part 300.530(d)(5). By agreeing to the change in placement, the grandparent "gave the IEP team, rather than the District's school board, control of the situation." As the district did not violate the student's rights, the judgment was reversed. *Doe v. Todd County School Dist.*, 625 F.3d 459 (8th Cir. 2010).

◆ A District of Columbia student who was eligible for special education taunted a substitute teacher and refused to follow instructions. Because he had two prior infractions in the same school year, he was suspended for 54 days and placed in an alternative educational setting. A manifestation determination review found his behavior was not a manifestation of his disability. After a hearing officer reduced the suspension to 10 days, an assistant district superintendent increased it to 45 days. Another hearing officer found that the alternative placement was not appropriate under the IDEA and reduced the suspension to 11 days. **When the district challenged that decision, the D.C. Circuit upheld it because the alternative placement denied the student a FAPE.** The hearing officer did not exceed his authority in modifying the suspension. *District of Columbia v. Doe*, 611 F.3d 888 (D.C. Cir. 2010).

◆ An Ohio student with ADD received interventions in grades one and two but was determined not to need an IEP. In third grade, she became physically aggressive and was referred to a mental health agency. Later, she was suspended for threatening behavior. Her mother requested a manifestation determination review and an evaluation, which found her eligible for special education. Her mother then filed a due process request for various IDEA violations. A hearing officer awarded compensatory education for the delay in identifying the student as IDEA-eligible. **A federal court agreed that the district should have conducted a manifestation determination before suspending the student.** It also ordered the discipline wiped from her record. *Jackson v. Northwest Local School Dist.*, No. 1:09-cv-300, 2010 WL 3452333 (S.D. Ohio 8/3/10).

◆ Along with several friends, an emotionally disabled Virginia student vandalized his school by shooting the building and some school buses with paintball guns. The principal recommended that he be expelled, which triggered an IDEA manifestation determination review. The review committee found his behavior was not a manifestation of his disability. A hearing officer recommended suspending the student for the rest of the year. His parents objected and sought due process. The hearing officer found no IDEA violation, and a federal court agreed. **There was no IDEA requirement that the review committee members know the student personally.** And the student was not drawn into the vandalism by his friends. Rather, he had been an instigator. *Fitzgerald v. Fairfax County School Board*, 556 F.Supp.2d 543 (E.D. Va. 2008).

◆ A Pennsylvania student who was eligible for a Section 504 plan but not an IEP under the IDEA caused a bomb scare at his school. The school district denied his parents' request for a manifestation determination hearing and expelled the student. The parents sued the school district in a federal court, which held **a manifestation determination is required for discipline under the IDEA, but not Section 504**. While a manifestation determination is one way to comply with Section 504 requirements, the law does not mandate this. As a result, the student had not been denied due process by the failure to conduct a manifestation determination. *Centennial School Dist. v. Phil L.*, 559 F.Supp.2d 634 (E.D. Pa. 2008).

◆ Classmates called a learning disabled New York student "faggot" and "PLC," which stood for "prescriptive learning class." A fight broke out between the student and a classmate, and the student was suspended for five days. The district notified him of a hearing to consider a longer suspension. The superintendent accepted the hearing officer's recommendation for another five-day suspension pending a manifestation hearing. The school's committee on special education found the student's behavior was not a manifestation of his disability, and the superintendent then planned to suspend him for the rest of the year. The student sued the school district in a federal district court, which found that **"PLC" was a reference to his learning disability, making the incident "related to" his disability**. Also, the district treated the manifestation determination "dismissively" and did not afford adequate due process. *Coleman v. Newburgh Enlarged City School Dist.*, 319 F.Supp.2d 446 (S.D.N.Y. 2004).

After the student graduated, he sued the district for his attorneys' fees. The Second Circuit held he had to exhaust his administrative remedies and was not entitled to fees. He had no right to graduate at a particular time from a particular school, even if he was a superior athlete on the verge of graduation. *Coleman v. Newburgh Enlarged City School Dist.*, 503 F.3d 198 (2d Cir. 2007).

C. Delinquency and Juvenile Justice

A federal regulation at 34 C.F.R. Part 300.535(a) explains that special education protections do not shield students who commit crimes or juvenile offenses from law enforcement efforts. The regulation states "[n]othing in this part prohibits an agency from reporting a crime committed by a child with a disability to appropriate authorities or prevents [s]tate law enforcement and judicial authorities from exercising their responsibilities with regard to the application of Federal and State law to crimes committed by a child with a disability." In the following case, the Court of Appeals of Michigan rejected a student's claim that this regulation violated his due process rights.

Court Decisions

♦ A Michigan student had Tourette's Disorder and related disabilities. He received special education services and had a behavioral plan. After the school district issued him several suspensions, it petitioned a state court to find him guilty of school incorrigibility under Section 712A.2 of the state code. This section made school incorrigibility an offense for juveniles who were "willfully and repeatedly" absent or who repeatedly violated school rules and regulations.

The court upheld the petition, and the student appealed to the Court of Appeals of Michigan. The court held the petition was properly filed and that the prosecutor had been neutral. **Despite the provision of behavioral plan services, the court found the student engaged in repeated and escalating misconduct** that disturbed others. It was not error for the county court to assume jurisdiction over the student, and the agency did not have to provide his special education and disciplinary records prior to filing a juvenile petition. In a separate proceeding, an administrative law judge had found the juvenile petition was not a change in placement. Since the student did not appeal from that finding, he could not attack it later. In any event, he was never removed from school for more than 10 consecutive school days or a series of removals totaling more than 10 school days in one school year. So the court found a manifestation determination hearing was unnecessary. Section 712A.2 did not require evidence of willful violations and did not exempt violations based on a juvenile's disability. **The IDEA does not prevent schools from reporting crimes by disabled students to appropriate officials.** As sufficient evidence supported an adjudication of guilt, the judgment was affirmed. *In re Nicholas Papadelis*, No. 291536, 2010 WL 3447892 (Mich. Ct. App. 9/2/10).

♦ A Georgia school district assigned a one-on-one assistant to an aggressive autistic student for an after-school daycare program and also devised a behavior intervention plan for him. A custodian with a special needs son received training and served as the assistant, but often had to be away to attend to his own child. On a day when the custodian was absent, the student became agitated and left the building. Eventually, several staff members placed him in his time-out room, where he hit the window and kicked the walls. A police officer handcuffed him until his father could come and pick him up. The father later sued for disability discrimination under Section 504 and the ADA, but **a federal court found no evidence of intentional discrimination against the student**. At most, staff members acted negligently. *J.D.P. v. Cherokee County, Georgia School Dist.*, 735 F.Supp.2d 1348 (N.D. Ga. 2010).

♦ A New Mexico student with a specific learning disability skipped classes 136 times in a semester, used drugs and alcohol, was arrested for attacking family members and sent to a juvenile detention center. The center evaluated her and recommended "placement in reg-ed with support." The student's school district accepted the form as an "interim IEP" when the student returned to school in fall, where she was to repeat grade nine. The district did not revise the "interim IEP" prior to the school year and did not update her last functioning IEP. During the next term, the student had serious disciplinary problems and 65 unexcused absences. The school suspended her for fighting, and she failed all her fall classes. A hearing officer found that the district did not deny the student a FAPE. The student enrolled in ninth grade at a different high school. This time, she consistently attended school and earned a 4.0 grade point average for the school year. But the student resumed skipping classes, and she used drugs and alcohol. She stopped attending school when her mother kicked her out of the house. The student appealed the administrative decision to a federal court.

The court held **any loss of educational opportunity suffered by the student was the result of her own behavior and not school errors**. On appeal, the U.S. Court of Appeals, Tenth Circuit, held any IDEA violation was immaterial because of her truancy and behavioral problems. The student had largely rejected the services offered to her, and the district was bound to provide her a FAPE if she decided to return to school. *Garcia v. Board of Educ. of Albuquerque Public Schools*, 520 F.3d 1116 (10th Cir. 2008).

♦ An Illinois student who received special education and related services was charged with lighting fireworks and throwing them at others. A juvenile court adjudicated him delinquent and placed him on probation. When he violated probation, his probation officer recommended a residential placement. His mother moved to a new school district, which was notified that it should appear in juvenile court regarding its potential liability for funding the student's placement. The juvenile court agreed with the probation officer that the student should be residentially placed, and ordered the district to fund the placement. The district challenged the decision in a state court and won. The Illinois Supreme Court held that **the student's placement was not made under the School Code, but under the Juvenile Court Act**. It was made to remedy a probation violation, not the student's educational needs. Also, the district was not given the opportunity to show that it could educate the student. The state had to fund the placement. *In re D.D.*, 819 N.E.2d 300 (Ill. 2004).

◆ A New York principal initiated a family court proceeding to determine if a student was in need of supervision based on 16 unexcused absences from school during a two-month period. The family court ordered the school's committee on special education to conduct an evaluation. It found that the student was emotionally disturbed and had a disability. After the court placed the student on probation for a year, he appealed. The New York Supreme Court, Appellate Division, ruled that the **adjudication of the student as a child in need of supervision did not constitute a change in placement** under the IDEA. The student's placement was not changed. He was simply ordered to attend school and participate in his IEP. *Erich D. v. New Milford Board of Educ.*, 767 N.Y.S.2d 488 (N.Y. App. Div. 2003).

III. PLACEMENT OF STUDENTS WITH DISABILITIES

Overview

The IDEA requires each local education agency to identify and evaluate students with disabilities in its jurisdiction. After a district identifies a student as disabled, it must develop and implement an individualized education program (IEP). The IEP must be reasonably calculated to provide educational benefits and where possible, to include the student with non-disabled students.

A. Identification and Evaluation

Parents may request the initial evaluation of a child for special education and related services, as may the state or the local educational agency (LEA). An evaluation is to take place within 60 days of receiving parental consent, or within a time frame established by the state. LEAs are exempt from the 60-day requirement in transfer cases or if a parent "repeatedly fails or refuses to produce the child for the evaluation."

Parents who have not allowed an evaluation of their children, or have refused special education and related services, will be barred from later asserting IDEA procedural protections in disciplinary cases. A special rule for eligibility determinations states that lack of appropriate instruction in reading or math may not be used to make an IDEA eligibility determination.

Lack of English proficiency is also specifically excluded from entering into eligibility determinations. When determining whether a child has a specific learning disability, LEAs may not consider a severe discrepancy between achievement and intellectual ability in oral expression, listening comprehension, written expression, basic reading skill, reading comprehension, mathematical calculation or mathematical reasoning.

Court Decisions

◆ The parents of a New York preschool student obtained three evaluations showing that their son had either an autism spectrum disorder, ADHD or serious social issues. They sought special education for him even though his teachers maintained that he made academic progress and his behavior problems were manageable. A due process hearing officer noted that the student's behavior did not adversely impact his education to a degree that indicated a need for special education. A federal court agreed, ruling that **all the parents could show was that because their son needed frequent redirection, he was not reaching his full academic potential**. But achievement of full academic potential is not the IDEA eligibility standard. And the record in this case did not demonstrate that the student's educational performance was adversely affected by his Asperger's syndrome. *A.J. v. Board of Educ., East Islip Union Free School Dist.*, 679 F.Supp.2d 299 (E.D.N.Y. 2010).

◆ After an evaluation, a Pennsylvania second-grader was thought to have ADHD. But there was no discrepancy between his ability and his achievement, so he was not placed in special education. By the seventh grade, the student's performance declined and at the end of the eighth grade, he was evaluated again and found to have ADHD. His performance continued to decline over the next two years, and he dropped out of school. The student's parents filed an IDEA action against the school district for failing to timely identify him as disabled. A federal court, and later the Third Circuit ruled against the parents, finding that **the school district did not rely solely on an ability/achievement analysis in determining that the student did not need special education at an earlier age**. The district did not violate its child-find duty under the IDEA. *Richard S. v. Wissahickon School Dist.*, 334 Fed.Appx. 508 (3d Cir. 2009).

◆ A California student had Pachygyria, a disorder associated with seizures, developmental delays and neuropsychiatric dysfunction. School evaluators, though highly experienced, had never before assisted a child with Pachygyria. They recommended a public school placement and determined that the student's behaviors and anxieties did not disrupt her ability to learn and participate in school activities. The parents, desiring a private school placement, sought due process and appealed an adverse decision to a federal court. **The court ruled that the evaluators' lack of familiarity with Pachygyria did not violate the IDEA and that the district offered the student an adequate academic program**. *Marcotte v. Palos Verdes Peninsula Unified School Dist.*, No. CV 08-1671 PSG (PLAx), 2009 WL 1873024 (C.D. Cal. 6/29/09).

◆ A New York student with ADHD was sexually abused by a cousin and was later suspended for fighting and drug possession. His grades dropped out of the honor roll range, but he continued to pass his classes. His parents placed him in a boarding school for troubled students. The committee on special education met and determined the student did not meet the IDEA criteria for severe emotional disturbance. His parents appealed, and the case reached the Second Circuit. The court held for the school district, ruling that **even if the student exhibited some of the symptomology for an emotional disturbance, his symptoms did not affect his academic performance**. Instead, drug use appeared to be at the root of his school problems. *Mr. and Mrs. N.C. v. Bedford Cent. School Dist.*, 300 Fed.Appx. 11 (2d Cir. 2008).

◆ A Pennsylvania student with autism spectrum disorder had a behavioral crisis while in a private school funded by the district. **A reevaluation led to an evaluation report that used boilerplate language, listing generic goals and principles that might work for any child rather than specifying the student's needs and issues.** The IEP also contained much of that boilerplate language. When the parents sought due process, a hearing officer determined that both the IEP and the private school placement were inappropriate. The case reached a federal court, which agreed that the IEP and the private school were inappropriate. A new IEP would have to be developed. *A.Y. and D.Y. v. Cumberland Valley School Dist.*, 569 F.Supp.2d 496 (M.D. Pa. 2008).

◆ A California student spent three years in foster care before reuniting with his mother as a five-year-old, just before beginning kindergarten. He acted out at school and was disciplined by his teacher four times in less than four months at a Los Angeles public school. His mother requested an initial special education assessment, which the district denied because of the student's limited school experience and the lack of general education interventions. The family moved out of the district, and the mother requested due process. A hearing officer held that the district had to pay for an independent educational evaluation, and a federal court agreed. **Although the district did not have to assess the student itself, it had an obligation to fund the independent evaluation.** *Los Angeles Unified School Dist. v. D.L.*, 548 F.Supp.2d 815 (C.D. Cal. 2008).

◆ A Texas student with ADHD received special education services until the fourth grade, after which he no longer needed them. He performed well in school but had behavioral problems through the seventh and eighth grades. He nevertheless passed all his classes and met the statewide standards required by the Texas Assessment of Knowledge and Skills. After he robbed a school concession stand he was placed in an alternative setting. His mother requested a due process hearing, alleging that the district failed to identify him as a student with a disability. The case reached the Fifth Circuit Court of Appeals, which held that even though the student had a qualifying disability (his ADHD), he did not need special education services as a result. **His behavioral problems resulted from non-ADHD occurrences, such as family problems.** *Alvin Independent School Dist. v. Patricia F.*, 503 F.3d 378 (5th Cir. 2007).

◆ A Maine elementary school student excelled academically but began having problems with peers and depression. She stayed in public school until sixth grade, when she skipped school, inflicted wounds on herself and had more peer problems. After attempting suicide, she was hospitalized and later diagnosed with Asperger's Syndrome. A school pupil evaluation team identified her as a qualified individual with a disability under Section 504, but determined she was ineligible for special education under the IDEA. She was offered 10 hours of weekly tutoring. Instead, her parents enrolled her in a private school.

In the lawsuit that arose over her education, **the First Circuit held that even though the child did not have academic needs, she could still be eligible for special education under the IDEA**. Here, the student's condition adversely affected her educational performance in nonacademic areas. Accordingly, the student was entitled to compensatory education for the period during which she was deemed ineligible. However, she was not entitled to tuition reimbursement for the private school placement. *Mr. I. v. Maine School Administrative Dist. No. 55*, 480 F.3d 1 (1st Cir. 2007).

◆ The foster parents of an HIV-positive Maryland student told her about her condition for the first time just before her fifth-grade year. Her behavior deteriorated sharply over the next two years. She cut herself, heard voices telling her to stab herself, and was hospitalized at five institutions, finally being diagnosed with a psychotic condition. She missed a lot of school, and her academic performance declined during sixth grade. Her mother requested an IEP meeting to determine her eligibility under the IDEA. The IEP team found that although the student engaged in inappropriate behavior or had inappropriate feelings, she did not qualify for special education because her condition caused no adverse educational impact. Eventually the dispute reached the Fourth Circuit, which held the student was eligible for special education. **Her emotional disturbance affected her educational performance**, despite contrary testimony from school district experts. *Board of Educ. of Montgomery County, Maryland v. S.G.*, 230 Fed.Appx. 330 (4th Cir. 2007).

◆ A Kentucky student was diagnosed with ADHD near the end of his fourth-grade year. His mother claimed the district should have identified him as IDEA-eligible earlier and requested a due process hearing. A hearing officer awarded the student 125 hours of compensatory education. A state appeals board affirmed the decision, but decided that the student's IEP team should determine how much compensatory education he should receive. On appeal, the Sixth Circuit held that the IEP team should not have been granted the authority to decide how much compensatory education the student was due. However, it rejected the mother's claim that the district should have referred the student for special education as early as kindergarten. **Children have different development rates and referring a child for special education too early can be damaging.** The court remanded the case for a re-determination of the compensatory education award. *Board of Educ. of Fayette County, Kentucky v. L.M.*, 478 F.3d 307 (6th Cir. 2007).

◆ The mother of a Florida student attending regular classes under a Section 504 plan sought other accommodations for him. After his fourth-grade year, she requested a due process hearing. After consenting to a less-than-full evaluation of her son, she agreed to a full evaluation. However, a school psychologist conducted only intellectual and process tests, based on his supervisor's instructions. These tests found the student had normal intelligence and did not qualify as an exceptional student. An administrative law judge found that the board had done all that could be expected to define the student's needs. **A Florida District Court of Appeal held the school district violated the IDEA and state law by making insufficient efforts to evaluate the student. His IDEA rights were not "extinguished by his mother's failure immediately to accede to the School Board's every suggestion."** The case was remanded with instructions to order the board to perform a complete evaluation of the student. *M.H. v. Nassau County School Board*, 918 So.2d 316 (Fla. Dist. Ct. App. 2005).

B. Child Find Obligation

The IDEA's "child find" obligation requires the states, through their local educational agencies (LEAs), to "identify, locate, and evaluate all children with disabilities residing within their boundaries." The child find obligation is triggered as an individualized duty to a child when an educational agency "has knowledge" that the child has a disability. Under the pre-2004 IDEA, students who were not declared eligible for IDEA services often made successful claims for IDEA procedural protections when their schools sought to discipline them.

Under current 20 U.S.C. § 1415(k)(5)(b), a school may be deemed to have knowledge that a child is disabled only if: (i) before the behavior leading to discipline, the child's parent "has expressed concern in writing" to a teacher or to supervisory or administrative personnel that the child is in need of special education or related services; (ii) the child's parent has requested an individual initial evaluation to determine if the child has a disability; or (iii) the child's teacher, or other school personnel, "has expressed specific concerns about a pattern of behavior demonstrated by the child, directly to the director of special education of such agency or to other supervisory personnel of the agency."

The "child find" duty of each state applies to children with disabilities who are homeless or wards of a state. LEAs must "conduct a thorough and complete child find process" to determine the number of parentally placed students with disabilities attending private schools in the LEA.

The child find process must be designed to ensure the equitable participation of parentally placed private school children. Local educational agencies must "undertake activities" for parentally placed private school students similar to activities for public school students. Services to parentally placed students may be provided at private schools, including religious schools, "to the extent consistent with law." Under the IDEA, LEAs and private schools must have "timely and meaningful consultation" for that purpose.

Court Decisions

◆ A California ninth-grade student had poor grades and scored below the first percentile on standardized tests. A school counselor attributed her performance to "transitional year difficulties." At the end of the student's tenth-grade year, she had failed her academic classes. Teachers said she was "like a stick of furniture" in class and said that her work was "gibberish and incomprehensible." They also reported the student played with dolls, colored with crayons and sometimes urinated on herself in her classroom. As the student's mother was "reluctant to have the child looked at," the school district "decided not to push" a special education evaluation. A third-party counselor recommended that the district test the student for learning disabilities, but she was instead promoted to grade eleven. Early in the school year, the mother requested an assessment and an IEP meeting. Later, the district found the student IDEA-eligible. The parent sought a due process hearing, resulting in a decision in her favor. After a federal court upheld the decision, the case reached the U.S. Court of Appeals, Ninth Circuit.

On appeal, the district asserted there was no parental right to file a claim unless an IDEA notice provision specifically applied. The court reviewed 20 U.S.C. § 1415(b)(6)(A) and held **a party may present a complaint to a court or hearing officer with respect to any matter relating to identification, evaluation or placement of a child**. As a result, the court held the child-find claim advanced by the parent was recognizable under the IDEA. *Compton Unified School Dist. v. Addison*, 598 F.3d 1181 (9th Cir. 2010).

◆ The parents of a Connecticut student with a nonverbal learning disability believed their school district should have diagnosed their son as IDEA-eligible for the fourth grade. However, the district did not find him eligible until it created an IEP for his sixth-grade year. The parents placed their son in a private school and eventually sued for tuition reimbursement. A federal district court held they failed to prove that district officials "overlooked clear signs of disability and were negligent in failing to order testing." **The IDEA child find provision does not impose liability for every failure to identify a child with a disability, and nonverbal learning disabilities are difficult to identify.** On appeal, the Second Circuit found the student's Connecticut Mastery Test scores indicated he was performing at goal in math and reading and was "proficient" in writing. And his lowest grade before being removed for a private school placement was a C+. The judgment for the school board was affirmed. *A.P. v. Woodstock Board of Educ.*, 370 Fed.Appx. 202 (2d Cir. 2010).

◆ The mother of Nevada preschool twins with speech and other developmental difficulties took them to a free screening session at a private learning center, which referred them to their school district. The district referred the mother to a "Child Find Day" about six weeks later and did not give her a copy of her IDEA procedural safeguards. The children were not responsive at the Child Find Day, and assessments were scheduled for two months later. Meanwhile, the private center determined that the children had autism. The district eventually agreed with that diagnosis. A hearing officer determined that the district had failed to timely evaluate the children, but on appeal, the Ninth Circuit held that **the delay between when the twins were evaluated and began receiving services was reasonable**. As a result, the mother was entitled to be reimbursed only for the $1,670 she spent on private evaluations. *JG v. Douglas County School Dist.*, 552 F.3d 786 (9th Cir. 2009).

♦ A student moved with her family to Delaware from New York. She had an accommodation plan under Section 504. At the end of her third-grade school year, she failed math and did not meet requirements for promotion to grade four. Upon learning the student would be retained in grade three, her parents sought a full range of assessments. One indicated a severe discrepancy in reading comprehension. Although an IEP was offered, the parents placed the child in a Christian school and requested a due process hearing for reimbursement from the district for their costs. The case reached the U.S. Court of Appeals, Third Circuit. It found the evidence at the time the parents sought an evaluation did not show their child's Section 504 plan was failing. Her grades were improving in all subjects. School officials could not have known that the student would later fail to advance in grade and fail a state test. While some of her programs were available to others, it appeared to the court that her curriculum was tailored to her needs. Her teacher "provided extra support at every turn."

Although the parents argued that the IEP put into place by the district was deficient, the court disagreed. **A lower court had properly found the student had no other IDEA-qualifying disabilities in math and writing**, as the parents claimed. And the district court found the IEP addressed her reading comprehension and had "significant provisions" devoted to her non-qualifying areas of concern, including math. Since the IEP was adequately drafted to provide a free appropriate public education, the court affirmed the denial of private school tuition reimbursement. *Anello v. Indian River School Dist.*, 355 Fed.Appx. 594 (3d Cir. 2009).

♦ An Ohio student was diagnosed with ADD, ADHD, oppositional defiant disorder and absence seizures. He was finally diagnosed with Asperger's syndrome in eighth grade. A dispute arose over the student's IEP, and his parents filed an IDEA action, asserting that the district's failure to diagnose Asperger's syndrome amounted to a violation of the act. **A federal court held that the district's failure to correctly label the student's disabilities did not violate the IDEA.** The student received special education from his second-grade year to the present. **The IDEA does not require schools to place students in specific categories. It only requires that they be given an appropriate education**, which the student received. *Pohorecki v. Anthony Wayne Local School Dist.*, 637 F.Supp.2d 547 (N.D. Ohio 2009).

♦ A federal court held **the IDEA child find obligation is triggered whenever a school has reason to suspect a child has a disability and requires special education to address it**. But discussions about a District of Columbia student did not satisfy the IDEA's requirement of a written request for an evaluation. Oral expressions of concern by parents about the educational performance of their children do not trigger a school's child find duty. *Reid v. District of Columbia*, 310 F.Supp.2d 137 (D.D.C. 2004).

C. Least Restrictive Environment

The IDEA requires placing students with disabilities with non-disabled peers to the extent possible. This is known as the least restrictive environment (LRE) requirement. Each IEP must explain the extent to which a child will not participate in regular education classes. In analyzing the LRE requirement, many courts rely on Oberti v. Board of Educ. of Borough of Clementon School Dist., *995 F.2d 1204 (3d Cir. 1993).* Oberti *evaluated whether the district made reasonable efforts to accommodate a student in regular classes, whether appropriate supplemental aids and services were made available, and the possible negative effects for other students if the student remained in regular education classes. While the IDEA has a strong preference for placements in the LRE, the U.S. Court of Appeals, Seventh Circuit, held in* Beth B. v. Van Clay, *282 F.3d 493 (7th Cir. 2002), that the Act does not require a regular classroom placement that would provide an unsatisfactory education.*

In McLaughlin v. Holt Public Schools Board of Educ., *320 F.3d 663 (6th Cir. 2003), the Sixth Circuit found an IDEA regulation requiring placement "as close as possible to the child's home" did not apply if a necessary program was unavailable at a neighborhood school.*

Teacher Scenarios

Disruption causes accident: Should teacher have stepped in earlier?..*308*

Court Decisions

♦ An 18-year-old Pennsylvania student with multiple disabilities was non-verbal and not toilet trained. Her district proposed placing her in a full-time life skills class and in mainstream school assemblies, lunch, homeroom and recess. Her parents requested a due process hearing, asserting the placement was too restrictive. A hearing officer agreed with them and ordered compensatory education, but an appeals panel held that the student required a regular education setting only for lunch, recess, physical education, homeroom, music, art and a single academic class. The award of compensatory education was reversed. A federal district court and later the Third Circuit upheld that decision, noting that **the student was making progress in her life skills class and her frequent loud vocalizations had a negative effect on other students**. *A.G. v. Wissahickon School Dist.*, 374 Fed.Appx. 330 (3d Cir. 2010).

◆ A New Hampshire student with mental retardation, orthopedic impairment and other disabilities attended a rehabilitation day center for four years under an IEP. When she was 19, the IEP team recommended a continued placement there. But her parents refused to consent to the IEP and withdrew her from school. They sought a home- and community-based program to help her with basic life skills and community interaction. The case reached the First Circuit, which ruled for the school district. It found **the student's behavior appeared to be improving and the day center was a less restrictive placement than the home service setting the parents wanted**. Further, the IEP called for a significant increase in services in the area of pre-vocational skills. *Lessard v. Lyndeborough Cooperative School Dist.*, 592 F.3d 267 (1st Cir. 2010).

◆ A 14-year-old Arizona student suffered a traumatic brain injury that confined him to a wheelchair and made him dependent on caregivers for daily activities. He was considered the most severely disabled student in his school district. His IEP team determined that he had a better chance of achieving his IEP goals if he were placed at a particular private day school 35 miles away. His parents objected, seeking instead to keep him in his neighborhood school with his non-disabled peers. A special education hearing officer found that the student failed to respond despite the district's best efforts and that the private day placement was best for him. The Arizona Court of Appeals agreed. **The student's severe disability made continued mainstreaming inappropriate.** *Stallings v. Gilbert Unified School Dist. No. 41*, No. 1 CA-CV 08-0625, 2009 WL 3165452 (Ariz. Ct. App. 10/1/09).

◆ A Connecticut school district behavioral consultant notified the parents of a student with Down syndrome and other impairments that because of his behavior problems it was becoming more difficult to keep the student in a regular classroom. A performance and planning team drafted an IEP that called for only 60% regular classroom placement instead of the 80% urged by the parents. The district hired a consultant who recommended gradually increasing the student's time in regular classrooms to 80%, and the district agreed to increase the time to 74%. However, the parents were determined to achieve 80% time in regular classrooms. A federal district court and the Second Circuit eventually upheld the IEP, noting that while mainstreaming is an important objective, it has to be weighed against the need for an appropriate education. **Mandating a percentage of time in regular classes would be inconsistent with the individualized approach of the IDEA.** *P. v. Newington Board of Educ.*, 546 F.3d 111 (2d Cir. 2008).

◆ The mother of a Kansas student with Down syndrome challenged the IEP proposed for his entry into high school, as it would require a long bus ride to a high school in another town. She sought to place him in the high school in their town. An educational cooperative serving eight school districts ran a "level program" or "cluster system" using a functional educational approach. A hearing officer and a federal court found that the Level IV program at the distant high school was the least restrictive placement and that the neighborhood school had no teachers qualified to teach the student. The student's inability to focus in regular classrooms was documented, and the Level IV program provided a continuum of placements and support services. **Although neighborhood placements are preferred under the IDEA and implicate the least restrictive environment, they are not an enforceable right.** *M.M. v. Unified School Dist. No. 368*, No. 07-2291-JTM, 2008 WL 4950987 (D. Kan. 11/18/08).

◆ A New York student with autism-spectrum disorders began to withdraw from reality. Her mother removed her from the private day school placement specified by her IEP and placed her in an unapproved private school in Connecticut. The following year, the district recommended a public school placement. The mother rejected the IEP and sought tuition reimbursement. A federal court found the IEP inadequate. But the Second Circuit reversed, finding considerable evidence to support the school district. **The student's recent social progress indicated she could make educational progress in an environment consistent with the IDEA's preference for mainstreaming.** *Cabouli v. Chappaqua Cent. School Dist.*, 202 Fed.Appx. 519 (2d Cir. 2006).

◆ A New Jersey school district placed a student with profound sensorineural hearing loss in a public school for deaf children outside the district. The next year, it proposed placing her in a self-contained school for the deaf located in the neighborhood school she would have attended if not for her special needs. It did not explain why it failed to propose that placement previously, or what now made it appropriate. The case reached the Third Circuit, which **found the school district's emphasis on least restrictive environment misplaced**. The district did not show the new placement would provide meaningful educational benefit. As the neighborhood school would offer only minimal mainstreaming opportunities, the school district was not allowed to change the placement. *S.H. v. State-Operated School Dist. of City of Newark*, 336 F.3d 260 (3d Cir. 2003).

D. Change in Placement and the 'Stay-Put' Provision

The IDEA requires school districts to provide parents of students with disabilities prior written notice of any proposed change in placement. If the parents wish to contest the change in placement, a hearing must be granted. During the pendency of review proceedings, the child is to remain in the "then-current" educational placement. This is the IDEA "stay-put" provision.

Court Decisions

◆ The parents of a Texas student with disabilities disagreed with the district's proposed IEP for grade two and placed her in a private school. They sought due process and obtained a ruling from the hearing officer that the district did not make an appropriate placement. Thus, the parents were entitled to tuition reimbursement. **By the time the administrative ruling was issued, the school year was nearly over.** When the district appealed to a federal court, the parents did not ask for tuition reimbursement for another school year. As a result, when the court ruled on the case over a year later, it held that they were not entitled to tuition reimbursement. However, the Fifth Circuit reversed, finding that **another year of tuition was due under the stay-put provision.** *Houston Independent School Dist. v. V.P.*, 582 F.3d 576 (5th Cir. 2009).

◆ A Pennsylvania student had a specific learning disability. His parents and the school district disagreed on a placement after his third-grade year. Over the next two years, his third-grade IEP became his stay-put placement under the IDEA. The district proposed providing itinerant learning support primarily in a regular classroom instead of the daily hour of resource room support specified in the third-grade IEP. The parents rejected that proposal, arguing that it amounted to a change in placement. In the lawsuit that followed, the Third Circuit held that the district provided the same services to the student in the inclusive setting, on a daily basis and with the same special education teacher. Thus, **providing the itinerant learning support was not a change in placement that violated the IDEA's stay-put provision.** *In re Educ. Assignment of Joseph R.*, 318 Fed.Appx. 113 (3d Cir. 2009).

◆ A Virginia special education student with an emotional disability attended a gifted and talented program in an elementary school. He persuaded a classmate to place a threatening note in another student's computer file stating "death awaits you." The district assembled a manifestation determination review committee, which found no relationship between the student's disabilities and the threatening note. It recommended expelling the student, but the district instead transferred him to a gifted and talented program at a nearby school for the remainder of the year. His parents objected to the transfer decision and requested a due process hearing. The hearing officer ruled against the parents, and the Fourth Circuit affirmed, noting that **the student's transfer to a nearly identical program at a nearby school did not implicate the IDEA's stay-put provision.** The court also held his IEP was appropriate. *A.W. v. Fairfax County School Board*, 372 F.3d 674 (4th Cir. 2004).

The student later used his cell phone to take pictures up a classmate's skirt without her knowledge. The school suspended the student for 10 days and recommended expelling him. The IEP team determined his misconduct was not a manifestation of his disability. A hearing officer then ruled he should be suspended for 18 days and reassigned to another school. The school board agreed and offered interim services, but the parents appealed to a federal court, seeking money damages. The court dismissed their lawsuit, noting that they failed to exhaust their administrative remedies. *A.W. v. Fairfax County School Board*, 548 F.Supp.2d 219 (E.D. Va. 2008).

◆ Florida triplets with autism received IDEA Part C services from the state's early intervention program until they turned three. When they "aged out" of Part C eligibility and the responsibility for their special education needs passed to IDEA Part B, their school district became obligated to provide them with IEPs. Because their school district did not have their IEPs in place, their parents sought to use the IDEA's stay-put provision to continue their individual family service plans (IFSPs). A federal court held **a student's Part C placement is not his or her current educational placement for stay-put purposes.** The Eleventh Circuit later affirmed the judgment, ruling the IDEA did not provide for the continued provision of services to the triplets pursuant to their IFSPs. *D.P. v. School Board of Broward County*, 483 F.3d 725 (11th Cir. 2007).

◆ An Ohio school district made addendums to a student's IEP in three consecutive months during his sixth-grade year. The third addendum sought to phase out a point reward system used to reinforce his behavior. The addendum also stated if the target behavior was not maintained, the original IEP would be reinstated. The parents did not learn that the addendum was being implemented until the district sent them a certified letter several days after the IEP meeting. A due process hearing officer found that the student's sixth-grade IEP included the third addendum, rendering it the student's "stay-put" placement pending the outcome of the due process hearing. A state appeals court held that the district did not provide adequate notice that the final addendum would be implemented. The court remanded the case for a determination of **whether the addendum fundamentally changed the student's IEP and whether the stay-put provision was implicated.** *Stancourt v. Worthington City School Dist. Board of Educ.*, 841 N.E.2d 812 (Ohio Ct. App. 2005).

After further consideration by the trial court, the case returned to the Ohio Court of Appeals. It noted the addendum was neither a fundamental change in nor an elimination of a basic element of the IEP. The original IEP called for a behavior plan that would eventually thin reinforcers. The court affirmed the judgment for the school district, holding that **not every change to an IEP constitutes a change in placement.** *Stancourt v. Worthington City School Dist.*, Nos. 07AP-835, 07AP-836, 2008 WL 4151623 (Ohio Ct. App. 9/9/08).

◆ The parents of a Michigan student with disabilities asserted the IEP offered by their school district denied him a free appropriate public education. They requested a hearing to challenge the IEP, then placed their son in a private school. The hearing officer dismissed the case upon learning of the unilateral placement. A state-level review officer upheld that decision, as did a federal district court. The court noted that the school district did not violate the IDEA by failing to annually update the student's IEP. **Once an IDEA action has been commenced, the student's most recent IEP continues to operate under the stay-put provision until conclusion of the appeal or litigation.** *Kuszewski v. Chippewa Valley School Dist.*, 56 Fed.Appx. 655 (6th Cir. 2003).

◆ In a Missouri case, the Eighth Circuit found the stay-put provision requires that a student remain in his or her "then-current educational placement" during the pendency of any IDEA action. **The transfer of a student to a different school building for fiscal reasons did not constitute a change of placement.** *Hale v. Poplar Bluff R-I School Dist.*, 280 F.3d 831 (8th Cir. 2002).

E. Other Placement Issues

1. Behavior Problems

Teacher Scenarios

'Teacher hit me,' autistic student says:
Mom sues 311

Court Decisions

◆ A Texas student with autism and other disorders regressed significantly in the summer before her ninth-grade year. Her IEP was revised, but her behavior and academic problems increased. She ran away from school and had sexual contact with other students in a lavatory. Her parents sought to place her at a residential school and a hearing officer agreed with their decision. A federal district court also affirmed the residential placement, awarding over $110,000 in tuition plus $36,000 in attorneys' fees to the parents. But the Fifth Circuit found **the parents had not yet shown that the residential placement was necessary for educational (rather than medical or behavioral) reasons**. The court returned the case to the lower court for further proceedings. *Richardson Independent School Dist. v. Michael Z.*, 580 F.3d 286 (5th Cir. 2009).

◆ A New York school district offered an autistic student support from a special education teacher for part of the day and a program assistant for the rest of the day. However, he had behavioral and lack-of-focus problems and his parents placed him in a private school. They sued for tuition reimbursement, alleging that the district violated the IDEA because it failed to offer a functional behavioral assessment (FBA). A hearing officer found that the district should have offered an FBA, but a state review officer reversed. The case reached the U.S. Court of Appeals, Second Circuit, which observed that three key district officials had testified that an FBA was not necessary. **The IEP adequately addressed the student's behavior, and the parents were not entitled to tuition reimbursement.** *A.C. and M.C. v. Board of Educ. of Chappaqua Cent. School Dist.*, 553 F.3d 165 (2d Cir. 2009).

◆ A Pennsylvania student with worsening psychological problems attended private schools at the district's expense. After she was kicked out of a residential school in New Mexico, her parents placed her in a psychiatric residential treatment center that provided no educational services. Her parents sought reimbursement for the costs. The case reached the Third Circuit, which held that **the district did not have to pay for the treatment center placement because her admission there was necessitated by her acute medical condition**. And her medical and educational needs could be separated. Further, once the student's condition stabilized, the district began providing services again. *Mary v. School Dist. of Philadelphia*, 575 F.3d 235 (3d Cir. 2009).

◆ The mother of a New York student with Asperger's disorder signed him up for a private school before the school district prepared an IEP for the upcoming year. The IEP, when completed, maintained his "other health impaired" classification, but placed him in a more restrictive special education class. The mother sought tuition reimbursement and a hearing officer found that the district's failure to obtain a functional behavior analysis (FBA) entitled the mother to tuition reimbursement. A review officer reversed, and a federal court agreed that the lack of an FBA was not fatal to the IEP. **School districts must consider using positive behavioral interventions and supports as well as other strategies to address behavior, so the mere failure to conduct an FBA did not violate the IDEA.** *Connor v. New York City Dep't of Educ.*, No. 08 Civ. 7710 (LBS), 2009 WL 3335760 (S.D.N.Y. 10/13/09).

◆ A Minnesota student with emotional and behavioral disabilities was suspended several times for fighting with other girls. Her suspensions added up to more than 10 days out of class. The district offered home-schooling services, but the student's mother rejected the offer. After conducting a functional behavioral assessment, the district offered to place the student in an emotional behavioral disability setting that included boys. The mother rejected this placement as well, preferring an all-girl setting. An administrative law judge held the district denied the student an appropriate education because of the suspensions and the district's failure to modify her IEP. But the Eighth Circuit found **the mixed-gender setting was appropriate given that all the student's serious behavior problems involved altercations with girls**. *M.M. v. Special School Dist. No. 1*, 512 F.3d 455 (8th Cir. 2008).

◆ A Minnesota student with a behavior disorder was escorted by paraprofessionals to a separate room when he needed to calm down. His IEP called for a written behavior intervention plan (BIP), but none was created by the relevant deadline. The dispute reached the Eighth Circuit, which held that **nothing in state or federal law required a written BIP in a student's IEP**. The school responded to the student's behavioral incidents using set procedures, and there was no substantive or procedural violation of the IDEA. *School Board of Independent School Dist. No. 11 v. Renollett*, 440 F.3d 1007 (8th Cir. 2006).

2. Extended School Year Services

Court Decisions

◆ A dispute arose between a New Jersey school district and the parents of a student over extended school year services (ESY) and transportation. A federal court ruled for the district on the ESY and transportation claims, but it awarded 17 days of compensatory education due to the district's failure to serve the student for the same number of days at the start of his fifth-grade year. The family then sought costs and attorneys' fees of $118,787. The court modified the award but still granted them all their costs and $71,850 in attorneys' fees. Even though they were successful on only one claim, their claims were all related. *L.T. v. Mansfield Township School Dist.*, No. 04-1381 (NLH), 2009 WL 1971329 (D.N.J. 7/1/09).

♦ A Pennsylvania school district offered an incoming kindergartner with autism an IEP that included applied behavioral analysis (ABA) therapy and verbal behavior (VB) services in an autistic support class. But the IEP reduced the student's ABA therapy from his early intervention IEP and also reduced his occupational therapy. His parents challenged the IEP and reached a settlement in which the student was to receive two hours of ABA and VB therapy a day. The district then provided three hours of therapy a day, exceeding interim IEP requirements. Later, the district proposed reducing the ABA/VB therapy for the rest of the school year and a summer extended school year program. A federal court held the district could provide less than three hours of ABA therapy a day and did not have to provide over 1.5 hours a day in the summer. **It had already provided more ABA therapy than the interim IEP required.** *Travis G. v. New Hope-Solebury School Dist.*, 544 F.Supp.2d 435 (E.D. Pa. 2008).

♦ A multiply disabled 11-year-old Massachusetts student had attended a seven-week summer program called "Active Healing" at district expense since her kindergarten year. But the program was not approved by the state. After a seizure caused the student to regress, her mother sought a 12-week extended evaluation at Active Healing. The district refused to pay for the evaluation because the program was unapproved, and the mother sought administrative review. A hearing officer ruled that the district had to pay for the evaluation, but a federal court disagreed. **Despite the past history of the district funding the summer program, it could not be ordered to pay for the extended evaluation at an unapproved program.** *Manchester-Essex Regional School Dist. v. Bureau of Special Educ. Appeals*, 490 F.Supp.2d 49 (D. Mass. 2007).

♦ The IEPs for a Kentucky student with cerebral palsy and delayed cognitive development addressed his ongoing behavior issues. His parents believed he was regressing and sought direct occupational therapy for him as well as a summer placement. Ultimately, the district rejected extended school year (ESY) programming for the student's next school year. The parents unilaterally placed the student in a residential facility that offered summer programs and requested a due process hearing. A hearing officer ruled for the district, but an appeals board and a federal district court reversed his decision. On further appeal, **the Sixth Circuit reversed the lower court decision, holding ESY programming was the exception, not the rule**. The parents would have to show that ESY was necessary to avoid something more than "adequately recoupable regression." *Kenton County School Dist. v. Hunt*, 384 F.3d 269 (6th Cir. 2004).

♦ A Virginia student with autism received ESY services prior to entering kindergarten. In kindergarten, he progressed in all but two of the 27 goals stated in his IEP. His parents sought to continue the one-on-one services he received during the summer, but were unable to agree with their school district on an IEP. A hearing officer and a federal court both ruled that the purpose of ESY services was to make reasonable progress on unmet goals. The court found that the district's IEP was adequate. The Fourth Circuit Court of Appeals held that **ESY services are necessary only when the regular school year benefits to a student will be significantly jeopardized in the absence of summer programming**. The court remanded the case to the hearing officer for a redetermination of the appropriateness of ESY services using the correct standard. *J.H. v. Henrico County School Board*, 326 F.3d 560 (4th Cir. 2003).

3. Transfer Students

The IDEA allows schools to conduct an evaluation of any student who transfers from a school outside the state before becoming obligated to develop a new IEP. When parents repeatedly refuse a school's efforts to conduct an individual evaluation of a child, the school is relieved of the obligation to convene an IEP meeting and is not considered in violation of the IDEA.

Court Decisions

♦ A New Jersey couple moved to Montana after a doctor determined that their child's performance had an autistic component. An IEP had been crafted to provide the child with speech/language therapy while he was in New Jersey. The IEP team at his new school refused to consider a New Jersey doctor's evaluation and reduced the student's speech/language therapy. After two months, the IEP team referred the student to a child development center for free autism testing. Five months later, a report came back confirming that his behavior was consistent with autism spectrum disorder. At this point, the school year was almost over. The IEP team met to develop an IEP for the next year and determined that the student did not need extended school year services. The parents brought an IDEA challenge that reached the Ninth Circuit. The court of appeals held that the **referral of the student to the child development center did not comply with the IDEA. The school district failed to meet its obligation to evaluate the student.** *N.B. and C.B. v. Hellgate Elementary School Dist.*, 541 F.3d 1202 (9th Cir. 2008).

♦ A California student with a cochlear implant received one-on-one deaf and hard of hearing services in his family's home. When his family moved to Nevada, the school district there offered the services in his neighborhood school under an interim IEP. His parents objected, asserting the location violated the California IEP.

They hired a private service provider and sought reimbursement from the Nevada school district. A hearing officer and then a federal district court held that the school district had offered comparable services to the transfer student. **The IDEA did not require the Nevada district to adopt the California IEP in its exact form.** *Sterling A. v. Washoe County School Dist.*, No. 3:07-CV-002450LRH-RJJ, 2008 WL 4865570 (D. Nev. 11/10/08).

◆ A Louisiana school district transferred a student with deafness from his neighborhood school to a cluster school located about four miles farther away from his home. His parents claimed the transfer was a change in placement under the IDEA that required the district to give them prior written notice. They requested a due process hearing. A federal court upheld the decision to transfer the student. The parents appealed. The U.S. Court of Appeals, Fifth Circuit, held that **the change in a school site at which an IEP is implemented is not a "change in placement" under the IDEA**. The few changes the student experienced as a result of the transfer to the new school did not amount to a change in placement. Riding a special bus for disabled students instead of a regular school bus and sharing a transliterator with another student instead of having his own were not fundamental changes to his IEP. *Veazey v. Ascension Parish School Board*, 121 Fed.Appx. 552 (5th Cir. 2005).

◆ When a student with autism moved to Rhode Island, his new school district assembled an IEP team and proposed an interim IEP within two weeks of the parents' first contact. The district wanted to place the student in a newly established self-contained classroom that used a modified version of the TEACCH method. The parents asserted that only DTT methodology was appropriate. They rejected the IEP and notified the district that they would be placing their son in a private school. They then rejected a second IEP developed by the district. A due process hearing officer ruled for the parents, but the First Circuit Court of Appeals ruled for the district, noting that **the IDEA did not require the best possible education for students with disabilities**. Here, the IEP was reasonably calculated to provide an appropriate education. The classroom was half the size of the student's previous placement, and the teachers had extensive experience and training with autistic children. Further, many of the elements of DTT would be available through the use of the TEACCH method, including considerable one-on-one instruction. *L.T. on Behalf of N.B. v. Warwick School Committee*, 361 F.3d 80 (1st Cir. 2004).

◆ A Seattle first-grade student with mild mental retardation and Down syndrome was assigned to a unique classroom combining special education and general education students. Just before the start of the next school year, her mother moved and sought a regular education placement for her daughter. The new district offered a temporary placement in a self-contained special education class until it could perform an evaluation. Two months into the school year, the student had yet to attend class, and the district offered a temporary placement of four hours of special education with at least an hour of regular education. It proposed increasing time in the regular education classroom as appropriate.

A due process hearing officer upheld the district's temporary placement as the closest approximation to the student's last IEP. A federal court and the Ninth Circuit agreed with the hearing officer that the district's placement was appropriate. **The temporary placement was not a "take it or leave it" proposition, but was rather designed to get as close to the student's previous unique placement as possible pending an evaluation.** The temporary IEP conferred educational benefits on the student. *Ms. S. and her Daughter G. v. Vashon Island School Dist.*, 337 F.3d 1115 (9th Cir. 2003).

◆ A California school district that became responsible for the education of a student with autism when he turned three years old did not have to replicate the individualized family service plan designed for him by the regional center that was formerly responsible for his education. The Ninth Circuit held that the status quo necessarily changed when responsibility for his education shifted to the district. According to the Ninth Circuit, the hearing officer and district court had properly analogized the case to that of an incoming transfer student. **When a student transfers from one public agency to another, the receiving agency is required only to provide a program that conforms with the last agreed-upon placement, not provide the exact same program.** *Johnson v. Special Educ. Hearing Office*, 287 F.3d 1176 (9th Cir. 2002).

F. Residency Issues

The IDEA mandate to provide a free appropriate public education extends to all children with a disability residing in the area served by a local educational agency. Disputes among school districts and other agencies are generally resolved through interagency agreements. Occasionally, parents fail to establish a clear domicile, raising residency issues.

Court Decisions

◆ A Kansas school district provided two children special education for some time. It determined they were not district residents because they did not sleep at their mother's rental unit. As a result, the district demanded the immediate withdrawal of the children from school. The parent requested an IDEA hearing and submitted an affidavit of residency. When it was learned that the children again stopped sleeping within district boundaries, the district filed a state court action against the parent and her boyfriend for fraud, seeking to recover the costs of serving the children while they were nonresidents. The mother sued the school district and special education director in a federal district court under the IDEA, Rehabilitation Act, and constitutional provisions. The court held for the district on a challenge to the district admissions policy and the constitutional claims. It found the boyfriend had no standing to maintain any claims pertaining to the children and the district's special education services director was entitled to qualified immunity. After a trial, the court dismissed the IDEA claim.

On appeal, the U.S. Court of Appeals, Tenth Circuit, affirmed the judgment on the IDEA claim but vacated the judgment on all the others. The district court again held for the district and director, and a second appeal went to the Tenth Circuit. It found the parent had abandoned the IDEA claims. The lower court had correctly held she lacked standing to challenge the nonresident admissions policy, since **she never actually sought admission for the children as nonresidents**. Even if the parent had standing, there was evidence that her children were absent from school due to illness and not due to the district's conduct. *D.L. v. Unified School Dist. No. 497*, 596 F.3d 768 (10th Cir. 2010).

◆ The mother of a Michigan special education student sought to enroll him in a neighboring school district, which had accepted 67 applications from nonresidents under the state's school choice law. However, because the process was less streamlined for special education students due to the higher costs, the two districts were unable to reach an agreement and the neighboring district rejected the student's application. His mother sued for discrimination, and the case reached the Sixth Circuit. The court of appeals held that the school choice law did not violate equal protection. **There was a rational reason for the stricter transfer requirements for special education students.** *Clark v. Banks*, 193 Fed.Appx. 510 (6th Cir. 2006).

IV. RELATED SERVICES

Overview

Related services include the provision of sign-language interpreters, transportation, speech pathology, psychological and counseling services, and physical and occupational therapy. The IDEA requires school districts to provide services that are necessary for students with disabilities to receive educational benefits, but excludes medical services from coverage except where required for evaluation or diagnostic purposes. See 20 U.S.C. § 1402 (26).

A. Generally

Court Decisions

◆ An Iowa student suffered a spinal cord injury that left him quadriplegic and ventilator dependent. For several years, his family provided personal attendant services at school. A family member or nurse performed catheterization, tracheostomy suctioning, repositioning and respiratory observation during the school day. When the student entered the fifth grade, his mother requested that the district provide him with continuous, one-on-one nursing services during the school day. The district refused, and the family filed a request for due process. An administrative law judge held the school district was obligated to reimburse the family for nursing costs incurred during the current school year and to provide the disputed services in the future. The case reached the U.S. Supreme Court, which held that the requested services were related services, not medical services. The court based its decision in the IDEA definition of related services, its holding in *Irving Independent School Dist. v. Tatro*, and the IDEA purpose of making special education available to all disabled students. Adopting a bright-line, physician/non-physician standard, the Court held that **since the disputed services could be performed by someone other than a physician, the district was obligated to provide them**. *Cedar Rapids Community School Dist. v. Garret F. by Charlene F.*, 526 U.S. 66 (1999).

◆ A West Virginia student with medical problems suffered abuse and neglect at the hands of his parents. He was placed in foster care. A state court conducted a review of his pending abuse and neglect petition and ordered his school board to provide and pay for a full-time nurse even though the board received no notice or opportunity to appear at the review hearing. The Supreme Court of Appeals of West Virginia issued an order for the board, finding that it should have been given notice and an opportunity to help shed light on the best interests of the student. **School records showed that the student had not suffered a seizure in two years and that he had not had a full-time nurse assigned to him for four of his 11 years in the school system.** *State of West Virginia v. Beane*, 680 S.E.2d 46 (W. Va. 2009).

◆ **The U.S. Supreme Court ruled that clean intermittent catheterization (CIC) is a related service not subject to the "medical service" exclusion of the IDEA.** The parents of an eight-year-old girl born with spina bifida brought suit against their local Texas school district after the district refused to provide CIC for the child while she attended school. The parents pursued administrative and judicial avenues to force the district to train staff to perform the simple procedure. After a U.S. district court held against the parents, they appealed to the U.S. Court of Appeals, Fifth Circuit, which reversed the district court ruling. The school district then appealed. The U.S. Supreme Court affirmed the court of appeals' ruling that CIC is a supportive related service, not a medical service excluded from the IDEA. *Irving Independent School Dist. v. Tatro*, 468 U.S. 883, 104 S.Ct. 3371, 82 L.Ed.2d 664 (1984).

◆ A Tennessee student with profound bilateral hearing loss received a cochlear implant at the age of 14 months. Her school district later developed an IEP for her, offering to place her in a new collaborative program that was being developed with Head Start. The program also served low-income students, many of whom did not have disabilities. The school district also proposed to discontinue the mapping service (optimization of the implant) it had been providing for the student. The parents objected and requested a hearing. A hearing officer held that the district's placement met IDEA requirements, but ruled that it had to continue the mapping services. **A federal court held that

the 2004 IDEA Amendments excluded the mapping of a cochlear implant as a related service under the IDEA. The regulations clarified that position in October 2006, so the district had to pay for mapping the implant until that time. *A.U. v. Roane County Board of Educ.*, 501 F.Supp.2d 1134 (E.D. Tenn. 2007).

◆ **A Virginia school board did not have to reimburse a disabled student for hospitalization costs that were paid years earlier by his father's group health insurance**, even though the payments counted against the lifetime medical benefits limit of the policy. The father made several requests to recover the $200,000 cost of the hospitalization from the board, but he did not request a due process hearing for almost 10 years. The hearing officer held the action was barred by a one-year Virginia statute of limitations. A federal district court affirmed. The Fourth Circuit agreed that the action was untimely. Also, the student was now an adult and was no longer covered by his father's insurance policy. He had his own Medicaid coverage, and this insurance was not affected by the decrease in lifetime medical benefits to his father's plan. *Emery v. Roanoke City School Board*, 432 F.3d 294 (4th Cir. 2005).

B. Level or Location of Services

Court Decisions

◆ A Pennsylvania student with learning disabilities received special education in reading, math and writing. In the sixth grade, his parents placed him in a private school and sought tuition reimbursement as well as compensatory education for the prior two years. After a federal court upheld the student's sixth-grade IEP, the U.S. Court of Appeals, Third Circuit, agreed that it addressed his deficiencies. **A lack of occupational therapy in the student's seventh-grade IEP was attributable to the delay by the parents in providing an occupational therapy evaluation.** Once they did so, a revised IEP provided for reevaluation of his potential needs within 30 days of his return to a district school. *Souderton Area School Dist. v. J.H.*, 351 Fed.Appx. 755 (3d Cir. 2009).

◆ A California student with multiple disabilities could not swallow food, instead receiving nutrition through a surgical opening in his stomach called a gastrostomy tube or "G-tube." His mother claimed he developed a severe reflux disorder from liquids, necessitating that he be fed only pureed foods. She used a syringe plunger even though standard medical practice called for using a gravity methodology. A dispute arose over the method of feeding her son. She kept him at home for a while, then sought compensatory education. A federal district court ultimately ruled that the mother could not dictate the method to be used to feed her son. **No doctor prescribed the plunge method, and the mother never provided evidence that the gravity method would not work.** No compensatory education was due. *C.N. v. Los Angeles Unified School Dist.*, No. CV 07-03642 MMM (SSx), 2008 WL 4552951 (C.D. Cal. 10/9/08).

◆ A Maryland student with disabilities received two types of medication from the school nurse under an agreement signed by her treating/prescribing psychiatrist. When teachers and other staff members observed that the student was lethargic and drowsy, the psychiatrist prescribed another medication. However, the student's fatigue continued. The nurse sought clarification from the doctor on giving the student medication when symptoms contraindicated further drug administration. The parents told the doctor not to provide further information to the nurse or other district employees regarding the student's medical condition and treatment. The district then refused to continue medicating the student. When the parents challenged that decision, they lost. The Court of Appeals of Maryland held that the dispute was about medical treatment and not special education. **The nurse could not be forced to medicate the student without free communication with the doctor.** *John A. v. Board of Educ. for Howard County*, 400 Md. 363, 929 A.2d 136 (Md. 2007).

◆ A Georgia student with a disability complained that words became fuzzy or three dimensional when he tried to read. A behavioral optometrist diagnosed accommodative and convergence disorder and recommended visual therapy to reduce vision loss. The district refused to pay for such therapy on the grounds that the student was receiving a free appropriate public education. The parents paid for the therapy, then sought due process. An administrative hearing officer and a federal court found that the parents were entitled to reimbursement for the therapy as a related service. The Eleventh Circuit agreed. **Although the student's condition had not yet caused poor academic performance, it did prevent him from receiving a free appropriate public education.** *DeKalb County School Dist. v. M.T.V.*, 164 Fed.Appx. 900 (11th Cir. 2006).

◆ The IEP of an Illinois third-grade student with Down syndrome called for 30 minutes of weekly direct occupational therapy (OT). The therapist who provided OT services to the student received her master's degree before the start of the school year, but did not obtain her license until near the end of the year. Using the results of the student's triennial evaluation, the district proposed an IEP for the student's fourth-grade year that called for 30 minutes of monthly OT consultation and less physical therapy than the parents desired. They rejected the IEP and obtained independent evaluations. A due process hearing officer agreed with the district's denial of reimbursement for the independent evaluations. Although she rejected the parents' claims of IEP deficiencies for nine of 11 areas identified, she held the district should provide 60 minutes weekly of direct OT services as compensatory services during the fourth grade because the occupational therapist was unlicensed and improperly supervised. A federal court upheld the IEP, but ordered the district to provide OT services.

The Seventh Circuit agreed that **60 minutes of direct OT services each week was appropriate given the failure of the district in the third-grade year to properly supervise the unlicensed occupational therapist.** However, the parents were not entitled to reimbursement for the independent evaluations because the district's evaluations had been appropriate. *Evanston Community Consolidated School Dist. No. 65 v. Michael M.*, 356 F.3d 798 (7th Cir. 2004).

◆ A hearing-impaired Louisiana student attended a public school with the assistance of a cued speech transliterator to supplement spoken information in his classes. Although other hearing-impaired students in the district who used American Sign Language attended their neighborhood schools, the cued speech transliterator served at a centralized location. The student achieved substantial academic benefit there, but his parents decided he should attend his neighborhood school for social reasons. The school district denied a transfer request by the parents. A hearing officer upheld the decision, but a federal district court held the student was entitled to attend his neighborhood school with the transliterator. The Fifth Circuit reversed the judgment. The student's IEP satisfied the IDEA, and his parents were seeking the neighborhood placement for primarily social reasons. **They did not have veto power over the district's decision to provide the transliterator only at the central location.** *White v. Ascension Parish School Board*, 343 F.3d 373 (5th Cir. 2003).

◆ A South Dakota student who suffered epileptic seizures was provided transportation to and from school by her district as a related service under the IDEA. She was accompanied by a nurse during the ride. Although parents could designate different pick-up and drop-off sites within a specific school area boundary, students were not transported outside the boundary unless it was necessary to obtain an educational benefit under an IEP. The district denied a request by the student's mother to drop her off at a day care center outside the boundary. The state Office of Special Education ordered the district to pay for transportation to the day care center, but a hearing examiner ruled it was not necessary. A federal court agreed, and the Eighth Circuit affirmed the decision that **the district did not have to provide transportation to the day care center**. The request was for the mother's own convenience and was not necessary to provide the student with educational benefit. *Fick v. Sioux Falls School Dist. 49-5*, 337 F.3d 968 (8th Cir. 2003).

C. Provision of Related Services at Private Schools

Court Decisions

◆ A New York first-grader with ADHD sought a 1:1 aide at his private school, and administrative rulings agreed that the aide would be sent to the private school. The district then sought a court ruling that the aide should be provided only at the public school. The Supreme Court, Appellate Division, held state law permitted a school district to provide services at a private school. It ruled that the decision must be made on a case-by-case basis, with the student's needs in the least restrictive environment serving as a guide. The New York Court of Appeals affirmed the judgment, finding **the state's dual enrollment statute was intended to offer private school students with disabilities "equal access to the full array of specialized public school programs."** *Board of Educ. of Bay Shore Union Free School Dist. v. Thomas K.*, 14 N.Y.3d 289 (N.Y. 2010).

◆ The parents of a student at the Delaware School for the Deaf became concerned when he began performing below grade level. They requested a general education placement with a full-time American Sign Language interpreter and a private school placement with a small class size. The school district responded that a sign-language interpreter would be provided only if the student attended district schools. After the parents placed their son in a private school, a hearing officer held that the district should have provided a sign-language interpreter. A federal district court reversed the judgment. **Nothing in the IDEA or its regulations conferred upon parentally placed private school students an individual right to receive special education and related services that they would receive in public schools.** The IDEA only required school districts to allocate a proportional share of IDEA funds to private schools, which the district had done here. *Board of Educ. of Appoquinimink School Dist. v. Johnson*, 543 F.Supp.2d 351 (D. Del. 2008).

◆ An Arizona student attended a school for the deaf from grades one through five and a public school from grades six through eight. During his public school attendance, a sign-language interpreter was provided by the school district. The student's parents enrolled him in a parochial high school for ninth grade and asked the school district to continue providing a sign-language interpreter. The school district refused, and the student's parents filed an IDEA action.

The case reached the U.S. Supreme Court, which held the Establishment Clause did not exclude religious institutions from publicly sponsored benefits. If this were the case, religious groups would not enjoy police and fire protection or have use of public roads and sidewalks. Government programs that neutrally provide benefits to broad classes of citizens are not subject to Establishment Clause prohibition simply because some religiously affiliated institutions receive an attenuated financial benefit. **Providing a sign-language interpreter under the IDEA was part of a general program for distribution of benefits in a neutral manner to qualified students.** A sign-language interpreter, unlike an instructor or counselor, was ethically bound to transmit everything said in the way it was intended. The Court reversed the decision. *Zobrest v. Catalina Foothills School Dist.*, 509 U.S. 1 (1993).

V. TUITION REIMBURSEMENT

Overview

If a school district is unable to provide special education services to a student with a disability in its own facilities, it must locate an appropriate program in another district, hospital or institution. *When a private placement is required, the district may become responsible for tuition and other costs.*

A. Private School Tuition Claims

Court Decisions

◆ A student attended Oregon public schools through grade 11. He had problems paying attention and finishing work, but he was able to pass his classes with help at home from family members. The school district evaluated him but found him ineligible for special education and related services. After he experienced multiple behavioral problems, a psychologist determined that he had ADHD, depression and other issues. His parents enrolled him in a three-week wilderness program and then a private residential school. They then requested a due process hearing. A hearing officer found the student was eligible for special education under the IDEA but held the school district only had to pay for the residential placement, not the wilderness program or the evaluation.

On appeal, the Ninth Circuit agreed with the student that he was not categorically barred from seeking tuition reimbursement. The U.S. Supreme Court agreed to review the case and took the opportunity to reaffirm its ruling in *Burlington School Committee v. Dep't of Educ.*, this chapter. In *Burlington*, the Court first approved of private school tuition reimbursement awards as a special education remedy. In this case, the Court found the district's failure to provide an IEP of any kind was at least as serious a violation of its IDEA responsibilities as a failure to provide an adequate IEP. **The Court rejected the district's argument that the student had to receive special education and related services from the district before advancing any claim for tuition reimbursement.** The 1997 IDEA amendments did not mandate a different result from *Burlington*, and the judgment was affirmed. *Forest Grove School Dist. v. T.A.*, 129 S.Ct. 2484 (U.S. 2009).

The case was returned to a federal court, which held the district did not have to pay the student's tuition. It reasoned that the parents had failed to notify the district of their private school selection until well after making it. Moreover, the district had found that the student did not need special education or even a Section 504 plan. And the parents seemingly chose the private school because of the student's drug use and behavioral problems. *Forest Grove School Dist. v. T.A.*, 675 F.Supp.2d 1063 (D. Or. 2009).

◆ An adopted student in Maryland with learning disabilities and emotional disturbance exhibited suicidal tendencies and clinical depression. Her IEP team placed her in a private special education day school. She later self-mutilated and attempted suicide. Her parents placed her in a residential school, even though a school psychologist found that she should be placed in a therapeutic school for students with serious emotional issues. The parents sought reimbursement, but a federal court and later the Fourth Circuit ruled against them. **The placement was based on the parents' desire to ensure the student did not harm herself. It was not made for educational reasons and was not the least restrictive environment** because she made progress in the day school when her mental health issues stabilized. *Shaw v. Weast*, 364 Fed.Appx. 47 (4th Cir. 2010).

◆ An Oregon student with ADHD and depression made progress in school but engaged in defiant and risky behavior at home. Her parents sought a more restrictive placement for her, but the school district ruled it out because she was earning good grades when she did her work. Her parents unilaterally placed her in a residential facility, but she was expelled for having sex with another student. Her parents then placed her in an out-of-state facility and sought tuition reimbursement, which the Ninth Circuit denied. It held **the student did not require residential placement for any educational reason. She was not disruptive in class and was well regarded by teachers.** *Ashland School Dist. v. Parents of Student R.J.*, 588 F.3d 1004 (9th Cir. 2009).

◆ A Virginia student with autism and a significant communication disorder made little progress in public schools, mastering only one IEP objective in six years. His parents requested a due process hearing, suggesting a one-on-one Lindamood-Bell Center placement. After a hearing, the school board acknowledged the student should be classified as having multiple disabilities but refused to provide one-on-one instruction. The parents placed him in the Lindamood-Bell program for four years and then sought tuition reimbursement. A hearing officer found three of the IEPs were invalid but also found the center to be an inappropriate placement. **A federal court agreed, but the Fourth Circuit vacated and remanded the case for a year-by-year IEP analysis.** If the center was appropriate, tuition reimbursement might be awarded. *M.S. v. Fairfax County School Board*, 553 F.3d 315 (4th Cir. 2009).

◆ The parents of a Colorado three-year-old with autism rejected the draft IEP offered by their school, which would have placed their son in an integrated setting, and kept their son at home with the one-on-one therapy program he had been receiving. The district failed to finalize the IEP for that year. The next year, the parents again rejected the district's IEP calling for an integrated placement with five hours of discrete trial training a week. The school district finalized that IEP, but the parents selected a private school, then sought tuition reimbursement. A hearing officer held for the school district, but a federal court found the parents entitled to tuition for the first year because the district failed to finalize the IEP. The Tenth Circuit reversed the judgment, noting that IDEA procedural violations were not sufficient for the parents to prevail in this case. **A procedural violation must result in lost educational opportunities to justify an award of tuition.** The court remanded the case (returned it to the district court) for further consideration of that issue. *Sytsema v. Academy School Dist. No. 20*, 538 F.3d 1306 (10th Cir. 2008).

When the case returned to the district court, it held that the unfinished IEP failed to offer the student needed one-on-one services. As a result, the parents were entitled to an award of their tuition costs. *Sytsema v. Academy*

School Dist. No. 20, No. 03-cv-2582-RPM, 2009 WL 3682221 (D. Colo. 10/30/09).

◆ A Georgia school district failed to assess a student for special education for four years despite requests from his teachers. When it finally did evaluate the student, it determined that he had an IQ of 63. A reevaluation of the student when he turned 16 found his IQ was 82 – the low end of average. However, the student was still at a third-grade level in reading and math. Eventually, his parents obtained an independent educational evaluation diagnosing dyslexia. The parents pursued a due process proceeding under the IDEA, and a hearing officer gave them a choice of additional support at the public school or a private school placement with reimbursement limited to $15,000 a year. The parents chose the private school, and the district appealed. A federal district court removed the tuition cap and ordered the school district to pay annual tuition of $34,150. On further appeal, the Eleventh Circuit held that **while the IDEA has a preference for public school placements, a private school placement may be an appropriate compensatory education remedy where a school denies a student a FAPE**. *Draper v. Atlanta Independent School System*, 518 F.3d 1275 (11th Cir. 2008).

◆ A South Carolina ninth-grader with a learning disability attended special education classes. Her parents disagreed with the IEP devised by their school district. The IEP called for mainstreaming in regular education classes for most subjects. The parents requested a due process hearing and unilaterally placed the student in a private school. A hearing officer held that the IEP was adequate. After the student raised her reading comprehension three full grades in one year at the private school, the parents sued the district for tuition reimbursement. A U.S. district court held the educational program and achievement goals of the proposed IEP were "wholly inadequate" under the IDEA. Even though the private school was not approved by the state education department, it provided the student with an excellent education that complied with IDEA substantive requirements. The parents were entitled to tuition reimbursement.

The U.S. Supreme Court held that the failure of the school district to provide an appropriate placement entitled the parents to tuition reimbursement, even though the private school was not on any state list of approved schools. This was because the district denied the student FAPE and the private education provided to her was found appropriate by the district court. South Carolina did not release a list of approved schools to the public. Under the IDEA, parents may unilaterally place children in private schools at their own risk. To recover tuition costs, parents must show that the placement proposed by the school district violates the IDEA, and that the private school placement is appropriate. The Court upheld lower court decisions for the parents. *Florence County School Dist. Four v. Carter*, 510 U.S. 7 (1993).

◆ The U.S. Supreme Court held that the parents of a child with a disability did not waive their claim for reimbursement of the expenses involved in unilaterally placing their child in a private school during the pendency of proceedings to review the child's IEP. The case involved a learning disabled child who was placed in a public school special education program against the wishes of his parents. The parents requested a due process hearing and, prior to the resolution of their complaint, placed their child in a private residential school recommended by specialists. The parents then sought reimbursement for their expenses. A federal appeals court found the IDEA stay-put provision to be "directory" rather than "mandatory." It decided that this "status quo" provision did not bar claims for reimbursement. The U.S. Supreme Court held that to bar reimbursement claims in cases of unilateral parent placement was contrary to the IDEA, which favors proper interim placements for disabled children. However, **parents who unilaterally change a child's placement during the pendency of proceedings do so at their own financial risk**. If the courts ultimately determine a child's IEP is appropriate, the parents are barred from obtaining reimbursement for any interim period in which the placement violated the IDEA. The Court affirmed the appellate court ruling. *Burlington School Committee v. Dep't of Educ.*, 471 U.S. 359, 105 S.Ct. 1996, 85 L.Ed.2d 385 (1985).

B. Parental Conduct

The IDEA discourages unilateral conduct by school districts and parents alike. The IDEA allows for the reduction or denial of reimbursement to parentally placed private school students, if the parents fail to give at least 10 days notice of the intended placement, do not make the child available to designated school employees for an assessment and evaluation before the child's removal from public school, or if a judge so rules.

In M.C. ex rel. Mrs. C. v. Voluntown Board of Educ., *226 F.3d 60, 68 (2d Cir. 2000), the U.S. Court of Appeals, Second Circuit, found that "courts have held uniformly that reimbursement is barred where parents unilaterally arrange for private educational services without ever notifying the school board of their dissatisfaction with their child's IEP." And in* Frank G. v. Board of Educ. of Hyde Park, *459 F.3d 356 (2d Cir. 2006), the court held it is inequitable to permit reimbursement when parents have not timely requested it.*

Court Decisions

◆ The mother of a Delaware student with disabilities placed him in a private school after a dispute about his IEP. The district agreed to fund the placement for one year and began the formal IEP process for the next year. However, the mother failed to return a form requesting permission to evaluate her son until midway through the summer. She also claimed she could not attend an IEP meeting because of scheduling conflicts. She then returned her son to the private school and refused to further participate in the IEP process, asserting that a free appropriate public education (FAPE) was denied because the IEP was not in place at the start of the school year. A federal district court ultimately ruled against her when she sued for tuition reimbursement, noting that **the delays were at least partly her fault and did not deny her son FAPE**. On appeal, the Third Circuit affirmed, noting that not all procedural violations of the IDEA result in a denial of FAPE. Here, the parents' non-cooperation caused the delay. *C.H. v. Cape Henlopen School Dist.*, 606 F.3d 59 (3d Cir. 2010).

◆ A New York school department's committee on special education developed an IEP for a student with autism. The IEP stated that the student would attend school in District 75 (a group of schools for students with disabilities) but did not specify which school he would attend. Instead, a citywide placement officer would make that determination. The student's parents objected to the school that was eventually proposed, but instead of visiting a second school they enrolled their son in a private school. When they sought tuition reimbursement, a federal court and later the Second Circuit ruled against them. Under the circumstances, **the IDEA did not require the school district to name the particular location for receiving special education services**. *T.Y. v. New York City Dep't of Educ.*, 584 F.3d 412 (2d Cir. 2009).

◆ The parents of a New Hampshire student became concerned that she needed special education, and their school district found she had a learning disability in math. An IEP team suggested a private school placement, which the parents agreed to. The following year, the parents requested due process, claiming the district had denied her a free appropriate public education (FAPE) for the past five years. They withdrew the student from school and began homeschooling her. The district threatened to file truancy charges against them unless they registered her as a home-schooled student. When the case finally reached a federal district court, **the court held that the parents acted unreasonably during the IEP process; thus, any delay in developing an IEP did not violate the IDEA**. Also, the truancy threat did not amount to a denial of FAPE. *Kasenia R. v. Brookline School Dist.*, 588 F.Supp.2d 175 (D.N.H. 2008).

◆ The parents of a Maine student placed her in a private residential facility before the district could evaluate her. They then demanded a due process hearing and met with the district to consider her eligibility for IDEA services. The hearing was delayed while an independent evaluation was conducted. At an IEP meeting, the parents insisted on a therapeutic residential placement while the district asserted that a nonresidential public school setting would be appropriate. The parents challenged the district's placement, claiming it failed to offer the student a finalized IEP. A federal district court and the First Circuit ruled for the district, noting that the IEP was never finalized because the parents disrupted the IEP process. **Their fixation on a residential placement at district expense caused the breakdown of the IEP process.** *C.G. and B.S. v. Five Town Community School Dist.*, 513 F.3d 279 (1st Cir. 2008).

◆ A New York student began to experience anxiety about school after being bullied there. He was diagnosed with severe anxiety and depression, and the school's committee on special education found him eligible under the IDEA with emotional disturbance. The district developed an IEP specifying individualized counseling, resource room services and test modifications. The parents later withdrew their consent for the IEP and sought home tutoring. The district then recommended several alternative high school placements. The parents unilaterally placed their son in an unapproved private school without informing the district, then rejected the district's recommendations. When they sought tuition reimbursement, the Second Circuit ruled against them. **The private school lacked a therapeutic setting and an administrative hearing officer had found it inappropriate.** *Gagliardo v. Arlington Cent. School Dist.*, 489 F.3d 105 (2d Cir. 2007).

VI. TRANSITION AND GRADUATION

Overview

Transition services describe "a results-oriented process, that is focused on improving the academic and functional achievement of the child with a disability ..." The IDEA requires a statement of a student's transition service needs for the IEP of each student with a disability no later than the age of 14, or earlier if appropriate. See 34 C.F.R. Part 222.50. Introductory language in the 2004 IDEA Amendments declared an increased emphasis on the provision of effective transition services for disabled students, in view of their increasing graduation rates.

A. Transition Plans

Court Decisions

◆ A New York preschooler received 30-35 hours per week of home-based Applied Behavioral Analysis (ABA) therapy from his school district, with speech and occupational therapy. The committee on special education (CSE) recommended a special education placement but without the ABA sessions. His parents rejected the IEP and sought due process. A hearing officer ruled for the school district, and the Second Circuit held the district did not have to provide home-based ABA therapy. **Appropriate supports and services were included in the IEP to ease the student's transition to school.** And the parents failed to show that the CSE had predetermined a kindergarten placement. *T.S. and S.P. v. Mamaroneck Union Free School Dist.*, 554 F.3d 247 (2d Cir. 2009).

◆ A New Hampshire school district prepared an IEP for an 18-year-old student that was nearly 60 pages long and contained nine pages of transition services. The parents rejected the IEP but refused to make any modifications to the plan or even to specify which parts of it were objectionable other than to say they disagreed with the behavior aspects of the IEP. The district unsuccessfully tried to put the rest of the IEP into effect and then filed an administrative due process request. A hearing officer ruled for the school district, and a federal district court affirmed the judgment, ruling **the district did not have to comply with the parents' unspecified vision of a perfect IEP**. The district had offered the student a detailed and comprehensive IEP that more than adequately addressed his needs. The mother appealed to the U.S. Court of Appeals, First Circuit. The court agreed with school officials that the student's IEP should be put into effect. **The IDEA does not require transition plans to be articulated as a separate component of an IEP. Nor were behavior plans necessary unless certain disciplinary actions had been taken.** Thus, the first proposed IEP, which discussed a behavior plan, did not violate the IDEA. *Lessard v. Wilton Lyndeborough Coop. School Dist.*, 518 F.3d 18 (1st Cir. 2008).

◆ After a Pennsylvania student with disabilities turned 16, his new IEP left sections of his mandatory transition plan largely blank, instead noting that he would meet with a school counselor to discuss his prerequisites for college and other issues. At the next IEP team meeting, the district offered the student an alternative special education day placement at an in-state private school. His parents instead opted for a residential school in New York. When they sought tuition reimbursement, the district failed to submit the due process request for more than three months. However, a hearing officer still ruled in favor of the district, finding the proposed placement appropriate. A federal court and the Third Circuit affirmed the judgment. **The dispute over the transition plan and the delay in submitting the due process request did not add up to an IDEA violation where the proposed IEP was appropriate.** *Sinan v. School Dist. of Philadelphia*, 293 Fed.Appx. 912 (3d Cir. 2008).

◆ An Illinois student with Rett Syndrome engaged in self-injurious behavior and sometimes struck others. In her first year of high school, she head-butted two staff members, breaking their noses. The district sought a special education setting, but the parents objected, instead settling for keeping the student at home. Eventually she was returned to her neighborhood school, where she made limited academic progress. When the district again tried to place the student in a special education setting, the parents requested a hearing, asserting that the IEP meeting was a sham to mask a "predetermined placement." A hearing officer, a federal court and the Seventh Circuit all ruled for the district. The parents received a meaningful opportunity to participate in the development and review of their daughter's IEP. **While the district did not include a transition plan in the IEP, the student was unable to benefit from one at the time**, so the lack of a transition plan did not violate the IDEA. *Board of Educ. of Township High School Dist. No. 211 v. Ross*, 486 F.3d 267 (7th Cir. 2007).

B. Graduation

The 2004 IDEA amendments relieved schools of a duty to seek an evaluation before terminating the eligibility of a student who has graduated with a regular diploma or become too old to be eligible for a free appropriate public education (FAPE). When an eligible child graduates or "ages out" of school, the school district must give the child a summary of his or her academic achievement and functional performance, with recommendations for assistance in meeting the child's postsecondary goals.

Court Decisions

◆ An Indiana school district offered special education to a learning disabled student until his parents decided to home school him. They sought to reintegrate him into public schools and obtained private evaluations showing that he had autism. But the school district did not identify an autism spectrum disorder until the student was 17 and awarded him a diploma at age 19. His parents challenged the graduation, asserting he should continue to receive special education. A federal court, using the stay-put provisions of the IDEA, ordered the district to continue educating the student in a college preparatory program. **The parents' challenge to the validity and good faith of the decision to graduate their son warranted a stay-put placement.** *Tindell v. Evansville-Vanderburgh School Corp.*, No. 309-cv-00159-SEB-WGH, 2010 WL 557058 (S.D. Ind. 2/10/10).

◆ An Illinois sophomore with Type 1 diabetes and a social anxiety disorder began missing school and took classes at a community college. She sought reimbursement for her tuition there, but a federal court and the Seventh Circuit ruled against her. The student had a Section 504 plan in place for her diabetes but was not IDEA eligible. **There was no medical evidence that she stopped attending high school because her anxiety had worsened, and she was unable to establish a medical basis for her better attendance and performance at the community college.** As a result, the parents' request for community college tuition reimbursement was properly denied. *Loch v. Edwardsville School Dist. No. 7*, 327 Fed.Appx. 647 (7th Cir. 2009).

◆ The parents of a California student waited until after he graduated to file a Section 504 claim against the school district. Appeal reached the Ninth Circuit. It held that despite differences between Section 504 and the IDEA, **a party seeking relief that is also available under the IDEA must exhaust administrative remedies to the same extent as for IDEA claims**. *Fraser v. Tamalpais Union High School Dist.*, 281 Fed.Appx. 746 (9th Cir. 2008).

◆ An Oregon student with a Section 504 plan had ADHD but did not qualify for an IEP. He was suspended for accessing a school database to change his grades. A hearing was conducted to consider expulsion, but his father claimed he received improper notice and thought the meeting was just for fact-finding. The school district agreed to further investigate, and the family filed a Section 504 complaint, challenging the suspension and seeking restoration of class credit. A hearing officer ordered the district to give the student the opportunity to recover lost credits. The student graduated with a regular diploma but sued the district under Section 504 and the IDEA, seeking to modify his final grades and requesting money damages. A federal court dismissed the case, holding that **even though he had graduated, he should still have pursued administrative remedies** before suing. *Ruecker v. Sommer*, 567 F.Supp.2d 1276 (D. Or. 2008).

◆ A 19-year-old Florida student had Asperger's syndrome and was non-verbal. His senior-year IEP identified writing as a priority need. At an IEP meeting held three months before the end of the year, the district proposed eliminating goals requiring him to complete written work. It also advised the parents their son would graduate at the end of the year, if he received all of his academic credits. The parents rejected the proposal to graduate their son and to eliminate his written work. They requested a new IEP meeting or mediation and new evaluations. Days before graduation, the board advised the parents it would hold an IEP meeting to discuss a diploma and review the IEP. It then informed them the graduation ceremony was the day before the IEP meeting.

An administrative law judge rejected the parents' request for stay-put relief, but a federal district court held their due process request before graduation triggered the stay-put provision. The board appealed to the Eleventh Circuit. It rejected the district court's finding that the board had misled the parents by scheduling an IEP meeting the day after their son's graduation. There was no evidence that the board did not intend to hold the meeting if the student failed to graduate. **The district court should not have back-dated a stay-put injunction.** The court vacated the decision and instructed the district court to decide if a preliminary order should be issued. *Sammons v. Polk County School Board*, 165 Fed.Appx. 750 (11th Cir. 2006).

The case returned to the district court, which held that the student, now 22, was not entitled to stay-put protection or compensatory education. *Sammons v. Polk County School Board*, No. 8:04-cv-2657-T-24-EAJ, 2007 WL 4358266 (M.D. Fla. 12/10/07).

◆ A Washington student became pregnant as a high school senior. She failed a quiz near the end of the year and was barred from the graduation ceremony. The district superintendent later met with the family and suggested a Section 504 plan to increase the student's point total for the failed course. A resulting increase in points for the class allowed her to graduate. She and her family sued the district and school officials, alleging discrimination and due process violations. A jury found that the district violated the student's due process rights and awarded her $5,000, with over $31,000 in attorneys' fees and costs. However, the jury found no discrimination. On appeal, the Court of Appeals of Washington found that **no state or federal law created an entitlement for students to attend graduation ceremonies**. The student received an opportunity to meet with the principal to resolve her grievance prior to the ceremony. She was not deprived of any interest protected by the Constitution. *Nieshe v. Concrete School Dist.*, 128 Wash.App. 1029 (Wash. Ct. App. 2005).

◆ The parents of a Pennsylvania student with dyslexia, memory disorder and ADHD agreed with their school district on a 12th-grade IEP that called for transition services in a college preparatory program in Maryland. The district did not provide the transition services, but at the end of the year, it recommended that the student be graduated. The parents objected, and the IEP team met without the parents to finalize an IEP for a thirteenth year of services that also did not include transition services. A due process hearing officer found that the student had received a free appropriate public education, but a state special education appeals panel reversed. The Commonwealth Court of Pennsylvania upheld the panel's decision. **The district had failed to provide agreed-upon transition services, then scheduled the student's graduation.** The court ordered the district to provide the student with a year of compensatory education in the college preparatory program. *Susquehanna Township School Dist. v. Frances J.*, 823 A.2d 249 (Pa. Commw. Ct. 2003).

◆ A federal district court held that an Illinois school district improperly decided to graduate a high school student with multiple disabilities on the basis of his accumulation of required credits instead of his progress toward his individualized goals. As the district committed several violations of the IDEA with respect to the student's educational program and IEPs, it was required to reimburse him for private school costs and provide compensatory education at a private school until he reached age 22. The violations included designing IEPs with vague and immeasurable goals, not changing IEP goals from year to year despite regression, and failure to develop a timely transition plan. **To be eligible for graduation, the student had to meet general graduation requirements and make progress on his IEP goals and objectives.** *Kevin T. v. Elmhurst Community School Dist. No. 205*, 2002 WL 433061 (N.D. Ill. 2002)..

VII. SCHOOL LIABILITY

A. IDEA Claims

1. Compensatory Education

Compensatory education is the belated provision of necessary educational or related services to a student to which the student was entitled, but which the education agency failed to provide. Compensatory education may be awarded to students who are over the statutory age of entitlement (usually 21) to prohibit education agencies from indefinitely delaying the provision of necessary services until the student is beyond school age

Teacher Scenarios

Special ed: When parents don't step up, do teachers have to step in? 309

Court Decisions

◆ The parents of an 11-year-old Pennsylvania student who had never attended public schools requested an evaluation for special education after obtaining a private evaluation. They did not sign the consent forms for a public evaluation, instead enrolling the student in a private school recommended by their evaluator. Eventually the district was able to conduct an evaluation and prepare an IEP, which the parents rejected. They sought compensatory education for the delay, claiming that they had asked for an evaluation during the student's kindergarten year. The case reached the Third Circuit, which ruled against the parents. It noted that **they were not entitled to compensatory education because they had no intention of placing their son in public school. There was no evidence they had asked for an evaluation during kindergarten.** *P.P. v. West Chester Area School Dist.*, 585 F.3d 727 (3d Cir. 2009).

◆ A Texas student with multiple disabilities had an IEP that included a goal to initiate communications about his need to go to the bathroom. The district used a voice-output device for him to communicate this need and gave a device to the parents for home use, explaining its proper use to his mother. The student regressed in his ability to use the device at home and in his extended school year program, and he wet the bed every morning. His parents challenged the IEP's schedule of in-home and parent training. A hearing officer noted that the district provided only four of ten scheduled training sessions, and ordered 150 minutes of compensatory training. But a federal district court ruled that **the student's regression in toilet training was not a failure to implement a significant portion of the IEP**. The award of compensatory training was reversed. *Clear Creek Independent School Dist. v. J.K.*, 400 F.Supp.2d 991 (S.D. Tex. 2005).

◆ A District of Columbia student with multiple disabilities had received special education for some time. An evaluation team determined that he was making progress but that he required new evaluations. However, they were not performed. After six months, the student's mother requested a due process hearing. A hearing officer determined the district failed to provide the student with a FAPE, but limited compensatory education to the two-month period prior to the hearing request. The mother appealed. A federal court noted that **the district had failed to show it was providing the services required by the IEP and did not conduct a reevaluation required by the IDEA**. Accordingly, the court held the student was entitled to compensatory education for the entire three-year period at issue. *Argueta v. Government of District of Columbia*, 355 F.Supp.2d 408 (D.D.C. 2005).

◆ A 19-year-old Tennessee student with no hands, one foot and cerebral palsy was dropped while school district attendants were attempting to move him from his wheelchair. His parents received his complete academic record for the first time and filed a due process complaint. A federal district court held the system violated the IDEA by not relaying information from the student's assessments. After he received a special education diploma, the Sixth Circuit ordered the district court to decide whether the case was moot. The district court held **the compensatory education claim was based on an assertion that the school system had denied a FAPE at a time when the student remained eligible for services**. Though he was now 24 and had a special education diploma, his compensatory education request involved past violations and the case was not moot. On appeal, the Sixth Circuit agreed, and found an IDEA procedural violation. *Barnett v. Memphis City Schools*, 113 Fed.Appx. 124 (6th Cir. 2004).

2. Monetary Damages, Costs and Fees

In Ortega v. Bibb County School Dist., *397 F.3d 1321 (11th Cir. 2005), the Eleventh Circuit restated a longstanding rule that tort-type personal injury claims for damages are unavailable under the IDEA. But attorneys representing students often add claims alleging disability discrimination and tort damages to IDEA actions. Claims involving any matter relating to the identification, evaluation or placement of a child, or the provision of a free appropriate public education, are subject to the IDEA's administrative exhaustion requirement.*

Court Decisions

◆ The parents of a New York student with disabilities sought private school tuition reimbursement. After winning at administrative and federal court levels, they sued to recover $29,350 in fees for assistance provided by an educational consultant throughout the process. A federal court awarded only $8,650 in fees, allowing only those charges accumulated between the hearing request and the administrative ruling. Appeal reached the U.S. Supreme Court. It found that nothing in the IDEA made clear to the states that accepting federal funds would make them responsible for reimbursing parents for expert witness fees. Expert witness fees could not be deemed costs so as to be reimbursable. *Arlington Cent. School Dist. Board of Educ. v. Murphy*, 548 U.S. 291 (2006).

◆ A Pennsylvania student had academic difficulty during her school career. By the fifth grade, she was receiving 45 minutes of daily learning support. In the second half of the year, the district reevaluated her and found her ineligible for special education. A due process hearing officer ruled that the district violated the IDEA and ordered compensatory education as well as reimbursement for an independent education evaluation. A review panel largely affirmed the decision. When the district appealed to a federal district court, the parents sought money damages. **The court ruled that the IDEA does not permit compensatory damages but ruled they might be available under Section 504.** The case would move forward. *Breanne C. v. Southern York County School Dist.*, 665 F.Supp.2d 504 (M.D. Pa. 2009).

◆ The mother of a Nevada student with autism took her son to a childhood autism program ordered by a hearing officer as compensatory education. The district was required to pay "all out-of-pocket expenses" – nearly $65,000. When the mother sought an additional $26,515 to fully compensate her for wages and benefits she lost while transporting her son to the program, the Supreme Court of Nevada held that she was not entitled to them. **Out-of-pocket expenses did not include lost income.** *Gumm v. Nevada Dep't of Educ.*, 113 P.3d 853 (Nev. 2005).

B. Discrimination Claims

The Americans with Disabilities Act (ADA), 42 U.S.C. § 12101, et seq., and Section 504 of the Rehabilitation Act of 1973, 29 U.S.C. § 794, are federal statutes prohibiting discrimination against persons with disabilities. Both acts require schools and their employees to make "reasonable accommodations" for qualified individuals with disabilities, but no institution is required to lower its academic standards in order to do so. As the Eighth Circuit Court of Appeals held in Sonkowsky v. Board of Educ. for Independent School Dist. No. 721, *327 F.3d 675 (8th Cir. 2003),* **to create liability under Section 504 or the ADA, there must be evidence of bad faith or gross misjudgment by school officials.**

Court Decisions

◆ Hawaii sisters were diagnosed as autistic when they were pre-schoolers. According to their parent, the Hawaii Department of Education (DOE) found the girls eligible for special education but did not implement or design IEPs for them. He alleged the school system "warehoused" them in their first years of school. A federal district court dismissed the family's discrimination case, finding Section 504 of the Rehabilitation Act created no private right of action to enforce the requirement to provide a free appropriate public education (FAPE), and no evidence of intentional discrimination based on disability.

On appeal, the U.S. Court of Appeals, Ninth Circuit, noted a distinction between FAPE under the IDEA and Section 504. **To establish Section 504 liability, the family had to show the DOE intentionally discriminated against the students or was deliberately indifferent to their rights.** Evidence supported the claim that the girls could not access the benefits of a public education without autism-specific services. There was evidence that the DOE was on notice that they required services but failed to provide them. Failure to act despite knowledge of the likelihood of harm was evidence of deliberate indifference. Rejecting the DOE's arguments regarding claims under Section 504 and regulations published under Section 504, the court returned the case to the district court. *Mark H. v. Hamamoto*, 620 F.3d 1090 (9th Cir. 2010).

◆ A Kentucky student with diabetes attended her neighborhood school, which did not have a nurse working there. Because the student required insulin shots, her mother arranged to have someone give them to her. However, the mother then sought to have the school district hire a nurse for the neighborhood school. The district instead offered to transfer the student to a nearby school where a nurse worked. The mother rejected this option because of the extra transportation time it would involve. She later sued the district in a federal district court for Rehabilitation Act and ADA violations. The court ruled against her, noting that **the school district had offered a reasonable accommodation, which the mother had refused.** *B.M. v. Board of Educ. of Scott County, Kentucky*, Civ. No. 5:07-153-JHM, 2008 WL 4073855 (E.D. Ky. 8/29/08).

◆ A disabled Wisconsin student with physical deformities endured verbal attacks and mockery by other students. Two boys in shop class also threw pieces of wood at him, causing injury. After they were suspended, he was allowed to leave classes early to avoid them. A third shop student then threw safety glasses at the student, causing a concussion and cracked teeth. That student was also suspended. The disabled student sued the school board and the shop teacher in a federal district court for violating his equal protection and due process rights by failing to protect him from his fellow students. **The court held he could not prove intentional discrimination by the board or teacher.** The shop teacher did not treat him differently than non-disabled students. There were also no ADA or Rehabilitation Act violations. *Werth v. Board of Directors of the Public Schools of City of Milwaukee*, 472 F.Supp.2d 1113 (E.D. Wis. 2007).

◆ A Pennsylvania student began having behavioral problems in elementary school and was diagnosed with ADHD and oppositional defiant disorder. He took medication that helped him in class, and he performed at grade level in reading, writing, math, science and social studies. In grade seven, the district found him eligible for a Section 504 accommodation plan. The student's behavior deteriorated; he threatened to shoot a teacher and burn down the school, and he was suspended. His parents asserted that the district had failed him under both the IDEA and Section 504. After a hearing officer found the school district had adequately addressed the student's attention and organization problems, the parents sued. **A federal court held that the student did not have a serious emotional disturbance so as to be entitled to IDEA disciplinary protections like a manifestation determination.** He understood the consequences of his behavior, and the school district accommodated his needs. *Brendan K. v. Easton Area School Dist.*, No. 05-4179, 2007 WL 1160377 (E.D. Pa. 4/16/07).

◆ A Massachusetts student with Asperger's syndrome applied for admission to an agricultural high school, seeking entry into its landscaping program. He scored only 32 of 55 possible points under the school's admissions policy and was placed on the waiting list. The school admitted 16 other students with IEPs, and at least 25 other students with IEPs ranked ahead of him on the waiting list. His claimed the school discriminated against him on the basis of his disability. A federal district court found no discrimination. **The school's admissions policy was neutral**, and other disabled students had been selected under its criteria. The school did not have to modify its admissions requirements because that would constitute a fundamental change in its program. *Cordeiro v. Driscoll*, No. 06-10854-DPW, 2007 WL 763907 (D. Mass. 3/8/07).

◆ The parents of an Arkansas student with mental retardation and serious heart disease said a group of non-disabled students pretended to befriend their son, then confined him in a dog cage and forced him to eat dog feces. They also stole from him, sexually abused him and exposed him to non-disabled peers. The parents claimed they discussed the bullying with school officials repeatedly, but that the district did nothing to stop the abuse. In the family's federal district court lawsuit, the district sought to have the claims dismissed for failure to exhaust administrative remedies, but a federal district court refused to do so. **As there was some evidence that the district acted with bad faith or gross misjudgment, the court held the case should proceed.** *R.P. v. Springdale School Dist.*, No. 06-5014, 2007 WL 552117 (W.D. Ark. 2/21/07).

◆ A Wyoming student with cerebral palsy attended school in a district that initially did not have accessible buildings. The district hired a full-time aide to assist her during the school day. During her entire school career, the student continued to have accessibility issues. The district did not make accessible seating in the school gym available, and locked her out of a school building because an accessible door was not working. Also, during her senior year, her aide frequently missed school due to a personal situation. When the student sued the district under Section 504 and the ADA, the district sought to have the case dismissed. The court refused to do so, noting that **the mere hiring of the full-time aide did not mean that the district had not intentionally discriminated against the student**. A trial would have to be held. *Swenson v. Lincoln County School Dist.*, 260 F.Supp.2d 1136 (D. Wyo. 2003).

C. Negligence and Civil Rights Claims

In order to hold school districts liable for negligence, there must be some act or omission that creates a foreseeable risk of harm. Civil rights actions require an injured party to show violation of a clearly established right, and often, "conscience-shocking" conduct.

Teacher Scenarios

How far does teacher have to go to protect mainstreamed student?......................310

Court Decisions

◆ A New York student with a history of behavior problems that included aggression at home, setting fires, stealing and threatening others attended school under an IEP. He made better social progress after being placed in a community residence and displayed no aggressive behaviors for two years. When he was 11 years old, he called a kindergartner his girlfriend while on a school bus. Her mother asked that they be separated. Later, he exposed himself to the kindergartner and forced her to touch him. Her mother sued the district for negligence. The Court of Appeals of New York ruled that she could not recover for her daughter's injuries because **the molestation by the 11-year-old was not foreseeable**. His past conduct did not indicate any sexually aggressive behavior. *Brandy B. v. Eden Cent. School Dist.*, 934 N.E.2d 304 (N.Y. 2010).

◆ An Illinois autistic student had daily tantrums, an eating disorder and episodes of running on impulse. A doctor prescribed a service dog, which was obtained two years later. This calmed the student greatly. However, at a preschool IEP meeting, district officials told his mother the service dog could not accompany him to school because even though the dog was hypoallergenic, another student was highly allergic to dogs. The family sought a preliminary injunction to temporarily allow the student to bring the dog to school. **The Appellate Court of Illinois agreed with the family that the student would suffer irreparable harm if he could not have the service dog in class, and it issued an order in his favor based on state law.** *Kalbfleisch v. Columbia Community Unit School Dist., Unit No. 4*, 920 N.E.2d 651 (Ill. App. Ct. 2009).

Later, the family sought an order that would allow the dog to accompany the student to school. The Appellate Court of Illinois held **the dog met the state's definition of a "service animal" even though the commands to assist the student came from staff members and not the student himself**. The student could bring the dog to school. *K.D. v. Villa Grove Community Unit School Dist. No. 302*, 936 N.E.2d 690 (Ill. App. Ct. 2010).

◆ A New York City special education teacher initiated a Type Three referral to remove an aggressive student from her class, and she contemplated quitting because of his behavior. Her supervisors told her to "hang in there" because referral could take up to 60 days. Forty-one days after initiating the referral, the student attacked another child and the teacher intervened, sustaining injuries. She sued the city for negligence, alleging that a "special relationship" supported her claim. A jury awarded her over $512,000, and appeal reached the state's highest court. **According to the New York Court of Appeals, no special relationship existed between the teacher and the board that would create a cause of action for negligence.** *DiNardo v. City of New York*, 13 N.Y.3d 872, 921 N.E.2d 585, 893 N.Y.S.2d 818 (N.Y. 2009).

◆ An assistant principal in North Carolina called a disabled student's mother to report some sexual experimentation between the student and another boy. The mother believed the contact was not consensual and she sued the school board for negligence, also asserting state constitutional claims. The school board sought immunity, but the North Carolina Supreme Court held the lawsuit could proceed. **Sovereign immunity was created by the courts, but constitutional rights trumped them.** And granting immunity to the board would leave the student and his mother without an adequate state remedy. *Craig v. New Hanover County Board of Educ.*, 678 S.E.2d 351 (N.C. 2009).

◆ A North Carolina teacher's aide allegedly force-fed a student to the point of choking on several occasions, used abusive language and pulled his hair. The student stopped eating and had to be hospitalized. His parents sued the aide, the school board, administrators and a teacher for claims including infliction of emotional distress. The teacher sought immunity, but the state courts rejected her claim. Her job was not created by the state constitution or laws, so she was denied public official immunity. While teachers served a vital role in public education, they did not meet the test for public official immunity.

Turning to the federal claims, **the court held the test for public official immunity starts with an inquiry into whether the official has violated clearly established rights of which a reasonable person would have known at the time of the violation.** Under both the state and U.S. Constitutions, the court found there is a liberty interest in the integrity of the human body. A right to be free from state-created brutal, harmful or demeaning intrusions into personal privacy and bodily security was recognized in 1980 by the Fourth Circuit. The complaint alleged the teacher knew of and might have witnessed the repeated abuse of the student. As there was evidence of the teacher's continued inaction in the face of widespread abuse, and the claims involved clearly established constitutional rights of which she would have known, the court held she could not claim immunity for the federal law claims. *Farrell v. Transylvania County Board of Educ.*, 682 S.E.2d 224 (N.C. Ct. App. 2009).

◆ The mother of a Virginia child with cerebral palsy and a seizure disorder became concerned that the student's teacher was improperly confining her to a wheelchair for most of the day. She hid recording equipment in the child's wheelchair, got information that corroborated her concerns and then sued the teacher, the school board and the superintendent for violating her child's right to bodily integrity under the Due Process Clause. The defendants sought immunity, but the Fourth Circuit held that they were not entitled to it. **The student had a clearly established right to be free from bodily restraint, and the mother alleged that the confinement was intentional and excessive.** If staff members indeed restrained the child for hours at a time as alleged, they would have violated clearly established law. The court remanded the case for further proceedings. *H.H. v. Moffett*, 335 Fed.Appx. 306 (4th Cir. 2009).

◆ A disabled California student had an IEP that called for full-time adult supervision. She had held hands with a male student on more than one occasion and went with him unsupervised to a greenhouse on campus, where he made sexual advances toward her. Her family sued the district for negligence and lost. The California Court of Appeal held that **the student's IEP did not require the district to supervise her every minute she was on campus.** Further, the hand-holding did not make it foreseeable that the male student would make sexual advances towards her during one brief, unsupervised period. *M.P. v. Chico Unified School Dist.*, No. 138462, 2009 WL 226005 (Cal. Ct. App. 2/2/09).

◆ A Minnesota student with an emotional-behavioral disorder and a history of sexually inappropriate behavior was supposed to sit alone behind the bus driver, and his transportation form included that directive. However, the form did not detail his past history. He was allowed to move back in the bus at some point, and he sexually assaulted another student. When the other student sued the district, the Minnesota Court of Appeals held that **the district had immunity with respect to its decision to withhold the student's prior history of sexual misbehavior.** But as for the failure to follow directions and keep the student in the seat behind the driver, the bus service had no immunity. *J.W. v. 287 Intermediate Dist.*, 761 N.W.2d 896 (Minn. Ct. App. 2009).

◆ A disabled female student in Ohio rode the bus home every afternoon with three disabled male students. No bus aide accompanied them because none was required by any of the students' IEPs. The student was abused by a male student during the rides home. A bus aide present on the morning drive eventually discovered the abuse, and the parents ultimately sued the district for her injuries. They claimed that the motor vehicle exception to immunity allowed them to sue, while the district asserted that the exception applied only to the action of driving the bus. On appeal, the Ohio Supreme Court held **immunity protected the school district. The motor vehicle exception applied only to the driving of the bus and not the supervision of students by the driver.** *Doe v. Marlington Local School Dist. Board of Educ.*, 907 N.E.2d 706 (Ohio 2009).

◆ A 15-year-old Tennessee student with depression, ADHD, bipolar disorder and schizophrenia jumped off a moving school bus after the driver refused to allow him to get off at a location that was not designated as a bus stop. The student died from the fall. His mother sued school officials, claiming disability discrimination and civil rights violations. A federal district court and the U.S. Court of Appeals, Sixth Circuit, ruled against her. The Sixth Circuit held **the school board had no policy or custom of deliberate indifference to student rights, and its conduct was not the moving force or cause of the death.** *Hill v. Bradley County Board of Educ.*, 295 Fed.Appx. 740 (6th Cir. 2008).

◆ A learning-disabled Colorado high school student told her mother she did not want to attend school anymore because boys teased her. The mother told the principal that certain boys were "bothering" her daughter. Later, the student told a school counselor that one boy had repeatedly called her to ask for oral sex and that two boys had coerced her into sexual conduct. The school resource officer then investigated, but the mother refused to cooperate on "advice of counsel." The district attorney then declined to prosecute the case because of the difficulty of proving the activity was not consensual and because of the trauma to which the student would be subjected. The student had a psychotic episode that required hospitalization. The family moved away, and they sued the school district under Title IX. A federal court and the Tenth Circuit ruled for the district, finding that **the district did not have actual**

knowledge of the sexual harassment until the student told the counselor about it. Nor did the district have a policy of allowing student-on-student sexual harassment. Finally, the district was not required to discipline the boys for sexual harassment. *Rost v. Steamboat Springs RE-2 School Dist.*, 511 F.3d 1114 (10th Cir. 2008).

◆ An Ohio school aide supervised an autistic student who had previously injured fellow students on the bus. The aide rode with the student on the bus, and was hit and bitten by the student on one occasion. Later, the aide accompanied the student on a field trip to a bowling alley, where the aide intervened to protect another student from the autistic student's attack. The aide was injured. She sued the school board for negligence and civil rights violations, asserting a "state created danger" theory. A federal court and the Sixth Circuit ruled in favor of the school board, noting that **the school district did not create the danger or increase the risk to the aide**. The board was simply attempting to discharge its duties under the IDEA. *Hunt v. Sycamore Community School Dist. Board of Educ.*, 542 F.3d 529 (6th Cir. 2008).

◆ A Kentucky special education student with profound mental disabilities fell while wearing roller skates during a field trip and broke his ankle. The parents then sued the school board and the teacher. A state trial court held the board and teacher were entitled to immunity. The Court of Appeals of Kentucky agreed. **Public employees have qualified immunity where they perform acts involving the exercise of discretion and judgment, if those acts are taken in good faith and within the scope of employment authority.** In this case, the teacher had to exercise discretion and her personal judgment a number of times during the day, including on how to implement the student's IEP and how to supervise him. She also acted in good faith and within the course and scope of her employment. *Pennington v. Greenup County Board of Educ.*, No. 2006-CA-001942-MR, 2008 WL 1757209 (Ky. Ct. App. 4/18/08).

◆ A Michigan student with multiple disabilities, including a seizure disorder, had to be harnessed into seats when traveling in a vehicle or a wheelchair. During a field trip, the student suffered a seizure and became unresponsive on a school bus. Later, he suffered another seizure on the bus, and neither the attendant nor the driver could perform CPR. Emergency responders arrived 10 minutes later and took the student to a hospital, where he died the next day. Litigation in the state court system reached the Michigan Court of Appeals. It found **the board was entitled to immunity because school officials did not act with "gross negligence," which is defined as conduct so reckless as to amount to a disregard for safety**. *Lofton v. Detroit Board of Educ.*, No. 276449, 2008 WL 4414255 (Mich. Ct. App. 9/30/08).

◆ A Nevada student had tuberous sclerosis, which is a neurological disease that causes tumors. He also had autism and was non-verbal. An IDEA lawsuit was brought on his behalf against his school district and teacher. In it, he alleged that his teacher slapped him repeatedly and body-slammed him into a chair. The student also claimed that school officials knew about his teacher's violent conduct but did nothing to prevent it. The teacher and the school district asked for qualified immunity, but a federal court and the Ninth Circuit refused to grant it. **The court held that no reasonable special education teacher would believe it was lawful to seriously beat a disabled four-year-old.** The case was allowed to proceed. *Preschooler II v. Clark County School Board of Trustees*, 479 F.3d 1175 (9th Cir. 2007).

D. Abuse and Neglect

Court Decisions

◆ A Minnesota student took a student to her resource room as a result of a behavior incident, as specified in her IEP. On the way, she denied the student lavatory use, causing the student to have an accident. An investigation found that the lavatory incident was merely a lapse in judgment, so the teacher was not disciplined. The student's mother sued the school district for claims including child abuse and neglect. A federal court and the Eighth Circuit ruled against her, noting that the mother failed to allege anything done by the teacher that was "shocking to the contemporary conscience" and that there was no due process or Fourth Amendment violation. **The student's IEP, which included a behavior intervention plan, stated she was to be taken to her resource room if she had a behavior incident.** The teacher was complying with this instruction at the time of the accident. *C.N. v. Willmar Public Schools, ISD No. 347*, 591 F.3d 624 (8th Cir. 2010).

◆ A Georgia student with emotional and behavioral issues and ADHD made suicidal comments to staff members but told a school psychologist he was just kidding. He was hospitalized for two weeks and released. The school placed him in its time-out room for most of two days due to disruptive behavior. He made suicidal threats again. After picking a fight with another student, the student was sent to the time-out room again, and he hanged himself. His parents sued the school system and state department of education, but the Georgia Court of Appeals found **no official disregarded his rights in a manner that could be deemed deliberately indifferent**. *King v. Pioneer Regional Educ. Service Agency*, 688 S.E.2d 7 (Ga. Ct. App. 2009).

◆ The family of an Ohio student with Down Syndrome sued their district and several employees, alleging that a substitute teacher did not monitor their child's classroom on many occasions and that the student was assaulted by a known abuser as a result. The Court of Appeals of Ohio granted the district immunity because the **failure to monitor was within the scope of the employees' official job duties**. But the individual employees might be liable for their "recklessness." The court returned the case to the trial court for consideration of that issue. *E.F. v. Oberlin City School Dist.*, No. 09CA009640, 2010 WL 1227703 (Ohio Ct. App. 3/31/10).

◆ A Florida student with autism sued his former teacher and school board based on five incidents of corporal punishment. He claimed that she violated his due process rights and the Rehabilitation Act by abusing him in class, and he pointed to her suspension and later conviction on one count of child abuse. But the court found four of the incidents were related to the student's refusal to go to a "cool-down room" or his calling the teacher names or threatening her. The fifth incident involved her tripping him, which was not corporal punishment. In each case of corporal punishment, **the teacher used restraint on the student only until he calmed down or agreed to comply with her instructions**. *T.W. v. School Board of Seminole County, Florida*, 610 F.3d 588 (11th Cir. 2010).

◆ A Minnesota student's IEP team determined she was ineligible for extended school year services, but it provided curb-to-curb transportation and an aide for one summer. The next summer, it required the student to use general education transportation without an aide. A driver sexually abused her, and the parents sued the school district for violating Section 504. A federal district court and the Eighth Circuit held for the district, as **discontinuation of the aide and abuse by the driver did not amount to discrimination. The district did not act with bad faith or gross misjudgment.** School officials had followed the IEP, which stated that the student was ineligible for ESY and related services. *M.Y. v. Special School Dist. No. 1*, 544 F.3d 885 (8th Cir. 2008).

VIII. TEACHER SCENARIOS

Sharpen Your Judgment

Is teacher required to 'handle' service dog?

"Sean has autism. He needs his dog, so why can't he bring it to school anymore?" Sean Alan's mother asked teacher Chase Ford as soon as she walked into the classroom.

"Thanks for meeting with me, Ms. Alan," Chase said. "I know the service dog helps Sean, but the problem is, he isn't really capable of handling the dog. So this isn't working."

"Wait a minute," Ms. Alan said. "Sean is autistic. Are you holding that against him now? That doesn't sit well with me – at all!"

"No, of course not," Chase reassured Ms. Alan. "The dog barks at other students – and sniffs them too. I have to handle the dog so everyone stays safe at school. Let's find a solution that works for everyone."

"I don't care about everyone else." Ms. Alan said. "And I'm not about to let you take away something that clearly helps him!

"I'll see you in court before I let that happen," she continued as she stormed out.

Ms. Alan sued, claiming the school denied an IEP request which would allow Sean to have the dog.

Did the judge agree?

Sharpen Your Judgment – The Decision

Yes, the judge agreed that Sean had a right to take his service dog to school.

The judge noted that barking and sniffing other students may have caused distractions. But when probed for more info about the extent of the distractions, the teacher admitted that the dog wasn't a "consistent problem" but an "occasional" issue.

The teacher also admitted that having the service dog at school helped Sean. With his dog at school, Sean calmed down after tantrums more quickly.

Sean also stopped running away from the teacher and the class during transition times, such as lunch, when his dog was with him.

The bottom line: Sean's dog had been trained to benefit a child with autism – and Sean's an autistic child who had shown improvement with the dog's help, the court found. For this reason, Sean had a right to take his service animal to school.

Analysis

It's not always easy to deal with challenges for special ed students.

But don't be too quick to dismiss an IEP accommodation – even if it isn't perfect.

Cite: *K.D. v. Villa Grove Community Unit School.*

Sharpen Your Judgment

Did teacher make right call with disabled student?

"Mrs. Kraven," said teacher Jacklyn Perris into her cell phone. "Thanks for calling me back. How's Alice?"

"In the hospital with two broken legs," said her mother. "She'll be out of school for weeks. What else did you expect when you let a girl with brittle bones go outside when it's icy?"

"But the office checked and found it wasn't icy outside. Does Alice say she slipped on ice?"

"She's not sure why she fell. But how could there not be ice after a freak snowstorm?"

"That's why the office put salt down before they decided to let the students go outside during lunch."

"But Alice isn't like the other kids! Any little stumble can be dangerous for her! That's why she needs an IEP to keep her inside on bad days."

"We've been over this," said Jacklyn quietly. "The team decided Alice doesn't qualify for special ed. But I pulled her aside that day and reminded her to be careful."

"That wasn't enough," said Mrs. Kraven.

Alice's parents' sued, arguing Alice should have had an IEP to keep her from getting hurt, and that the teacher violated the IDEA by not keeping her safe inside. Did she?

Sharpen Your Judgment – The Decision

No, the teacher didn't violate the IDEA.

Alice has a serious health condition that can affect her education, but she and her parents can't sue under special ed law for two reasons.

First, the IDEA guarantees a "free and appropriate public education" – not the right to sue for personal injury after an accident.

Second, lawsuits are a last resort under that law. Procedures like meetings, mediations and hearings are required first. Alice and her parents hadn't gone through them before suing.

Analysis: Include disabled students

The judge pointed out that if it was really a question of keeping Alice safe at school, the answer was for teachers to keep Alice from doing anything – because a fall is so likely to hurt her that even crossing a room is risky.

But the IDEA's goal is to include disabled students in regular school life – not isolate them.

It can be hard to get the safety-inclusion balance right with fragile students – special ed or not. This teacher did a good job. She made sure the weather didn't pose extra risks to Alice, then reminded her to be careful – and got the message across in a way that didn't single her out in front of the others.

Cite: *Edwards v. School Dist. of Baraboo.*

Parents say teacher crossed the line by restraining student who acted up

The defense: 'We just followed the recommendation'

"That's my pencil, jerk. Give it back or I'll smack you."

Even though teacher Alex Washington had his back to the room, he knew who was shouting. It was the unmistakable voice of Robert Sklarz.

Alex had heard it before. Robert had emotional problems identified in his IEP. Alex remembered reading it and the recommended action to take with Robert when trouble broke out:

"Separate him from other students and remove him from the classroom as soon as possible."

Alex turned toward the students as he spoke: "All right, calm down now. No one's going to smack anyone. Robert, what seems to be ..."

"Yesterday, I was missing my pencil," Robert broke in. "Now, today, this jerk shows up with it." He nodded toward Lawrence Avent.

"He's crazy," Lawrence countered. "This pencil's mine. Besides, there must be a million that look like this one."

Before Alex could make his way closer to the two boys, Robert lunged at Lawrence, screaming, "Crazy? I'll show you who's crazy, punk!"

Alex got between the two just in time and wrapped his arms around Robert while coaxing the student toward the door.

"Easy, Robert," the teacher said in an even voice. "Come with me and we'll get this straightened out."

That only seemed to raise Robert's anger, as he struggled to reach Lawrence.

"I'll get you," he scowled.

Eventually, Alex calmed Robert down and managed to get a staffer to take the boy to the principal's office.

Three days later ...

Three days later, Alex sat across from principal Maria Ashe, who asked, "So that's exactly how the situation developed with Robert Sklarz?"

"Exactly as you see it in my notes," Alex nodded. "I did what was recommended in the IEP – separated him from the others and moved him out of the classroom."

"Well, his parents say he ended up at the doctor's with an injured back," Maria explained. "They say you used unauthorized corporal punishment with their son.

"How likely is it that he got injured when you grabbed him?"

"I did put him in a bear hug," Alex admitted. "Just to stop him, not punish him."

"How else was I supposed to make sure he didn't 'lose it' totally and make things worse? Other teachers have had problems with him like this before."

"I know," Maria agreed. "But it's never resulted in an injury before, and the parents are upset about it. After I spoke to them on the phone, they said something about seeing a lawyer and pursuing legal action."

'He violated policy'

Eventually, the parents sued the teacher and the district over the student's injury.

The foundation of the parents' argument in court: The district has a policy against force and corporal punishment, and the teacher violated the policy.

The district argued:

- the teacher used the force necessary to maintain order and follow the requirements of the IEP, and
- there was no intent on the part of the teacher to injure the student or use corporal punishment.

Was the teacher right?

Decision: Yes. A court noted the district in fact did have a policy banning corporal punishment, but the student's IEP implied that force was necessary to follow the plan's mandates.

The two were not contradictory. The use of reasonable force was for the purpose of maintaining order and restraining the student, and not for punishment.

Cite: *Loy v. Dodgeville School Dist.*

Discussion points for teachers and principals:

A tense classroom situation and the pieces of an Individualized Education Plan can combine to make for some tricky and difficult decisionmaking for a teacher. In those instances, courts consider whether the teacher:

■ made a best and reasonable effort to follow the IEP, and

■ dealt with the situation in a balanced way aimed at maintaining classroom order and controlling the student.

Mother says school has to permit deaf son's service dog

IEP team denied it because of other students' allergies

Teacher Mary Clementee smiled as she sat down to eat lunch with the Special Ed director in the teacher's lounge.

"It's nice to see you can still smile," said the director. "I heard Zach Bilinski tried to bring his service dog in again and you sent him to the office."

The teacher nodded. "His mother thinks he needs the dog 24-7 to alert him to the dangers he can't hear."

"But didn't we spend hours at Zach's IEP meetings explaining why the dog can't be at school?"

The teacher said, "Zach's mom is so worried that I don't think she even heard what we said about Felipe's allergies or Wanda's fear. Wanda can't even focus if a dog's in the room."

"But, isn't the bottom line that Zach doesn't need the dog for any educational reason?"

"That's not his mother's bottom line," the teacher pointed out.

Mother not happy with the IEP

Mary was grading papers at the end of the day when Zach's mother stormed in.

"How can you put his life at risk this way?" she asked.

"Hi, Mrs. Bilinski," said the teacher. "Sit down and we'll talk."

When she was seated, the teacher said, "You know we agreed on many things for Zach's IEP to help him learn, and I think you'll agree it's been working.

"His grades have shot up since he's had a full-time sign-language interpreter, a hearing student to take notes for him and plenty of time for tests. His IEP -"

"Forget about the IEP!" interrupted his mother. "As his teacher, don't you care if he's safe? You know he can't hear sirens. What if there's an emergency and he's all alone?"

"That's why we put flashing alarm lights in the bathroom," the teacher reminded her.

"But he needs the dog, too," his mother insisted. "You're his teacher. Why aren't you looking out for his best interests?"

The mother sued for the accommodation. Did she win?

Decision: No, the mother didn't win. Considering the hardships the service dog posed – without providing educational benefit for Zach – it couldn't come to school.

Key: It can be tough to say no to parents' requests, but you also have to keep your other students in mind.

Cite: *Cave v. East Meadow Union Free School.*

Mom claims teacher was out of line: Students voted to remove classmate

Teacher insists autistic student constantly disrupts lessons

Teacher Susan Allan was nervous as she walked into the principal's office for the scheduled meeting with a mad parent.

Mike Hill's mother was already seated in one of the chairs – and she skipped the niceties of small talk. "It's not OK to embarrass my son in front of the entire class just because he's autistic!"

"I didn't mean to –" Susan started to say before the principal interrupted.

"Why don't we start at the beginning?" the principal suggested. "Ms. Hill, please tell me exactly what happened."

Vote to kick student out of class

"I'd be happy to," Ms. Hill said. "My son Mike was upset because he got in trouble for misbehaving during class.

"Mike said the teacher called him to the front of the class," Ms. Hill continued. "He sat in a chair while she held a vote."

"A vote?" the principal asked.

"Yes, a vote to kick him out of class," Ms. Hill confirmed and glared at Susan accusingly. "How could you?"

"I didn't mean to embarrass Mike," Susan said. "He wouldn't settle down. He's constantly disrupting lessons – and it isn't fair to the rest of the class."

"Isn't fair to the rest of the class?" Ms. Hill repeated. "That's all you have to say? I'm calling my attorney."

Ms. Hill filed a lawsuit, claiming the defendants violated the Individuals with Disabilities Act (IDEA) and the Americans with Disabilities Act (ADA).

School officials asked the court to dismiss her claims. Did it?

Decision: No, the judge refused to grant summary judgment.

Key: More information was needed to determine whether school officials violated the IDEA and the ADA, the judge noted, so a trial was needed.

Note: Rather than face a costly trial, the school suspended the teacher for one year and agreed to pay $350,000 to settle the claim.

Cite: *Barton v. St. Lucie County School Board.*

Learning-disabled student acts up: Should punishment be less severe?

Teacher must make the call on classroom disruption

Teacher Gail Dunlap decided she'd keep a close eye on Daniel Hamilton and Robert Croce.

The two students had been at each other all week, especially after Robert figured out that Daniel was struggling with a reading disability. That's when the teasing had started.

A sample of Robert's taunts: "Hey, Dumb Dan, my little sister in first grade can read better than you."

The first time Gail overheard one of the taunts, she spoke to Daniel first: "I want you to let me know if he says anything like that again, and I'll handle it."

Then she took Robert aside and warned him: "We don't allow that sort of thing in this classroom. If it continues, you'll be paying a visit to the principal's office. Do we understand each other?"

Robert uttered a sullen "yes," but the teacher feared it wouldn't end there. She turned out to be right.

A shout – a punch

Later in the week, while Gail huddled for a moment with a student who had a question, she heard a shout from behind her. It was Daniel Hamilton's voice:

"I've had it with you and your mouth. Let's see what your big mouth thinks about this," he exclaimed as he landed a punch squarely on the face of Robert Croce.

Daniel kept swinging angrily as Robert, nose bloodied, tried to block the attack.

The teacher managed to separate the boys.

"Daniel, stand right there," she ordered him while she applied paper towels to Robert's face.

What caused it?

"... And that's what happened," Gail concluded in a next-day meeting with Daniel's parents and principal Alex Meltzer.

"So this other kid had been on my son about his reading disability?" Daniel's mother asked.

"Well, I heard him taunting Daniel one time, and I put a stop to it right away," the teacher explained. "We're assuming it continued and that's why Daniel reacted the way he did."

"And knowing all that, you still recommended that Daniel be punished for hitting another student?" the mother shot back.

"My recommendation was based strictly on school policy," the teacher answered.

"That's correct," the principal noted. "When there's a physical confrontation, teachers are supposed to figure out who started the fight and recommend punishment for that student ..."

"But the other kid started it," the father interrupted.

"Not by our definition," the principal said. "The one who threw the first punch is the one who started the fight."

"Look," the mother said, "we all know Daniel has a reading disability, and we all know that's what led to the fight – his reaction to the problem with the disability.

"If you punish him for that, we'll be forced to sue."

The decision

The parents ended up suing to lift the punishment.

Did the court's decision back the school?

Decision: No. A judge ordered the school to lift the punishment for fighting.

The decision rested on two main reasons:

- The student had a documented disability that had to be taken into account as a factor.
- In a general sense, the disability did lead to the confrontation. In other words, it was reasonable to assume that had there been no reading disability, there would have been no fight.

Given the disability, the judge said, the school had to reconsider and rescind the punishment for the student's actions.

Cite: *Coleman v. Newburgh Enlarged City School Dist.*

Discussion points for teachers and principals:

Consider and discuss so you're ready to make the right decisions:

■ If a student with any type of disability breaks rules or violates policies, how should the disability be taken into account when determining the appropriate punishment?

■ Do your school's policies cover responses to rule-breaking by a student with a disability?

Dealing with difficult students: When to draw the line

Did teacher react correctly in tense situation?

When student Nick Woodruff ignored the request, teacher Adrian Fernandez pondered his next move.

The teacher was well-read on Nick's IEP detailing the student's mild autism that resulted in his sometimes ignoring requests and getting out of control.

The teacher decided to repeat the request: "Nick, I said I want you to shut down your computer now and get ready for phys-ed with the rest of the class."

Still, the student ignored him and kept tapping at the keyboard.

With that, the teacher leaned over, put his hand on the computer mouse and started the shutdown procedure.

That's when the student shouted, "Don't you ever do that," and swung a balled fist at the teacher's face.

He responds

The blow grazed the teacher's chin, and the student recoiled his fist and appeared to get ready to swing again.

The teacher thrust his arm out and slammed his palm into the student's chest to back him out of striking range. The move worked, as the student's next blow hit only air. But the force of the teacher's hand pushed the student off this seat and onto the floor.

The teacher moved toward the student to help him up, but that only made the boy more angry.

"Don't hit me again. You can't do that," the boy screamed and sobbed as he ran out of the classroom.

A week later ...

At the meeting a week later, principal Nora Lily began, "Just to be sure we know what happened, Adrian, tell me why you pushed Nick Woodruff."

"Sure," the teacher nodded. "Nick had already taken one swing at me and looked like he was getting ready to try it again.

"I wasn't so much trying to push or strike him as I was trying to move him away from me so I didn't get hit."

"OK, and you'd read Nick's IEP about his tendency to ignore requests and use violence?" the principal asked.

"Yes, and I checked it to see if it said anything about how we should react. It didn't say anything about not responding."

"Nick's parents claim you did more than 'respond,'" the principal explained. "They say what you did amounted to corporal punishment."

"I can see how it might look that way to someone who wasn't there, but nothing I did was aimed at punishing Nick," the teacher insisted. "That's all."

"That's clear to me," the principal agreed. "We just have to make sure we can explain that in case this grows into something bigger than it is."

"Such as?" the teacher asked.

"We could end up in an administrative hearing, or who knows? The parents may take this all the way to court."

The decision

Eventually the parents did sue, and the case went to court.

Did the court find the teacher's actions justifiable?

Decision: Yes. A judge threw out the case, noting the teacher had acted appropriately.

The judge based the decision on three key factors:

- The teacher was fully acquainted with the student's IEP and made decisions based on its content.
- The teacher's explanation about his action was reasonable – that he used force to control the situation and not to punish the student.
- The force used by the teacher obviously wasn't of the type intended to injure the student, and, in fact, the student suffered no injury.

Cite: *Fessler v. Giles County Board of Educ.*

Discussion points for teachers and principals:

Consider and discuss so you're ready to make the right decisions:

■ What's the district's policy about controlling and containing a violent student?

■ Does the student have an IEP? If so, what does it say regarding violent acts?

■ How have previous incidents of violence been handled – rightly or wrongly – in your district?

Sharpen Your Judgment
Student excluded from field trip – for ADHD?

"I got your email. What's the latest with James Reid?" Coach Vinny Travo asked as he walked into Principal Heather Marks' office.

"James' parents are suing," Heather told him. "According to them, you wouldn't let James go on the Minnesota Vikings field trip because he has ADHD – and he's a Green Bay Packers fan."

"That's ridiculous," Vinny said. "James misbehaved – and that has nothing to do with having ADHD or being a Packers fan.

"Just look at his discipline record," Vinny continued. "He has a habit of ignoring the rules. What am I supposed to do – allow it?"

"Not at all," Heather said. "He's had more than 25 write-ups this school year. I think the discipline was warranted."

"His parents are trying to game the system by playing the disability card," Vinny said. "I would never exclude a student based on a disability – or a football team."

"We'll see how it plays out in court," Heather said.

James' parents sued, claiming he was excluded from the trip because of his disability.

Did the judge agree?

Sharpen Your Judgment – The Decision

No, the judge sided with the school.

James' parents claimed that he was excluded from the Minnesota Vikings field trip for two reasons: He has ADHD and he's a Green Bay Packers fan.

The school argued James was excluded from the bus trip for yet another disciplinary problem. The school pointed to his long list of infractions as proof.

That swayed the judge. James' parents might have had a valid argument, if not for his long history of behavior problems.

When school officials take students off campus to special field trips, the teachers must be able to keep students in line, the judge explained. Because James didn't follow the rules in school, the discipline was justified, the court ruled.

Analysis: Look at the history of behavior

It's natural for parents to want to make excuses for poor behavior – and ADHD might seem like a good reason.

But schools can discipline students who have a history of poor behavior, in spite of ADHD problems. Document the behavior to show the logic behind the decision.

Cite: *Sonkowsky v. Board of Educ. for Independent School Dist. No. 721*

They commit same offense but don't get same punishment

Parent wants to know why one got tougher treatment

The two boys fidgeted nervously as teacher Tom Hansen spoke to them.

"Your answers on the science test are remarkably alike – even the wrong ones are the same.

"Is there something you two want to tell me before this gets you into deeper trouble?"

An uncomfortable silence hung in the air for about a minute before one of the boys, Josh Legrew, spoke up in a faltering voice:

"OK, OK, we cheated," he said. "I let Michael look at my answers because I owed him a favor."

Though he suspected as much, the teacher still was a little surprised at the confession by Josh, one of the top students in the class.

"Is that true, Michael?" the teacher followed up.

"Yes, it's true. I might as well admit it now that this punk has rolled over on me," he said while nodding toward Josh.

"All right then," the teacher sighed, "we'll be talking about the punishment for you two."

Why the difference?

A few days later, the teacher sat across a table from Michael's angry father.

"Let me understand," the father said. "Two boys together cheat on a test, and you're recommending that my son gets worse punishment than the other kid?"

"That's right," the teacher answered. "The cheating is a first offense for the other boy, Josh. But this is the third time I've caught Michael cheating."

"And the fact that Josh is a perfect little boy while my Michael has ADHD has nothing to do with your decision, right?" the father said.

"No, it doesn't," the teacher replied.

He sues

The father eventually sued the school and the teacher, arguing that the son was being unfairly punished, partly because of his ADHD, and that students had to be punished equally for equal offenses.

Did the school win?

Decision: Yes. A judge ruled the same offenses don't require the same punishments, and schools are allowed to take circumstances into account, including a student's disciplinary record.

Key: The teacher had a complete record of the boy's disciplinary actions and a clear reason for choosing different levels of punishment for the same offense.

Cite: *Schneider v. Corvallis School Dist.*

Disruption causes accident: Should teacher have stepped in earlier?

Mom accuses teacher of trying to punish student

Teacher Amy Hill was grading papers at her desk when TA Kay Harris said, "Look outside."

The students had been rambunctious all day – and now a light snow had started to fall. "What are we in for when the kids get back from lunch?" Amy asked, knowing the weather would rile them up even more.

"As if the residual Halloween sugar-buzz isn't enough to handle," Kay said.

Just then, students filed into the room.

And as expected, they were excited about the first snowfall of the year. They were already picking teams for the anticipated snowball fight after school.

"OK, class," Amy said. "Let's settle down and get our work done. Then you can talk about the snow. Deal?"

The class settled down, and Amy started her lesson. But just as she began, students in one corner of the class burst into giggles.

'Let's stay focused, please'

Amy put her book down. "I know you're excited. But let's stay focused on our work. We have a lot to get done today. If you pay attention I may let you have a few minutes of free time." She turned around to write on the board.

The giggling continued. Amy walked to the snickering section of the room. "What's going on here?"

One of the girls in class spoke up. "Tell Tommy to quit that. He stinks!"

A handful of students burst into uncontrollable laughter, which prompted Tommy to pass gas again – loudly. Then, he laughed.

"Stop it!" the girl shrieked at Tommy. But he didn't stop. Amy motioned for her TA to take over the class, and Amy took Tommy into the hallway.

Following his IEP

Amy sighed as she looked at Tommy, a high-functioning autistic student. He had been mainstreamed into her class.

Tommy usually responded well to the instructions in his IEP. So Amy followed it to the letter.

"I have taken you out of class because you're disturbing your classmates," she explained. "Do you need to use the restroom? Or do you want to go back to class?"

He slapped the classroom door.

"I expect you to go to work, Tommy," Amy said as they walked back into class.

But the talk didn't help. Tommy walked straight to the girl who'd complained – and passed gas again.

She stood up and screamed. The boys in the class stood up, pointed and howled. "Dude, you just took a dump all over yourself!"

Sure enough, when Amy turned around, she saw that Tommy needed to be cleaned up. So Kay took him to the restroom.

Mom's mad

Tommy's mother sued Amy personally, claiming she refused to allow Tommy to use the restroom to punish him for misbehaving in class – and it made him have an embarrassing accident in front of his classmates.

The teacher argued that Tommy was trying to get a laugh out of classmates. His accident was really an accident. She didn't deny him restroom privileges. She asked the court to dismiss the charges. Did it?

Decision: Yes, the judge dismissed the claim. The teacher removed Tommy from the situation, but he never asked to use the restroom, so the teacher didn't punish him, the court ruled.

Key: Courts recognize when teachers follow IEPs. This teacher removed the student from class and talked to him.

Following a student's IEP can't be considered punishment because it's the previously agreed-upon plan, the court explained.

Cite: *Bess v. Kanawha Board of Educ.*

Discussion points for teachers and principals:

It's a fact: Disruptions will happen. But when disruptions become legal hassles, teachers' actions often determine the court's decisions. This teacher took the right steps – following the student's IEP by:

■ removing the student from class, and

■ asking the student how he would like to proceed.

Special ed: When parents don't step up, do teachers have to step in?

Teacher honored Mom's request – so why's she suing?

Teacher Kay Brown looked up from the stack of papers she was grading when she heard a knock on her classroom door. "Come on in," she said.

Susy Hill's mother walked into the classroom. "We need to talk about Susy," she said.

"Sure, no problem," Kay said, moving the stack of tests as she retrieved a file. "This is my planning period, so it's a good time to talk about what it's going to be like to have an IEP for the first time. Are you happy with it?"

"Yes, I see some improvement," Ms. Hill said. "But you shouldn't have waited so long to finally get Susy on an IEP."

"Waited so long?" Kay asked. "I'm sure I made recommendations to have her tested at school earlier this year. Remember?"

Teacher made recommendation

"You mentioned testing briefly, but I think Susy would've been better off if she'd had an IEP earlier," Ms. Hill said. "Why did you let her slip through the cracks?"

"Let's look at the file," Kay said. "At parent-teacher conferences, I made recommendations to have the school test Susy. And when you said 'no' repeatedly, the school referred her to an outside specialist."

"I took her to the specialist – like you said. The specialist agreed that she has a disability, so why did you wait for me to ask about an IEP?" Ms. Hill asked accusingly. "You should've been clear about Susy's needs right from the start."

Kay was stunned. "I thought I was specific about her educational needs," Kay said.

"You weren't," Ms. Hill shot back quickly.

Documentation is reviewed

"Why don't we take a look at Susy's file?" Kay suggested, trying to find a positive angle. "Let's start from the beginning. We can look at where we started.

"Then we'll assess where we've helped Susy improve," Kay continued. "Maybe we can find tweaks that will help even more. We can suggest them at the next IEP meeting."

"The only thing I want to discuss is your failure," Ms. Hill said insistently. "You dropped the ball, and Susy suffered."

Kay knew Ms. Hill wanted to play the blame game. "OK, let's discuss the information I shared with you," she said, flipping through the file.

"First, I let you know that Susy failed every subject," Kay said. "In this report, I stated that her classwork was 'incomprehensible.' I told you that she often refused to come into the classroom.

"I told you she should be tested," Kay continued. "But you said 'no' over and over so we didn't want to push the matter."

"I don't care about the report. You'll be hearing from my lawyer," Ms. Hill said.

She sued, claiming the school ignored Susy's disabilities and violated the IDEA. Did the judge agree?

Decision: Yes, the district court ruled that the school's inaction violated the IDEA and on appeal, the appellate court affirmed the decision.

Key: While her mother was reluctant to have Susy tested, school officials had warning signs indicating that Susy's disabilities interfered with her education, so they still had a "child find" obligation under the IDEA.

Officials didn't test Susy at school, and they didn't act quickly when the specialist confirmed that she needed an IEP.

Instead, they waited for Susy's mother to "explicitly request an educational assessment" even though they knew Susy displayed signs of a disability, which violated the IDEA, the court explained.

Cite: *Compton Unified School Dist. v. Addison.*

Discussion points for teachers and principals:

Some parents aren't ready to accept that their child may have a disability. But parents' reluctance to testing doesn't relieve schools of "child find" obligations under the IDEA.

Best practices include:

■ Referring the student for an initial evaluation at school.

■ Documenting the parent's response to the test and results.

How far does teacher have to go to protect mainstreamed student?

Special ed student sexually assaulted: How did it happen?

Teacher Kay Harris sighed, thankful that her students were at lunch. Teaching special ed students is rewarding, but it's exhausting, she thought.

At least non-disabled student-tutors helped Kay in the classroom. They made life a lot easier.

She reached for her bag and noticed one of her student-tutors was standing at the door. "Oh! Hi, Anne," Kay said. "I didn't know you were still here."

"Can I talk to you?" Anne whispered.

"Of course," Kay said, fighting the urge to sneak a peek at her watch. "What's on your mind today?"

"I don't know how to tell you this," Anne said, "but it's important."

Kay pointed to a desk. "Why don't you have a seat and tell me about it?" she prodded gently.

Peer-tutor took advantage of student

"Well, Eddie did something to Gina," Anne started, "and I'm mad about it. You'll be mad, too."

Kay's internal alarm starting beeping. Eddie was a student-tutor who mentored the special ed students – and Gina's a student with mental retardation.

But Kay hadn't noticed anything unusual today. "What happened, Anne?" she asked.

"Eddie was working with Gina," Anne said.

"Yes," Kay agreed. "Go on. Tell me why you're upset."

"Gina was working at the puzzle table, and Eddie, um, he unzipped his jeans and pulled it out," she whispered.

"It?" Kay's eyebrows shot up.

"Yes, it!" Anne stammered and continued, "then I saw Eddie make Gina use her hand on him."

"Where was I while this was happening?" Kay asked, closing her eyes and rubbing her temples.

"You were teaching the money counting lesson at the back table," Anne said.

"You probably didn't see because Eddie kept Gina's hand under the puzzle table," Anne continued. "I only noticed because I heard Eddie making noises."

The investigation

Kay and Anne reported the incident, and school officials launched a full investigation, which revealed Eddie's history of sexually harassing female classmates.

After Eddie admitted he'd taken advantage of Gina, he was arrested.

But Gina's parents weren't satisfied. They sued, saying the special ed teacher knew Gina was more likely to be sexually assaulted than a non-disabled student.

Gina's parents claimed they told the teacher not to let Gina work one-on-one with male tutors. They said the teacher had a responsibility to protect Gina, but failed to do so.

The teacher argued she didn't know about Eddie's prior discipline record. She also pointed out that she didn't leave Gina alone in the classroom with a male tutor. She asked the court to dismiss the charges, saying she was entitled to qualified immunity.

Was she?

Decision: No, the court refused to dismiss the claim and grant qualified immunity to the teacher.

Key: The court noted this teacher knew special ed students have an increased risk of being sexually assaulted.

She also knew the student's parents specifically said their daughter wasn't allowed to work one-on-one with male tutors, the court pointed out.

Considering these factors, the teacher should've provided a higher level of supervision while the student worked with the male tutor, the court explained. Because the teacher failed to provide adequate supervision, she wasn't entitled to qualified immunity, the court ruled.

Cite: *Schroeder v. San Diego Unified School Dist.*

Discussion points for teachers and principals:

This case shows, "I didn't know" won't fly when safety's on the line. When teachers give students authoritative roles, safety issues can't slip through the cracks. Teachers should:

■ double-check students' disciplinary records, and

■ refuse to let students who aren't responsible enough to handle authority tutor their classmates.

Sharpen Your Judgment

'Teacher hit me,' autistic student says: Mom sues

Teacher Rich Wells walked into Principal Heather Marks' office with a grin. "Happy Monday!" he sang out and laughed. "That's not a phrase I normally use. I told you my team would win the Super Bowl!"

"Yeah, yeah," Heather said. "I hate to bust your football bubble, but we need to talk. Jim Leon's mom is suing."

"Why?" he asked. "I shouldn't be surprised. She is, um, should we say – a bit difficult?"

"She's claiming you have been hitting Jim's knees – as punishment," Heather said.

"What? I would never hit a student, especially a student with autism and an IEP!" Rich said. "You know that's not true. I've had trouble with her before – but this is crazy!"

"Jim's mom said he told her that you hit him on the knees," Heather said.

"This is ridiculous," Rich said. "I just can't imagine why Jim said that."

"I'm sorry about all of this," Heather said. "You realize we're going to have to conduct an investigation, right?"

Jim's mom sued, claiming the teacher abused him. School officials asked the court to dismiss the claim.

Did the judge agree?

Sharpen Your Judgment – The Decision

Yes, the judge dismissed the claim.

Jim's mom claimed he said the teacher hit his knees. She took pictures and showed them to the court. In them, his knees were red.

School officials acknowledged the pictures showed Jim's hurt knees, but argued they didn't show the teacher hitting Jim.

The court said the pictures proved Jim had "red and slightly swollen knees." But it agreed they didn't prove the teacher did it.

Because of the seriousness of the claim, the court ordered a medical examiner to question Jim alone. During the interview, Jim said:

- He liked "lots of stuff" about the "good" teacher, and
- Jim's mom told him to say the teacher hit him.

In light of Jim's answers, the court dismissed the claims.

Analysis: In a tough spot

Sometimes difficult parents can be frustrating. In such instances, it's important to remain calm, cooperate with investigations and remember that the truth will come out.

Cite: *G.C. v. School Board of Seminole County.*

8 Interscholastic Athletics

TOPICS

I. HIGH SCHOOL ATHLETICS 315

II. DISCRIMINATION AND EQUITY 319

III. ISSUES IN COACHING 323

CHAPTER EIGHT
Interscholastic Athletics

I. HIGH SCHOOL ATHLETICS

Overview

A. Eligibility Rules and Restrictions

State athletic association eligibility rules requiring a sit-out period for athletes transferring into a district from a neighboring school district, private school or from out of state may be enforced if they are reasonably related to the prevention of recruiting student-athletes. Many courts, including the Louisiana Court of Appeal, have held there is no constitutional right to play varsity sports. Challenges by students with disabilities are considered in Section II C., below.

1. Transfer Students

Court Decisions

◆ A Louisiana student transferred to a different public high school. He asked the Louisiana High School Athletic Association (LHSAA) to rule on his eligibility. The LHSAA determined there had not been a bona fide change of residence under its "transfer rule" and that he was ineligible to play football during his first year at the new school. His parents sued the LHSAA in a state court for an order allowing him to compete in varsity athletics at his new school. The case was dismissed on a legal technicality, and by the time an appeal reached the state court of appeal the student had graduated from high school. For this reason, the court held the claim for an order against the LHSAA requiring the association to allow his participation in sports was moot.

As for the student's challenge to the transfer rule and the LHSAA's eligibility ruling, the court found **LHSAA actions were "internal affairs of a voluntary association."** According to the court, an amateur organization conducting sports competitions maintained exclusive authority over a specific class of amateur athletes. While the lower court had incorrectly declined to consider claims for damages for alleged deprivation of constitutional rights, the court of appeal rejected the constitutional issues. LHSAA investigations and the enforcement of its rules were not "state action." Even if the LHSAA was deemed a "state actor," the court held "[a] student's interest in participating in a single year of interscholastic athletics amounts to an expectation, not a constitutionally protected claim of entitlement." The possibility of obtaining a college athletic scholarship was speculative and was not a protected property interest. As the student had no due process right to interscholastic athletic participation and did not advance a valid equal protection claim, the court affirmed the judgment on those claims. *Menard v. Louisiana High School Athletic Ass'n*, 30 So.3d 790 (La. Ct. App. 2009).

◆ An Oklahoma student athlete's parent made a negative comment about the basketball coach after a game and later refused to discuss the incident with the district superintendent. The parents were then barred from school property. The student quit the team and two months later transferred to a different school. The Oklahoma Secondary School Activities Association (OSSAA) denied the student's request for a waiver from its transfer rule, which bars transfer students from playing varsity sports for one year unless the OSSAA grants a waiver. A state court granted the family's petition for relief from the OSSAA ruling.

On appeal, the Supreme Court of Oklahoma noted that OSSAA rules explicitly bar hardship waivers when circumstances indicate discontent with the school in which eligibility has been established. **Participation in interscholastic athletics is not a right but a privilege subject to OSSAA eligibility rules.** Courts do not generally interfere in a voluntary association's internal affairs unless a member's financial or property rights are involved or there is evidence of a serious mistake or wrongdoing. No such mistake had occurred here, and the lower court committed error in ruling otherwise. *Morgan v. Oklahoma Secondary School Activities Ass'n*, 207 P.3d 362 (Okla. 2009).

◆ A student athlete at Barren County High School violated the school's alcohol policy and was declared ineligible for interscholastic athletic competition for the next school year. His family moved, and he enrolled at Glasgow High School. He asked the Kentucky High School Athletic Association (KHSAA) to declare him eligible for interscholastic athletics there based on a bona fide change in address exception to KHSAA's transfer rule. The KHSAA denied the request. While the student had established a new address, he was still ineligible under the penalty imposed at Barren High School. A Kentucky court granted the student's request for a restraining order barring the KHSAA's enforcement of the decision. The order was made in an *ex parte* proceeding, in which the KHSAA did not receive notice or an opportunity to appear. The Court of Appeals of Kentucky refused to disturb the order, and the KHSAA appealed. On appeal to the Supreme Court of Kentucky, the court noted that when the party being restrained is brought to court, the order has served its purpose and should be extinguished. **The correct way to challenge the restraining order was to ask the court issuing it to dissolve the order.** The court vacated the court of appeals' order. *Kentucky High School Athletic Ass'n v. Edwards*, 256 S.W.3d 1 (Ky. 2008).

◆ The U.S. Court of Appeals, Eleventh Circuit, affirmed a court ruling against a Georgia high school football coach and former players who alleged harm when the state high school association forfeited their games for a season. The association found that **the school improperly included a nonresident player on the team**. The lower court rejected student claims based on lost opportunities to receive college scholarships. Students have no constitutional right to participate in athletics. As the coach was not discharged or demoted, his constitutional rights were also not violated. *Stewart v. Bibb County Board of Educ.*, 195 Fed.Appx. 927 (11th Cir. 2006).

◆ The Louisiana High School Athletic Association (LHSAA) received a complaint about a student residency issue. The student's parents claimed that two LHSAA officers demanded to search their house and threatened to immediately declare the student ineligible from athletic participation if they refused. They let the officers search the house. The LHSAA commissioner held that the student's school violated its transfer and change of residence rules by letting the student play basketball. The student sued the district in a state court, which dismissed the case. On appeal, the Court of Appeal of Louisiana found **the student's claim to "an opportunity for an athletic scholarship to college" was a speculative and uncertain expectation, not a protected property interest**. The student had no due process rights to participate in interscholastic sports. The court found her equal protection claim did not specifically allege how she was treated differently from others. The state high school athletic association was not a state actor that could be held liable for an unlawful search of a private home. However, the complaint stated sufficient facts to support a claim for invasion of privacy under state law. The court reversed that part of the judgment. *Johansen v. Louisiana High School Athletic Ass'n*, 916 So.2d 1081 (La. Ct. App. 2005).

◆ A Kansas parent claimed that a public high school athletic director recruited his son extensively. The student attended the school for two half-days and then decided to transfer. He sent the athletic director a "limited eligibility transfer form" that would allow him to remain eligible for non-varsity sports after a transfer. The director refused to sign the eligibility form, asserting that the transfer was athletically motivated. The state athletic association approved the denial, relying on statements by school officials, who declared that the parent considered his son's athletic opportunities when making the transfer decision. The parent claimed the transfer was not motivated by athletics, and he sued. The court considered the parent's request for a preliminary injunction and noted that the student would not suffer any irreparable harm if it failed to intervene. He would miss only 18 weeks of basketball eligibility and could still practice with the football team. The board had a legitimate basis for denying the eligibility request. **As there is no recognized property interest in playing non-varsity sports, the court found no equal protection violation.** *Love v. Kansas State High School Activities Ass'n*, 2004 WL 2357879 (D. Kan. 2004).

2. Other Rules

State laws typically vest state athletic associations with broad powers to interpret their own rules. Constitutional claims generally fail, as many court decisions have held there is no constitutionally protected interest to participate in interscholastic athletics or other extracurricular activities.

Court Decisions

◆ West Virginia state athletic association rules imposed a two-game suspension on any student-athlete who was ejected from a basketball game. After being ejected from a game, a student-athlete had physical contact with a referee, triggering another rules violation. He sued the West Virginia Secondary Schools Activities Commission (SSAC), seeking an order to prevent enforcement of the two-game suspension. Meanwhile, his school suspended him for four games. By the time the court held a hearing, the parties had reached an agreement by which he would miss three games. Despite the agreement, the court proceeded to consider an SSAC rule regarding the forfeiture of games involving suspended players. The court struck down the rule and another SSAC rule based on its lack of provisions for administrative review. The SSAC appealed to the Supreme Court of Appeals of West Virginia, which reversed. **The lower court's attempt to declare an SSAC rule on multi-game suspensions unconstitutional was improper.** The SSAC was not a state actor, and no due process right was implicated. *Mayo v. West Virginia Secondary Schools Activities Comm'n*, 223 W.Va. 88, 672 S.E.2d 224 (W.Va. 2008).

◆ A Delaware student played varsity basketball and remained in the school district when his mother moved to Georgia. She executed a power of attorney authorizing the basketball coach and a lawyer to make decisions regarding her son. After the lawyer came to the school for a copy of the student's transcript, the school investigated his relationship with the student. The principal concluded that the power of attorney was insufficient and that the student was not a resident. The principal informed the Delaware Interscholastic Athletic Association (DIAA) that the school had used an ineligible player, and stated that the school planned to forfeit all the games in which the student participated. He asked the DIAA to waive the applicable forfeiture penalties. The DIAA denied the waiver request, and the state education board (SBE) upheld that decision. A court then issued a letter opinion which explained that **Delaware law vested the DIAA with the power to decide all controversies involving its rules, regulations and waivers.** State law provided for appeals of DIAA decisions to the SBE, but declared that "the decision of the SBE shall be final and not subject to further appeal." *Cape Henlopen School Dist. v. Delaware Interscholastic Athletic Ass'n*, No. 08A-01-003 ESB, 2009 WL 388944 (Del. Super. 1/28/09).

◆ The Oklahoma Secondary School Activities Association required private schools to obtain a majority vote of members for admission. However, any public school that applied for membership was automatically admitted. The Christian Heritage Academy twice sought to join the association. Both its applications were rejected, even after it reduced its boundaries to reduce its competitive advantage. The academy sued the association for equal protection violations. The case reached the U.S. Court of Appeals, Tenth Circuit, which held that the association violated the Equal Protection Clause. **There was no legitimate purpose for the different admission rules.** The association was a state actor because 98% of its members were public schools. Its directors were public school employees and its authority to determine eligibility and hold playoffs was granted by the state. The association treated the academy differently from public schools with comparable student populations and locations. *Christian Heritage Academy v. Oklahoma Secondary School Activities Ass'n*, 483 F.3d 1025 (10th Cir. 2007).

◆ A West Virginia student who had been home-schooled sought to participate on a middle school wrestling team. The West Virginia Secondary School Activities Commission (WVSSAC) denied the request, and the case reached the state supreme court of appeals. The court noted that WVSSAC rules required students to maintain a 2.0 grade average to remain eligible for interscholastic sports. Students also had to do passing work in four subjects per week in which they could earn credit toward graduation. Home-schooled students were evaluated only once per year. The court held school boards should not be required to spend funds to support home-schooled student participation in interscholastic sports. Participation in extracurricular activities did not rise to the level of a fundamental or constitutional right under the West Virginia Constitution.

Excluding home-schooled students from interscholastic sports did not violate equal protection. Like the parents of private school students, the parents of home-schooled children voluntarily chose not to participate in the state's public school system. In making this choice, these parents agreed to forgo the privileges of a public school education, one of which was the opportunity to qualify for interscholastic sports. The court held that the WVSSAC did not exceed its authority in issuing the eligibility rules. *Jones v. West Virginia State Board of Educ.*, 218 W.Va. 52, 622 S.E.2d 289 (W.Va. 2005).

◆ A Pennsylvania student was home-schooled for her seventh- and eighth-grade years. A school district allowed her to play interscholastic basketball both years. The student ended her home school program in grade nine and enrolled in a state-chartered and certified "cyber charter school." The school district let the student play on an interscholastic basketball team, but it later excluded her for failing to meet district requirements. Her family sued. The case reached the U.S. Court of Appeals, Third Circuit, which noted that the district's interscholastic sports participation requirements included verifiable attendance documentation. All of the student's attendance and class time was self-verified, under a curriculum provided by the University of Missouri. As her attendance was not verified by certified instructors and her curriculum was not approved by the state board of education, the school district could find her ineligible for interscholastic sports. **The decision denying the student's participation in interscholastic sports did not violate her constitutional rights.** *Angstadt v. Midd-West School Dist.*, 377 F.3d 338 (3d Cir. 2004).

B. Athletic and Extracurricular Suspensions

In addition to refusing to recognize any constitutional right to participate in interscholastic athletics or other extracurricular activities, the courts have rejected the argument that the possibility of obtaining a college athletic scholarship is an interest protected by any constitutional provision.

Court Decisions

◆ Upset that his son was not playing a particular position, a parent approached a coach during a high school baseball game. A harsh exchange of words followed, and school officials banned the parent from all athletic events for one year. The parent sued the school board in a federal court for constitutional rights violations. After the court denied him temporary relief, he filed a notice of dismissal. The school district opposed dismissal because it appeared that the parent had filed a complaint with the Ohio Civil Rights Commission. Under federal rules, this meant he lost the right to voluntary dismissal. **The court exercised its discretion to dismiss the case, even though he would simply be pursuing his claims with the state.** *Pennington v. Lake Local Schools Board of Educ.*, 257 F.R.D. 629 (N.D. Ohio 2009).

◆ A Kentucky high school student admitted to the school principal that he had been drinking alcohol before coming to a school dance. The school board excluded him from playing basketball and all other extracurricular activities. He sued the board and principal, asserting that the discipline was arbitrary and capricious. He further alleged discrimination and due process violations. A court dismissed the complaint, and the student appealed. The Court of Appeals of Kentucky noted that students have no fundamental or vested property right to participate in interscholastic athletics. For that reason, the student's constitutional claims had been properly dismissed. **A school board may suspend or expel a student for violating lawful school regulations.** However, the student claimed that the board acted arbitrarily and capriciously in denying his opportunity to participate in interscholastic athletics. The court held that he stated a viable claim for arbitrary and capricious action by the board and principal. Thus, the case required a trial. *Critchelow v. Breckinridge County Board of Educ.*, 2006 WL 3456658 (Ky. Ct. App. 2006).

◆ Parents told school officials that a Washington student-athlete and several other football players were drinking alcohol at a school dance. A staff member saw a beer container in the student's car, and a search of the car yielded an empty beer carton, cigars and tobacco. The school suspended the student for 10 days for violating a school policy against drinking alcohol as a member of the football team. He appealed the discipline, and the athletic board suspended him from a football game and five wrestling matches. He had to forfeit his football letter and individual honors and was recommended for alcohol evaluation and treatment. The principal upheld both the academic and athletic sanctions pursuant to an informal conference, as did a district hearing officer and the school board. When the student sued, a state court held for the district. The state court of appeals held that **interscholastic sports participation is a privilege, not a constitutionally protected property or liberty interest**. The district provided the student with more process than required under the circumstances by applying the state law procedures for short-term academic suspensions. It was not required to provide him with the kind of protections he would receive for an expulsion proceeding. The judgment for the district was affirmed. *Taylor v. Enumclaw School Dist. No. 216*, 133 P.3d 492 (Wash. Ct. App. 2006).

◆ A Pennsylvania coach suspected that a student was taking drugs and required him to take a drug test. A drug treatment facility determined that the student had no drug abuse problem, but he claimed that the principal did not reinstate him to swim and water polo teams despite the evaluation results. He claimed the coach cut a lock off his locker, performed a search, and seized his property. His family sued. A court held that the privacy expectations of student/athletes are even lower than those of the general student population. The coach suspected the student was using drugs because his behavior was unusual. There was an immediate concern for safety. The student did not assert a valid Fourth Amendment claim based on the locker search. His First Amendment claim failed, as he was not prevented from associating with team members. The removal of a student from school athletic teams did not implicate any due process rights. **Students do not have a due process property interest in any particular component of a public education**, such as extracurricular activities participation. There was also no due process violation based on the disclosure of medical information. The results of the drug testing were only revealed to the student's parents and his medical condition was not indicated. The court held for the district and school officials on all the claims. *Dominic J. v. Wyoming Valley West High School*, 362 F.Supp.2d 560 (M.D. Pa. 2005).

C. Drug Testing

Drug testing by urinalysis has been deemed a "search" under the Fourth Amendment to the U.S. Constitution. Testing limited to potential interscholastic sports participants has met with widespread court approval. For search cases involving a broader student population, see Chapter Five.

Courts have held student-athletes to a higher standard of conduct than the general student population in drug testing cases, due to the representative role they play and their reduced expectations of privacy. In the next case, a California school district could not justify expanding a mandatory random drug testing program for student athletes to include a broader range of participants in competitive recreational activities under the state constitution.

Court Decisions

◆ A California school board expanded a random drug testing program that had been previously limited to student-athletes. Anecdotal evidence indicated that students, including those taking music, were using drugs and alcohol. Although the superintendent later said he had little reason to suspect students involved in competitive recreational activities (CRAs) used substances at a higher rate than others, he wanted to test as many students as possible. When the policy was approved, it applied to CRAs such as choir, band, science bowl, "tri-mathalon," mock trial and the Future Farmers of America. Some CRA activities were used for student class grades and some satisfied state university admissions requirements. The expanded testing program covered 56.8% of high school students in the district. No procedure was in the testing program for challenging a positive test result. Consequences for a false positive were limited to CRA eligibility, and results were not shared with law enforcement agencies.

Parents of two honor roll students sued the school district in a state superior court for violation of their privacy rights under the state constitution. The court granted the students' request for a preliminary order halting the testing. Appeal went to the state court of appeal. It found the district offered "vague and shifting justifications" for testing CRA participants, and held the policy intruded upon privacy interests protected by the state constitution. Privacy rights were implicated by testing urine samples and requiring parents to disclose medications a child might be taking. **"Unlike the federal Constitution, the California Constitution contains an explicit guarantee of the right to privacy."** A state supreme court decision had held the California Constitution creates "a legal and enforceable right of privacy for every Californian." CRA participants were not shown to have reduced expectations of privacy in comparison to others. Some CRAs were curricular and some fulfilled college admissions requirements. The court held the superior court did not abuse its discretion in finding the students were entitled to injunctive relief. They were likely to prevail in further court activity by showing a sufficient expectation of privacy to pursue state constitutional claims. *Brown v. Shasta Union High School Dist.*, No. C061972, 2010 WL 3442147 (Cal. Ct. App. 9/2/10).

◆ After a 2000 survey indicated that 50% of student-athletes in a Washington school district self-identified as drug and/or alcohol users, the district began a random testing program. Participants had to agree to be tested for drug use as a condition of playing extracurricular sports. Drug test results under the program were not sent to law enforcement agencies. Students who tested positive were suspended from sports, but not from school. Parents of several students who played high school sports sued the school district, asserting the policy violated the state constitution. A state court upheld the policy, and the parents appealed.

The Supreme Court of Washington found "stark differences" between the Fourth Amendment and the Washington Constitution, which prohibits a search of a person "without authority of law." Under *New Jersey v. T.L.O.*, 469 U.S. 325 (1985), school officials may search students based on reasonable grounds for suspecting the search will turn up evidence of a violation of school rules. In *Vernonia School Dist. 47J v. Acton*, below, the Supreme Court upheld a random, suspicionless drug testing program for student-athletes. The Washington court found the Supreme Court "never adequately explained why individual suspicion was needed in *T.L.O.* but not in *Acton*." **The state constitution provided greater protection than the Fourth Amendment**, and as students had a fundamental privacy interest in their bodily functions, the judgment was reversed. *York v. Wahkiakum School Dist. No. 200*, 178 P.3d 995 (Wash. 2008).

◆ An Oregon school district responded to increased student drug use by instituting a random drug testing policy for all students wishing to participate in varsity athletics. Each student-athlete was to submit a consent form authorizing a test at the beginning of the season and weekly random testing thereafter. Students who refused testing were suspended from sports for the rest of the season. A seventh-grader who wanted to play football refused to sign the drug-testing consent form and was suspended from sports for the season. His parents sued the district, arguing that the policy violated the Fourth Amendment and the Oregon Constitution. A court upheld the policy, but the Ninth Circuit held that it violated both the U.S. and Oregon Constitutions.

On appeal, the U.S. Supreme Court stated that the reasonableness of a student search under the Fourth Amendment is determined by balancing the interests between the government and individual. **Students have a lesser expectation of privacy than the general populace, and student-athletes have an even lower expectation of privacy in the locker room.** The invasion of privacy in this case was no worse than what was typically encountered in public restrooms. Positive test results were disclosed to only a few school employees. The insignificant invasion of student privacy was outweighed by the district's important interest in addressing drug use by students who risked physical harm while playing sports. The Court vacated and remanded the decision of the court of appeals. *Vernonia School Dist. 47J v. Acton*, 515 U.S. 646 (1995).

◆ In 2002, the Supreme Court expanded the reach of its *Vernonia* decision in *Board of Educ. of Independent School Dist. 92 of Pottawatomie County v. Earls*. The Court held that an Oklahoma school district with no discernible drug problem could implement a program of testing for all students seeking to participate in extracurricular activities. **The Court found no reason to limit random drug testing to student-athletes**, extending *Vernonia* to cover all extracurricular activities participants. For a full summary of the case, please see Chapter Five, Section II.B. *Board of Educ. of Independent School Dist. 92 of Pottawatomie County v. Earls*, 536 U.S. 822 (2002).

II. DISCRIMINATION AND EQUITY

Overview

Federal civil rights laws forbid discrimination based on sex, race or disability in federally funded school athletic programs. All public school entities must also comply with the Equal Protection Clause.

A. Gender Equity

Title IX of the Education Amendments of 1972, 20 U.S.C. § 1681(a), prohibits sex discrimination and exclusion from participation in any educational program on the basis of sex by any program or activity receiving federal funding. Federal regulations at 34 C.F.R. Part 106.41 provide guidance on equal athletic opportunities for members of both sexes. In determining whether equal opportunities exist, the U.S. Department of Education's Office for Civil Rights (OCR) considers several factors including: (1) whether selection of sports and levels of competition accommodate both sexes; (2) the provision of equipment or supplies; (3) the scheduling of games and practices; (4) travel and per diem allowances; (5) coaching and tutoring opportunities; (6) coaching and tutoring assignments and compensation; (7) provision of locker rooms, practice and competitive facilities; (8) provision of medical and training facilities and services; and publicity. See 34 C.F.R. Part 106.41(c).

Court Decisions

◆ As the only female on her school's freshman football team, a Wisconsin student claimed discrimination by her head coach. She said he denied her access to the girls' locker room and kept snacks and practice schedules in the boys' locker room, where she was not allowed to go. According to the student, the coach told her to get her haircut "like a boy." After her mother complained to school officials that the coach was not letting her child obtain her equipment, the student practiced without pads and injured a shoulder and clavicle. She sued the school district and coach in a federal district court for civil rights violations.

The court held that to impose Title IX liability on a federal funding recipient, the institution must have actual notice of discrimination by employees and yet have "deliberate indifference" to it. There was evidence that when other players came to practice without equipment, the usual response was to find appropriate gear. The district did not contest the coach's departure from this general rule or his hostility to the mother's complaints. The student made out a valid equal protection claim against the coach. A state law claim against the coach for disregarding a known danger also deserved further consideration. But the student did not show the district had notice of any discriminatory acts, particularly the denial of her access to the girls' locker room. As the district had no actual notice of the coach's allegedly discriminatory actions, the Title IX claim against it was dismissed. The student did not show the district created a dangerous situation, but claimed only that no official stopped her from harming herself by practicing without pads. This did not support her due process claim against the school district. *Elborough v. Evansville Community School Dist.*, 636 F.2d 812 (W.D. Wis. 2009).

◆ California high school girls sued their school district in a federal court, asserting Title IX violations. They produced evidence that the difference between their enrollment numbers and the percentage of girls participating in sports was from 6.7 to 10.3 % in the three most recent school years. The court found a 6.7 % difference represented 47 girls or at least one competitive team. Thus, the district failed the substantial proportionality inquiry of Title IX's regulations. The court also found that female athletic participation rates at the high school were not expanding. As a result, the district failed the second part of the regulatory test. Finally, the district failed the third part of the regulatory test because it discontinued a viable field hockey program twice due to its inability to retain a coach. **Student interest and ability, not the ability to retain a coach, determined whether the test was met.** As the district failed each part of the Title IX regulatory compliance test, the court found the district was not in compliance with Title IX. *Ollier v. Sweetwater Union High School Dist.*, 604 F.Supp.2d 1264 (S.D. Cal. 2009).

◆ Two female Tennessee students enrolled in a weightlifting/conditioning class along with 35 boys. The principal removed the girls from the class out of concern for inappropriate behavior by males, and a staff member told them to report to the guidance office to work as helpers. One student objected. A state official contacted the district's director of schools, and within a few days the principal permitted the student to return to the class. She missed only three days of class, earned an A grade, and graduated. However, she claimed the stress of being removed from the class made her unable to eat and that she contracted mononucleosis as a result. The family sued the school board and officials in a federal court for violating the Equal Protection Clause and Title IX, claiming $1 million in damages. After the court granted the board's dismissal motion, the U.S. Court of Appeals, Sixth Circuit, affirmed. **The principal was not executing an official policy of the board at the time he ordered her removal, and did not act as a board policy maker.** Here, the board took immediate corrective action on her behalf as soon as the director of schools learned about the incident. As the board had no prior notice of the student's claim, it could not be found deliberately indifferent to known acts of discrimination. *Phillips v. Anderson County Board of Educ.*, 259 Fed.Appx. 842 (6th Cir. 2008).

◆ The Michigan High School Athletic Association (MHSAA) scheduled girls' basketball, volleyball and soccer seasons during non-traditional seasons throughout the state. Female student-athletes sued the MHSAA for violating the Equal Protection Clause, Title IX and the state Civil Rights Act. A federal court noted that psychological harm was done to female athletes in the form of a message that they were subordinate to males. The scheduling created many disadvantages for girls, including lost scholarships and the inability to participate in "March Madness" events and tournaments. The court prohibited the MHSAA from continuing to schedule girls' sports in disadvantageous seasons. The Sixth Circuit then held that **competition in non-traditional seasons harmed girls, particularly by sending them a message that they were "second class" or were less valued than boys.** The MHSAA's evidence did not establish that separate seasons for boys and girls maximized opportunities for their participation. Female athletes were always required to play in disadvantageous seasons. The scheduling differences were properly found to be discriminatory, as boys' and girls' schedules were separate and treated unequally. *Communities for Equity v. Michigan High School Athletic Ass'n*, 459 F.3d 676 (6th Cir. 2006).

◆ A Wisconsin boy wanted to participate on the girls' gymnastics team at his high school. He filed a state court action against the Wisconsin Interscholastic Athletic Association (WIAA), alleging constitutional and Title IX claims. The student challenged a WIAA rule prohibiting all interscholastic activity involving boys and girls competing against each other, except as permitted by law and board of control interpretations. He added Wisconsin statutory and constitutional claims for injunctive relief. The court denied any relief, noting that the WIAA is a private, voluntary association. As the WIAA was not a public entity, no equal protection suit could be brought against it. The WIAA received no federal funds and could not be sued under Title IX. The student appealed to the Court of Appeals of Wisconsin, which found that **he failed to offer any evidence that the WIAA was engaged in action traditionally reserved to the state.** His equal protection and Title IX claims could not succeed. The court affirmed the judgment for the WIAA. *Bukowski v. Wisconsin Interscholastic Ass'n*, 726 N.W.2d 356 (Table) (Wis. Ct. App. 2006).

◆ New York state and regional championships for girls' soccer were held in the fall, and 649 of 714 schools offering soccer scheduled it accordingly. Some districts scheduled girls' soccer in spring to avoid jeopardizing field hockey programs. Two districts scheduled boys' soccer in fall, and the boys' teams remained eligible for state and regional competition. Girls' soccer was the only sport held outside the state championship season in either district. The families of two students who sought to play girls' soccer for district schools sued the districts for Title IX violations. A federal court held that the scheduling of girls' soccer seasons in spring violated Title IX. The districts appealed to the Second Circuit, which noted that a Title IX policy interpretation required equivalent treatment, benefits and opportunities, and the accommodation of interests and abilities of both sexes.

The court held that the scheduling of girls' soccer in spring created a disparity that had a negative impact on girls. It sent girls the message that they were not expected to succeed and that the school did not value their athletic ability as much as it valued the ability of boys.

There was no reason why soccer and field hockey could not be played in the same season. The court affirmed the judgment and ordered the district court to consider whether boys and girls received equal opportunities for post-season competition. *McCormick v. School Dist. of Mamaroneck*, 370 F.3d 275 (2d Cir. 2004).

◆ The Minnesota State High School League recognized girls hockey as a varsity sport in 1994, many years after it began sponsoring boys hockey. Boys hockey tournaments took place in professional sports arenas, including the Target and Xcel Energy Centers. The league selected Ridder Arena, home of the University of Minnesota women's hockey team, to be the site of the 2004 girls tournament. A group representing girls hockey team members and their parents sued the league for Title IX and state Human Rights Act violations. The court denied a motion for a preliminary order to venue the girls tournament at the Xcel Energy Center, as **neither Title IX nor state law required the identical treatment of boys and girls athletics**. Instead, the laws required "equivalent treatment and equal accommodation."

In later court proceedings, the court found there were differences in the way the league handled tournaments. Other girls sports events were held at Xcel, and a boys tournament there drew smaller or comparable crowds than girls' events. The girls raised the issue of what message the choice of venue sent to female hockey players and fans. The evidence could lead a jury to find the league's scheduling policy violated Title IX, so the court ordered a trial. Less than a month after the decision, the parties announced a settlement under which the 2006 girls tournament would be held at Xcel. *Mason v. Minnesota State High School League*, No. 03-6462(JRT/FLN), 2004 WL 1630968 (D. Minn. 2004).

◆ A male Rhode Island high school student desired to compete as a member of his school's girls' field hockey team. However, the regulations of the Rhode Island Interscholastic League forbade boys from participating on girls' athletic teams. A federal court denied his request for an injunction based on the Fourteenth Amendment's Equal Protection Clause. He then sued the league, seeking an injunction based on the state constitution's equal protection provisions. The trial court granted the injunction, but the Rhode Island Supreme Court vacated the injunction. Gender classifications under the state constitution need only serve important governmental objectives and be substantially related to the achievement of those objectives. **Safety concerns and physical differences between the sexes justified the rule.** *Kleczek v. Rhode Island Interscholastic League*, 612 A.2d 734 (R.I. 1992).

B. Race Discrimination

Title VI of the Civil Rights Act of 1964 prohibits intentional race discrimination in any program that receives federal funds. Title VI is based on the Equal Protection Clause, and many discrimination complaints allege violations of Title VI, the Equal Protection Clause, and analogous state laws.

Court Decisions

◆ As a freshman, an Illinois student played for the varsity football team. He received a disciplinary referral for wearing his pants too low, in violation of the school dress code. The school referred him for discipline for failing to follow instructions to leave an area where some other students were fighting. His father learned that the student was at risk of being placed on disciplinary probation. The student finished his sophomore year at the high school but then moved with his father outside the district's boundaries. The father presented administrators with false documents showing that the family still lived in the district. The district allowed the student to work out with the football team during his junior year, but it barred him from Illinois High School Association games. The family moved back into the district, and the student was allowed to play football his senior year. But the family sued for constitutional rights violations. **A federal court found no evidence that other students were disciplined for wearing their pants too low.** But there was evidence that Caucasian students involved in the fighting incident were also disciplined, and 12 Caucasian students were placed on disciplinary probation in the student's sophomore year. The student apparently received the same treatment as others. The court held for the school district. *Bryant v. Board of Educ., Dist. 228*, No. 06 C 5697, 2008 WL 1702162 (N.D. Ill. 2008).

◆ The U.S. Court of Appeals, Eleventh Circuit, held that a lower court properly ruled against an Alabama student who filed an equal protection lawsuit based on his expulsion for striking two football coaches who removed him from a football game. **The claims failed because the student was unable to show that he was treated any differently than others.** He was not "similarly situated" to two other students who were not expelled, as their conduct involved horseplay and lesser misconduct. *Davis v. Houston County, Alabama Board of Educ.*, 291 Fed.Appx. 251 (11th Cir. 2008).

◆ Thirteen suburban Chicago school districts withdrew from the South Inter-Conference Association after over 30 years of membership. They formed two new athletic conferences, excluding two school districts in Thornton, Illinois that served mostly African-American students. The Thornton districts alleged a racially motivated conspiracy among the 13 districts, resulting in three racially segregated conferences. They joined several Thornton parents and students in a federal court action against the 13 districts. The Thornton parties **included a racially charged statement by a board member of one of the 13 districts accusing African-Americans of ruining neighborhoods in Chicago's south suburbs**. They also referenced apartheid, white flight and a racial Mason-Dixon line. Rejecting a claim by the Thornton parties that a reference to *Brown v. Board of Education* stated the grounds of their lawsuit, the court found there was no basis for any of the statements. As a result, the court struck them from the complaint. The lengthy statement by the board member was redundant and served no purpose but to scandalize the conduct of the 13 districts. His remarks might be inadmissible hearsay and had to be stricken. *Board of Educ. of Thornton Township High School Dist. 205 v. Board of Educ. of Argo Community High School Dist. 217*, No. 06 C 2005, 2006 WL 1896068 (N.D. Ill. 2006).

♦ A Mississippi student's parent claimed that the school's head football coach called her son "nigger" and "fat black ass" during team practices. A teammate allegedly repeated these epithets, and along with another player, hit her son's helmet with rocks during practice. The coach allegedly did nothing and the principal took no action when she reported this. In a later practice, the teammate allegedly lunged at the student and gouged his eye, causing permanent injury. When the principal investigated the incident, no one admitted seeing an assault.

The parent sued the school district, coaching staff and school officials in a federal district court, alleging deprivation of her son's civil rights. The court dismissed the claims, and the parent appealed to the U.S. Court of Appeals, Fifth Circuit. It found the teammate was not a "state actor" and thus could not be liable for civil rights violations filed under 42 U.S.C. § 1983. The Due Process Clause did not require coaches to protect the student from the teammate because there was no "special relationship" between the coaches and student. While the conduct of school officials in this case was "morally reprehensible," the teammate's actions could not be attributed to them. **Use of racial epithets, without evidence of harassment or other deprivation of established rights, does not constitute an equal protection violation.** The school investigated the incident, and while its response may have been inadequate, it did not show inaction creating an equal protection violation. Apart from the racial epithets, the parent produced no evidence of bias by school officials. The judgment was affirmed. *Priester v. Lowndes County*, 354 F.3d 414 (5th Cir. 2004).

The case returned to the district court, which found that the student had alleged sufficient facts to avoid pretrial judgment on his discrimination claims against the district. Disputed fact issues surrounded his expulsion, including whether he had shoved the coach and threatened to kill the teammates while disobeying instructions to avoid a confrontation. This required a trial. *Priester v. Starkville School Dist.*, No. 1: 03CV90, 2005 WL 2347285 (N.D. Miss. 2005).

C. Students with Disabilities

In PGA Tour v. Martin, *532 S.Ct. 661 (U.S. 2001), the Supreme Court held the Americans with Disabilities Act (ADA) requires an individualized inquiry to determine whether a requested modification is reasonable and necessary for the disabled individual, and whether the modification would fundamentally alter the nature of the competition.*

Court Decisions

♦ A 19-year-old Mississippi senior with learning disabilities transferred to another school and sought a temporary restraining order that would allow him to play basketball. He sued the state athletic association under the ADA, the IDEA and the Constitution. A federal court refused to grant him relief, finding no justification for disrupting the status quo. **The state high school athletic association had found that the transfer was made for athletic reasons**, and he failed to show a substantial likelihood of success on the merits of his claims. The student essentially argued that if he was not allowed to play varsity basketball, he would be less likely to get a professional contract. This could be remedied by an award of money damages, undercutting the claim that he would be irreparably injured in the absence of a court order. On appeal, the U.S. Court of Appeals, Fifth Circuit, rejected the student's arguments. His primary argument was financial and the court rejected claims under federal disability laws and provisions of the U.S. Constitution. *Newsome v. Mississippi High School Activities Ass'n*, 326 Fed.Appx. 878 (5th Cir. 2009).

♦ A New Jersey student with learning disabilities was recruited for football by several NCAA Division I schools. The NCAA ruled that a number of his high school special education classes did not satisfy its core course requirement and declared him ineligible during his freshman season. He sued the NCAA, the universities and the ACT/Clearinghouse, which administers college entrance examinations. After he died, his estate continued the litigation. His mother later revealed to the NCAA and the universities that he had been in and out of drug treatment and mental health programs and that his death resulted from an apparent drug overdose. The court sanctioned the mother and her attorneys, finding that the failure to disclose the information was willful and in bad faith.

The U.S. Court of Appeals, Third Circuit, held that the alleged discrimination took place during the 1995-96 school year, when the student was deemed ineligible for football under NCAA rules. The evidence of any substance abuse by the student in 1995-96 was minimal. **His substance abuse was irrelevant for purposes of establishing liability.** The district court's contrary ruling was reversed. The case was returned to the district court for a determination of whether the NCAA and the universities violated the ADA and Rehabilitation Act. *Bowers v. NCAA*, 475 F.3d 524 (3d Cir. 2007).

♦ A Colorado student was diagnosed with attention deficit disorder (ADD) at age eight. He received medication and attended a speech class for grade four. By middle school, his special education program ended, and he stopped taking medication for ADD. In high school, his academic modifications were limited to additional time for tests and homework, and the provision of class notes. He missed several weeks of school in ninth grade due to a sinus infection, and he repeated grade nine. His parents divorced near this time. When the student reached grade 12, state athletic association rules barred him from playing football as he was in his ninth consecutive semester of high school attendance. The association denied his request for a hardship waiver, and he sought a state court order to declare its eight-semester rule violated a state anti-discrimination act. The court denied his request for preliminary relief. On appeal, the Court of Appeals of Colorado found evidence that he repeated grade nine because of his parents' divorce, problems adjusting to a new school, and his sinus infection. **A single failed year of school was a temporary and short-term event that did not render the student "disabled" under state law or the ADA.** The trial court had properly denied his request for temporary relief. *Tesmer v. Colorado High School Activities Ass'n*, 140 P.3d 249 (Colo. Ct. App. 2006).

◆ Under either Section 504 or the ADA, **a person with disabilities may be excluded from a program if participation presents a direct threat to the health and safety of others**. In a Kentucky case, a school district properly excluded a student with hemophilia and hepatitis B from participation on the junior varsity basketball team while trying to determine if he presented a serious health risk to others. The U.S. Court of Appeals, Sixth Circuit, reasoned that Congress created a narrow exception to the broad prohibition against discrimination contained in the ADA, where an individual with disabilities presents a direct threat to the health and safety of others. School officials had never removed the student from the team but had placed him on hold status while awaiting medical advice. The action was appropriate in view of the potential liability faced by the school if a competitor became infected as a result of his participation. The student had also voluntarily chosen not to participate. *Doe v. Woodford County Board of Educ.*, 213 F.3d 921 (6th Cir. 2000).

III. ISSUES IN COACHING

Overview

Coaches typically receive a salary supplement for their coaching duties under separate contracts. In these cases, their property interests in their coaching assignments are limited to the term of the supplemental contract and severable from teaching contracts. Under these circumstances, coaching duties do not have the same statutory protections as regular teaching assignments.

A Texas school athletic administrator was unable to convince the state court of appeals that the Texas Whistleblower Act protected him from being demoted after he reported a violation of state interscholastic rules.

Alabama's Supreme Court has held that teachers under contract for supplemental non-teaching duties like coaching do not require notice of non-renewal for such contracts under the state Teacher Tenure Act.

A. Employment

Court Decisions

◆ A Texas high school administrator served as athletic director and director of extracurricular activities. He learned that a high school football player might be in violation of a state University Interscholastic League (UIL) residency rule. The administrator discussed the problem with other school officials. With district approval, he submitted a written report to the UIL, and the football team was barred from playoff games. About five weeks later, the district reassigned the administrator to an athletic trainer position. After a hearing, the district reinstated him to the extracurricular activities job. But he was not reinstated as an athletic director and he sued the district under the Texas Whistleblower's Act. On appeal, the Supreme Court of Texas held **the elements of the state Whistleblower Act could be considered in order to determine both a court's jurisdiction and any liability issues**. It returned the case to the lower court for a determination of whether the administrator had stated a Whistleblower violation. *Galveston Independent School Dist. v. Jaco*, 303 S.W.3d 699 (Tex. 2010).

Upon its third review of the case, the court of appeals explained that the Whistleblower Act pertained to the good faith reporting by a public employee of a "violation of law" by the employing governmental entity. According to the school district, the trial court should not have denied pretrial judgment, since UIL rules were not laws. **Agreeing with the district, the court found no state law requiring the UIL to have a residency rule.** UIL rules were not "adopted" by the legislature, but were submitted by the UIL to the state commissioner of education for approval. As UIL rules were not "laws" under the Whistleblower Act and to do so would lead to absurd results, the court held for the district. *Galveston Independent School Dist. v. Jaco*, 331 S.W.3d 182 (Tex. Ct. App. 2011).

◆ Many complaints were made about an Iowa high school basketball coach's threatening and intimidating treatment of players and his use of profanity. Five players quit the varsity team during his first year. The district renewed the coach's contract, but it also extended his probationary status and notified him of "major concerns" with the boys' basketball program. In the coach's fourth season, he was again the subject of numerous student and parent complaints. Fifteen families wrote letters, complaining that he told injured players not to see their doctors, ignored athletic association rules, set a poor example for ethical behavior and created a negative environment that damaged student self-esteem and confidence.

The district superintendent specifically forbade the coach from correcting players outside the presence of an assistant coach, counselor or parent. In a basketball game held the next year, a player failed to follow coaching instructions. After the game, the coach and player met briefly in a hallway with no other adult present. Administrators ruled that the coach had violated the directive. The school fired the coach, and the Supreme Court of Iowa noted that **the school board had appropriately considered the coach's entire history, as well as the final incident, when voting to terminate his coaching contract**. The coach had been informed throughout his career about the need to respect his players, and the superintendent had specifically notified him that failure to do so could lead to termination. Just cause existed for contract termination. *Board of Directors* *of Ames Community School Dist. v. Cullinan*, 745 N.W.2d 487 (Iowa 2008).

◆ Tennessee's highest court held school directors have the authority to transfer tenured teachers, including those with coaching responsibilities. For this reason, a tenured teacher who head-coached a high school girls' basketball team for 17 years could be transferred – as to his coaching responsibilities – without regard to a collective bargaining agreement. **The statutory term "teacher" did not extend to contracts for coaching duties, as there was no certification of coaches in the state.** An arbitrator had incorrectly held that a master contract governed the renewal of the coaching contract in this case. Year-to-year appointments were not entitled to the benefits of the collective bargaining process. *Lawrence County Educ. Ass'n v. Lawrence County Board of Educ.*, 244 S.W.3d 302 (Tenn. 2007).

◆ An inner-city Alabama high school basketball coach was a tenured science teacher with 20 years of teaching experience. Before the start of the 2004-05 basketball season, he agreed with players to use a "one-minute drill" or "circle" as a form of discipline in practices. The "drill" consisted of the team encircling the rules violator, then hitting or kicking him for up to one minute. The coach looked on and timed the hitting with a stopwatch. The punishment was used 11 times in a six-week period. After the media reported a player's injuries, the school district placed the coach on administrative leave. A hearing officer found the coach engaged in serious misconduct but did not recommend canceling his contract. Instead, the coach was barred from coaching for four years, suspended without pay for 30 days, and ordered to apologize to all players and parents.

The case reached the Supreme Court of Alabama, which noted that at his hearing, the coach acknowledged his mistake and promised it would never happen again. Players uniformly stated that he was a positive influence in their lives. **The Alabama Teacher Tenure Act permitted consideration of a teacher's employment history, including matters occurring in previous years.** The coach had no prior disciplinary record, and parents and students expressed a strong and almost unanimous desire for him to remain. The coach had been able to improve grades and make college a realistic goal for his players. The hearing officer had attempted to balance a number of vital concerns. That decision was upheld. *Ex parte Dunn*, 962 So.2d 814 (Ala. 2007).

◆ A nontenured Alabama teacher was the faculty sponsor for a junior varsity cheerleading squad. Parents complained about unfairness in cheerleading tryouts. The principal investigated and gave the teacher a questionnaire. She responded to the questionnaire and raised her own questions about the tryouts. The principal decided not to renew the teacher's contract, and she sued the school board for speech and due process violations. A federal court held for the board, and the Eleventh Circuit affirmed. A public employee who does not speak as a citizen on a matter of public concern has no First Amendment claim based on his or her employer's reaction to the speech. Public employees are not speaking as "citizens" when they speak about their official duties. **The teacher's responses to the questionnaire were unprotected.** *Gilder-Lucas v. Elmore County Board of Educ.*, 186 Fed.Appx. 885 (11th Cir. 2006).

◆ During a job interview with an Indiana school board, a coach disclosed his criminal convictions, including one for conspiracy to distribute marijuana. He assured the board he had "turned his life around," and the board hired him. The coach was then offered additional positions teaching special education and coaching the girls' basketball team. He obtained a limited one-year teaching license to teach special education. Near the end of the coach's term, an interim district superintendent recommended not renewing his teaching contract due to the expiration of his limited teaching license. The non-renewal of the coach's contract was reported in the media. The board voted to immediately remove him as the girls' basketball coach. He resigned as football coach and sued the board for denial of his equal protection and due process rights.

The Seventh Circuit ruled against him. His sole argument was that the board had singled him out by requiring him to take drug tests. He stated that the district athletic director had been caught stealing from the school but was not required to submit to drug testing. The court held that **the coach and athletic director were not "similarly situated" and could not be compared for purposes of an Equal Protection claim.** The athletic director was never prosecuted for any crimes, while the coach had a felony drug conviction. *Ott v. Edinburgh Community School Corp.*, 189 Fed.Appx. 507 (7th Cir. 2006).

◆ A Mississippi teacher's football coaching duties included summer work, but he refused to attend eight of 24 summer workouts. The school board voted not to renew his primary teaching contract for the next year as a result. After a state chancery court upheld the decision, the teacher appealed to the Court of Appeals of Mississippi. He argued that his coaching rider did not permit the non-renewal of his teaching contract, and that the rider was not enforceable because it required him to work for no pay, in violation of state and federal wage laws. The court held **state law did not prohibit school boards from including riders or attachments in school employment contracts**. The teacher's rider was valid, and the trial court did not commit error by finding that he failed to perform his duties by skipping the summer workouts. There was no merit to his argument that the extended time period specified in his coaching rider violated state and federal wage laws. Federal regulations published under the Fair Labor Standards Act exempt teachers and those with coaching duties from coverage. There was no merit to a claim that the rider applied only to cases of resignation or involuntary termination. The employment contract and rider referred to a single teacher/coach position. As the teacher had defiantly chosen not to attend the summer workouts, the court upheld the judgment for the school district. *Smith v. Petal School Dist.*, 956 So.2d 273 (Miss. Ct. App. 2006).

◆ After working for six years for his district, an Alabama teacher transferred to a high school to teach physical education and coach basketball. He discovered that the girls' team did not receive the same funding or access to equipment and facilities as boys' teams. He claimed that his job was made difficult by lack of adequate funding, equipment and facilities, and he began complaining to supervisors. He stated that the district did not respond to his complaints and gave him negative evaluations before removing him as girls' coach. He sued the school board in a federal court, claiming the loss of his supplemental coaching contracts constituted unlawful retaliation in violation of Title IX. The court dismissed the case, and the Eleventh Circuit affirmed this.

The U.S. Supreme Court stated that **Title IX covers retaliation against a person for complaining about sex discrimination**. "Retaliation is, by definition an intentional act," and is a form of discrimination, since the person who complains is treated differently than others. Without finding that actual discrimination had occurred, the Court held that the teacher was entitled to attempt to show that the board was liable. A private right of action for retaliation was within the statute's prohibition of intentional sex discrimination. Title IX did not require the victim of retaliation to also be the victim of discrimination. Teachers and coaches were often in the best position to vindicate the rights of students by identifying discrimination and notifying administrators. A reasonable school board would realize it could not cover up violations of Title IX by retaliating against teachers. The Court reversed the judgment. *Jackson v. Birmingham Board of Educ.*, 544 U.S. 167 (2005).

B. Defamation

Coaches, like other public school officials and teachers, are considered "public officials" in defamation cases. This means that to prevail, they must show that defamatory statements were made with "actual malice." And they must prove the other elements of a defamation claim. Since actual malice is difficult to prove, defamation claimants typically face an uphill battle.

Court Decisions

◆ Several parents of players on a Utah high school basketball team accused their coach of giving preferential treatment to the team's star player, criticized his demeanor and questioned his use of team funds. The administration eventually dismissed the coach from his head coaching duties, citing "his refusal to promise that he would not deny team membership and playing time to the women in retaliation against the Parents." The coach sued the parents for defamation, and a trial court agreed with the parents that the coach was a "public official." This meant he was required to show they made their statements with "actual malice" to prevail on his defamation claims.

The Supreme Court of Utah explained that **persons who are deemed to be public officials or public figures "surrender a sizeable measure of their right to recover damages from those who defame them."** Statements directed at public officials or public figures require proof that the speaker had actual malice. However, the coach did not occupy a position with such "apparent importance" that he had "public official" status. Despite the increasing popularity of athletics, the court rejected the parents' claim that coaches should be treated as public officials. Unlike those in "policy-making positions," Utah teachers and coaches did not surrender their ability to protect their reputations by accepting their jobs. However, the court agreed with the parents that they could be entitled to a conditional privilege based on family relationships. The case was returned to the district court, which was to decide whether the parents' statements were defamatory under the new standard explained by the supreme court. *O'Connor v. Burningham*, 165 P.3d 1214 (Utah 2007).

◆ Michigan High School Athletic Association rules required transfer students to sit out of interscholastic athletic competition for two semesters if a transfer was "athletically motivated." A star student-athlete told his football coach and others he was considering a transfer because "the program was in disarray." The student's mother told the principal the transfer was academically motivated, but the principal filed a complaint with the state athletic association, asserting the transfer was athletically motivated. Two newspapers interviewed school officials, then published articles speculating that the transfer was athletically motivated. The student sued the school district, principal, coach and the district athletic director for defamation and other claims. The case reached the Court of Appeals of Michigan, which held **the principal, coach and athletic director were entitled to speak to reporters who were already aware of the story**. The trial court had properly dismissed defamation and invasion of privacy claims based on governmental immunity. Statements to the association were limited to furthering the district's interest and were made in a proper manner. And the statements to the reporters were not defamation, as there was no evidence that they caused any special harm. The student himself openly spoke about his transfer at school. *Cassise v. Walled Lake Consolidated Schools*, No. 257299, 2006 WL 445960 (Mich. Ct. App. 2006).

◆ A Louisiana student and her mother were spectators at a game. She claimed a coach physically and verbally threatened them and called the police to have them removed from the gym. The student sued the school board and coach in a federal court, claiming "threatening and abusive language is actionable" in actions for federal civil rights violations under 42 U.S.C. § 1983. The coach moved for dismissal, asserting there was no viable Section 1983 claim, and that she was also entitled to qualified immunity. The court agreed with the coach, stating that **the Due Process Clause "does not transform every tort committed by a state actor into a constitutional violation."** Even in a state custodial situation, "the use of words, no matter how violent, does not comprise a Section 1983 violation." The court rejected the student's claim alleging harm to her reputation. The conduct she alleged did not raise a valid constitutional claim. Any harm to reputation was not a deprivation of a constitutional liberty or property interest recognized by state or federal law. *Paige v. Tangipahoa Parish School Board*, No. 04-354, 2005 WL 943636 (E.D. La. 2005).

♦ A Minnesota school district decided not to rehire a varsity football coach. A newspaper published articles quoting sources who said the coach was "known for his temper, inappropriate comments and foul language, which people claim he uses to intimidate players." While news accounts did not identify the source of these comments, one statement was attributed to a former assistant coach. The head coach sued the school district for defamation, breach of contract and other claims. A court twice denied motions by the coach to identify staff members who allegedly defamed him, then held for the district and employees.

The case eventually reached the state supreme court, which recited the elements for a defamation claim, which are: (1) a false and defamatory statement (2) in an unprivileged publication to a third party that (3) harmed the plaintiff's reputation in the community. **Public officials must also demonstrate that the statement was made with "actual malice." In Minnesota, public school teachers and coaches are deemed public officials.** Since the speaker was anonymous, the court held that his or her identity would necessarily lead to relevant evidence on the issue of actual malice. The district court had found that the statements, if false, were defamatory. The court reversed, finding that if any school employee was the source of the statements, there was probable cause to believe the speaker had relevant information. *Weinberger v. Maplewood Review*, 668 N.W.2d 667 (Minn. 2003).

C. Liability

Coaches typically avoid liability for student injuries, unless there is a showing of willful or wanton misconduct. For additional cases involving liability in the context of school athletics, see Chapter One.

Court Decisions

♦ A Tennessee cheerleading sponsor worked in a school cafeteria and was not a certified teacher. She supervised the cheerleading squad for over two years without incident. A cheerleader then broke her arm during a practice when she landed on the floor while attempting a "basket toss" maneuver. At the time of the injury, the sponsor had left the practice for other duties. The cheerleader sued the school board and sponsor for negligence. After a court awarded pretrial judgment to the board and sponsor, the cheerleader appealed. The Court of Appeals of Tennessee held that **the cheerleader failed to show that the sponsor's experience was inadequate or fell below an established standard of care**. Thus, the negligent hiring claim failed. But there was a dispute concerning the sponsor's level of supervision over the squad. While she said she told the squad not to perform stunts in her absence, the cheerleader said there was no such warning. A trial was required on that issue. *Britt v. Maury County Board of Educ.*, 2008 WL 4427190 (Tenn. Ct. App. 9/29/08).

♦ A Pennsylvania junior high school wrestling coach directed a 152-pound wrestler to "live wrestle" a 240-pound teammate during a practice. "Live wrestling" simulated actual competitive conditions, with both wrestlers giving their best efforts. Pennsylvania Interscholastic Athletic Association (PIAA) rules limited wrestling to competitors in their own weight class or one class above. The teammate was three PIAA weight classes above the wrestler, and he injured the wrestler's leg when he collapsed on him. The wrestler sued the school district and employees in a federal court, which held for the district.

The wrestler appealed to the U.S. Court of Appeals, Third Circuit, which explained that **to hold the coach liable for a constitutional violation, it had to be shown that he deprived the wrestler of a federal right in a way that was foreseeable and fairly direct**. In this case, the coach had paired mismatched wrestlers simply because there was no partner for the teammate. The coach apparently had done this previously. As there was at least circumstantial evidence of deliberate indifference to the wrestler's federally protected rights, the court returned the case to the lower court. However, the claims against the school district failed. State agencies are not liable for constitutional violations of their employees, except for policy makers, or where the agency itself has an official policy or custom of violating federally protected rights. *Patrick v. Great Valley School Dist.*, 296 Fed.Appx, 258 (3d Cir. 2008).

♦ Four Tennessee student-athletes claimed their varsity football head coach humiliated and degraded them, used inappropriate language and required them to participate in a year-round conditioning program that violated school rules. They claimed he hit a player in the helmet and threw away college recruiting letters that were sent to "disfavored players." One of them typed a petition that said "I hate Coach Euverard and I don't want to play for him." Eighteen players signed the petition. When the coach learned of this, he summoned players into his office one by one to interview them. Players who signed the petition were allowed to stay on the team if they apologized and said they wanted to play for the head coach. Four players who did not apologize and accept the coach were taken off the team. They sued the coach, school board and other officials for First Amendment violations. A federal district court denied the officials' motion for qualified immunity, and they appealed. The U.S. Court of Appeals, Sixth Circuit, noted that the petition was a direct challenge to the coach's authority, and it would harm team unity and divide teammates into groups. **The petition was reasonably likely to cause substantial disruption to the team and therefore was not protected.** There was no First Amendment violation as the players had implicitly agreed to accept their coach's authority by turning out for the team. *Lowery v. Euverard*, 497 F.3d 584 (6th Cir. 2007).

♦ An Ohio student was injured when a batted ball ricocheted off an L-screen that had been placed in front of him for protection. He was hospitalized and doctors implanted four titanium plates and screws into his head. He sued the school district and coach for negligence, claiming that the coach failed to properly supervise the batting cage and did not provide protective helmets for pitchers. The complaint did not allege malice, bad faith or reckless conduct or claim damages from the coach individually. A court awarded pretrial judgment to the school district and the student appealed. The case reached the state supreme court, which held teachers and coaches have wide discretion to determine what supervision is necessary for student safety. The coach's decisions reflected his discretion. He instructed pitchers regarding the L-screen as well as general guidance on game preparations. **The coach's direction represented the exercise of his judgment and discretion in the use of equipment or facilities in connection with his position.** As the injury resulted from the coach's judgment or discretion, the district could claim immunity. There was no suggestion of reckless conduct, malice or bad faith. *Elston v. Howland Local Schools*, 113 Ohio St.3d 314, 865 N.E.2d 845 (Ohio 2007).

◆ A Texas cross country coach had his team warm up on the paved shoulder of a two-lane state highway. He followed the team in his personal vehicle. The warmup took place about 7:00 a.m., in low-light conditions. After warming up, the team gathered on the shoulder of the eastbound lane of the highway. The coach parked on the westbound shoulder and activated his emergency flashers. An oncoming vehicle drove onto the eastbound shoulder, striking and killing a team member. The team member's parent sued the school board and coach in a state court, alleging that the coach negligently operated his emergency flashers. The court held that the board and coach were entitled to immunity under the Texas Tort Claims Act. The state court of appeals affirmed the judgment. Government units can be liable for property damage, personal injury and death in cases involving the use or operation of a motor vehicle. But the activation of the emergency flashers on the coach's car did not create a waiver of immunity under the Act. Even if it did, there was no evidence that the death arose from this use. The student was killed by the vehicle that struck him. **The coach's actions were supervisory in nature and did not involve the operation or use of a motor vehicle.** *Morales v. Barnette*, 219 S.W.3d 477 (Tex. Ct. App. 2007).

◆ A Michigan middle school wrestling coach injured a student when he performed a maneuver in practice without prior warning. The student sued, and a state court denied pretrial judgment to the coach, finding that he was grossly negligent in performing the maneuver without prior notice. The case reached the Supreme Court of Michigan, which held that even if the coach had grabbed the student from behind and took him to the mat as alleged, this did not produce injury. **The injury occurred when the coach and student were engaged in wrestling activity.** The student testified that after he completed a body roll, he did what he had been coached to do – brace his arm and try to escape. This was what caused the injury. As the lack of adequate notice of the initial maneuver was not a basis for injury, the court reversed the judgment. *Jefferson Middle School v. Nadeau*, 477 Mich. 1109, 729 N.W.2d 840 (Mich. 2007).

◆ A Texas basketball coach and an athletic trainer were blamed for the death of a student who collapsed after completing a two-mile run with her team. The student's parents claimed the coach and trainer failed to perform CPR or give her other necessary medical attention and that their delays caused her death. They sued the district, coach and trainer in a federal district court. **The court held that to show a school employee has violated a constitutional interest in bodily integrity, there must be proof of deliberate indifference toward the victim.** The family had alleged only negligence, not deliberate indifference. The coach attended to the student about five minutes after she finished running, and the trainer saw her about 12 minutes later. As this was not "conscious disregard" for her health and safety, the employees had qualified immunity. The district was entitled to immunity for the constitutional and state law claims. *Livingston v. DeSoto Independent School Dist.*, 391 F.Supp.2d 463 (N.D. Tex. 2005).

◆ A 15-year-old Mississippi student became fatigued at a football practice on a hot August day. He told the coach he felt weak and needed a water break, but the coach thought he was "faking it" and refused the request for a break. After allegedly suffering a heatstroke, the student sued the district and coach in a state court for negligence. The court held a trial and found the student suffered damages of $350,000, including $68,000 in medical bills. However, the court found the coach and district were entitled to immunity under the Mississippi Torts Claims Act (MTCA) because their conduct was discretionary. The student appealed to the Supreme Court of Mississippi. The court explained that government entities and their employees are entitled to MTCA immunity against all claims based on the exercise of discretionary duties. Here, the coach was in the best position to know his team and had to motivate and discipline players. **Imposing liability on the coach and district would result in their loss of control over high school football programs due to the risk of lawsuits.** Since the coach's actions were discretionary within the meaning of the MTCA, the supreme court affirmed the judgment for the district and coach. *Harris v. McCray*, 867 So.2d 188 (Miss. 2003).

◆ A 14-year-old California student told two coaches of her great fear of diving into shallow water. They allowed her to swim the first leg of team relay races during the first meets of the season, which allowed her to start in the water. Minutes before the start of a meet, a coach told her that she could not start the relay and would have to dive into the pool. She panicked and begged him to change the rotation to allow her to start from the water. He refused and allegedly threatened to exclude her from the meet. She broke her neck on a practice dive, and later sued the school district and coach. She presented evidence from a certified water safety instructor that the dive she tried was ultra-hazardous if done by an inadequately trained swimmer. A state court held for the district and coach, but the state supreme court ruled that the case required a trial. **The court held a school district generally has no duty**

to protect a student from the inherent risks in a sport. But sports instructors and coaches have a duty not to increase the risks of sports participation beyond what is inherent in the sport. The trial court had to credit the student's expert and her statements concerning the lack of instruction, her fear of diving into shallow water, and her claim that the coach threatened her if she did not dive. *Kahn v. East Side Union High School Dist.*, 31 Cal.4th 990, 4 Cal.Rptr.3d 103, 75 P.3d 30 (Cal. 2003).

◆ A Nebraska high school football player was struck on his head during a game. He felt dizzy and disoriented, but stayed in the game a few plays before taking himself out. Coaches observed he was short of breath but attributed this to hyperventilation. As the student made normal eye contact and had normal speech and movement, no medical attention was sought. The student later asked to return to the game, and coaches allowed him to do so. He suffered a headache the entire weekend, but coaches denied he said anything about it the next week. They allowed him to practice with the team, and he suffered a closed-head traumatic brain injury. The student sued the school district in a state court for personal injuries. After the court dismissed the case, the Nebraska Supreme Court held it should not have discredited testimony by expert witnesses.

Certified athletic trainers who taught state-required courses for coaching endorsements had testified for the student that Nebraska **high school coaches should know that headache, dizziness and disorientation are symptomatic of a concussion.** The case then returned to the trial court. It heard testimony that little training or literature was available to coaches about head injury at the time of the injury. The court dismissed the case, as the coaching staff complied with the duty of care required of a reasonably prudent person with a state coaching endorsement. The supreme court later affirmed this decision. *Cerny v. Cedar Bluffs Junior/Senior Public School*, 268 Neb. 958, 679 N.W.2d 198 (Neb. 2004).

D. Misconduct

Court Decisions

◆ A California freshman made her varsity softball team. This achievement and her relationship with the team's head coach "stirred up some resentment among the other softball team members." Rumors began that she was having a lesbian relationship with the coach. The principal warned the coach to avoid favoritism, "maintain a proper professional distance" and avoid being alone with the student. After the coach disobeyed the warning, the district did not renew her probationary contract. The student claimed that students continued calling her "homo" and that teachers who witnessed the harassment did nothing to stop it. However, she reported only one incident to the school, and when she did, a vice principal met with the student and a harasser. The new coach then dismissed her from the team, stating that she had been a "cancer on the team." She sued the district, principal, vice principal and other staff.

A court awarded pretrial judgment to the district and staff, and the Court of Appeal of California affirmed. Here, the student had been rude and disrespectful to the new head coach, an assistant coach and her teammates. Only one potentially harassing remark was ever reported to the school, and the vice principal responded to it. **The student sought damages for "school yard insults and name calling," most of which were never brought to the school's attention.** She did not show harassment so severe, pervasive and objectively offensive that it denied her equal access to education under Title IX. *Ashby v. Hesperia Union School Dist.*, 2004 WL 2699940 (Cal. Ct. App. 2004).

◆ A Pennsylvania coach suspected that a member of the high school swim team was pregnant. He repeatedly asked her if this was true. She consistently denied it but eventually agreed to take a pregnancy test. The result was positive and, after learning that there was no medical reason to prevent the student from swimming competitively, the coach let her remain on the team. However, she alleged that after her baby was born, the coach attempted to alienate her from her peers, refused to speak with her and retaliated against her by removing her from competition. She sued him for civil rights violations. A federal district court held that the coach was entitled to qualified immunity.

On appeal, the Third Circuit found that **requiring a student to submit to a pregnancy test, if proven, would be an unlawful search and seizure.** A reasonable swim coach would not have forced a student to take a pregnancy test. Because the coach did not "justify his failure to respect the boundaries of reasonableness," he was not entitled to qualified immunity on the student's Fourth Amendment claim. This aspect of the district court's judgment was reversed and remanded. The court also reversed and remanded the student's claims based on violations of her constitutional privacy rights and state law. Her pregnancy was entitled to privacy protection under the Due Process Clause. The coach was not entitled to qualified immunity, since current law put him on notice that the compelled disclosure of personal information was not objectively reasonable. *Gruenke v. Seip*, 225 F.3d 290 (3d Cir. 2000).

INDEX

Abuse and neglect, 26-28
Academic practices, 237-265
    admissions and attendance, 258-262
        age requirements, 260-262
        race-related issues, 258-260
    compulsory attendance, 262-265
        attendance policies, 264-265
        home school programs, 263-264
        truancy, 262-263
    curriculum and grading, 245-249
        bilingual education, 247-248
        curriculum, 246-247
        grading, 248-249
    educational malpractice, 257-258
    reform legislation, 237-245
        charter schools, 240-245
        No Child Left Behind Act, 237-238
        state reform acts, 239-240
    student records, 249-255
        electronic records, 254-255
        media requests, 252-254
        parental rights, 249-252
        student rights, 249-252
        video records, 254-255
    testing, 256-257

Building and grounds, 34
    building entry policies, 34
    intruders, 34
    visitors, 34
Bullying, 22-23

Defamation, 28-30
Discrimination, 172-174
    race, 172-173
    religion, 174
Dress code
    employees, 114-115
    students, 106-109

Field trips, 12-13
Freedom of speech and association, 97-124
    academic freedom, 116-118
    bullying, 99-101
    Confederate flags, 103-104
    dress code, 106-111
    employees, 111-116
    gang affiliation, 110-111
    Internet and technology cases, 101-103
    non-school publications, 105-106
    parents, 118-121
    personal appearance, 106-111
    student publications, 104-105
    threats, 99-101
    use of school facilities, 121-124

Immunity, 4-5, 7-8, 11, 12, 14, 15-16, 18, 20, 23-24, 31-32, 33-34
Intentional conduct, 18-30
    employees, 18-20
    parents, 24-26
    students, 21-24
Interscholastic athletics, 315-328
    coaching, 323-328
    discrimination, 319-323
        gender, 319-321
        race, 321-322
        students with disabilities, 322-323
    drug testing, 318-319
    eligibility rules, 315-317
    suspensions, 317-318

Negligence, 3-6
    accidents off school grounds, 16-18
    accidents on school grounds, 15-16
    defenses, 4-6
    elements, 3-4
    generally, 13-14

Physical education classes, 10-11

Religion
    commencement ceremonies, 66-67
    curriculum, 63-65
    employees, 78-79
    Equal Access Act, 73-74
    Establishment Clause issues, 61-71
    financial assistance and voucher programs, 79-80
    immunization, 70-71
    literature and symbols, 75-77
    music performances, 65-66
    Pledge of Allegiance, 67-69
    prayer, 61-63
    released-time programs, 69, 70
    student groups, 72-73
    textbooks, 65
    use of school facilities, 71-77

School athletics, 6-10
    assumption of risk, 8-9
    employees, 9-10
    parents, 9-10
    participants, 6-9
    spectators, 9-10
Sexual harassment, 165-170
    by staff, 168-169
    by students, 166-168
    sexting, 165-166
Shop class injuries, 11-12
Student discipline, 183-214
    cell phones and electronic devices, 194-196
    corporal punishment, 210-214
    drug-sniffing dogs, 208-209
    drugs, alcohol and weapons, 189-192
    due process, 183-187
    expulsions and suspensions, 183-197
    fighting, 193-194

Miranda warnings, 206-208
    search and seizure, 197-210
        off-campus searches, 200-201
        random searches, 205-206
        strip searches, 201-204
    zero-tolerance policies, 187-188
Students with disabilities, 170-172, 271-301
    discipline, 275-279
    graduation, 294-295
    harassment, 170-172
    IDEA requirements, 271-272
    IEPs, 272-274, 275
    placement, 279-288
        child find obligation, 281-282
        extended school year services, 285-286
        identification and evaluation, 279-281
        least restrictive environment, 282-283
        stay-put provision, 283-285
        transfer students, 286-287
    related services, 288-290
    school liability, 295-301
    transition, 293-294
    tuition reimbursement, 290-293
Suicide, 28

Teacher scenarios
    accidents/incidents off school grounds, 50
    allergies, 35
    athletics, 38
    bullying, 49, 51, 135, 220, 221, 222
    cell phones, 130
    cheerleading, 37, 39
    child abuse, 53, 54, 55
    class scheduling issues, 266
    custody-related issues, 157
    defamation, 56, 126
    difficult parents, 53
    dress codes, 51, 139, 144
    due process, 215, 268
    electronic devices, 217
    emergency drill, 44
    expulsions, 219
    field trips, 43, 48
    fighting, 35
    grading, 148, 266
    graduation ceremonies, 145
    harassment, 52, 175, 176
    hate speech, 128
    Internet postings, 137, 138
    intruders, 36
    investigations, 136, 215, 216, 230, 231
    issues with parents, 158, 159, 160
    laboratory accidents, 45
    lesson plans, 155
    monkey bars, 47
    negligence, 36, 45
    physical education class injuries, 39, 40, 41
    playground accidents, 48
    Pledge of Allegiance, 85, 86
    proms, 50

promwear, 155, 177
race discrimination, 178
recess, 46
religion, 81, 82, 88, 91, 92, 94
    athletic events, 93
    church camp invitations, 90
    graduation, 83, 84
    holiday cards, 89
    holiday program, 86, 87
safety equipment, 42, 43
school banners, 126
school plays, 42
science experiments, 37
sexual assault, 179, 310
sexual harassment, 175
special education, 309
stairways, 49
student clubs, 140, 177
student expression, 127, 129, 132, 141, 142, 144, 146, 151, 153, 154, 156, 220
student newspapers, 142
student protests, 143
student records, 267
student searches, 224, 225, 226, 227, 228, 229
student use of school PA system, 161
students with disabilities, 302, 303, 304, 305, 306, 307, 308, 310
suicide, 55, 56
T-shirts, 147, 149, 150, 152, 154
talent show, 125
teacher polling of students, 159
testing, 267
textbooks, 88
texting in class, 223
threats, 134, 135, 220, 222, 224
transportation, 57
use of force by teachers, 231, 232, 233, 311
weapons, 133
zero-tolerance policies, 218

Transportation, 30-32
    bus accidents, 30-32